## *1000 YEARS OF IRISH PROSE*

For a country its size, Ireland produces an abundance of good writing as readers of this book will discover. One reason, perhaps, is that in Ireland the writer has been held in esteem by his countrymen right through history. Even today — censorship notwithstanding — he may be said to occupy the place of honor Americans reserve for the successful politician, businessman or athlete.

About 75 years ago, at a low point in Irish history, there began to appear a parade of Irish writers who were to alter the course of literature in the English language. It started with Standish O'Grady, got its greatest impetus from Yeats, and continues to this day. The high points of this "Literary Revival" are represented here in 640 pages by some of the very best of these writers.

This anthology is unique in that it can be read straight through from beginning to end. The first four of its six sections give, in roughly chronological order, a picture of the different phases through which the Revival has passed since the 1880's: *first*, the rediscovery of the glories of the Celtic past; *second*, a new awareness of the poetry and drama implicit in everyday Irish life; *third*, the determination to make a new Ireland by violent revolution; *fourth*, the disillusioned realism of the post-revolutionary period. The *fifth* and *sixth* sections are devoted to humor and experimental writing, respectively.

The selections picked by the editors either are complete or are longer than those found in the average anthology. Such major writers as Yeats, George Moore, Synge, Joyce, Standish O'Grady, James Stephens, Liam O'Flaherty and Frank O'Connor are represented by more than one selection. Important pronouncements on political and social questions by AE, Douglas Hyde, Padraic Pearse, and James Connolly serve to remind the reader that good Irish writing is not confined to belles-lettres. About one-third of the 43 selections by 30 authors have never been published in the U.S. before.

This is the first time that the very essence of the Irish Literary Revival has been placed between the covers of a single volume. It is a pioneer undertaking and should prove something of a landmark.

# 1000 YEARS OF IRISH PROSE

THE LITERARY REVIVAL

EDITED WITH AN INTRODUCTION BY
VIVIAN MERCIER AND
DAVID H. GREENE

*The Universal Library*

GROSSET & DUNLAP

NEW YORK

1000 YEARS OF IRISH PROSE. COPYRIGHT 1952

BY THE DEVIN-ADAIR COMPANY

PERMISSION TO REPRODUCE MATERIAL FROM THIS BOOK MUST BE OBTAINED IN WRITING FROM SPECIAL COPYRIGHT OWNERS AS LISTED ON THE ACKNOWLEDGMENT PAGES.

DRAMATIC RIGHTS TO THE PLAYS INCLUDED IN THIS BOOK ARE CONTROLLED BY SAMUEL FRENCH, INC., 25 WEST 45 ST., NEW YORK

UNIVERSAL LIBRARY EDITION 1961

BY ARRANGEMENT WITH THE DEVIN-ADAIR COMPANY

PRINTED IN THE UNITED STATES OF AMERICA

# ACKNOWLEDGMENTS

We gratefully acknowledge the advice and assistance of the following people: Padraic Colum, Oscar Cargill, John V. Kelleher, Horace Reynolds, Sean O'Casey, Daniel Corkery, Sean O'Faolain, John Slocum, James Laughlin, Conor Cruise O'Brien, Patrick K. Lynch, Desmond Ryan, Seamus Murphy, Seumas O'Sullivan, Sean Hendrick, Henry B. MacCurdy, Alphonsus Sweeney, Frank O'Connor, Peter Kavanagh, the staffs of The New York Public and The New York University libraries, our publisher Devin Garrity and his staff, and our wives Gina Mercier and Catherine Greene.

Permission to reprint material, hereby acknowledged, was kindly given by the following: The Macmillan Company for 'Maelshaughlinn at the Fair' from *Castle Conquer* (copyright 1923), 'Cathleen Ni Houlihan,' from *The Hour Glass and Other Plays* (copyright 1904, 1931), 'The Two Gods' from *The Crock of Gold* (copyright 1912, 1940), 'The Unworthy Princess' from *Here Are Ladies* (copyright 1913), 'The Shadow of a Gunman' (copyright 1925), and 'The Resurrection' from *Wheels & Butterflies* (copyright 1934); Random House for 'Preface to The Playboy of the Western World,' 'In the Shadow of the Glen,' and the first part of 'The Aran Islands' from *The Complete Works of John M. Synge* (copyright 1935), 'The Sirens' from *Ulysses* (copyright 1918, 1919, 1920 by Margaret Anderson; 1934 by The Modern Library); Alfred A. Knopf for 'The Bridal Night' from *Crab Apple Jelly* (copyright 1944) and 'First Confession' from *Traveller's Samples* (copyright 1951); Harcourt, Brace for 'Going into Exile' from *Spring Sowing and Other Stories* (copyright 1926); The Viking Press for 'Dead King' from *A Portrait of the Artist as a Young Man* (copyright 1916 by B. W. Huebsch, 1944 by Nora Joyce) and 'Midsummer Night Madness' from *Midsummer Night Madness and Other Stories* (copyright 1932); Charles Scribner's Sons for 'The Fate of the Sons of Usnach' taken from *Cuchulain of Muirthemne;* Professor Daniel Corkery and The Devin-Adair Co. for 'Rock-of-the-Mass' from *The Wager and Other Stories* (copyright 1950); Mr. Diarmuid Russell for 'The Dublin Strike'; Senator Margaret Pearse and The Talbot Press for 'The Coming Revolution' and 'At the Grave of O'Donovan Rossa' from *The*

*Collected Works of Padraic H. Pearse;* Mr. Desmond Ryan and The Irish Transport and General Workers' Union for 'What is our Programme?'; Mrs. Alan Cameron (Elizabeth Bowen) for 'An Evening in Anglo-Ireland' from *The Last September* (copyright 1929); Mr. Edward Sheehy and Mr. Seumas O'Sullivan for *God Send Sunday;* Mr. Liam O'Flaherty and Jacques Chambrun Inc. for 'The Wounded Cormorant' from *The Tent and Other Stories;* Mr. Austin Clarke for 'Gormlai and Cormac' from *The Singing Men at Cashel;* Mr. Michael McLaverty and the editors of *Irish Writing* for 'Six Weeks on and Two Ashore'; Mr. Francis Stuart and The Devin-Adair Co. for 'The Varied Shapes of Violence' from *Redemption* (copyright 1950); the estate of Miss Edith Somerville and Longmans, Green and Co., for 'The Holy Island' from some *Experiences of an Irish R. M.;* Mr. Michael O'Kelly for 'The Man with the Gift' from *The Golden Barque and The Weaver's Grave;* Mr. Patrick Kavanagh and Brandt and Brandt for 'The Grey Dawn' from *The Green Fool;* Mrs. Margaret O'Flaherty (Margaret Barrington) for 'Village Without Men' from *They Go, The Irish;* Mr. Brian O'Nolan (Flann O'Brien) and Pantheon Books for 'Mad Sweeny *versus* Jem Casey' from *At Swim-Two-Birds;* Mr. Brian O'Nolan (Myles na gCopaleen) and the editors of *Irish Writing* for 'Drink and Time in Dublin'; Mr. C. D. Medley for 'A Letter to Rome' from *The Untilled Field;* Mr. Oliver St. John Gogarty for 'Tall Hats and Churns' from *As I Was Going Down Sackville Street* (copyright 1937); Appleton-Century-Crofts for 'A Theological Fork' from *Hail and Farewell* (copyright 1911, 1912, 1914, 1925).

D. H. G.
V. M.

# CONTENTS

Acknowledgments .................................................... v
Introduction .......... David H. Greene and Vivian Mercier   ix

## OLD EIRE AND THE ANCIENT WAYS

| | | |
|---|---|---|
| Cathleen Ni Houlihan | W. B. Yeats | 3 |
| The Bardic History of Ireland | Standish O'Grady | 14 |
| The Knighting of Cuculain | Standish O'Grady | 30 |
| The Duel of Cuculain and Fardia | Standish O'Grady | 34 |
| The Death of Cuculain | Standish O'Grady | 39 |
| The Fate of the Sons of Usnach | Lady Gregory | 44 |
| The Two Gods | James Stephens | 73 |
| The Necessity for De-Anglicising Ireland | Douglas Hyde | 79 |

## THE LIVING WORLD FOR TEXT

| | | |
|---|---|---|
| Preface to The Playboy of the Western World | J. M. Synge | 93 |
| The Aran Islands | J. M. Synge | 94 |
| In the Shadow of the Glen | J. M. Synge | 142 |
| The Emigrant | Shan F. Bullock | 157 |
| A Letter to Rome | George Moore | 163 |
| A Theological Fork | George Moore | 175 |
| Dead King | James Joyce | 191 |
| Maelshaughlinn at the Fair | Padraic Colum | 203 |
| Rock-of-the-Mass | Daniel Corkery | 208 |

## OUR OWN RED BLOOD

| | | |
|---|---|---|
| The Dublin Strike | AE (George Russell) | 227 |
| The Coming Revolution | Padraic Pearse | 234 |
| At the Grave of O'Donovan Rossa | Padraic Pearse | 238 |
| What is Our Programme? | James Connolly | 240 |
| Proclamation of the Irish Republic | | 245 |
| The Shadow of a Gunman | Sean O'Casey | 247 |
| An Evening in Anglo-Ireland | Elizabeth Bowen | 294 |
| Midsummer Night Madness | Sean O'Faolain | 310 |
| God Send Sunday | Edward Sheehy | 344 |

## TURN ASIDE AND BROOD

| | | |
|---|---|---|
| Going Into Exile | Liam O'Flaherty | 369 |
| The Wounded Cormorant | Liam O'Flaherty | 379 |
| Gormlai and Cormac | Austin Clarke | 382 |
| The Bridal Night | Frank O'Connor | 406 |
| Six Weeks on and Two Ashore | Michael McLaverty | 413 |
| The Varied Shapes of Violence | Francis Stuart | 423 |

## WHERE MOTLEY IS WORN

| | | |
|---|---|---|
| The Holy Island | Somerville and Ross | 447 |
| The Unworthy Princess | James Stephens | 463 |
| The Man with the Gift | Seumas O'Kelly | 467 |
| Tall Hats and Churns | Oliver St. John Gogarty | 476 |
| The Grey Dawn | Patrick Kavanagh | 487 |
| Village Without Men | Margaret Barrington | 497 |
| Drink and Time in Dublin | Myles na gCopaleen | 509 |
| First Confession | Frank O'Connor | 516 |

## NO COUNTRY FOR OLD MEN

| | | |
|---|---|---|
| The Sirens | James Joyce | 527 |
| Mad Sweeny *versus* Jem Casey | Flann O'Brien | 563 |
| The Resurrection | W. B. Yeats | 583 |
| Notes on the Authors | | 595 |

# INTRODUCTION

When the publisher asked us to edit a two-volume collection modestly entitled *1000 Years of Irish Prose*, we had no hesitation in ignoring the mathematics of the thing and deciding to devote the first volume to the period of the Literary Revival, as our subtitle indicates. Having temporarily disposed of approximately 930 of our 1000 years, we faced the question of what kind of book this would be. Would it be one of those Cabinets or Treasuries one can still pick up at secondhand bookstores in broken sets and faded grandeur—Irish harps on the cover and blind Carolan for a frontispiece—designed to show the world what the Irish have always known, that half of the great writers in English literature, and a few other literatures besides, were Irishmen? If so, we had only to assemble snippets from as many writers as we could find who could safely be described as Irish, and our 'green branch hung with many a bell' would impress more by its length and variety than by the quality of its contents. Or would it be full of what Tom Broadbent in *John Bull's Other Island* called 'Irish charm,' which is to say saints, leprechauns, and 'the mist that does be on the bog'? If we scorned these conventional approaches, there was the chance that we might end up by thrusting at our readers one of those anthologies which present only what is unfamiliar and should have remained so.

Having scouted the terrain, in this instance an Irish bog where the ghost of Justin McCarthy dogged our footsteps, we came to the conclusion that we would be hanged for one thing as quickly as another and that we might satisfy more readers if we first satisfied ourselves. So our principles were formulated: first, no snippets. Second, we would offer what we considered the most readable and the most significant—if there is any distinction between the two—in Irish prose writing from the point where the Literary Revival may be said to have begun to the present day. We also decided that we were dealing with a body of writing which for the greater part of our period, say up to the death of Yeats, was informed by certain ideals held in common by most of the men and women who were doing the writing, that in fact we were dealing with a movement.

We are aware of the fact that the Literary Revival has recently been called a thing more of shadow than of substance and that one Dublin wit described the whole affair as nothing more than a group of writers who lived in the same town and hated each other cordially. We not only believe that the Literary Revival was a movement but also that its ideals were defined and its destination charted very largely by one man. There is more truth than irony in Sean O'Casey's description of William Butler Yeats as 'The Great Founder.'

Yeats, as you will see, is represented here by two plays which indicate the two extremes to which his career as a writer took him. *Cathleen Ni Houlihan*, which was first performed in 1902 with Maude Gonne in the title role, marks the real beginning of the Irish National Theatre. Nobody, even in 1902, pretended it was a great play, but it gave life once again to the Poor Old Woman who is Ireland herself and had an effect upon its audiences which neither they nor Yeats could ever forget.

> Did that play of mine send out
> Certain men the English shot?

In 1907, for example, he was able to silence a hostile audience which would not let him speak in defense of Synge's *Playboy* by shouting at them, 'The author of *Cathleen Ni Houlihan* addresses you.' Mary Colum, who was in that audience, tells us that 'The audience, remembering that passionately patriotic play, forgot its antagonism for a few minutes, and Yeats got his cheers.'

The other play of Yeats which we have chosen is *The Resurrection*, first performed at the Abbey Theatre in 1934. It is based on the strange philosophical system Yeats expounded in *A Vision* when his song was no longer 'a coat covered with embroideries out of old mythologies' and he had become a poet of major proportions and a Nobel prize winner. By this time the movement he had founded and was still dominating had gone through almost as many phases of existence as his twenty-eight phases of the moon, and even the Poor Old Woman, as we shall see presently, was finding the going much rougher.

Since we were anthologizing the prose writing of a distinct literary movement and its aftermath, we arranged the selections not in chronological order but in such a way as to show their relationship to each other and to the whole. The book is therefore divided into as many sections as the material itself suggested. And since the gigantic figure of Yeats dominated so much of modern Irish literature we have drawn our section headings from his poetry. But before we examine the literature itself, let us consider briefly what conditions helped to produce it and what sort of men its authors were.

## II

The new period of British colonization of Ireland which began under Queen Elizabeth and continued to the end of the seventeenth century created a fundamental schism in Irish life which has persisted to the present day. Where the old Anglo-Norman colonists of the twelfth century and after were largely assimilated by the prevailing Gaelic culture, and in any case shared the religion of the people they invaded, the new colonists set out to destroy the Gaelic culture they found *in situ;* they felt the less sympathy for it because it was associated in their minds with the Roman Catholic religion, which was regarded by both Scottish and English settlers as an abominable heresy. Thus, as in the Spanish conquest of South America, the normally selfish outlook of a colonizing group was reinforced by religious bigotry—as well as by genuine religious idealism. Intermarriage between colonizers and colonized, which had been the chief agency of Norman-Gaelic assimilation, was now out of the question. Religion, culture, political and economic status went hand in hand. Even in present-day Ireland the rough-and-ready equation of an Irish-Gaelic name with Roman Catholicism and peasant origins is more often right than wrong.

The eighteenth century was the century *par excellence* of Protestant Ascendancy in Ireland. Thanks to the destruction of the Gaelic aristocracy in the wars of the preceding century and the oppressive Penal Laws which denied most civil rights to Catholics, the Protestant aristocracy and middle class were left free to create an Anglo-Irish culture of their own if they could; but the competition offered by England was too strong. Too many of their best brains—Sheridan, Goldsmith, Burke—gravitated to London. The attempt to found an Anglo-Irish state met with no better success; the Irish Parliament, which had won itself some genuine independence of Britain in 1782, was extinguished by the Act of Union of 1800.

The events of the eighteenth century made it abundantly clear that if there was ever to be a distinctively Irish culture again, the Protestants alone could never provide it. The base of their cultural pyramid was altogether too narrow, while its apex was constantly being lopped off to be put to English uses. London had always been their cultural capital; when it became their political capital too, there seemed no possibility that the term 'Anglo-Irish' could ever come to have a valid meaning. Yet in retrospect we can see that nineteenth-century Irish history contains two seemingly contradictory trends. On the one hand, Protestantism, except in the North-east, steadily lost more and more of its economic and political power; the Irish Catholics, having found leaders among themselves for the first time in over a hundred years, regained their civil rights under Daniel O'Connell in 1829 and won back the ownership of the soil under Michael Davitt in the years 1879–1903. On the other hand, step by step with the decline of their economic and political power—perhaps even because of it—Irish Protestants developed a steadily growing interest in the Gaelic heritage of their adopted country. The Young Ireland movement begun by Thomas Davis and others in 1842 sought to base a nationalist movement of all creeds and classes upon a common interest in Irish history and tradition, but it came too soon; what the mass of the Irish people needed, as the Great Famine of 1846–1848 was soon to demonstrate, was a system of land tenure that would give them enough to eat. Until Ireland became a country of peasant proprietors, only the Protestants and a relatively few well-to-do Catholics were in a position to care for cultural—as opposed to political—nationalism. By 1893, when Douglas Hyde and others founded the non-political Gaelic League for the revival of the Irish language and the whole culture that went with it, times had changed: culture need no longer fear outright hunger as a competitor.

It will be convenient, as well as historically correct, to abandon here the embarrassing classifications of 'Catholic' and 'Protestant.' Instead we can speak of the Catholics as Irish, and separate the Protestants into Anglo-Irish—those whose loyalties were divided between Ireland and England—and Unionists—those, mainly in the four north-eastern counties of Antrim, Down, Derry and Armagh where there is still a Protestant majority, who gave undivided allegiance to the British crown.

As readers of Daniel Corkery's *The Hidden Ireland* know, Ireland was still producing Gaelic poets of genius in the eighteenth century; by the beginning of the nineteenth it seemed as though the Irish language might disappear for ever; before it did, a number of poets, Irish and Anglo-Irish, determined to translate at least some of its finer lyrics. We must also give credit to the historians, who were actually the first to translate Irish texts into English. But the real scope and grandeur of the Gaelic heritage was not made clear until about the middle of the nineteenth century, when the growth of modern philology made possible the editing and translation of the texts in Old Irish (i.e., the language as written before 900 A. D.). Not until the scholars, historians and translators had done their work could the great writers of the early part of the Revival —Yeats, Synge, Lady Gregory, Standish O'Grady—accomplish their astonishing feat of recreating, for readers of modern English, a literature and a mythology which had been moribund for nearly a thousand years. In the process they took a great step toward the healing of the schism, for it must be stressed that those whose names are singled out above, and the overwhelming majority of their first coadjutors, were Anglo-Irish. Two further steps were necessary to make the new literature representative, not of a narrow group only, nor of a glorious period in the remote past, but of the whole Irish people as it exists here and now. First, the new respect for the Gaelic past of Ireland must lead to a new respect for the Irish peasantry who were its legitimate heirs. Second, the country people themselves, or at least the more articulate among them, must become conscious of their heritage. These two steps were taken with astonishing rapidity. Half-a-dozen years after the founding of the Irish Literary Theatre in 1899, the 'peasant play' had become an established literary genre. Only twenty-five years after Synge paid his first visit to the Aran Islands to study the Irish language and observe the ways of the islanders who spoke it, one of those islanders, Liam O'Flaherty, published his first novel in English, beginning a literary career which was to win him a worldwide reputation—as wide as the distance from Hollywood to Moscow.

Since the earliest of our selections dates from 1878, the first to be considered among the movements which give the period its complexity and vigor is the Home Rule Movement. Founded in 1870 by Isaac Butt, an Anglo-Irish lawyer, it was dominated by the figure of an Anglo-Irish landlord, Charles Stuart Parnell, who became Chairman of the Irish Party at Westminster in 1878. Its object was to win, through the efforts of the Members of Parliament elected by Irish constituencies to the British House of Commons, a measure of self-government for Ireland that in retrospect appears little more liberating than U. S. statehood. By 1890 it had already become clear that nothing short of a reform of the House of Lords would force such a measure through the British legislature. In this year Parnell was cited as the adulterous co-respondent in the divorce action of Captain O'Shea, M. P., against his wife Kitty. The suit was not defended and the subsequent scandal ended Parnell's leadership and tore the Irish Party in pieces. Parnell died in the following year. Some of the repercussions of the scandal on Irish feeling may be read of in the selection from Joyce that we have titled 'Dead King.' An English Liberal Government that was prepared to abolish the veto of the House of Lords if necessary finally passed a Home Rule Act in 1914, but the implementing of its provisions was postponed until after World War I. By 1920 the Unionists of the six counties which now make up Northern Ireland were ready to accept the Home Rule program that they had solemnly sworn to resist to the death in 1912, while the rest of Ireland had lost all interest in Home Rule and was crying out for nothing less than national sovereignty, preferably as a Republic.

National sovereignty and complete separation from England had always been the aim of some Irishmen in every period since the Anglo-Norman invasion. The Irish Republican Brotherhood, a secret society founded in 1858, which had organized the abortive Fenian uprising of 1867, was still in being during our period, though few suspected its existence, while fewer still dreamed that Irishmen would ever rise in arms against Britain again. The Brotherhood in Dublin contained one indispensable link with the past, Tom Clarke, the old Fenian. In New York's Clan na Gael was another, John Devoy. But the final inspiration of the 1916 Rising, its Commander-in-Chief and President of the Provisional Government, was an ascetic schoolmaster and Gaelic enthusiast who joined the IRB as late as 1913, Padraic Pearse. Had Pearse not been a military and political leader, his rhetorical gift would still have won him a place in our anthology.

The IRB members as a group—whatever their individual opinions might be—were agreed that it would be time enough to decide exactly what shape the new Ireland ought to take *after* an All-Ireland Republic had fought its way out of the British Empire. But the leaders of a number of social and economic movements that were also at work during our period had determined to change the face of Ireland in their own time, even if the Union with Great Britain lasted till Doomsday.

The Land League, founded 1879, was the first of these movements to succeed; under the leadership of its founder Michael Davitt, a former Fenian and the son of an evicted tenant farmer, the tenant farmers of Ireland became a disciplined, organized army; they invented and used the technique of the boycott to bring recalcitrant landlords to heel. Helped by the Irish Party, they gained from the Land Act of 1881 the 'three F's'—fair rent, fixity of tenure, and free sale. The landlords, fearing that their rents would be progressively reduced by similar Acts in the future, began to favor a system of land purchase, whereby the British Government would finance the tenants' purchase of their estates. Wyndham's Land Act of 1903 was the most sweeping of the measures which implemented this policy of purchase; Davitt (d. 1906) lived to write a book entitled, quite accurately, *The Fall of Feudalism in Ireland*.

A movement that was predominantly urban and middle-class to begin with was Arthur Griffith's *Sinn Féin* (Gaelic for 'Ourselves'), founded in 1905. Griffith possessed the imagination of the utterly unimaginative; being in favor of an independent Ireland, he set about imagining what such an Ireland would be like: very like England, it turned out, with a merchant navy and many industries and two houses of parliament and even a king. Ireland was to form part of a dual monarchy with Britain, as Hungary did with Austria, and this end was to be achieved by passive resistance, as it had been in Hungary. The Irish were simply to start governing themselves one day, setting up their own executive, legislature and judiciary, and thenceforward to ignore the organs of British government in Ireland. For ten years and more Sinn Féin was a skeleton organization, chiefly advocating the development of native industries, until the execution of the 1916 leaders, coupled with the threat of conscription, turned the majority of the Irish people into separatists almost overnight. After the gory defeat of the Easter Rising, few wanted open war with Britain, but all sought a program more radical than that of the Irish Parliamentary Party, which had discredited itself by allowing Home Rule to be shelved while urging Irishmen to enlist in the British Army. Sinn Féin provided that program and the rudiments of a political machine. In the General

Election of December 1918 Sinn Féin candidates won 73 of the 106 Irish seats, refused to go to Westminster, and set up their own parliament, Dáil Eireann, in Dublin the next month. Eamon De Valera was elected President of the Irish Republic and he made Griffith his Minister for Home Affairs. Guerrilla warfare between the British forces in Ireland and the Irish Republican Army soon followed. The Truce of June 1921 led to the Anglo-Irish Treaty of December 1921, which Griffith signed as one of the plenipotentiaries. When the Dáil ratified the Treaty in spite of the opposition of De Valera and many others, Griffith became head of the Provisional Government set up to carry out the terms of the Treaty, and so first President of the Irish Free State. He died August 13, 1922, at the height of the civil war between his government and the De Valera party.

Two further politico-economic movements must be briefly mentioned, Trade Unionism and Agricultural Co-operation. The leading figure in the former was James Connolly, who with James Larkin introduced industrial—as opposed to craft—unionism into Ireland. Their Irish Transport and General Workers' Union is still the biggest in Ireland. When this union lost the bitterly fought Dublin Tramways strike in 1913, partly because the Dublin Metropolitan Police intervened aggressively on the employers' side, Connolly and Larkin founded the Irish Citizen Army, a workers' organization to protect the workers. The British Government was hardly in a position to suppress a private army of this type as long as it countenanced the Ulster Volunteers, formed in 1913 to resist Home Rule. The Irish Volunteers, later known as the Irish Republican Army, were organized the same year at the instigation of the IRB, ostensibly to defend Home Rule, but with the hope that they might ultimately play a much more aggressive role, as the Dublin units in fact did by carrying out the Easter Rising of 1916.

The Irish Agricultural Organization Society, founded by the Tory Sir Horace Plunkett, sought to promote farmers' and consumers' co-operatives, and to teach better farming methods in general. One of its organizers, AE, became the leading apostle for an entire national economy based on rural self-help, similar to the 'distributism' favored by G. K. Chesterton.

In a period that saw the formation of entirely new social classes and the growth of more daring national aspirations, no cultural movement could remain merely cultural and apolitical. Douglas Hyde resigned from the presidency of the Gaelic League in 1915, when the 'non-political' clause was voted out of its constitution, but in fact most of its members had always felt that the existence of the Irish language was one of the most compelling arguments for the independence of the Irish nation. In the League's early days its branches combined the gaiety of social clubs with the fervor of Communist cells. No conscientious listing of political and social movements, such as we have sought to give here, could lay claim to completeness while omitting to mention the more-than-cultural significance of the Gaelic League.

### III

To be typical of the authors who made their mark on Irish literature in the period 1880–1905 a man (or woman) must be born into an Anglo-Irish, Protestant family; Edward Martyn and George Moore are the chief exceptions to this rule, but they resemble Lady Gregory and the partnership of Somerville and Ross in belonging to the land-owning class. If our hypothetical author is not the son of a landlord, he must be the son or grandson of a Church of Ireland clergyman, like O'Grady, Yeats, Hyde and Synge. If of clerical descent, he is almost certain to have attended Trinity College, Dublin (O'Grady, Hyde, Synge). He is more at home in the countryside or in Dublin than in the provincial towns and cities, and has lived or studied for some time outside Ireland. His political views may belong anywhere from extreme Toryism leftwards, so long as they stop short of physical-force separatism, which would involve his seeking the blood of his friends and relations. Oddly, even if his politics are nationalist, he plays no part in the Irish Parliamentary Party's efficient machine. He usually draws his subject-matter from the myths, legends, folklore and history of Ireland's past rather than from contemporary Irish life. If he cannot make his living by writing or allied pursuits like editing, he does not seek another form of livelihood, but makes up the deficit with income from land or investments which he has inherited. (These generalizations do not apply to writers born in the province of Ulster, where a different social pattern already existed. AE and Shan F. Bullock, both Protestants, came of tenant-farming rather than land-owning parents; they had to earn their own livings from an early age, so that writing was for them an avocation.)

In contrast, the typical writer to win a reputation in the years 1905–25 is born into a Catholic family. Among the writers of that generation included in this anthology there are only two exceptions to this rule, Sean O'Casey and James Stephens; Lennox Robinson would be another; others would be hard to find outside the ranks of the poets. Our author may have been born in Dublin, like Joyce, O'Casey and Pearse, but is more likely to have seen the light in Cork or some little country town (Colum, O'Kelly, Connolly). He may or may not have had a college education, but it is a better than even chance that he must sooner or later earn his entire livelihood for a period as a primary—or secondary—school teacher (Joyce, Pearse, Corkery). He has been at some time an enthusiastic member of the Gaelic League, is probably a member or fellow-traveler of Sinn Féin, and, if he also belongs to the Volunteers or the Citizen Army, stands a reasonable chance of dying a violent death, like Pearse and Connolly. The writers of the previous generation would regard him as coming, at best, from the lower middle class. He may regard himself (Connolly, O'Casey) as belonging to the working class. Whatever his background, he has got to earn his living.

If his artistic life runs true to type, he will be a playwright, or at least write one play. Even Pearse, included here for his political writings, wrote several plays. The Abbey Theatre dominates the cultural landscape in this generation, only to lose its commanding position in the next. Our writer will draw his material from contemporary life, of which he is likely to be extremely critical.

Much that has been said of the writer of 1905–25 is true of his successor who came into prominence in the period 1925–50. He is typically a Catholic, born into a family more poor than rich; the small towns, however, are on the wane. If he was not born in Dublin or Cork, the chances are that he was born on a small farm (O'Flaherty, Kavanagh). He may even have been a native speaker of Gaelic like Liam O'Flaherty; at any rate he probably possesses a fluency in spoken Irish that even the fanatical Gaels of earlier generations might envy.

The writers of this third literary generation who were old enough at the time all took the De Valera (Republican) side in the Civil War; when their cause was defeated, several of them

(O'Faolain, O'Connor, Francis Stuart) spent some time in prison. Failure must have been hard to accept in those days, when we realize that almost all the earlier movements described above had met with astonishing success; thus we can say of the typical author of this period that he is likely to be a disillusioned realist or else prone to resolve the contradictions of the real world by transplanting them to a realm of comic fantasy. He may possibly have Socialist sympathies, be a 'bad Catholic,' and have had at least one of his books banned in the Republic of Ireland. Writing of one kind or another, eked out with a certain number of radio talks, may well provide him with his entire living, though many writers still do, or have done, their stint as teachers (O'Faolain, McLaverty, Clarke). Novels and volumes of short stories are likely to outnumber plays and books of verse in his creative output. If he has to earn his living solely by writing, his non-fiction titles may eventually outnumber all the rest put together. In fact, the Irish writer of today does not differ markedly from his counterpart in other countries. He regards his writing as a job, a profession; the amateurism of the early Revival, when writing was either a vocation or an avocation, has become a thing of the past. Much of the earlier writing undeniably bore the marks of its non-professional origin, but an astonishingly large proportion of it succeeded in being amateur without being amateurish.

The Anglo-Irish of the privileged classes, who initiated the Literary Revival, could not expect to retain permanently the cultural leadership that they had assumed in the movement's early days. What they could and did do—Synge perhaps most successfully of all —was to provide models that the Catholic Irish author could feel were native to Ireland and worthy of imitation. Even Joyce, who scorned purely Irish models in favor of European ones, learned more than he was prepared to admit from Yeats and Synge. You will find their cadences in *Finnegans Wake* if you read it aloud; nor should we forget that Joyce thought it worth while to translate into Italian Yeats' *The Countess Cathleen* and Synge's *Riders to the Sea*.

## IV

The literary movement which these forces and these writers produced is unique, if only for the fact that it achieved two things which could easily have cancelled each other. It made articulate the ideals of a people who were in the process of achieving political independence and of re-establishing their national identity, and at the same time it produced a literature capable of commanding respect independently of its geographical and political orientation. One does not need to be Irish or care a hoot for the most distressful country that ever yet was seen to realize that the Irish Literary Revival marks one of those rare moments in history when the writers were equal to the times and the times were worthy of the writers.

'A healthy nation,' wrote Bernard Shaw in 1906, 'is as unconscious of its nationality as a healthy man of his bones. But if you break a nation's nationality it will think of nothing else but getting it set again.' Small wonder that nationalism, the chief concern of the nation, became the chief inspiration of its writers. And yet the writers of the Revival managed to avoid the fate which befell the poets of *The Nation*—nationalists of a previous generation—who were similarly motivated: they inspired an insurgent nation by epitomizing its ideals, but they never became its propagandists. In fact they sometimes challenged the nationalist and his methods. The leading character in Sean O'Casey's *The Shadow of a Gunman* says, 'I draw the line when I hear the gunmen blowin' about dyin' for the people, when it's the people that are dyin' for the gunmen! With all due respect for the gunmen, I don't want them to die for me.'

This note of scepticism toward nationalist ideals, so conspicuous in a literature essentially nationalistic, did not escape the notice of friend or enemy. John Eglinton, himself a product of the movement, remarked that after 1916, the year of the Easter Rising, the Irish people did not wish to have their name associated with the so-called Irish Renaissance. From the enemy camp the Chief Secretary for Ireland, testifying before a Royal Commission set up in 1916 to investigate the causes of the Easter Rising, pointed out that while the writers on the whole fueled the fire that burned in Irish hearts for a free Ireland, at the same time they 'made fun of mad political enterprises and lashed with savage satire some historical aspects of the Irish Revolutionary. . . . This critical tone and temper was the deadly foe of that wild sentimental passion which has once more led too many brave young fellows to a certain doom in the belief that any revolution in Ireland is better than none.' And he added that if the World War had not intervened, this new critical temper might have prevailed to convince the people of the madness of insensate revolt. One can only add that such confidence in the power of poets to convince revolutionists must have been rare in English officials.

The writers, it seemed, were fighting their own war of independence in liberating themselves from the role of propagandist which they felt had been thrust upon them by circumstance and tradition. How else can one explain their determination to cut loose from the romantic conception of Ireland which they inherited from writers of previous generations. For example, where popular poets of the nineteenth century wrote patriotic love lyrics to Cathleen Ni Houlihan, the traditional symbol of Ireland, writers of the twentieth century too frequently wrote of her in the mood of Stephen Dedalus, who called her 'an old sow that eats her farrow.' There is a great gap between James Clarence Mangan's immortal 'Dark Rosaleen,'

> My Dark Rosaleen!
> My own Rosaleen!
> To hear your sweet and sad complaints,
> My life, my love, my saint of saints,
> My Dark Rosaleen!

and Louis MacNeice's insolent lines about the same lady:

> She is both a bore and a bitch;
>   Better close the horizon,
> Send her no more fantasy, no more longings which
>   Are under a fatal tariff.
> For common sense is the vogue
>   And she gives her children neither sense nor money
> Who slouch around the world with a gesture and a brogue
>   And a faggot of useless memories.

James Joyce, going further in this as in most things, portrayed Cathleen as the milk woman of *Ulysses*, with old shrunken paps, serving Haines and Mulligan, 'Her conqueror and her gay betrayer, their common cuckquean,' and probably as Kate Strong the scavenger woman of *Finnegans Wake,* whose cottage is full of 'Droppings of biddies, stinkend pusshies, moggies duggies, rotten witchawubbles, festering rubbages and beggars bullets.'

This repudiation of the cult of Cathleen reminds one of what Larry Doyle in *John Bull's Other Island* says about his fellow countryman. 'He can't be intelligently political: he dreams of what the Shan Van Vocht said in ninety-eight. If you want to interest him in Ireland you've got to call the unfortunate island Kathleen ni Hoolihan and pretend she's a little old woman. It saves thinking. It saves working. It saves everything except imagination.' Modern Irish writers have something of Larry Doyle's power of facing facts. If Cathleen Ni Houlihan sometimes impresses them as being 'an oul' bitch,' they prefer to call her just that.

Another function which they accepted unwillingly, if they ever accepted it, was the defense of the national character. They were expected to proclaim to the world that the 'stage Irishman' of tradition was a lie, or at least a travesty of the national character. But while they effectively demolished the myth of the 'stage Irishman,' they proceeded to create caricatures, when it pleased them, which were hardly much different from what they had demolished. Consequently Synge's patricidal Playboy and the wastrels of O'Casey's plays and O'Flaherty's stories of Dublin slum life were considered strange contributions to a literature which was expected to tell the world that all Irishmen were not ludicrous plowboys and bog-trotting Jeeter Lesters. And the price which had to be paid for this 'irresponsibility' was the *Playboy* riots, the 'demonstrations' over O'Casey's *The Plough and the Stars,* and the hostility of many American-Irish—*ipsis Hibernicis Hiberniores*—who insisted on evaluating Christy Mahon, Joxer Daly, and Gypo Nolan not as artistic creations but in terms of the effect they might have upon audiences outside Ireland. Small wonder that some of the writers have been denounced not as bad writers but as bad Irishmen, who have done a disservice to their country.

One gets a clear idea of the intensity of this pressure upon the writers in William Carleton, an Irish novelist of a hundred years ago, in whose *Traits and Stories of the Irish Peasantry,* as Daniel Corkery has said, under-educated Ireland discovered its own image. Carleton was quite as sensitive as any Irishman of his time to the ridicule implicit in the traditional treatment of Irish character on the English stage. But as a novelist he complained about what he called the 'pseudo-patriots' who were 'of the opinion that every writer, professing to depict our national character and manners, should make it a point of conscience to suppress all that is calculated to "lessen us in the eyes of the world," as they are pleased to term it, and only to give to the public the bright and favourable side. It is unnecessary to dwell upon the moral dishonesty and meanness of a principle, at once so disgraceful to literature and so repugnant to truth.' It remains only to be said that, despite his defiance, Carleton himself at times gave way to the 'pseudo-patriots' whose influence he deplored.

In fairness to the 'pseudo-patriots' it should be said that the Irish, who have lived through centuries of political indignity and of seeing themselves represented in caricatures, have a justifiable resentment at being laughed at through 'foreign jaws' or, what is worse, through the jaws of the native writer writing for an English public to whom such caricatures were amusing. Therefore it is sometimes difficult for them to realize that it is more important in our time, when nobody cares much about small nations anyway, that Ireland should produce a writer of genius like Synge, even if he took for his theme 'the villainy of Mayo and the fools that is there,' than a hundred poets like the one who wrote 'Bless the Dear Old Verdant Land.' Today students in American universities and people of culture everywhere are interested in modern Irish literature not because it either flatters or lessens the Irish in the eyes of the world, but because its achievement is formidable and significant. It produced two dramatists of genius in Synge and O'Casey, the most original and most controversial novelist of our generation in Joyce, and William Butler Yeats, whom T. S. Eliot described as 'the greatest poet of our time.'

Although the writers of the Revival who were of Ascendancy stock were at times critical of revolutionary methods, refused to look at Ireland through the sentimental mist of tradition, and considered themselves as something more than mere adjuncts of a political movement, they were basically sympathetic to nationalist ideals and in touch with the march of historical events. Being Irishmen all, they had a singleness of purpose which seemed at times to have been compounded of a medley of opposites. Yeats censured Maude Gonne's revolutionary zeal because she 'taught to ignorant men most violent ways'; he lashed out at Paudeen, and called Ireland a 'blind bitter land.' But he also wrote *Cathleen Ni Houli-*

*han*, saw Pearse summoning Cuchulain to his side in the terrible beauty that was born in 1916, and insisted on being accounted

> True brother of a company
> That sang, to sweeten Ireland's wrong. . . .

It was his achievement that he was able to discriminate between political and literary ideals. He could acknowledge the accomplishment of The Young Irelanders, the poets of *The Nation*, who were the real founders of modern Irish literature because they wrote for Irishmen on the basis of their own culture. But at the same time he could reject their influence because they subordinated literary to political ideals and in the end amounted to inferior poets. Yeats was right,

> Because, to him who ponders well,
> My rhymes more than their rhyming tell
> Of things discovered in the deep,
> Where only body's laid asleep.

Daniel Corkery has defined Irish literature as 'the literature written in the Irish language and that alone'; in his terminology all the selections we have included in this book would be rated 'Anglo-Irish,' though less than half of them were written by Anglo-Irish authors. This leads us to the paradoxical conclusion that the literature which expresses to the full the richness and tumult and glory of Irish life over the past seventy years—years during which Ireland made greater contributions to Western civilization than at any time since the beginning of the Danish invasions—does not itself deserve to be called Irish. Anybody who confined his reading about this period to works originally written in Gaelic would form a very meager idea indeed of its true depth and complexity. Ignoring Gaelic culture, as the Anglo-Irish did for so long, certainly impoverished Irish life to a degree that made literature or any other contribution to civilization by Ireland next to impossible; but to ignore that part of Ireland's heritage which finds expression in the English language would be an equal or even greater impoverishment. Ireland is not yet so rich in culture that she can afford to throw any of her inheritance away: Irish and British between them have squandered enough of it already. Ireland's greatest age in the past resulted from the marriage of two very different cultures—Latin Christianity and Gaelic paganism: is it then shameful to admit that her greatest age in modern times flowered from the cross-fertilization of Catholic Gaeldom with Protestant Englishry? Nowhere else in Europe, perhaps nowhere in the world, have Protestantism and Catholicism come to terms with such happy results—each borrowing the virtues of the other—as they did in Southern Ireland within the period covered by this book.

## V

The first section of this book takes its title from 'To the Rose upon the Rood of Time,'

> I would before my time to go
> Sing of Old Eire and the ancient ways

and celebrates the discovery of the Celtic past by offering, after Yeats' *Cathleen Ni Houlihan,* Standish O'Grady's renderings from the Red Branch (or Ulster) cycle of heroic tales which center on the hero Cuchulain, and his essay on the bardic history of Ireland. The effect these translations had upon the early writers of the Revival is acknowledged by AE's tribute to O'Grady: 'It was he who made me proud and conscious of my country.' Lady Gregory's *Cuchulain of Muirthemne,* which Synge described as 'part of my daily bread,' gives us our next selection—'The Fate of the Sons of Usnach'—also taken from the Red Branch cycle. For a freer use of Celtic mythology we offer James Stephens' portrayal of the victory of Angus Og over Pan, the Celtic god of love over the Greek, in the contention for the hand of Caitilin, from *The Crock of Gold.* Douglas Hyde's lecture delivered before The Irish Literary Society in 1892 on 'The Necessity for De-Anglicising Ireland' advocates a more pedestrian kind of return to the Celtic past by urging Irishmen to stop aping English manners and Anglicizing their names. Such a selection, we felt, would best illustrate Hyde's role as grass-roots propagandist of the Gaelic revival.

The title of the second section comes from 'In Memory of Major Robert Gregory,'

> And that enquiring man John Synge comes next,
> That dying chose the living world for text.

Here the interest is not in the dead Ireland of Cuchulain and Angus Og but the living Ireland of the average Irishman—the countryman in Synge, Shan F. Bullock, and Daniel Corkery, the country priest in George Moore's 'A Letter to Rome,' or Joyce's Dubliners fighting over the ghost of Parnell. The selection from *Hail and Farewell* is offered not only because it gives a truer picture of Moore's position than his short story but because it is obviously as artful a work of fiction as any short story he wrote.

In 'Our Own Red Blood,' its title from 'The Rose Tree,'

> 'But where can we draw water,'
> Said Pearse to Connolly,
> 'When all the wells are parched away?
> O plain as plain can be
> There's nothing but our own red blood
> Can make a right Rose Tree,'

we have a further kind of de-Anglicization—revolution: AE's two important utterances on the great Dublin strike of 1913, which has been called the first step on the road to Easter Week; Padraic Pearse's two notable speeches; James Connolly's famous editorial in *The Workers' Republic* which called for revolution so emphatically that he had to be kidnapped by the IRB and prevented from letting the cat out of the bag; and the Proclamation of the Irish Republic, probably composed by Pearse and Connolly. Sean O'Casey's *The Shadow of a Gunman* needs no comment beyond the fact that it dramatized the trench-coated figure in the slouch hat. The same figure appears in Elizabeth Bowen's 'An Evening in Anglo-Ireland with Undertones of War,' our title for a selection from her novel *The Last September*, and in Sean O'Faolain's 'Midsummer Night Madness,' both of which describe the impact of revolution upon the Big House, as O'Casey describes its effect on the slums. Edward Sheehy's story 'God Send Sunday,' which has not previously been published in this country, deals with the period of the Civil War.

In the next section it is not only upon love's bitter mystery that men brood, as in 'Who Goes With Fergus?'

> And no more turn aside and brood
> Upon love's bitter mystery . . .

but upon the new Ireland which some of them have viewed with disillusionment. Liam O'Flaherty, best known in this country for the movie which John Ford made of *The Informer*—not the best of his novels—is represented by his story 'Going Into Exile,' with its picture of an Irish mother who watches her son and daughter disappearing down the road on their way to exile in the New World. 'The Wounded Cormorant' is one of O'Flaherty's animal sketches, which are distinguished from his other works mostly by the fact that they deal directly with animals and not with the animal in man. Austin Clarke's 'Gormlai and Cormac,' our title for a passage taken from his prose romance *The Singing Men at Cashel*, is medieval in setting, like so much of his work, but has a modern application, one gathers. Frank O'Connor's 'Bridal Night' has, in addition to pathos, a note of impatience with Irish rural life, as does 'Six Weeks on and Two Ashore' by Michael McLaverty, a Catholic from Ulster. Francis Stuart's 'The Varied Shapes of Violence' is from his best novel *Redemption* and has for its setting Ireland after World War II.

In the next section, 'Where Motley Is Worn,' its title from 'Easter 1916,' the bitterness has yielded to humor, though it is frequently pointed with satire and even mockery. Somerville and Ross, who seem to have been oblivious to the Literary Revival, lead off with a story from *The Experiences of an Irish R. M.* 'The Holy Island' should prove that Somerville and Ross had an understanding of the peasant's attitude toward the law which Mr. Yeates their hero seems never to have acquired. James Stephens' 'The Unworthy Princess' distils all the calculated naïveté which is his hallmark. Seumas O'Kelly's 'The Man With The Gift,' while not as well known as 'The Weaver's Grave,' has a slyness all its own. 'First Confession,' from Frank O'Connor's most recent collection of short stories, is offered because it exhibits another side of his talent—an ability to write farce. No anthology of Irish writing would be complete without something from Oliver St. John Gogarty: 'Tall Hats and Churns' is our title for a selection from *As I Was Going Down Sackville Street*. Patrick Kavanagh's 'The Grey Dawn,' from his autobiography *The Green Fool*, is, we think, something of a documentary. Margaret Barrington's 'Village Without Men' is a visualization of another Danish invasion of Ireland. Myles na gCopaleen's 'Drink and Time in Dublin' was inspired by the movie *The Lost Weekend*. Myles na gCopaleen (Myles of the little horses) is a pen name, snatched from the pages of *The Collegians*, of Gerald Griffin, by Brian O'Nolan, *alias* (also) Flann O'Brien, who writes a humorous column in *The Irish Times*.

The title of the last section is from 'Sailing to Byzantium,'

> That is no country for old men. The young
> In one another's arms, birds in the trees . . .

The 'young' represented in this section are experimenters. The group is headed, naturally, by Joyce who, according to the story, may have come too late to influence Yeats, but not Flann O'Brien, whose *At Swim-Two-Birds*, a book-within-a-book-within-a-book, gives us 'Mad Sweeny *versus* Jem Casey.' The title of our last item, *The Resurrection*, suggests to us at least the possibility that if romantic Ireland did not die with O'Leary, it did with Yeats; and that if in the Ireland of today 'conduct and work grow coarse, and coarse the soul'—to misapply a line from one of his last poems—there are, as Myles na gCopaleen remarked, other Toms, other Moores, and one can hope that another Literary Revival is just around the corner.

Now for some apologies, or at least explanations. We are aware that in order to give substantial space to our thirty writers we had to exclude many others who deserve to be included. The most obvious omission is Paul Vincent Carroll. But three-act plays are the affliction of all anthologists, and neither *Shadow and Substance* nor *The White Steed* could be accommodated. The same thing was true of Lennox Robinson and Denis Johnston. We would also have liked to include a part of *John Bull's Other Island*, but Shaw always refused to allow any of his work to be anthologized.

As for ignoring, in our political section, De Valera, Arthur Griffith, and Michael Collins, we have little to explain. Both Griffith and Collins were more than articulate, but Griffith's best writing never rose above *ad hoc* journalism, and Collins was dead before he had had a chance to express himself adequately. Mr. De Valera's famous radio talk in defense of Irish wartime neutrality, however impressive it may have sounded when he delivered it, does not seem so impressive when seen in type.

We have not included any translations from contemporary Gaelic prose because we have found no qualities in such translations that are not already present in the English originals of certain bilingual authors. The Irish of Padraic O Conaire, for instance, has won high praise for its colloquial vigor, but the available translations sound academic and stilted. Maurice O'Sullivan's autobiographic *Twenty Years A-Growing* lost none of its vitality in translation, but there is little in the life it describes that is unfamiliar to readers of Liam O'Flaherty.

If our readers should wonder why, having included Ireland's 'Declaration of Independence,' the 1916 Proclamation of the Irish Republic, we have not included the preamble to Ireland's constitution, we can only say that the government of southern Ireland adopted two constitutions during its first twenty years and neither was accepted by the people with anything approaching unanimity. Probably no Irish children have ever been made to learn the preamble of either. What Irish children do learn by heart—Emmet's speech from the dock—awaits our next volume.

DAVID H. GREENE
VIVIAN MERCIER

*Part I*

# OLD EIRE AND THE ANCIENT WAYS

*I would, before my time to go,
Sing of Old Eire and the ancient ways . . .*
W. B. YEATS

WILLIAM BUTLER YEATS

# Cathleen Ni Houlihan[1]

### CHARACTERS

PETER GILLANE
MICHAEL GILLANE............*his son, going to be married*
PATRICK GILLANE.............*a lad of twelve, Michael's brother*
BRIDGET GILLANE.............*Peter's wife*
DELIA CAHEL................*engaged to Michael*
THE POOR OLD WOMAN
NEIGHBOURS

SCENE. *Interior of a cottage close to Killala, in 1798.* BRIDGET *is standing at a table undoing a parcel.* PETER *is sitting at one side of the fire,* PATRICK *at the other.*

*Peter.* What is that sound I hear?

*Patrick.* I don't hear anything. *[He listens]* I hear it now. It's like cheering. *[He goes to the window and looks out]* I wonder what they are cheering about. I don't see anybody.

*Peter.* It might be a hurling.

*Patrick.* There's no hurling to-day. It must be down in the town the cheering is.

*Bridget.* I suppose the boys must be having some sport of their own. Come over here, Peter, and look at Michael's wedding-clothes.

*Peter. [shifts his chair to table].* Those are grand clothes, indeed.

*Bridget.* You hadn't clothes like that when you married me, and no coat to put on of a Sunday more than any other day.

*Peter.* That is true, indeed. We never thought a son of our own would be wearing a suit of that sort for his wedding, or have so good a place to bring a wife to.

*Patrick. [who is still at the window].* There's an old woman coming down the road. I don't know is it here she is coming.

*Bridget.* It will be a neighbour coming to hear about Michael's wedding. Can you see who it is?

---
[1] First performed April 2, 1902 at the Hall of St. Theresa's, Clarendon St., Dublin, by W. G. Fay's Irish National Dramatic Company.

*Patrick.* I think it is a stranger, but she's not coming to the house. She's turned into the gap that goes down where Maurteen and his sons are shearing sheep. *[He turns towards* BRIDGET*]* Do you remember what Winny of the Cross Roads was saying the other night about the strange woman that goes through the country whatever time there's war or trouble coming?

*Bridget.* Don't be bothering us about Winny's talk, but go and open the door for your brother. I hear him coming up the path.

*Peter.* I hope he has brought Delia's fortune with him safe, for fear her people might go back on the bargain and I after making it. Trouble enough I had making it.

(PATRICK *opens the door and* MICHAEL *comes in*)

*Bridget.* What kept you, Michael? We were looking out for you this long time.

*Michael.* I went round by the priest's house to bid him be ready to marry us to-morrow.

*Bridget.* Did he say anything?

*Michael.* He said it was a very nice match, and that he was never better pleased to marry any two in his parish than myself and Delia Cahel.

*Peter.* Have you got the fortune, Michael?

*Michael.* Here it is.

(MICHAEL *puts bag on table and goes over and leans against chimney-jamb.* BRIDGET, *who has been all this time examining the clothes, pulling the seams and trying the lining of the pockets, etc., puts the clothes on the dresser*)

*Peter. [getting up and taking the bag in his hand and turning out the money].* Yes, I made the bargain well for you, Michael. Old John Cahel would sooner have kept a share of this a while longer. 'Let me keep the half of it until the first boy is born,' says he. 'You will not,' says I. 'Whether there is or is not a boy, the whole hundred pounds must be in Michael's hands before he brings your daughter to the house.' The wife spoke to him then, and he gave in at the end.

*Bridget.* You seem well pleased to be handling the money, Peter.

*Peter.* Indeed, I wish I had had the luck to get a hundred pounds, or twenty pounds itself, with the wife I married.

*Bridget.* Well, if I didn't bring much I didn't get much. What had you the day I married you but a flock of hens and you feeding them, and a few lambs and you driving them to the market at Ballina? *[She is vexed and bangs a jug on the dresser]* If I brought no fortune, I worked it out in my bones, laying down the baby, Michael that is standing there now, on a stook of straw, while I dug the potatoes, and never asking big dresses or anything but to be working.

*Peter.* That is true, indeed.

(*He pats her arm*)

*Bridget.* Leave me alone now till I ready the house for the woman that is to come into it.

*Peter.* You are the best woman in Ireland, but money is good, too. *[He begins handling the money again and sits down]* I never thought to see so much money within my four walls. We can do great things now we have it. We can take the ten acres of land we have the chance of since Jamsie Dempsey died, and stock it. We will go to the fair at Ballina to buy the stock. Did Delia ask any of the money for her own use, Michael?

*Michael.* She did not, indeed. She did not seem to take much notice of it, or to look at it at all.

*Bridget.* That's no wonder. Why would she look at it when she had yourself to look at, a fine, strong young man? It is proud she must be to get you; a good steady boy that will make use of the money, and not be running through it or spending it on drink like another.

*Peter.* It's likely Michael himself was not thinking much of the fortune either, but of what sort the girl was to look at.

*Michael.* *[coming over towards the table].* Well, you would like a nice comely girl to be beside you, and to go walking with you. The fortune only lasts for a while, but the woman will be there always.

*Patrick.* *[turning round from the window].* They are cheering again down in the town. Maybe they are landing horses from Enniscrone. They do be cheering when the horses take the water well.

*Michael.* There are no horses in it. Where would they be going and no fair at hand? Go down to the town, Patrick, and see what is going on.

*Patrick.* [*opens the door to go out, but stops for a moment on the threshold*]. Will Delia remember, do you think, to bring the greyhound pup she promised me when she would be coming to the house?

*Michael.* She will surely.

(PATRICK *goes out, leaving the door open*)

*Peter.* It will be Patrick's turn next to be looking for a fortune, but he won't find it so easy to get it and he with no place of his own.

*Bridget.* I do be thinking sometimes, now things are going so well with us, and the Cahels such a good back to us in the district, and Delia's own uncle a priest, we might be put in the way of making Patrick a priest some day, and he so good at his books.

*Peter.* Time enough, time enough. You have always your head full of plans, Bridget.

*Bridget.* We will be well able to give him learning, and not to send him tramping the country like a poor scholar that lives on charity.

*Michael.* They're not done cheering yet.

(*He goes over to the door and stands there for a moment, putting up his hand to shade his eyes*)

*Bridget.* Do you see anything?

*Michael.* I see an old woman coming up the path.

*Bridget.* Who is it, I wonder? It must be the strange woman Patrick saw a while ago.

*Michael.* I don't think it's one of the neighbours anyway, but she has her cloak over her face.

*Bridget.* It might be some poor woman heard we were making ready for the wedding and came to look for her share.

*Peter.* I may as well put the money out of sight. There is no use leaving it out for every stranger to look at.

(*He goes over to a large box in the corner, opens it and puts the bag in and fumbles at the lock*)

*Michael.* There she is, father! [*An* OLD WOMAN *passes the window slowly. She looks at* MICHAEL *as she passes*] I'd sooner a stranger not to come to the house the night before my wedding.

*Bridget.* Open the door, Michael; don't keep the poor woman waiting.

(*The* OLD WOMAN *comes in.* MICHAEL *stands aside to make way for her*)

*Old Woman.* God save all here!

*Peter.* God save you kindly!

*Old Woman.* You have good shelter here.

*Peter.* You are welcome to whatever shelter we have.

*Bridget.* Sit down there by the fire and welcome.

*Old Woman.* [*warming her hands*]. There is a hard wind outside.

(MICHAEL *watches her curiously from the door.* PETER *comes over to the table*)

*Peter.* Have you travelled far today?

*Old Woman.* I have travelled far, very far; there are few have travelled so far as myself, and there's many a one that doesn't make me welcome. There was one that had strong sons I thought were friends of mine, but they were shearing their sheep, and they wouldn't listen to me.

*Peter.* It's a pity indeed for any person to have no place of their own.

*Old Woman.* That's true for you indeed, and it's long I'm on the roads since I first went wandering.

*Bridget.* It is a wonder you are not worn out with so much wandering.

*Old Woman.* Sometimes my feet are tired and my hands are quiet, but there is no quiet in my heart. When the people see me quiet, they think old age has come on me and that all the stir has gone out of me. But when the trouble is on me I must be talking to my friends.

*Bridget.* What was it put you wandering?

*Old Woman.* Too many strangers in the house.

*Bridget.* Indeed you look as if you'd had your share of trouble.

*Old Woman.* I have had trouble indeed.

*Bridget.* What was it put the trouble on you?

*Old Woman.* My land that was taken from me.

*Peter.* Was it much land they took from you?

*Old Woman.* My four beautiful green fields.

*Peter.* [Aside to BRIDGET] Do you think could she be the widow Casey that was put out of her holding at Kilglass a while ago?

*Bridget.* She is not. I saw the widow Casey one time at the market in Ballina, a stout fresh woman.

*Peter.* [To OLD WOMAN] Did you hear a noise of cheering, and you coming up the hill?

*Old Woman.* I thought I heard the noise I used to hear when my friends came to visit me.

(*She begins singing half to herself*)

> I will go cry with the woman,
> For yellow-haired Donough is dead,
> With a hempen rope for a neckcloth,
> And a white cloth on his head,—

*Michael.* [coming from the door]. What is it that you are singing, ma'am?

*Old Woman.* Singing I am about a man I knew one time, yellow-haired Donough that was hanged in Galway.

(*She goes on singing, much louder*)

> I am come to cry with you, woman,
> My hair is unwound and unbound;

> I remember him ploughing his field,
> Turning up the red side of the ground,
> And building his barn on the hill
> With the good mortared stone;
> O! we'd have pulled down the gallows
> Had it happened in Enniscrone!

*Michael.* What was it brought him to his death?

*Old Woman.* He died for love of me: many a man has died for love of me.

*Peter.* [*Aside to* BRIDGET] Her trouble has put her wits astray.

*Michael.* Is it long since that song was made? Is it long since he got his death?

*Old Woman.* Not long, not long. But there were others that died for love of me a long time ago.

*Michael.* Were they neighbours of your own, ma'am?

*Old Woman.* Come here beside me and I'll tell you about them. [MICHAEL *sits down beside her on the hearth*] There was a red man of the O'Donells from the north, and a man of the O'Sullivans from the south, and there was one Brian that lost his life at Clontarf by the sea, and there were a great many in the west, some that died hundreds of years ago, and there are some that will die to-morrow.

*Michael.* Is it in the west that men will die to-morrow?

*Old Woman.* Come nearer, nearer to me.

*Bridget.* Is she right, do you think? Or is she a woman from beyond the world?

*Peter.* She doesn't know well what she's talking about, with the want and the trouble she has gone through.

*Bridget.* The poor thing, we should treat her well.

*Peter.* Give her a drink of milk and a bit of the oaten cake.

*Bridget.* Maybe we should give her something along with that, to bring her on her way. A few pence, or a shilling itself, and we with so much money in the house.

*Peter.* Indeed I'd not begrudge it to her if we had it to spare, but if we go running through what we have, we'll soon have to break the hundred pounds, and that would be a pity.

*Bridget.* Shame on you, Peter. Give her the shilling, and your blessing with it, or our own luck will go from us.

(PETER *goes to the box and takes out a shilling*)

*Bridget.* [*To the* OLD WOMAN] Will you have a drink of milk, ma'am?

*Old Woman.* It is not food or drink that I want.

*Peter.* [*offering the shilling*]. Here is something for you.

*Old Woman.* That is not what I want. It is not silver I want.

*Peter.* What is it you would be asking for?

*Old Woman.* If anyone would give me help he must give me himself, he must give me all.

(PETER *goes over to the table staring at the shilling in his hand in a bewildered way, and stands whispering to* BRIDGET)

*Michael.* Have you no one to care for you in your age, ma'am?

*Old Woman.* I have not. With all the lovers that brought me their love I never set out the bed for any.

*Michael.* Are you lonely going the roads, ma'am?

*Old Woman.* I have my thoughts and I have my hopes.

*Michael.* What hopes have you to hold to?

*Old Woman.* The hope of getting my beautiful fields back again; the hope of putting the strangers out of my house.

*Michael.* What way will you do that, ma'am?

*Old Woman.* I have good friends that will help me. They are gathering to help me now. I am not afraid. If they are put down to-day they will get the upper hand to-morrow. [*She gets up*] I must be going to meet my friends. They are coming to help me and I must be there to welcome them. I must call the neighbours together to welcome them.

*Michael.* I will go with you.

*Bridget.* It is not her friends you have to go and welcome, Michael; it is the girl coming into the house you have to welcome. You have plenty to do; it is food and drink you have to bring to the house. The woman that is coming home is not coming with empty hands; you would not have an empty house before her. *[To the* OLD WOMAN*]* Maybe you don't know, ma'am, that my son is going to be married to-morrow.

*Old Woman.* It is not a man going to his marriage that I look to for help.

*Peter.* *[To* BRIDGET*].* Who is she, do you think, at all?

*Bridget.* You did not tell us your name yet, ma'am.

*Old Woman.* Some call me the Poor Old Woman, and there are some that call me Cathleen, the daughter of Houlihan.[1]

*Peter.* I think I knew some one of that name once. Who was it, I wonder? It must have been some one I knew when I was a boy. No, no; I remember, I heard it in a song.

*Old Woman.* *[who is standing in the doorway].* They are wondering that there were songs made for me; there have been many songs made for me. I heard one on the wind this morning.

(*She sings*)
>Do not make a great keening
>When the graves have been dug to-morrow.
>Do not call the white-scarfed riders
>To the burying that shall be to-morrow.
>
>Do not spread food to call strangers
>To the wakes that shall be to-morrow;
>Do not give money for prayers
>For the dead that shall die to-morrow . . .

they will have no need of prayers, they will have no need of prayers.

*Michael.* I do not know what that song means, but tell me something I can do for you.

*Peter.* Come over to me, Michael.

*Michael.* Hush, father, listen to her.

*Old Woman.* It is a hard service they take that help me. Many that are red-cheeked now will be pale-cheeked; many that have been free to walk the hills and the bogs and the rushes will be sent to walk hard streets in far countries; many a good plan will

---
[1] A traditional personification of Ireland.

be broken; many that have gathered money will not stay to spend it; many a child will be born and there will be no father at its christening to give it a name. They that have red cheeks will have pale cheeks for my sake, and for all that, they will think they are well paid.

(*She goes out; her voice is heard outside singing*)

> They shall be remembered for ever,
> They shall be alive for ever,
> They shall be speaking for ever,
> The people shall hear them for ever.

*Bridget.* [*To* PETER] Look at him, Peter; he has the look of a man that has got the touch. [*Raising her voice*] Look here, Michael, at the wedding-clothes. Such grand clothes as these are. You have a right to fit them on now; it would be a pity to-morrow if they did not fit. The boys would be laughing at you. Take them, Michael, and go into the room and fit them on.

(*She puts them on his arm*)

*Michael.* What wedding are you talking of? What clothes will I be wearing to-morrow?

*Bridget.* These are the clothes you are going to wear when you marry Delia Cahel to-morrow.

*Michael.* I had forgotten that.

(*He looks at the clothes and turns towards the inner room, but stops at the sound of cheering outside*)

*Peter.* There is the shouting come to our own door. What is it has happened?

(PATRICK *and* DELIA *come in*)

*Patrick.* There are ships in the Bay; the French are landing at Killala![1]

(PETER *takes his pipe from his mouth and his hat off, and stands up. The clothes slip from* MICHAEL'S *arm*)

---
[1] This was the French expedition under General Humbert sent to assist the Irish rebels, but it proved too little and too late.

*Delia.* Michael! *[He takes no notice]* Michael! *[He turns towards her]* Why do you look at me like a stranger?

(*She drops his arm.* BRIDGET *goes over towards her*)

*Patrick.* The boys are all hurrying down the hillside to join the French.

*Delia.* Michael won't be going to join the French.

*Bridget.* *[To* PETER*]* Tell him not to go, Peter.

*Peter.* It's no use. He doesn't hear a word we're saying.

*Bridget.* Try and coax him over to the fire.

*Delia.* Michael! Michael! You won't leave me! You won't join the French, and we going to be married!

(*She puts her arms about him, he turns towards her as if about to yield.* OLD WOMAN'S *voice outside*)

>    They shall be speaking for ever,
>    The people shall hear them for ever.

(MICHAEL *breaks away from* DELIA, *stands for a second at the door, then rushes out, following the* OLD WOMAN'S *voice.* BRIDGET *takes* DELIA, *who is crying silently, into her arms*)

*Peter.* *[To* PATRICK, *laying a hand on his arm]* Did you see an old woman going down the path?

*Patrick.* I did not, but I saw a young girl, and she had the walk of a queen.

CURTAIN

# STANDISH O'GRADY

# The Bardic History of Ireland[1]

## DAWN

THERE IS not perhaps in existence a product of the human mind so extraordinary as the Irish annals. From a time dating for more than three thousand years before the birth of Christ, the stream of Hibernian history flows down uninterrupted, copious and abounding, between accurately defined banks, with here and there picturesque meanderings, here and there flowers lolling on those delusive waters, but never concealed in mists or lost in a marsh. As the centuries wend their way, king succeeds king with a regularity most gratifying, and fights no battle, marries no wife, begets no children, does no doughty deed of which a contemporaneous note was not taken, and which has not been incorporated in the annals of his country. To think that this mighty fabric of recorded events, so stupendous in its dimensions, so clean and accurate in its details, so symmetrical and elegant, should be after all a mirage and delusion, a gorgeous bubble, whose glowing rotundity, whose rich hues, azure, purple, amethyst and gold, vanish at a touch and are gone, leaving a sorry remnant over which the patriot disillusionized may grieve.

Early Irish history is the creation mainly of the bards. Romances and poems supplied the great blocks with which the fabric was reared. These the chroniclers fitted into their places, into the interstices pouring shot-rubbish, and grouting. The bardic intellect, revolving round certain ideas for centuries, and round certain material facts, namely, the mighty barrows of their ancestors, produced gradually a vast body of definite historic lore, life-like kings and heroes, real-seeming queens. The mechanical intellect followed with perspicuous arrangement, with a thirst for accuracy, minuteness, and verisimilitude. With such quarrymen and such builders the work went on apace, and anon a fabric huge rose like an exhalation, and like an exhalation its towers and pinnacles of empurpled mist are blown asunder and dislimn.

[1] From *History of Ireland: Critical and Philosophical*, Volume I, London and Dublin, 1881.

Doubtless the legendary blends at some point with the historic narrative. The cloud and mist somewhere condense into the clear stream of indubitable fact. But how to discern under the rich and teeming mythus of the bards, the course of that slender and doubtful rivulet, or beneath the piled rubbish and dust of the chroniclers, discover the tiny track which elsewhere broadens into the highway of a nation's history. In this minute, circumstantial, and most imposing body of history, where the certain legend exhibits the form of plain and probable narrative, and the certain fact displays itself with a mythical flourish, how there to fix upon any one point and say here is the first truth. It is a task perilous and perplexing.

Descartes commenced his investigations into the nature of the soul, by assuming the certainty of his own existence. Standing upon this adamantine foothold, he sought around him for ground equally firm, which should support his first step in the quagmire of metaphysics. But in the early Irish history, what one solid and irrefutable fact appears upon which we can put foot or hand and say, 'This, at all events, is certain; this that I hold is not mist; this that I stand on is neither water nor mire?' Running down the long list of Milesian kings, chiefs, brehons, and bards, where first shall we pause, arrested by some substantial form in this procession of empty ghosts—how distinguish the man from the shadow, when over all is diffused the same concealing mist, and the eyes of the living and the dead look with the same pale glare? Eocha of the heavy sighs, how shall we certify or how deny the existence of that melancholy man, or of Tiernmas, who introduced the worship of fire? Lara of the ships, did he really cross the sea to Gaul, and return thence to give his name to Leinster, and beget Leinster kings? Ugainey More, did he rule to the Torrian sea, holding sea-coast towns in fee, or was he a prehistoric shadow thrown into the past from the stalwart figure of Niall of the Hostages? Was Morann a real brehon, or fabulous as the collar that threatened to strangle him in the utterances of unjust judgments? Was Ferkeirtney a poet, having flesh and bones and blood, and did Bricrind, the satirist, really compose those bitter ranns[1] for the Ultonians? or were both as ghostly as the prime druid, Amergin, who came into the island with the sons of Milesius, and in a manner beyond all praise, collected the histories of the conquered peoples? Or do we wrong

---

[1] Verses.

that venerable man whose high-sounding name clung for ages around the estuary of the Avoca?

One thing at all events we cannot deny—that the national record is at least lively. Clear noble shapes of kings and queens, chieftains, brehons, and bards gleam in the large rich light shed abroad over the triumphant progress of the legendary tale. We see Duns[1] snow-white with roofs striped crimson and blue, chariots cushioned with noble skins, with bright bronze wheels and silver poles and yokes. The lively-hearted, resolute steeds gallop past, bearing the warrior and his charioteer with the loud clangour of rattling spears and darts. As in some bright young dawn, over the dewy grass, and in the light of the rising sun, superhuman in size and beauty, their long, yellow hair curling on their shoulders, bound around the temples with torcs of gold, clad in white linen tunics, and loose brattas of crimson silk fastened on the breast with huge wheel brooches of gold, their long spears musical with running rings; with naked knees and bare crown, they cluster round their kings, the chieftains and knights of the heroic age of Ireland.

The dawn of history is like the dawn of the day. The night of the pre-historic epoch grows rare, its dense weight is relaxed; flakes of fleeting and uncertain light wander and vanish; vague shapes of floating mist reveal themselves, gradually assuming form and colour; faint hues of crimson, silver, and gold strike here and there, and the legendary dawn grows on. But the glory of morn though splendid is unsubstantial; the glory of changing and empurpled mist—vapours that conceal the solid face of nature, the hills, trees, streams, and the horizon, holding between us and the landscape a concealing veil, through whose close woof the eye cannot penetrate, and over all a weird strange light.

In the dawn of the history of all nations we see this deceptive light, those glorious and unearthly shapes; before Grecian history, the gods and demigods who fought around Ilium; before Roman, the strong legends of Virginius and Brutus; in the dawn of Irish history, the Knights of the Red Branch, and all the glory that surrounded the Court of Concobar Mac Nessa, High King of the Ultonians.

But of what use these concealing glories, these cloudy warriors, and air-built palaces? Why not pass on at once to credible history?

A nation's history is made for it by circumstances, and the irre-

---
[1] Fortified dwellings.

sistible progress of events; but their legends, they make for themselves. In that dim twilight region, where day meets night, the intellect of man, tired by contact with the vulgarity of actual things, goes back for rest and recuperation, and there sleeping, projects its dreams against the waning night and before the rising of the sun.

The legends represent the imagination of the country; they are that kind of history which a nation desires to possess. They betray the ambition and ideals of the people and, in this respect, have a value far beyond the tale of actual events and duly recorded deeds, which are no more history than a skeleton is a man. Nay, too, they have their own reality. They fill the mind with an adequate and satisfying pleasure. They present a rhythmic completeness and a beauty not to be found in the fragmentary and ragged succession of events in time. Achilles and Troy appear somehow more real than Histiaeus and Miletus, Cuculain[1] and Emain Macha than Brian Boru and Kincora.

Such is the effect produced by a sympathetic and imaginative study of the bardic literature, the critical faculty being for a time held in abeyance, but with its inevitable reappearance and reassertion of its rights, that gorgeous world, with all its flashing glories, dissolves like a dream, or is held together only by a resolute suppression of all disturbing elements. If we endeavour to realise, vividly and as a whole, the early ages and personages of Irish history, piercing below the annals, studying them in connection with the imaginative literature, using everywhere a strict and critical eye, and demanding that verisimilitude and underlying harmony which we look for in modern historical romance, imagination itself wavers and fails. Here is a splendid picture, complete in all its parts, fully satisfying the imagination; but yonder is another, and the two will not harmonize; or here is a fact stated, and the picture contradicts the fact. So contemplated, the historic track, clear and definite in the annals, viewed through the medium of the bardic literature, is doubtful and elusive in the extreme. Spite its splendid appearance in the annals, it is thin, legendary, evasive. Looked at with the severe eyes of criticism, the broad walled highway of the old historians, on which pass many noble figures of kings and queens, brehons, bards, kerds and warriors, legislators and druids, real-seeming antique shapes of men and women, marked by many a cairn, piled above heroes, illustrious with battles, elections, con-

---
[1] Pronounced Coo-húll-in.

ventions, melts away into thin air. The glare of bardic light flees away; the broad, firm highway is torn asunder and dispersed; even the narrow, doubtful track is not seen; we seem to foot it hesitatingly, anxiously, from stepping-stone to stepping-stone set at long distance in some quaking Cimmerian waste. But all around, in surging, tumultuous motion, come and go the gorgeous, unearthly beings that long ago emanated from bardic minds, a most weird and mocking world. Faces rush out of the darkness, and as swiftly retreat again. Heroes expand into giants, and dwindle into goblins, or fling aside the heroic form and gambol as buffoons; gorgeous palaces are blown asunder like a smoke-wreath; kings, with wand of silver and ard-roth[1] of gold, move with all their state from century to century; puissant heroes, whose fame reverberates through and sheds a glory over epochs, approach and coalesce; battles are shifted from place to place and century to century; buried monarchs reappear, and run a new career of glory. The explorer visits an enchanted land where he is mocked and deluded. Everything seems blown loose from its fastenings. All that should be most stable is whirled round and borne away like foam or dead leaves in a storm.

But with the cessation of this creative bardic energy, what a deposit and residuum for the annalists. Consider the great work of the Four Masters, as it treats of this period, that strange sarcophagus filled with the imagined dust of visionary hosts. There lies a vast silent land, a land of the dead, a vast continent of the dead, lit with pale phosphoric radiance. The weird light that surges round us elsewhere has passed away from that land. The phantasmal energy has ceased there—the transmutation scenes that mock, the chaos, and the whirlwind. There, too, at one time, the same phantasmagoria prevailed, real-seeming warriors thundered, kings glittered, kerds wrought, harpers harped, chariots rolled. But all that has passed away. Reverent hands, to whom that phantasmal world was real, decently composed and laid aside in due order the relics and anatomies of those airy nations, building over each hero his tomb, and setting up his gravestone, piously graving the year of his death and birth, and his battles. There they repose in their multitudes in ordered and exact numbers and relation, reaching away into the dim past to the edge of the great deluge, and beyond it; there the Queen Ceasair and her comrades, pre-Noachian wander-

---
[1] The royal orb.

ers; there Fintann, who lived on both sides of the great flood, and roamed the depths when the world was submerged; there Partholanus and his ill-starred race—the chroniclers know them all; there the children of Nemed in their own Golgotha, their stones all carefully lettered, these not so ancient as the rest, only three thousand years before the birth of Christ; there the Clan Fomor, a giant race, and the Firbolgs with their correlatives, Fir-Domnan and Fir-Gaileen—the Tuatha De Danaan, whom the prudent annalist condemns to a place amongst the dead—a divine race, they will not die—they flee afar, preferring their phantasmal life; even the advent of the Talkend [1] will not slay them, though their glory suffers eclipse before the new faith. The children of Milith are there with their long ancestry reaching to Egypt and the Holy Land—Heber, Heremon, Amergin, Ir, with all their descendants, each beneath his lettered stone; Tiernmas and Moh Corb, Ollav Fohla, their lines descending through many centuries; all put away and decently composed for ever. No confusion now, no dissolving scenes or aught that shocks and disturbs, no conflicting events and incredible re-appearances. Chronology is respected. The critical and historical intellect has provided that all things shall be done rightly and in order, that the obits and births and battles should be natural and imposing, and worthy of the annals of an ancient people.

And thus, regarding the whole from a point of view sufficiently remote, a certain epic completeness and harmony characterizes that vast panoramic succession of ages and races.

### Rath[2] and Cairn Germs of the History

Scattered over the surface of every country in Europe may be found sepulchral monuments, the remains of pre-historic times and nations, and of a phase of life and civilization which has long since passed away. No country in Europe is without its cromlechs and dolmens, huge earthen tumuli, great flagged sepulchres, and enclosures of tall pillar-stones. The men by whom these works were made, so interesting in themselves, and so different from anything of

---

[1] St. Patrick.
[2] An enclosure (usually circular) made by a strong earthen wall, and serving as a fort and place of residence for the chief of a tribe. N. E. D.

the kind erected since, were not strangers and aliens, but our own ancestors, and out of their rude civilization our own has slowly grown. Of that elder phase of European civilization no record or tradition has been anywhere bequeathed to us. Of its nature, and the ideas and sentiments whereby it was sustained, nought may now be learned save by an examination of those tombs themselves, and of the dumb remnants, from time to time exhumed out of their soil—rude instruments of clay, flint, brass, and gold, and by speculations and reasonings founded upon these, archaeological gleanings, meagre and sapless.

For after the explorer has broken up, certainly desecrated, and perhaps destroyed those noble sepulchral raths; after he has disinterred the bones laid there once by pious hands, and the urn with its unrecognisable ashes of king or warrior, and by the industrious labour of years hoarded his fruitless treasure of stone celt and arrow-head, of brazen sword and gold fibula and torque; and after the savant has rammed many skulls with sawdust, measuring their capacity, and has adorned them with some obscure label, and has tabulated and arranged the implements and decorations of flint and metal in the glazed cases of the cold gaunt museum, the imagination, unsatisfied and revolted, shrinks back from all that he has done. Still we continue to inquire, receiving from him no adequate response—who were those ancient chieftains and warriors for whom an affectionate people raised those strange tombs? What life did they lead? What deeds perform? How did their personality affect the minds of their people and posterity? How did our ancestors look upon those great tombs, certainly not reared to be forgotten, and how did they—those huge monumental pebbles and swelling raths—enter into and affect the civilization or religion of the times?

We see the cromlech with its massive slab and immense supporting pillars, but we vainly endeavour to imagine for whom it was first erected, and how that greater than cyclopean house affected the minds of those who made it, or those who were reared in its neighbourhood or within reach of its influence. We see the stone cist with its great smooth flags, the rocky cairn, and huge barrow and massive walled cathair,[1] but the interest which they invariably excite is only aroused to subside again unsatisfied. From this department of European antiquities the historian retires baf-

---
[1] A circular stone fort.

fled, and the dry savant is alone master of the field, but a field which, as cultivated by him alone, remains barren, or fertile only in things the reverse of exhilarating. An antiquarian museum is more melancholy than a tomb.

But there is one country in Europe, in which, by virtue of a marvellous strength and tenacity of the historical intellect, and of filial devotedness of the memory of their ancestors, there have been preserved down into the early phases of mediaeval civilization, and then committed to the sure guardianship of manuscript, the hymns, ballads, stories, and chronicles, the names, pedigrees, achievements, and even characters, of those ancient kings and warriors over whom those massive cromlechs were erected and great cairns piled. There is not a conspicuous sepulchral monument in Ireland, the traditional history of which is not recorded in our ancient literature, and of the heroes in whose honour they were raised. In the rest of Europe there is not a single barrow, dolmen, or cist of which the ancient traditional history is recorded; in Ireland there is hardly one of which it is not. And these histories are in many cases as rich and circumstantial as that of men of the greatest eminence who have lived in modern times. Granted that the imagination which for centuries followed with eager interest the lives of these heroes, beheld as gigantic what was not so, as romantic and heroic what was neither one nor the other, still the great fact remains, that it was beside and in connection with the mounds and cairns that this history was elaborated, and elaborated concerning them and concerning the heroes to whom they were sacred.

On the plain of Tara, beside the little stream Nemna, itself famous as that which first turned a mill-wheel in Ireland, there lies a barrow, not itself very conspicuous in the midst of others, all named and illustrious in the ancient literature of the country. The ancient hero there interred is to the student of the Irish bardic literature a figure as familiar and clearly seen as any personage in the *Biographia Britannica*. We know the name he bore as a boy and the name he bore as a man. We know the names of his father and his grandfather, and of the father of his grandfather; of his mother, and the father and mother of his mother, and the pedigrees and histories of each of these. We know the name of his nurse, and of his children, and of his wife, and the character of his wife, and of the father and mother of his wife, and where they lived and were buried. We know all the striking events of his boyhood and manhood, the names of his horses and his weapons, his own character and his friends, male and female. We know his battles, and the names of those whom he slew in battle, and how he was himself slain, and by whose hands. We know his physical and spiritual characteristics, the device upon his shield, and how that was originated, carved, and painted, and by whom. We know the colour of his hair, the date of his birth and of his death, and his relations, in time and otherwise, with the remainder of the princes and warriors with whom, in that mound-raising period of our history, he was connected, in hostility or friendship; and all this enshrined in ancient song, the transmitted traditions of the people who raised that barrow, and who laid within it sorrowing their brave ruler and defender. That mound is the tomb of Cuculain, once king of the district in which Dundalk stands to-day, and the ruins of whose earthen fortification may still be seen two miles from that town.

This is a single instance, and used merely as an example, but one out of a multitude almost as striking. There is not a king of Ireland, described as such in the ancient annals, whose barrow is not mentioned in these or other compositions, and every one of which may at the present day be identified where the ignorant plebeian or the ignorant patrician has not destroyed them. The early history of Ireland clings around and grows out of the Irish barrows until, with almost the universality of that primeval forest from which Ireland took one of its ancient names, the whole isle and all within it was clothed with a nobler raiment, invisible, but not the less real, of a full and luxuriant history, from whose presence, all-embracing, no part was free. Of the many poetical and rhetorical titles lavished upon this country, none is truer than that which calls her the Isle of Song. Her ancient history passed unceasingly into the realm of artistic representation; the history of one generation became the poetry of the next, until the whole island was illuminated and coloured by the poetry of the bards. Productions of mere fancy and imagination these songs are not, though fancy and imagination may have coloured and shaped all their subject matter, but the names are names of men and women who once lived and died in Ireland, and over whom their people raised the swelling rath and reared the rocky cromlech. In the sepulchral monuments their names were preserved, and in their performance of sacred rites and the holding of games, fairs, and assemblies in their honour, the memory of their achievements kept fresh, till the traditions that clung around these places were enshrined in tales which were finally incorporated in the *Leabhar na Huidhre*[1] and the *Book of Leinster*.[2]

Pre-historic narrative is of two kinds—in one the imagination is at work consciously, in the other unconsciously. Legends of the former class are the product of a lettered and learned age. The story floats loosely in a world of imagination. The other sort of pre-historic narrative clings close to the soil and to visible and tangible objects. It may be legend, but it is legend believed in as history, never consciously invented, and growing out of certain spots of the earth's surface, and supported by and drawing its life from the soil like a natural growth.

Such are the early Irish tales that cling around the mounds and cromlechs as that by which they are sustained, which was originally their source, and sustained them afterwards in a strong enduring life. It is evident that these cannot be classed with stories that float vaguely in an ideal world, which may happen in one place as well as another, and in which the names might be disarrayed without changing the character and consistency of the tale, and its relations, in time or otherwise, with other tales.

Foreigners are surprised to find the Irish claim for their own country an antiquity and a history prior to that of the neighbouring countries. Herein lie the proof and the explanation. The traditions and history of the mound-raising period have in other countries passed away. Foreign conquest, or less intrinsic force of imagination, and pious sentiment have suffered them to fall into oblivion; but in Ireland they have been all preserved in their original fulness and vigour, hardly a hue has faded, hardly a minute circumstance or articulation been suffered to decay.

The enthusiasm with which the Irish intellect seized upon the grand moral life of Christianity, and ideals so different from, and so hostile to, those of the heroic age, did not consume the traditions or destroy the pious and reverent spirit in which men still looked back upon those monuments of their own pagan teachers and kings, and the deep spirit of patriotism and affection with which the mind still clung to the old heroic age, whose types were war-

---

[1] *The Book of the Dun Cow*, a MS compilation of the 12th century.
[2] A similar MS compilation of the 12th century.

like prowess, physical beauty, generosity, hospitality, love of family and nation, and all those noble attributes which constituted the heroic character as distinguished from the saintly. The Danish conquest, with its profound modification of Irish society, and consequent disruption of old habits and conditions of life, did not dissipate it; nor the more dangerous conquest of the Normans, with their own innate nobility of character, chivalrous daring, and continental grace and civilization; nor the Elizabethan convulsions and systematic repression and destruction of all native phases of thought and feeling. Through all these storms, which successively assailed the heroic literature of ancient Ireland, it still held itself undestroyed. There were still found generous minds to shelter and shield the old tales and ballads, to feel the nobleness of that life of which they were the outcome, and to resolve that the soil of Ireland should not, so far as they had the power to prevent it, be denuded of its raiment of history and historic romance, or reduced again to primeval nakedness. The fruit of the persistency and unquenched love of country and its ancient traditions, is left to be enjoyed by us. There is not through the length and breadth of the country a conspicuous rath or barrow of which we cannot find the traditional history preserved in this ancient literature. The mounds of Tara, the great barrows along the shores of the Boyne, the raths of Slieve Mish, Rathcrogan, and Teltown, the stone caiseals[1] of Aran and Innishowen, and those that alone or in smaller groups stud the country over, are all, or nearly all, mentioned in this ancient literature, with the names and traditional histories of those over whom they were raised.

The indigenous history of the surrounding nations commences with the Christian ages—that of Ireland runs back into the pre-Christian. The Irish bards, unlike those of Gaul, Britain and, we may add, Germany, handed over to the monks and mediaeval scholars an immense mass of mingled history, tradition, and mythology, which the monks and Christianized bards were compelled to accept, and which to a certain extent, they have verified and established as indubitable.

The literary monuments in which is enshrined the ancient history of Ireland, though chronologically later than the corresponding monuments of Greece and of the Norse nations, are yet in fact more archaic. They cling close to and encircle the mounded tombs

---
[1] Stone buildings or forts.

of gods and heroes. Other literatures have floated far away from that to which they owe their genesis. They resemble the full course of a stream which has had its source far away. The stream of the Irish bardic literature still lingers in the mountains which gave it birth. It is near the well-head.

The stone-circle, rath, mound, cromlech, pillar-stone, so far as I know, appear in no literature to-day except the ancient literature of Ireland.

The pre-Christian period of Irish history presents difficulties from which the corresponding period in the histories of other countries is free. The surrounding nations escape the difficulty by having nothing to record. The Irish historian is immersed in perplexity on account of the mass of material ready to his hand. The English have lost utterly all record of those centuries before which the Irish historian stands with dismay and hesitation, not through deficiency of materials, but through their excess. Had nought but the chronicles been preserved, the task would have been simple. We would then have had merely to determine approximately the date of the introduction of letters, and allowing a margin on account of the bardic system and the commission of family and national history to the keeping of rhymed and alliterated verse, fix upon some reasonable point, and set down in order the old successions of kings and the battles and other remarkable events. But in Irish history there remains, demanding treatment, that other immense mass of literature of an imaginative nature, illuminating with anecdote and tale the events and personages mentioned simply and without comment by the chronicler. It is this poetic literature which constitutes the stumbling-block, as it constitutes also the glory, of early Irish history, for it cannot be rejected and it cannot be retained. It cannot be rejected, because it contains historical matter which is consonant with and illuminates the dry lists of the chronologist, and it cannot be retained, for popular poetry is not history; and the task of distinguishing in such literature the fact from the fiction—where there is certainly fact and certainly fiction—is one of the most difficult to which the intellect can apply itself. That this difficulty has not been hitherto surmounted by Irish writers is no just reproach. For the last century, intellects of the highest attainments, trained and educated to the last degree, have been vainly endeavouring to solve a similar question in the far less copious and less varied heroic literature of Greece. Yet the labours of Wolf,

Grote, Mahaffy, Geddes, and Gladstone, have not been sufficient to set at rest the small question, whether it was one man or two or many who composed the *Iliad* and *Odyssey*, while the reality of the achievements of Achilles and even his existence might be denied or asserted by a scholar without general reproach. When this is the case with regard to the great heroes of the *Iliad*, I fancy it will be some time before the same problem will have been solved for the minor characters, and as it affects Thersites, or that eminent artist who dwelt at home in Hyla, being by far the most excellent of leather-cutters. When, therefore, Greek still meets Greek in an interminable and apparently bloodless conflict over the disputed body of the *Iliad* and still no end appears, surely it would be madness for any one to sit down and gaily distinguish true from false in the immense and complex mass of the Irish bardic literature, having in his ears this century-lasting struggle over a single Greek poem and a single small phase of the semi-historic life of Hellas. . . .[1]

## Importance of the Mythical Period in the History of Nations

So absolute is the tyranny of the imagination over the minds of men, that it is often precisely those portions of the history of a people which are not historical that attract the most profound attention and arouse the deepest feelings. Even within the limits of the historical period it is the imaginative treatment of persons and events which takes the strongest hold upon the world. It is the Socrates of Plato's dialogues, the Marc Antony of Shakespeare's drama and of Plutarch's anecdotes, the Alfred of pretty Anglo-Saxon myths, whom we really see and think of, and not the Socrates, Marc Antony, and Alfred of positive undeniable history. The legend-making faculty, and what is akin to it, never cease and never can cease. Romance, epic, drama, and artistic representation are at all times the points to which history continually aspires— there only its final development and efflorescence. Archaeology culminates in history, history culminates in art.

This is true of persons and events falling within the scope of the most undeniable history, but it is when the great permanent

---
[1] Two irrelevant paragraphs are omitted here.

universal feelings of a nation or race project themselves into appropriate types of human personality, moving freely in a congenial atmosphere and world, that the power of imagination is rightly known and its profound and penetrating effect fully felt. While perpetually teased and hampered by the critical and historical instinct, it works as it were in chains, and its results are proportionately trivial. To express the whole nature of a race or nation, the artist needs that absolute freedom which is only supplied by a complete escape from positive history and unyielding despotic fact. Then the results become so typical, and of such enduring value and importance, that not the historian alone, but all eager and vivid minds are irresistibly attracted thither by influences similar to those which attract us in storms, in the sea, in running water, in revolutionary epochs, and in all that seems to indicate abounding life, movement, and freedom.

Such an escape from the actual is supplied to some more favoured or more gifted nations in the possession of a great mythical age lying behind their progress through time, imparting to their lives its own greatness and glory, inspiring life and hope and a buoyancy which laughs at obstacles and will not recognise defeat. The very lawlessness and audacity of conception which characterise such imagined ages are ever welcome. They prove overflowing youth and hope, and point to a maturity of power. The Greek race performed mightier achievements than the fabled labours of Heracles or of the mountain-rending Titans. The gigantic conceptions of heroism and strength, with which the forefront of Irish history is thronged, prove the great future of this race and land, of which the mere contemplation of the actual results of time might cause even the patriot to despair.

To the Greek bards who shaped the mythology of Hellas we must remotely attribute all the enormous influence which Greece has exercised on the world. But for them, the Greece that we know would not have been; without them the *Iliad* and *Odyssey* would never have arisen, nor the Athenian drama, nor Greek art, nor architecture. All of these, as we find them, are concerned with the gods and heroes who were the creations of pre-historic bards. It was they, namely these pre-historic unremembered Greeks, who supplied the types, and the fire, ideality, and creative impulses. The great age of Hellas was not an accident, but an emergence into light, and a bursting as it were into flower of that which was generated and nursed in earlier obscurer centuries. Those rude elder forgotten bards were the root of all that floral magnificence of the Periclean and subsequent ages. That this is true of all the imaginative and artistic work of Greece is self-evident; but I believe it is no less true of Greek philosophy, and of the whole life of Hellas, as it exhibits itself in history. How all-controlling over the pre-historic Greek mind must have been the influence of the bards, the comparative study of the corresponding period of Irish history shows, with a clearness and fulness which cannot be elsewhere found. For centuries of the progress of the Hellenic mind, the great tides and currents were bardic, religious, and imaginative. From those ages it emerges into the litten spaces of history, bringing with it such powers and ambitions as accrued to it during the centuries of the predominance of the bards.

As compared with the history of Greece, that of our own land is of course a small thing, its real greatness lying in the promise of the future, not in the actualities of the past; of which future, that far off mythic age is a prophecy. But no more than Grecian is Irish history comprehensible without a knowledge of those gods, giants, and heroes, with whose crowded cycles its pre-historic ages are filled. No such visible results have flowed to the world from the labours of the Irish bards as what has indirectly accrued from those of Orpheus, Musaeus, and the other spiritual progenitors of the Greek race. The development of the Irish mind under the influence of the bards was interrupted by the advent of Christianity at a very early age, impelled by the force of all the existing civilization of Europe. Had the intellectual and spiritual sovereignty of the Irish bards continued for a few centuries longer, I, for one, regarding the wonderful imaginative power evinced in the whole conception of that vast epos which forms the bardic history of Ireland, and the innumerable defined lofty or beautiful characters which it contains, feel as confident as one can well be concerning anything not actually realized, that results would have been forthcoming which would now be portion of the intellectual wealth of mankind.

Yet were the labours of the Irish bards considerable and well worthy of attention, and their influence upon the history of this nation deep and far-reaching. In the first place, they have left behind the still extant imaginative literature, monuments of antiquity in the highest degree interesting and important. No other European country supplies records exhibiting phases of thought and civilization so archaic, as are revealed with regard to the Irish race, in this unique literature. Thus a great hiatus in European, and, more particularly, in Grecian history, is partially filled. We find in it a stage of mental and social development corresponding to that of Hellas in the centuries that preceded the age of Homer, and of which all monuments have been swept away.

Again, we must remember that the intellectual influence exercised by Ireland over the north-west of Europe, during the sixth, seventh, and eighth centuries, is distinctly, though indirectly, traceable to the bards. It is not in the nature of things that a savage and untutored race should suddenly burst upon the world and assume the spiritual control of peoples who had been for centuries in contact with Roman influence. When the Christian missionaries landed in Ireland, they found a people whose intellectual, moral, and imaginative powers had been for many generations stimulated and aroused by their native bards. But for them the Ireland of those centuries would have been impossible.

But perhaps the most valuable work achieved for Ireland by those ancient shapers of legend and heroic tale, is like all that is best done in the world, incapable of being definitely grasped and clearly exhibited. Their best work is probably hidden in the blood and brain of the race to this day. Those antique singing men, with their imagined gods and superhuman heroes, breathed into the land and people the gallantry and chivalrousness, the prevailing ideality, the love of action and freedom, the audacity and elevation of thought, which, underneath all rudeness and grotesquerie, characterizes those remnants of their imaginings, and which we would believe no intervening centuries have been powerful wholly to annul. Theirs, not the monks', was the *perfervidum ingenium Scotorum*.[1]

I would also add when I consider the extraordinary stimulus which the perusal of that literature gives to the imagination, even in centuries like these, and its wealth of elevated and intensely human characters that, as I anticipate, with the revival of Irish literary energy and the return of Irish self-esteem, the artistic craftsmen of the future will find therein, and in unfailing abundance, the material of persons and sentiments fit for the highest purposes of epic and dramatic literature and of art, pictorial and sculptural. . . .

---

[1] Over-enthusiastic genius of the Irish.

# The Knighting of Cuculain[1]

THEN IN THE PRESENCE of his court, and his warriors, and the youths who were the comrades and companions of Cuculain, Concobar presented the young hero with his weapons of war, after he had taken the vows of the Red Branch, and having also bound himself by certain *gaesa*.[2] But Cuculain looked narrowly upon the weapons, and he struck the spears together, and clashed the sword upon the shield, and he brake the spears in pieces and the sword, and made chasms in the shield.

'These are not good weapons, O my King,' said the boy.

Then the King presented him with others that were larger and stronger, and these, too, the boy brake into little pieces.

'These are still worse, O son of Nessa,' said the boy, 'and it is not seemly, O Chief of the Red Branch, that on the day that I am to receive my arms I should be made a laughing-stock before the Clanna Rury, being yet but a boy.'

But Concobar Mac Nessa exulted exceedingly when he beheld the amazing strength and the waywardness of the boy, and beneath delicate brows his eyes glittered like glittering swords as he glanced rapidly round on the crowd of martial men that surrounded him; but amongst them all he seemed himself a bright torch of valour and war, more pure and clear than polished steel. But he beckoned to one of his knights, who hastened away and returned, bringing Concobar's own shield and spears and sword out of the Tayta Brac, where they were kept, an equipment in reserve. And Cuculain shook them and bent them, and clashed them together, but they held firm.

'These are good arms, O son of Nessa,' said Cuculain.

Then there were led forward a pair of noble steeds and a war-car, and the king conferred them on Cuculain. Then Cuculain sprang into the chariot, and standing with legs apart, he stamped from side to side and shook and shook, and jolted the car until the axle brake, and the car itself was broken to pieces.

'This is not a good chariot, O my King,' said the boy.

---

[1] From *History of Ireland: Heroic Period*, London and Dublin, 1878. This and the two following selections, episodes in the life of the greatest of Irish mythical heroes, come from the Red Branch (or Ulster) cycle of tales.
[2] Tabus. More correctly *geasa*.

30

# THE KNIGHTING OF CUCULAIN

Then there were led forward three chariots, and all these he brake in succession.

'These are not good chariots, O Chief of the Red Branch,' said Cuculain. 'No brave warrior would enter the battle or fight from such rotten foothold.'

Then the King called to his son Cowshra Mend Macha and bade him take Laeg, and harness to the war-chariot, of which he had the care, the wondrous grey steed, and that one which had been given him by Kelkar, the son of Uther, and to give Laeg a charioteering equipment to be charioteer of Cuculain. For now it was apparent to all the nobles and to the King that a lion of war had appeared amongst them, and that it was for him that Macha had sent these omens.

Then Cuculain's heart leaped in his breast when he heard the thunder of the great war-car and the mad whinnying of the horses that smelt the battle afar. Soon he beheld them with his eyes, and the charioteer with the golden fillet of his office, erect in the car, struggling to subdue their fury. A grey long-maned steed, whale-bellied, broad-chested, behind one yoke, a black, tufty-maned steed behind the other.

Like a hawk swooping along the face of a cliff when the wind is high, or like the rush of the March wind over the smooth plain, or like the fleetness of the stag roused from his lair by the hounds, and covering his first field, was the rush of those steeds when they had broken through the restraint of the charioteer, as though they galloped over fiery flags, so that the earth shook and trembled with the velocity of their motion, and all the time the great car brayed and shrieked as the wheels of solid and glittering bronze went round, for there were demons that had their abode in that car.

The charioteer restrained the steeds before the assembly, but nay-the-less a deep purr, like the purr of a tiger, proceeded from the axle. Then the whole assembly lifted up their voices and shouted for Cuculain, and he himself, Cuculain, the son of Sualtam, sprang into his chariot, all armed, with a cry as of a warrior springing into his chariot in the battle, and he stood erect and brandished his spears, and the war-sprites of the Gael shouted along with him, for the Bocanahs and Bananahs and the Geniti Glindi, the wild people of the glens, and the demons of the air, roared around him, when first the great warrior of the Gael, his battle-arms in his hands, stood equipped for war in his chariot before all the warriors of his tribe, the kings of the Clanna Rury and the people of Emain Macha. Then Cuculain bid Laeg let the steeds go, and they flew away rapidly, and three times they encircled Emain Macha. Then said Cuculain:

'Where leads the great road yonder?'

'To Ath-na-Forary and the border of the Crave Rue,'[1] said Laeg.

'And wherefore is it called "the Ford of the Watchings?"' said Cuculain.

'Because,' said Laeg, 'there is always one of the king's knights there keeping ward and watch over the gate of the province.'

'Guide thither my horses,' said Cuculain, 'for I have sworn not to lay aside my arms to-day until I have wetted them in the blood of one of the enemies of my tribe; and who is it who is over the garrison this day?'

'It is Konal Karna who commands there this day,' said Laeg.

Now, as they were drawing near to the ford, the watchman heard the rolling of the chariot and the trampling of the horses, and they sent word to Konal that a war-chariot was approaching from Emain Macha, but Konal came out of the Dun with his people, and when he saw Cuculain in the war-car of the king, and his glittering weapons around him, he began to laugh, and said, 'Is it arms the boy has taken?'

And Cuculain said, 'Indeed it is, and I have sworn not let them back into the Tayta Brac until I have wetted them in the blood of one of the enemies of Ulla.'[2]

Then Konal ceased laughing and said, 'You shall not do this, Setanta, for you shall not be permitted,' and he held back the horses, but Cuculain forced the horses onwards, and Konal fell back.

Then cried Konal to his charioteer, 'Harness my horses, for if this mad boy ventures into the territory of the enemy and meets with hurt I shall never be forgiven by the Ultonians.' Now the territories of Mid-Erin were hostile to Concobar through the expatriation and defeat of Fergus.

But the horses were quickly yoked, and Konal Karna dashed through the ford, and straightway he came up to Cuculain and

---
[1] Red Branch, name of the Ulster Order of Knighthood.
[2] Ulster.

drove for a while abreast of the boy, urging him to return. Then Cuculain stood up on both feet with his legs far apart in the car, and raising high above his head in his hands a large stone which Laeg had picked from the highway, he dashed it with all his force on the pole of Konal Karna's chariot, and the pole was broken in twain, and the chariot fell down, and the chief of the Red Branch, Konal Karna, the beauty of the Ultonians, was rolled out of the chariot upon the road, and was defiled with dust.

'Do you think that I can throw straight?' cried Cuculain; 'and now that you remind me, it is one of the vows of our order never to go with insecure trappings, rotten chariot-poles, or the like.'

Then Konal got up out of the dust, and swore that if a step would save Cuculain's head from the men of Meath he would not take it.

But Cuculain laughed again, and Laeg urged on the steeds. Now as they drew near the Boyne and the point where it receives the waters of the Mattok there was a great Dun. In this Dun lived three brothers, the three sons of Nectan, renowned amongst the tribes of Meath for valour and strength. Then as they drew nigh the Dun, Cuculain shouted insults and challenges with a loud voice, for the brothers had seen the war-car of Concobar Mac Nessa far away, and their own chariots were prepared, and they had despatched messengers on every side to cut off the retreat of the men of Ulla. Then Laeg checked the horses, and Cuculain descended upon the ground, and fitted an iron bullet to his sling, and he slung and killed the first of the warriors, and slung again and killed the second, and he slung the third time with all his might against the warrior, who was almost upon them, his strong shield held before him, while he crouched down in the chariot, and the iron bullet passed through the bronze shield and through his forehead, and went out behind. Then Cuculain drew his sword, and ran and cut off the heads of the slain, and sprang into the chariot, and Laeg flogged the steeds, who flew northwards again, swifter than the wind, for already they saw signals and fires, and horsemen galloping across the country to intercept their passage to the north. But they escaped out of the jaws of the enemy, and reached Ath-na-Forary, and when Konal saw the heads of the men of Meath, and recognised who were those warriors, he was filled with wonder, and he sent men of war to conduct him back to Emain Macha, and the whole city came out to welcome the young knight. Then his arms were hung up in the Tayta Brac, but Cuculain himself went back to his comrades, and he slept with them, and did not go out with the Red Branch.

# The Duel of Cuculain and Fardia[1]

THEN AROSE Cuculain, the unconquerable, striding through the forest, and he wondered which of the great champions of Meave should be brought against him that day; and when he came out into the open, he beheld the whole south country filled with a vast multitude, as it had been the Aenech[2] of Taylteen or the great Feis[3] of Tara when the authority of the Ard-Rie[4] is supreme, and all the tribes of Erin gather together with their kings. But he saw not at first who was the champion that had come out against him, and he advanced through the willows, and came to the edge of the ford, and looked across, and he saw Fardia, son of Daman, of the Fir-bolgs, and Fardia looked upon Cuculain, and Cuculain looked upon Fardia.

Then Cuculain blushed, and his neck and face above, and his temples waxed fiery red, and then again, paler than the white flower of the thorn, and his under jaw fell, and he stood like one stupefied; but Fardia held his shield unmoved, with his spears resting on the ground, and beneath the heavy cathbarr[5] his brows stronger than brass.

But Cuculain sent forth a voice hoarse and untuned, and said:

'Is it Fardia Mac Daman of the Fir-bolgs, for there is a mist before my eyes?'

But Fardia answered not.

Then said Cuculain:

'Art thou come out to meet me in arms to-day seeking to slay me?'

And Fardia answered sternly:

'Go back, O Cuculain, to thine own people, and cease to bar the

---
[1] From *History of Ireland: Heroic Period*, London & Dublin, 1878.
[2] A fair.
[3] A festival.
[4] High King.
[5] A helmet or headpiece. In modern Gaelic *cathbharr*.

# THE DUEL OF CUCULAIN AND FARDIA

gates of the north against our host, and I shall not slay thee nor dishonour thee, but if thou remainest, I shall slay thee here at the ford. Therefore, I bid thee go back into the province.'

But Cuculain answered him, and his voice became like the voice of a young girl, or the accents of one seeking an alms.

'And is it thou alone of all this great host that has come out against thy friend, seeking to slay me or dishonour me? There are the battle-standards of all the warrior-tribes of Erin, save only the Ultonians, the banners of the children of Ith and Heber, all the far-spreading clans of Heremon, the children of Amergin and Brega of Donn and Biela, and the Desie of Temair; there are the warlike clans of the Fomoroh, and the remnant of the people of Partholan, the Clanna Nemedh from the great harbour southwards, the children of Orba, the Ernai, and the Osree, the Gamaradians, and the Clan Dega. Could no champion be sought out of this great host that covers the green plains of Conaul Murthemney to the limits of the furthest hills to come out against me, but that thou alone shouldst stand forth against thy friend? Persist not, O son of Daman, but retire, and I will meet three champions instead of one from this day forward. We parted with mutual gifts and with tears, why does thy spear now thirst after my blood, and why dost thou seek to dishonour me?'

And Fardia made answer:

'Other champions, by their prowess, bear away many gifts, why should I ever have my hands empty? Bright as the sun is the brooch of Meave, which she has given me, the Royal Brooch of Cruhane, emblem of sovereignty amongst the Gael. Gems glitter along the rim. Like a level sunbeam in the forest is the shining delg[1] of it. I shall have honour while I live, and my clan after me shall be glorious to the end of time. Therefore, prepare for battle, O son of Sualtam; I remember thee not at all, or as one whom years since I met, and straight again forgot. Therefore, prepare thyself for battle, or I shall slay thee off thy guard.'

And Cuculain said:

'O Fardia, I believe thee not. Full well dost thou remember. Beneath the same rug we slept, and sat together at the feast, and side by side we went into the red battle. Together we consumed cities, and drave away captives. Together we practised feats of arms before the warrior-queen, grieving when either got any hurt. To-

---
[1] A brooch. In modern Gaelic *dealg*.

gether we kept back the streaming foe in the day of disaster, when the battle-torrent roared over us, either guarding the other more than himself.'

Then beneath his lowering brows the hot tears burst forth from the eyes of the son of Daman, and fell continuously from his beard, and he answered with a voice most stern, but that held within it a piteous tone like a vessel in which the careless eye sees not the hidden flaw, but at a touch, lo, it is broken. So sounded the stern voice of the warrior.

'Go back now, O Cuculain, to thy pleasant Dun—Dun Dalgan upon the sea. Go back now, for I would not slay thee, and rule over Murthemney and the rough headland of thy sires, and Meave will not waste thy territory or injure aught that is thine. And care no more for the Red Branch, for they have forsaken thee, and given thee over to destruction, who have conspired against thee, trusting in thy great heart that thou wouldst be slain on the marches of the province, holding the gates of the north against their foes, for Hound is thy name and Royal Hound thy nature. Therefore, go back, O Cuculain, and save thy young life; return now to thy infant son and thy sweet bride. Go back, O Cuculain, for sweet is life, the life of the warrior, and very dark and sorrowful and empty is the grave.'

'I will not go back, O Fardia Mac Daman, but here on the marches, while there is blood in my veins, and while reason like a king rebelled against but unsubdued, holds the sovereignty of my mind, shall I contest the borders of my nation, though forsaken and alone. My people have indeed abandoned me and conspired for my destruction; but there is no power in Erin to dissolve my knightship to the son of Nessa and my kinship with the Crave Rue. Though they hate me, yet cannot I eject the love out of my heart. And not the kings alone and the might of the Crave Rue, but the women and the young children of Ulla are under my protection, and all the unwarlike tribes, and this the sacred soil of Ulla upon which I stand. And this too well I know, that no power in the earth or in the air can keep the Red Branch my foe for ever, and that loud and deep will be their sorrow when the red pyre flames beneath me. And seek not to terrify me with death, O son of Daman, for of yore too our minds did not agree, for dark and sorrowful death is not, but a passage to the land of the ever young, the Tiernanog. There shall I see the Tuatha face to face, and there the heroic sons of Milith and himself, a mighty shade, and there all the noblest of the earth. There hatred and scorn are not known, nor the rupturing of friendships, but sweet love rules over all.'

'Go back, O Cuculain, go back now again, for I would not slay thee. Think no more of the son of Nessa and the Red Branch, than whom the race of Milith hath produced naught fiercer or more baleful. Rooted out and cast down shall be the Red Branch in this foray, whether thou, O Cuculain, survivest or art slain. Go back, O son of Sualtam, return to thine own Dun. Once indeed thou wast obedient to me and served me, and polished my armour, and tied up my spears submissive to my commands. Therefore go back; add not thy blood to the bloody stream.'

'Revilest thou my nation, O son of Daman. Talk no more now, but prepare thyself for battle and for death. I will not obey thee or retire before thee, nor shalt thou at all dishonour me as thou hast most foully dishonoured thyself. This indeed I well know, that I shall be slain at the ford when my strength has passed away, or my mind is overthrown; but by thee, O son of Daman, I shall not meet my death. Once indeed I was subservient to thee, because I was younger than thee. Therefore was I then as a servant unto thee, but not now; and which of us twain shall die I know, and it is thou, O Fardia, son of Daman.'

Therewith then they fought, and Cuculain had no weapon save only his colg,[1] for the Gae Bulg, the rude spear which he had fashioned, he dropped upon the shore, and Fardia discharged his javelins at the same time, for he was ambidexter, and quick as lightning. Cuculain avoided them, and they stuck trembling in the thither bank, and quick to right and left Cuculain severed the leathern thongs[2] rushing forward. Then drew Fardia his mighty sword that made a flaming crescent as it flashed most bright and terrible, and rushed headlong upon Cuculain, and they met in the midst of the ford. But straightway there arose a spray and a mist from the trampling of the heroes, and through the mist their forms moved hugely, like two giants of the Fomoroh contending in a storm. But the war-demons too contended around them fighting, the Bocanahs and Bananahs, the wild people of the glens and the demons of the air, and the fiercer and more blood-thirsty of the

---

[1] A sword.
[2] The Irish fastened leather thongs to their javelins with which to pull them back if they missed the mark.

Tuatha de Danan, and screeched in the clamour of the warriors, the clash of the shields and the clatter of land (*sic*) and meeting colg. But the warriors of Meave turned pale, and the war-steeds brake loose, and flew through the plain with the war-cars, and the women and camp-followers brake forth and fled, and the upper water of the divine stream gathered together for fear, and reared itself aloft like a steed that has seen a spectre, with jags of torn water and tossing foam. But Cuculain was red all over, like a garment raised out of the dyeing-vat, and Fardia's great sword made havoc in his unarmoured flesh. Three times Cuculain closed with the Firbolg, seeking to get within the ponderous shield, and three times the son of Daman cast him off, as the cliffs of Eyrus cast off a foaming billow of the great sea; but when the fourth time he was rushing on like a storm, he heard as it were the voice of Laeg, the son of Riangowra, taunting and insulting him, and himself he saw, standing in the river ford on the left, for he was accustomed to revile Cuculain. Yet this time too the Fir-bolg cast him off, and advanced upon Cuculain to slay him. Then stepped back Cuculain quickly, and the men of Meave shouted, for Cuculain's shield was falling to pieces. But again rushed forward the hound of Ulla, stooping, with the Gae Bulg in his hand, using it like a spearman in the battle, and he drove Fardia through the ford and upon the hither bank, pressed against the shield, but Fardia himself too retreated back. But when the Fir-bolgs saw what was done they feared mightily for their champion, and raised a sudden howl of lamentation and rage, and rushed forward, breaking through the guards. Which when Fergus MacRoy beheld, he sprang down from his chariot, shouting dreadfully, and put his hand into the hollow of his shield, and took out his battlestone, and smote Imchall, the son of Dega, with the battlestone upon the head, and he fell rushing forward amongst the first. But Cormac Conlingas and Mainey Lamgarf ran thither with the queen's spearmen restraining the Firbolgs.

But, meantime, Cuculain lifted suddenly the Gae Bulg above his head, and plunged it into Fardia; but it passed through the upper rim of the brazen shield, and through the strong bones of his breast beneath his beard, and he fell backward with a crash, and grasped with out-stretched hands at the ground, and his spirit went out of him, and he died.

But Cuculain plucked out the spear, and stood above him, panting, as a hound pants returning from the chase, and the war-demons passed out of him, and he looked upon Fardia, and a great sorrow overwhelmed him, and he lamented and moaned over Fardia, joining his voice to the howl of the people of Fardia, the great-hearted children of Mac Erc, and he took off the cathbarr from the head of Fardia, and unwound his yellow hair, tress after bright tress, most beautiful, shedding many tears, and he opened the battle-dress and took out the queen's brooch—that for which his friend had come to slay him—and he cursed the lifeless metal, and cast it from him into the air, southwards over the host, and men saw it no more.

# The Death of Cuculain[1]

More terrible than at any other time was the son of Sualtam in those battles which he entered in the naked majesty of his irresistible strength, shorn of his glory, and having lost his magic attributes, for this time he went to war like one who has devoted himself to death. Around him the shadows thickened, but like a light in darkness, his valour shone the brighter as before his fast-lessening warriors he charged the armies of the great Queen. Over the plains of Murthemney, between Dundalgan and the Boyne, pealed the voice of the son of Sualtam, shouting amid his warriors, and ever the southern host gave way before him, and their battalions were confused.

Then northward in the hills collected the people of Ulla, the unwarlike tribes, seeing afar that one hero, and the fast-lessening ranks of the Ultonians, where the great champion of the north fought on against the immense overflowing host of the Four Provinces.

But as the Ultonians grew less in the dread conflict, the southern warriors precipitated themselves upon Cuculain, and like a great rock over which rolls some mighty billow of the western sea, so was Cuculain often submerged in their overflowing tide; and as with the down-sinking billow the same rock reappears in its invincible greatness, and the white brine runs down its stubborn ribs, so

---

[1] From *History of Ireland: Cuculain and His Contemporaries*, London & Dublin, 1880.

the son of Sualtam perpetually reappeared scattering and destroying his foes. Then crashed his battle mace through opposing shields; then flew the foam-flakes from his lips over his reddened garments; baleful shone his eyes beneath his brows, and his voice died away in his throat till it became a hoarse whisper. Often, too, Laeg charged with the war-car, and extricated him surrounded, and the mighty steeds tramped down opposing squadrons, and many a southern hero was transfixed with the chariot-spear, or divided by the brazen scythes.

It was on the eighth day, two hours after noon, that Cuculain raising his eyes beheld where the last of the Red Branch were overwhelmed, and he and Laeg were abandoned and alone, and he heard Laeg shouting, for he was surrounded by a battalion, and Cuculain hastened back to defend him, and sprang into the chariot, bounding over the rim, and extended Fabane above him on the left. There he intercepted three javelins cast against the charioteer by a Lagenian hand; but Erc, son of Cairbre Nia-far, pursued him, and at the same time cast his spear from the right. Through Cuculain it passed, breaking through the battle-shirt and the waist-piece, and it pierced his left side between the hip-bone and the lowest rib, and transfixed Laeg in the stomach above the navel. Then fell the reins from the hands of Laeg.

'How is it with thee, O Laeg?' said then Cuculain.

And Laeg answered:

'I have had enough this time, O my dear master. Truly thou hast fulfilled thy vow, for it was through thee that I have been slain.'

Then Cuculain cut through the spear-tree with his colg, and tore forth the tree out of himself; but meantime, Lewy Mac Conroi stabbed black Shanglan with his red hands, driving the spear through his left side, behind the shoulder, and Shanglan fell, overturning the war-car, and Cuculain sprang forth, but as he sprang, Lewy Mac Conroi pierced him through the bowels. Then fell the great hero of the Gael.

Thereat the sun darkened, and the earth trembled, and a wail of agony from immortal mouths shrilled across the land, and a pale panic smote the vast host of Meave when, with a crash, fell that pillar of heroism, and that flame of the warlike valour of Erin was extinguished. Then, too, from his slain comrade brake forth the Liath Macha, for, like a housewife's thread, the divine steed brake the traces, and the brazen chains, and the yoke, and bounded forth neighing, and three times he encircled the heroes, trampling down the host of Meave. Afar then retreated the host, and the Liath Macha, wearing still the broken collar, went back into the realms of the unseen, and entered his house upon the Boyne, where, since the ancient days, was his mysterious dwelling-place.

But Cuculain kissed Laeg, and Laeg, dying, said:

'Farewell, O dear master, and schoolfellow. Till the end of the world no servant will ever have a better master than thou hast been to me.'

And Cuculain said:

'Farewell, O dear Laeg. The gods of Erin have deserted us, and the Clan Cailitin are now abroad, and what will happen to us henceforward I know not. But true and faithful thou hast ever been to me, and it is now seventeen years since we plighted friendship, and no angry word has ever passed between us since then.'

Then the spirit went out of Laeg, and he died, and Cuculain, raising his eyes, saw thence north-westward, about two hundred yards, a small lake called Loch-an-Tanaigte, and he tore forth from himself the bloody spear, and went staggering, and at times he fell, nevertheless he reached the lake, and stooped down and drank a deep draught of the pure cold water, keen with frost, and the burning fever in his veins was allayed. After that he arose, and saw northwards from the lake a tall pillar-stone, the grave of a warrior slain there in some ancient war, and its name was Carrig-an-Compan. When Cuculain first saw it there was standing upon it a grey-necked crow, which retired as he approached. With difficulty he reached it, and he leaned awhile against the pillar, for his mind wandered, and he knew nothing for a space.

After that he took off his brooch, and, removing the torn bratta,[1] he passed it round the top of the pillar, where there was an indentation in the stone, and passed the ends under his arms and around his breast, tying with languid hands a loose knot, which soon was made fast by the weight of the dying hero. But the host of Meave, when they beheld him, retired again, for they said that he was immortal, and that Lu Lamfada would once more come down out of fairyland to his aid, and that they would wreak a terrible vengeance. So afar they retreated, when they beheld him standing with the drawn sword in his hand, and the rays of the set-

---

[1] A cloak. In modern Gaelic *brat*.

ting sun bright on his panic-striking helmet. So stood Cuculain, even in death-pangs, a terror to his enemies, and the bulwark of his nation.

Now, as Cuculain stood dying, a stream of blood trickled from his wounds, and ran in devious ways down to the lake, and poured its tiny red current into the pure water; and as Cuculain looked upon it, thinking many things in his deep mind, there came forth an otter out of the reeds of the lake and approached the pebbly strand, where the blood flowed into the water, having been attracted thither by the smell, and at the point where the blood flowed into the lake, he lapped up the life-blood of the hero, looking up from time to time, after the manner of a dog feeding. Which seeing, Cuculain gazed upon the otter, and he smiled for the last time, and said:

'O thou greedy water-dog, often in my boyhood have I pursued thy race in the rivers and lakes of Murthemney; but now thou hast a full eric,[1] who drinkest the blood of me dying. Nor do I grudge thee this thy bloody meal. Drink on, thou happy beast. To thee, too, doubtless, there will some time be an hour of woe.'

Then to Cuculain appeared a vision, and he deemed that he saw Laeg approaching, riding alone on black Shanglan, and he was glad therefor, and he deemed that Laeg applied healing salves to his wounds. And Cuculain said:

'Go now straightway to Emain Macha, O Laeg, and say to Concobar that I here in Murthemney will contend till I perish against the invaders of Ulla, and give my benediction to my uncle, the great King of the Ultonians, and to all the Red Branch; and go to Emer and tell her not to weep for me, but to let her grief be of short duration, and that I will remember her while life endures.'

Then to Cuculain it seemed that Laeg, frowning, said:

'Surely, O Cu, thy peerless and noble wife, beautiful Emer, thou wouldst never forget.'

After that Cuculain dreamed that Laeg went off to Emain Macha, and that he heard the sound of the hoofs afar, going northwards, and a terrible loneliness and desolation came over his mind, and again he saw the faces of that wandering clan, and they laughed around him and taunted him, and said:

'Thus shalt thou perish, O Hound, and thus shall all like thee be forsaken and deserted, and they shall perish in loneliness and sor-

---
[1] A blood fine or pecuniary compensation for the crime of murder.

# THE DEATH OF CUCULAIN

row. And early death and desolation shall be their lot, for we are powerful over men and over gods, and the kingdom that is seen, and the kingdom that is unseen belong to us,' and they ringed him round, and chaunted obscene songs, and triumphed.

Nevertheless they terrified him not, for a deep spring of stern valour was open in his soul and the might of his unfathomable spirit sustained him.

Then was Cuculain aware that the Clan Cailitin had retired, as though in fear, and there stood beside him a child, having a strange aspect, and he took Cuculain by the hand, and said:

'Regard not these children of evil, O my brother, their dominion is but for a time.'

And Cuculain said:

'What god art thou who hast conquered the Clan Cailitin?'

Thus perished Cuculain—'mild, handsome, invincible,' *coev, aulin, cinlaca*.

LADY GREGORY

# The Fate of the Sons of Usnach[1]

Now it was one Fedlimid, son of Doll, was harper to King Conchubar, and he had but one child, and this is the story of her birth.

Cathbad, the Druid, was at Fedlimid's house one day. 'Have you got knowledge of the future?' said Fedlimid. 'I have a little,' said Cathbad. 'What is it you are wanting to know?' 'I was not asking to know anything,' said Fedlimid, 'but if you know of anything that may be going to happen me, it is as well for you to tell me.'

Cathbad went out of the house for a while, and when he came back he said: 'Had you ever any children?' 'I never had,' said Fedlimid, 'and the wife I have had none, and we have no hope ever to have any; there is no one with us but only myself and my wife.' 'That puts wonder on me,' said Cathbad, 'for I see by Druid signs that it is on account of a daughter belonging to you, that more blood will be shed than ever was shed in Ireland since time and race began. And great heroes and bright candles of the Gael will lose their lives because of her.' 'Is that the foretelling you have made for me?' said Fedlimid, and there was anger on him, for he thought the Druid was mocking him; 'if that is all you can say, you can keep it for yourself; it is little I think of your share of knowledge.' 'For all that,' said Cathbad, 'I am certain of its truth, for I can see it all clearly in my own mind.'

The Druid went away, but he was not long gone when Fedlimid's wife was found to be with child. And as her time went on, his vexation went on growing, that he had not asked more questions of Cathbad, at the time he was talking to him, and he was under a smouldering care by day and by night, for it is what he was thinking, that neither his own sense and understanding or the share of friends he had, would be able to save him, or to make a back against the world, if this misfortune should come upon him, that would bring such great shedding of blood upon the earth; and it is the thought that came, that if this child should be born, what he had to do was to put her far away, where no eye would see her, and no ear hear word of her.

---

[1] From *Cuchulain of Muirthemne*, London, 1902. The story of Deirdre is the great love tale of the Red Branch (or Ulster) cycle. It has provided Yeats, Synge, AE, Stephens and numerous others with a theme for tragedy, epic or romance.

FATE OF THE SONS OF USNACH 45

The time of the delivery of Fedlimid's wife came on, and it was a girl-child she gave birth to. Fedlimid did not allow any living person to come to the house or to see his wife, but himself alone.

But just after the child was born, Cathbad, the Druid, came in again, and there was shame on Fedlimid when he saw him, and when he remembered how he would not believe his words. But the Druid looked at the child and he said: 'Let Deirdre be her name; harm will come through her.

'She will be fair, comely, bright-haired; heroes will fight for her, and kings go seeking for her.'

And then he took the child in his arms, and it is what he said: 'O Deirdre, on whose account many shall weep, on whose account many women shall be envious, there will be trouble on Ulster for your sake, O fair daughter of Fedlimid.

'Many will be jealous of your face, O flame of beauty; for your sake heroes shall go to exile. For your sake deeds of anger shall be done in Emain; there is harm in your face, for it will bring banishment and death on the sons of kings.

'In your fate, O beautiful child, are wounds, and ill-doings, and shedding of blood.

'You will have a little grave apart to yourself; you will be a tale of wonder for ever, Deirdre.'

Cathbad went away then, and he sent Levarcham, daughter of Aedh, to the house; and Fedlimid asked her would she take the venture of bringing up the child, far away where no eye would see her, and no ear hear of her. Levarcham said she would do that, and that she would do her best to keep her the way he wished.

So Fedlimid got his men, and brought them away with him to a mountain, wide and waste, and there he bade them to make a little house, by the side of a round green hillock, and to make a garden of apple-trees behind it, with a wall about it. And he bade them put a roof of green sods over the house, the way a little company might live in it, without notice being taken of them.

Then he sent Levarcham and the child there, that no eye might see, and no ear hear of Deirdre. He put all in good order before them, and he gave them provisions, and he told Levarcham that food and all she wanted would be sent from year to year as long as she lived.

And so Deirdre and her foster-mother lived in the lonely place among the hills without the knowledge or the notice of any strange person, until Deirdre was fourteen years of age. And Deirdre grew straight and clean like a rush on the bog, and she was comely beyond comparison of all the women of the world, and her movements were like the swan on the wave, or the deer on the hill. She was the young girl of the greatest beauty and of the gentlest nature of all the women of Ireland.

Levarcham, that had charge of her, used to be giving Deirdre every knowledge and skill that she had herself. There was not a blade of grass growing from root, or a bird singing in the wood, or a star shining from heaven, but Deirdre had the name of it. But there was one thing she would not have her know, she would not let her have friendship with any living person of the rest of the world outside their own house.

But one dark night of winter, with black clouds overhead, a hunter came walking the hills, and it is what happened, he missed the track of the hunt, and lost his way and his comrades.

And a heaviness came upon him, and he lay down on the side of the green hillock by Deirdre's house. He was weak with hunger and going, and perished with cold, and a deep sleep came upon him. While he was lying there a dream came to the hunter, and he thought that he was near the warmth of a house of the Sidhe,[1] and the Sidhe inside making music, and he called out in his dream, 'If there is any one inside, let them bring me in, in the name of the Sun and the Moon.' Deirdre heard the voice, and she said to Levarcham, 'Mother, mother, what is that?' But Levarcham said, 'It is nothing that matters; it is the birds of the air gone astray, and trying to find one another. But let them go back to the branches of the wood.' Another troubled dream came on the hunter, and he cried out a second time. 'What is that?' asked Deirdre again. 'It is nothing that matters,' said Levarcham. 'The birds of the air are looking for one another; let them go past to the branches of the wood.' Then a third dream came to the hunter, and he cried out a third time, if there was any one in the hill to let him in for the sake of the Elements, for he was perished with cold and overcome with hunger. 'Oh! what is that, Levarcham?' said Deirdre. 'There is nothing there for you to see, my child, but only the birds of the air, and they lost to one another, but let them go past us to the branches of the wood. There is no place or shelter for them here to-night.' 'Oh, mother,' said Deirdre, 'the bird asked to come in for the sake of

---

[1] Fairies, pronounced *shee*.

the Sun and the Moon, and it is what you yourself told me, that anything that is asked like that, it is right for us to give it. If you will not let in the bird that is perished with cold and overcome with hunger, I myself will let it in.' So Deirdre rose up and drew the bolt from the leaf of the door, and let in the hunter. She put a seat in the place for sitting, food in the place for eating, and drink in the place for drinking, for the man who had come into the house. 'Come now and eat food, for you are in want of it,' said Deirdre. 'Indeed it is I was in want of food and drink and warmth when I came into this house; but by my word, I have forgotten that since I saw yourself,' said the hunter. 'How little you are able to curb your tongue,' said Levarcham. 'It is not a great thing for you to keep your tongue quiet when you get the shelter of a house and the warmth of a hearth on a dark winter night.' 'That is so,' said the hunter, 'I may do that much, to keep my mouth shut; but I swear by the oath my people swear by, if some others of the people of the world saw this great beauty that is hidden away here, they would not leave her long with you.' 'What people are those?' said Deirdre. 'I will tell you that,' said the hunter; 'they are Naoise, son of Usnach, and Ainnle and Ardan, his two brothers.' 'What is the appearance of these men, if we should ever see them?' said Deirdre. 'This is the appearance that is on those three men,' said the hunter: 'the colour of the raven is on their hair, their skin is like the swan on the wave, their cheeks like the blood of the speckled red calf, and their swiftness and their leap are like the salmon of the stream and like the deer of the grey mountain; and the head and shoulders of Naoise are above all the other men of Ireland.' 'However they may be,' said Levarcham, 'get you out from here, and take another road; and by my word, little is my thankfulness to yourself; or to her that let you in.' 'You need not send him out for telling me that,' said Deirdre, 'for as to those three men, I myself saw them last night in a dream, and they hunting upon a hill.'

The hunter went away, but in a little time after he began to think to himself how Conchubar, High King of Ulster, was used to lie down at night and to rise up in the morning by himself, without a wife or any one to speak to; and that if he could see this great beauty it was likely he would bring her home to Emain, and that he himself would get the good-will of the king for telling him there was such a queen to be found on the face of the world.

So he went straight to King Conchubar at Emain Macha, and he sent word in to the king that he had news for him, if he would hear it. The king sent for him to come in. 'What is the reason of your journey?' he said. 'It is what I have to tell you, King,' said the hunter, 'that I have seen the greatest beauty that ever was born in Ireland, and I am come to tell you of it.'

'Who is this great beauty, and in what place is she to be seen, when she was never seen before you saw her, if you did see her?' 'I did see her, indeed,' said the hunter, 'but no other man can see her, unless he knows from me the place where she is living.' 'Will you bring me to the place where she is, and you will have a good reward?' said the king. 'I will bring you there,' said the hunter. 'Let you stay with my household tonight,' said Conchubar, 'and I myself and my people will go with you early on the morning of to-morrow.' 'I will stay,' said the hunter, and he stayed that night in the household of King Conchubar.

Then Conchubar sent to Fergus and to the other chief men of Ulster, and he told them of what he was about to do. Though it was early when the songs and the music of the birds began in the woods, it was earlier yet when Conchubar, king of Ulster, rose up with his little company of near friends, in the fresh spring morning of the fresh and pleasant month of May, and the dew was heavy on every bush and flower as they went out towards the green hill where Deirdre was living.

But many a young man of them that had a light, glad, leaping step when they set out, had but a tired, slow, failing step before the end, because of the length and the roughness of the way. 'It is down there below,' said the hunter, 'in the house in that valley, the woman is living, but I myself will not go nearer it than this.'

Conchubar and his troop went down then to the green hillock where Deirdre was, and they knocked at the door of the house. Levarcham called out that neither answer nor opening would be given to any one at all, and that she did not want disturbance put on herself or her house. 'Open,' said Conchubar, 'in the name of the High King of Ulster.' When Levarcham heard Conchubar's voice, she knew there was no use trying to keep Deirdre out of sight any longer, and she rose up in haste and let in the king, and as many of his people as could follow him.

When the king saw Deirdre before him, he thought in himself that he never saw in the course of the day, or in the dreams of the night, a creature so beautiful, and he gave her his full heart's weight of love there and then. It is what he did; he put Deirdre up on the shoulders of his men, and she herself and Levarcham were brought away to Emain Macha.

With the love that Conchubar had for Deirdre, he wanted to marry her with no delay, but when her leave was asked, she would not give it, for she was young yet, and she had no knowledge of the duties of a wife, or the ways of a king's house. And when Conchubar was pressing her hard, she asked him to give her a delay of a year and a day. He said he would give her that, though it was hard for him, if she would give him her certain promise to marry him at the year's end. She did that, and Conchubar got a woman teacher for her, and nice, fine, pleasant, modest maidens to be with her at her lying down and at her rising up, to be companions to her. And Deirdre grew wise in the works of a young girl, and in the understanding of a woman; and if any one at all looked at her face, whatever colour she was before that, she would blush crimson red. And it is what Conchubar thought, that he never saw with the eyes of his body a creature that pleased him so well.

One day Deirdre and her companions were out on a hill near Emain Macha, looking around them in the pleasant sunshine, and they saw three men walking together. Deirdre was looking at the men and wondering at them, and when they came near, she remembered the talk of the hunter, and the three men she saw in her dream, and she thought to herself that these were the three sons of Usnach, and that this was Naoise, that had his head and shoulders above all the men of Ireland. The three brothers went by without turning their eyes at all upon the young girls on the hillside, and they were singing as they went, and whoever heard the low singing of the sons of Usnach, it was enchantment and music to them, and every cow that was being milked and heard it, gave two-thirds more of milk. And it is what happened, that love for Naoise came into the heart of Deirdre, so that she could not but follow him. She gathered up her skirt and went after the three men that had gone past the foot of the hill, leaving her companions there after her.

But Ainnle and Ardan had heard talk of the young girl that was at Conchubar's Court, and it is what they thought, that if Naoise their brother would see her, it is for himself he would have her, for she was not yet married to the king. So when they saw Deirdre coming after them, they said to one another to hasten their steps, for they had a long road to travel, and the dusk of night coming on. They did so, and Deirdre saw it, and she cried out after them, 'Naoise, son of Usnach, are you going to leave me?' 'What cry was that came to my ears, that it is not well for me to answer, and not easy for me to refuse?' said Naoise. 'It was nothing but the cry of Conchubar's wild ducks,' said his brothers; 'but let us quicken our steps and hasten our feet, for we have a long road to travel, and the dusk of the evening coming on.' They did so, and they were widening the distance between themselves and her. Then Deirdre cried, 'Naoise! Naoise! son of Usnach, are you going to leave me?' 'What cry was it that came to my ears and struck my heart, that it is not well for me to answer, or easy for me to refuse?' said Naoise. 'Nothing but the cry of Conchubar's wild geese,' said his brothers; 'but let us quicken our steps and hasten our feet, the darkness of night is coming on.' They did so, and were widening the distance between themselves and her. Then Deirdre cried the third time, 'Naoise! Naoise! Naoise! son of Usnach, are you going to leave me?' 'What sharp, clear cry was that, the sweetest that ever came to my ears, and the sharpest that ever struck my heart, of all the cries I ever heard?' said Naoise. 'What is it but the scream of Conchubar's lake swans,' said his brothers. 'That was the third cry of some person beyond there,' said Naoise, 'and I swear by my hand of valour,' he said, 'I will go no further until I see where the cry comes from.' So Naoise turned back and met Deirdre, and Deirdre and Naoise kissed one another three times, and she gave a kiss to each of his brothers. And with the confusion that was on her, a blaze of red fire came upon her, and her colour came and went as quickly as the aspen by the stream. And it is what Naoise thought to himself, that he never saw a woman so beautiful in his life; and he gave Deirdre, there and then, the love that he never gave to living thing, to vision, or to creature, but to herself alone.

Then he lifted her high on his shoulder, and he said to his brothers to hasten their steps; and they hastened them.

'Harm will come of this,' said the young men. 'Although there should harm come,' said Naoise, 'I am willing to be in disgrace while I live. We will go with her to another province, and there is not in Ireland a king who will not give us a welcome.' So they called their people, and that night they set out with three times fifty men, and three times fifty women, and three times fifty greyhounds, and Deirdre in their midst.

They were a long time after that shifting from one place to another all around Ireland, from Essruadh in the south, to Beinn Etair in the east again, and it is often they were in danger of being destroyed by Conchubar's devices. And one time the Druids raised a wood before them, but Naoise and his brothers cut their way through it. But at last they got out of Ulster and sailed to the country of Alban, and settled in a lonely place; and when hunting on the mountains failed them, they fell upon the cattle of the men of Alban, so that these gathered together to make an end of them. But the sons of Usnach called to the king of Scotland, and he took them into his friendship, and they gave him their help when he went out into battles or to war.

But all this time they had never spoken to the king of Deirdre, and they kept her with themselves, not to let any one see her, for they were afraid they might get their death on account of her, she being so beautiful.

But it chanced very early one morning, the king's steward came to visit them, and he found his way into the house where Naoise and Deirdre were, and there he saw them asleep beside one another. He went back then to the king, and he said: 'Up to this time there has never been found a woman that would be a fitting wife for you; but there is a woman on the shore of Loch Ness now, is well worthy of you, king of the East. And what you have to do is to make an end of Naoise, for it is of his wife I am speaking.' 'I will not do that,' said the king; 'but go to her,' he said, 'and bid her to come and see me secretly.' The steward brought her that message, but Deirdre sent him away, and all that he had said to her, she told it to Naoise afterwards. Then when she would not come to him, the king sent the sons of Usnach into every hard fight, hoping they would get their death, but they won every battle, and came back safe again. And after a while they went to Loch Eitche, near the sea, and they were left to themselves there for a while in peace and quietness. And they settled and made a dwelling house for themselves by the side of Loch Ness, and they could kill the salmon of the stream from out their own door, and the deer of the grey hills from out their window. But when Naoise went to the court of the king, his clothes were splendid among the great men of the army of Scotland, a cloak of bright purple, rightly shaped, with a fringe of bright gold; a coat of satin with fifty hooks of silver; a brooch on which were a hundred polished gems; a gold-hilted sword in his hand, two blue-green spears of bright points, a dagger with the colour of yellow gold on it, and a hilt of silver. But the two children they had, Gaiar and Aebgreine, they gave into the care of Manannan, Son of the Sea. And he cared them well in Emhain of the Apple Trees, and he brought Bobaras the poet to give learning to Gaiar. And Aebgreine of the Sunny Face he gave in marriage afterwards to Rinn, son of Eochaidh Juil of the Land of Promise.

Now it happened after a time that a very great feast was made by Conchubar, in Emain Macha, for all the great among his nobles, so that the whole company were easy and pleasant together. The musicians stood up to play their songs and to give poems, and they gave out the branches of relationship and of kindred. These are the names of the poets that were in Emain at the time, Cathbad, the Druid, son of Conall, son of Rudraige; Geanann of the Bright Face, son of Cathbad; Ferceirtne, and Geanann Black-Knee, and many others, and Sencha, son of Ailell.

They were all drinking and making merry until Conchubar, the king, raised his voice and spoke aloud, and it is what he said: 'I desire to know from you, did you ever see a better house than this house of Emain, or a hearth better than my hearth in any place you were ever in?' 'We did not,' they said. 'If that is so,' said Conchubar, 'do you know of anything at all that is wanting to you?' 'We know of nothing,' said they. 'That is not so with me,' said Conchubar. 'I know of a great want that is on you, the want of the three best candles of the Gael, the three noble sons of Usnach, that ought not to be away from us for the sake of any woman in the world, Naoise, Ainnle, and Ardan; for surely they are the sons of a king, and they would defend the High Kingship against the best men of Ireland.' 'If we had dared,' said they, 'it is long ago we would have said it, and more than that, the province of Ulster would be equal to any other province in Ireland, if there was no Ulsterman in it but those three alone, for it is lions they are in hardness and in bravery.' 'If that is so,' said Conchubar, 'let us send word by a messenger to Alban, and to the dwelling-place of the sons of Usnach, to ask them back again.' 'Who will go there with the message?' said they all. 'I cannot know that,' said Conchubar, 'for there is *geasa,* that is bonds, on Naoise not to come back with any man only one of the three, Conall Cearnach, or Fergus, or Cuchulain, and I will know now,' said he, 'which one of those three loves me best.' Then he called Conall to one side, and he asked him, 'What would you do with me if I should send you for the sons of Usnach, and if they were destroyed through me—a thing I do not mean to do?' 'As I am not going to undertake it,' said Conall, 'I will say that it is not one alone I would kill, but any Ulsterman I would lay hold of that had harmed them would get shortening of life from me and the sorrow of death.' 'I see well,' said Conchubar, 'you are no friend of mine,' and he put Conall away from him. Then he called Cuchulain to him, and asked him the same as he did the other. 'I give my word, as I am not going,' said Cuchulain, 'if you want that of me, and that you think to kill them when they come, it is not one person alone that would die for it, but every Ulsterman I could lay hold of would get shortening of life from me and the sorrow of death.' 'I see well,' said Conchubar, 'that you are no friend of mine.' And he put Cuchulain from him. And then he called Fergus to him, and asked him the same question, and Fergus said, 'Whatever may happen, I promise your blood will be safe from me, but besides yourself there is no Ulsterman that would try to harm them, and that I would lay hold of, but I would give him shortening of life and the sorrow of death.' 'I see well,' said Conchubar, 'it is yourself must go for them, and it is to-morrow you must set out, for it is with you they will come, and when you are coming back to us westward, I put you under bonds to go first to the fort of Borach, son of Cainte, and give me your word now that as soon as you get there, you will send on the sons of Usnach to Emain, whether it be day or night at the time.' After that the two of them went in together, and Fergus told all the company how it was under his charge they were to be put.

Then Conchubar went to Borach and asked had he a feast ready prepared for him. 'I have,' said Borach, 'but although I was able to make it ready, I was not able to bring it to Emain.' 'If that is so,' said Conchubar, 'give it to Fergus when he comes back to Ireland, for it is *geasa* on him not to refuse your feast.' Borach promised he would do that, and so they wore away that night.

So Fergus set out in the morning, and he brought no guard nor helpers with him, but himself and his two sons, Fair-Haired Iollan, and Rough-Red Buinne, and Cuillean, the shield-bearer, and the shield itself. They went on till they got to the dwelling-place of the sons of Usnach, and to Loch Eitche in Alba. It is how the sons of Usnach lived; they had three houses, and the house where they made ready the food, it is not there they would eat it, and the house where they would eat it, it is not there they would sleep.

When Fergus came to the harbour he let a great shout out of him. And it is how Naoise and Deirdre were, they had a chessboard between them, and they playing on it. Naoise heard the shout, and he said, 'That is the shout of a man of Ireland.' 'It is not, but the cry of a man of Alban,' said Deirdre. She knew at the first it was Fergus gave the shout, but she denied it. Then Fergus let another shout out of him. 'That is an Irish shout,' said Naoise again. 'It is not, indeed,' said Deirdre, 'let us go on playing.' Then Fergus gave the third shout, and the sons of Usnach knew this time it was the shout of Fergus, and Naoise said to Ardan to go out and meet him. Then Deirdre told him that she herself knew at the first shout that it was Fergus. 'Why did you deny it, then, Queen?' said Naoise. 'Because of a vision I saw last night,' said Deirdre. 'Three birds I saw coming to us from Emain Macha, and three drops of honey in their mouths, and they left them with us, and three drops of our blood they brought away with them.' 'What meaning do you put on that, Queen?' said Naoise. 'It is,' said Deirdre, 'Fergus that is coming to us with a message of peace from Conchubar, for honey is not sweeter than a message of peace sent by a lying man.' 'Let that pass,' said Naoise. 'Is there anything in it but troubled sleep and the melancholy of woman? And it is a long time Fergus is in the harbour. Rise up, Ardan, to be before him, and bring him with you here.' And Ardan went down to meet him, and gave a fond kiss to himself and to his two sons. And it is what he said: 'My love to you, dear comrades.' After that he asked news of Ireland, and they gave it to him, and then they came to where Naoise and Ainnle and Deirdre were, and they kissed Fergus and his two sons, and they asked news of Ireland from them. 'It is the best news I have for you,' said Fergus, 'that Conchubar, king of Ulster, has sworn by the earth beneath him, by the high heaven above him, and by the sun that travels to the west, that he will have no rest by day nor sleep by night, if the sons of Usnach, his own foster-brothers, will not come back to the land of their home and the country of their birth; and he has sent us to ask you there.' 'It is better for them to stop here,' said Deirdre, 'for they have a greater sway in Scotland than

Conchubar himself has in Ireland.' 'One's own country is better than any other thing,' said Fergus, 'for no man can have any pleasure, however great his good luck and his way of living, if he does not seen his own country every day.' 'That is true,' said Naoise, 'for Ireland is dearer to myself than Alban, though I would get more in Alban than in Ireland.' 'It will be safe for you to come with me,' said Fergus. 'It will be safe indeed,' said Naoise, 'and we will go with you to Ireland; and though there were no trouble beneath the sun, but a man to be far from his own land, there is little delight in peace and a long sleep to a man that is an exile. It is a pity for the man that is an exile; it is little his honour, it is great his grief, for it is he will have his share of wandering.'

It was not with Deirdre's will Naoise said that, and she was greatly against going with Fergus. And she said: 'I had a dream last night of the three sons of Usnach, and they bound and put in the grave by Conchubar of the Red Branch.' But Naoise said: 'Lay down your dream, Deirdre, on the heights of the hills, lay down your dream on the sailors of the sea, lay down your dream on the rough grey stones, for we will give peace and we will get it from the king of the world and from Conchubar.' But Deirdre spoke again, and it is what she said: 'There is the howling of dogs in my ears; a vision of the night is before my eyes, I see Fergus away from us, I see Conchubar without mercy in his dun; I see Naoise without strength in battle; I see Ainnle without his loud-sounding shield; I see Ardan without shield or breastplate, and the Hill of Atha without delight. I see Conchubar asking for blood; I see Fergus caught with hidden lies; I see Deirdre crying with tears, I see Deirdre crying with tears.'

'A thing that is unpleasing to me, and that I would never give in to,' said Fergus, 'is to listen to the howling of dogs, and to the dreams of women; and since Conchubar the High King has sent a message of friendship, it would not be right for you to refuse it.' 'It would not be right, indeed,' said Naoise, 'and we will go with you to-morrow.' And Fergus gave his word, and he said, 'If all the men of Ireland were against you, it would not profit them, for neither shield nor sword or a helmet itself would be any help or protection to them against you, and I myself to be with you.' 'That is true,' said Naoise, 'and we will go with you to Ireland.'

They spent the night there until morning, and then they went where the ships were, and they went on the sea, and a good many of their people with them, and Deirdre looked back on the land of Alban, and it is what she said: 'My love to you, O land to the east, and it goes ill with me to leave you; for it is pleasant are your bays and your harbours and your wide flowery plains and your green-sided hills; and little need was there for us to leave you.' And she made this complaint: 'Dear to me is that land, that land to the east, Alban, with its wonders; I would not have come from it hither but that I came with Naoise.

'Dear to me, Dun Fiodhaigh and Dun Fionn; dear is the dun above them; dear to me Inis Droignach, dear to me Dun Suibhne.

'O Coill Cuan! Ochone! Coill Cuan! where Ainnle used to come. My grief! it was short I thought his stay there with Naoise in Western Alban. Glen Laoi, O Glen Laoi, where I used to sleep under soft coverings; fish and venison and badger's flesh, that was my portion in Glen Laoi.

'Glen Masan, my grief! Glen Masan! high its hart's-tongue, bright its stalks; we were rocked to pleasant sleep over the wooded harbour of Masan.

'Glen Archan, my grief! Glen Archan, the straight valley of the pleasant ridge; never was there a young man more light-hearted than my Naoise used to be in Glen Archan.

'Glen Eitche, my grief! Glen Eitche, it was there I built my first house; beautiful were the woods on our rising; the home of the sun is Glen Eitche.

'Glen-da-Rua, my grief! Glen-da-Rua, my love to every man that belongs to it; sweet is the voice of the cuckoo on the bending branch on the hill above Glen-da-Rua.

'Dear to me is Droighin over the fierce strand, dear are its waters over the clean sand; I would never have come out from it at all but that I came with my beloved!'

After she had made that complaint they came to Dun Borach, and Borach gave three fond kisses to Fergus and to the sons of Usnach along with him. It was then Borach said he had a feast laid out for Fergus, and that it was *geasa* for him to leave it until he would have eaten it. But Fergus reddened with anger from head to foot, and it is what he said: 'It is a bad thing you have done, Borach, laying out a feast for me, and Conchubar to have made me give my word that as soon as I would come to Ireland, whether it would be by day or in the night-time, I would send on the sons of

Usnach to Emain Macha.' 'I hold you under bonds,' said Borach, 'to stop and use the feast.'

Then Fergus asked Naoise what should he do about the feast. 'You must choose,' said Deirdre, 'whether you will forsake the children of Usnach or the feast, and it would be better for you to refuse the feast than to forsake the sons of Usnach.' 'I will not forsake them,' said he, 'for I will send my two sons, Fair-Haired Iollan and Rough-Red Buinne, with them, to Emain Macha.' 'On my word,' said Naoise, 'that is a great deal to do for us; for up to this no other person ever protected us but ourselves.' And he went out of the place in great anger; and Ainnle, and Ardan, and Deirdre, and the two sons of Fergus followed him, and they left Fergus dark and sorrowful after them. But for all that, Fergus was full sure that if all the provinces of Ireland would go into one council, they would not consent to break the pledge he had given.

As for the sons of Usnach, they went on their way by every short road, and Deirdre said to them, 'I will give you a good advice, Sons of Usnach, though you may not follow it.' 'What is that advice, Queen?' said Naoise. 'It is,' said she, 'to go to Rechrainn, between Ireland and Scotland, and to wait there until Fergus has done with the feast; and that will be the keeping of his word to Fergus, and it will be the lengthening of your lives to you.' 'We will not follow that advice,' said Naoise; and the children of Fergus said it was little trust she had in them, when she thought they would not protect her, though their hands might not be so strong as the hands of the sons of Usnach; and besides that, Fergus had given them his word. 'Alas! it is sorrow came on us with the word of Fergus,' said Deirdre, 'and he to forsake us for a feast,' and she made this complaint: 'It is grief to me that ever I came from the east on the word of the unthinking son of Rogh. It is only lamentations I will make. Och! it is very sorrowful my heart is!

'My heart is heaped up with sorrow; it is to-night my great hurt is. My grief! my dear companions, the end of your days is come.'

And it is what Naoise answered her: 'Do not say that in your haste, Deirdre, more beautiful than the sun. Fergus would never have come for us eastward to bring us back to be destroyed.'

And Deirdre said, 'My grief! I think it too far for you, beautiful sons of Usnach, to have come from Alban of the rough grass; it is lasting will be its life-long sorrow.'

After that they went forward to Finncairn of the watchtower on sharp-peaked Slieve Fuad, and Deirdre stayed after them in the valley, and sleep fell on her there.

When Naoise saw that Deirdre was left after them, he turned back as she was rising out of her sleep, and he said, 'What made you wait after us, Queen?' 'Sleep that was on me,' said Deirdre; 'and I saw a vision in it.' 'What vision was that?' said Naoise. 'It was,' she said, 'Fair-Haired Iollan that I saw without his head on him, and Rough-Red Buinne with his head on him; and it is without help of Rough-Red Buinne you were, and it is with the help of Fair-Haired Iollan you were.' And she made this complaint:

'It is a sad vision has been shown to me, of my four tall, fair, bright companions; the head of each has been taken from him, and no help to be had one from another.'

But when Naoise heard this he reproached her, and said, 'O fair, beautiful woman, nothing does your mouth speak but evil. Do not let the sharpness and the great misfortune that come from it fall on your friends.' And Deirdre answered him with kind, gentle words, and it is what she said: 'It would be better to me to see harm come on any other person than upon any one of you three, with whom I have travelled over the seas and over the wide plains; but when I look on you, it is only Buinne I can see safe and whole, and I know by that his life will be longest among you; and indeed it is I that am sorrowful to-night.'

After that they came forward to the high willows, and it was then Deirdre said, 'I see a cloud in the air, and it is a cloud of blood; and I would give you a good advice, sons of Usnach,' she said. 'What is that advice?' said Naoise. 'To go to Dundealgan where Cuchulain is, until Fergus has done with the feast, and to be under the protection of Cuchulain, for fear of the treachery of Conchubar.' 'Since there is no fear on us, we will not follow that advice,' said Naoise. And Deirdre complained, and it is what she said: 'O Naoise, look at the cloud I see above us in the air; I see a cloud over green Macha, cold and deep red like blood. I am startled by the cloud that I see here in the air; a thin, dreadful cloud that is like a clot of blood. I give a right advice to the beautiful sons of Usnach not to go to Emain to-night, because of the danger that is over them.

'We will go to Dundealgan, where the Hound of the Smith is; we will come to-morrow from the south along with the Hound, Cuchulain.'

But Naoise said in his anger to Deirdre, 'Since there is no fear on us, we will not follow your advice.' And Deirdre turned to the grandsons of Rogh, and it is what she said: 'It is seldom until now, Naoise, that yourself and myself were not of the one mind. And I say to you, Naoise, that you would not have gone against me like this, the day Manannan gave me the cup in the time of his great victory.'

After that they went on to Emain Macha. 'Sons of Usnach,' said Deirdre, 'I have a sign by which you will know if Conchubar is going to do treachery on you.' 'What sign is that?' said Naoise. 'If you are let come into the house where Conchubar is, and the nobles of Ulster, then Conchubar is not going to do treachery on you. But if it is in the House of the Red Branch you are put, then he is going to do treachery on you.'

After that they came to Emain Macha, and they took the handwood and struck the door, and the doorkeeper asked who was there. They told him that it was the sons of Usnach, and Deirdre, and the two sons of Fergus were there.

When Conchubar heard that, he called his stewards and serving men to him, and he asked them how was the House of the Red Branch for food and for drink. They said that if all the seven armies of Ulster would come there, they would find what would satisfy them. 'If that is so,' said Conchubar, 'bring the sons of Usnach into it.'

It was then Deirdre said, 'It would have been better for you to follow my advice, and never to have come to Emain, and it would be right for you to leave it, even at this time.' 'We will not,' said Fair-Haired Iollan, 'for it is not fear or cowardliness was ever seen on us, but we will go to the house.' So they went on to the House of the Red Branch, and the stewards and the serving-men with them, and well-tasting food was served to them, and pleasant drinks, till they were all glad and merry, except only Deirdre and the sons of Usnach; for they did not use much food or drink, because of the length and the greatness of their journey from Dun Borach to Emain Macha. Then Naoise said, 'Give the chessboard to us till we go playing.' So they gave them the chessboard and they began to play.

It was just at that time Conchubar was asking, 'Who will I send that will bring me word of Deirdre, and that will tell me if she has the same appearance and the same shape she had before, for if she has, there is not a woman in the world has a more beautiful shape or appearance than she has, and I will bring her out with edge of blade and point of sword in spite of the sons of Usnach, good though they be. But if not, let Naoise have her for himself.' 'I myself will go there,' said Levarcham, 'and I will bring you word of that.' And it is how it was, Deirdre was dearer to her than any other person in the world; for it was often she went through the world looking for Deirdre and bringing news to her and from her. So Levarcham went over to the House of the Red Branch, and near it she saw a great troop of armed men, and she spoke to them, but they made her no answer, and she knew by that it was none of the men of Ulster were in it, but men from some strange country that Conchubar's messengers had brought to Emain.

And then she went in where Naoise and Deirdre were, and it is how she found them, the polished chessboard between them, and they playing on it; and she gave them fond kisses, and she said: 'You are not doing well to be playing; and it is to bring Conchubar word if Deirdre has the same shape and appearance she used to have that he sent me here now; and there is grief on me for the deed that will be done in Emain to-night, treachery that will be done, and the killing of kindred, and the three bright candles of the Gael to be quenched, and Emain will not be the better of it to the end of life and time,' and she made this complaint sadly and wearily:

'My heart is heavy for the treachery that is being done in Emain this night; on account of this treachery, Emain will never be at peace from this out.

'The three that are most king-like to-day under the sun; the three best of all that live on the earth, it is grief to me to-night they to die for the sake of any woman. Naoise and Ainnle whose deeds are known, and Ardan, their brother; treachery is to be done on the young, bright-faced three; it is not I that am not sorrowful to-night.'

When she had made this complaint, Levarcham said to the sons of Usnach and to the children of Fergus to shut close the doors and the windows of the house and to do bravery. 'And oh, sons of Fergus,' she said, 'defend your charge and your care bravely till Fergus comes, and you will have praise and a blessing for it.' And she cried with many tears, and she went back to where Conchubar was, and he asked news of Deirdre of her. And Levarcham said, 'It is good news and bad news I have for you.' 'What news is that?' said Conchubar. 'It is the good news,' she said, 'the three sons of Usnach to have come to you and to be over there, and they are the three that are bravest and mightiest in form and in looks and in countenance, of all in the world; and Ireland will be yours from this out, since the sons of Usnach are with you; and the news that is worst with me is, the woman that was best of the women of the world in form and in looks, going out of Emain, is without the form and without the appearance she used to have.'

When Conchubar heard that, much of his jealousy went backward, and he was drinking and making merry for a while, until he thought on Deirdre again the second time, and on that he asked, 'Who will I get to bring me word of Deirdre?' But he did not find any one would go there. And then he said to Gelban, the merry, pleasant son of the king of Lochlann: 'Go over and bring me word if Deirdre has the same shape and the same appearance she used to have, for if she has, there is not on the ridge of the world or on the waves of the earth, a woman more beautiful than herself.'

So Gelban went to the House of the Red Branch, and he found the doors and the windows of the fort shut, and fear came on him. And it is what he said: 'It is not an easy road for any one that would get to the sons of Usnach, for I think there is very great anger on them.' And after that he found a window that was left open by forgetfulness in the house, and he was looking in. Then Deirdre saw him through the window, and when she saw him looking at her, she went into a red blaze of blushes, and Naoise knew that some one was looking at her from the window, and she told him that she saw a young man looking in at them. It is how Naoise was at that time, with a man of the chessmen in his hand, and he made a fair throw over his shoulder at the young man, that put the eye out of his head. The young man went back to where Conchubar was. 'You were merry and pleasant going out,' said Conchubar, 'but you are sad and cheerless coming back.' And then Gelban told him the story from beginning to end. 'I see well,' said Conchubar, 'the man that made that throw will be king of the world, unless he has his life shortened. And what appearance is there on Deirdre?' he said. 'It is this,' said Gelban, 'although Naoise put out my eye, I would have wished to stay there looking at her with the other eye, but for the haste you put on me; for there is not in the world a woman is better of shape or of form than herself.'

When Conchubar heard that, he was filled with jealousy and with envy, and he bade the men of his army that were with him, and that had been drinking at the feast, to go and attack the place where the sons of Usnach were. So they went forward to the House of the Red Branch, and they gave three great shouts around it, and they put fires and red flames to it. When the sons of Usnach heard the shouts, they asked who those men were that were about the house. 'Conchubar and the men of Ulster,' they all said together. 'Is it the pledge of Fergus you would break?' said Fair-Haired Iollan. 'On my word,' said Conchubar, 'there will be sorrow on the sons of Usnach, Deirdre to be with them.' 'That is true,' said Deirdre, 'Fergus had deceived you.' 'By my oath,' said Rough-Red Buinne, 'if he betrayed, we will not betray.' It was then Buinne went out and killed three-fifths of the fighting men outside, and put great disturbance on the rest; and Conchubar asked who was there, and who was doing destruction on his men like that. 'It is I, myself, Rough-Red Buinne, son of Fergus,' said he. 'I will give you a good gift if you will leave off,' said Conchubar. 'What gift is that?' said Rough-Red Buinne. 'A hundred of land,' said Conchubar. 'What besides?' said Rough-Red Buinne. 'My own friendship and my counsel,' said Conchubar. 'I will take that,' said Rough-Red Buinne. It was a good mountain that was given him as a reward, but it turned barren in the same night, and no green grew on it again for ever, and it used to be called the Mountain of the Share of Buinne.

Deirdre heard what they were saying. 'By my word,' she said, 'Rough-Red Buinne has forsaken you, and in my opinion, it is like the father the son is.' 'I give my word,' says Fair-Haired Iollan, 'that is not so with me; as long as this narrow, straight sword stays in my hand, I will not forsake the sons of Usnach.'

After that, Fair-Haired Iollan went out, and made three courses around the house, and killed three-fifths of the heroes outside, and he came in again where Naoise was, and he playing chess, and Ainnle with him. So Iollan went out the second time, and made three other courses round the fort, and he brought a lighted torch with him on the lawn, and he went destroying the hosts, so that they dared not come to attack the house. And he was a good son, Fair-Haired Iollan, for he never refused any person on the ridge of the world anything that he had, and he never took wages from any person but only Fergus.

It was then Conchubar said: 'What place is my own son, Fiacra the Fair?' 'I am here, High Prince,' said Fiacra. 'By my word,' said Conchubar, 'it is on the one night yourself and Iollan were born, and as it is the arms of his father he has with him, let you take my arms with you, that is, my shield, the Ochain, my two spears, and my great sword, the Gorm Glas, the Blue Green—and do bravery and great deeds with them.'

Then Fiacra took Conchubar's arms, and he and Fair-Haired Iollan attacked one another, and they made a stout fight, one against the other. But however it was, Fair-Haired Iollan put down Fiacra, so that he made him lie under the shelter of his shield, till it roared for the greatness of the strait he was in; for it was the way with the Ochain, the shield of Conchubar, to roar when the person on whom it would be was in danger; and the three chief waves of Ireland, the Wave of Tuagh, the Wave of Cliodna, and the Wave of Rudraige, roared in answer to it.

It was at that time Conall Cearnach was at Dun Sobairce, and he heard the Wave of Tuagh. 'True it is,' said Conall, 'Conchubar is in some danger, and it is not right for me to be here listening to him.'

Conall rose up on that, and he put his arms and his armour on him, and came forward to where Conchubar was at Emain Macha, and he found the fight going on on the lawn, and Fiacra, the son of Conchubar, greatly pressed by Fair-Haired Iollan, and neither the king of Ulster nor any other person dared to go between them. But Conall went aside, behind Fair-Haired Iollan, and thrust his sword through him. 'Who is it has wounded me behind my back?' said Fair-Haired Iollan. 'Whoever did it, by my hand of valour, he would have got a fair fight, face to face, from myself.' 'Who are you yourself?' said Conall. 'I am Iollan, son of Fergus, and are you yourself Conall?' 'It is I,' said Conall. 'It is evil and it is heavy the work you have done,' said Iollan, 'and the sons of Usnach under my protection.' 'Is that true?' said Conall. 'It is true, indeed,' said Iollan. 'By my hand of valour,' said Conall, 'Conchubar will not get his own son alive from me to avenge it,' and he gave a stroke of the sword to Fiacra, so that he struck his head off, and he left them so. The clouds of death came upon Fair-Haired Iollan then, and he threw his arms towards the fortress, and called out to Naoise to do bravery, and after that he died.

It is then Conchubar himself came out and nineteen hundred

men with him, and Conall said to him: 'Go up now to the doorway of the fort, and see where your sister's children are lying on a bed of trouble.' And when Conchubar saw them he said: 'You are not sister's children to me; it is not the deed of sister's children you have done me, but you have done harm to me with treachery in the sight of all the men of Ireland.' And it is what Ainnle said to him: 'Although we took well-shaped, soft-handed Deirdre from you, yet we did a little kindness to you at another time, and this is the time to remember it. That day your ship was breaking up on the sea, and it full of gold and silver, we gave you up our own ship, and ourselves went swimming to the harbour.' But Conchubar said: 'If you did fifty good deeds to me, surely this would be my thanks; I would not give you peace, and you in distress, but every great want I could put on you.'

And then Ardan said: 'We did another little kindness to you, and this is the time to remember it; the day the speckled horse failed you on the green of Dundealgan, it was we gave you the grey horse that would bring you fast on your road.'

But Conchubar said: 'If you had done fifty good deeds to me, surely this would be my thanks; I would not give you peace, and you in distress, but every great want I could put on you.'

And then Naoise said: 'We did you another good deed, and this is the time to remember it; we have put you under many benefits; it is strong our right is to your protection.

'The time when Murcael, son of Brian, fought the seven battles at Beinn Etair, we brought you, without fail, the heads of the sons of the king of the South-East.'

But Conchubar said: 'If you had done me fifty good deeds, surely this is my thanks; I would not give you peace in your distress, but every great want I could put upon you.

'Your death is not a death to me now, young sons of Usnach, since he that was innocent fell by you, the third best of the horsemen of Ireland.'

Then Deirdre said: 'Rise up, Naoise, take your sword, good son of a king, mind yourself well, for it is not long that life will be left in your fair body.'

It is then all Conchubar's men came about the house, and they put fires and burning to it. Ardan went out then, and his men, and put out the fires and killed three hundred men. And Ainnle went out in the third part of the night, and he killed three hundred, and did slaughter and destruction on them.

And Naoise went out in the last quarter of the night, and drove away all the army from the house.

He came into the house after that, and it is then Deirdre rose up and said to him: 'By my word, it is well you won your way; and do bravery and valour from this out, and it was bad advice you took when you ever trusted Conchubar.'

As for the sons of Usnach, after that they made a good protection with their shields, and they put Deirdre in the middle and linked the shields around her, and they gave three leaps out over the walls of Emain, and they killed three hundred men in that sally.

When Conchubar saw that, he went to Cathbad, the Druid, and said to him: 'Go, Cathbad, to the sons of Usnach, and work enchantment on them; for unless they are hindered they will destroy the men of Ulster for ever if they go away in spite of them; and I give the word of a true hero, they will get no harm from me, but let them only make agreement with me.' When Cathbad heard that, he agreed, believing him, and he went to the end of his arts and his knowledge to hinder the sons of Usnach, and he worked enchantment on them, so that he put the likeness of a dark sea about them, with hindering waves. And when Naoise saw the waves rising he put up Deirdre on his shoulder, and it is how the sons of Usnach were, swimming on the ground as they were going out of Emain; yet the men of Ulster did not dare to come near them until their swords had fallen from their hands. But after their swords fell from their hands, the sons of Usnach were taken. And when they were taken, Conchubar asked of the children of Durthacht to kill them. But the children of Durthacht said they would not do that. There was a young man with Conchubar whose name was Maine, and his surname Rough-Hand, son of the king of the fair Norwegians, and it is Naoise had killed his father and his two brothers; Athrac and Triathrach were their names. And he said he himself would kill the sons of Usnach. 'If that is so,' said Ardan, 'kill me the first, for I am younger than my brothers, so that I will not see my brothers killed.' 'Let him not be killed but myself,' said Ainnle. 'Let that not be done,' said Naoise, 'for I have a sword that Manannan, son of Lir, gave me, and the stroke of it leaves nothing after it, track nor trace; and strike the three of us together, and we will die at the one time.' 'That is well,' said they all, 'and let you lay down your heads,' they said. They did that, and Maine gave a strong quick blow of the sword on the three necks together on the block, and struck the three heads off them with one stroke; and the men of Ulster gave three loud sorrowful shouts, and cried aloud about them there.

As for Deirdre, she cried pitifully, wearily, and tore her fair hair, and she was talking on the sons of Usnach and on Alban, and it is what she said:

'A blessing eastward to Alban from me; good is the sight of her bays and valleys, pleasant was it to sit on the slopes of her hills, where the sons of Usnach used to be hunting.

'One day, when the nobles of Scotland were drinking with the sons of Usnach, to whom they owed their affection, Naoise gave a kiss secretly to the daughter of the lord of Duntreon. He sent her a frightened deer, wild, and a fawn at its foot; and he went to visit her coming home from the host of Inverness. When myself heard that, my head filled full of jealousy; I put my boat on the waves, it was the same to me to live or to die. They followed me swimming, Ainnle and Ardan, that never said a lie; they turned me back again, two that would give battle to a hundred; Naoise gave me his true word, he swore three times with his arms as witness, he would never put vexation on me again, until he would go from me to the hosts of the dead.

'Och! if she knew to-night, Naoise to be under a covering of clay, it is she would cry her fill, and it is I would cry along with her.'

After she had made this complaint, seeing they were all taken up with one another, Deirdre came forward on the lawn, and she was running round and round, up and down, from one to another, and Cuchulain met her, and she told him the story from first to last, how it had happened to the sons of Usnach. It is sorrowful Cuchulain was for that, for there was not in the world a man was dearer to him than Naoise. And he asked who killed him. 'Maine Rough-Hand,' said Deirdre. Then Cuchulain went away, sad and sorrowful, to Dundealgan.

After that Deirdre lay down by the grave, and they were digging earth from it, and she made this lament after the sons of Usnach:

# FATE OF THE SONS OF USNACH

'Long is the day without the sons of Usnach; it was never wearisome to be in their company; sons of a king that entertained exiles; three lions of the Hill of the Cave.

'Three darlings of the women of Britain; three hawks of Slieve Cuilenn; sons of a king served by valour, to whom warriors did obedience. The three mighty bears; three lions of the fort of Conrach; three sons of a king who thought well of their praise; three nurslings of the men of Ulster.

'Three heroes not good at homage; their fall is a cause of sorrow; three sons of the sister of a king; three props of the army of Cuailgne.

'Three dragons of Dun Monad, the three valiant men from the Red Branch; I myself will not be living after them, the three that broke hard battles.

'Three that were brought up by Aoife, to whom lands were under tribute; three pillars in the breach of battle; three pupils that were with Scathach.

'Three pupils that were with Uathach; three champions that were lasting in might; three shining sons of Usnach; it is weariness to be without them.

'The High King of Ulster, my first betrothed, I forsook for love of Naoise; short my life will be after him; I will make keening at their burial.

'That I would live after Naoise let no one think on the earth; I will not go on living after Ainnle and after Ardan.

'After them I myself will not live; three that would leap through the midst of battle; since my beloved is gone from me I will cry my fill over his grave.

'O young man, digging the new grave, do not make the grave narrow; I will be along with them in the grave, making lamentation and ochones!

'Many the hardship I met with along with the three heroes; I suffered want of house, want of fire, it is myself that used not to be troubled.

'Their three shields and their spears made a bed for me often. O young man, put their three swords close over their grave.

'Their three hounds, their three hawks, will be from this time without huntsmen; three helpers of every battle; three pupils of Conall Cearnach.

'The three leashes of those three hounds have brought a sigh from my heart; it is I had the care of them, the sight of them is a cause of grief.

'I was never one day alone to the day of the making of this grave, though it is often that myself and yourselves were in loneliness.

'My sight is gone from me with looking at the grave of Naoise; it is short till my life will leave me, and those who would have keened me do not live.

'Since it is through me they were betrayed I will be tired out with sorrow; it is a pity I was not in the earth before the sons of Usnach were killed.

'Sorrowful was my journey with Fergus, betraying me to the Red Branch; we were deceived all together with his sweet, flowery words. I left the delights of Ulster for the three heroes that were bravest; my life will not be long, I myself am alone after them.

'I am Deirdre without gladness, and I at the end of my life; since it is grief to be without them, I myself will not be long after them.'

After that complaint Deirdre loosed out her hair, and threw herself on the body of Naoise before it was put in the grave and gave three kisses to him, and when her mouth touched his blood, the colour of burning sods came into her cheeks, and she rose up like one that had lost her wits, and she went on through the night till she came to where the waves were breaking on the strand. And a fisherman was there and his wife, and they brought her into their cabin and sheltered her, and she neither smiled nor laughed, nor took food, drink, or sleep, nor raised her head from her knees, but crying always after the sons of Usnach.

But when she could not be found at Emain, Conchubar sent Levarcham to look for her, and to bring her back to his palace, that he might make her his wife. And Levarcham found her in the fisherman's cabin, and she bade her come back to Emain, where she would have protection and riches and all that she would ask. And she gave her this message she brought from Conchubar: 'Come up to my house, O branch with the dark eyelashes, and there need be no fear on your fair face, of hatred or of jealousy or of reproach.' And Deirdre said: 'I will not go up to his house, for it is not land or earth or food I am wanting, or gold or silver or horses, but leave to go to the grave where the sons of Usnach are lying,

'I do not sleep through the night; my senses are scattered away from me, I do not care for food or drink. I have no welcome to-day for the pleasant drink of nobles, or ease, or comfort, or delight, or a great house, or the palace of a king.

'Do not break the strings of my heart as you took hold of my young youth, Conchubar; though my darling is dead, my love is strong to live. What is country to me, or land, or lordship? What are swift horses? What are jewels and gold? Och! it is I will be lying to-night on the strand like the beautiful sons of Usnach.'

So Levarcham went back to Conchubar to tell him what way Deirdre was, and that she would not come with her to Emain Macha.

And when she was gone, Deirdre went out on the strand, and she found a carpenter making an oar for a boat, and making a mast for it, clean and straight, to put up a sail to the wind. And when she saw him making it, she said: 'It is a sharp knife you have, to cut the oar so clean and so straight, and if you will give it to me,' she said, 'I will give you a ring of the best gold in Ireland for it, the ring that belonged to Naoise, and that was with him through the battle and through the fight; he thought much of it in his lifetime; it is pure gold, through and through.' So the carpenter took the ring in his hand, and the knife in the other hand, and he looked at them together, and he gave her the knife for the ring, and for her asking and her tears. Then Deirdre went close to the waves, and she said: 'Since the other is not with me now, I will spend no more of my lifetime without him.' And with that she drove the black knife into her side, but she drew it out again and threw it in the sea to her right hand, the way no one would be blamed for her death.

Then Conchubar came down to the strand and five hundred men along with him, to bring Deirdre away to Emain Macha, but all he found before him was her white body on the ground, and it without life. And it is what he said:

'A thousand deaths on the time I brought death on my sister's children; now I am myself without Deirdre, and they themselves are without life.

'They were my sister's children, the three brothers I vexed with blows, Naoise, and Ainnle, and Ardan; they have died along with Deirdre.'

And they took her white, beautiful body, and laid it in a grave, till I give the three honey kisses to their three white, beauti[ful] bodies.' And she made this complaint:

'Make keening for the heroes that were killed on their coming [to] Ireland; stately they used to be, coming to the house, the thr[ee] great sons of Usnach.

'The sons of Usnach fell in the fight like three branches tha[t] were growing straight and nice, and they destroyed in a heav[y] storm that left neither bud nor twig of them.

'Naoise, my gentle, well-learned comrade, make no delay in cry[]ing him with me; cry for Ardan that killed the wild boars, cry for Ainnle whose strength was great.

'It was Naoise that would kiss my lips, my first man and my first sweetheart; it was Ainnle would pour out my drink, and it was Ardan would lay my pillow.

'Though sweet to you is the mead that is drunk by the soft-living son of Ness, the food of the sons of Usnach was sweeter to me all through my lifetime.

'Whenever Naoise would go out to hunt through the woods or the wide plains, all the meat he would bring back was better to me than honey.

'Though sweet to you are the sounds of pipes and of trumpets, it is truly I say to the king, I have heard music that is sweeter.

'Delightful to Conchubar, the king, are pipes and trumpets; but the singing of the sons of Usnach was more delightful to me.

'It was Naoise had the deep sound of the waves in his voice; it was the song of Ardan that was good, and the voice of Ainnle towards their green dwelling-place.

'Their birth was beautiful and their blossoming, as they grew to the strength of manhood; sad is the end to-day, the sons of Usnach to be cut down.

'Dear were their pleasant words, dear their young, high strength; in their going through the plains of Ireland there was a welcome before the coming of their strength.

'Dear their grey eyes that were loved by women, many looked on them as they went; when they went freely searching through the woods, their steps were pleasant on the dark mountain.

'I do not sleep at any time, and the colour is gone from my face; there is no sound can give me delight since the sons of Usnach do not come.

and a flagstone was raised over her grave, and over the grave of the sons of Usnach, and their names were written in Ogham,[1] and keening was made for their burial.

And as to Fergus, son of Rogh, he came on the day after the children of Usnach were killed, to Emain Macha. And when he found they had been killed and his pledge to them broken, he himself, and Cormac Conloingeas, Conchubar's own son, and Dubthach, the Beetle of Ulster, with their men, made an attack on Conchubar's house and men, and a great many were killed by them, and Emain Macha was burned and destroyed.

And after doing that, they went into Connaught, to Ailell and to Maeve at Cruachan, and they were made welcome there, and they took service with them and fought with them against Ulster because of the treachery that was done by Conchubar. And that is the way Fergus and the others came to be on the side of the men of Connaught in the war for the Brown Bull of Cuailgne.

And Cathbad laid a curse on Emain Macha, on account of that great wrong. And it is what he said, that none of the race of Conchubar should have the kingdom, to the end of life and time.

And that came true, for the most of Conchubar's sons died in his own lifetime, and when he was near his death, he bade the men of Ulster bring back Cormac Conloingeas out of Cruachan, and give him the kingdom.

So they sent messengers to Cormac, and he set out and his three troops of men with him, and he left his blessing with Ailell and with Maeve, and he promised them a good return for all the kind treatment they had given him. And they crossed the river at Athluain, and there they saw a red woman at the edge of the ford, and she washing her chariot and her harness. And after that they met a young girl coming towards them, and a light green cloak about her, and a brooch of precious stones at her breast. And Cormac asked her was she coming with them, and she said she was not, and it would be better for himself to turn back, for the ruin of his life was come.

And he stopped for the night at the House of the Two Smiths on the hill of Bruighean Mor, the great dwelling-place.

But a troop of the men of Connaught came about the house in the night, for they were on the way home after destroying and

---

[1] An ancient Irish alphabet of twenty characters.

robbing a district of Ulster, and they thought to make an end of Cormac before he would get to Emain.

And it chanced there was a great harper, Craiftine, living close by, and his wife, Sceanb, daughter of Scethern, a Druid of Connaught, loved Cormac Conloingeas, and three times she had gone to meet him at Athluain, and she planted three trees there—Grief, and Dark, and Dumbness.

And there was great hatred and jealousy of Cormac on Craiftine, so when he knew the men of Connaught were going to make an attack on him, he went outside the house with his harp, and played a soft sleepy tune to him, the way he had not the strength to rouse himself up, and himself and the most of his people were killed. And Amergin, that had gone with the message to him, made his grave and his mound, and the place is called Cluain Duma, the Lawn of the Mound.

JAMES STEPHENS

# The Two Gods[1]

CAITILIN NI MURRACHU WAS SITTING alone in the little cave behind Gort na Cloca Mora. Her companion had gone out as was his custom to walk in the sunny morning and to sound his pipe in desolate, green spaces whence, perhaps, the wanderer of his desire might hear the guiding sweetness. As she sat she was thinking. The last few days had awakened her body, and had also awakened her mind, for with the one awakening comes the other. The despondency which had touched her previously when tending her father's cattle came to her again, but recognisably now. She knew the thing which the wind had whispered in the sloping field and for which she had no name—it was Happiness. Faintly she shadowed it forth, but yet she could not see it. It was only a pearl-pale wraith, almost formless, too tenuous to be touched by her hands, and too aloof to be spoken to. Pan had told her that he was the giver of happiness, but he had given her only unrest and fever and a longing which could not be satisfied. Again there was a want, and she could not formulate, or even realise it with any closeness. Her newborn Thought had promised everything, even as Pan, and it had given— she could not say that it had given her nothing or anything. Its limits were too quickly divinable. She had found the Tree of Knowledge, but about on every side a great wall soared blackly enclosing her in from the Tree of Life—a wall which her thought was unable to surmount even while instinct urged that it must topple before her advance, but instinct may not advance when thought has schooled it in the science of unbelief; and this wall will not be conquered until Thought and Instinct are wed, and the first son of that bridal will be called The Scaler of the Wall.

So, after the quiet weariness of ignorance, the unquiet weariness of thought had fallen upon her. That travail of mind which, through countless generations, has throed to the birth of an ecstasy, the prophecy which humanity has sworn must be fulfilled, seeing through whatever mists and doubtings the vision of a gaiety wherein the innocence of the morning will not any longer be strange to our maturity.

While she was so thinking Pan returned, a little disheartened that

[1] From *The Crock of Gold*, London, 1912.

he had found no person to listen to his pipings. He had been seated but a little time when suddenly, from without, a chorus of birds burst into joyous singing. Limpid and liquid cadenzas, mellow flutings, and the sweet treble of infancy met and danced and piped in the airy soundings. A round, soft tenderness of song rose and fell, broadened and soared, and then the high flight was snatched, eddied a moment, and was borne away to a more slender and wonderful loftiness, until, from afar, that thrilling song turned on the very apex of sweetness, dipped steeply and flashed its joyous return to the exultations of its mates below, rolling an ecstasy of song which for one moment gladdened the whole world and the sad people who moved thereon; then the singing ceased as suddenly as it began, a swift shadow darkened the passage, and Angus Óg came into the cave.

Caitilin sprang from her seat affrighted, and Pan also made a half movement towards rising, but instantly sank back again to his negligent, easy posture.

The god was slender and as swift as a wind. His hair swung about his face like golden blossoms. His eyes were mild and dancing and his lips smiled with quiet sweetness. About his head there flew perpetually a ring of singing birds, and when he spoke his voice came sweetly from a centre of sweetness.

'Health to you, daughter of Murrachu,' said he, and he sat down.

'I do not know you, sir,' the terrified girl whispered.

'I cannot be known until I make myself known,' he replied. 'I am called Infinite Joy, O daughter of Murrachu, and I am called Love.'

The girl gazed doubtfully from one to the other.

Pan looked up from his pipes.

'I also am called Love,' said he gently, "and I am called Joy.'

Angus Óg looked for the first time at Pan.

'Singer of the Vine,' said he, 'I know your names—they are Desire and Fever and Lust and Death. Why have you come from your own place to spy upon my pastures and my quiet fields?'

Pan replied mildly.

'The mortal gods move by the Immortal Will, and, therefore, I am here.'

'And I am here,' said Angus.

'Give me a sign,' said Pan, 'that I must go.'

Angus Óg lifted his hand and from without there came again the triumphant music of the birds.

'It is a sign,' said he, 'the voice of Dana speaking in the air,' and, saying so, he made obeisance to the great mother.

Pan lifted his hand, and from afar there came the lowing of the cattle and the thin voices of the goats.

'It is a sign,' said he, 'the voice of Demeter speaking from the earth,' and he also bowed deeply to the mother of the world.

Again Angus Óg lifted his hand, and in it there appeared a spear, bright and very terrible.

But Pan only said, 'Can a spear divine the Eternal Will?' and Angus Óg put his weapon aside, and he said—

'The girl will choose between us, for the Divine Mood shines in the heart of man.'

Then Caitilin Ni Murrachu came forward and sat between the gods, but Pan stretched out his hand and drew her to him, so that she sat resting against his shoulder and his arm was about her body.

'We will speak the truth to this girl,' said Angus Óg.

'Can the gods speak otherwise?' said Pan, and he laughed with delight.

'It is the difference between us,' replied Angus Óg. 'She will judge.'

'Shepherd Girl,' said Pan, pressing her with his arm, 'you will judge between us. Do you know what is the greatest thing in the world—because it is of that you will have to judge.'

'I have heard,' the girl replied, 'two things called the greatest things. You,' she continued to Pan, 'said it was Hunger, and long ago my father said that Commonsense was the greatest thing in the world.'

'I have not told you,' said Angus Óg, 'what I consider is the greatest thing in the world.'

'It is your right to speak,' said Pan.

'The greatest thing in the world,' said Angus Óg, 'is the Divine Imagination.'

'Now,' said Pan, 'we know all the greatest things and we can talk of them.'

'The daughter of Murrachu,' continued Angus Óg, 'has told us what you think and what her father thinks, but she has not told us what she thinks herself. Tell us, Caitilin Ni Murrachu, what you think is the greatest thing in the world.'

So Caitilin Ni Murrachu thought for a few moments and then replied timidly.

'I think that Happiness is the greatest thing in the world,' said she.

Hearing this they sat in silence for a little time, and then Angus Óg spoke again—

'The Divine Imagination may only be known through the thoughts of His creatures. A man has said Commonsense and a woman has said Happiness are the greatest things in the world. These things are male and female, for Commonsense is Thought and Happiness is Emotion, and until they embrace in Love the will of Immensity cannot be fruitful. For, behold, there has been no marriage of humanity since time began. Men have but coupled with their own shadows. The desire that sprang from their heads they pursued, and no man has yet known the love of a woman. And women have mated with the shadows of their own hearts, thinking fondly that the arms of men were about them. I saw my son dancing with an Idea, and I said to him, "With what do you dance, my son?" and he replied, "I make merry with the wife of my affection," and truly she was shaped as a woman is shaped, but it was an Idea he danced with and not a woman. And presently he went away to his labours, and then his Idea arose and her humanity came upon her so that she was clothed with beauty and terror, and she went apart and danced with the servant of my son, and there was great joy of that dancing—for a person in the wrong place is an Idea and not a person. Man is Thought and woman is Intuition, and they have never mated. There is a gulf between them and it is called Fear, and what they fear is, that their strengths shall be taken from them and they may no longer be tyrants. The Eternal has made love blind, for it is not by science, but by intuition alone, that he may come to his beloved: but desire, which is science, has many eyes and sees so vastly that he passes his love in the press, saying there is no love, and he propagates miserably on his own delusions. The finger tips are guided by God, but the devil looks through the eyes of all creatures so that they may wander in the errors of reason and justify themselves of their wanderings. The desire of a man shall be Beauty, but he has fashioned a slave in his mind and called it Virtue. The desire of a woman shall be Wisdom, but she has formed a beast in her blood and called it Courage: but the real virtue is courage, and the real courage is liberty, and the real liberty is wisdom, and Wisdom is the son of Thought and Intuition; and his names also are Innocence and Adoration and Happiness.'

When Angus Óg had said these words he ceased, and for a time there was silence in the little cave. Caitilin had covered her face with her hands and would not look at him, but Pan drew the girl closer to his side and peered sideways, laughing at Angus.

'Has the time yet come for the girl to judge between us?' said he.

'Daughter of Murrachu,' said Angus Óg, 'will you come away with me from this place?'

Caitilin then looked at the god in great distress.

'I do not know what to do,' said she. 'Why do you both want me? I have given myself to Pan, and his arms are about me.'

'I want you,' said Angus Óg, 'because the world has forgotten me. In all my nation there is no remembrance of me. I, wandering on the hills of my country, am lonely indeed. I am the desolate god forbidden to utter my happy laughter. I hide the silver of my speech and the gold of my merriment. I live in the holes of the rocks and the dark caves of the sea. I weep in the morning because I may not laugh, and in the evening I go abroad and am not happy. Where I have kissed a bird has flown; where I have trod a flower has sprung. But Thought has snared my birds in his nets and sold them in the market-places. Who will deliver me from Thought, from the base holiness of Intellect, the maker of chains and traps? Who will save me from the holy impurity of Emotion, whose daughters are Envy and Jealousy and Hatred, who plucks my flowers to ornament her lusts and my little leaves to shrivel on the breasts of infamy? Lo, I am sealed in the caves of nonentity until the head and the heart shall come together in fruitfulness, until Thought has wept for Love, and Emotion has purified herself to meet her lover. Tir-na-nÓg is the heart of a man and the head of a woman. Widely they are separated. Self-centred they stand, and between them the seas of space are flooding desolately. No voice can shout across those shores. No eye can bridge them, nor any desire bring them together until the blind god shall find them on the wavering stream—not as an arrow searches straightly from a bow, but gently, imperceptibly as a feather on the wind reaches the ground on a hundred starts; not with the compass and the chart, but by the breath of the Almighty which blows from all quarters without care and without ceasing. Night and day it urges from the outside to the inside. It gathers ever to the centre. From the far without to the deep within, trembling from the body to the soul until the head of a woman and the heart of a man are filled with the Divine Imagination. Hymen, Hymenæa! I sing to the ears that are stopped, the eyes that are sealed, and the minds that do not labour. Sweetly I sing on the hillside. The blind shall look within and not without; the deaf shall hearken to the murmur of their own veins, and be enchanted with the wisdom of sweetness; the thoughtless shall think without effort as the lightning flashes, that the hand of Innocence may reach to the stars, that the feet of Adoration may dance to the Father of Joy, and the laugh of Happiness be answered by the Voice of Benediction.'

Thus Angus Óg sang in the cave, and ere he had ceased Caitilin Ni Murrachu withdrew herself from the arms of her desires. But so strong was the hold of Pan upon her that when she was free her body bore the marks of his grip, and many days passed away before these marks faded.

Then Pan arose in silence, taking his double reed in his hand, and the girl wept, beseeching him to stay to be her brother and the brother of her beloved, but Pan smiled and said—

'Your beloved is my father and my son. He is yesterday and tomorrow. He is the nether and the upper millstone, and I am crushed between until I kneel again before the throne from whence I came,' and, saying so, he embraced Angus Óg most tenderly and went his way to the quiet fields, and across the slopes of the mountains, and beyond the blue distances of space.

And in a little time Caitilin Ni Murrachu went with her companion across the brow of the hill, and she did not go with him because she had understood his words, nor because he was naked and unashamed, but only because his need of her was very great, and, therefore, she loved him, and stayed his feet in the way, and was concerned lest he should stumble.

DOUGLAS HYDE

# The Necessity for De-Anglicising Ireland[1]

WHEN WE SPEAK of "The Necessity for De-Anglicising the Irish Nation," we mean it, not as a protest against imitating what is *best* in the English people, for that would be absurd, but rather to show the folly of neglecting what is Irish, and hastening to adopt, pell-mell, and indiscriminately, everything that is English, simply because it *is* English.

This is a question which most Irishmen will naturally look at from a National point of view, but it is one which ought also to claim the sympathies of every intelligent Unionist, and which, as I know, does claim the sympathy of many.

If we take a bird's-eye view of our island to-day, and compare it with what it used to be, we must be struck by the extraordinary fact that the nation which was once, as every one admits, one of the most classically learned and cultured nations in Europe, is now one of the least so; how one of the most reading and literary peoples has become one of the *least* studious and most *un*-literary, and how the present art products of one of the quickest, most sensitive, and most artistic races on earth are now only distinguished for their hideousness.

I shall endeavour to show that this failure of the Irish people in recent times has been largely brought about by the race diverging during this century from the right path, and ceasing to be Irish without becoming English. I shall attempt to show that with the bulk of the people this change took place quite recently, much more recently than most people imagine, and is, in fact, still going on. I should also like to call attention to the illogical position of men who drop their own language to speak English, of men who translate their euphonious Irish names into English monosyllables, of men who read English books, and know nothing about Gaelic literature, nevertheless protesting as a matter of sentiment that they hate the country which at every hand's turn they rush to imitate.

---

[1] Delivered before the Irish National Literary Society in Dublin, November 25, 1892.

I wish to show you that in Anglicising ourselves wholesale we have thrown away with a light heart the best claim which we have upon the world's recognition of us as a separate nationality. What did Mazzini say? What is Goldwin Smith never tired of declaiming? What do the *Spectator* and *Saturday Review* harp on? That we ought to be content as an integral part of the United Kingdom because we have lost the notes of nationality, our language and customs.

It has always been very curious to me how Irish sentiment sticks in this half-way house—how it continues to apparently hate the English, and at the same time continues to imitate them; how it continues to clamour for recognition as a distinct nationality, and at the same time throws away with both hands what would make it so. If Irishmen only went a little farther they would become good Englishmen in sentiment also. But—illogical as it appears—there seems not the slightest sign or probability of their taking that step. It is the curious certainty that come what may Irishmen will continue to resist English rule, even though it should be for their good, which prevents many of our nation from becoming Unionists upon the spot. It is a fact, and we must face it as a fact, that although they adopt English habits and copy England in every way, the great bulk of Irishmen and Irishwomen over the whole world are known to be filled with a dull, ever-abiding animosity against her, and—right or wrong—to grieve when she prospers, and joy when she is hurt. Such movements as Young Irelandism, Fenianism, Land Leagueism, and Parliamentary obstruction seem always to gain their sympathy and support. It is just because there appears no earthly chance of their becoming good members of the Empire that I urge that they should not remain in the anomalous position they are in, but since they absolutely refuse to become the one thing, that they become the other; cultivate what they have rejected, and build up an Irish nation on Irish lines.

But you ask, why should we wish to make Ireland more Celtic than it is—why should we de-Anglicise it at all?

I answer because the Irish race is at present in a most anomalous position, imitating England and yet apparently hating it. How can it produce anything good in literature, art, or institutions as long as it is actuated by motives so contradictory? Besides, I believe it is our Gaelic past which, though the Irish race does not recognise it just at present, is really at the bottom of the Irish heart, and prevents us becoming citizens of the Empire, as, I think, can be easily proved.

To say that Ireland has not prospered under English rule is simply a truism; all the world admits it, England does not deny it. But the English retort is ready. You have not prospered, they say, because you would not settle down contentedly, like the Scotch, and form part of the Empire. 'Twenty years of good, resolute, grandfatherly government,' said a well-known Englishman, will solve the Irish question. He possibly made the period too short, but let us suppose this. Let us suppose for a moment—which is impossible—that there were to arise a series of Cromwells in England for the space of one hundred years, able administrators of the Empire, careful rulers of Ireland, developing to the utmost our national resources, whilst they unremittingly stamped out every spark of national feeling, making Ireland a land of wealth and factories, whilst they extinguished every thought and every idea that was Irish, and left us, at last, after a hundred years of good government, fat, wealthy, and populous, but with all our characteristics gone, with every external that at present differentiates us from the English lost or dropped; all our Irish names of places and people turned into English names; the Irish language completely extinct; the O's and the Macs dropped; our Irish intonation changed, as far as possible, by English schoolmasters into something English; our history no longer remembered or taught; the names of our rebels and martyrs blotted out; our battlefields and traditions forgotten; the fact that we were not of Saxon origin dropped out of sight and memory, and let me now put the question—How many Irishmen are there who would purchase material prosperity at such a price? It is exactly such a question as this and the answer to it that shows the difference between the English and Irish race. Nine Englishmen out of ten would jump to make the exchange, and I as firmly believe that nine Irishmen out of ten would indignantly refuse it.

And yet this awful idea of complete Anglicisation, which I have here put before you in all its crudity, is, and has been, making silent inroads upon us for nearly a century.

Its inroads have been silent, because, had the Gaelic race perceived what was being done, or had they been once warned of what was taking place in their own midst, they would, I think, never have allowed it. When the picture of complete Anglicisation is drawn for them in all its nakedness Irish sentimentality becomes suddenly a power and refuses to surrender its birthright.

What lies at the back of the sentiments of nationality with which the Irish millions seem so strongly leavened, what can prompt them to applaud such sentiments as:

> They say the British Empire owes much to Irish hands,
> That Irish valour fixed her flag o'er many conquered lands;
> And ask if Erin takes no pride in these her gallant sons,
> Her Wolseleys and her Lawrences, her Wolfes and Wellingtons.
>
> Ah! these were of the Empire—we yield them to her fame,
> And ne'er in Erin's orisons are heard their alien name;
> But those for whom her heart beats high and benedictions swell,
> They died upon the scaffold and they pined within the cell.

Of course it is a very composite feeling which prompts them; but I believe that what is largely behind it is the half unconscious feeling that the race which at one time held possession of more than half Europe, which established itself in Greece, and burned infant Rome, is now—almost extirpated and absorbed elsewhere—making its last stand for independence in this island of Ireland; and do what they may the race of to-day cannot wholly divest itself from the mantle of its own past. Through early Irish literature, for instance, can we best form some conception of what that race really was, which, after overthrowing and trampling on the primitive peoples of half Europe, was itself forced in turn to yield its speech, manners, and independence to the victorious eagles of Rome. We alone of the nations of Western Europe escaped the claws of those birds of prey; we alone developed ourselves naturally upon our own lines outside of and free from all Roman influence; we alone were thus able to produce an early art and literature, *our* antiquities can best throw light upon the pre-Romanised inhabitants of half Europe, and—we are our father's sons.

There is really no exaggeration in all this, although Irishmen are sometimes prone to overstating as well as to forgetting. Westwood himself declares that, were it not for Irishmen, these islands would possess no primitive works of art worth the mentioning; Jubainville asserts that early Irish literature is that which best throws light upon the manners and customs of his own ancestors the Gauls; and Zimmer, who has done so much for Celtic philology, has declared that only a spurious criticism can make an attempt to doubt about the historical character of the chief persons of our two epic cycles, that of Cuchullain and that of Finn. It is useless elaborating this point; and Dr. Sigerson has already shown in his opening lecture the debt of gratitude which in many respects Europe owes to ancient Ireland. The dim consciousness of this is one of those things which are at the back of Irish national sentiment, and our business, whether we be Unionists or Nationalists, should be to make this dim consciousness an active and potent feeling, and thus increase our sense of self-respect and of honour.

What we must endeavour to never forget is this, that the Ireland of to-day is the descendant of the Ireland of the seventh century, then the school of Europe and the torch of learning. It is true that Northmen made some minor settlements in it in the ninth and tenth centuries, it is true that the Normans made extensive settlements during the succeeding centuries, but none of those broke the continuity of the social life of the island. Dane and Norman drawn to the kindly Irish breast issued forth in a generation or two fully Irishised, and more Hibernian than the Hibernians themselves, and even after the Cromwellian plantation the children of numbers of the English soldiers who settled in the south and midlands, were, after forty years' residence, and after marrying Irish wives, turned into good Irishmen, and unable to speak a word of English, while several Gaelic poets of the last century have, like Father English, the most unmistakably English names. In two points only was the continuity of the Irishism of Ireland damaged. First, in the north-east of Ulster, where the Gaelic race was expelled and the land planted with aliens, whom our dear mother Erin, assimilative as she is, has hitherto found it difficult to absorb, and in the ownership of the land, eight-ninths of which belongs to people many of whom always lived, or live, abroad, and not half of whom Ireland can be said to have assimilated.

During all this time the continuation of Erin's national life centred, according to our way of looking at it, not so much in the Cromwellian or Williamite landholders who sat in College Green, and governed the country, as in the mass of the people whom Dean Swift considered might be entirely neglected, and looked upon as hewers of wood and drawers of water; the men who, nevertheless, constituted the real working population, and who were living on in the hopes of better days; the men who have since made America, and have within the last ten years proved what an important factor they may be in wrecking or in building the British Empire. These are the men of whom our merchants, artisans, and farmers mostly consist, and in whose hands is to-day the making or marring of an Irish nation. But, alas, *quantum mutatus ab illo!* What the battleaxe of the Dane, the sword of the Norman, the wile of the Saxon were unable to perform, we have accomplished ourselves. We have at last broken the continuity of Irish life, and just at the moment when the Celtic race is presumably about to largely recover possession of its own country, it finds itself deprived and stript of its Celtic characteristics, cut off from the past, yet scarcely in touch with the present. It has lost since the beginning of this century almost all that connected it with the era of Cuchullain and of Ossian, that connected it with the Christianisers of Europe, that connected it with Brian Boru and the heroes of Clontarf, with the O'Neills and O'Donnells, with Rory O'More, with the Wild Geese, and even to some extent with the men of '98. It has lost all that they had—language, traditions, music, genius, and ideas. Just when we should be starting to build up anew the Irish race and the Gaelic nation—as within our own recollection Greece has been built up anew—we find ourselves despoiled of the bricks of nationality. The old bricks that lasted eighteen hundred years are destroyed; we must now set to, to bake new ones, if we can, on other ground and of other clay. Imagine for a moment the restoration of a German-speaking Greece.

The bulk of the Irish race really lived in the closest contact with the traditions of the past and the national life of nearly eighteen hundred years, until the beginning of this century. Not only so, but during the whole of the dark Penal times they produced amongst themselves a most vigorous literary development. Their schoolmasters and wealthy farmers, unwearied scribes, produced innumerable manuscripts in beautiful writing, each letter separated from another as in Greek, transcripts both of the ancient literature of their sires and of the more modern literature produced by themselves. Until the beginning of the present century there was no county, no barony, and, I may almost say, no townland which did not boast of an Irish poet, the people's representative of those ancient bards who died out with the extirpation of the great Milesian families. The literary activity of even the eighteenth century among the Gaels was very great, not in the South alone, but also in Ulster—the number of poets it produced was something astonishing. It did not, however, produce many works in Gaelic prose, but it propagated translations of many pieces from the French, Latin, Spanish, and English. Every well-to-do farmer could read and write Irish, and many of them could understand even archaic Irish. I have myself heard persons reciting the poems of Donogha More O'Daly, Abbot of Boyle, in Roscommon, who died sixty years before Chaucer was born. To this very day the people have a word for archaic Irish, which is much the same as though Chaucer's poems were handed down amongst the English peasantry, but required a special training to understand. This training, however, nearly every one of fair education during the Penal times possessed, nor did they begin to lose their Irish training and knowledge until after the establishment of Maynooth and the rise of O'Connell. These two events made an end of the Gaelicism of the Gaelic race, although a great number of poets and scribes existed even down to the forties and fifties of the present century, and a few may linger on yet in remote localities. But it may be said, roughly speaking, that the ancient Gaelic civilisation died with O'Connell, largely, I am afraid, owing to his example and his neglect of inculcating the necessity of keeping alive racial customs, language, and traditions, in which with the one notable exception of our scholarly idealist, Smith O'Brien, he has been followed until a year ago by almost every leader of the Irish race.

Thomas Davis and his brilliant band of Young Irelanders came just at the dividing of the line, and tried to give to Ireland a new literature in English to replace the literature which was just being discarded. It succeeded and it did not succeed. It was a most brilliant effort, but the old bark had been too recently stripped off the Irish tree, and the trunk could not take as it might have done to a fresh one. It was a new departure, and at first produced a violent effect. Yet in the long run it failed to properly leaven our peasantry who might, perhaps, have been reached upon other lines. I say they *might* have been reached upon other lines because it is quite certain that even well on into the beginning of this century, Irish poor scholars and schoolmasters used to gain the greatest favour and applause by reading out manuscripts in the people's houses at night, some of which manuscripts had an antiquity of a couple of hundred years or more behind them, and which, when they got illegible from age, were always recopied. The Irish peasantry at that time were all to some extent cultured men, and many of the better off ones were scholars and poets. What have we now left of all that? Scarcely a trace. Many of them read newspapers indeed, but who reads, much less recites, an epic poem, or chants an elegiac or even a hymn?

Wherever Irish throughout Ireland continued to be spoken, there the ancient MSS. continued to be read, there the epics of Cuchullain, Conor MacNessa, Déirdre, Finn, Oscar, and Ossian continued to be told, and there poetry and music held sway. Some people may think I am exaggerating in asserting that such a state of things existed down to the present century, but it is no exaggeration. I have myself spoken with men from Cavan and Tyrone who spoke excellent Irish. Carleton's stories bear witness to the prevalence of the Irish language and traditions in Ulster when he began to write. My friend Mr. Lloyd has found numbers in Antrim who spoke good Irish. And, as for Leinster, my friend Mr. Cleaver informed me that when he lived in Wicklow a man came by from the County Carlow in search of work who could not speak a word of English. Old labourers from Connacht, who used to go to reap the harvest in England and take shipping at Drogheda, told me that at that time, fifty years ago, Irish was spoken by every one round that town. I have met an old man in Wicklow, not twenty miles from Dublin, whose parents always repeated the Rosary in Irish. My friend Father O'Growny, who has done and is doing so much for the Irish language and literature at Maynooth, tells me that there, within twenty miles of Dublin, are three old people who still speak Irish. O'Curry found people within seven miles of Dublin city who had never heard English in their youth at all, except from the car-drivers of the great town. I gave an old man in the street who begged from me, a penny, only a few days ago, saying, 'Sin pighin agad,' and when he answered in Irish I asked him where he was from, and he said from *Newna (n' Eamhain)*, *i.e.*, Navan. Last year I was in Canada and out hunting with some Red Indians, and we spent a night in the last white man's house in the last settlement on the brink of the primeval forest; and judging from a peculiarly Hibernian physiognomy that the man was Irish, I addressed him in Gaelic, and to the intense astonishment both of whites and Indians we entered into a conversation which none of them understood; and it turned out that he was from within three miles of Kilkenny, and had been forty years in

## THE NECESSITY FOR DE-ANGLICISING IRELAND

that country without forgetting the language he had spoken as a child, and I, although from the centre of Connacht, understood him perfectly. When my father was a young boy in the county Leitrim, not far from Longford, he seldom heard the farm labourers and tenants speak anything but Irish amongst themselves. So much for Ulster and Leinster, but Connacht and Munster were until quite recently completely Gaelic. In fact, I may venture to say, that, up to the beginning of the present century, neither man, woman, nor child of the Gaelic race, either of high blood or low blood, existed in Ireland who did not either speak Irish or understand it. But within the last ninety years we have, with an unparalleled frivolity, deliberately thrown away our birthright and Anglicised ourselves. None of the children of those people of whom I have spoken know Irish, and the race will from henceforth be changed; for as Monsieur Jubainville says of the influence of Rome upon Gaul, England 'has definitely conquered us, she has even imposed upon us her language, that is to say, the form of our thoughts during every instant of our existence.' It is curious that those who most fear West Britonism have so eagerly consented to imposing upon the Irish race what, according to Jubainville, who in common with all the great scholars of the continent, seems to regret it very much, is 'the form of our thoughts during every instant of our existence.'

So much for the greatest stroke of all in our Anglicisation, the loss of our language. I have often heard people thank God that if the English gave us nothing else they gave us at least their language. In this way they put a bold face upon the matter, and pretend that the Irish language is not worth knowing, and has no literature. But the Irish language *is* worth knowing, or why would the greatest philologists of Germany, France, and Italy be emulously studying it, and it *does* possess a literature, or why would a German savant have made the calculation that the books written in Irish between the eleventh and seventeenth centuries, and still extant, would fill a thousand octavo volumes.

I have no hesitation at all in saying that every Irish-feeling Irishman, who hates the reproach of West-Britonism, should set himself to encourage the efforts which are being made to keep alive our once great national tongue. The losing of it is our greatest blow, and the sorest stroke that the rapid Anglicisation of Ireland has inflicted upon us. In order to de-Anglicise ourselves we must at once arrest the decay of the language. We must bring pressure upon our politicians not to snuff it out by their tacit discouragement merely because they do not happen themselves to understand it. We must arouse some spark of patriotic inspiration among the peasantry who still use the language, and put an end to the shameful state of feeling—a thousand-tongued reproach to our leaders and statesmen—which makes young men and women blush and hang their heads when overheard speaking their own language.[1] Maynooth has at last come splendidly to the front, and it is now incumbent upon every clerical student to attend lectures in the Irish language and history during the first three years of his course. But in order to keep the Irish language alive where it is still spoken— which is the utmost we can at present aspire to—nothing less than a house-to-house visitation and exhortation of the people themselves will do, something—though with a very different purpose— analogous to the procedure that James Stephens adopted throughout Ireland when he found her like a corpse on the dissecting table. This and some system of giving medals or badges of honour to every family who will guarantee that they have always spoken Irish amongst themselves during the year. But, unfortunately, distracted as we are and torn by contending factions, it is impossible to find either men or money to carry out this simple remedy, although to a dispassionate foreigner—to a Zeuss, Jubainville, Zimmer, Kuno Meyer, Windisch, or Ascoli, and the rest—this is of greater importance than whether Mr. Redmond or Mr. MacCarthy lead the largest wing of the Irish party for the moment, or Mr. So-

---

[1] As an instance of this, I mention the case of a young man I met on the road coming from the fair of Tuam, some ten miles away. I saluted him in Irish, and he answered me in English. "Don't you speak Irish," said I. "Well, I declare to God, sir," he said, "my father and mother hasn't a word of English, but still, I don't speak Irish." This was absolutely true for him. There are thousands upon thousands of houses all over Ireland to-day where the old people invariably use Irish in addressing the children, and the children as invariably answer in English, the children understanding Irish but not speaking it, the parents understanding their children's English but unable to use it themselves. In a great many cases, I should almost say most, the children are not conscious of the existence of two languages. I remember asking a gossoon a couple of miles west of Ballaghaderreen in the Co. Mayo, some questions in Irish and he answered them in English. At last I said to him, *"Nach labhrann tu Gaedheilg?"* (*i.e.*, "Don't you speak Irish?") and his answer was, "And isn't it Irish I'm spaking?" "No *a-chuisle*," said I, "it's not Irish you're speaking, but English." "Well then," said he, "that's how I spoke it ever!" He was quite unconscious that I was addressing him in one language and he answering in another. On a different occasion I spoke Irish to a little girl in a house near Kilfree Junction, Co. Sligo, into which I went while waiting for a train. The girl answered me in Irish until her brother came in. "Arrah now, Mary," said he, with what was intended to be a most bitter sneer; "and isn't that a credit to you!" And poor Mary—whom I had with difficulty persuaded to begin—immediately hung her head and changed to English. This is going on from Malin Head to Galway, and from Galway to Waterford, with the exception possibly of a few spots in Donegal and Kerry, where the people are wiser and more national.

and-So succeed with his election petition. To a person taking a bird's-eye view of the situation a hundred or five hundred years hence, believe me, it will also appear of greater importance than any mere temporary wrangle, but, unhappily, our countrymen cannot be brought to see this.

We can, however, insist, and we *shall* insist if Home Rule be carried, that the Irish language, which so many foreign scholars of the first calibre find so worthy of study, shall be placed on a par with—or even above—Greek, Latin, and modern languages, in all examinations held under the Irish Government. We can also insist, and we *shall* insist, that in those baronies where the children speak Irish, Irish shall be taught, and that Irish-speaking schoolmasters, petty sessions clerks, and even magistrates be appointed in Irish-speaking districts. If all this were done, it should not be very difficult, with the aid of the foremost foreign scholars, to bring about a tone of thought which would make it disgraceful for an educated Irishman—especially of the old Celtic race, MacDermotts, O'Conors, O'Sullivans, MacCarthys, O'Neills—to be ignorant of his own language—would make it at least as disgraceful as for an educated Jew to be quite ignorant of Hebrew.

*Part II*

# THE LIVING WORLD FOR TEXT

*And that enquiring man John Synge comes next,
That dying chose the living world for text . . .*
　　　　　　　　　　　　W. B. YEATS

J. M. SYNGE

# Preface to The Playboy of the Western World[1]

IN WRITING *The Playboy of the Western World*, as in my other plays, I have used one or two words only that I have not heard among the country people of Ireland, or spoken in my own nursery before I could read the newspapers. A certain number of the phrases I employ I have heard also from herds and fishermen along the coast from Kerry to Mayo, or from beggar-women and ballad-singers nearer Dublin; and I am glad to acknowledge how much I owe to the folk-imagination of these fine people. Anyone who has lived in real intimacy with the Irish peasantry will know that the wildest sayings and ideas in this play are tame indeed, compared with the fancies one may hear in any little hillside cabin in Geesala, or Carraroe, or Dingle Bay. All art is a collaboration; and there is little doubt that in the happy ages of literature, striking and beautiful phrases were as ready to the story-teller's or the playwright's hand, as the rich cloaks and dresses of his time. It is probable that when the Elizabethan dramatist took his ink-horn and sat down to his work he used many phrases that he had just heard, as he sat at dinner, from his mother or his children. In Ireland, those of us who know the people have the same privilege. When I was writing *The Shadow of the Glen*, some years ago, I got more aid than any learning could have given me from a chink in the floor of the old Wicklow house where I was staying, that let me hear what was being said by the servant girls in the kitchen. This matter, I think, is of importance, for in countries where the imagination of the people, and the language they use, is rich and living, it is possible for a writer to be rich and copious in his words, and at the same time to give the reality, which is the root of all poetry, in a comprehensive and natural form. In the modern literature of towns, however, richness is found only in sonnets, or prose poems, or in one or two elaborate books that are far away from the profound and common interests of life. One has, on one side, Mallarmé and Huysmans producing this literature; and on the other, Ibsen and Zola dealing with the reality of life in joyless and pallid words. On

[1] From *The Playboy of the Western World*, Dublin, 1907.

the stage one must have reality, and one must have joy; and that is why the intellectual modern drama has failed, and people have grown sick of the false joy of the musical comedy, that has been given them in place of the rich joy found only in what is superb and wild in reality. In a good play every speech should be as fully flavoured as a nut or apple, and such speeches cannot be written by anyone who works among people who have shut their lips on poetry. In Ireland, for a few years more, we have a popular imagination that is fiery and magnificent, and tender; so that those of us who wish to write start with a chance that is not given to writers in places where the springtime of the local life has been forgotten, and the harvest is a memory only, and the straw has been turned into bricks.

*January* 21, 1907

# The Aran Islands[1]

I AM in Aranmor,[2] sitting over a turf fire, listening to a murmur of Gaelic that is rising from a little public-house under my room.

The steamer which comes to Aran sails according to the tide, and it was six o'clock this morning when we left the quay of Galway in a dense shroud of mist.

A low line of shore was visible at first on the right between the movement of the waves and fog, but when we came further it was lost sight of, and nothing could be seen but the mist curling in the rigging, and a small circle of foam.

There were few passengers; a couple of men going out with young pigs tied loosely in sacking, three or four young girls who sat in the cabin with their heads completely twisted in their shawls, and a builder, on his way to repair the pier at Kilronan, who walked up and down and talked with me.

In about three hours Aran came in sight. A dreary rock appeared at first sloping up from the sea into the fog; then, as we drew nearer, a coast-guard station and the village.

---

[1] From *The Aran Islands*, London and Dublin, 1907.
[2] Aranmor is the largest of the three islands that make up the Aran group. The others are Inishmaan and Inishere.

A little later I was wandering out along the one good roadway of the island, looking over low walls on either side into small flat fields of naked rock. I have seen nothing so desolate. Grey floods of water were sweeping everywhere upon the limestone, making at times a wild torrent of the road, which twined continually over low hills and cavities in the rock or passed between a few small fields of potatoes or grass hidden away in corners that had shelter. Whenever the cloud lifted I could see the edge of the sea below me on the right, and the naked ridge of the island above me on the other side. Occasionally I passed a lonely chapel or schoolhouse, or a line of stone pillars with crosses above them and inscriptions asking a prayer for the soul of the person they commemorated.

I met few people; but here and there a band of tall girls passed me on their way to Kilronan, and called out to me with humorous wonder, speaking English with a slight foreign intonation that differed a good deal from the brogue of Galway. The rain and cold seemed to have no influence on their vitality, and as they hurried past me with eager laughter and great talking in Gaelic, they left the wet masses of rock more desolate than before.

A little after midday when I was coming back one old half-blind man spoke to me in Gaelic, but, in general, I was surprised at the abundance and fluency of the foreign tongue.

In the afternoon the rain continued, so I sat here in the inn looking out through the mist at a few men who were unlading hookers that had come in with turf from Connemara, and at the long-legged pigs that were playing in the surf. As the fishermen came in and out of the public-house underneath my room, I could hear through the broken panes that a number of them still used the Gaelic, though it seems to be falling out of use among the younger people of this village.

The old woman of the house had promised to get me a teacher of the language, and after a while I heard a shuffling on the stairs, and the old dark man I had spoken to in the morning groped his way into the room.

I brought him over to the fire, and we talked for many hours. He told me that he had known Petrie and Sir William Wilde, and many living antiquarians, and had taught Irish to Dr. Finck and Dr. Pedersen, and given stories to Mr. Curtin of America. A little after middle age he had fallen over a cliff, and since then he had had little eyesight, and a trembling of his hands and head.

As we talked he sat huddled together over the fire, shaking and blind, yet his face was indescribably pliant, lighting up with an ecstasy of humour when he told me anything that had a point of wit or malice, and growing sombre and desolate again when he spoke of religion or the fairies.

He had great confidence in his own powers and talent, and in the superiority of his stories over all other stories in the world. When we were speaking of Mr. Curtin, he told me that this gentleman had brought out a volume of his Aran stories in America, and made five hundred pounds by the sale of them.

'And what do you think he did then?' he continued; 'he wrote a book of his own stories after making that lot of money with mine. And he brought them out, and the divil a halfpenny did he get for them. Would you believe that?'

Afterwards he told me how one of his children had been taken by the fairies.

One day a neighbour was passing, and she said, when she saw it on the road, 'That's a fine child.'

Its mother tried to say 'God bless it,' but something choked the words in her throat.

A while later they found a wound on its neck, and for three nights the house was filled with noises.

'I never wear a shirt at night,' he said, 'but I got up out of my bed, all naked as I was, when I heard the noises in the house, and lighted a light, but there was nothing in it.'

Then a dummy[1] came and made signs of hammering nails in a coffin.

The next day the seed potatoes were full of blood, and the child told his mother that he was going to America.

That night it died, and 'Believe me,' said the old man, 'the fairies were in it.'

When he went away, a little bare-footed girl was sent up with turf and the bellows to make a fire that would last for the evening.

She was shy, yet eager to talk, and told me that she had good spoken Irish, and was learning to read it in the school, and that she had been twice to Galway, though there are many grown women in the place who have never set a foot upon the mainland.

---

[1] A deaf mute.

The rain has cleared off, and I have had my first real introduction to the island and its people.

I went out through Killeany—the poorest village in Aranmor—to a long neck of sandhill that runs out into the sea towards the south-west. As I lay there on the grass the clouds lifted from the Connemara mountains and, for a moment, the green undulating foreground, backed in the distance by a mass of hills, reminded me of the country near Rome. Then the dun top-sail of a hooker swept above the edge of the sandhill and revealed the presence of the sea.

As I moved on a boy and a man came down from the next village to talk to me, and I found that here, at least, English was imperfectly understood. When I asked them if there were any trees in the island they held a hurried consultation in Gaelic, and then the man asked if 'tree' meant the same thing as 'bush,' for if so there were a few in sheltered hollows to the east.

They walked on with me to the sound which separates this island from Inishmaan—the middle island of the group—and showed me the roll from the Atlantic running up between two walls of cliff.

They told me that several men had stayed on Inishmaan to learn Irish, and the boy pointed out a line of hovels where they had lodged running like a belt of straw round the middle of the island. The place looked hardly fit for habitation. There was no green to be seen, and no sign of the people except these beehive-like roofs, and the outline of a Dun that stood out above them against the edge of the sky.

After a while my companions went away and two other boys came and walked at my heels, till I turned and made them talk to me. They spoke at first of their poverty, and then one of them said—

'I dare say you do have to pay ten shillings a week in the hotel?'

'More,' I answered.

'Twelve?'

'More.'

'Fifteen?'

'More still.'

Then he drew back and did not question me any further, either thinking that I had lied to check his curiosity, or too awed by my riches to continue.

Repassing Killeany I was joined by a man who had spent twenty years in America, where he had lost his health and then returned, so long ago that he had forgotten English and could hardly make me understand him. He seemed hopeless, dirty, and asthmatic, and after going with me for a few hundred yards he stopped and asked for coppers. I had none left, so I gave him a fill of tobacco, and he went back to his hovel.

When he was gone, two little girls took their place behind me and I drew them in turn into conversation.

They spoke with a delicate exotic intonation that was full of charm, and told me with a sort of chant how they guide 'ladies and gintlemins' in the summer to all that is worth seeing in their neighborhood, and sell them pampooties and maidenhair ferns, which are common among the rocks.

We were now in Kilronan, and as we parted they showed me holes in their own pampooties, or cowskin sandals, and asked me the price of new ones. I told them that my purse was empty, and then with a few quaint words of blessing they turned away from me and went down to the pier.

All this walk back had been extraordinarily fine. The intense insular clearness one sees only in Ireland, and after rain, was throwing out every ripple in the sea and sky, and every crevice in the hills beyond the bay.

This evening an old man came to see me, and said he had known a relative of mine who passed some time on this island forty-three years ago.

'I was standing under the pier-wall mending nets,' he said, 'when you came off the steamer, and I said to myself in that moment, if there is a man of the name of Synge left walking the world, it is that man yonder will be he.'

He went on to complain in curiously simple yet dignified language of the changes that have taken place here since he left the island to go to sea before the end of his childhood.

'I have come back,' he said, 'to live in a bit of a house with my sister. The island is not the same at all to what it was. It is little good I can get from the people who are in it now, and anything I have to give them they don't care to have.'

From what I hear this man seems to have shut himself up in a world of individual conceits and theories, and to live aloof at his trade of net-mending, regarded by the other islanders with respect and half-ironical sympathy.

A little later when I went down to the kitchen I found two men from Inishmaan who had been benighted on the island. They seemed a simpler and perhaps a more interesting type than the people here, and talked with careful English about the history of the Duns, and the Book of Ballymote, and the Book of Kells, and other ancient MSS., with the names of which they seemed familiar.

In spite of the charm of my teacher, the old blind man I met the day of my arrival, I have decided to move on to Inishmaan, where Gaelic is more generally used, and the life is perhaps the most primitive that is left in Europe.

I spent all this last day with my blind guide, looking at the antiquities that abound in the west or north-west of the island.

As we set out I noticed among the groups of girls who smiled at our fellowship—old Mourteen says we are like the cuckoo with its pipit—a beautiful oval face with the singularly spiritual expression that is so marked in one type of the West Ireland women. Later in the day, as the old man talked continually of the fairies and the women they have taken, it seemed that there was a possible link between the wild mythology that is accepted on the islands and the strange beauty of the women.

At midday we rested near the ruins of a house, and two beautiful boys came up and sat near us. Old Mourteen asked them why the house was in ruins, and who had lived in it.

'A rich farmer built it a while since,' they said, 'but after two years he was driven away by the fairy host.'

The boys came on with us some distance to the north to visit one of the ancient beehive dwellings that is still in perfect preservation. When we crawled in on our hands and knees, and stood up in the gloom of the interior, old Mourteen took a freak of earthly humour and began telling what he would have done if he could have come in there when he was a young man and a young girl along with him.

Then he sat down in the middle of the floor and began to recite old Irish poetry, with an exquisite purity of intonation that brought tears to my eyes though I understood but little of the meaning.

On our way home he gave me the Catholic theory of the fairies.

When Lucifer saw himself in the glass he thought himself equal with God. Then the Lord threw him out of Heaven, and all the angels that belonged to him. While He was 'chucking them out,' an archangel asked Him to spare some of them, and those that were falling are in the air still, and have power to wreck ships, and to work evil in the world.

From this he wandered off into tedious matters of theology, and repeated many long prayers and sermons in Irish that he had heard from the priests.

A little further on we came to a slated house, and I asked him who was living in it.

'A kind of a schoolmistress,' he said; then his old face puckered with a gleam of pagan malice.

'Ah, master,' he said, 'wouldn't it be fine to be in there, and to be kissing her?'

A couple of miles from this village we turned aside to look at an old ruined church of the Ceathair Aluinn (The Four Beautiful Persons), and a holy well near it that is famous for cures of blindness and epilepsy.

As we sat near the well a very old man came up from a cottage near the road, and told me how it had become famous.

'A woman of Sligo had a son who was born blind, and one night she dreamed that she saw an island with a blessed well in it that could cure her son. She told her dream in the morning, and an old man said it was of Aran she was after dreaming.

'She brought her son down by the coast of Galway, and came out in a curagh, and landed below where you see a bit of a cove.

'She walked up then to the house of my father—God rest his soul —and she told them what she was looking for.

'My father said that there was a well like what she had dreamed of, and that he would send a boy along with her to show her the way.

'"There's no need, at all," said she; "haven't I seen it all in my dream?"

'Then she went out with the child and walked up to this well, and she kneeled down and began saying her prayers. Then she put her hand out for the water, and put it on his eyes, and the moment it touched him he called out: "O mother, look at the pretty flowers!"'

After that Mourteen described the feats of poteen drinking and fighting that he did in his youth, and went on to talk of Diarmid, who was the strongest man after Samson, and of one of the beds of Diarmid and Grainne,[1] which is on the east of the island. He says that Diarmid was killed by the druids, who put a burning shirt on him—a fragment of mythology that may connect Diarmid with the legend of Hercules, if it is not due to the "learning" in some hedge-school master's ballad.

Then we talked about Inishmaan.

'You'll have an old man to talk with you over there,' he said, 'and tell you stories of the fairies, but he's walking about with two sticks under him this ten year. Did ever you hear what it is goes on four legs when it is young, and on two legs after that, and on three legs when it does be old?'

I gave him the answer.

'Ah, master,' he said, 'you're a cute one, and the blessing of God be on you. Well, I'm on three legs this minute, but the old man beyond is back on four; I don't know if I'm better than the way he is; he's got his sight and I'm only an old dark man.'

I am settled at last on Inishmaan in a small cottage with a continual drone of Gaelic coming from the kitchen that opens into my room.

Early this morning the man of the house came over for me with a four-oared curagh—that is, a curagh with four rowers and four oars on either side, as each man uses two—and we set off a little before noon.

It gave me a moment of exquisite satisfaction to find myself moving away from civilisation in this rude canvas canoe of a model that has served primitive races since men first went on the sea.

We had to stop for a moment at a hulk that is anchored in the bay, to make some arrangements for the fish-curing of the middle island, and my crew called out as soon as we were within earshot that they had a man with them who had been in France a month from this day.

When we started again, a small sail was run up in the bow, and we set off across the sound with a leaping oscillation that had no resemblance to the heavy movement of a boat.

The sail is only used as an aid, so the men continued to row after it had gone up, and as they occupied the four cross-seats I lay on the canvas at the stern and the frame of slender laths, which bent and quivered as the waves passed under them.

---

[1] Grainne, the betrothed of the hero Finn, compelled Diarmid to elope with her. Finn pursued them relentlessly until the death of Diarmid.

When we set off it was a brilliant morning of April, and the green, glittering waves seemed to toss the canoe among themselves, yet as we drew nearer this island a sudden thunderstorm broke out behind the rocks we were approaching, and lent a momentary tumult to this still vein of the Atlantic.

We landed at a small pier, from which a rude track leads up to the village between small fields and bare sheets of rock like those in Aranmor. The youngest son of my boatman, a boy of about seventeen, who is to be my teacher and guide, was waiting for me at the pier and guided me to his house, while the men settled the curagh and followed slowly with my baggage.

My room is at one end of the cottage, with a boarded floor and ceiling, and two windows opposite each other. Then there is the kitchen with earth floor and open rafters, and two doors opposite each other opening into the open air, but no windows. Beyond it there are two small rooms of half the width of the kitchen with one window apiece.

The kitchen itself, where I will spend most of my time, is full of beauty and distinction. The red dresses of the women who cluster round the fire on their stools give a glow of almost Eastern richness, and the walls have been toned by the turf-smoke to a soft brown that blends with the grey earth-colour of the floor. Many sorts of fishing-tackle, and the nets and oil-skins of the men, are hung upon the walls or among the open rafters; and right overhead, under the thatch, there is a whole cowskin from which they make pampooties.

Every article on these islands has an almost personal character, which gives this simple life, where all art is unknown, something of the artistic beauty of mediæval life. The curaghs and spinning-wheels, the tiny wooden barrels that are still much used in the place of earthenware, the home-made cradles, churns, and baskets, are all full of individuality, and being made from materials that are common here, yet to some extent peculiar to the island, they seem to exist as a natural link between the people and the world that is about them.

The simplicity and unity of the dress increases in another way the local air of beauty. The women wear red petticoats and jackets of the island wool stained with madder, to which they usually add a plaid shawl twisted round their chests and tied at their backs. When it rains they throw another petticoat over their heads with the waistband round their faces, or, if they are young, they use a heavy shawl like those worn in Galway. Occasionally other wraps are worn, and during the thunderstorm I arrived in I saw several girls with men's waistcoats buttoned round their bodies. Their skirts do not come much below the knee, and show their powerful legs in the heavy indigo stockings with which they are all provided.

The men wear three colours: the natural wool, indigo, and a grey flannel that is woven of alternate threads of indigo and the natural wool. In Aranmor many of the younger men have adopted the usual fisherman's jersey, but I have only seen one on this island.

As flannel is cheap—the women spin the yarn from the wool of their own sheep, and it is then woven by a weaver in Kilronan for fourpence a yard—the men seem to wear an indefinite number of waistcoats and woollen drawers one over the other. They are usually surprised at the lightness of my own dress, and one old man I spoke to for a minute on the pier, when I came ashore, asked me if I was not cold with 'my little clothes.'

As I sat in the kitchen to dry the spray from my coat, several men who had seen me walking up came in to talk to me, usually murmuring on the threshold, 'The blessing of God on this place,' or some similar words.

The courtesy of the old woman of the house is singularly attractive, and though I could not understand much of what she said—she has no English—I could see with how much grace she motioned each visitor to a chair, or stool, according to his age, and said a few words to him till he drifted into our English conversation.

For the moment my own arrival is the chief subject of interest, and the men who come in are eager to talk to me.

Some of them express themselves more correctly than the ordinary peasant, others use the Gaelic idioms continually and substitute 'he' or 'she' for 'it,' as the neuter pronoun is not found in modern Irish.

A few of the men have a curiously full vocabulary, others know only the commonest words in English, and are driven to ingenious devices to express their meaning. Of all the subjects we can talk of war seems their favourite, and the conflict between America and Spain is causing a great deal of excitement. Nearly all the families have relations who have had to cross the Atlantic, and all eat of the flour and bacon that is brought from the United States, so they have a vague fear that 'if anything happened to America,' their own island would cease to be habitable.

Foreign languages are another favourite topic, and as these men are bilingual they have a fair notion of what it means to speak and think in many different idioms. Most of the strangers they see on the islands are philological students, and the people have been led to conclude that linguistic studies, particularly Gaelic studies, are the chief occupation of the outside world.

'I have seen Frenchmen, and Danes, and Germans,' said one man, 'and there does be a power of Irish books along with them, and they reading them better than ourselves. Believe me there are few rich men now in the world who are not studying the Gaelic.'

They sometimes ask me the French for simple phrases, and when they have listened to the intonation for a moment, most of them are able to reproduce it with admirable precision.

When I was going out this morning to walk round the island with Michael, the boy who is teaching me Irish, I met an old man making his way down to the cottage. He was dressed in miserable black clothes which seemed to have come from the mainland, and was so bent with rheumatism that, at a little distance, he looked more like a spider than a human being.

Michael told me it was Pat Dirane, the story-teller old Mourteen had spoken of on the other island. I wished to turn back, as he appeared to be on his way to visit me, but Michael would not hear of it.

'He will be sitting by the fire when we come in,' he said; 'let you not be afraid, there will be time enough to be talking to him by and by.'

He was right. As I came down into the kitchen some hours later old Pat was still in the chimney-corner, blinking with the turf smoke.

He spoke English with remarkable aptness and fluency, due, I believe, to the months he spent in the English provinces working at the harvest when he was a young man.

After a few formal compliments he told me how he had been crippled by an attack of the 'old hin' (*i.e.* the influenza), and had been complaining ever since in addition to his rheumatism.

While the old woman was cooking my dinner he asked me if I liked stories, and offered to tell one in English, though he added, it would be much better if I could follow the Gaelic. Then he began:

There were two farmers in County Clare. One had a son, and the other, a fine rich man, had a daughter.

The young man was wishing to marry the girl, and his father told him to try and get her if he thought well, though a power of gold would be wanting to get the like of her.

'I will try,' said the young man.

He put all his gold into a bag. Then he went over to the other farm, and threw in the gold in front of him.

'Is that all gold?' said the father of the girl.

'All gold,' said O'Conor (the young man's name was O'Conor).

'It will not weigh down my daughter,' said the father.

'We'll see that,' said O'Conor.

Then they put them in the scales, the daughter in one side and the gold in the other. The girl went down against the ground, so O'Conor took his bag and went out on the road.

As he was going along he came to where there was a little man, and he standing with his back against the wall.

'Where are you going with the bag?' said the little man.

'Going home,' said O'Conor.

'Is it gold you might be wanting?' said the man.

'It is, surely,' said O'Conor.

'I'll give you what you are wanting,' said the man, 'and we can bargain in this way—you'll pay me back in a year the gold I give you, or you'll pay me with five pounds cut off your own flesh.'

That bargain was made between them. The man gave a bag of gold to O'Conor, and he went back with it, and was married to the young woman.

They were rich people, and he built her a grand castle on the cliffs of Clare, with a window that looked out straight over the wild ocean.

One day when he went up with his wife to look out over the wild ocean, he saw a ship coming in on the rocks, and no sails on her at all. She was wrecked on the rocks, and it was tea that was in her, and fine silk.

O'Conor and his wife went down to look at the wreck, and when the lady O'Conor saw the silk she said she wished a dress of it.

They got the silk from the sailors, and when the Captain came up to get the money for it, O'Conor asked him to come again and take his dinner with them. They had a grand dinner, and they drank after it, and the Captain was tipsy. While they were still drinking, a letter came to O'Conor, and it was in the letter that a friend of his was dead, and that he would have to go away on a long journey. As he was getting ready the Captain came to him.

'Are you fond of your wife?' said the Captain.

'I am fond of her,' said O'Conor.

'Will you make me a bet of twenty guineas no man comes near her while you'll be away on the journey?' said the Captain.

'I will bet it,' said O'Conor; and he went away.

There was an old hag who sold small things on the road near the castle, and the lady O'Conor allowed her to sleep up in her room in a big box. The Captain went down on the road to the old hag.

'For how much will you let me sleep one night in your box?' said the Captain.

'For no money at all would I do such a thing,' said the hag.

'For ten guineas?' said the Captain.

'Not for ten guineas,' said the hag.

'For twelve guineas?' said the Captain.

'Not for twelve guineas,' said the hag.

'For fifteen guineas?' said the Captain.

'For fifteen I will do it,' said the hag.

Then she took him up and hid him in the box. When night came the lady O'Conor walked up into her room, and the Captain watched her through the hole that was in the box. He saw her take off her two rings and put them on a kind of a board that was over her head like a chimney-piece, and take off her clothes, except her shift, and go up into her bed.

As soon as she was asleep the Captain came out of his box, and he had some means of making a light, for he lit the candle. He went over to the bed where she was sleeping without disturbing her at all, or doing any bad thing, and he took the two rings off the board, and blew out the light, and went down again into the box.

He paused for a moment, and a deep sigh of relief rose from the men and women who had crowded in while the story was going on, till the kitchen was filled with people.

As the Captain was coming out of his box the girls, who had appeared to know no English, stopped their spinning and held their breath with expectation.

The old man went on—

When O'Conor came back the Captain met him, and told him that he had been a night in his wife's room, and gave him the two rings.

O'Conor gave him the twenty guineas of the bet. Then he went up into the castle, and he took his wife up to look out of the window over the wild ocean. While she was looking he pushed her from behind, and she fell down over the cliff into the sea.

An old woman was on the shore, and she saw her falling. She went down then to the surf and pulled her out all wet and in great disorder, and she took the wet clothes off her, and put on some old rags belonging to herself.

When O'Conor had pushed his wife from the window he went away into the land.

After a while the lady O'Conor went out searching for him, and when she had gone here and there a long time in the country, she heard that he was reaping in a field with sixty men.

She came to the field and she wanted to go in, but the gate-man would not open the gate for her. Then the owner came by, and she told him her story. He brought her in, and her husband was there, reaping, but he never gave any sign of knowing her. She showed him to the owner, and he made the man come out and go with his wife.

Then the lady O'Conor took him out on the road where there were horses, and they rode away.

When they came to the place where O'Conor had met the little man, he was there on the road before them.

'Have you my gold on you?' said the man.

'I have not,' said O'Conor.

'Then you'll pay me the flesh off your body,' said the man.

They went into a house, and a knife was brought, and a clean white cloth was put on the table, and O'Conor was put upon the cloth.

Then the little man was going to strike the lancet into him, when says lady O'Conor—

'Have you bargained for five pounds of flesh?'

'For five pounds of flesh,' said the man.

'Have you bargained for any drop of his blood?' said lady O'Conor.

'For no blood,' said the man.

'Cut out the flesh,' said lady O'Conor, 'but if you spill one drop of his blood I'll put that through you.' And she put a pistol to his head.

The little man went away and they saw no more of him.

When they got home to their castle they made a great supper, and they invited the Captain and the old hag, and the old woman that had pulled the lady O'Conor out of the sea.

After they had eaten well the lady O'Conor began, and she said they would all tell their stories. Then she told how she had been saved from the sea, and how she had found her husband.

Then the old woman told her story, the way she had found the lady O'Conor wet, and in great disorder, and had brought her in and put on her some old rags of her own.

The lady O'Conor asked the Captain for his story, but he said they would get no story from him. Then she took her pistol out of her pocket, and she put it on the edge of the table, and she said that any one that would not tell his story would get a bullet into him.

Then the Captain told the way he had got into the box, and come over to her bed without touching her at all, and had taken away the rings.

Then the lady O'Conor took the pistol and shot the hag through the body, and they threw her over the cliff into the sea.

That is my story.

It gave me a strange feeling of wonder to hear this illiterate native of a wet rock in the Atlantic telling a story that is so full of European associations.

The incident of the faithful wife takes us beyond Cymbeline to the sunshine on the Arno, and the gay company who went out from Florence to tell narratives of love. It takes us again to the low vineyards of Würzburg on the Main, where the same tale was told in the middle ages, of the 'Two Merchants and the Faithful Wife of Ruprecht von Würzburg.'

The other portion, dealing with the pound of flesh, has a still wider distribution, reaching from Persia and Egypt to the *Gesta*

*Romanorum*, and the *Pecorone* of Ser Giovanni, a Florentine notary.

The present union of the two tales has already been found among the Gaels, and there is a somewhat similar version in Campbell's *Popular Tales of the Western Highlands*.

Michael walks so fast when I am out with him that I cannot pick my steps, and the sharp-edged fossils which abound in the limestone have cut my shoes to pieces.

The family held a consultation on them last night, and in the end it was decided to make me a pair of pampooties, which I have been wearing to-day among the rocks.

They consist simply of a piece of raw cowskin, with the hair outside, laced over the toe and round the heel with two ends of fishing-line that work round and are tied above the instep.

In the evening, when they are taken off, they are placed in a basin of water, as the rough hide cuts the foot and stocking if it is allowed to harden. For the same reason the people often step into the surf during the day, so that their feet are continually moist.

At first I threw my weight upon my heels, as one does naturally in a boot, and was a good deal bruised, but after a few hours I learned the natural walk of man, and could follow my guide in any portion of the island.

In one district below the cliffs, towards the north, one goes for nearly a mile jumping from one rock to another without a single ordinary step; and here I realised that toes have a natural use, for I found myself jumping towards any tiny crevice in the rock before me, and clinging with an eager grip in which all the muscles of my feet ached from their exertion.

The absence of the heavy boot of Europe has preserved to these people the agile walk of the wild animal, while the general simplicity of their lives has given them many other points of physical perfection. Their way of life has never been acted on by anything much more artificial than the nests and burrows of the creatures that live round them, and they seem, in a certain sense, to approach more nearly to the finer types of our aristocracies—who are bred artificially to a natural ideal—than to the labourer or citizen, as the wild horse resembles the thoroughbred rather than the hack or carthorse. Tribes of the same natural development are, perhaps, frequent in half-civilised countries, but here a touch of the refinement of old societies is blended, with singular effect, among the qualities of the wild animal.

While I am walking with Michael some one often comes to me to ask the time of day. Few of the people, however, are sufficiently used to modern time to understand in more than a vague way the convention of the hours, and when I tell them what o'clock it is by my watch they are not satisfied, and ask how long is left them before the twilight.

The general knowledge of time on the island depends, curiously enough, on the direction of the wind. Nearly all the cottages are built, like this one, with two doors opposite each other, the more sheltered of which lies open all day to give light to the interior. If the wind is northerly the south door is opened, and the shadow of the door-post moving across the kitchen floor indicates the hour; as soon, however, as the wind changes to the south the other door is opened, and the people, who never think of putting up a primitive dial, are at a loss.

This system of doorways has another curious result. It usually happens that all the doors on one side of the village pathway are lying open with women sitting about on the thresholds, while on the other side the doors are shut and there is no sign of life. The moment the wind changes everything is reversed, and sometimes when I come back to the village after an hour's walk there seems to have been a general flight from one side of the way to the other.

In my own cottage the change of the doors alters the whole tone of the kitchen, turning it from a brilliantly-lighted room looking out on a yard and laneway to a sombre cell with a superb view of the sea.

When the wind is from the north the old woman manages my meals with fair regularity, but on the other days she often makes my tea at three o'clock instead of six. If I refuse it she puts it down to simmer for three hours in the turf, and then brings it in at six o'clock full of anxiety to know if it is warm enough.

The old man is suggesting that I should send him a clock when I go away. He'd like to have something from me in the house, he says, the way they wouldn't forget me, and wouldn't a clock be as handy as another thing, and they'd be thinking on me whenever they'd look on its face.

The general ignorance of any precise hours in the day makes it impossible for the people to have regular meals.

They seem to eat together in the evening, and sometimes in the morning, a little after dawn, before they scatter for their work, but during the day they simply drink a cup of tea and eat a piece of bread, or some potatoes, whenever they are hungry.

For men who live in the open air they eat strangely little. Often when Michael has been out weeding potatoes for eight or nine hours without food, he comes in and eats a few slices of homemade bread, and then he is ready to go out with me and wander for hours about the island.

They use no animal food except a little bacon and salt fish. The old woman says she would be very ill if she ate fresh meat.

Some years ago, before tea, sugar, and flour had come into general use, salt fish was much more the staple article of diet than at present, and, I am told, skin diseases were very common, though they are now rare on the islands.

No one who has not lived for weeks among these grey clouds and seas can realise the joy with which the eye rests on the red dresses of the women, especially when a number of them are to be found together, as happened early this morning.

I heard that the young cattle were to be shipped for a fair on the mainland, which is to take place in a few days, and I went down on the pier, a little after dawn, to watch them.

The bay was shrouded in the greys of coming rain, yet the thinness of the cloud threw a silvery light on the sea, and an unusual depth of blue to the mountains of Connemara.

As I was going across the sandhills one dun-sailed hooker glided slowly out to begin her voyage, and another beat up to the pier. Troops of red cattle, driven mostly by the women, were coming up from several directions, forming, with the green of the long tract of grass that separates the sea from the rocks, a new unity of colour.

The pier itself was crowded with bullocks and a great number of the people. I noticed one extraordinary girl in the throng who seemed to exert an authority on all who came near her. Her curiously-formed nostrils and narrow chin gave her a witch-like expression, yet the beauty of her hair and skin made her singularly attractive.

When the empty hooker was made fast its deck was still many feet below the level of the pier, so the animals were slung down by a rope from the mast-head, with much struggling and confusion.

Some of them made wild efforts to escape, nearly carrying their owners with them into the sea, but they were handled with wonderful dexterity, and there was no mishap.

When the open hold was filled with young cattle, packed as tightly as they could stand, the owners with their wives or sisters, who go with them to prevent extravagance in Galway, jumped down on the deck, and the voyage was begun. Immediately afterwards a rickety old hooker beat up with turf from Connemara, and while she was unlading all the men sat along the edge of the pier and made remarks upon the rottenness of her timber till the owners grew wild with rage.

The tide was now too low for more boats to come to the pier, so a move was made to a strip of sand towards the south-east, where the rest of the cattle were shipped through the surf. Here the hooker was anchored about eighty yards from the shore, and a curagh was rowed round to tow out the animals. Each bullock was caught in its turn and girded with a sling of rope by which it could be hoisted on board. Another rope was fastened to the horns and passed out to a man in the stern of the curagh. Then the animal was forced down through the surf and out of its depth before it had much time to struggle. Once fairly swimming, it was towed out to the hooker and dragged on board in a half-drowned condition.

The freedom of the sand seemed to give a stronger spirit of revolt, and some of the animals were only caught after a dangerous struggle. The first attempt was not always successful, and I saw one three-year-old lift two men with his horns, and drag another fifty yards along the sand by his tail before he was subdued.

While this work was going on a crowd of girls and women collected on the edge of the cliff and kept shouting down a confused babble of satire and praise.

When I came back to the cottage I found that among the women who had gone to the mainland was a daughter of the old woman's, and that her baby of about nine months had been left in the care of its grandmother.

As I came in she was busy getting ready my dinner, and old Pat Dirane, who usually comes at this hour, was rocking the cradle. It is made of clumsy wicker-work, with two pieces of rough wood fastened underneath to serve as rockers, and all the time I am in my room I can hear it bumping on the floor with extraordinary violence. When the baby is awake it sprawls on the floor, and the old woman sings it a variety of inarticulate lullabies that have much musical charm.

Another daughter, who lives at home, has gone to the fair also, so the old woman has both the baby and myself to take care of as well as a crowd of chickens that live in a hole beside the fire. Often when I want tea, or when the old woman goes for water, I have to take my own turn at rocking the cradle.

One of the largest Duns, or pagan forts, on the islands, is within a stone's throw of my cottage, and I often stroll up there after a dinner of eggs or salt pork, to smoke drowsily on the stones. The neighbours know my habit, and not infrequently some one wanders up to ask what news there is in the last paper I have received, or to make inquiries about the American war. If no one comes I prop my book open with stones touched by the Fir-bolgs, and sleep for hours in the delicious warmth of the sun. The last few days I have almost lived on the round walls, for, by some miscalculation, our turf has come to an end, and the fires are kept up with dried cow-dung—a common fuel on the island—the smoke from which filters through into my room and lies in blue layers above my table and bed.

Fortunately the weather is fine, and I can spend my days in the sunshine. When I look round from the top of these walls I can see the sea on nearly every side, stretching away to distant ranges of mountains on the north and south. Underneath me to the east there is the one inhabited district of the island, where I can see red figures moving about the cottages, sending up an occasional fragment of conversation or of old island melodies.

The baby is teething, and has been crying for several days. Since his mother went to the fair they have been feeding him with cow's milk, often slightly sour, and giving him, I think, more than he requires.

This morning, however, he seemed so unwell they sent out to look for a foster-mother in the village, and before long a young woman, who lives a little way to the east, came in and restored him his natural food.

A few hours later, when I came into the kitchen to talk to old Pat, another woman performed the same kindly office, this time a person with a curiously whimsical expression.

Pat told me a story of an unfaithful wife, which I will give further down, and then broke into a moral dispute with the visitor, which caused immense delight to some young men who had come down to listen to the story. Unfortunately it was carried on so rapidly in Gaelic that I lost most of the points.

This old man talks usually in a mournful tone about his ill-health, and his death, which he feels to be approaching, yet he has occasional touches of humour that remind me of old Mourteen on the north island. To-day a grotesque twopenny doll was lying on the floor near the old woman. He picked it up and examined it as if comparing it with her. Then he held it up: 'Is it you is after bringing that thing into the world,' he said, 'woman of the house?'

Here is the story:[1]

One day I was travelling on foot from Galway to Dublin, and the darkness came on me and I ten miles from the town I was wanting to pass the night in. Then a hard rain began to fall and I was tired walking, so when I saw a sort of a house with no roof on it up against the road, I got in the way the walls would give me shelter.

As I was looking round I saw a light in some trees two perches off, and thinking any sort of a house would be better than where I was, I got over a wall and went up to the house to look in at the window.

I saw a dead man laid on a table, and candles lighted, and a woman watching him. I was frightened when I saw him, but it was raining hard, and I said to myself, if he was dead he couldn't hurt me. Then I knocked on the door and the woman came and opened it.

'Good evening, ma'am,' says I.

'Good evening kindly, stranger,' says she. 'Come in out of the rain.'

Then she took me in and told me her husband was after dying on her, and she was watching him that night.

'But it's thirsty you'll be, stranger,' says she. 'Come into the parlour.'

Then she took me into the parlour—and it was a fine clean house—and she put a cup, with a saucer under it, on the table before me with fine sugar and bread.

When I'd had a cup of tea I went back into the kitchen where

---

[1] The story which follows is the source of Synge's play, *In the Shadow of the Glen*.

the dead man was lying, and she gave me a fine new pipe off the table with a drop of spirits.

'Stranger,' says she, 'would you be afeard to be alone with himself?'

'Not a bit in the world, ma'am,' says I; 'he that's dead can do no hurt.'

Then she said she wanted to go over and tell the neighbours the way her husband was after dying on her, and she went out and locked the door behind her.

I smoked one pipe, and I leaned out and took another off the table. I was smoking it with my hand on the back of my chair—the way you are yourself this minute, God bless you—and I looking on the dead man, when he opened his eyes as wide as myself and looked at me.

'Don't be afraid, stranger,' said the dead man; 'I'm not dead at all in the world. Come here and help me up and I'll tell you all about it.'

Well, I went up and took the sheet off of him, and I saw that he had a fine clean shirt on his body, and fine flannel drawers.

He sat up then, and says he—

'I've got a bad wife, stranger, and I let on to be dead the way I'd catch her goings on.'

Then he got two fine sticks he had to keep down his wife, and he put them at each side of his body, and he laid himself out again as if he was dead.

In half an hour his wife came back and a young man along with her. Well, she gave him his tea, and she told him he was tired, and he would do right to go and lie down in the bedroom.

The young man went in and the woman sat down to watch by the dead man. A while after she got up and 'Stranger,' says she, 'I'm going in to get the candle out of the room; I'm thinking the young man will be asleep by this time.' She went into the bedroom, but the divil a bit of her came back.

Then the dead man got up, and he took one stick, and he gave the other to myself. We went in and saw them lying together with her head on his arm.

The dead man hit him a blow with the stick so that the blood out of him leapt up and hit the gallery.

That is my story.

In stories of this kind he always speaks in the first person, with minute details to show that he was actually present at the scenes that are described.

At the beginning of this story he gave me a long account of what had made him be on his way to Dublin on that occasion, and told me about all the rich people he was going to see in the finest streets of the city.

A week of sweeping fogs has passed over and given me a strange sense of exile and desolation. I walk round the island nearly every day, yet I can see nothing anywhere but a mass of wet rock, a strip of surf, and then a tumult of waves.

The slaty limestone has grown black with the water that is dripping on it, and wherever I turn there is the same grey obsession twining and wreathing itself among the narrow fields, and the same wail from the wind that shrieks and whistles in the loose rubble of the walls.

At first the people do not give much attention to the wilderness that is round them, but after a few days their voices sink in the kitchen, and their endless talk of pigs and cattle falls to the whisper of men who are telling stories in a haunted house.

The rain continues; but this evening a number of young men were in the kitchen mending nets, and the bottle of poteen was drawn from its hiding-place.

One cannot think of these people drinking wine on the summit of this crumbling precipice, but their grey poteen, which brings a shock of joy to the blood, seems predestined to keep sanity in men who live forgotten in these worlds of mist.

I sat in the kitchen part of the evening to feel the gaiety that was rising, and when I came into my own room after dark, one of the sons came in every time the bottle made its round, to pour me out my share.

It has cleared, and the sun is shining with a luminous warmth that makes the whole island glisten with the splendour of a gem, and fills the sea and sky with a radiance of blue light.

I have come out to lie on the rocks where I have the black edge of the north island in front of me, Galway Bay, too blue almost to look at, on my right, the Atlantic on my left, a perpendicular cliff under my ankles, and over me innumerable gulls that chase each other in a white cirrus of wings.

A nest of hooded crows is somewhere near me, and one of the old birds is trying to drive me away by letting itself fall like a stone every few moments, from about forty yards above me to within reach of my hand.

Gannets are passing up and down above the sound, swooping at times after a mackerel, and further off I can see the whole fleet of hookers coming out from Kilronan for a night's fishing in the deep water to the west.

As I lie here hour after hour, I seem to enter into the wild pastimes of the cliff, and to become a companion of the cormorants and crows.

Many of the birds display themselves before me with the vanity of barbarians, performing in strange evolutions as long as I am in sight, and returning to their ledge of rock when I am gone. Some are wonderfully expert, and cut graceful figures for an inconceivable time without a flap of their wings, growing so absorbed in their own dexterity that they often collide with one another in their flight, an incident always followed by a wild outburst of abuse. Their language is easier than Gaelic, and I seem to understand the greater part of their cries, though I am not able to answer. There is one plaintive note which they take up in the middle of their usual babble with extraordinary effect, and pass on from one to another along the cliff with a sort of an inarticulate wail, as if they remembered for an instant the horror of the mist.

On the low sheets of rock to the east I can see a number of red and grey figures hurrying about their work. The continual passing in this island between the misery of last night and the splendour of to-day, seems to create an affinity between the moods of these people and the moods of varying rapture and dismay that are frequent in artists, and in certain forms of alienation. Yet it is only in the intonation of a few sentences or some old fragment of melody that I catch the real spirit of the island, for in general the men sit together and talk with endless iteration of the tides and fish, and of the price of kelp in Connemara.

After Mass this morning an old woman was buried. She lived in the cottage next mine, and more than once before noon I heard a faint echo of the keen. I did not go to the wake for fear my presence might jar upon the mourners, but all last evening I could hear the strokes of a hammer in the yard, where, in the middle of a little crowd of idlers, the next of kin laboured slowly at the coffin. To-day, before the hour for the funeral, poteen[1] was served to a number of men who stood about upon the road, and a portion was brought to me in my room. Then the coffin was carried out sewn loosely in sailcloth, and held near the ground by three cross-poles lashed upon the top. As we moved down to the low eastern portion of the island, nearly all the men, and all the oldest women, wearing petticoats over their heads, came out and joined in the procession.

While the grave was being opened the women sat down among the flat tombstones, bordered with a pale fringe of early bracken, and began the wild keen, or crying for the dead. Each old woman, as she took her turn in the leading recitative, seemed possessed for the moment with a profound ecstasy of grief, swaying to and fro, and bending her forehead to the stone before her, while she called out to the dead with a perpetually recurring chant of sobs.

All round the graveyard other wrinkled women, looking out from under the deep red petticoats that cloaked them, rocked themselves with the same rhythm, and intoned the inarticulate chant that is sustained by all as an accompaniment.

The morning had been beautifully fine, but as they lowered the coffin into the grave, thunder rumbled overhead and hailstones hissed among the bracken.

In Inishmaan one is forced to believe in a sympathy between man and nature, and at this moment when the thunder sounded a death-peal of extraordinary grandeur above the voices of the women, I could see the faces near me stiff and drawn with emotion.

When the coffin was in the grave, and the thunder had rolled away across the hills of Clare, the keen broke out again more passionately than before.

This grief of the keen is no personal complaint for the death of one woman over eighty years, but seems to contain the whole passionate rage that lurks somewhere in every native of the island. In this cry of pain the inner consciousness of the people seems to lay itself bare for an instant, and to reveal the mood of beings who feel their isolation in the face of a universe that wars on them with winds and seas. They are usually silent, but in the presence of death all outward show of indifference or patience is forgotten, and they

---

[1] Illegally distilled whiskey.

shriek with pitiable despair before the horror of the fate to which they all are doomed.

Before they covered the coffin an old man kneeled down by the grave and repeated a simple prayer for the dead.

There was an irony in these words of atonement and Catholic belief spoken by voices that were still hoarse with the cries of pagan desperation.

A little beyond the grave I saw a line of old women who had recited in the keen sitting in the shadow of a wall beside the roofless shell of the church. They were still sobbing and shaken with grief, yet they were beginning to talk again of the daily trifles that veil from them the terror of the world.

When we had all come out of the graveyard, and two men had rebuilt the hole in the wall through which the coffin had been carried in, we walked back to the village, talking of anything, and joking of anything, as if merely coming from the boat-slip, or the pier.

One man told me of the poteen drinking that takes place at some funerals.

'A while since,' he said, 'there were two men fell down in the graveyard while the drink was on them. The sea was rough that day, the way no one could go to bring the doctor, and one of the men never woke again, and found death that night.'

The other day the men of this house made a new field. There was a slight bank of earth under the wall of the yard, and another in the corner of the cabbage garden. The old man and his eldest son dug out the clay, with the care of men working in a gold-mine, and Michael packed it in panniers—there are no wheeled vehicles on this island—for transport to a flat rock in a sheltered corner of their holding, where it was mixed with sand and seaweed and spread out in a layer upon the stone.

Most of the potato-growing of the island is carried on in fields of this sort—for which the people pay a considerable rent—and if the season is at all dry, their hope of a fair crop is nearly always disappointed.

It is now nine days since rain has fallen, and the people are filled with anxiety, although the sun has not yet been hot enough to do harm.

The drought is also causing a scarcity of water. There are a few springs on this side of the island, but they come only from a little distance, and in hot weather are not to be relied on. The supply for this house is carried up in a water-barrel by one of the women. If it is drawn off at once it is not very nauseous, but if it has lain, as it often does, for some hours in the barrel, the smell, colour, and taste are unendurable. The water for washing is also coming short, and as I walk round the edges of the sea, I often come on a girl with her petticoats tucked up round her, standing in a pool left by the tide and washing her flannels among the sea-anemones and crabs. Their red bodices and white tapering legs make them as beautiful as tropical sea-birds, as they stand in a frame of seaweeds against the brink of the Atlantic. Michael, however, is a little uneasy when they are in sight, and I cannot pause to watch them. This habit of using the sea water for washing causes a good deal of rheumatism on the island, for the salt lies in the clothes and keeps them continually moist.

The people have taken advantage of this dry moment to begin the burning of the kelp,[1] and all the islands are lying in a volume of grey smoke. There will not be a very large quantity this year, as the people are discouraged by the uncertainty of the market, and do not care to undertake the task of manufacture without a certainty of profit.

The work needed to form a ton of kelp is considerable. The seaweed is collected from the rocks after the storms of autumn and winter, dried on fine days, and then made up into a rick, where it is left till the beginning of June.

It is then burnt in low kilns on the shore, an affair that takes from twelve to twenty-four hours of continuous hard work, though I understand the people here do not manage well and spoil a portion of what they produce by burning it more than is required.

The kiln holds about two tons of molten kelp, and when full it is loosely covered with stones, and left to cool. In a few days the substance is as hard as the limestone, and has to be broken with crowbars before it can be placed in curaghs for transport to Kilronan, where it is tested to determine the amount of iodine it contains, and is paid for accordingly. In former years good kelp would bring seven pounds a ton, now four pounds are not always reached.

In Aran even manufacture is of interest. The low flame-edged kiln, sending out dense clouds of creamy smoke, with a band of

---

[1] Seaweeds which are burnt for the sake of the substances found in the ashes. N.E.D.

red and grey clothed workers moving in the haze, and usually some petticoated boys and women who come down with drink, forms a scene with as much variety and colour as any picture from the East.

The men feel in a certain sense the distinction of their island, and show me their work with pride. One of them said to me yesterday, 'I'm thinking you never saw the like of this work before this day?'

'That is true,' I answered, ' I never did.'

'Bedad, then,' he said, 'isn't it a great wonder that you've seen France and Germany, and the Holy Father, and never seen a man making kelp till you come to Inishmaan.'

All the horses from this island are put out on grass among the hills of Connemara from June to the end of September, as there is no grazing here during the summer.

Their shipping and transport is even more difficult than that of the horned cattle. Most of them are wild Connemara ponies, and their great strength and timidity make them hard to handle on the narrow pier, while in the hooker itself it is not easy to get them safely on their feet in the small space that is available. They are dealt with in the same way as the bullocks I have spoken of already, but the excitement becomes much more intense, and the storm of Gaelic that rises the moment a horse is shoved from the pier, till it is safely in its place, is indescribable. Twenty boys and men howl and scream with agitation, cursing and exhorting, without knowing, most of the time, what they are saying.

Apart, however, from this primitive babble, the dexterity and power of the men are displayed to more advantage than in anything I have seen hitherto. I noticed particularly the owner of a hooker from the north island that was loaded this morning. He seemed able to hold up a horse by his single weight when it was swinging from the masthead, and preserved a humorous calm even in moments of the wildest excitement. Sometimes a large mare would come down sideways on the backs of the other horses, and kick there till the hold seemed to be filled with a mass of struggling centaurs, for the men themselves often leap down to try and save the foals from injury. The backs of the horses put in first are often a good deal cut by the shoes of the others that arrive on top of them, but otherwise they do not seem to be much the worse, and as they are not on their way to a fair, it is not of much consequence in what condition they come to land.

There is only one bit and saddle in the island, which are used by the priest, who rides from the chapel to the pier when he has held the service on Sunday.

The islanders themselves ride with a simple halter and a stick, yet sometimes travel, at least in the larger island, at a desperate gallop. As the horses usually have panniers, the rider sits sideways over the withers, and if the panniers are empty they go at full speed in this position without anything to hold to.

More than once in Aranmor I met a party going out west with empty panniers from Kilronan. Long before they came in sight I could hear a clatter of hoofs, and then a whirl of horses would come round a corner at full gallop with their heads out, utterly indifferent to the slender halter that is their only check. They generally travel in single file with a few yards between them, and as there is no traffic there is little fear of an accident.

Sometimes a woman and a man ride together, but in this case the man sits in the usual position, and the woman sits sideways behind him, and holds him round the waist.

Old Pat Dirane continues to come up every day to talk to me, and at times I turn the conversation to his experiences of the fairies.

He has seen a good many of them, he says, in different parts of the island, especially in the sandy districts north of the slip. They are about a yard high with caps like the 'peelers' [1] pulled down over their faces. On one occasion he saw them playing ball in the evening just above the slip, and he says I must avoid that place in the morning or after nightfall for fear they might do me mischief.

He has seen two women who were 'away' with them, one a young married woman, the other a girl. The woman was standing by a wall, at a spot he described to me with great care, looking out towards the north.

Another night he heard a voice crying out in Irish, *'mháthair tá mé marbh'* ('O mother, I'm killed'), and in the morning there was blood on the wall of his house, and a child in a house not far off was dead.

---

[1] Policemen so called after their founder Sir Robert Peel.

Yesterday he took me aside, and said he would tell me a secret he had never yet told to any person in the world.

'Take a sharp needle,' he said, 'and stick it in under the collar of your coat, and not one of them will be able to have power on you.'

Iron is a common talisman with barbarians, but in this case the idea of exquisite sharpness was probably present also, and, perhaps, some feeling for the sanctity of the instrument of toil, a folk-belief that is common in Brittany.

The fairies are more numerous in Mayo than in any other county, though they are fond of certain districts in Galway, where the following story is said to have taken place.

'A farmer was in great distress as his crops had failed, and his cow had died on him. One night he told his wife to make him a fine new sack for flour before the next morning; and when it was finished he started off with it before the dawn.

'At that time there was a gentleman who had been taken by the fairies, and made an officer among them, and it was often people would see him and her riding on a white horse at dawn and in the evening.

'The poor man went down to the place where they used to see the officer, and when he came by on his horse, he asked the loan of two hundred and a half of flour, for he was in great want.

'The officer called the fairies out of a hole in the rocks where they stored their wheat, and told them to give the poor man what he was asking. Then he told him to come back and pay him in a year, and rode away.

'When the poor man got home he wrote down the day on a piece of paper, and that day year he came back and paid the officer.'

When he had ended his story the old man told me that the fairies have a tenth of all the produce of the country, and make stores of it in the rocks.


It is a Holy Day, and I have come up to sit on the Dun while the people are at Mass.

A strange tranquillity has come over the island this morning, as happens sometimes on Sunday, filling the two circles of sea and sky with the quiet of a church.

The one landscape that is here lends itself with singular power to this suggestion of grey luminous cloud. There is no wind, and no definite light. Aranmor seems to sleep upon a mirror, and the hills of Connemara look so near that I am troubled by the width of the bay that lies before them, touched this morning with individual expression one sees sometimes in a lake.

On these rocks, where there is no growth of vegetable or animal life, all the seasons are the same, and this June day is so full of autumn that I listen unconsciously for the rustle of dead leaves.

The first group of men are coming out of the chapel, followed by a crowd of women, who divide at the gate and troop off in different directions, while the men linger on the road to gossip.

The silence is broken; I can hear far off, as if over water, a faint murmur of Gaelic.

In the afternoon the sun came out and I was rowed over for a visit to Kilronan.

As my men were bringing round the curagh to take me off a headland near the pier, they struck a sunken rock, and came ashore shipping a quantity of water. They plugged the hole with a piece of sacking torn from a bag of potatoes they were taking over for the priest, and we set off with nothing but a piece of torn canvas between us and the Atlantic.

Every few hundred yards one of the rowers had to stop and bail, but the hole did not increase.

When we were about half way across the sound we met a curagh coming towards us with its sails set. After some shouting in Gaelic, I learned that they had a packet of letters and tobacco for myself. We sidled up as near as was possible with the roll, and my goods were thrown to me wet with spray.

After my weeks in Inishmaan, Kilronan seemed an imposing centre of activity. The half-civilised fishermen of the larger island are inclined to despise the simplicity of the life here, and some of them who were standing about when I landed asked me how at all I passed my time with no decent fishing to be looking at.

I turned in for a moment to talk to the old couple in the hotel, and then moved on to pay some other visits in the village.

Later in the evening I walked out along the northern road, where I met many of the natives of the outlying villages, who had come down to Kilronan for the Holy Day, and were now wandering home in scattered groups.

The women and girls, when they had no men with them, usually tried to make fun with me.

'Is it tired you are, stranger?' said one girl. I was walking very slowly, to pass the time before my return to the east.

'Bedad, it is not, little girl,' I answered in Gaelic, 'it is lonely I am.'

'Here is my little sister, stranger, who will give you her arm.'

And so it went. Quiet as these woman are on ordinary occasions, when two or three of them are gathered together in their holiday petticoats and shawls, they are as wild and capricious as the women who live in towns.

About seven o'clock I got back to Kilronan, and beat up my crew from the public-houses near the bay. With their usual carelessness they had not seen to the leak in the curagh, nor to an oar that was losing the brace that holds it to the toll-pin, and we moved off across the sound at an absurd pace with a deepening pool at our feet.

A superb evening light was lying over the island, which made me rejoice at our delay. Looking back there was a golden haze behind the sharp edges of the rock, and a long wake from the sun, which was making jewels of the bubbling left by the oars.

The men had had their share of porter and were unusually voluble, pointing out things to me that I had already seen, and stopping now and then to make me notice the oily smell of mackerel that was rising from the waves.

They told me that an evicting party is coming to the island tomorrow morning, and gave me a long account of what they make and spend in a year, and of their trouble with the rent.

'The rent is hard enough for a poor man,' said one of them, 'but this time we didn't pay, and they're after serving processes on every one of us. A man will have to pay his rent now, and a power of money with it for the process, and I'm thinking the agent will have money enough out of them processes to pay for his servant-girl and his man all the year.'

I asked afterwards who the island belonged to.

'Bedad,' they said, 'we've always heard it belonged to Miss ——, and she is dead.'

When the sun passed like a lozenge of gold flame into the sea the cold became intense. Then the men began to talk among themselves, and losing the thread, I lay half in a dream looking at the pale oily sea about us, and the low cliffs of the island sloping up past the village with its wreath of smoke to the outline of Dun Conor.

Old Pat was in the house when I arrived, and he told a long story after supper:

There was once a widow living among the woods, and her only son living along with her. He went out every morning through the trees to get sticks, and one day as he was lying on the ground he saw a swarm of flies flying over what the cow leaves behind her. He took up his sickle and hit one blow at them, and hit that hard he left no single one of them living.

That evening he said to his mother that it was time he was going out into the world to seek his fortune, for he was able to destroy a whole swarm of flies at one blow, and he asked her to make him three cakes the way he might take them with him in the morning.

He started the next day a while after the dawn, with his three cakes in his wallet, and he ate one of them near ten o'clock.

He got hungry again by midday and ate the second, and when night was coming on him he ate the third. After that he met a man on the road who asked him where he was going.

'I'm looking for some place where I can work for my living,' said the young man.

'Come with me,' said the other man, 'and sleep tonight in the barn, and I'll give you work to-morrow to see what you're able for.'

The next morning the farmer brought him out and showed him his cows and told him to take them out to graze on the hills, and to keep good watch that no one should come near them to milk them. The young man drove out the cows into the fields, and when the heat of the day came on he lay down on his back and looked up into the sky. A while after he saw a black spot in the north-west, and it grew larger and nearer till he saw a great giant coming towards him.

He got up on to his feet and he caught the giant round the legs with his two arms, and he drove him down into the hard ground above his ankles, the way he was not able to free himself. Then the giant told him to do him no hurt, and gave him his magic rod, and told him to strike on the rock, and he would find his beautiful black horse, and his sword and his fine suit.

The young man struck the rock and it opened before him, and he found the beautiful black horse, and the giant's sword and the suit lying before him. He took out the sword alone, and he struck one blow with it and struck off the giant's head. Then he put back the sword into the rock, and went out again to his cattle, till it was time to drive them home to the farmer.

When they came to milk the cows they found a power of milk in them, and the farmer asked the young man if he had seen nothing out on the hills, for the other cow-boys had been bringing home the cows with no drop of milk in them. And the young man said he had seen nothing.

The next day he went out again with the cows. He lay down on his back in the heat of the day, and after a while he saw a black spot in the north-west, and it grew larger and nearer, till he saw it was a great giant coming to attack him.

'You killed my brother,' said the giant; 'come here, till I make a garter of your body.'

The young man went to him and caught him by the legs and drove him down into the hard ground up to his ankles.

Then he hit the rod against the rock, and took out the sword and struck off the giant's head.

That evening the farmer found twice as much milk in the cows as the evening before, and he asked the young man if he had seen anything. The young man said that he had seen nothing.

The third day the third giant came to him and said, 'You have killed my two brothers; come here, till I make a garter of your body.'

And he did with this giant as he had done with the other two, and that evening there was so much milk in the cows it was dropping out of their udders on the pathway.

The next day the farmer called him and told him he might leave the cows in the stalls that day, for there was a great curiosity to be seen, namely, a beautiful king's daughter that was to be eaten by a great fish, if there was no one in it that could save her. But the young man said such a sight was all one to him, and he went out with the cows on to the hills. When he came to the rock he hit it with his rod and brought out the suit and put it on him, and brought out the sword and strapped it on his side, like an officer, and he got on the black horse and rode faster than the wind till he came to where the beautiful king's daughter was sitting on the shore in a golden chair, waiting for the great fish.

When the great fish came in on the sea, bigger than a whale, with two wings on the back of it, the young man went down into the surf and struck at it with his sword and cut off one of its wings. All the sea turned red with the bleeding of it, till it swam away and left the young man on the shore.

Then he turned his horse and rode faster than the wind till he came to the rock, and he took the suit off him and put it back in the rock, with the giant's sword and the black horse, and drove the cows down to the farm.

The man came out before him and said he had missed the greatest wonder ever was, and that a noble person was after coming down with a fine suit on him and cutting off one of the wings from the great fish.

'And there'll be the same necessity on her for two mornings more,' said the farmer, 'and you'd do right to come and look on it.'

But the young man said he would not come.

The next morning he went out with his cows, and he took the sword and the suit and the black horse out of the rock, and he rode faster than the wind till he came where the king's daughter was sitting on the shore. When the people saw him coming there was great wonder on them to know if it was the same man they had seen the day before. The king's daughter called out to him to come and kneel before her, and when he kneeled down she took her scissors and cut off a lock of hair from the back of his head and hid it in her clothes.

Then the great fish came in from the sea, and he went down into the surf and cut the other wing off from it. All the sea turned red with the bleeding out of it, till it swam away and left them.

That evening the farmer came out before him and told him of the great wonder he had missed, and asked him would he go the next day and look on it. The young man said he would not go.

The third day he came again on the black horse to where the king's daughter was sitting on a golden chair waiting for the great fish. When it came in from the sea the young man went down before it, and every time it opened its mouth to eat him, he struck into its mouth, till his sword went out through its neck, and it rolled back and died.

Then he rode off faster than the wind, and he put the suit and the sword and the black horse into the rock, and drove home the cows.

The farmer was there before him and he told him that there was to be a great marriage feast held for three days, and on the third day the king's daughter would be married to the man that killed the great fish, if they were able to find him.

A great feast was held, and men of great strength came and said it was themselves were after killing the great fish.

But on the third day the young man put on the suit, and strapped the sword to his side like an officer, and got on the black horse and rode faster than the wind, till he came to the palace.

The king's daughter saw him, and she brought him in and made him kneel down before her. Then she looked at the back of his head and she saw the place where she had cut off the lock with her own hand. She led him in to the king, and they were married, and the young man was given all the estate.

That is my story.


Two recent attempts to carry out evictions on the island came to nothing, for each time a sudden storm rose, by, it is said, the power of a native witch, when the steamer was approaching, and made it impossible to land.

This morning, however, broke beneath a clear sky of June, and when I came into the open air the sea and rocks were shining with wonderful brilliancy. Groups of men, dressed in their holiday clothes, were standing about, talking with anger and fear, yet showing a lurking satisfaction at the thought of the dramatic pageant that was to break the silence of the seas.

About half-past nine the steamer came in sight, on the narrow line of sea-horizon that is seen in the centre of the bay, and immediately a last effort was made to hide the cows and sheep of the families that were most in debt.

Till this year no one on the island would consent to act as bailiff, so that it was impossible to identify the cattle of the defaulters. Now, however, a man of the name of Patrick has sold his honour, and the effort of concealment is practically futile.

This falling away from the ancient loyalty of the island has caused intense indignation, and early yesterday morning, while I was dreaming on the Dun, this letter was nailed on the doorpost of the chapel:

'Patrick, the devil, a revolver is waiting for you. If you are missed with the first shot, there will be five more that will hit you.

'Any man that will talk with you, or work with you, or drink a pint of porter in your shop, will be done with the same way as yourself.'

As the steamer drew near I moved down with the men to watch the arrival, though no one went further than about a mile from the shore.

Two curaghs from Kilronan with a man who was to give help in identifying the cottages, the doctor, and the relieving officer, were drifting with the tide, unwilling to come to land without the support of the larger party. When the anchor had been thrown it gave me a strange throb of pain to see the boats being lowered, and the sunshine gleaming on the rifles and helmets of the constabulary who crowded into them.

Once on shore the men were formed in close marching order, a word was given, and the heavy rhythm of their boots came up over the rocks. We were collected in two straggling bands on either side of the roadway, and a few moments later the body of magnificent armed men passed close to us, followed by a low rabble, who had been brought to act as drivers for the sheriff.

After my weeks spent among primitive men this glimpse of the newer types of humanity was not reassuring. Yet these mechanical police, with the commonplace agents and sheriffs, and the rabble they had hired, represented aptly enough the civilisation for which the homes of the island were to be desecrated.

A stop was made at one of the first cottages in the village, and the day's work began. Here, however, and at the next cottage, a compromise was made, as some relatives came up at the last moment and lent the money that was needed to gain a respite.

In another case a girl was ill in the house, so the doctor interposed, and the people were allowed to remain after a merely formal eviction. About midday, however, a house was reached where there was no pretext for mercy, and no money could be procured. At a sign from the sheriff the work of carrying out the beds and utensils was begun in the middle of a crowd of natives who looked on in absolute silence, broken only by the wild imprecations of the woman of the house. She belonged to one of the most primitive families on the island, and she shook with uncontrollable fury as she saw the strange armed men who spoke a language she could not understand driving her from the hearth she had brooded on for thirty years. For these people the outrage to the hearth is the supreme catastrophe. They live here in a world of grey, where there are wild rains and mists every week in the year, and their warm chimney corners, filled with children and young girls, grow into the consciousness of each family in a way it is not easy to understand in more civilised places.

The outrage to a tomb in China probably gives no greater shock to the Chinese than the outrage to a hearth in Inishmaan gives to the people.

When the few trifles had been carried out, and the door blocked with stones, the old woman sat down by the threshold and covered her head with her shawl.

Five or six other women who lived close by sat down in a circle round her, with mute sympathy. Then the crowd moved on with the police to another cottage where the same scene was to take place, and left the group of desolate women sitting by the hovel.

There were still no clouds in the sky, and the heat was intense. The police when not in motion lay sweating and gasping under the walls with their tunics unbuttoned. They were not attractive, and I kept comparing them with the islandmen, who walked up and down as cool and fresh-looking as the sea-gulls.

When the last eviction had been carried out a division was made: half the party went off with the bailiff to search the inner plain of the island for the cattle that had been hidden in the morning, the other half remained on the village road to guard some pigs that had already been taken possession of.

After a while two of these pigs escaped from the drivers and began a wild race up and down the narrow road. The people shrieked and howled to increase their terror, and at last some of them became so excited that the police thought it time to interfere. They drew up in double line opposite the mouth of a blind laneway where the animals had been shut up. A moment later the shrieking began again in the west and the two pigs came in sight, rushing down the middle of the road with the drivers behind them.

They reached the line of the police. There was a slight scuffle, and then the pigs continued their mad rush to the east, leaving three policemen lying in the dust.

The satisfaction of the people was immense. They shrieked and hugged each other with delight, and it is likely that they will hand down these animals for generations in the tradition of the island.

Two hours later the other party returned, driving three lean cows before them, and a start was made for the slip. At the public-house the policemen were given a drink while the dense crowd that was following waited in the lane. The island bull happened to be in a field close by, and he became wildly excited at the sight of the cows and of the strangely-dressed men. Two young islanders sidled up to me in a moment or two as I was resting on a wall, and one of them whispered in my ear—

'Do you think they could take fines of us if we let out the bull on them?'

In face of the crowd of women and children, I could only say it was probable, and they slunk off.

At the slip there was a good deal of bargaining, which ended in all the cattle being given back to their owners. It was plainly of no use to take them away, as they were worth nothing.

When the last policeman had embarked, an old woman came forward from the crowd and, mounting on a rock near the slip, began a fierce rhapsody in Gaelic, pointing at the bailiff and waving her withered arms with extraordinary rage.

'This man is my own son,' she said; 'it is I that ought to know him. He is the first ruffian in the whole big world.'

Then she gave an account of his life, coloured with a vindictive fury I cannot reproduce. As she went on the excitement became so intense I thought the man would be stoned before he could get back to his cottage.

On these islands the women live only for their children, and it is hard to estimate the power of the impulse that made this old woman stand out and curse her son.

In the fury of her speech I seem to look again into the strangely reticent temperament of the islanders, and to feel the passionate spirit that expresses itself, at odd moments only, with magnificent words and gestures.

Old Pat has told me a story of the goose that lays the golden eggs, which he calls the Phœnix:

A poor widow had three sons and a daughter. One day when her sons were out looking for sticks in the wood they saw a fine speckled bird flying in the trees. The next day they saw it again, and the eldest son told his brothers to go and get sticks by themselves, for he was going after the bird.

He went after it, and brought it in with him when he came home in the evening. They put it in an old hencoop, and they gave it some of the meal they had for themselves;—I don't know if it ate the meal, but they divided what they had themselves; they could do no more.

That night it laid a fine spotted egg in the basket. The next night it laid another.

At that time its name was in the papers and many heard of the bird that laid the golden eggs, for the eggs were of gold, and there's no lie in it.

When the boys went down to the shop the next day to buy a stone of meal, the shopman asked if he could buy the bird of them. Well, it was arranged in this way. The shopman would marry the boys' sister—a poor simple girl without a stitch of good clothes—and get the bird with her.

Some time after that one of the boys sold an egg of the bird to a gentleman that was in the country. The gentleman asked him if he had the bird still. He said that the man who had married his sister was after getting it.

'Well,' said the gentleman, 'the man who eats the heart of that bird will find a purse of gold beneath him every morning, and the man who eats its liver will be king of Ireland.'

The boy went out—he was a simple poor fellow—and told the shopman.

Then the shopman brought in the bird and killed it, and he ate the heart himself and he gave the liver to his wife.

When the boy saw that, there was grèat anger on him, and he went back and told the gentleman.

'Do what I'm telling you,' said the gentleman. 'Go down now and tell the shopman and his wife to come up here to play a game of cards with me, for it's lonesome I am this evening.'

When the boy was gone he mixed a vomit and poured the lot of it into a few naggins of whiskey, and he put a strong cloth on the table under the cards.

The man came up with his wife and they began to play.

The shopman won the first game and the gentleman made them drink a sup of the whiskey.

They played again and the shopman won the second game. Then the gentleman made him drink a sup more of the whiskey.

As they were playing the third game the shopman and his wife got sick on the cloth, and the boy picked it up and carried it into the yard, for the gentleman had let him know what he was to do. Then he found the heart of the bird and he ate it, and the next morning when he turned in his bed there was a purse of gold under him.

That is my story.

When the steamer is expected I rarely fail to visit the boat-slip, as the men usually collect when she is in the offing, and lie arguing among their curaghs till she has made her visit to the south island, and is seen coming towards us.

This morning I had a long talk with an old man who was rejoicing over the improvement he had seen here during the last ten or fifteen years.

Till recently there was no communication with the mainland except by hookers, which were usually slow, and could only make the voyage in tolerably fine weather, so that if an islander went to a fair it was often three weeks before he could return. Now, however, the steamer comes here twice in the week, and the voyage is made in three or four hours.

The pier on this island is also a novelty, and is much thought of, as it enables the hookers that still carry turf and cattle to discharge and take their cargoes directly from the shore. The water round it, however, is only deep enough for a hooker when the tide is nearly full, and will never float the steamer, so passengers must still come to land in curaghs. The boat-slip at the corner next the south island is extremely useful in calm weather, but it is exposed to a heavy roll from the south, and is so narrow that the curaghs run some danger of missing it in the tumult of the surf.

In bad weather four men will often stand for nearly an hour at the top of the slip with a curagh in their hands, watching a point of rock towards the south where they can see the strength of the waves that are coming in.

The instant a break is seen they swoop down to the surf, launch their curagh, and pull out to sea with incredible speed. Coming to land is attended with the same difficulty, and, if their moment is badly chosen, they are likely to be washed sideways and swamped among the rocks.

This continual danger, which can only be escaped by extraordinary personal dexterity, has had considerable influence on the local character, as the waves have made it impossible for clumsy, foolhardy, or timid men to live on these islands.

When the steamer is within a mile of the slip, the curaghs are put out and range themselves—there are usually from four to a dozen—in two lines at some distance from the shore.

The moment she comes in among them there is a short but desperate struggle for good places at her side. The men are lolling on their oars talking with the dreamy tone which comes with the rocking of the waves. The steamer lies to, and in an instant their faces become distorted with passion, while the oars bend and quiver with the strain. For one minute they seem utterly indifferent to their own safety and that of their friends and brothers. Then the sequence is decided, and they begin to talk again with the dreamy tone that is habitual to them, while they make fast and clamber up into the steamer.

While the curaghs are out I am left with a few women and very old men who cannot row. One of these old men, whom I often talk with, has some fame as a bone-setter, and is said to have done remarkable cures, both here and on the mainland. Stories are told of how he has been taken off by the quality in their carriages through the hills of Connemara, to treat their sons and daughters, and come home with his pockets full of money.

Another old man, the oldest on the island, is fond of telling me anecdotes—not folk-tales—of things that have happened here in his lifetime.

He often tells me about a Connaught man who killed his father with the blow of a spade when he was in passion, and then fled to this island and threw himself on the mercy of some of the natives with whom he was said to be related. They hid him in a hole—which the old man has shown me—and kept him safe for weeks, though the police came and searched for him, and he could hear their boots grinding on the stones over his head. In spite of a reward which was offered, the island was incorruptible, and after much trouble the man was safely shipped to America.

This impulse to protect the criminal is universal in the west. It seems partly due to the association between justice and the hated English jurisdiction, but more directly to the primitive feeling of these people, who are never criminals yet always capable of crime, that a man will not do wrong unless he is under the influence of a passion which is as irresponsible as a storm on the sea. If a man has killed his father, and is already sick and broken with remorse, they can see no reason why he should be dragged away and killed by the law.

Such a man, they say, will be quiet all the rest of his life, and if you suggest that punishment is needed as an example, they ask, 'Would any one kill his father if he was able to help it?' [1]

Some time ago, before the introduction of police, all the people of the islands were as innocent as the people here remain to this day. I have heard that at that time the ruling proprietor and magistrate of the north island used to give any man who had done wrong a letter to a jailer in Galway, and send him off by himself to serve a term of imprisonment.

As there was no steamer, the ill-doer was given a passage in some chance hooker to the nearest point on the mainland. Then he walked for many miles along a desolate shore till he reached the town. When his time had been put through he crawled back along the same route, feeble and emaciated, and had often to wait many weeks before he could regain the island. Such at least is the story.

It seems absurd to apply the same laws to these people and to the criminal classes of a city. The most intelligent man on Inishmaan has often spoken to me of his contempt of the law, and of the increase of crime the police have brought to Aranmor. On this island, he says, if men have a little difference, or a little fight, their friends take care it does not go too far, and in a little time it is forgotten. In Kilronan there is a band of men paid to make out cases for themselves; the moment a blow is struck they come down and arrest the man who gave it. The other man he quarrelled with has to give evidence against him; whole families come down to the court and swear against each other till they become bitter enemies. If there is a conviction the man who is convicted never forgives. He waits his time, and before the year is out there is a cross summons, which the other man in turn never forgives. The feud continues to grow, till a dispute about the colour of a man's hair may end in a murder, after a year's forcing by the law. The mere

---

[1] This is the story upon which Synge based his play *The Playboy of the Western World*.

fact that it is impossible to get reliable evidence in the island—not because the people are dishonest, but because they think the claim of kinship more sacred than the claims of abstract truth—turns the whole system of sworn evidence into a demoralising farce, and it is easy to believe that law dealings on this false basis must lead to every sort of injustice.

While I am discussing these questions with the old men the curaghs begin to come in with cargoes of salt, and flour, and porter.

To-day a stir was made by the return of a native who had spent five years in New York. He came on shore with half a dozen people who had been shopping on the mainland, and walked up and down on the slip in his neat suit, looking strangely foreign to his birthplace, while his old mother of eighty-five ran about on the slippery seaweed, half crazy with delight, telling every one the news.

When the curaghs were in their places the men crowded round him to bid him welcome. He shook hands with them readily enough, but with no smile of recognition.

He is said to be dying.

Yesterday—a Sunday—three young men rowed me over to Inishere, the south island of the group.

The stern of the curagh was occupied, so I was put in the bow with my head on a level with the gunnel. A considerable sea was running in the sound, and when we came out from the shelter of this island, the curagh rolled and vaulted in a way not easy to describe.

At one moment, as we went down into the furrow, green waves curled and arched themselves above me; then in an instant I was flung up into the air and could look down on the heads of the rowers, as if we were sitting on a ladder, or out across a forest of white crests to the black cliff of Inishmaan.

The men seemed excited and uneasy, and I thought for a moment that we were likely to be swamped. In a little while, however, I realised the capacity of the curagh to raise its head among the waves, and the motion became strangely exhilarating. Even, I thought, if we were dropped into the blue chasm of the waves, this death, with the fresh sea saltness in one's teeth, would be better than most deaths one is likely to meet.

When we reached the other island, it was raining heavily, so that we could not see anything of the antiquities or people.

For the greater part of the afternoon we sat on the tops of empty barrels in the public-house, talking of the destiny of Gaelic. We were admitted as travellers, and the shutters of the shop were closed behind us, letting in only a glimmer of grey light, and the tumult of the storm. Towards evening it cleared a little and we came home in a calmer sea, but with a dead head-wind that gave the rowers all they could do to make the passage.

On calm days I often go out fishing with Michael. When we reach the space above the slip where the curaghs are propped, bottom upwards, on the limestone, he lifts the prow of the one we are going to embark in, and I slip underneath and set the centre of the foremost seat upon my neck. Then he crawls under the stern and stands up with the last seat upon his shoulders. We start for the sea. The long prow bends before me so that I see nothing but a few yards of shingle at my feet. A quivering pain runs from the top of my spine to the sharp stones that seem to pass through my pampooties, and grate upon my ankles. We stagger and groan beneath the weight; but at last our feet reach the slip, and we run down with a half-trot like the pace of barefooted children.

A yard from the sea we stop and lower the curagh to the right. It must be brought down gently—a difficult task for our strained and aching muscles—and sometimes as the gunnel reaches the slip I lose my balance and roll in among the seats.

Yesterday we went out in the curagh that had been damaged on the day of my visit to Kilronan, and as we were putting in the oars the freshly-tarred patch stuck to the slip which was heated with the sunshine. We carried up water in the bailer—the 'supeen,' a shallow wooden vessel like a soup-plate—and with infinite pains we got free and rode away. In a few minutes, however, I found the water spouting up at my feet.

The patch had been misplaced, and this time we had no sacking. Michael borrowed my pocket scissors, and with admirable rapidity cut a square of flannel from the tail of his shirt and squeezed it into the hole, making it fast with a splint which he hacked from one of the oars.

During our excitement the tide had carried us to the brink of the rocks, and I admired again the dexterity with which he got his oars into the water and turned us out as we were mounting on a wave that would have hurled us to destruction.

With the injury to our curagh we did not go far from the shore. After a while I took a long spell at the oars, and gained a certain dexterity, though they are not easy to manage. The handles overlap by about six inches—in order to gain leverage, as the curagh is narrow—and at first it was almost impossible to avoid striking the upper oar against one's knuckles. The oars are rough and square, except at the ends, so one cannot do so with impunity. Again, a curagh with two light people in it floats on the water like a nutshell, and the slightest inequality in the stroke throws the prow round at least a right angle from its course. In the first half-hour I found myself more than once moving towards the point I had come from, greatly to Michael's satisfaction.

This morning we were out again near the pier on the north side of the island. As we paddled slowly with the tide, trolling for pollock, several curaghs, weighed to the gunnel with kelp, passed us on their way to Kilronan.

An old woman, rolled in red petticoats, was sitting on a ledge of rock that runs into the sea at the point where the curaghs were passing from the south, hailing them in quavering Gaelic, and asking for a passage to Kilronan.

The first one that came round without a cargo turned in from some distance and took her away.

The morning had none of the supernatural beauty that comes over the island so often in rainy weather, so we basked in the vague enjoyment of the sunshine, looking down at the wild luxuriance of the vegetation beneath the sea, which contrasts strangely with the nakedness above it.

Some dreams I have had in this cottage seem to give strength to the opinion that there is a psychic memory attached to certain neighbourhoods.

Last night, after walking in a dream among buildings with strangely intense light on them, I heard a faint rhythm of music beginning far away on some stringed instrument.

It came closer to me, gradually increasing in quickness and volume with an irresistibly definite progression. When it was quite near the sound began to move in my nerves and blood, and to urge me to dance with them.

I knew that if I yielded I would be carried away to some moment of terrible agony, so I struggled to remain quiet, holding my knees together with my hands.

The music increased continually, sounding like the strings of harps, tuned to a forgotten scale, and having a resonance as searching as the strings of the 'cello.

Then the luring excitement became more powerful than my will, and my limbs moved in spite of me.

In a moment I was swept away in a whirlwind of notes. My breath and my thoughts and every impulse of my body, became a form of the dance, till I could not distinguish between the instruments and the rhythm and my own person or consciousness.

For a while it seemed an excitement that was filled with joy, then it grew into an ecstasy where all existence was lost in a vortex of movement. I could not think there had ever been a life beyond the whirling of the dance.

Then with a shock the ecstasy turned to an agony and rage. I struggled to free myself, but seemed only to increase the passion of the steps I moved to. When I shrieked I could only echo the notes of the rhythm.

At last with a moment of uncontrollable frenzy I broke back to consciousness and awoke.

I dragged myself trembling to the window of the cottage and looked out. The moon was glittering across the bay, and there was no sound anywhere on the island.

I am leaving in two days, and old Pat Dirane has bidden me good-bye. He met me in the village this morning and took me into 'his little tint,' a miserable hovel where he spends the night.

I sat for a long time on his threshold, while he leaned on a stool behind me, near his bed, and told me the last story I shall have from him—a rude anecdote not worth recording. Then he told me with careful emphasis how he had wandered when he was a young man, and lived in a fine college, teaching Irish to the young priests!

They say on the island that he can tell as many lies as four men: perhaps the stories he has learned have strengthened his imagination.

When I stood up in the doorway to give him God's blessing, he leaned over on the straw that forms his bed, and shed tears. Then he turned to me again, lifting up one trembling hand, with the mitten worn to a hole on the palm, from the rubbing of his crutch.

'I'll not see you again,' he said, with tears trickling on his face, 'and you're a kindly man. When you come back next year I won't be in it. I won't live beyond the winter. But listen now to what I'm telling you; let you put insurance on me in the city of Dublin, and it's five hundred pounds you'll get on my burial.'

This evening, my last in the island, is also the evening of the 'Pattern'—a festival something like 'Pardons' of Brittany.

I waited especially to see it, but a piper who was expected did not come, and there was no amusement. A few friends and relations came over from the other island and stood about the public-house in their best clothes, but without music dancing was impossible.

I believe on some occasions when the piper is present there is a fine day of dancing and excitement, but the Galway piper is getting old, and is not easily induced to undertake the voyage.

Last night, St. John's Eve, the fires were lighted and boys ran about with pieces of the burning turf, though I could not find out if the idea of lighting the house fires from the bonfires is still found on the island.

I have come out of an hotel full of tourists and commercial travellers, to stroll along the edge of Galway bay, and look out in the direction of the islands. The sort of yearning I feel towards those lonely rocks is indescribably acute. This town, that is usually so full of wild human interest, seems in my present mood a tawdry medley of all that is crudest in modern life. The nullity of the rich and the squalor of the poor give me the same pang of wondering disgust; yet the islands are fading already and I can hardly realise that the smell of the seaweed and the drone of the Atlantic are still moving round them.

One of my island friends has written to me:—

DEAR JOHN SYNGE,—I am for a long time expecting a letter from you and I think you are forgetting this island altogether.

Mr.——died a long time ago on the big island and his boat was on anchor in the harbour and the wind blew her to Black Head and broke her up after his death.

Tell me are you learning Irish since you went. We have a branch of the Gaelic League here now and the people is going on well with the Irish and reading.

I will write the next letter in Irish to you. Tell me will you come to see us next year and if you will you'll write a letter before you. All your loving friends is well in health.—*Mise do chara go buan*.[1]

Another boy I sent some baits to has written to me also, beginning his letter in Irish and ending it in English:

DEAR JOHN,—I got your letter four days ago, and there was pride and joy on me because it was written in Irish, and a fine, good, pleasant letter it was. The baits you sent are very good, but I lost two of them and half my line. A big fish came and caught the bait, and the line was bad and half of the line and the baits went away. My sister has come back from America, but I'm thinking it won't be long till she goes away again, for it is lonesome and poor she finds the island now.—I am your friend. . . .

Write soon and let you write in Irish, if you don't I won't look on it.

# In the Shadow of the Glen[2]

SCENE. *The last cottage at the head of a long glen in County Wicklow.*

(*Cottage kitchen; turf fire on the right; a bed near it against the wall with a body lying on it covered with a sheet. A door is at the other end of the room, with a low table near it, and stools, or wooden chairs. There are a couple of glasses on the table, and a bottle of whisky, as if for a wake, with two cups, a teapot, and a home-made cake. There is another small door near the bed.* NORA BURKE *is moving about the room, settling a few things, and lighting candles on the table, looking now and then at the bed with an uneasy look. Some one knocks softly at the door. She takes up a stocking with money from the table and puts it in her pocket. Then she opens the door.*)

*Tramp* [*outside*]. Good evening to you, lady of the house.

*Nora.* Good evening kindly, stranger, it's a wild night, God help you, to be out in the rain falling.

*Tramp.* It is, surely, and I walking to Brittas from the Aughrim fair.

*Nora.* Is it walking on your feet, stranger?

---
[1] I am your friend forever.
[2] First performed at the Molesworth Hall, Dublin, October 8, 1903.

## IN THE SHADOW OF THE GLEN

*Tramp.* On my two feet, lady of the house, and when I saw the light below I thought maybe if you'd a sup of new milk and a quiet decent corner where a man could sleep. [*He looks in past her and sees the dead man.*] The Lord have mercy on us all!

*Nora.* It doesn't matter anyway, stranger, come in out of the rain.

*Tramp* [*coming in slowly and going towards the bed*]. Is it departed he is?

*Nora.* It is, stranger. He's after dying on me, God forgive him, and there I am now with a hundred sheep beyond on the hills, and no turf drawn for the winter.

*Tramp* [*looking closely at the dead man*]. It's a queer look is on him for a man that's dead.

*Nora* [*half-humorously*]. He was always queer, stranger, and I suppose them that's queer and they living men will be queer bodies after.

*Tramp.* Isn't it a great wonder you're letting him lie there, and he not tidied, or laid out itself?

*Nora* [*coming to the bed*]. I was afeard, stranger, for he put a black curse on me this morning if I'd touch his body the time he'd die sudden, or let any one touch it except his sister only, and it's ten miles away she lives in the big glen over the hill.

*Tramp* [*looking at her and nodding slowly*]. It's a queer story he wouldn't let his own wife touch him, and he dying quiet in his bed.

*Nora.* He was an old man, and an odd man, stranger, and it's always up on the hills he was, thinking thoughts in the dark mist. [*She pulls back a bit of the sheet.*] Lay your hand on him now, and tell me if it's cold he is surely.

*Tramp.* Is it getting the curse on me you'd be, woman of the house? I wouldn't lay my hand on him for the Lough Nahanagan and it filled with gold.

*Nora* [*looking uneasily at the body*]. Maybe cold would be no sign of death with the like of him, for he was always cold, every day since I knew him,—and every night, stranger,—[*she covers up his face and comes away from the bed*]; but I'm thinking it's dead he is surely, for he's complaining a while back of a pain in his heart, and this morning, the time he was going off to Brittas for three days or four, he was taken with a sharp turn. Then he went into his bed and he was saying it was destroyed he was, the time the shadow was going up through the glen, and when the sun set on the bog beyond he made a great lep, and let a great cry out of him, and stiffened himself out the like of a dead sheep.

*Tramp* [*crosses himself*]. God rest his soul.

*Nora* [*pouring him out a glass of whisky*]. Maybe that would do you better than the milk of the sweetest cow in County Wicklow.

*Tramp.* The Almighty God reward you, and may it be to your good health.

(*He drinks.*)

*Nora* [*giving him a pipe and tobacco*]. I've no pipes saving his own, stranger, but they're sweet pipes to smoke.

*Tramp.* Thank you kindly, lady of the house.

*Nora.* Sit down now, stranger, and be taking your rest.

*Tramp* [*filling a pipe and looking about the room*]. I've walked a great way through the world, lady of the house, and seen great wonders, but I never seen a wake till this day with fine spirits, and good tobacco, and the best of pipes, and no one to taste them but a woman only.

*Nora.* Didn't you hear me say it was only after dying on me he was when the sun went down, and how would I go out into the glen and tell the neighbours, and I a lone woman with no house near me?

*Tramp* [*drinking*]. There's no offence, lady of the house?

*Nora.* No offence in life, stranger. How would the like of you, passing in the dark night, know the lonesome way I was with no house near me at all?

*Tramp* [*sitting down*]. I knew rightly. [*He lights his pipe so that there is a sharp light beneath his haggard face.*] And I was thinking, and I coming in through the door, that it's many a lone woman would be afeard of the like of me in the dark night, in a place wouldn't be as lonesome as this place, where there aren't two living souls would see the little light you have shining from the glass.

*Nora* [*slowly*]. I'm thinking many would be afeard, but I never knew what way I'd be afeard of beggar or bishop or any man of you at all. [*She looks towards the window and lowers her voice.*] It's other things than the like of you, stranger, would make a person afeard.

*Tramp* [*looking round with a half-shudder*]. It is surely, God help us all!

*Nora* [*looking at him for a moment with curiosity*]. You're saying that, stranger, as if you were easy afeard.

*Tramp* [*speaking mournfully*]. Is it myself, lady of the house, that does be walking round in the long nights, and crossing the hills when the fog is on them, the time a little stick would seem as big as your arm, and a rabbit as big as a bay horse, and a stack of turf as big as a towering church in the city of Dublin? If myself was easy afeard, I'm telling you, it's long ago I'd have been locked into the Richmond Asylum, or maybe have run up into the back hills with nothing on me but an old shirt, and been eaten by the crows the like of Patch Darcy—the Lord have mercy on him—in the year that's gone.

*Nora* [*with interest*]. You knew Darcy?

*Tramp.* Wasn't I the last one heard his living voice in the whole world?

*Nora.* There were great stories of what was heard at that time, but would any one believe the things they do be saying in the glen?

*Tramp.* It was no lie, lady of the house. . . . I was passing below on a dark night the like of this night, and the sheep were lying under the ditch and every one of them coughing, and choking, like an old man, with the great rain and the fog. Then I heard a thing talking—queer talk, you wouldn't believe at all, and you out of your dreams,—and 'Merciful God,' says I, 'if I begin hearing the like of that voice out of the thick mist, I'm destroyed surely.' Then I run, and I run, and I run, till I was below in Rathvanna. I got drunk that night, I got drunk in the morning, and drunk the day after,—I was coming from the races beyond—and the third day they found Darcy. . . . Then I knew it was himself I was after hearing, and I wasn't afeard any more.

*Nora* [*speaking sorrowfully and slowly*]. God spare Darcy, he'd always look in here and he passing up or passing down, and it's very lonesome I was after him a long while [*she looks over at the bed and lowers her voice, speaking very clearly*], and then I got happy again—if it's ever happy we are, stranger,—for I got used to being lonesome.

(*A short pause; then she stands up.*)

*Nora.* Was there any one on the last bit of the road, stranger, and you coming from Aughrim?

*Tramp.* There was a young man with a drift of mountain ewes, and he running after them this way and that.

*Nora* [*with a half-smile*]. Far down, stranger?

*Tramp.* A piece only.

(*She fills the kettle and puts it on the fire.*)

*Nora.* Maybe, if you're not easy afeard, you'd stay here a short while alone with himself.

*Tramp.* I would surely. A man that's dead can do no hurt.

*Nora* [*speaking with a sort of constraint*]. I'm going a little back to the west, stranger, for himself would go there one night and another and whistle at that place, and then the young man you're after seeing—a kind of a farmer has come up from the sea to live in a cottage beyond—would walk round to see if there was a thing we'd have to be done, and I'm wanting him this night, the way he can go down into the glen when the sun goes up and tell the people that himself is dead.

*Tramp* [*looking at the body in the sheet*]. It's myself will go for him, lady of the house, and let you not be destroying yourself with the great rain.

*Nora.* You wouldn't find your way, stranger, for there's a small path only, and it running up between two sluigs where an ass and cart would be drowned. [*She puts a shawl over her head.*] Let you be making yourself easy, and saying a prayer for his soul, and it's not long I'll be coming again.

*Tramp* [*moving uneasily*]. Maybe if you'd a piece of a grey thread and a sharp needle—there's great safety in a needle, lady of the house—I'd be putting a little stitch here and there in my old coat, the time I'll be praying for his soul, and it going up naked to the saints of God.

*Nora* [*takes a needle and thread from the front of her dress and gives it to him*]. There's the needle, stranger, and I'm thinking you won't be lonesome, and you used to the back hills, for isn't a dead man itself more company than to be sitting alone, and hearing the winds crying, and you not knowing on what thing your mind would stay?

*Tramp* [*slowly*]. It's true, surely, and the Lord have mercy on us all!

(NORA *goes out. The* TRAMP *begins stitching one of the tags in his coat, saying the De Profundis under his breath. In an instant the sheet is drawn slowly down, and* DAN BURKE *looks out. The* TRAMP *moves uneasily, then looks up, and springs to his feet with a movement of terror.*)

*Dan* [*with a hoarse voice*]. Don't be afeard, stranger; a man that's dead can do no hurt.

*Tramp* [*trembling*]. I meant no harm, your honour; and won't you leave me easy to be saying a little prayer for your soul?

(*A long whistle is heard outside.*)

*Dan* [*sitting up in his bed and speaking fiercely*]. Ah, the devil mend her. . . . Do you hear that, stranger? Did ever you hear another woman could whistle the like of that with two fingers in her mouth? [*He looks at the table hurriedly.*] I'm destroyed with the drouth, and let you bring me a drop quickly before herself will come back.

*Tramp* [*doubtfully*]. Is it not dead you are?

*Dan.* How would I be dead, and I as dry as a baked bone, stranger?

*Tramp* [*pouring out the whisky*]. What will herself say if she smells the stuff on you, for I'm thinking it's not for nothing you're letting on to be dead?

*Dan.* It is not, stranger, but she won't be coming near me at all, and it's not long now I'll be letting on, for I've a cramp in my back, and my hip's asleep on me, and there's been the devil's own fly itching my nose. It's near dead I was wanting to sneeze, and you blathering about the rain, and Darcy [*bitterly*]—the devil choke him—and the towering church. [*Crying out impatiently.*] Give me that whisky. Would you have herself come back before I taste a drop at all?

(TRAMP *gives him the glass.*)

*Dan* [*after drinking*]. Go over now to that cupboard, and bring me a black stick you'll see in the west corner by the wall.

*Tramp* [*taking a stick from the cupboard*]. Is it that?

*Dan.* It is, stranger; it's a long time I'm keeping that stick for I've a bad wife in the house.

*Tramp* [*with a queer look*]. Is it herself, master of the house, and she a grand woman to talk?

*Dan.* It's herself, surely, it's a bad wife she is—a bad wife for an old man, and I'm getting old, God help me, though I've an arm to me still. [*He takes the stick in his hand.*] Let you wait now a short while, and it's a great sight you'll see in this room in two hours or three. [*He stops to listen.*] Is that somebody above?

*Tramp* [*listening*]. There's a voice speaking on the path.

*Dan.* Put that stick here in the bed and smooth the sheet the way it was lying. [*He covers himself up hastily.*] Be falling to sleep now and don't let on you know anything, or I'll be having your life. I wouldn't have told you at all but it's destroyed with the drouth I was.

*Tramp* [*covering his head*]. Have no fear, master of the house. What is it I know of the like of you that I'd be saying a word or putting out my hand to stay you at all?

(*He goes back to the fire, sits down on a stool with his back to the bed and goes on stitching his coat.*)

*Dan* [*under the sheet, querulously*]. Stranger.

*Tramp* [*quickly*]. Whisht, whisht. Be quiet, I'm telling you, they're coming now at the door.

(NORA *comes in with* MICHAEL DARA, *a tall, innocent young man, behind her.*)

*Nora.* I wasn't long at all, stranger, for I met himself on the path.

*Tramp.* You were middling long, lady of the house.

*Nora.* There was no sign from himself?

*Tramp.* No sign at all, lady of the house.

*Nora* [*to* MICHAEL]. Go over now and pull down the sheet, and look on himself, Michael Dara, and you'll see it's the truth I'm telling you.

*Michael.* I will not, Nora, I do be afeard of the dead.

(*He sits down on a stool next the table facing the* TRAMP. NORA *puts the kettle on a lower hook of the pothooks, and piles turf under it.*)

*Nora* [*turning to* TRAMP]. Will you drink a sup of tea with myself and the young man, stranger, or [*speaking more persuasively*] will you go into the little room and stretch yourself a short while on the bed. I'm thinking it's destroyed you are walking the length of that way in the great rain.

*Tramp.* Is it go away and leave you, and you having a wake, lady of the house? I will not surely. [*He takes a drink from his glass which he has beside him.*] And it's none of your tea I'm asking either.

(*He goes on stitching.* NORA *makes the tea.*)

*Michael* [*after looking at the* TRAMP *rather scornfully for a moment*]. That's a poor coat you have, God help you, and I'm thinking it's a poor tailor you are with it.

*Tramp.* If it's a poor tailor I am, I'm thinking it's a poor herd does be running back and forward after a little handful of ewes the way I seen yourself running this day, young fellow, and you coming from the fair.

(NORA *comes back to the table.*)

*Nora* [*to* MICHAEL *in a low voice*]. Let you not mind him at all, Michael Dara, he has a drop taken and it's soon he'll be falling asleep.

*Michael.* It's no lie he's telling; I was destroyed surely. They were that wilful they were running off into one man's bit of oats, and another man's bit of hay, and tumbling into the red bogs till it's more like a pack of old goats than sheep they were. Mountain ewes is a queer breed, Nora Burke, and I'm not used to them at all.

*Nora* [*settling the tea things*]. There's no one can drive a mountain ewe but the men do be reared in the Glen Malure, I've heard them say, and above by Rathvanna, and the Glen Imaal, men the like of Patch Darcy, God spare his soul, who would walk through five hundred sheep and miss one of them, and he not reckoning them at all.

*Michael* [*uneasily*]. Is it the man went queer in his head the year that's gone?

*Nora.* It is surely.

*Tramp* [*plaintively*]. That was a great man, young fellow, a great man I'm telling you. There was never a lamb from his own ewes he wouldn't know before it was marked, and he'd run from this to the city of Dublin and never catch for his breath.

*Nora* [*turning round quickly*]. He was a great man surely, stranger, and isn't it a grand thing when you hear a livin' man sayin' a good word of a dead man, and he mad dying?

*Tramp.* It's the truth I'm saying, God spare his soul.

(*He puts the needle under the collar of his coat, and settles himself to sleep in the chimney-corner.* NORA *sits down at the table; their backs are turned to the bed.*)

*Michael* [*looking at her with a queer look*]. I heard tell this day, Nora Burke, that it was on the path below Patch Darcy would be passing up and passing down, and I heard them say he'd never pass it night or morning without speaking with yourself.

*Nora* [*in a low voice*]. It was no lie you heard, Michael Dara.

*Michael.* I'm thinking it's a power of men you're after knowing if it's in a lonesome place you live itself.

*Nora* [*giving him his tea*]. It's in a lonesome place you do have to be talking with some one, and looking for some one, in the evening of the day, and if it's a power of men I'm after knowing they were fine men, for I was a hard child to please, and a hard girl to please [*she looks at him a little sternly*], and it's a hard woman I am to please this day, Michael Dara, and it's no lie I'm telling you.

*Michael* [*looking over to see that the* TRAMP *is asleep, and then pointing to the dead man*]. Was it a hard woman to please you were when you took himself for your man?

*Nora.* What way would I live and I an old woman if I didn't marry a man with a bit of a farm, and cows on it, and sheep on the back hills?

*Michael* [*considering*]. That's true, Nora, and maybe it's no fool you were, for there's good grazing on it, if it is a lonesome place, and I'm thinking it's a good sum he's left behind.

*Nora* [*taking the stocking with money from her pocket, and putting it on the table*]. I do be thinking in the long nights it was a big fool I was that time, Michael Dara, for what good is a bit of a farm with cows on it, and sheep on the back hills, when you do be sitting looking out from a door the like of that door, and seeing nothing but the mists rolling down the bog, and the mists again, and they rolling up the bog, and hearing nothing but the wind crying out in the bits of broken trees were left from the great storm, and the streams roaring with the rain.

*Michael* [*looking at her uneasily*]. What is it ails you, this night, Nora Burke? I've heard tell it's the like of that talk you do hear from men and they after being a great while on the back hills.

*Nora* [*putting out the money on the table*]. It's a bad night, and a wild night, Michael Dara, and isn't it a great while I am at the foot of the back hills, sitting up here boiling food for himself, and food for the brood sow, and baking a cake when the night falls? [*She puts up the money, listlessly, in little piles on the table.*] Isn't it a long while I am sitting here in the winter and the summer, and the fine spring, with the young growing behind me and the old passing, saying to myself one time, to look on Mary Brien who wasn't that height [*holding out her hand*], and I a fine girl growing up, and there she is now with two children, and another coming on her in three months or four.

(*She pauses.*)

*Michael* [*moving over three of the piles*]. That's three pounds we have now, Nora Burke.

*Nora* [*continuing in the same voice*]. And saying to myself another time, to look on Peggy Cavanagh, who had the lightest hand at milking a cow that wouldn't be easy, or turning a cake, and there she is now walking round on the roads, or sitting in a dirty old house, with no teeth in her mouth, and no sense and no more hair than you'd see on a bit of a hill and they after burning the furze from it.

*Michael.* That's five pounds and ten notes, a good sum, surely! . . . It's not that way you'll be talking when you marry a young man, Nora Burke, and they were saying in the fair my lambs were the best lambs, and I got a grand price, for I'm no fool now at making a bargain when my lambs are good.

*Nora.* What was it you got?

*Michael.* Twenty pound for the lot, Nora Burke. . . . We'd do right to wait now till himself will be quiet awhile in the Seven Churches, and then you'll marry me in the chapel of Rathvanna, and I'll bring the sheep up on the bit of a hill you have on the back mountain, and we won't have anything we'd be afeard to let our minds on when the mist is down.

*Nora* [*pouring him out some whisky*]. Why would I marry you, Mike Dara? You'll be getting old and I'll be getting old, and in a little while I'm telling you, you'll be sitting up in your bed—the way himself was sitting—with a shake in your face, and your teeth falling, and the white hair sticking out round you like an old bush where sheep do be leaping a gap.

(DAN BURKE *sits up noiselessly from under the sheet, with his hand to his face. His white hair is sticking out round his head.*)

*Nora* [*goes on slowly without hearing him*]. It's a pitiful thing to be getting old, but it's a queer thing surely. It's a queer thing to see an old man sitting up there in his bed with no teeth in him, and a rough word in his mouth, and his chin the way it would take the bark from the edge of an oak board you'd have building a door. . . . God forgive me, Michael Dara, we'll all be getting old, but it's a queer thing surely.

*Michael.* It's too lonesome you are from living a long time with an old man, Nora, and you're talking again like a herd that would be coming down from the thick mist [*he puts his arm round her*], but it's a fine life you'll have now with a young man, a fine life surely. . . .

(DAN *sneezes violently.* MICHAEL *tries to get to the door, but before he can do so,* DAN *jumps out of bed in queer white clothes, with his stick in his hand, and goes over and puts his back against it.*)

*Michael.* Son of God deliver us.

(*Crosses himself, and goes backward across the room.*)

*Dan* [*holding up his hand at him*]. Now you'll not marry her the time I'm rotting below in the Seven Churches, and you'll see the thing I'll give you will follow you on the back mountains when the wind is high.

*Michael* [*to* NORA]. Get me out of it, Nora, for the love of God. He always did what you bid him, and I'm thinking he would do it now.

*Nora* [*looking at the* TRAMP]. Is it dead he is or living?

*Dan* [*turning towards her.*] It's little you care if it's dead or living I am, but there'll be an end now of your fine times, and all the talk you have of young men and old men, and of the mist coming up or going down. [*He opens the door.*] You'll walk out now from that door, Nora Burke, and it's not to-morrow, or the next day, or any day of your life, that you'll put in your foot through it again.

*Tramp* [*standing up.*] It's a hard thing you're saying for an old man, master of the house, and what would the like of her do if you put her out on the roads?

*Dan.* Let her walk round the like of Peggy Cavanagh below, and be begging money at the cross-road, or selling songs to the men.

[*To* NORA.] Walk out now, Nora Burke, and it's soon you'll be getting old with that life, I'm telling you; it's soon your teeth'll be falling and your head'll be the like of a bush where sheep do be leaping a gap.

(*He pauses: she looks round at* MICHAEL.)

*Michael* [*timidly*]. There's a fine Union below in Rathdrum.

*Dan.* The like of her would never go there.... It's lonesome roads she'll be going and hiding herself away till the end will come, and they find her stretched like a dead sheep with the frost on her, or the big spiders, maybe, and they putting their webs on her, in the butt of a ditch.

*Nora* [*angrily*]. What way will yourself be that day, Daniel Burke? What way will you be that day and you lying down a long while in your grave? For it's bad you are living, and it's bad you'll be when you're dead. [*She looks at him a moment fiercely, then half turns away and speaks plaintively again.*] Yet, if it is itself, Daniel Burke, who can help it at all, and let you be getting up into your bed, and not be taking your death with the wind blowing on you, and the rain with it, and you half in your skin.

*Dan.* It's proud and happy you'd be if I was getting my death the day I was shut of yourself. [*Pointing to the door.*] Let you walk out through that door, I'm telling you, and let you not be passing this way if it's hungry you are, or wanting a bed.

*Tramp* [*pointing to* MICHAEL]. Maybe himself would take her.

*Nora.* What would he do with me now?

*Tramp.* Give you the half of a dry bed, and good food in your mouth.

*Dan.* Is it a fool you think him, stranger, or is it a fool you were born yourself? Let her walk out of that door, and let you go along with her, stranger—if it's raining itself—for it's too much talk you have surely.

*Tramp* [*going over to* NORA]. We'll be going now, lady of the house—the rain is falling, but the air is kind and maybe it'll be a grand morning by the grace of God.

IN THE SHADOW OF THE GLEN 155

*Nora.* What good is a grand morning when I'm destroyed surely, and I going out to get my death walking the roads?

*Tramp.* You'll not be getting your death with myself, lady of the house, and I knowing all the ways a man can put food in his mouth. . . . We'll be going now, I'm telling you, and the time you'll be feeling the cold, and the frost, and the great rain, and the sun again, and the south wind blowing in the glens, you'll not be sitting up on a wet ditch, the way you're after sitting in this place, making yourself old with looking on each day, and it passing you by. You'll be saying one time, 'It's a grand evening, by the grace of God,' and another time, 'It's a wild night, God help us, but it'll pass surely.' You'll be saying—

*Dan* [*goes over to them crying out impatiently*]. Go out of that door, I'm telling you, and do your blathering below in the glen.

(NORA *gathers a few things into her shawl.*)

*Tramp* [*at the door*]. Come along with me now, lady of the house, and it's not my blather you'll be hearing only, but you'll be hearing the herons crying out over the black lakes, and you'll be hearing the grouse and the owls with them, and the larks and the big thrushes when the days are warm, and it's not from the like of them you'll be hearing a talk of getting old like Peggy Cavanagh, and losing the hair off you, and the light of your eyes, but it's fine songs you'll be hearing when the sun goes up, and there'll be no old fellow wheezing, the like of a sick sheep, close to your ear.

*Nora.* I'm thinking it's myself will be wheezing that time with lying down under the Heavens when the night is cold; but you've a fine bit of talk, stranger, and it's with yourself I'll go. [*She goes towards the door, then turns to* DAN.] You think it's a grand thing you're after doing with your letting on to be dead, but what is it at all? What way would a woman live in a lonesome place the like of this place, and she not making a talk with the men passing? And what way will yourself live from this day, with none to care for you? What is it you'll have now but a black life, Daniel Burke, and it's not long I'm telling you, till you'll be lying again under that sheet, and you dead surely.

(*She goes out with the* TRAMP. MICHAEL *is slinking after them, but* DAN *stops him.*)

*Dan.* Sit down now and take a little taste of the stuff, Michael Dara. There is a great drouth on me, and the night is young.

*Michael* [*coming back to the table*]. And it's very dry I am, surely, with the fear of death you put on me, and I after driving mountain ewes since the turn of the day.

*Dan* [*throwing away his stick*]. I was thinking to strike you, Michael Dara, but you're a quiet man, God help you, and I don't mind you at all.

(*He pours out two glasses of whiskey, and gives one to* MICHAEL.)

*Dan.* Your good health, Michael Dara.

*Michael.* God reward you, Daniel Burke, and may you have a long life, and a quiet life, and good health with it.

(*They drink.*)

CURTAIN

SHAN F. BULLOCK

# The Emigrant[1]

She leant out of the carriage window and saw the van-door close; then called to the porter if her box were safe and sound.

'Aw, ay,' said he, and slouched up, wiping the wet from his hand on his corduroys; 'aw, ay; it'll follow ye safe to Clogheen, anyhow. Good-bye, an' God speed ye!'

'Good-bye,' she said, and gave him her hand. 'But aren't the rest o' ye comin'?' she called.

The station-master came and gave her a parting word; then two or three town loiterers; then the station-master's wife, with a shawl over her head, and picking her way through the puddles; last of all came a man—the girl's father, one could see—running stiffly, and glancing back often at the horse and cart standing forlorn outside the gate.

'Good-bye, Mary,' he said, 'an' God be with ye, me girl.' He held her hand for a second or two and his lips kept moving whilst she answered bravely. 'Ye'ill write from New York?'

'I will—aw, at once.'

'Do—don't keep us waitin',' he said; then stood back with the others, and blinked at the driving rain. She pulled a handkerchief from a battered brown hand-bag, and nervously wiped her lips.

'Ah,' called she, 'ye all thought yes'd see me cryin'. Ah, I tricked ye rightly.'

'Ah, no,' answered the porter; 'we knew ye'd be brave.'

'Ay, ay,' assented the rest, and shifted their legs; 'ay, ay.'

'Away ye go,' shouted the guard; the engine shrieked; Mary shook out her handkerchief and called good-bye; her friends waved an arm; she had started for the States.

'They thought I'd cry,' said she, as she sat back and fell to plucking at the fingers of her woollen gloves. 'They thought I'd cry—och, no!'

She was brave; yet her lips were quivering, and her eyes were turned mournfully on the fields and hedges and the cottages here and there shining white through the grey drift of the rain.

'We'll soon be at it,' she said presently. 'Ah, Lord, the day it is! An' the state I'm in; och, och.' She stooped and wrung the water

[1] From *Ring o' Rushes*, New York, 1896.

from her bedraggled skirt. 'An' me hair that tattered; aw, it's shockin'! But I didn't cry,' she said, and flashed her black eyes at me. 'Och, no. Whisht! we're gettin' near it. Aw, there it is; there they are! Good-bye, *muther!* Good-bye, *Patsey,* an' *Johnny,* an' *Lizzie!* Good-bye *all!*'

I stood up, and over her hat caught a glimpse of the group gathered on the street before the cottage: the mother in her nightcap, the children bare-legged, all waving their arms and caps, and crying their farewells.

'Good-bye,' cried Mary back through the rain; 'och, good-bye!'

That was the last of them she would see, she said, as she sat down again, the last, till the Lord knew when. She was for the States? asked some one. Ah, she was; she could get work there; she could do nothing at home. Sure, it was better to go than to be a burden on them all. Ah, yes; she had been out before an' had come home to settle, but—but, and her handkerchief went fast to her lips —well, things had turned out troublesome. She'd do better out there; there were too many at home, and her mother was poorly. Ah, an', sure, times were shockin' bad.

'Ay, ay,' the men went in chorus; 'they are, they are'; then looked mournfully at her red cheeks, and from one to another passed the word that she was a brave girl, so she was; a brave girl; and God speed her, said they, as one by one they went out clumsily at Glann station, and left Mary and me together.

It was fair-day at Glann; therefore did the train settle itself by the platform for a long rest.

'The guard mebbe's gone to see the fair,' said Mary; and I laughed, stamped vigorously (for it was cold) across the carriage floor, wiped the window, and looked out.

Down the further bank of the railway, along a narrow path which had started beyond the fields somewhere near the town, was coming a little procession of six men, bearing a coffin on a rough hurdle made of ash poles. The men were bare-headed; a single bunch of wild-flowers lay atop the streaming coffin; there were no mourners, nor anywhere could one see any sign of sorrow or curiosity. They came on down, the men with their pitiful burden, crossed a track, came to a siding, slid the coffin into a fish-van, shut the door, pulled their soft felt hats from their pockets, mopped their faces, then took shelter behind the van and lit their pipes.

# THE EMIGRANT

There wanted only a bottle to make the scene complete, and I was confidently watching for it, when right at my elbow arose a great sobbing.

'Aw, aw,' cried Mary; 'did ye see? Did ye see? Och! What a way to be trated! An' such a day for a buryin'! All out in the wet—the wet an' the cowld. Aw, poor crature! Aw, muther, muther, ye'll die, ye'ill die! I'll niver see ye again, nor father, nor no one. Aw, it's cruel to lave ye. I'll go back; I'll go back!'

Her sobs were pitiful. Loiterers began to gather round the door. It was only a poor girl going to America, I explained; they would pity her, I was sure. Ah, they would, said they, and went, all but one: a big, sunburnt fellow dressed in rough tweed, who came forward and asked my leave. For what? Ah, he knew the girl; came in, went over and laid a rough hand on Mary's shoulder.

'Ah, don't,' she said. 'I'll go home, I'll go home.'

'What ails ye, Mary, at all?' said he, and shook her again. She turned.

'Ah, God A'mighty, James!' she cried; and her tears went. 'It's you. Where are ye goin'? What brings ye? Who towld ye?'

James sat down heavily, and began beating his boot with his stick. Ah, he'd been to the fair, had sold early, was waiting for a train to take him home.

'Where are ye goin'?' he said over his shoulder. 'What wur ye bleartin' about?'

Mary hung her head and did not answer.

'Where are ye goin'?' he said again.

She looked up at him quickly, almost defiantly.

'To the States.'

He nodded; began again the tattoo on his boot, and before another word came the train had started.

'We're goin',' said Mary. 'Hurry an' say good-bye, or they'll shut ye in.'

'No matter,' he answered; 'I'll stay where I am.'

The maid sat apart from the man, and answered his abrupt, mannerless questions as bravely as she might.

Why was she going? Ah, he knew; there was no need to ask.

Why had she not told him? Better not; what was the use? All was over between them.

The man eyed her wonderingly. Over? he repeated. Over? Did

she not know he was ready to make it up, and—to do his best? Ay, yes, she knew; still—

Still, what? It was better to go, she said, and looked tearfully out at the flying fields.

Yes, it was better to go; I agreed with Mary. He was a lout, for certain; a good-for-nothing, by all chance. She would lose nothing by leaving him. There, there, sitting beside her, was the trouble about which she had spoken. She had come home to settle down with him; but things had been troublesome. Ah, yes. One knew it all. He had been easy-going and lazy; wanted things to turn up, felt no inclination to hurry into married cares. Aw, sure, he could wait awhile; and if he, then Mary. Something like that it had been; anyhow, Mary had not settled. They had quarrelled, and now she was leaving him for better or worse. She was wise. Had the man no bowels? Had he nothing for her but hard questions and pitying looks? Would he not, before he went, say one kind word to this girl who had trusted in his word and manhood, and finding them wanting was now leaving him for ever? Did there not some golden memory linger about his heart? Not one. He was wooden to the core. He would sit on there, tapping his boot and staring at his big freckled hands, neither hurt nor sorry, but just wondering that a girl could be such a fool; the train would stop, and with a nod and a flabby shake of the hand, he would take himself out into the rain. And good riddance!

The train slowed; Mary's lips began to quiver. The train stopped; I gathered in my legs, so that the fellow might pass without touching me. He raised his head and looked out at the sky.

'Ah, I may as well g'wan to the junction,' he drawled; 'it'll be all the same; one could do nothin' such a day, anyhow.'

'Yis,' said Mary, and not cheerlessly. 'Sure, ye may as well.'

We sat silent all the way to Clogheen, and there we parted: Mary, so it was set down, to catch a train north, James one back home, and I to do my work in the town.

Two hours afterwards I met the two in the rain-swept streets, and in my surprise stopped short before them. Mary looked up and laughed.

'Ah,' said she, 'I'm here yit; that train went without me.'

'Oh,' said I; 'that's very bad; why, the next won't be here for hours. And you're drenched? But—but—' and I looked at James as he stood, slightly flushed and dripping wet, blankly staring across the street.

'Ah, yis,' Mary answered. 'James missed his, too; I'm not goin' at all; sure, we've made it up.'

I put my watch slowly back into my pocket and nodded. 'James has promised me,' she went on, and her eyes fell; 'an' we're goin' to get marr'ed come harvest-time; an' he'll try hard for a place at the big house above. An'—an'—God knows, Sir, I'm not sorry, for me heart was sore at lavin' home.'

They knew their own business best; but there fell an awkward silence, so I asked James concerning his prospects. Did he see his way clearly?

Ah, he did; and began tapping his boots. Sure, there was always a way if one could only wait till it came. 'Isn't she better here, anyway, whatever comes,' said he, and gave me a moment's glimpse at his face, 'than out yonder wid the strangers? Sure, 'twas madness av her to think o' it; sure, Providence sent me to Glann fair.'

Providence? And had Providence sent also that dismal procession to the fish-van, that Mary might see it and sob for her friends, and her James, and the home of her heart?

'And you, Mary?' I asked. 'Are *you* quite satisfied?'

'Ah, yis,' said she mournfully. 'Ah, I hope so.'

I took her into a shop and bought her a little wedding gift—a silver brooch, shaped like a harp and set with green marble, then wished them more happiness than I ever hoped they would have, and went my way.

Three hours afterwards saw me at Clogheen station again, and there was Mary, standing dejected by her little yellow box.

'Not gone home yet, Mary?' I asked.

Her handkerchief fluttered out.

'No-o, Sir. I—was lookin' for ye. I—I wanted to give ye back this'; and she held out the brooch. 'I'll niver wear it. Och, it's all over. I—I'm goin' on to catch the ship.'

It was well. I determined that this time neither Providence nor emotion should hinder her going.

'Ah, no,' she sobbed; ''twas only foolishness. Me heart was sore at lavin' them all; an' the sight o' that coffin an' James comin' like that— Och, I cudn't bear it! But 'twas foolish av me; it's better for me to go.'

I took the brooch, pinned it on her jacket, and spoke a foolish word or two by way of comfort. She would, I hoped, wear it for my sake, if not for . . .

'Aw, Sir,' she burst out, 'if he'd only been *steady!* for I liked him well. Och, och!'

She turned and looked down the platform; there sat James, drunk and asleep.

GEORGE MOORE

# A Letter to Rome[1]

ONE MORNING the priest's housekeeper mentioned, as she gathered up the breakfast things, that Mike Mulhare had refused to let his daughter Catherine marry James Murdoch until he had earned the price of a pig.

'This is bad news,' said the priest, and he laid down the newspaper.

'And he waiting for her all the summer! Wasn't it in February last that he came out of the poorhouse? And the fine cabin he has built for her! He'll be so lonesome in it that he'll be going——'

'To America!' said the priest.

'Maybe it will be going back to the poorhouse he'll be, for he'll never earn the price of his passage at the relief works.'

The priest looked at her for a moment as if he did not catch her meaning. A knock came at the door, and he said:

'The inspector is here, and there are people waiting for me.' And while he was distributing the clothes he had received from Manchester, he argued with the inspector as to the direction the new road should take; and when he came back from the relief works, his dinner was waiting. He was busy writing letters all the afternoon; and it was not until he had handed them to the postmistress that he was free to go to poor James Murdoch, who had built a cabin at the end of one of the famine roads in a hollow out of the way of the wind.

From a long way off the priest could see him digging his patch of bog.

And when he caught sight of the priest he stuck his spade in the ground and came to meet him, almost as naked as an animal, bare feet protruding from ragged trousers; there was a shirt, but it was buttonless, and the breast-hair trembled in the wind—a likely creature to come out of the hovel behind him.

'It has been dry enough,' he said, 'all the summer; and I had a thought to make a drain. But 'tis hard luck, your reverence, and after building this house for her. There's a bit of smoke in the house now, but if I got Catherine I wouldn't be long making a

---

[1] From *The Untilled Field*, London, 1903. Text from Carra Edition, New York, 1923.

chimney. I told Mike he should give Catherine a pig for her fortune, but he said he would give her a calf when I bought the pig, and I said, "Haven't I built a fine house, and wouldn't it be a fine one to rear him in?"'

And together they walked through the bog, James talking to the priest all the way, for it was seldom he had anyone to talk to.

'Now I mustn't take you any further from your digging.'

'Sure there's time enough,' said James. 'Amn't I there all day?'

'I'll go and see Mike Mulhare myself,' said the priest.

'Long life to your reverence.'

'And I will try to get you the price of the pig.'

'Ah, 'tis your reverence that's good to us.'

The priest stood looking after him, wondering if he would give up life as a bad job and go back to the poorhouse; and while thinking of James Murdoch he became conscious that the time was coming for the priests to save Ireland. Catholic Ireland was passing away; in five-and-twenty years Ireland would be a Protestant country if—(he hardly dared to formulate the thought)—if the priests did not marry. The Greek priests had been allowed to retain their wives in order to avert a schism. Rome had always known how to adapt herself to circumstances; there was no doubt that if Rome knew Ireland's need of children she would consider the revocation of the decree of celibacy, and he returned home remembering that celibacy had only been made obligatory in Ireland in the twelfth century.

Ireland was becoming a Protestant country! He drank his tea mechanically, and it was a long time before he took up his knitting. But he could not knit, and laid the stocking aside. Of what good would his letter be? A letter from a poor parish priest asking that one of the most ancient decrees should be revoked! It would be thrown into the waste-paper basket. The cardinals are men whose thoughts move up and down certain narrow ways, clever men no doubt, but clever men are often the dupes of conventions. All men who live in the world accept the conventions as truths. It is only in the wilderness that the truth is revealed to man. 'I must write the letter! Instinct,' he said, 'is a surer guide than logic, and my letter to Rome was a sudden revelation.'

As he sat knitting by his own fireside his idea seemed to come out of the corners of the room. 'When you were at Rathowen,' his idea said, 'you heard the clergy lament that the people were leaving the country. You heard the bishop and many eloquent men speak on the subject. Words, words, but on the bog road the remedy was revealed to you.

'That if each priest were to take a wife about four thousand children would be born within the year, forty thousand children would be added to the birth-rate in ten years. Ireland can be saved by her priesthood!'

The truth of this estimate seemed beyond question, and yet, Father MacTurnan found it difficult to reconcile himself to the idea of a married clergy. 'One is always the dupe of prejudice,' he said to himself and went on thinking. 'The priests live in the best houses, eat the best food, wear the best clothes; they are indeed the flower of the nation, and would produce magnificent sons and daughters. And who could bring up their children according to the teaching of our holy church as well as priests?'

So did his idea unfold itself, and very soon he realized that other advantages would accrue, beyond the addition of forty thousand children to the birth-rate, and one advantage that seemed to him to exceed the original advantage would be the nationalization of religion, the formation of an Irish Catholicism suited to the ideas and needs of the Irish people.

In the beginning of the century the Irish lost their language, in the middle of the century the characteristic aspects of their religion. It was Cardinal Cullen who had denationalized religion in Ireland. But everyone recognized his mistake. How could a church be nationalized better than by the rescission of the decree of celibacy? The begetting of children would attach the priests to the soil of Ireland; and it could not be said that anyone loved his country who did not contribute to its maintenance. The priests leave Ireland on foreign missions, and every Catholic who leaves Ireland, he said, helps to bring about the very thing that Ireland has been struggling against for centuries—Protestantism.

His idea talked to him every evening, and, one evening, it said, 'Religion, like everything else, must be national,' and it led him to contrast cosmopolitanism with parochialism. 'Religion, like art, came out of parishes,' he said. He felt a great force to be behind him. He must write! He must write . . .

He dropped the ink over the table and over the paper, he jotted down his ideas in the first words that came to him until midnight; and when he slept his letter floated through his sleep.

'I must have a clear copy of it before I begin the Latin translation.'

He had written the English text thinking of the Latin that would come after, very conscious of the fact that he had written no Latin since he had left Maynooth, and that a bad translation would discredit his ideas in the eyes of the Pope's secretary, who was doubtless a great Latin scholar.

'The Irish priests have always been good Latinists,' he murmured, as he hunted through the dictionary.

The table was littered with books, for he had found it necessary to create a Latin atmosphere, and one morning he finished his translation and walked to the whitening window to rest his eyes before reading it over. But he was too tired to do any more, and he laid his manuscript on the table by his bedside.

'This is very poor Latin,' he said to himself some hours later, and the manuscript lay on the floor while he dressed. It was his servant who brought it to him when he had finished his breakfast, and, taking it from her, he looked at it again.

'It is as tasteless,' he said, 'as the gruel that poor James Murdoch is eating.' He picked up *St. Augustine's Confessions*. 'Here is idiom,' he muttered, and he continued reading till he was interrupted by the wheels of a car stopping at his door. It was Meehan! None had written such good Latin at Maynooth as Meehan.

'My dear Meehan, this is indeed a pleasant surprise.'

'I thought I'd like to see you. I drove over. But—I am not disturbing you. . . . You've taken to reading again. St. Augustine! And you're writing in Latin!'

Father James's face grew red, and he took the manuscript out of his friend's hand.

'No, you mustn't look at that.'

And then the temptation to ask him to overlook certain passages made him change his mind.

'I was never much of a Latin scholar.'

'And you want me to overlook your Latin for you. But why are you writing Latin?'

'Because I am writing to the Pope. I was at first a little doubtful, but the more I thought of this letter the more necessary it seemed to me.'

'And what are you writing to the Pope about?'

'You see Ireland is going to become a Protestant country.'

# A LETTER TO ROME

'Is it?' said Father Meehan, and he listened a little while. Then, interrupting his friend, he said:

'I've heard enough. Now, I strongly advise you not to send this letter. We have known each other all our lives. Now, my dear Mac-Turnan——'

Father Michael talked eagerly, and Father MacTurnan sat listening. At last Father Meehan saw that his arguments were producing no effect, and he said:

'You don't agree with me.'

'It isn't that I don't agree with you. You have spoken admirably from your point of view, but our points of view are different.'

'Take your papers away, burn them!'

Then, thinking his words were harsh, he laid his hand on his friend's shoulder and said:

'My dear MacTurnan, I beg of you not to send this letter.'

Father James did not answer; the silence grew painful, and Father Michael asked Father James to show him the relief works that the Government had ordered.

But important as these works were, the letter to Rome seemed more important to Father Michael, and he said:

'My good friend, there isn't a girl that would marry us; now is there? There isn't a girl in Ireland who would touch us with a forty-foot pole. Would you have the Pope release the nuns from their vows?'

'I think exceptions should be made in favour of those in Orders. But I think it would be for the good of Ireland if the secular clergy were married.'

'That's not my point. My point is that even if the decree were rescinded we shouldn't be able to get wives. You've been living too long in the waste, my dear friend. You've lost yourself in dreams. We shouldn't get a penny. "Why should we support that fellow and his family?" is what they'd be saying.'

'We should be poor, no doubt,' said Father James. 'But not so poor as our parishioners. My parishioners eat yellow meal, and I eat eggs and live in a good house.'

'We are educated men, and should live in better houses than our parishioners.'

'The greatest saints lived in deserts.'

And so the argument went on until the time came to say goodbye, and then Father James said:

'I shall be glad if you will give me a lift on your car. I want to go to the post-office.'

'To post your letter?'

'The idea came to me—it came swiftly like a lightning-flash, and I can't believe that it was an accident. If it had fallen into your mind with the suddenness that it fell into mine, you would believe that it was an inspiration.'

'It would take a good deal to make me believe I was inspired,' said Father Michael, and he watched Father James go into the post-office to register his letter.

At that hour a long string of peasants returning from their work went by. The last was Norah Flynn, and the priest blushed deeply for it was the first time he had looked on one of his parishioners in the light of a possible spouse; and he entered his house frightened; and when he looked round his parlour he asked himself if the day would come when he should see Norah Flynn sitting opposite to him in his armchair. His face flushed deeper when he looked towards the bedroom door, and he fell on his knees and prayed that God's will might be made known to him.

During the night he awoke many times, and the dream that had awakened him continued when he had left his bed, and he wandered round and round the room in the darkness, seeking a way. At last he reached the window and drew the curtain, and saw the dim dawn opening out over the bog.

'Thank God,' he said, 'it was only a dream—only a dream.'

And lying down he fell asleep, but immediately another dream as horrible as the first appeared, and his housekeeper heard him beating on the walls.

'Only a dream, only a dream,' he said.

He lay awake, not daring to sleep lest he might dream. And it was about seven o'clock when he heard his housekeeper telling him that the inspector had come to tell him they must decide what direction the new road should take. In the inspector's opinion it should run parallel with the old road. To continue the old road two miles further would involve extra labour; the people would have to go further to their work, and the stones would have to be drawn further. The priest held that the extra labour was of secondary importance. He said that to make two roads running parallel with each other would be a wanton humiliation to the people.

But the inspector could not appreciate the priest's arguments.

He held that the people were thinking only how they might earn enough money to fill their bellies.

'I don't agree with you, I don't agree with you,' said the priest. 'Better go in the opposite direction and make a road to the sea.'

'You see, your reverence, the Government don't wish to engage upon any work that will benefit any special class. These are my instructions.'

'A road to the sea will benefit no one. . . . I see you are thinking of the landlord. But there isn't a harbour; no boat ever comes into that flat, waste sea.'

'Well, your reverence, one of these days a harbour may be made. An arch would look well in the middle of the bog, and the people wouldn't have to go far to their work.'

'No, no. A road to the sea will be quite useless; but its futility will not be apparent—at least, not so apparent—and the people's hearts won't be broken.'

The inspector seemed a little doubtful, but the priest assured him that the futility of the road would satisfy English ministers.

'And yet these English ministers,' the priest reflected, 'are not stupid men; they're merely men blinded by theory and prejudice, as all men are who live in the world. Their folly will be apparent to the next generation, and so on and so on for ever and ever, world without end.'

'And the worst of it is,' the priest said, 'while the people are earning their living on these roads, their fields will be lying idle, and there will be no crops next year.'

'We can't help that,' the inspector answered, and Father MacTurnan began to think of the cardinals and the transaction of business in the Vatican; cardinals and ministers alike are the dupes of convention. Only those who are estranged from habits and customs can think straightforwardly.

'If, instead of insisting on these absurd roads, the Government would give me the money, I'd be able to feed the people at a cost of about a penny a day, and they'd be able to sow their potatoes. And if only the cardinals would consider the rescission of the decree on its merits, Ireland would be saved from Protestantism.'

Some cardinal was preparing an answer—an answer might be even in the post. Rome might not think his letter worthy of an answer.

A few days afterwards the inspector called to show him a letter he had just received from the Board of Works. Father James had to go to Dublin, and in the excitement of these philanthropic activities the emigration question was forgotten. Six weeks must have gone by when the postman handed him a letter.

'This is a letter from Father Moran,' he said to the inspector who was with him at the time. 'The Bishop wishes to see me. We will continue the conversation to-morrow. It is eight miles to Rathowen, and how much further is the Palace?'

'A good seven,' said the inspector. 'You're not going to walk it, your reverence?'

'Why not? In four hours I shall be there.' He looked at his boots first, and hoped they would hold together; and then he looked at the sky, and hoped it would not rain.

There was no likelihood of rain; no rain would fall today out of that soft dove-coloured sky full of sun; ravishing little breezes lifted the long heather, the rose-coloured hair of the knolls, and over the cutaway bog wild white cotton was blowing. Now and then a yellow-hammer rose out of the coarse grass and flew in front of the priest, and once a pair of grouse left the sunny hillside where they were nesting with a great whirr; they did not go far, but alighted in a hollow, and the priest could see their heads above the heather watching him.

'The moment I'm gone they'll return to their nest.'

He walked on, and when he had walked six miles he sat down and took a piece of bread out of his pocket. As he ate it his eyes wandered over the undulating bog, brown and rose, marked here and there by a black streak where the peasants had been cutting turf. The sky changed very little; it was still a pale, dove colour; now and then a little blue showed through the grey, and sometimes the light lessened; but a few minutes after the sunlight fluttered out of the sky again and dozed among the heather.

'I must be getting on,' he said, and he looked into the brown water, fearing he would find none other to slake his thirst. But just as he stooped he caught sight of a woman driving an ass who had come to the bog for turf, and she told him where he would find a spring, and he thought he had never drunk anything so sweet as this water.

'I've got a good long way to go yet,' he said, and he walked studying the lines of the mountains, thinking he could distinguish one hill from the other; and that in another mile or two he would be out of the bog. The road ascended, and on the other side there were a few pines. Some hundred yards further on there was a green sod. But the heather appeared again, and he had walked ten miles before he was clear of whins and heather.

As he walked he thought of his interview with the Bishop, and was nearly at the end of his journey when he stopped at a cabin to mend his shoe. And while the woman was looking for a needle and thread, he mopped his face with a great red handkerchief that he kept in the pocket of his threadbare coat—a coat that had once been black, but had grown green with age and weather. He had outwalked himself, and would not be able to answer the points that the Bishop would raise. The woman found him a scrap of leather, and it took him an hour to patch his shoe under the hawthorn tree.

He was still two miles from the Palace, and arrived footsore, covered with dust, and so tired that he could hardly rise from the chair to receive Father Moran when he came into the parlour.

'You seem to have walked a long way, Father MacTurnan.'

'I shall be all right presently. I suppose his Grace doesn't want to see me at once.'

'Well, that's just it. His Grace sent me to say he would see you at once. He expected you earlier.'

'I started the moment I received his Grace's letter. I suppose his Grace wishes to see me regarding my letter to Rome.'

The secretary hesitated, coughed, and went out, and Father MacTurnan wondered why Father Moran looked at him so intently. He returned in a few minutes, saying that his Grace was sorry that Father MacTurnan had had so long a walk, and he hoped he would rest awhile and partake of some refreshment. . . . The servant brought in some wine and sandwiches, and the secretary returned in half an hour. His Grace was now ready to receive him. . . .

Father Moran opened the library door, and Father MacTurnan saw the Bishop—a short, alert man, about fifty-five, with a sharp nose and grey eyes and bushy eyebrows. He popped about the room giving his secretary many orders, and Father MacTurnan wondered if the Bishop would ever finish talking to his secretary. He seemed to have finished, but a thought suddenly struck him, and he followed his secretary to the door, and Father MacTurnan began to fear that the Pope had not decided to place the Irish clergy on the same footing as the Greek. If he had, the Bishop's interest in these many various matters would have subsided: his mind would be engrossed by the larger issue.

As he returned from the door his Grace passed Father MacTurnan without speaking to him, and going to his writing-table he began to search amid his papers. At last Father MacTurnan said:

'Maybe your Grace is looking for my letter to Rome?'

'Yes,' said his Grace, 'do you see it?'

'It's under your Grace's hand, those blue papers.'

'Ah, yes,' and his Grace leaned back in his armchair, leaving Father MacTurnan standing.

'Won't you sit down, Father MacTurnan?' he said casually. 'You've been writing to Rome, I see, advocating the revocation of the decree of celibacy. There's no doubt the emigration of Catholics is a very serious question. So far you have got the sympathy of Rome, and I may say of myself; but am I to understand that it was your fear for the religious safety of Ireland that prompted you to write this letter?'

'What other reason could there be?'

Nothing was said for a long while, and then the Bishop's meaning began to break in on his mind; his face flushed, and he grew confused.

'I hope your Grace doesn't think for a moment that——'

'I only want to know if there is anyone—if your eyes ever went in a certain direction, if your thoughts ever said, "Well, if the decree were revoked—"'

'No, your Grace, no. Celibacy has been no burden to me—far from it. Sometimes I feared that it was celibacy that attracted me to the priesthood. Celibacy was a gratification rather than a sacrifice.'

'I am glad,' said the Bishop, and he spoke slowly and emphatically, 'that this letter was prompted by such impersonal motives.'

'Surely, your Grace, His Holiness didn't suspect——'

The Bishop murmured an euphonious Italian name, and Father MacTurnan understood that he was speaking of one of the Pope's secretaries.

'More than once,' said Father MacTurnan, 'I feared if the decree were revoked, I shouldn't have had sufficient courage to comply with it.'

And then he told the Bishop how he had met Norah Flynn on

the road. An amused expression stole into the Bishop's face, and his voice changed.

'I presume you do not contemplate making marriage obligatory; you do not contemplate the suspension of the faculties of those who do not take wives?'

'It seems to me that exception should be made in favour of those in orders, and of course in favour of those who have reached a certain age like your Grace.'

The Bishop coughed, and pretended to look for some paper which he had mislaid.

'This was one of the many points that I discussed with Father Michael Meehan.'

'Oh, so you consulted Father Meehan,' the Bishop said, looking up.

'He came in the day I was reading over my Latin translation before posting it. I'm afraid the ideas that I submitted to the consideration of His Holiness have been degraded by my very poor Latin. I should have wished Father Meehan to overlook my Latin, but he refused. He begged of me not to send the letter.'

'Father Meehan,' said his Grace, 'is a great friend of yours. Yet nothing he could say could shake your resolution to write to Rome?'

'Nothing,' said Father MacTurnan. 'The call I received was too distinct and too clear for me to hesitate.'

'Tell me about this call.'

Father MacTurnan told the Bishop that the poor man had come out of the workhouse because he wanted to be married, and that Mike Mulhare would not give him his daughter until he had earned the price of a pig. 'And as I was talking to him I heard my conscience say, "No one can afford to marry in Ireland but the clergy." We all live better than our parishioners.'

And then, forgetting the Bishop, and talking as if he were alone with his God, he described how the conviction had taken possession of him—that Ireland would become a Protestant country if the Catholic emigration did not cease. And he told how this conviction had left him little peace until he had written his letter.

The priest talked on until he was interrupted by Father Moran.

'I have some business to transact with Father Moran now,' the Bishop said, 'but you must stay to dinner. You've walked a long way, and you are tired and hungry.'

'But, your Grace, if I don't start now, I shan't get home until nightfall.'

'A car will take you back, Father MacTurnan. I will see to that. I must have some exact information about your poor people. We must do something for them.'

Father MacTurnan and the Bishop were talking together when the car came to take Father MacTurnan home, and the Bishop said:

'Father MacTurnan, you have borne the loneliness of your parish a long while.'

'Loneliness is only a matter of habit. I think, your Grace, I'm better suited to the place than I am for any other. I don't wish any change if your Grace is satisfied with me.'

'No one will look after the poor people better than yourself, Father MacTurnan. But,' he said, 'it seems to me there is one thing we have forgotten. You haven't told me if you have succeeded in getting the money to buy the pig.'

Father MacTurnan grew very red. . . . 'I had forgotten it. The relief works——'

'It's not too late. Here's five pounds, and this will buy him a pig.'

'It will indeed,' said the priest, 'it will buy him two!'

He had left the Palace without having asked the Bishop how his letter had been received at Rome, and he stopped the car, and was about to tell the driver to go back. But no matter, he would hear about his letter some other time. He was bringing happiness to two poor people, and he could not persuade himself to delay their happiness by one minute. He was not bringing one pig, but two pigs, and now Mike Mulhare would have to give him Norah and a calf; and the priest remembered that James Murdoch had said —'What a fine house this will be to rear them in.' There were many who thought that human beings and animals should not live together; but after all, what did it matter if they were happy? And the priest forgot his letter to Rome in the thought of the happiness he was bringing to two poor people. He could not see Norah Mulhare that night; but he drove down to the famine road, and he and the driver called till they awoke James Murdoch. The poor man came stumbling across the bog, and the priest told him the news.

# A Theological Fork[1]

The castle hall was empty and grey, only the autumn dusk in the Gothic window; and the shuffle of the octogenarian butler sounded very dismal as he pottered across the tessellated pavement. On learning from him that Mr. Martyn was still writing, I wandered from the organ into the morning-room, and sat by the fire, waiting for Edward's footstep. It came towards me about half an hour afterwards, slow and ponderous, not at all like the step of the successful dramatist; and my suspicions that his third act was failing him were aggravated by his unwillingness to tell me about the alterations he was making in it. All he could tell me was that he had been in Maynooth last summer, and had heard the priests declaring that they refused to stultify themselves; and as the word seemed to him typical of the country he would put it frequently into the mouths of his politicians.

How drama was to arise out of the verb, to stultify, did not seem clear, and in the middle of my embarrassment he asked me where I had been all the afternoon, brightening up somewhat when I told him that I had been to Coole. In a curious detached way he is always eager for a gossip, and we talked of Yeats and Lady Gregory for a long time, and of our walk round the lake, Edward rousing from my description of the swans to ask me where I had left the poet.

At the gate.

Why didn't you ask him to stay for dinner? And while I sought for an answer, he added: Maybe it's just as well you didn't, for to-day is Friday and the salmon I was expecting from Galway hasn't arrived.

But Yeats and I aren't Catholics.

My house is a Catholic house, and those who don't care to conform to the rule——

Your dogmatism exceeds that of an Archbishop; and I told him that I had heard my father say that the Archbishop of Tuam, Dr. McHale, had meat always on his table on Friday, and when asked how this was, answered that he didn't know who had gotten dispensations and who hadn't. Edward muttered that he was not to

---

[1] From *Hail And Farewell: Ave*, London, 1911. Text from N.Y. edition of 1925.

be taken in by such remarks about dispensations; he knew very well I had never troubled to ask for one.

Why should I, since I'm not a Catholic?

If you aren't a Catholic, why don't you become a Protestant?

In the first place, one doesn't become a Protestant, one discovers oneself a Protestant; and it seems to me that an Agnostic has as much right to eat meat on Friday as a Protestant.

Agnosticism isn't a religion. It contains no dogma.

It comes to this, then: that you're going to make me dine off a couple of boiled eggs. And I walked about the room, indignant, but not because I care much about my food—two eggs and a potato are more agreeable to me in intelligent society than grouse would be in stupid. But two eggs and a potato forced down my throat on a theological fork in a Gothic house that had cost twenty thousand pounds to build—two eggs and a potato, without hope of cheese! The Irish do not eat cheese, and I am addicted to it, especially to Double Gloucester. In my school-days that cheese was a wonderful solace in my life, but after leaving school I asked for it in vain, and gave up hope of ever eating it again. It was not till the 'nineties that a waiter mentioned it. Stilton, sir; Chester, Double Gloucester —— Double Gloucester! You have Double Gloucester! I thought it extinct. You have it? Then bring it, I cried, and so joyfully that he couldn't drag himself from my sight. An excellent cheese, I told him, but somewhat fallen from the high standard it had assumed in my imagination. Even so, if there had been a slice of Double Gloucester in the larder at Tillyra, I should not have minded the absence of the salmon, and if Edward had pleaded that his servants would be scandalised to see any one who was supposed to be a Catholic eat meat on Fridays, I should have answered: But everybody knows I'm not a Catholic. I've written it in half a dozen books. And if Edward had said: But my servants don't read your books; I shall be obliged if you'll put up with fasting fare for once, I would have eaten an egg and a potato without murmur or remark. But to be told I must dine off two eggs and a potato, so that his conscience should not be troubled during the night, worried me, and I am afraid I cast many an angry look across the table. An apple-pie came up and some custards, and these soothed me; he discovered some marmalade in a cupboard, and Edward is such a sociable being when his pipe is alight, that I forgave his theological prejudices for the sake of his aesthetic. We peered into reproductions of Fra Angelico's frescoes, and studied Leonardo's sketches for draperies. Edward liked Ibsen from the beginning, and will like him to the end, and Swift. But he cannot abide Schumann's melodies. We had often talked of these great men and their works, but never did he talk as delightfully as on that Friday evening right on into Saturday morning. Nor was it till Sunday morning that his soul began to trouble him again. As I was finishing breakfast, he had the cheek to ask me to get ready to go to Mass.

But, Edward, I don't believe in the Mass. My presence will be only——

Will you hold your tongue, George? . . . and not give scandal, he answered, his voice trembling with emotion.

Everybody knows that I don't believe in the Mass.

If you aren't a Catholic, why don't you become a Protestant? And he began pushing me from behind.

I have told you before that one may become a Catholic, but one discovers oneself a Protestant. But why am I going to Gort?

Because you had the bad taste to describe our church in *A Drama in Muslin*, and to make such remarks about our parish priest that he said, if you showed yourself in Ardrahan again, he'd throw dirty water over you.

If you send me to Gort, I shall be able to describe Father ——'s church.

Will you not be delaying?

One word more. It isn't on account of my description of Father ——'s church that you won't take me to Ardrahan: the real reason is because, at your request, mind you, I asked Father —— not to spit upon your carpet when he came to dinner at Tillyra. You were afraid to ask a priest to refrain from any of his habits, and left the room.

I only asked you to draw his attention to the spittoon.

Which I did; but he said such things were only a botheration, and my admonitions on the virtue of cleanliness angered him so that he never——

You'll be late for Mass. And you, Whelan; now, are you listening to me? Do you hear me? You aren't to spare the whip. Away you go; you'll only be just in time. And you, Whelan, you're not to delay putting up the horse. Do you hear me?

Whelan drove away rapidly, and when I looked back I saw my friend hurrying across the park, tumbling into the sunk fence in anxiety not to miss the *Confiteor*, and Whelan, who saw the accident, too, feared that the masther is after hurting himself. Happily this was not so. Edward was soon on his feet again, running across the field like a hare, the driver said—out of politeness, I suppose.

Hardly like a hare, I said, hoping to draw a more original simile from Whelan's rustic mind; but he only coughed a little, and shook up the reins which he held in a shapeless, freckled hand.

Do you like the parish priest at Gort better than Father——at Ardrahan?

They're well matched, Whelan answered—a thick-necked, long-bodied fellow with a rim of faded hair showing under a bowler-hat that must have been about the stables for years, collecting dust along the corn-bin and getting greasy in the harness-room. One reasoned that it must have been black once upon a time, and that Whelan must have been a young man long ago; and one reasoned that he must have shaved last week, or three weeks ago, for there was a stubble on his chin. But in spite of reason, Whelan seemed like something that had always been, some old rock that had lain among the bramble since the days of Finn MacCoole, and his sullenness seemed as permanent as that of the rocks, and his face, too, seemed like a worn rock, for it was without profile, and I could only catch sight of a great flabby ear and a red, freckled neck, about which was tied a woollen comforter that had once been white.

He answered my questions roughly, without troubling to turn his head, like a man who wishes to be left to himself; and acquiescing in his humour, I fell to thinking of Father James Browne, the parish priest of Carnacun in the 'sixties, and of the day that he came over to Moore Hall in his ragged cassock and battered biretta, with McHale's Irish translation of Homer under his arm, saying that the Archbishop had caught the Homeric ring in many a hexameter. My father smiled at the priest's enthusiasm, but I followed this tall, gaunt man, of picturesque appearance, whose large nose with tufted nostrils I remember to this day, into the Blue Room to ask him if the Irish were better than the Greek. He was a little loth to say it was not, but this rustic scholar did not carry patriotism into literature, and he admitted, on being pressed, that he liked the Greek better, and I listened to his great rotund voice pouring through his wide Irish mouth while he read me some eight or ten lines of Homer, calling my attention to the famous line that echoes the clash of the wave on the beach and the rustle of the shingle as the wave sinks back. My curiosity about McHale's translation interested him in me, and it was arranged soon after between him and my father that he should teach me Latin, and I rode a pony over every morning to a thatched cottage under ilex-trees, where the pleasantest hours of my childhood were spent in a parlour lined with books from floor to ceiling, reading there a little Virgil, and persuading an old priest into talk about Quintilian and Seneca. One day he spoke of Propertius, and the beauty of the name led me to ask Father James if I might read him, and not receiving a satisfactory answer, my curiosity was stimulated and Caesar studied diligently for a month.

Shall I know enough Latin in six months to read Propertius?

It will be many years before you will be able to read him. He is a very difficult writer.

Could Martin Blake read Propertius?

Martin Blake was Father James's other pupil, and these Blakes are neighbours of ours, and live on the far side of Carnacun. Father James was always telling me of the progress Martin was making in the Latin language, and I was always asking Father James when I should overtake him, but he held out very little hope that it would be possible for me ever to outdo Martin in scholarship. He may have said this because he could not look upon me as a promising pupil, or he may have been moved by a hope to start a spirit of emulation in me. He was a wise old man, and the reader will wonder how it was that, with such a natural interest in languages and such excellent opportunities, I did not become a classical scholar; the reader's legitimate curiosity shall be satisfied.

One day Father James said the time would come when I would give up hunting—everything, for the classics, and I rode home, elated, to tell my mother the prophecy. But she burst out laughing, leaving me in no doubt whatever that she looked upon Father James's idea of me as an excellent joke; and the tragedy of it all is that I accepted her casual point of view without consideration, carrying it almost at once into reality, playing truant instead of going to my Latin lesson. Father James, divested of his scholarship, became a mere priest in my eyes. I think that I avoided him, and am sure that I hardly ever saw him again, except at Mass.

A strange old church is Carnacun, built in the form of a cross, with whitewashed walls and some hardened earth for floor; and I should be hard set to discover in my childhood an earlier memory than the panelled roof, designed and paid for by my father, who had won the Chester Cup some years before. The last few hundred pounds of his good-fortune were spent in pitch-pine rafters and boards, and he provided a large picture of the *Crucifixion*, painted by my cousin, Jim Browne, who happened to be staying at Moore Hall at the time, from Tom Kelly the lodge-keeper, the first nude model that ever stood up in Mayo (Mayo has always led the way—Ireland's vanbird for sure). It was taken in great pomp from Moore Hall to Carnacun; and the hanging of it was a great and punctilious affair. A board had to be nailed at the back whereby a rope could be attached to hoist it into the roof, and lo! Mickey Murphy drove a nail through one of the gilt leaves which served as a sort of frame for the picture. My father shouted his orders to the men in the roof that they were to draw up the picture very slowly, and, lest it should sway and get damaged in the swaying, strings were attached to it. My father and mother each held a string, and the third may have been held by Jim Browne, or perhaps I was allowed to hold it.

Some time afterwards a *Blessed Virgin* and a *St. Joseph* came down from Dublin, and they were painted and gilded by my father, and so beautifully, that they were the admiration of every one for a very long while, and it was Jim Browne's *Crucifixion* and these anonymous statues that awakened my first aesthetic emotions. I used to look forward to seeing them all the way from Moore Hall to Carnacun—a bleak road as soon as our gate-lodge was passed: on one side a hill that looked as if it had been peeled; on the other some moist fields, divided by small stone walls, liked by me in those days, for they were excellent practice for my pony. Along this road our tenantry used to come from their villages, the women walking on one side (the married women in dark blue cloaks, the girls hiding their faces behind their shawls, carrying their boots in their hands, which they would put on in the chapel-yard), the men walking on the other side, the elderly men in traditional swallow-tail coats, knee-breeches, and worsted stockings; the young men in corduroy trousers and frieze coats. As we passed, the women curtseyed in their red petticoats; the young men lifted their round bowler-hats; but the old men stood by, their tall hats in their hands. At the bottom of every one was a red handkerchief, and I remember wisps of grey hair floating in the wind Our tenantry met the tenantry of Clogher and Tower Hill, and

## A THEOLOGICAL FORK

they all collected round the gateway of the chapel to admire the carriages of their landlords. We were received like royalty as we turned in through the gates and went up the wooden staircase leading to the gallery, frequented by the privileged people of the parish—by us, and by our servants, the postmaster and postmistress from Ballyglass, and a few graziers. In the last pew were the police, and after the landlords these were the most respected.

As soon as we were settled in our pew the acolytes ventured from the sacristy tinkling their bells, the priest following, carrying the chalice covered with the veil. As the ceremony of the Mass was never of any interest to me, I used to spend my time looking over the pew into the body of the church, wondering at the herd of peasantry, trying to distinguish our own serfs among those from the Tower Hill and Clogher estates. Pat Plunket, a highly respectable tenant (he owned a small orchard), I could always discover; he knelt just under us, and in front of a bench, the only one in the body of the church, and about him collected those few that had begun to rise out of brutal indigence. Their dress and their food were slightly different from the commoner kind. Pat Plunket and Mickey Murphy, the carpenter, not the sawyer, were supposed to drink tea and eat hot cakes. The others breakfasted off Indian-meal porridge. And to Pat Plunket's bench used to come a tall woman, whose grace of body the long blue-black cloak of married life could not hide. I liked to wonder which among the men about her might be her husband. And a partial memory still lingers of a cripple that was allowed to avail himself of Pat Plunket's bench. His crutches were placed against the wall, and used to catch my eye, suggesting thoughts of what his embarrassment would be if they were taken away whilst he prayed. A great unknown horde of peasantry from Ballyglass and beyond it knelt in the left-hand corner, and after the Communion they came up the church with a great clatter of brogues to hear the sermon, leaving behind a hideous dwarf whom I could not take my eyes off, so strange was his waddle as he moved about the edge of the crowd, his huge mouth grinning all the time.

Our pew was the first on the right-hand side, and the pew behind us was the Clogher pew, and it was filled with girls—Helena, Livy, Lizzy, and May—the first girls I ever knew; and these are now under the sod—all except poor Livy, an old woman whom I sometimes meet out with her dog by the canal. In the first pew on the left was a red landlord with a frizzled beard and a perfectly handsome wife, and behind him was Joe McDonnell from Carnacun House, a great farmer, and the wonder of the church, so great was his belly. I can see these people dimly, like figures in the background of a picture; but the blind girl is as clear in my memory as if she were present. She used to kneel behind the Virgin's altar and the Communion rails, almost entirely hidden under an old shawl, grown green with age; and the event of every Sunday, at least for me, was to see her draw herself forward when the Communion bell rang, and lift herself to receive the wafer that the priest placed upon her tongue, and having received it, she would sink back, overcome, overawed, and I used to wonder at her piety, and think of the long hours she spent sitting by the cabin-fire waiting for Sunday to come round again. On what roadside was that cabin? And did she come, led by some relative or friend, or finding her way down the road by herself? Questions that interested me more than anybody else, and it was only at the end of a long inquiry that I learnt that she came from one of the cabins opposite Carnacun House. Every time we passed that cabin I used to look out for her, thinking how I might catch sight of her in the doorway; but I never saw her except in the chapel. Only once did we meet her as we drove to Ballyglass, groping her way, doubtless, to Carnacun. Where else would she be going? And hearing our horses' hoofs she sank closer to the wall, overawed, into the wet among the falling leaves.

As soon as the Communion was over Father James would come forward, and thrusting his hands under the alb (his favourite gesture) he would begin his sermon in Irish (in those days Irish was the language of the country among the peasantry), and we would sit for half an hour, wondering what were the terrible things he was saying, asking ourselves if it were pitchforks or ovens, or both, that he was talking; for the peasantry were groaning aloud, the women not infrequently falling on their knees, beating their breasts; and I remember being perplexed by the possibility that some few tenantry might be saved, for if that happened how should we meet them in heaven? Would they look another way and pass us by without lifting their hats and crying: Long life to yer honour?

My memories of Carnacun Chapel and Father James Browne were interrupted by a sudden lurching forward of the car, which nearly flung me into the road. Whelan apologised for himself and his horse, but I damned him, for I was annoyed at being awakened from my dream. There was no hope of being able to pick it up again, for the chapel bell was pealing down the empty landscape, calling the peasants from their desolate villages. It seemed to me that the Carnacun bell used to cry across the moist fields more cheerfully; there was a menace in the Gort bell as there is in the voice of a man who fears that he may not be obeyed, and this gave me an interest in the Mass I was going to hear. It would teach me something of the changes that had happened during my absence. The first thing I noticed as I approached the chapel was the smallness of the crowd of men about the gateposts; only a few figures, and they surly and suspicious fellows, resolved not to salute the landlord, yet breaking away with difficulty from traditional servility. Our popularity had disappeared with the laws that favoured us, but Whelan's appearance counted for something in the decaying sense of rank among the peasantry, and I mentally reproached Edward for not putting his servant into livery. It interested me to see that the superstitions of Carnacun were still followed: the peasants dipped their fingers in a font and sprinkled themselves, and the only difference that I noticed between the two chapels was one for the worse; the windows at Gort were not broken, and the happy, circling swallows did not build under the rafters. It was easier to discover differences in the two congregations. My eyes sought vainly the long dark cloak of married life, nor did I succeed in finding an old man in knee-breeches and worsted stockings, nor a girl drawing her shawl over her head.

The Irish language is inseparable from these things, I said, and it has gone. The sermon will be in English, or in a language as near English as those hats and feathers are near the fashions that prevail in Paris.

The Gort peasants seemed able to read, for they held Prayerbooks, and as if to help them in their devotion a harmonium began to utter sounds as discordant as the red and blue glass in the windows, and all the time the Mass continued very much as I remembered it, until the priest lifted his alb over his head and placed it upon the altar (Father James used to preach in the vestment, I said to myself); and very slowly and methodically the Gort priest tried to explain the mystery of Transubstantiation to the peasants, and they listened to him with such indifference that it were difficult not to think that Father James's sermons, based on the fear of the devil, were more suitable to Ireland.

A Mass only rememberable for a squealing harmonium, some panes in terrifying blues and reds, and my own great shame. However noble my motive may have been, I had knelt and stood with the congregation; I had even bowed my head, making believe by this parade that I accepted the Mass as a truth. It could not be right to do this, even for the sake of the Irish Literary Theatre, and I left the chapel asking myself by what strange alienation of the brain had Edward come to imagine that a piece of enforced hypocrisy on my part could be to any one's advantage.

It seemed to me that mortal sin had been committed that morning; a sense of guilt clung about me. Edward was consulted. Could it be right for me who did not believe in the Mass to attend Mass? He seemed to acquiesce that it might not be right, but when Sunday came round again my refusal to get on the car so frightened him that I relinquished myself to his scruples, to his terror, to his cries. The reader will judge me weak, but it should be remembered that he is my oldest friend, and it seemed to me that we should never be the same friends again if I refused; added to which he had been telling me all the week that he was getting on finely with his third act, and for the sake of a hypothetical act I climbed up on the car.

Now, Whelan, don't delay putting up the horse. Mind you're in time for Mass, and don't leave the chapel until the last Gospel has been read.

Must he wait for Benediction? I cried ironically.

Edward did not answer, possibly because he does not regard Benediction as part of the liturgy, and is, therefore, more or less indifferent to it. The horse trotted and Whelan clacked his tongue, a horrible noise from which I tried to escape by asking him questions.

Are the people quiet in this part of the country?

Quiet enough, he answered, and I thought I detected a slightly contemptuous accent in the syllables.

Not much life in the country? I hear the hunting is going to be stopped?

Parnell never told them to stop the hunting.

You're a Parnellite?

He was a great man.

The priests went against him, I said, because he loved another man's wife.

And O'Shea not living with her at the time.

Even if he had been, I answered, Ireland first of all, say I. He was a great man.

He was that.

And the priest at Gort—was he against him?

Wasn't he every bit as bad as the others?

Then you don't care to go to his church?

I'd just as lief stop away.

It's strange, Whelan; it's strange that Mr. Martyn should insist on my going to Gort to Mass. Of what use can Mass be to any one if he doesn't wish to hear it?

Whelan chuckled, or seemed to chuckle.

He will express no opinion, I said to myself, and abstractions don't interest him. So, turning to the concrete, I spoke of the priest who was to say Mass, and Whelan agreed that he had gone again Parnell.

Well, Whelan, it's a great waste of time going to Gort to hear a Mass one doesn't want to hear, and I have business with Mr. Yeats.

Maybe you'd like me to turn into Coole, sur?

I was thinking we might do that . . . only you won't speak to Mr. Martyn about it, will you? Because, you see, Whelan, every one has his prejudices, and I am a great friend of Mr. Martyn, and wouldn't like to disappoint him.

Wouldn't like to contrairy him, sur?

That's it, Whelan. Now, what about your dinner? You don't mind having your dinner in a Protestant house?

It's all one to me, sur.

The dinner is the main point, isn't it, Whelan?

Begad it is, sur, and he turned the horse in through the gates.

Just go round, I said, and put the horse up and say nothing to anybody.

Yes, sur.

After long ringing the maidservant opened the door and told me that Lady Gregory had gone to church with her niece; Mr. Yeats was composing. Would I take a seat in the drawing-room and wait till he was finished? He must have heard the wheels of the car coming round the gravel sweep, for he was in the room before the servant left it—enthusiastic, though a little weary. He had written five lines and a half, and a pause between one's rhymes is an excellent thing, he said. One could not but admire him, for even in early morning he was convinced of the importance of literature in our national life. He is nearly as tall as a Dublin policeman, and preaching literature he stood on the hearthrug, his feet set close together. Lifting his arms above his head (the very movement that Raphael gives to Paul when preaching at Athens), he said what he wanted to do was to gather up a great mass of speech. It did not seem to me clear why he should be at pains to gather up a great mass of speech to write so exiguous a thing as *The Shadowy Waters;* but we live in our desires rather than in our achievements, and Yeats talked on, telling me that he was experimenting, and did not know whether his play would come out in rhyme or in blank verse; he was experimenting. He could write blank verse almost as easily as prose, and therefore feared it; some obstacle, some dam was necessary. It seemed a pity to interrupt him, but I was interested to hear if he were going to accept my end, and allow the lady to drift southward, drinking yellow ale with the sailors, while the hero sought salvation alone in the North. He flowed out into a torrent of argument and explanation, very ingenious, but impossible to follow. Phrase after phrase rose and turned and went out like a wreath of smoke, and when the last was spoken and the idea it had borne had vanished, I asked him if he knew the legend of Diarmuid and Grania. He began to tell it to me in its many variants, surprising me with unexpected dramatic situations, at first sight contradictory and incoherent, but on closer scrutiny revealing a psychology in germ which it would interest me to unfold. A wonderful hour of literature that was, flowering into a resolution to write an heroic play together. As we sat looking at each other in silence, Lady Gregory returned from church.

She came into the room quickly, with a welcoming smile on her face, and I set her down here as I see her: a middle-aged woman, agreeable to look upon, perhaps for her broad, handsome, intellectual brow enframed in iron-grey hair. The brown, wide-open eyes are often lifted in looks of appeal and inquiry, and a natural wish to sympathise softens her voice till it whines. It modulated, however, very pleasantly as she yielded her attention to Yeats, who insisted on telling her how two beings so different as myself and Whelan had suddenly become united in a conspiracy to deceive Edward, Whelan because he could not believe in the efficacy of a

Mass performed by an anti-Parnellite, and I because—Yeats hesitated for a sufficient reason, deciding suddenly that I had objected to hear Mass in Gort because there was no one in the church who had read Villiers de l'Isle Adam except myself; and he seemed so much amused that the thought suddenly crossed my mind that perhaps the *cocasseries* of Connaught were more natural to him than the heroic moods which he believed himself called upon to interpret. His literature is one thing and his conversation is another, divided irreparably. Is this right? Lady Gregory chattered on, telling stories faintly farcical, amusing to those who knew the neighbourhood, but rather wearisome for one who didn't, and I was waiting for an opportunity to tell her that an heroic drama was going to be written on the subject of Diarmuid and Grania.

When my lips broke the news, a cloud gathered in her eyes, and she admitted that she thought it would be hardly wise for Yeats to undertake any further work at present; and later in the afternoon she took me into her confidence, telling me that Yeats came to Coole every summer because it was necessary to get him away from the distractions of London, not so much from social as from the intellectual distractions that Arthur Symons had inaugurated. The Savoy rose up in my mind with its translations from Villiers de l'Isle Adam, Verlaine, and Maeterlinck; and I agreed with her that alien influences were a great danger to the artist. All Yeats's early poems, she broke in, were written in Sligo, and among them were twenty beautiful lyrics and Ireland's one great poem, *The Wanderings of Usheen*—all these had come straight out of the landscape and the people he had known from boyhood.

For seven years we have been waiting for a new book from him; ever since *The Countess Cathleen* we have been reading the publisher's autumn announcement of *The Wind among the Reeds*. The volume was finished here last year; it would never have been finished if I had not asked him to Coole; and though we live in an ungrateful world, I think somebody will throw a kind word after me some day, if for nothing else, for *The Wind among the Reeds*.

I looked round, thinking that perhaps life at Coole was arranged primarily to give him an opportunity of writing poems. As if she had read my thoughts, Lady Gregory led me into the back drawing-room, and showed me the table at which he wrote, and I admired the clean pens, the fresh ink, and the spotless blotter; these were her special care every morning. I foresaw the strait sofa lying across the window, valued in some future time because the poet had reclined upon it between his rhymes. Ah me! the creeper that rustles an accompaniment to his melodies in the pane will awaken again, year after year, but one year it will awaken in vain. . . . My eyes thanked Lady Gregory for her devotion to literature. Instead of writing novels she had released the poet from the quern of daily journalism, and anxious that she should understand my appreciation of her, I spoke of the thirty-six wild swans that had risen out of the lake while Yeats and I wandered all through the long evening seeking a new composition for *The Shadowy Waters*.

She did not answer me, and I followed her in silence back to the front room and sat listening to her while she told me that it was because she wanted poems from him that she looked askance at our project to write a play together on the subject of Diarmuid and Grania. It was not that the subject was unsuited to his genius, but she thought it should be written by him alone; the best of neither would transpire in collaboration, and she lamented that it were useless to save him from the intellectual temptations of Symons if he were to be tossed into more subtle ones. She laughed, as is her way when she cozens, and reminded me that we were of different temperaments and had arisen out of different literary traditions.

Mayo went to Montmartre, and Sligo turned into Fleet Street.

Suspicious in her cleverness, my remark did not altogether please her, and she said something about a man of genius and a man of talent coming together, speaking quickly under her breath, so that her scratch would escape notice at the time; and we were talking of our responsibilities towards genius when the door opened and Yeats came into the room.

He entered somewhat diffidently, I thought, with an invitation to me to go for a walk. Lady Gregory was appeased with the news that he had written five and a half lines that morning, and a promise that he would be back at six, and would do a little more writing before dinner. As he went away he told me that he might attain his maximum of nine lines that evening, if he succeeded in finishing the broken line. But S must never meet S; for his sake was inadmissible, and while seeking how he might avoid such a terrifying cacophony we tramped down wet roads and climbed over low walls into scant fields, finding the ruined castle we were in search of at the end of a long boreen among tall, wet grasses. The walls were intact and the stair, and from the top we stood watching the mist drifting across the grey country, Yeats telling how the wine had been drugged at Tara, myself thinking how natural it was that Lady Gregory should look upon me as a danger to Yeats's genius. As we descended the slippery stair an argument began in my head whereby our project of collaboration might be defended. Next time I went to Coole I would say to Lady Gregory: You see, Yeats came to me with *The Shadowy Waters* because he had entangled the plot and introduced all his ideas into it, and you will admit that the plot had to be disentangled? To conciliate her completely I would say that while Yeats was rewriting *The Shadowy Waters* I would spend my time writing an act about the many adventures that befell Diarmuid and Grania as they fled before Finn. Yeats had told me these adventures in the ruined castle; I had given to them all the attention that I could spare from Lady Gregory, who, I was thinking, might admit my help in the arrangement of some incidents in *The Shadowy Waters*, but would always regard our collaboration in *Diarmuid and Grania* with hostility. But for this partiality it seemed to me I could not blame her, so well had she put her case when she said that her fear was that my influence might break up the mould of his mind.

The car waited for me at the end of the boreen, and before starting I tried to persuade Yeats to come to Tillyra with me, but he said he could not leave Lady Gregory alone, and before we parted I learnt that she read to him every evening. Last summer it was *War and Peace*, and this summer she was reading Spenser's *Faerie Queene*, for he was going to publish a selection and must get back to Coole for the seventh canto.

Good-bye, and springing up on the car, I was driven by Whelan into the mist, thinking Yeats the most fortunate amongst us, he having discovered among all others that one who, by instinctive sympathy, understood the capacity of his mind, and could evoke it, and who never wearied of it, whether it came to her in elaborately wrought stanzas or in the form of some simple confession, the mood of last night related as they crossed the sward after breakfast. As the moon is more interested in the earth than in any other thing, there is always some woman more interested in a man's mind than in anything else, and willing to follow it sentence by sentence. A great deal of Yeats's work must come to her in fragments—a line and a half, two lines—and these she faithfully copies on her typewriter, and even those that his ultimate taste has rejected are treasured up, and perhaps will one day appear in a stately variorum edition.

Well she may say that the future will owe her something, and my thoughts moved back to the first time I saw her some twenty-five years ago. She was then a young woman, very earnest, who divided her hair in the middle and wore it smooth on either side of a broad and handsome brow. Her eyes were always full of questions, and her Protestant high-school air became her greatly and estranged me from her.

In her drawing-room were to be met men of assured reputation in literature and politics, and there was always the best reading of the time upon her tables. There was nothing, however, in her conversation to suggest literary faculty, and it was a surprise to me to hear one day that she had written a pamphlet in defence of Arabi Pasha, an Egyptian rebel. Some years after she edited her husband's memoirs, and did the work well. So at core she must have been always literary, but early circumstances had not proved favourable to the development of her gift, and it languished till she met Yeats. He could not have been long at Coole before he began to draw her attention to the beauty of the literature that rises among the hills and bubbles irresponsibly, and set her going from cabin to cabin taking down stories, and encouraged her to learn the original language of the country, so that they might add to the Irish idiom which the peasant had already translated into English, making in this way a language for themselves.

Yeats could only acquire the idiom by the help of Lady Gregory, for although he loves the dialect and detests the defaced idiom which we speak in our streets and parlours, he has little aptitude to learn that of the boreen and the market-place. She put her aptitude at his service, and translated portions of *Cathleen ni Houlihan* into Kiltartan (Kiltartan is the village in which she collects the dialect); and she worked it into the revised version of the stories from *The Secret Rose*, published by the Dun Emer Press, and thinking how happy their lives must be at Coole, implicated in literary partnership, my heart went out towards her in a sudden sympathy. She has been wise all her life through, I said; she knew him to be her need at once, and she never hesitated . . . yet she knew me before she knew him.

JAMES JOYCE

# Dead King[1]

A GREAT FIRE, banked high and red, flamed in the grate and under the ivytwined branches of the chandelier the Christmas table was spread. They had come home a little late and still dinner was not ready: but it would be ready in a jiffy, his mother had said. They were waiting for the door to open and for the servants to come in, holding the big dishes covered with their heavy metal covers.

All were waiting: Uncle Charles, who sat far away in the shadow of the window, Dante and Mr Casey, who sat in the easychairs at either side of the hearth, Stephen, seated on a chair between them, his feet resting on the toasted boss. Mr Dedalus looked at himself in the pierglass above the mantelpiece, waxed out his moustache ends and then, parting his coat tails, stood with his back to the glowing fire: and still from time to time he withdrew a hand from his coat tail to wax out one of his moustache ends. Mr Casey leaned his head to one side and, smiling, tapped the gland of his neck with his fingers. And Stephen smiled too for he knew now that it was not true that Mr Casey had a purse of silver in his throat. He smiled to think how the silvery noise which Mr Casey used to make had deceived him. And when he had tried to open Mr Casey's hand to see if the purse of silver was hidden there he had seen that the fingers could not be straightened out: and Mr Casey had told him that he had got those three cramped fingers making a birthday present for Queen Victoria.

Mr Casey tapped the gland of his neck and smiled at Stephen with sleepy eyes: and Mr Dedalus said to him:

—Yes. Well now, that's all right. O, we had a good walk, hadn't we, John? Yes . . . I wonder if there's any likelihood of dinner this evening. Yes. . . .Oh, well now, we got a good breath of ozone round the Head today. Ay, bedad.

He turned to Dante and said:

—You didn't stir out at all, Mrs Riordan?

Dante frowned and said shortly:

—No.

Mr Dedalus dropped his coat tails and went over to the sideboard. He brought forth a great stone jar of whisky from the locker and

[1] From *A Portrait of the Artist as a Young Man*, New York, 1916.

filled the decanter slowly, bending now and then to see how much he had poured in. Then replacing the jar in the locker he poured a little of the whisky into two glasses, added a little water and came back with them to the fireplace.

—A thimbleful, John, he said, just to whet your appetite.

Mr Casey took the glass, drank, and placed it near him on the mantelpiece. Then he said:

—Well, I can't help thinking of our friend Christopher manufacturing . . .

He broke into a fit of laughter and coughing and added:

—. . . manufacturing that champagne for those fellows.

Mr Dedalus laughed loudly.

—Is it Christy? he said. There's more cunning in one of those warts on his bald head than in a pack of jack foxes.

He inclined his head, closed his eyes, and, licking his lips profusely, began to speak with the voice of the hotel keeper.

—And he has such a soft mouth when he's speaking to you, don't you know. He's very moist and watery about the dewlaps, God bless him.

Mr Casey was still struggling through his fit of coughing and laughter. Stephen, seeing and hearing the hotel keeper through his father's face and voice, laughed.

Mr Dedalus put up his eyeglass and, staring down at him, said quietly and kindly:

—What are you laughing at, you little puppy, you?

The servants entered and placed the dishes on the table. Mrs Dedalus followed and the places were arranged.

—Sit over, she said.

Mr Dedalus went to the end of the table and said:

—Now, Mrs Riordan, sit over. John, sit you down, my hearty.

He looked round to where Uncle Charles sat and said:

—Now then, sir, there's a bird here waiting for you.

When all had taken their seats he laid his hand on the cover and then said quickly, withdrawing it:

—Now, Stephen.

Stephen stood up in his place to say the grace before meals:

*Bless us, O Lord, and these Thy gifts which through Thy bounty we are about to receive through Christ our Lord. Amen.*

All blessed themselves and Mr Dedalus with a sigh of pleasure lifted from the dish the heavy cover pearled around the edge with glistening drops.

Stephen looked at the plump turkey which had lain, trussed and skewered, on the kitchen table. He knew that his father had paid a guinea for it in Dunn's of D'Olier Street and that the man had prodded it often at the breastbone to show how good it was: and he remembered the man's voice when he had said:

—Take that one, sir. That's the real Ally Daly.

Why did Mr Barrett in Clongowes[1] call his pandybat[2] a turkey? But Clongowes was far away: and the warm heavy smell of turkey and ham and celery rose from the plates and dishes and the great fire was banked high and red in the grate and the green ivy and red holly made you feel so happy and when dinner was ended the big plum pudding would be carried in, studded with peeled almonds and sprigs of holly, with bluish fire running around it and a little green flag flying from the top.

It was his first Christmas dinner and he thought of his little brothers and sisters who were waiting in the nursery, as he had often waited, till the pudding came. The deep low collar and the Eton jacket made him feel queer and oldish: and that morning when his mother had brought him down to the parlour, dressed for mass, his father had cried. That was because he was thinking of his own father. And Uncle Charles had said so too.

Mr Dedalus covered the dish and began to eat hungrily. Then he said:

—Poor old Christy, he's nearly lopsided now with roguery.

—Simon, said Mrs Dedalus, you haven't given Mrs Riordan any sauce.

Mr Dedalus seized the sauceboat.

—Haven't I? he cried. Mrs Riordan, pity the poor blind.

Dante covered her plate with her hands and said:

—No, thanks.

Mr Dedalus turned to Uncle Charles.

—How are you off, sir?

—Right as the mail, Simon.

—You, John?

---

[1] Clongowes Wood College, County Kildare, the preparatory school which Stephen Dedalus is attending.
[2] The disciplinary rod.

—I'm all right. Go on yourself.

—Mary? Here, Stephen, here's something to make your hair curl.

He poured sauce freely over Stephen's plate and set the boat again on the table. Then he asked Uncle Charles was it tender. Uncle Charles could not speak because his mouth was full; but he nodded that it was.

—That was a good answer our friend made to the canon. What? said Mr Dedalus.

—I didn't think he had that much in him, said Mr Casey.

—*I'll pay your dues, father, when you cease turning the house of God into a pollingbooth.*

—A nice answer, said Dante, for any man calling himself a catholic to give to his priest.

—They have only themselves to blame, said Mr Dedalus suavely. If they took a fool's advice they would confine their attention to religion.

—It is religion, Dante said. They are doing their duty in warning the people.

—We go to the house of God, Mr Casey said, in all humility to pray to our Maker and not to hear election addresses.

—It is religion, Dante said again. They are right. They must direct their flocks.

—And preach politics from the altar, is it? asked Mr Dedalus.

—Certainly, said Dante. It is a question of public morality. A priest would not be a priest if he did not tell his flock what is right and what is wrong.

Mrs Dedalus laid down her knife and fork, saying:

—For pity sake and for pity sake let us have no political discussion on this day of all days in the year.

—Quite right, ma'am, said Uncle Charles. Now Simon, that's quite enough now. Not another word now.

—Yes, yes, said Mr Dedalus quickly.

He uncovered the dish boldly and said:

—Now then, who's for more turkey?

Nobody answered. Dante said:

—Nice language for any catholic to use!

—Mrs Riordan, I appeal to you, said Mrs Dedalus, to let the matter drop now.

Dante turned on her and said:

—And am I to sit here and listen to the pastors of my church being flouted?

—Nobody is saying a word against them, said Mr Dedalus, so long as they don't meddle in politics.

—The bishops and priests of Ireland have spoken, said Dante, and they must be obeyed.

—Let them leave politics alone, said Mr Casey, or the people may leave their church alone.

—You hear? said Dante, turning to Mrs Dedalus.

—Mr Casey! Simon! said Mrs Dedalus, let it end now.

—Too bad! Too bad! said Uncle Charles.

—What? cried Mr Dedalus. Were we to desert him at the bidding of the English people?

—He was no longer worthy to lead, said Dante. He was a public sinner.

—We are all sinners and black sinners, said Mr Casey coldly.

—*Woe be to the man by whom the scandal cometh!* said Mrs. Riordan. *It would be better for him that a millstone were tied about his neck and that he were cast into the depths of the sea rather than that he should scandalise one of these, my least little ones.* That is the language of the Holy Ghost.

—And very bad language if you ask me, said Mr Dedalus coolly.

—Simon! Simon! said Uncle Charles. The boy.

—Yes, yes, said Mr Dedalus. I meant about the . . . I was thinking about the bad language of that railway porter. Well now, that's all right. Here, Stephen, show me your plate, old chap. Eat away now. Here.

He heaped up the food on Stephen's plate and served Uncle Charles and Mr Casey to large pieces of turkey and splashes of sauce. Mrs Dedalus was eating little and Dante sat with her hands in her lap. She was red in the face. Mr Dedalus rooted with the carvers at the end of the dish and said:

—There's a tasty bit here we call the pope's nose. If any lady or gentleman . . .

He held a piece of fowl up on the prong of the carvingfork. Nobody spoke. He put it on his own plate, saying:

—Well, you can't say but you were asked. I think I had better eat it myself because I'm not well in my health lately.

He winked at Stephen and, replacing the dishcover, began to eat again.

There was a silence while he ate. Then he said:

—Well now, the day kept up fine after all. There were plenty of strangers down too.

Nobody spoke. He said again:

—I think there were more strangers down than last Christmas.

He looked round at the others whose faces were bent towards their plates and, receiving no reply, waited for a moment and said bitterly:

—Well, my Christmas dinner has been spoiled anyhow.

—There could be neither luck nor grace, Dante said, in a house where there is no respect for the pastors of the church.

Mr Dedalus threw his knife and fork noisily on his plate.

—Respect! he said. Is it for Billy with the lip or for the tub of guts up in Armagh? Respect!

—Princes of the church, said Mr Casey with slow scorn.

—Lord Leitrim's coachman, yes, said Mr Dedalus.

—They are the Lord's anointed, Dante said. They are an honour to their country.

—Tub of guts, said Mr Dedalus coarsely. He has a handsome face, mind you, in repose. You should see that fellow lapping up his bacon and cabbage of a cold winter's day. O Johnny!

He twisted his features into a grimace of heavy bestiality and made a lapping noise with his lips.

—Really, Simon, you should not speak that way before Stephen. It's not right.

—O, he'll remember all this when he grows up, said Dante hotly —the language he heard against God and religion and priests in his own home.

—Let him remember too, cried Mr Casey to her from across the table, the language with which the priests and the priests' pawns broke Parnell's heart and hounded him into his grave. Let him remember that too when he grows up.

—Sons of bitches! cried Mr Dedalus. When he was down they turned on him to betray him and rend him like rats in a sewer. Lowlived dogs! And they look it! By Christ, they look it!

—They behaved rightly, cried Dante. They obeyed their bishops and their priests. Honour to them!

—Well, it is perfectly dreadful to say that not even for one day in the year, said Mrs Dedalus, can we be free from these dreadful disputes!

Uncle Charles raised his hands mildly and said:

—Come now, come now, come now! Can we not have our opinions whatever they are without this bad temper and this bad language? It is too bad surely.

Mrs Dedalus spoke to Dante in a low voice but Dante said loudly:

—I will not say nothing. I will defend my church and my religion when it is insulted and spit on by renegade catholics.

Mr Casey pushed his plate rudely into the middle of the table and, resting his elbows before him, said in a hoarse voice to his host:

—Tell me, did I tell you that story about a very famous spit?

—You did not, John, said Mr Dedalus.

Why then, said Mr Casey, it is a most instructive story. It happened not long ago in the county Wicklow where we are now.

He broke off and, turning towards Dante, said with quiet indignation:

—And I may tell you, ma'am, that I, if you mean me, am no renegade catholic. I am a catholic as my father was and his father before him and his father before him again when we gave up our lives rather than sell our faith.

—The more shame to you now, Dante said, to speak as you do.

—The story, John, said Mr Dedalus smiling. Let us have the story anyhow.

—Catholic indeed! repeated Dante ironically. The blackest protestant in the land would not speak the language I have heard this evening.

Mr Dedalus began to sway his head to and fro, crooning like a country singer.

—I am no protestant, I tell you again, said Mr Casey flushing.

Mr Dedalus, still crooning and swaying his head, began to sing in a grunting nasal tone:

> *O, come all you Roman catholics*
> *That never went to mass.*

He took up his knife and fork again in good humour and set to eating, saying to Mr Casey:

—Let us have the story, John. It will help us to digest.

Stephen looked with affection at Mr Casey's face which stared across the table over his joined hands. He liked to sit near him at the fire, looking up at his dark fierce face. But his dark eyes were never fierce and his slow voice was good to listen to. But why was he then against the priests? Because Dante must be right then. But he had heard his father say she was a spoiled nun and that she had come out of the convent in the Alleghanies when her brother had got the money from the savages for the trinkets and the chainies. Perhaps that made her severe against Parnell. And she did not like him to play with Eileen because Eileen was a protestant and when she was young she knew children that used to play with protestants and the protestants used to make fun of the litany of the Blessed Virgin. *Tower of Ivory*, they used to say, *House of Gold!* How could a woman be a tower of ivory or a house of gold? Who was right then? And he remembered the evening in the infirmary in Clongowes, the dark waters, the light at the pierhead and the moan of sorrow from the people when they had heard.

Eileen had long white hands. One evening when playing tig she had put her hands over his eyes: long and white and thin and cold and soft. That was ivory: a cold white thing. That was the meaning of *Tower of Ivory*.

—The story is very short and sweet, Mr Casey said. It was one day down in Arklow, a cold bitter day, not long before the chief died. May God have mercy on him!

He closed his eyes wearily and paused. Mr Dedalus took a bone from his plate and tore some meat from it with his teeth, saying:

—Before he was killed, you mean.

Mr Casey opened his eyes, sighed and went on:

—It was down in Arklow one day. We were down there at a meeting and after the meeting was over we had to make our way to the railway station through the crowd. Such booing and baaing, man, you never heard. They called us all the names in the world. Well there was one old lady, and a drunken old harridan she was surely, that paid all her attention to me. She kept dancing along beside me in the mud bawling and screaming into my face: *Priest-hunter! The Paris Funds! Mr Fox! Kitty O'Shea!* [1]

—And what did you do, John? asked Mr Dedalus.

—I let her bawl away, said Mr. Casey. It was a cold day and to keep up my heart I had (saving your presence, ma'am) a quid of

---

[1] Kathleen O'Shea was the mistress of Parnell and wife of another Irish member of Parliament whose bringing of divorce proceedings caused Parnell's political downfall.

Tullamore in my mouth and sure I couldn't say a word in any case because my mouth was full of tobacco juice.

—Well, John?

—Well. I let her bawl away, to her heart's content, *Kitty O'Shea* and the rest of it till at last she called that lady a name that I won't sully this Christmas board nor your ears, ma'am, nor my own lips by repeating.

He paused. Mr Dedalus, lifting his head from the bone, asked:

—And what did you do, John?

—Do! said Mr Casey. She stuck her ugly old face up at me when she said it and I had my mouth full of tobacco juice. I bent down to her and *Phth!* says I to her like that.

He turned aside and made the act of spitting.

—*Phth!* says I to her like that, right into her eye.

He clapped a hand to his eye and gave a hoarse scream of pain.

—*O Jesus, Mary and Joseph!* says she. *I'm blinded! I'm blinded and drownded!*

He stopped in a fit of coughing and laughter, repeating:

—*I'm blinded entirely.*

Mr Dedalus laughed loudly and lay back in his chair while Uncle Charles swayed his head to and fro.

Dante looked terribly angry and repeated while they laughed:

—Very nice! Ha! Very nice!

It was not nice about the spit in the woman's eye.

But what was the name the woman had called Kitty O'Shea that Mr Casey would not repeat? He thought of Mr Casey walking through the crowds of people and making speeches from a wagonette. That was what he had been in prison for and he remembered that one night Sergeant O'Neill had come to the house and had stood in the hall, talking in a low voice with his father and chewing nervously at the chinstrap of his cap. And that night Mr Casey had not gone to Dublin by train but a car had come to the door and he had heard his father say something about the Cabinteely road.

He was for Ireland and Parnell and so was his father: and so was Dante too for one night at the band on the esplanade she had hit a gentleman on the head with her umbrella because he had taken off his hat when the band played *God save the Queen* at the end.

Mr Dedalus gave a snort of contempt.

—Ah, John, he said. It is true for them. We are an unfortunate priestridden race and always were and always will be till the end of the chapter.

Uncle Charles shook his head, saying:

—A bad business! A bad business:

Mr Dedalus repeated:

—A priestridden Godforsaken race!

He pointed to the portrait of his grandfather on the wall to his right.

—Do you see that old chap up there, John? he said. He was a good Irishman when there was no money in the job. He was condemned to death as a whiteboy. But he had a saying about our clerical friends, that he would never let one of them put his two feet under his mahogany.

Dante broke in angrily:

—If we are a priestridden race we ought to be proud of it! They are the apple of God's eye. *Touch them not,* says Christ, *for they are the apple of My eye.*

—And can we not love our country then? asked Mr Casey. Are we not to follow the man that was born to lead us?

—A traitor to his country! replied Dante. A traitor, an adulterer! The priests were right to abandon him. The priests were always the true friends of Ireland.

—Were they, faith? said Mr Casey.

He threw his fist on the table and, frowning angrily, protruded one finger after another.

—Didn't the bishops of Ireland betray us in the time of the union[1] when Bishop Lanigan presented an address of loyalty to the Marquess Cornwallis? Didn't the bishops and priests sell the aspirations of their country in 1829 in return for catholic emancipation?[2] Didn't they denounce the fenian movement[3] from the pulpit and in the confession box? And didn't they dishonour the ashes of Terence Bellew MacManus?[4]

His face was glowing with anger and Stephen felt the glow rise

---

[1] The Act of Union (1800) disestablished the Irish Parliament. Ireland received instead a number of seats in the British Parliament.
[2] The Catholic Emancipation Act (1829) admitted Catholics to Parliament, to Commissions in the Services, and to the Inner Bar.
[3] The Fenians were members of the Irish Republican Brotherhood, a secret revolutionary organization which attempted an uprising in 1867.
[4] A hero of the 1848 uprising.

to his own cheek as the spoken words thrilled him. Mr Dedalus uttered a guffaw of coarse scorn.

—O, by God, he cried, I forgot little old Paul Cullen! Another apple of God's eye!

Dante bent across the table and cried to Mr Casey:

—Right! Right! They were always right! God and morality and religion come first.

Mrs Dedalus, seeing her excitement, said to her:

—Mrs Riordan, don't excite yourself answering them.

—God and religion before everything! Dante cried. God and religion before the world!

Mr Casey raised his clenched fist and brought it down on the table with a crash.

—Very well then, he shouted hoarsely, if it comes to that, no God for Ireland!

—John! John! cried Mr Dedalus, seizing his guest by the coat sleeve.

Dante stared across the table, her cheeks shaking. Mr Casey struggled up from his chair and bent across the table towards her, scraping the air from before his eyes with one hand as though he were tearing aside a cobweb.

—No God for Ireland! he cried. We have had too much God in Ireland. Away with God!

—Blasphemer! Devil! screamed Dante, starting to her feet and almost spitting in his face.

Uncle Charles and Mr Dedalus pulled Mr Casey back into his chair again, talking to him from both sides reasonably. He stared before him out of his dark flaming eyes, repeating:

—Away with God, I say!

Dante shoved her chair violently aside and left the table, upsetting her napkinring which rolled slowly along the carpet and came to rest against the foot of an easychair. Mrs Dedalus rose quickly and followed her towards the door. At the door Dante turned round violently and shouted down the room, her cheeks flushed and quivering with rage:

—Devil out of hell! We won! We crushed him to death! Fiend!

The door slammed behind her.

Mr Casey, freeing his arms from his holders, suddenly bowed his head on his hands with a sob of pain.

—Poor Parnell! he cried loudly. My dead king!

He sobbed loudly and bitterly.

Stephen, raising his terrorstricken face, saw that his father's eyes were full of tears.

PADRAIC COLUM

# Maelshaughlinn at the Fair[1]

'Today,' Maelshaughlinn said, 'I'm the lonesome poor fellow, without father or mother, a girl's promise, nor my own little horse.' They walked along with him, and he began to tell them of his adventure.

Penitentially he began it, but he expanded with the swelling narrative. 'This time last week,' he said, 'when I was there playing for you all I had no thought of parting with my own little horse. The English wanted beasts for a war, and the farmers about here were making horses out of the sweepings of the knackers' yards, and taking horses out of ha'penny lucky-bags to sell them to them. Yesterday morning I took out my own little beast and faced for Arvach fair. I met the dealer on the road. He was an Englishman, and, above all nations on the face of the earth, the English are the easiest to deal with in regard of horses. I mentioned the price—it was an honest price, but none of our own people would have taken the offer in any reasonable way. An Irishman would have cursed into his hat, so that he might shake the curses out over my head. The Englishman took on to consider it, and my heart went threshing my ribs. Then he gave me my price; he paid me in hard, weighty, golden sovereigns, and went away, taking the little horse with him.

'I sat down on the side of the ditch to take a breath. Now you'll say that I ought to have gone back to work, and I'll say that I agree with you. But no man can be wise at all times. Anyway, I was sitting on a ditch, with a lark singing over every foot of ground, and nothing before me but the glory of the day. A girl came along the road, and, on my soul, I never saw a girl walking so finely. "She'll be a head above any girl in the fair," I said, "and may God keep the brightness on her head." "God save you, Maelshaughlinn," said the girl. "God save you, my jewel," said I. I stood up to look after her, for a fine woman walking finely is above all the sights that man ever saw. Then a few lads passed, whistling and swinging their sticks. "God give you a good day," said the lads. "God give you luck, boys," said I. And there was I, swinging my stick after the lads, and heading for the fair.

'"Never go into a fair where you've no business." That's an oul'

---

[1] From *Castle Conquer*, New York, 1923, re-edited by the author.

saying and a wise saying, but never forget that neither man nor immortal can be wise at all times. Satan fell from Heaven, Adam was cast out of Paradise, and even my uncle broke his pledge.

'When I came into the fair there was a fiddler playing behind a tinker's cart. I had a shilling to spend in the town, and so I went into Flynn's and asked for a cordial. A few most respectable men came in then, and I asked them to take a treat from me. Well, one drank and another drank, and then Rose Heffernan came into the shop with her brother. Young Heffernan sent the glasses round, and then I asked Rose to take a glass of wine, and I put down a sovereign on the counter. The fiddler was coming down the street, and I sent a young lad out to him with silver. I stood for a while talking with Rose, and I heard the word go round the shop concerning myself. It was soon settled that I had got a legacy. The people there never heard of any legacies except American legacies, and so they put my fortune down to an uncle who had died, they thought, in the States. Now I didn't want Rose to think that my money was a common legacy out of the States, so by half-words I gave them to understand that I had got my fortune out of Mexico. Mind you, I wasn't far out when I spoke of Mexico, for I had a grand-uncle who went out there, and his picture is in the house this present minute.

'Well, after the talk of the Mexican legacy went round, I couldn't take any treats from the people, though indeed plenty were offered me. I asked everyone to drink again. I think the crowds of the world stood before Flynn's counter. A big Connachtman held up what he said was a Mexican dollar, and I took it out of his hand and gave it to Rose Heffernan. I paid him for it too; it comes into my mind now that I paid him for it twice.

'There's not on the track of the sun a place to come near Arvach on the day of a fair. A man came along leading a black horse, and the size of the horse and the eyes of the horse would terrify you. There was a drift of sheep going by, and the fleece of each was worth gold. There were tinkers with their carts of shining tins, as ugly and as quarrelsome fellows as ever beat each other to death in a ditch, and there were the powerful men, with the tight mouths, and the eyes that could judge of a beast, and the dark handsome women from the mountains. To crown all, a piper came into the town by the other end, and his music was enough to put the blood like a mill-race through your heart. The music of the piper, I think, would have made the beasts walk out of the fair on their hind legs, if the music of the fiddler didn't charm them to be still. Judith O'Reilly and Baun Driscoll were on the road, and Rose Heffernan was talking to them. Judith O'Reilly has the best wit and the best discourse of any woman within the four seas of Ireland, and she said to the other girls as I came up, "Faith, girls, the good of the mission will be gone from us since Maelshaughlinn came into the fair, for the young women will be talking about him, and not about the sermon coming home from the mission." "It's not the best manners," said I, "to treat girls to a glass across a counter, but come into a shop," said I, "and let me pay for your fancy." Well, I got Baun Driscoll to ask for a net for her hair. They don't sell these nets less than by the dozen, so I bought a dozen nets for Baun's hair. I bought ear-rings and brooches, dream-books and fortune-books, buckles and combs, and I thought I had spent no more money than I'd thank you for picking off the ground. A tinker woman came in and offered to tell the girls their fortunes, and I had to cross her hand with silver.

'I came out on the street after that, and took a few turns through the fair. The noise and the crowd were getting on my mind, and I couldn't think with any satisfaction, so I went into Mrs. Molloy's, and sat for a while in the snug. I had peace and quiet there, and I began to plan out what I would do with my money. I had a notion of going into Clooney on Tuesday, and buying a few sheep to put on my little fields, and of taking a good craftsman home from the fair, a man who could put fine thatch on my little house so that Nannie would like to be looking at it. I made up my mind to have the doors and windows shining with paint, to plant a few trees before the door, and to have a growing calf in the garden before the house. In a while, I thought, I could have another little horse to be my comfort and my consolation. I wasn't drinking anything heavier than light ale, so I thought the whole thing out quietly. After a while I got up, bid good-bye to Mrs. Molloy, and stood at the door to watch the fair.

'There was a man just before me with the pea and thimble, and I never saw a trick-of-the-loop with less sense of the game. He was winning money right and left, but that was because the young fellows before him were like motherless calves. Just to expose the man I put down a few pence on the board. In a short time I had fleeced my showman. He took up his board and went away, leaving me shillings the winner.

'I stood on the edge of the pavement wondering what I could do that would be the beating of the things I had done already. By this time the fiddler and the piper were drawing nigh to each other, and there was a musician to the right of me, and a musician to the left of me. I sent silver to each, and told them to cease playing as I had something to say. I got up on a cart and shook my hat to get silence. I said "I'm going to bid the musicians play in the market square, and the man who gets the best worth out of his instrument will get a prize from me." The words were no sooner out of my mouth than men, women, and children made for the market square like two-year-olds let loose.

'You'd like the looks of the fiddler, but the piper was a black-a'vised fellow that kept a troop of tinkers about him. It was the piper who said "Master, what's the prize to be?" Before I had time to think the fiddler was up and talking. "He's of the oul' ancient race," said the fiddler, "and he'll give the prize that the Irish nobility gave to the musicians—a calf, the finest calf in the fair, a white calf with skin as soft as the fine mist on the ground, a calf so gentle that the smoothest field under it would look as rough as a bog." And the fiddler was that lifted out of himself that he nearly leapt over a cart. Somebody pushed in a young calf, and then I sat down on a stone, for there was no use in saying anything or trying to hear anything after that. The fiddler played first, and I was nearly taken out of my trouble when I heard him, for he was a real man of art, and he played as if he was playing before a king, with the light of heaven on his face. The piper was spending his silver on the tinkers, and they were all deep in drink when he began to play. At the first sound of his pipes an old tinkerwoman fell into a trance. It was powerful, but the men had to tie him up with a straw rope, else the horses would have kicked the slates off the market-house roof. Nobody was quiet after that. There was a thousand men before me offering to sell me ten thousand calves, each calf whiter than the one before. There was one party round the fiddler and another party round the piper. I think it was the fiddler that won; anyway, he had the strongest backing, for they hoisted the calf on to a cart, and they put the fiddler beside it, and the two of them would have got out of the crowd, only the tinkers cut the traces of the cart. I was saved by a few hardy men who carried me through the market-house and into Flynn's by a back way, and there I paid for the calf.

'When I came out of Flynn's the people were going home quiet enough. I got a lift on Fardy's cart, and everybody, I think, wanted me to come to Clooney on Tuesday next. I think I'd have got out of Arvach with safety, only a dead-drunk tinker wakened up and knew me, and he gave a screech that brought the piper hot-foot after me. First of all the piper cursed me. He had a bad tongue, and he put on me the blackest, bitterest curses you ever heard in your life. Then he lifted up the pipes, and he gave a blast that went through me like a spear of ice. The man that sold me the calf gave me a luck-penny back, and that's all the money I brought out of Arvach fair.

'"Never go into the fair where you have no business." That's a wise saying, and it's a saying that will be a guide to me for the rest of the days of my life.'

DANIEL CORKERY

# Rock-of-the-Mass[1]

I

DUNERLING EAST was its name, the model farm in all that countryside. Only after many years it had come to be so; and Michael Hodnett, the farmer who had made it so, lay fast asleep in his armchair on the right-hand side of the front door. As of its own weight his big strong-looking head had sunk itself deep into his deep chest. The sunshine of the October afternoon was depositing itself lavishly upon him, thickening upon him, it seemed, while slumber bound him there, so huge and lumpish, so inert, so old and fallen. Dunerling East just now was looking more model-like than ever before. The house itself had had all its sashes, its doors, its timber work painted afresh; its blinds and curtains had been renewed; its ivy growths trimmed; and the whole farm, even its farthest fields and screening thickets, spoke of the same well-being, the same skilful management. The sleeper might lawfully take his rest, his spirit had so indisputably established itself everywhere within the far-flung mearings. Even were he to pass away in his sleep, and stranger folk, as reckless as might be, to come into possession of the land, many years must needs go by before Dunerling East became hail-fellow-well-met with the farms round about it, shaggy and scraggy as they were, waterlogged in the bottoms and bleached or perished on the uplands, unsheltered by larch or beech.

All this cleaning up had been done in preparation for the first coming together, after many years, of all or nearly all that were left of the family. The arrival of Stephen Hodnett, the third youngest son, from the States had been the occasion. He had brought with him his young wife, and, as well, an elder sister of hers, a young widow, for whose distraction indeed the voyage had been undertaken. Of all the sons of the house this son, Stephen, perhaps had done best: he was now manager of a large bakery store in New York. But the brother next to him in years, Finnbarr, had done well too. He was come, also accompanied by his wife,

---
[1] From *The Wager and Other Stories*, New York, 1950. First Published in *The Stormy Hills*, Dublin, 1929.

from Kerry, where he managed a very successful creamery. The son to whom the care of the farm had fallen, to whom indeed the farm now legally belonged, Nicholas by name, had maintained it in the condition to which his father, this old man asleep in the chair, had brought it; perhaps he had even bettered it, but, of course, the land had been got into good heart long before it fell to his turn to till it. Nicholas, though older than Stephen or Finnbarr, had never married: he would wait until his father's death. The only other son of the house was up in Dublin—Father Philip Hodnett, a curate in St. Multose's parish. He was the one living member who was not at present in Dunerling East. Within the house lurked somewhere the eldest living of all the old man's family, Ellen, the second child born to him. She looked old enough to be the mother of those mentioned, even of Nicholas, the eldest of them. She was sixty and looked more. Her cheeks were thin and haggard, colourless, her hair grey, and her eyes stared blankly at the life moving before them as if it were but an insipid and shadowy thing when compared with what moved restlessly, perhaps even disastrously, within the labyrinths of her own brain. On her the mothering of the whole family had fallen when Michael Hodnett buried his wife in Inchigeela.

From the feet of the sleeping figure the ground fell away downwards to a bracken-covered stream. Beyond the bracken it rose again; much more suddenly however, so suddenly indeed that the red earth showed in patches through the tangled greenery. Those reddish patches looked like corbels supporting the cornice-like ledge of the upward-sloping grazing grounds above. Just now, along that sun-drenched ledge, a procession of shapely deep-uddered cattle was moving from left to right, the beasts in single file or in pairs or groups, deliberately pacing. Thirty-one milkers were to pass like that, making for the unseen bridgeway across the stream in the hollow. Presently they would dip from sight and again be discovered in the tree-covered passage trailing up towards the milking sheds, the rich sunshine catching their deep-coloured flanks and slipping swiftly and suddenly from their horns and moving limbs. Anyone who had ever come to know how deeply the sight of that afternoon ritual used to thrill the old man, now so sunken in his sleep, could hardly forbear from waking him to witness it.

Behind the cattle sauntered Nicholas. His head was bent, and in his right hand a sliver from a sally tree lazily switched the cattle along. Although a working day, he was dressed in his Sunday clothes. His gaiters were new, rich brown in colour, and had straps about them; his boots also were new and brown. All day since morning his visitors, his brothers Stephen and Finnbarr and their people, had been away motoring in the hills towards the west—around Keimaneigh and Gougane Barra—and he had found the idle day as long as a week. 'Stay where you are,' he had said to one of the labourers who were digging out potatoes in the fields behind the house; 'stay where you are, and I'll bring them in,' and he was glad of the chance to go through the fields one after another until he was come to where the impatient cattle were gathered, anxious and crying, about the fastened gate. Their time for milking was overdue, and they needed no urging towards the sheds. When they were safe across the bridge he left them to themselves: by that time the first of them were already head-bound in the stalls. Closing a gate behind them he made diagonally up the sloping field. At his approach his father suddenly raised his head.

' 'Tisn't Sunday?' he said, and then, recollecting himself: 'They haven't come back yet?'

'Any moment now,' Nicholas answered. He then turned his back on him and gazed across the countryside where a couple of roads could be picked out. The weather had been very fine for some weeks and little clouds of sunny dust wavered above them.

'Are the cows in?'

'I'm after bringing them across.'

'Is Finn after looking at them?'

'Yes, he'd get rid of the Kerry, he said.'

'Didn't I tell you! Didn't I tell you!'

He had filled up with passionate life. As he blurted out the words, he raised his heavy stick in his blob of a hand. Nicholas glanced away from him, and again searched the countryside with his eyes:

'They won't be long now: 'tis as good for us to be going in!'

He put his arm beneath his father's. He lifted him. The old man's right foot trailed uselessly along the ground. But his thoughts were on the cows:

' 'Tis often I do be thinking on the two beasts we had and we coming hither from Carrig-an-afrinn. Scraggy animals, scraggy, splintery things.'

II

Mrs. Muntleberry, the young American widow, and her sister, Stephen's wife, were both thoughtful gentle women; it was plain in their quiet eyes, their quiet faces. After the meal, homely in its way, but good, they now sat bent forward earnestly staring at the old man who was keeping himself so alert and upright in their midst, ruling the roomful with word, gesture, glance. Of his power of work, of his downrightness, they had, of course, often heard from Stephen: in Stephen himself they had found something of the same character: until today, however, they had not realized how timid in him were the strong traits of his father's character. They had been motoring in a world of rock-strewn hillsides; they had swung into glens that struck them cold, so bleak they were, so stern-looking even in the softest tide of the year. Carrig-an-afrinn they had not actually passed through: it would have meant threading slowly up many twisting narrow hillside bohereens in which their car could scarcely turn: perhaps also Stephen had not cared to have them actually come upon the bedraggled homestead—little else than a hut—from which the Hodnetts had risen. They had, however, gone as close to it as the main road allowed them, had seen, and felt almost in their bones, the niggardliness of life among those hillsides of tumultuously tumbled rocks. That wayfaring in bleak places had brought them to understand Stephen's father; even if he were no different this evening, had remained as he had been ever since their arrival—drowsing between sleep and waking, mumbling old songs, sometimes losing count of who they were— they would nevertheless because of this day's excursioning have more deeply understood the tough timber that was in him. But all the evening he had been quite different. The names of old places, of old families, had been in the air about him. He grew young to hear them, to bethink himself of them. They had aroused him. Stephen had forgotten many of them. He would say, ''Tis north from Inchimore,' and his father had enough to catch at: ''Tis the Sweeneys were north of Inchimore. 'Tis Keimcorravoola you're thinking of.' And of itself either the place name or the family name was enough to spur the old man's brain to all manner of recollections. So it had been with him all the evening, alert as they had never seen him, a new man, and not a bit modest about his powers when young, whether at fighting or hurley or farming. His stick was in the air about their heads: and once without warning he had brought it down on the table, making them all leap to their feet and grab at the dancing tea things—down with all his force lest they should not clearly understand how final had been the stroke with which he had felled a Twomey man in a faction fight at Ballyvourney. And when in speaking of some other ancient wrestling bout he referred to his adversary's trunk, how he had clasped it and could not be shaken off, the two women looked at himself, alert yet lumpish before them, noted his body's girth and depth, and felt that 'trunk' was indeed the right word to use of such bodies.

Finn's wife, the Kerry woman, was enjoying it heartily. Her Kerry eyes, deep hazel in colour, were dancing to watch the old man's antics, grotesque and unashamed, were dancing also to note the quiet, stilly, well-schooled Americans opening the doors of their minds to comprehend adequately this rough-hewn chunk of peasant human kind. The expression coming and going on the faces of the three sons, she also enjoyed. She watched to see how they took every gross countryside word and phrase that would unconcernedly break from the old man's lips. Her own Finn she held for the cleverest of them because he had the gift of slipping in some contrary word that would excite his father to still more energetic gestures or more emphatic expletives.

In time old Hodnett had exhausted the tale of the great deeds of his prime: a gentler mood descended on him: 'Like you'd shut that door, or like you'd tear a page out of a book and throw it from you, I put an end to all that folly and wildness. Listen now, let ye listen now, this is what happened and I coming over here from Carrig-an-afrinn.'

III

He told them how on that day which of all the days of his long life stood most clearly before his mind, he had made swiftly home from the fair at Macroom. Michael, his eldest son, a boy of about sixteen years at the time, had hastened down from the potato field on hearing the jolting of the returning cart. As usual with him he examined his father's face. He was at first relieved and then puzzled to discover from it that his father had scarcely taken any drink during that long day of absence from home, of boon companionship in the town. More than that, his father was going about in a sort of constraint, as if he had had something happen to him while away, or had come upon some tidings which now must be dwelt upon within himself. Yet he did not seem gloomy or rough, and he could be gloomy enough and rough enough when the fit was on him. Often and often after a long day in Macroom, he had turned in from the road, flung the reins on the horse's back, and without preface begun to heap malediction on the head of the villain pig buyers from Cork with whom he had been trafficking. To-day he was different:

'Is Johnny above?' he questioned his son as he loosed the horse from the shafts. The boy nodded.

'Up with you then. Up with you while there's light in it.'

The boy, climbing up to where he had left old Johnny, who was helping them to dig out the potatoes, was still wondering over the mood his father had returned in.

'What is he after getting?' the labourer asked him.

'Four ten.'

'He'd get more in Dunmanway last Friday.'

'He's satisfied. He says he is.'

Before long they saw himself coming through the gap. 'What way are they up along there?' he asked them, nodding his head towards the sloping ridges they had been digging.

'Small enough then,' his son answered.

The father stooped and picked up one of the potatoes. He began to rub it between his finger and thumb.

'They'll be different in Dunerling East,' his son said, complacently tossing his head.

As if that were the last thing he had expected to come from the boy's lips his father looked sharply at him.

Dunerling East was the farm he had been for several weeks negotiating the purchase of. It was ten miles away towards the east, ten miles farther from the hardness of the mountains, the cold rains, the winds, the mists. In those ten miles the barren hills that separate Cork from Kerry had space to stretch themselves out, to die away into gentle curves, to become soft and kind. So curiously his father had looked at him the boy wondered if something had not happened to upset the purchase. He was not surprised when his father, peering at him under his brows, spoke to him in a cold voice:

'The potatoes might be better. The grass too. And the cattle. Only the Hodnetts might be worse.'

Michael glanced at the labourer, then back at his father. He found him still skinning the potato with his hard thumb. But he could also see, young and all as he was, that his thought was not on the potato, big or little. The labourer had once more bent to his digging; and Michael, withdrawing his eyes slowly from his father's face, spat on his hands and gripped the spade: yet he could not resist saying:

'They're poor return for a man's labour.'

He scornfully touched the potatoes hither and thither with the tip of his spade, freeing them from the turfy earth, black and fibrous. They were indeed small.

The father seemed careless of their size. He stood there, a solid piece of humankind, huge, big-faced, with small round eyes, shrewd-looking, not unhumorous. He said: 'If I hadn't that fifty pound paid on it, I'd put Dunerling East out of my mind.'

He turned from them and made for the gap through which he had come. They questioned each other with their eyes and then stared after the earnest figure until the broken hillside swallowed it up.

It was a soft, still evening. Here and there a yellow leaf fell from the few scattered birch trees growing among the rocks which, on every side, surrounded the little patch of tilled earth. A robin was singing quietly, patiently—the robin's way. The air was moist; and because a break in the weather seemed near, they worked on, the two of them, until they could no longer see the potatoes. Then Johnny straightened his back, lit his bit of a pipe and shouldered his spade. Together both of them, taking long slow strides, made down towards the house. Suddenly the boy said:

'Look at himself!'

They saw him standing upright on one of the numerous ledges of rock which broke up through the surface of their stubble field. He had his back towards them. He was staring downwards, overlooking his own land, towards the straggling road, staring intently, although little except the general shape of the countryside could now be distinguished.

'Is it? Is it him at all, do you think?' old Johnny asked.

' 'Tis sure,' Michael answered. Then he cried out, sending the vowels travelling:

# ROCK-OF-THE-MASS

'Ho-o! Ho-o!'

His father turned and after a pause began to make towards them. Awkwardly they awaited him; they did not know what to say. He said:

' 'Tis at Carrig-an-afrinn I was looking.'

Carrig-an-afrinn was the name of the whole farm, a large district, mostly a hillside of rock and heather; they were standing in Carrig-an-afrinn: but they understood that what he had been looking at was Carrig-an-afrinn itself—the Rock of the Mass, the isolated pile of rock by the roadside from which the ploughland had got its name.

They walked beside him then.

'I'm after hearing a thing this day I never knew before,' he said, and then stopping up and examining their faces he added:

' 'Tis what I heard: In any place where a Mass was ever celebrated an angel is set on guard for ever and ever.'

' 'Twould be a likely thing,' the old labourer said.

'I never heard tell of it,' Michael said.

'Myself never heard tell of it,' his father snapped out.

' 'Twould be a likely thing,' old Johnny said again, 'remembering the nature of the Mass.'

'Who was it told you?'

'One who was well able!'

The three of them turned and looked downwards towards the rough altar-like pile of rock where Mass used to be said secretly for the people in the penal days when it was felony to celebrate Mass in public. Only the pile of rock was visible, and that not distinctly, so thick the light had become.

'You know very well that Mass was said there hundreds and hundreds of times.'

The father spoke to his son almost as if he had been contradicting him. He received no reply. Then he added in a suddenly-deepened voice:

'Likely that place is thick with angels.'

The labourer uncovered his head without a word.

In stillness they stood there on the lonely hillside; and in the darkening rocks and fields there was no sound, except of small things stirring at their feet. After a few seconds, the farmer faced again for the house. Without thought, it seemed, he avoided the rocky patches. Indeed even at midnight he could have walked unperplexed through those rockstrewn fields. The others heard his voice coming to them in the dusk over his shoulder:

' 'Tis a strange thing that I never heard of that wonder until I'm just leaving the place for good and all. A strange thing; and it frightens me.'

When they found themselves free of the fields and in the *poirse*, or laneway, that led up to their yard, he said again with sudden passion:

' 'Tis a small thing would make me break the bargain.'

The boy flared up:

'A queer thing you'd do then.'

'Queer!'

'It may be years and years before we have the chance of buying a place like Dunerling East.'

He spoke the name as if that of itself were worth the purchase money.

'Carrig-an-afrinn is not a bad farm at all.'

At this Michael burst out:

'Johnny, do you hear him? And he raging and swearing at them rocks as long as I remember—raging and swearing at them as if they were living men and they against him! And he praying to God to take us out of it before his eyes were blinded with the years. And now he'd stay in it!'

Of that incident and of the night that followed it, the old man, forty-four years after, remembered every detail—every word spoken and every thought that disturbed his rest.

IV

Having given them to understand all that has been here set down, he went on: 'I tell ye, I didn't shut an eye that night, only thinking and thinking and I twisting and turning in my bed. When I looked back through the years and thought of what a poor place Carrig-an-afrinn was—there was scarcely a poorer—'twas little less than a miracle to have me able to buy out a big place like this—a place that had been in the grip of the gentry for hundreds and hundreds of years. And up to that I always thought that I had no one to thank for it but myself—the strength of my own four bones, but after what I was told in Macroom that day, how did I know but that maybe it was in Carrig-an-afrinn itself the luck was? and that good fortune would follow whoever lived in it like good Christians, and that maybe secret friends would help them, and they at the ploughing or waiting up in the nights for a calf to come, or a young foal or a litter of bonamhs itself? Who knows? Who knows? And what puzzled me entirely was that I should be ignorant of all that until the very day, as you may say, I was settled on leaving it. It frightened me. While we were in Carrig-an-afrinn no great sickness befell us or misfortune, except a horse to break his leg or a cow to miscarry or a thing like that; and I thought of all the strong farmers I was after seeing in my time, and they having to sell off their places and scatter away with themselves into Cork or Dublin, or maybe to America itself. Sure this place itself, if ye saw it when we came hither, the dirty state 'twas in, the land gone back, exhausted, and the house and sheds broken, everything in wrack and ruin—'tisn't with a light heart ye'd undertake it. But of course only for that I couldn't have bought it all at all. So I said to myself, and I listening to the clock ticking at the foot of the bed, I'm undertaking that big place, and maybe 'twon't thrive with me. And if it fails me, where am I? That's what I said. If it fails me, where am I? I tell ye, I was broken with thinking on it. And all the time, and this is the queerest thing of all, I heard someone saying, "Carrig-an-afrinn, Carrig-an-afrinn. Carrig-an-afrinn, Carrig-an-afrinn." And not once or twice or three times, but all the night long, and I thinking and thinking. Of course, there was no one saying it at all, only maybe the beating of my own heart to be like a tune. But I was afraid. I thought maybe music might come rising up to me out of the *cummer*, and it thronged with angels, or a great light come striking in at the window. And sure enough at last I started up and I cried out, "There it is! There it is!" But 'twas no unnatural light at all, only the dawn of day breaking in on top of me. 'Tis how I was after dozing off for a little while unknown to myself, and I woke up suddenly in confusion and dread.

'That morning and I rising up my limbs were like wisps of straw. I was terrified of the long day before me, and that's the worst way a man can be. But when I came out and stood in the broad sun, and 'twas a morning of white frost, I drew in the air to myself, and I took courage to see my poor animals grazing so peacefully on the hill, just like what you see in a picture. If the big farms broke the men that were born to softness and luxury, Dunerling East wouldn't break me, and I reared hard and tough! That's what I said, with great daring in my breast.

'Not long after that we moved our handful of stock east to this place. I laughed to picture the two scraggy beasts, and all the deep feeding of Dunerling East to themselves. And that same evening myself and Michael, Michael that's dead, God rest him, went over and hither and in and out through the length and breadth of this estate and round by the boundary ditch; and 'tis a thing I will not forget till my dying day what he said to me, my son Michael, that same evening, and we killed from the exertion. He stopped and looked up at me before he spoke:

' "Look," he said, "why have you your hands like that?"

'My two hands, clenched, and stiff, *stiff*, like you'd have them in a fight, watching your opponent, watching to catch him off his guard, or for fear he'd spring on you. That's how I had my hands. And 'twas natural for me to have my hands like that, for what I was saying to myself was: I'll break it! I'll break it! And I was saying that because if I didn't break it I was sport for the world. Like a bully at a fair I was, going about my own land the first day I walked it!'

In recalling the labours of his prime he had become a new man. When they looked at him they saw not the stricken old creature whose days were now spent in the drowsy sun, but the indomitable peasant who had wrung enough from the rocks of Carrig-an-afrinn to buy out Dunerling East from the broken gentry, and who then had reclaimed Dunerling East from its hundred years of neglect. When he could not find words to fit his thought his left eye would close tight, and one big tooth, that he still retained in his upper gum, would dig itself into his lower lip, until the struggling words came to him. And they noticed that his two hands had clenched themselves long before he needed them clenched to illustrate how it was he had tackled the reclamation of the sluggish marshlands of Dunerling East. His own sons quailed before him. The two Americans had drawn together, shoulder touching shoulder: they watched him across the table with wide eyes, their faces drawn. The creamery manager from Kerry dared no longer to put in his jocose word. He wished rather to be able to draw off the old man's mind from this renewal of the unrelenting warfare of his manhood. But no such word could he find:

his father was abroad in a passion of fictitious energy: it would indeed be a potent word that could stay or hinder him. Every now and then the timbers of the heavy chair groaned beneath the movement of his awkward carcase. He was unconscious of it. It meant as little to him as his own exposing of the shifts, the meanness, the overreaching, the unintentional tyranny he had practised while he worked out his dream.

'My poor boy, Michael,' he went on, 'was the first to go. He was great for the work. For a boy that was slight and tender I never saw the equal of him. 'Twas how he had great spirit. A word was worse to him than a whip. When we'd be cutting the deep grass in the inches, half a dozen of us all in a line, and he'd fall behind, being young and soft, I'd say to him, "Ah, Michael," I'd say, "God be with the little fields of Carrig-an-afrinn, you could cut them with a scissors"; that would bring him into line I tell ye. The poor boy. 'Twas pleurisy he got first; and we thought nothing of it: maybe we didn't take it in time. But what chance was there to be taking him into Macroom to the doctor, or from one holy well to another? The time he died too, it could not be a worse time. Herself was after bringing little Stephen into the world—and before she was rightly fit the harvest was upon us; and 'twas the first real good harvest we got out of Dunerling East. When I looked at it standing I said: " 'Tis my doing and my boy's doing, and my boy is dead!" But herself was better than any man in a harvest field. Maybe she overworked herself. She wasn't the one to give in. The day she was laid in Inchigeela 'tis well if I didn't curse the day I came hither from Carrig-an-afrinn. Father O'Herlihy was standing by. "The Lord giveth and the Lord taketh away," he said, and his hand on my shoulder, and 'twas all I could do to say "Amen" to that. There I was with a houseful of them about me and only herself, that poor thing inside, only herself to do a ha'porth for them. I don't blame her for being as she is—knitting, knitting, knitting, or looking into the fire and thinking—I don't blame her at all. What she went through after that, pulling and hauling and slashing and digging, 'twould kill half a parish. Up at four in the morning getting the pigs' food ready, or the mash for the calves; and milking the cows, and keeping the children from mischief. The only other girl I had, she was second after Nicholas there, I lost her just when she was rising to be of use to me. 'Twas a fever she got from drinking bad water. And the two boys I lost after that, one of them was the terror of the countryside. He turned against herself inside; he was wild and fiery. Mind you, he dared me to my face. He said what no son of mine ever said to me. I won't repeat it. I won't repeat it. The eyes were blazing in his head. The delicacy was showing in him. The brains of that kind is a terror. He went off with himself and left me in the lurch. And then he came back— one twelvemonth after—and 'tis like herself inside he was. Only bitter, and the health wasted. The same as any labouring boy he walked in to me. Not a shirt to his back, or what you could call a shirt. He shamed me, the way he was. And he dying on his feet. 'Twas a dead man was patrolling the fields for months before he took to the bed entirely. And I daren't say a word to him because he had a tongue would raise blisters on a withered skull. The other poor boy, his name was Laurence, was a handsome boy. Everybody used to say he'd make a handsome priest. But sure at that time I couldn't dream of such a thing. It takes a power of money to make a priest. He died of pneumonia, and not a thing to happen to him only a bit of a pain in his side. Only for that I hadn't time to be thinking on it I'd be saying there was a curse on top of us; but no, because year after year the produce was getting better and better; and in spite of all the sickness and deaths and funerals— and funerals are the greatest robbers of all—the money began to rise up on me, and I could get in the help when I wanted it—'tis often I had a score of men at the harvesting, besides what neighbors would come of themselves. Those there (he nodded at his three sons, all of them sitting with bowed heads, with pipes in their mouths, not daring to break across his speech)—those there, they only knew the end of the story. Ah boys, ah boys, the softness comes out of the hard, like the apple from the old twisted bough, and 'tis only the softness ye knew of. And then in the end of it all, the great change in the laws came about and I bought out the land and 'twas my own, as you may say. The day I signed for it, a sort of lowness came over me, and I remembered my poor dead boy saying, and he my first born. "Look how you're holding your hands!" Let ye listen to me now; I cried down my eyes to my own self that night because herself was in the clay. That poor soul inside, you might as well be talking to a cock of last year's hay, dull with the weather and the sun, you'd only get "yes" and "no" for an answer. And the rest—those here—were too young. What I did was: to send over for old Johnny, old Johnny I would have helping me an odd time in Carrig-an-afrinn, to come over to me, that I wanted him. God knows all I wanted him for was to keep me in talk against that terrible fit of darkness and loneliness would fall on me again. He came over and together we walked the land, every perch of it. He knew what sort it was when we came hither, and 'tis he was the man could tell the difference. What he said was, now, let ye listen, let ye listen to what he said, and he only a poor ignorant man: "After all, 'twas only a rush in your hand!" Now that was what a wrestler would say of another in the old times, "He was only a rush in my hands," meaning by that that he had no trouble in breaking him. That was great praise and yet it couldn't rouse me for I was after walking the land field after field; and one field I found was the same as another. That's a strange thing to say. Maybe 'tis how I was old and I coming hither. 'Twas in Carrig-an-afrinn I grew up. There was never a man drove a handful of cattle of his own rearing to a fair that hadn't some favourite among them; and he sees the dealers come round them and strike them and push them, and knock them about, and he knows that they are all the same to him, that he sees no difference between one and the other, except one to be riper than another, or a thing like that. And 'twas so with me. I walked my fields and one was the same as another. There was no corner of them that I could make for when the darkness would fall on me. I knew 'twould be different in Carrig-an-afrinn. And that's what I was thinking of when old Johnny said to me that after all Dunerling East was like a rush in my hands. I opened my heart to him. I told him I felt like the steward of the place, and not like the owner of it. He said 'twasn't right for me to be saying a thing like that, that 'tis down on my two knees I should be and I thanking God, but that the heart of man was only a sieve. The very next day and I still going about like that, counting up the great improvements I was after making since I came in, and arguing with myself, and yet dissatisfied with myself, I wandered up the hillside opposite, and whatever turn I gave or however the sun was shining, 'twas about four o'clock in the evening, I saw Doughill and Douse rising up in the west and snug away down at the foot of Doughill I saw a little shoulder of a hill, and "Honour of God," I said, "if that isn't Carrig-an-afrinn itself!" Let ye listen to me, I fell down on my knees in thanksgiving like a pagan would be praying to the sun! And from that day forward I had a spot of land to turn to when the black fit would fall on me. Mind you, 'twas a good time I found it, for while I was breaking the place and wrestling with it I didn't think of anything else, only to be going ahead and going ahead. But 'twas different when I could pay for the help, and I had time to look around, and the rent wasn't half what it used to be. Ah, the soft comes out of the hard, and the little lambs from the hailstones. If Dunerling East is a good property now 'twas many the hot sweat fell into the sods of its ridges. But sure them that could witness to that, they're all dead, except that poor thing inside, God help her; and 'tis she took the burden as well as the next.'

V

His voice fell and the glow of exaltation vanished from his features.

'They're all dead?' Mrs. Muntleberry said, quietly.

'Dead!' the old man answered her, and having said it, his head kept on moving slightly up and down to some pulse in his brain.

'Then these,' she said again, and indicated the three sons with her eyes, 'these are a second crop.'

'A second crop,' he said, 'except that poor creature inside.'

They found it hard to break the silence that had fallen on them. Earlier in the evening both Stephen and Finnbarr had been, as one might say, themselves—Stephen, the bakery manager, a hustler, and Finn, the creamery manager, not unable to hustle also. But as the story went on, and, though they had heard it all in a fragmentary way before, they had scattered from the homestead without ever having made themselves one clear unified picture of what coming hither from Carrig-an-afrinn had meant for their father. They had never seen him clearly as one who would not be beaten, no matter who by his side fell worsted in the struggle. Only the oldest of them, Nicholas, the farmer, could recall any of the dead, and he was a soft quiet creature, strong of body, but inactive of brain. The one mood, however, had come upon all three; they were not much different from what they had been before they had scattered, from what they had been when Ellen would still them by whispering the one word: 'Himself.'

It was Finn who first rose. He went and lightly beat the inverted bowl of his pipe against the bars of the fire grate. Then drawing with his strong lips through the empty stem, head in the air, he took a few steps towards the window and drew back one of the heavy curtains. The colour, the glow had gone from the day. Instead there were now everywhere filmy veils of mist. Beyond the sunken stream the hillside looked near and the screens of trees, ash and beech, seemed tall and unsubstantial: in the twilight softness the homely features of farming and cattle trafficking were hidden away. The scene was gracious and tender. They all stared through the window.

'It looks fine, so it does,' Finn said.

'It does; it looks fine,' his wife added, letting the words die away. The old man was listening.

' 'Tis what a traveller said, and he a man that had recourse to all the places in the world, 'tis what he said: that it had the appearance of a gentleman's place out and out.'

Mrs. Muntleberry turned and let her eyes rest softly on his face: 'Still you liked Carrig-an-afrinn too?'

He lifted his head; such words he had not expected: 'Ah, ma'am, ah, ma'am,' he said, making an effort to move his trunk so that he might face her directly, 'Carrig-an-afrinn, Carrig-an-afrinn, the very name of it, the very name of it!' And he stared at her with a fixity of expression that frightened her, stared at her in blank hopelessness of saying even the first word of all the words that rioted within him. He recovered. He swept his hand across his brow, toying with his hair. 'They tell me Pat Leary, who's there ever since we came hither—there's only the one year between us—they tell me he sits in the *cummer* an odd hour at the foot of the rock where the Chalice used to stand. His work is done. He'll catch hold of plough nor snaffle no more, same as myself. 'Tis a great comfort to him to sit there.'

She was sorry she had brought Carrig-an-afrinn back to his thoughts.

'The heart is a sieve,' she said, watching him to see how he'd take old Johnny's word. But he was not so easily moved from mood to mood.

'You saw it to-day?' he questioned earnestly, 'You saw it to-day?'

'We went quite close to it. Did we see the Rock itself? Did we, Stephen?'

Stephen said as boldly as he could:

'Oh yes, we went quite close to it.'

'Ah, ma'am, Nicholas there, some day he's going to pack me into the motor car; and over with us to see it. It can't be long I have to stay.'

Before he had finished, almost indeed at the first word, Nicholas had risen and quietly taken down a shabby-looking old violin from the top of a heavy cupboard that stood in the corner. While they all looked at him he tuned it without a word, and to him tuning was no easy task. Then he stretched his two long legs out from the chair and began to play.

The instrument was almost toneless, and the player almost without skill. He played the old songs of the countryside, going straight from one to another, from a *caoine*[1] to a reel, from a love song to a lively rattle about cattle-dealing or horse racing. Nerveless, toneless, yet the playing was quiet; and it was the music itself, and not the instrument or musician was in the fiddler's mind. After a while this the Americans noticed. Then the scratching, the imperfect intonation, the incongruous transition from melody to melody disturbed them but little. He played on and on; and they were all thankful to him. The room darkened, but the sky was still bright. At last he lowered the fiddle, a string needed to be tightened. The others at once broke into talk. Mrs. Muntleberry was nearest to Nicholas. She had her eyes on the instrument. He noticed how at the word 'Carrig-an-afrinn' which was again on the lips of the old man, her head had raised itself. He whispered to her, without taking his eyes off his task:

'He'll never see Carrig-an-afrinn again.'

'No?' she whispered back, with a little gasp of surprise.

'Nor nobody else,' he went on; 'they're after blasting it away to make the road wider: 'tis how two lorries couldn't pass on it. I'm in dread of my life he'll find it out. 'Twould be terrible.'

She turned her eyes on the old man's face. The music had restored him again to confidence. His eyes were glowing. He had re-established his mastery. 'Let ye listen, let ye listen to me,' he was saying.

---

[1] *Keen,* lament for the dead.

*Part III*

# OUR OWN RED BLOOD

*O plain as plain can be
There's nothing but our own red blood
Can make a right Rose Tree.*
                    W. B. YEATS

AE (GEORGE RUSSELL)

# The Dublin Strike

### An Open Letter to the Employers[1]

Sirs,—I address this warning to you, the aristocracy of industry in this city, because, like all aristocracies, you tend to grow blind in long authority, and to be unaware that you and your class and its every action are being considered and judged day by day by those who have power to shake or overturn the whole social order, and whose restlessness in poverty to-day is making our industrial civilisation stir like a quaking bog. You do not seem to realise that your assumption that you are answerable to yourselves alone for your actions in the industries you control is one that becomes less and less tolerable in a world so crowded with necessitous life. Some of you have helped Irish farmers to upset a landed aristocracy in this island, an aristocracy richer and more powerful in its sphere than you are in yours, with its roots deep in history. They, too, as a class, though not all of them, were scornful or neglectful of the workers in the industry by which they profited; and to many who knew them in their pride of place and thought them all-powerful they are already becoming a memory, the good disappearing together with the bad. If they had done their duty by those from whose labour came their wealth, they might have continued unquestioned in power and prestige for centuries to come. The relation of landlord and tenant is not an ideal one, but any relations in a social order will endure if there is infused into them some of that spirit of human sympathy which qualifies life for immortality. Despotisms endure while they are benevolent, and aristocracies while 'noblesse oblige' is not a phrase to be referred to with a cynical smile. Even an oligarchy might be permanent if the spirit of human kindness, which harmonises all things otherwise incompatible, is present.

You do not seem to read history so as to learn its lessons. That you are an uncultivated class was obvious from recent utterances of some of you upon art. That you are incompetent men in the sphere in which you arrogate imperial powers is certain, because for many years, long before the present uprising of labour, your enterprises have been dwindling in the regard of investors, and

---
[1] Dublin, October 6, 1913.

this while you have carried them on in the cheapest labour market in these islands, with a labour reserve always hungry and ready to accept any pittance. You are bad citizens, for we rarely, if ever, hear of the wealthy among you endowing your city with the munificent gifts which it is the pride of merchant princes in other cities to offer, and Irishmen not of your city, who offer to supply the wants left by your lack of generosity, are met with derision and abuse. Those who have economic power have civic power also, yet you have not used the power that was yours to right what was wrong in the evil administration of this city. You have allowed the poor to be herded together so that one thinks of certain places in Dublin as of a pestilence. There are twenty thousand rooms, in each of which live entire families, and sometimes more, where no functions of the body can be concealed, and delicacy and modesty are creatures that are stifled ere they are born. The obvious duty of you in regard to these things you might have left undone, and it be imputed to ignorance or forgetfulness; but your collective and conscious action as a class in the present labour dispute has revealed you to the world in so malign an aspect that the mirror must be held up to you, so that you may see yourselves as every humane person sees you.

The conception of yourselves as altogether virtuous and wronged is, I assure you, not at all the one which onlookers hold of you. No doubt, you have rights on your side. No doubt, some of you suffered without just cause. But nothing which has been done to you cries aloud to Heaven for condemnation as your own actions. Let me show you how it seems to those who have followed critically the dispute, trying to weigh in a balance the rights and wrongs. You were within the rights society allows you when you locked out your men and insisted on the fixing of some principle to adjust your future relations with labour when the policy of labour made it impossible for some of you to carry on your enterprises. Labour desired the fixing of some such principle as much as you did. But, having once decided on such a step, knowing how many thousands of men, women and children, nearly one-third of the population of this city, would be affected, you should not have let one day have passed without unremitting endeavours to find a solution of the problem.

What did you do? The representatives of labour unions in Great Britain met you, and you made of them a preposterous, an impossible demand, and because they would not accede to it you closed the Conference: you refused to meet them further: you assumed that no other guarantees than those you asked were possible, and you determined deliberately, in cold anger, to starve out one-third of the population of this city, to break the manhood of the men by the sight of the suffering of their wives and the hunger of their children. We read in the Dark Ages of the rack and thumbscrew. But these iniquities were hidden and concealed from the knowledge of men in dungeons and torture-chambers. Even in the Dark Ages humanity could not endure the sight of such suffering, and it learnt of such misuse of power by slow degrees, through rumour, and when it was certain it razed its Bastilles to their foundations. It remained for the twentieth century and the capital city of Ireland to see an oligarchy of four hundred masters deciding openly upon starving one hundred thousand people, and refusing to consider any solution except that fixed by their pride. You, masters, asked men to do that which masters of labour in any other city in these islands had not dared to do. You insolently demanded of those men who were members of a trade union that they should resign from that union; and from those who were not members you insisted on a vow that they would never join it.

Your insolence and ignorance of the rights conceded to workers universally in the modern world were incredible, and as great as your inhumanity. If you had between you collectively a portion of human soul as large as a threepenny bit, you would have sat night and day with the representatives of labour, trying this or that solution of the trouble, mindful of the women and children, who at least were innocent of wrong against you. But no! You reminded labour you could always have your three square meals a day while it went hungry. You went into conference again with the representatives of the State, because, dull as you are, you know public opinion would not stand your holding out. You chose as your spokesman the bitterest tongue that ever wagged in this island, and then, when an award was made by men who have an experience in industrial matters a thousand times transcending yours, who have settled disputes in industries so great that the sum of your petty enterprises would not equal them, you withdraw again, and will not agree to accept their solution, and fall back again on your devilish policy of starvation. Cry aloud to Heaven for new souls! The souls you have got cast upon the screen of publicity appear like the horrid and writhing creatures enlarged from the insect world, and revealed to us by the cinematograph.

You may succeed in your policy and ensure your own damnation by your victory. The men whose manhood you have broken will loathe you, and will always be brooding and scheming to strike a fresh blow. The children will be taught to curse you. The infant being moulded in the womb will have breathed into its starved body the vitality of hate. It is not they—it is you who are blind Samsons pulling down the pillars of the social order. You are sounding the death-knell of autocracy in industry. There was autocracy in political life, and it was superseded by democracy. So surely will democratic power wrest from you the control of industry. The fate of you, the aristocracy of industry, will be as the fate of the aristocracy of land if you do not show that you have some humanity still among you. Humanity abhors, above all things, a vacuum in itself, and your class will be cut off from humanity as the surgeon cuts the cancer and alien growth from the body. Be warned ere it is too late.

## A Plea for the Workers[1]

I stand for the first time on a public platform in this country. The great generosity of English to Irish workers has obliterated the memory of many an ancient tale of wrong. I come from Dublin, where most extraordinary things have been happening. Humanity long dumb there has found a voice, it has its prophet and its martyrs. We no longer know people by the old signs and the old shams. People are to us either human or sub-human. They are either on the side of those who are fighting for human conditions in labour or they are with those who are trying to degrade it and thrust it into the abyss.

Ah! but I forgot; there has sprung up a third party, who are super-human beings, they have so little concern for the body at all, that they assert it is better for children to be starved than to be moved from the Christian atmosphere of the Dublin slums.[2]

---

[1] A speech delivered at the Royal Albert Hall, London, November 1, 1913.

[2] When English and Scottish sympathizers offered temporary homes to the children of the strikers, the 'super-human beings,' mostly pietistic women, objected on the grounds that the children would lose their religion by staying in non-Catholic homes. An angry mob actually prevented a party of several hundred children from boarding a ship at the North Wall and the two women in charge of the children were actually arrested for attempted kidnapping.

Dublin is the most Christian city in these islands. Its tottering tenements are holy. The spiritual atmosphere which pervades them is ample compensation for the diseases which are there and the food which is not there. If any poor parents think otherwise, and would send their children for a little from that earthly paradise, they will find the docks and railway stations barred by these superhuman beings and by the police, and they are pitched head-long out of the station, set upon and beaten, and their children snatched from them. A Dublin labourer has no rights in his own children. You see if these children were even for a little out of the slums, they would get discontented with their poor homes, so a very holy man has said. Once getting full meals, they might be so inconsiderate as to ask for them all their lives. They might destroy the interesting experiments carried on in Dublin for generations to find out how closely human beings can be packed together, on how little a human being can live, and what is the minimum wage his employer need pay him. James Larkin interrupted these interesting experiments towards the evolution of the underman and he is in gaol. You have no idea what the slums in Dublin are like. There are more than 20,000 families, each living in one room. Many of these dens are so horrible, so unsanitary, so overrun with vermin, that doctors tell me that the only condition on which a man can purchase sleep is that he is drugged with drink. The Psalmist says the Lord gives sleep to his beloved, but in these Dublin dens men and women must pay the devil his price for a little of that peace of God. It maddens one to think that man the immortal, man the divine, should exist in such degradation, that his heirship of the ages should be the life of a brute.

I beseech you not to forsake these men who are out on strike. They may have been to blame for many an action. The masters may perhaps justifiably complain of things done and undone. But if the masters have rights by the light of reason and for the moment, the men are right by the light of spirit and for eternity. This labour uprising in Ireland is the despairing effort of humanity to raise itself out of a dismal swamp of disease and poverty. James Larkin may have been an indiscreet leader. He may have committed blunders, but I believe in the sight of heaven the crimes are all on the other side. If our Courts of Justice were courts of humanity, the masters of Dublin would be in the dock charged with criminal conspiracy, their crime that they tried to starve out one-third of the people in Dublin, to break their hearts, and degrade their manhood, for the greatest crime against humanity is its own degradation.

The men have always been willing to submit their case to arbitration, but the masters refuse to meet them. They refuse to consult with your trades union leaders. They would not abide by the Askwith report. They refused to hear of prominent Irishmen acting as arbitrators. They said scornfully of the Peace Committee that it was only interfering. They say they are not fighting trades unionism, but they refuse point blank to meet the Trades Council in Dublin. They want their own way absolutely. These Shylocks of industry want their pound of flesh starved from off the bones of the workers. They think their employees have no rights as human beings, no spirit whose dignity can be abased.

You have no idea what labour in Ireland, which fights for the bare means of human support, is up against. The autocrats of industry can let loose upon them the wild beasts that kill in the name of the State. They can let loose upon them a horde of wild fanatics who will rend them in the name of God. The men have been deserted by those who were their natural leaders. For ten weeks the miserable creatures who misrepresent them in Parliament kept silent. When they were up for the first time in their lives against anything real they scurried back like rats to their hole. These cacklers about self-government had no word to say on the politics of their own city, but after ten weeks of silence they came out with six lines of a letter signed by all the six poltroons. They disclaimed all responsibility for what is happening in the city and county they represent. It was no concern of theirs; but they would agree to anything the Archbishop might say! Are they not heroic prodigies! Dublin is looking on these men with alien eyes. It was thought they were democrats; we have found out they were only democratic blatherers.

We are entering from to-day on a long battle in Ireland. The masters have flung down a challenge to the workers. The Irish aristocracy were equally scornful of the workers in the land, and the landlords of land are going or have gone. The landlords of industry will have disappeared from Ireland when the battle begun this year is ended. Democratic control of industry will replace the autocracy which exists to-day. We are working for the co-operative commonwealth to make it the Irish policy of the future, and I ask you to stand by the men who are beginning the struggle. There is good human material there.

I have often despaired over Dublin, which John Mitchel called a city of genteel dastards and bellowing slaves, but a man[1] has arisen who has lifted the curtain which veiled from us the real manhood in the city of Dublin. Nearly all the manhood is found among obscure myriads who are paid from five to twenty-five shillings per week. The men who will sacrifice anything for a principle get rarer and rarer above that limit of wealth. I am a literary man, a lover of ideas, but I have found few people in my life who would sacrifice anything for a principle. Yet in Dublin, when the masters issued that humiliating document, asking men—on penalty of dismissal—to swear never to join a trades union, thousands of men who had no connection with the Irish Transport Workers—many among them personally hostile to that organisation—refused to obey. They would not sign away their freedom, their right to choose their own heroes and their own ideas. Most of these men had no strike funds to fall back on. They had wives and children depending on them. Quietly and grimly they took through hunger the path to the Heavenly City. They stand silently about the streets. God alone knows what is passing in the heart of these men. Nobody in the Press in Dublin has said a word about it. Nobody has praised them, no one has put a crown upon their brows. Yet these men are the true heroes of Ireland to-day, they are the descendants of Oscar, Cuchulain, the heroes of our ancient stories. For all their tattered garments, I recognise in these obscure men a majesty of spirit. It is in these workers in the towns and in the men in the cabins in the country that the hope of Ireland lies. The poor have always helped each other, and it is they who listen eagerly to the preachers of a social order based on brotherhood and co-operation.

I am a literary man and not a manual worker. I am but a voice, while they are the deed and the being, but I would be ashamed ever in my life again to speak of an ideal if I did not stand by these men and say of them what I hold to be true. If you back them up to-day they will be able to fight their own battles to-morrow, and perhaps to give you an example. I beseech you not to forsake these men.

[1] James Larkin.

PADRAIC PEARSE

# The Coming Revolution[1]

NOVEMBER 1913

I HAVE come to the conclusion that the Gaelic League, as the Gaelic League, is a spent force; and I am glad of it. I do not mean that no work remains for the Gaelic League, or that the Gaelic League is no longer equal to work; I mean that the vital work to be done in the new Ireland will be done not so much by the Gaelic League itself as by men and movements that have sprung from the Gaelic League or have received from the Gaelic League a new baptism and a new life of grace. The Gaelic League was no reed shaken by the wind, no mere *vox clamantis*: it was a prophet and more than a prophet. But it was not the Messiah. I do not know if the Messiah has yet come, and I am not sure that there will be any visible and personal Messiah in this redemption: the people itself will perhaps be its own Messiah, the people labouring, scourged, crowned with thorns, agonising and dying, to rise again immortal and impassible. For peoples are divine and are the only things that can properly be spoken of under figures drawn from the divine epos.

If we do not believe in the divinity of our people we have had no business, or very little, all these years in the Gaelic League. In fact, if we had not believed in the divinity of our people, we should in all probability not have gone into the Gaelic League at all. We should have made our peace with the devil, and perhaps might have found him a very decent sort; for he liberally rewards with attorney-generalships, bank balances, villa residences, and so forth, the great and the little who serve him well. Now, we did not turn our backs upon all these desirable things for the sake of *is* and *tá*.[2] We did it for the sake of Ireland. In other words, we had one and all of us (at least, I had, and I hope that all you had) an ulterior motive in joining the Gaelic League. We never meant to be Gaelic Leaguers and nothing more than Gaelic Leaguers. We meant to do something for Ireland, each in his own way. Our

---

[1] From *Collected Works of Padraic H. Pearse: Political Writings and Speeches*, Dublin & London, 1922.
[2] *Is* and *tá* are the two forms of the verb *to be* in Gaelic and constitute a stumbling block for the beginner.

234

## THE COMING REVOLUTION

Gaelic League time was to be our tutelage: we had first to learn to know Ireland, to read the lineaments of her face, to understand the accents of her voice; to re-possess ourselves, disinherited as we were, of her spirit and mind, re-enter into our mystical birthright. For this we went to school to the Gaelic League. It was a good school, and we love its name and will champion its fame throughout all the days of our later fighting and striving. But we do not propose to remain schoolboys for ever.

I have often said (quoting, I think, Herbert Spencer) that education should be a preparation for complete living; and I say now that our Gaelic League education ought to have been a preparation for our complete living as Irish Nationalists. In proportion as we have been faithful and diligent Gaelic Leaguers, our work as Irish Nationalists (by which term I mean people who accept the ideal of, and work for, the realisation of an Irish Nation, by whatever means) will be earnest and thorough, a valiant and worthy fighting, not the mere carrying out of a ritual. As to what your work as an Irish Nationalist is to be, I cannot conjecture; I know what mine is to be, and would have you know yours and buckle yourself to it. And it may be (nay, it is) that yours and mine will lead us to a common meeting-place, and that on a certain day we shall stand together, with many more beside us, ready for a greater adventure than any of us has yet had, a trial and a triumph to be endured and achieved in common.

This is what I meant when I said that our work henceforward must be done less and less through the Gaelic League and more and more through the groups and the individuals that have arisen, or are arising, out of the Gaelic League. There will be in the Ireland of the next few years a multitudinous activity of Freedom Clubs, Young Republican Parties, Labour Organisations, Socialist Groups, and what not; bewildering enterprises undertaken by sane persons and insane persons, by good men and bad men, many of them seemingly contradictory, some mutually destructive, yet all tending towards a common objective, and that objective: the Irish Revolution.

For if there is one thing that has become plainer than another it is that when the seven men met in O'Connell Street to found the Gaelic League, they were commencing, had there been a Liancourt there to make the epigram, not a revolt, but a revolution. The work of the Gaelic League, its appointed work, was that; and the work is done. To every generation its deed. The deed of the generation that has now reached middle life was the Gaelic League, the beginning of the Irish Revolution. Let our generation not shirk *its* deed, which is to accomplish the revolution.

I believe that the national movement of which the Gaelic League has been the soul has reached the point which O'Connell's movement had reached at the close of the series of monster meetings. Indeed, I believe that our movement reached that point a few years ago—say, at the conclusion of the fight for Essential Irish; and I said so at the time. The moment was ripe then for a new Young Ireland Party, with a forward policy; and we have lost much by our hesitation. I propose in all seriousness that we hesitate no longer—that we push on. I propose that we leave Conciliation Hall behind us and go into the Irish Confederation.

Whenever Dr. Hyde, at a meeting at which I have had a chance of speaking after him, has produced his dove of peace, I have always been careful to produce my sword; and to tantalise him by saying that the Gaelic League has brought into Ireland 'Not Peace, but a Sword.' But this does not show any fundamental difference of outlook between my leader and me; for while he is thinking of peace between brother-Irishmen, I am thinking of the sword-point between banded Irishmen and the foreign force that occupies Ireland, and his peace is necessary to my war. It is evident that there can be no peace between the body politic and a foreign substance that has intruded itself into its system; between them war only until the foreign substance is expelled or assimilated.

Whether Home Rule means a loosening or a tightening of England's grip upon Ireland remains yet to be seen. But the coming of Home Rule, if come it does, will make no material difference in the nature of the work that lies before us; it will affect only the means we are to employ, our plan of campaign. There remains, under Home Rule as in its absence, the substantial task of achieving the Irish Nation. I do not think it is going to be achieved without stress and trial, without suffering and bloodshed; at any rate, it is not going to be achieved without *work*. Our business here and now is to get ourselves into harness for such work as has to be done.

I hold that before we can do any work, any *men's* work, we must first realise ourselves as men. Whatever comes to Ireland she needs men. And we of this generation are not in any real sense men, for we suffer things that men do not suffer, and we seek to redress grievances by means which men do not employ. We have, for instance, allowed ourselves to be disarmed; and, now that we have the chance of re-arming, we are not seizing it. Professor Eoin Mac Neill pointed out last week that we have at this moment an opportunity of rectifying the capital error we made when we allowed ourselves to be disarmed; and such opportunities, he reminds us, do not always come back to nations.

A thing that stands demonstrable is that nationhood is not achieved otherwise than in arms: in one or two instances there may have been no actual bloodshed, but the arms were there and the ability to use them. Ireland unarmed will attain just as much freedom as it is convenient for England to give her; Ireland armed will attain ultimately just as much freedom as she wants. These are matters which may not concern the Gaelic League, as a body; but they concern every member of the Gaelic League, and every man and woman of Ireland. I urged much of this five or six years ago in addresses to the Ard-Chraobh:[1] but the League was too busy with resolutions to think of revolution, and the only resolution that a member of the League could not come to was the resolution to be a man. My fellow-Leaguers had not (and have not) apprehended that the thing which cannot defend itself, even though it may wear trousers, is no man.

I am glad, then, that the North has 'begun.' I am glad that the Orangemen have armed, for it is a goodly thing to see arms in Irish hands. I should like to see the A. O. H.[2] armed. I should like to see the Transport Workers armed. I should like to see any and every body of Irish citizens armed. We must accustom ourselves to the thought of arms, to the sight of arms, to the use of arms. We may make mistakes in the beginning and shoot the wrong people; but bloodshed is a cleansing and a sanctifying thing, and the nation which regards it as the final horror has lost its manhood. There are many things more horrible than bloodshed; and slavery is one of them.

---
[1] The governing body of the Gaelic League.
[2] Ancient Order of Hibernians.

# At the Grave of O'Donovan Rossa[1]

It has seemed right, before we turn away from this place in which we have laid the mortal remains of O'Donovan Rossa, that one among us should, in the name of all, speak the praise of that valiant man, and endeavour to formulate the thought and the hope that are in us as we stand around his grave. And if there is anything that makes it fitting that I, rather than some other, I rather than one of the grey-haired men who were young with him and shared in his labour and in his suffering, should speak here, it is perhaps that I may be taken as speaking on behalf of a new generation that has been re-baptised in the Fenian faith, and that has accepted the responsibility of carrying out the Fenian programme. I propose to you then that, here by the grave of this unrepentant Fenian,[2] we renew our baptismal vows; that, here by the grave of this unconquered and unconquerable man, we ask of God, each one for himself, such unshakable purpose, such high and gallant courage, such unbreakable strength of soul as belonged to O'Donovan Rossa.

Deliberately here we avow ourselves, as he avowed himself in the dock, Irishmen of one allegiance only. We of the Irish Volunteers, and you others who are associated with us in today's task and duty, are bound together and must stand together henceforth in brotherly union for the achievement of the freedom of Ireland. And we know only one definition of freedom: it is Tone's definition, it is Mitchel's definition, it is Rossa's definition. Let no man blaspheme the cause that the dead generations of Ireland served by giving it any other name and definition than their name and their definition.

We stand at Rossa's grave not in sadness but rather in exaltation of spirit that it has been given to us to come thus into so close a communion with that brave and splendid Gael. Splendid and holy causes are served by men who are themselves splendid and holy. O'Donovan Rossa was splendid in the proud manhood of him, splendid in the heroic grace of him, splendid in the Gaelic strength and clarity and truth of him. And all that splendour and pride

---

[1] From *Collected Works of Padraic H. Pearse: Political Writings and Speeches*, Dublin & London, 1922. The speech was delivered at Glasnevin Cemetery, Dublin, August 1, 1915.
[2] The Fenians were members of the Irish Republican Brotherhood, a secret revolutionary organization which attempted an uprising in 1867.

and strength was compatible with a humility and a simplicity of devotion to Ireland, to all that was olden and beautiful and Gaelic in Ireland, the holiness and simplicity of patriotism of a Michael O'Clery[1] or of an Eoghan O'Growney.[2] The clear true eyes of this man almost alone in his day visioned Ireland as we of today would surely have her: not free merely, but Gaelic as well; not Gaelic merely, but free as well.

In a closer spiritual communion with him now than ever before or perhaps ever again, in a spiritual communion with those of his day, living and dead, who suffered with him in English prisons, in communion of spirit too with our own dear comrades who suffer in English prisons today, and speaking on their behalf as well as our own, we pledge to Ireland our love, and we pledge to English rule in Ireland our hate. This is a place of peace, sacred to the dead, where men should speak with all charity and with all restraint; but I hold it a Christian thing, as O'Donovan Rossa held it, to hate evil, to hate untruth, to hate oppression, and, hating them, to strive to overthrow them. Our foes are strong and wise and wary; but, strong and wise and wary as they are, they cannot undo the miracles of God who ripens in the hearts of young men the seeds sown by the young men of a former generation. And the seeds sown by the young men of '65 and '67 are coming to their miraculous ripening today. Rulers and Defenders of Realms had need to be wary if they would guard against such processes. Life springs from death; and from the graves of patriot men and women spring living nations. The Defenders of this Realm have worked well in secret and in the open. They think that they have pacified Ireland. They think that they have purchased half of us and intimidated the other half. They think that they have foreseen everything, think that they have provided against everything; but the fools the fools, the fools!—they have left us our Fenian dead, and while Ireland holds these graves, Ireland unfree shall never be at peace.

---

[1] Brother Michael O'Clery, 1575-1643, a Franciscan, chief author of *The Annals of The Four Masters*, a famous Gaelic historical compilation.
[2] Rev. Eugene O'Growney, 1863-1899, Professor of Irish at Maynooth 1891-1894.

# What Is Our Programme?[1]

WE ARE often asked the above question. Sometimes the question is not too politely put, sometimes it is put in frantic bewilderment, sometimes it is put in wrathful objurgation, sometimes it is put in tearful entreaty, sometimes it is put by Nationalists who affect to despise the Labour Movement, sometimes it is put by Socialists who distrust the Nationalists because of the anti-Labour record of many of their friends, sometimes it is put by our enemies, sometimes by our friends, and always it is pertinent, and worthy of an answer.

The Labour Movement is like no other movement. Its strength lies in being like no other movement. It is never so strong as when it stands alone. Other movements dread analysis and shun all attempts to define their objects. The Labour Movement delights in analysing, and is perpetually defining and re-defining its principles and objects.

The man or woman who has caught the spirit of the Labour Movement brings that spirit of analysis and definition into all his or her public acts, and expects at all times to answer the call to define their position. They cannot live on illusions, nor thrive by them; even should their heads be in the clouds they will make no forward step until they are assured that their feet rest upon the solid earth.

In this they are essentially different from the middle or professional classes, and the parties or movements controlled by such classes in Ireland. These always talk of realities, but nourish themselves and their followers upon the unsubstantial meat of phrases; always prate about being intensely practical but nevertheless spend their whole lives in following visions.

When the average non-Labour patriot in Ireland who boasts of his practicality is brought in contact with the cold world and its problems he shrinks from the contact, should his feet touch the solid earth he affects to despise it as a 'mere material basis,' and strives to make the people believe that true patriotism needs no

[1] From *The Workers' Republic*, Vol. I, No. 35, Dublin, January 22, 1916.

## WHAT IS OUR PROGRAMME?

foundation to rest upon other than the brainstorms of its poets, orators, journalists, and leaders.

Ask such people for a programme and you are branded as a carping critic; refuse to accept their judgment as the last word in human wisdom and you become an enemy to be carefully watched; insist that in the crisis of your country's history your first allegiance is to your country and not to any leader, executive, or committee, and you are forthwith a disturber, a factionist, a wrecker.

What is our programme! We at least, in conformity with the spirit of our movement, will try and tell it.

Our programme in time of peace was to gather into Irish hands in Irish trade unions the control of all the forces of production and distribution in Ireland. We never believed that freedom would be realised without fighting for it. From our earliest declaration of policy in Dublin in 1896 the editor of this paper has held to the dictum that our ends should be secured 'peacefully if possible, forcibly if necessary.' Believing so we saw what the world outside Ireland is realising to-day, that the destinies of the world and the fighting strength of armies are at the mercy of organised Labour as soon as that Labour becomes truly revolutionary. Thus we strove to make Labour in Ireland organised—and revolutionary.

We saw that should it come to a test in Ireland (as we hoped and prayed it might come), between those who stood for the Irish nation and those who stood for the foreign rule, the greatest civil asset in the hand of the Irish nation for use in the struggle would be the control of Irish docks, shipping, railways and production by Unions who gave sole allegiance to Ireland.

We realised that the power of the enemy to hurl his forces upon the forces of Ireland would lie at the mercy of the men who controlled the transport system of Ireland; we saw that the hopes of Ireland a Nation rested upon the due recognition of the identity of interest between that ideal and the rising hopes of Labour.

In Europe to-day we have seen the strongest governments of the world exerting every effort, holding out all possible sort of inducement to Organised Labour to use its organisation on the side of those governments in time of war. We have spent the best part of our lifetime striving to create in Ireland the working class spirit that would create an Irish organisation of Labour willing to do voluntarily for Ireland what those governments of Europe are beseeching their trade unions to do for their countries. And we have partly succeeded.

We have succeeded in creating an organisation that will willingly do more for Ireland than any trade union in the world has attempted to do for its national government. Had we not been attacked and betrayed by many of our fervent advanced patriots, had they not been so anxious to destroy us, so willing to applaud even the British Government when it attacked us, had they stood by us and pushed our organisation all over Ireland it would now be in our power at a word to crumple up and demoralise every offensive move of the enemy against the champions of Irish freedom.

Had we been able to carry out all our plans, as such an Irish organisation of Labour alone could carry them out, we could at a word have created all the conditions necessary to the striking of a successful blow whenever the military arm of Ireland wished to move.

Have we a programme? We are the only people that had a programme—that understood the mechanical conditions of modern war, and the dependence of national power upon industrial control.

What is our programme now? At the grave risk of displeasing alike the perfervid Irish patriot and the British 'competent military authority,' we shall tell it.

We believe that in times of peace we should work along the lines of peace to strengthen the nation, and we believe that whatever strengthens and elevates the Working Class strengthens the nation.

But we also believe that in times of war we should act as in war. We despise, entirely despise and loathe, all the mouthings and mouthers about war who infest Ireland in time of peace, just as we despise and loathe all the cantings about caution and restraint to which the same people treat us in times of war.

Mark well then our programme. While the war lasts and Ireland still is a subject nation we shall continue to urge her to fight for her freedom.

We shall continue, in season and out of season, to teach that the 'far-flung battle line' of England is weakest at the point nearest its heart, that Ireland is in that position of tactical advantage, that a defeat of England in India, Egypt, the Balkans or Flanders would not be so dangerous to the British Empire as any conflict of armed forces in Ireland, that the time for Ireland's Battle is NOW, the place for Ireland's Battle is HERE.

That a strong man may deal lusty blows with his fists against a host of surrounding foes and conquer, but will succumb if a child sticks a pin in his heart.

But the moment peace is once admitted by the British Government as being a subject ripe for discussion, *that moment our policy will be for peace* and in direct opposition to all talk or preparation for armed revolution.

We will be no party to leading out Irish patriots to meet the might of an England at peace. The moment peace is in the air we shall strictly confine ourselves, and lend all our influence to the work of turning the thought of Labour in Ireland to the work of peaceful reconstruction.

That is our programme. You can now compare it with the programme of those who bid you hold your hand now, and thus put it in the power of the enemy to patch up a temporary peace, turn round and smash you at his leisure, and then go to war again with the Irish question settled—in the graves of Irish patriots.

We fear that is what is going to happen. It is to our mind inconceivable that the British public should allow conscription to be applied to England and not to Ireland. Nor do the British Government desire it. But that Government will use the cry of the necessities of war to force conscription upon the people of England, and will then make a temporary peace, and turn round to force Ireland to accept the same terms as have been forced upon England.

The English public will gladly see this done—misfortune likes company. The situation will then shape itself thus: The Irish Volunteers who are pledged to fight conscription will either need to swallow their pledge, and see the young men of Ireland conscripted, or will need to resent conscription, and engage the military force of England at a time when England is at peace.

This is what the diplomacy of England is working for, what the stupidity of some of our leaders who imagine they are Wolfe Tones is making possible. It is our duty, it is the duty of all who wish to save Ireland from such shame or such slaughter to strengthen the hand of those of the leaders who are for action as against those who are playing into the hands of the enemy.

We are neither rash nor cowardly. We know our opportunity

when we see it, and we know when it has gone. We know that at the end of this war England will have at least an army of one million men, or *more than two soldiers for every adult male in Ireland*. And these soldiers veterans of the greatest war in history.

We shall not want to fight those men. We shall devote our attention to organising their comrades who return to civil life, to organising them into trade unions and Labour parties to secure them their rights in civil life.

Unless we emigrate to some country where there are men.

ANONYMOUS

# Proclamation of the Irish Republic[1]

## POBLACHT NA H EIREANN.
## THE PROVISIONAL GOVERNMENT
### OF THE
## IRISH REPUBLIC
## TO THE PEOPLE OF IRELAND.

IRISHMEN AND IRISHWOMEN: In the name of God and of the dead generations from which she receives her old tradition of nationhood, Ireland, through us, summons her children to her flag and strikes for her freedom.

Having organised and trained her manhood through her secret revolutionary organisation, the Irish Republican Brotherhood, and through her open military organisations, the Irish Volunteers and the Irish Citizen Army, having patiently perfected her discipline, having resolutely waited for the right moment to reveal itself, she now seizes that moment, and, supported by her exiled children in America and by gallant allies in Europe, but relying in the first on her own strength, she strikes in full confidence of victory.

We declare the right of the people of Ireland to the ownership of Ireland, and to the unfettered control of Irish destinies, to be sovereign and indefeasible. The long usurpation of that right by a foreign people and government has not extinguished the right, nor can it ever be extinguished except by the destruction of the Irish people. In every generation the Irish people have asserted their right to national freedom and sovereignty; six times during the past three hundred years they have asserted it in arms. Standing on that fundamental right and again asserting it in arms in the face of the world, we hereby proclaim the Irish Republic as a Sovereign Independent State, and we pledge our lives and the lives of our comrades-in-arms to the cause of its freedom, of its welfare, and of its exaltation among the nations.

---

[1] This is the Proclamation which was read by Padraic Pearse on the steps of the General Post Office, Dublin, on April 17, 1916, announcing the Rising of Easter Week.

The Irish Republic is entitled to, and hereby claims, the allegiance of every Irishman and Irishwoman. The Republic guarantees religious and civil liberty, equal rights and equal opportunities to all its citizens, and declares its resolve to pursue the happiness and prosperity of the whole nation and of all its parts, cherishing all the children of the nation equally, and oblivious of the differences carefully fostered by an alien government, which have divided a minority from the majority in the past.

Until our arms have brought the opportune moment for the establishment of a permanent National Government, representative of the whole people of Ireland and elected by the suffrages of all her men and women, the Provisional Government, hereby constituted, will administer the civil and military affairs of the Republic in trust for the people.

We place the cause of the Irish Republic under the protection of the Most High God, Whose blessing we invoke upon our arms, and we pray that no one who serves that cause will dishonour it by cowardice, inhumanity, or rapine. In this supreme hour the Irish nation must, by its valour and discipline and by the readiness of its children to sacrifice themselves for the common good, prove itself worthy of the august destiny to which it is called.

Signed on Behalf of the Provisional Government,
THOMAS J. CLARKE,
SEAN MAC DIARMADA, THOMAS MAC DONAGH,
P. H. PEARSE, EAMONN CEANNT,
JAMES CONNOLLY. JOSEPH PLUNKETT.

SEAN O'CASEY

# The Shadow of a Gunman[1]

CHARACTERS IN THE PLAY

DONAL DAVOREN
SEUMAS SHIELDS, *a pedlar*
TOMMY OWENS
ADOLPHUS GRIGSON
MRS. GRIGSON
MINNIE POWELL
} *Residents in the Tenement*

MR. MULLIGAN, *the landlord*
MR. MAGUIRE, *soldier of the I.R.A.*
MRS. HENDERSON } *Residents of an adjoining Tenement*
MR. GALLOGHER
AN AUXILIARY

SCENE. *A room in a tenement in Hilljoy Square, Dublin. Some hours elapse between the two acts. The period of the Play is May 1920.*

## ACT I

*A Return Room in a tenement house in Hilljoy Square. At the back two large windows looking out into the yard; they occupy practically the whole of the back wall space. Between the windows is a cupboard, on the top of which is a pile of books. The doors are open, and on these are hanging a number of collars and ties. Running parallel with the windows is a stretcher bed; another runs at right angles along the wall at right. At the head of this bed is a door leading to the rest of the house. The wall on the left runs diagonally, so that the fireplace—which is in the centre—is plainly visible. On the mantelshelf to the right is a statue of the Virgin, to the left a statue of the Sacred Heart, and in the centre a crucifix. Around the fireplace are a few common cooking utensils. In the centre of the room is a table, on which are a typewriter, a candle and candlestick, a bunch of wild flowers in a vase, writing materials and a number of books. There are two chairs, one near the fireplace and one at the table. The aspect of the place is one of absolute untidiness, engendered on the one hand by the congenital slovenliness of* SEUMAS SHIELDS, *and on the other by the temperament of* DONAL DAVOREN, *making it appear impossible to effect an improvement in such a place.*

---

[1] First performed at the Abbey Theater, Dublin, April 9, 1923.

DAVOREN *is sitting at the table typing. He is about thirty. There is in his face an expression that seems to indicate an eternal war between weakness and strength; there is in the lines of the brow and chin an indication of a desire for activity, while in his eyes there is visible an unquenchable tendency towards rest. His struggle through life has been a hard one, and his efforts have been handicapped by an inherited and self-developed devotion to 'the might of design, the mystery of colour, and the belief in the redemption of all things by beauty everlasting.' His life would drive him mad were it not for the fact that he never knew any other. He bears upon his body the marks of the struggle for existence and the efforts towards self-expression.*

SEUMAS SHIELDS, *who is in the bed next the wall to the right, is a heavily built man of thirty-five; he is dark-haired and sallow-complexioned. In him is frequently manifested the superstition, the fear and the malignity of primitive man.*

Davoren [*lilting an air as he composes*]:

> Or when sweet Summer's ardent arms outspread,
> Entwined with flowers,
> Enfold us, like two lovers newly wed,
> Thro' ravish'd hours—
> Then sorrow, woe and pain lose all their powers,
> For each is dead, and life is only ours.

(*A woman's figure appears at the window and taps loudly on one of the panes; at the same moment there is loud knocking at the door.*)

Voice of Woman at Window. Are you awake, Mr. Shields—Mr. Shields, are you awake? Are you goin' to get up today at all, at all?

Voice at the Door. Mr. Shields, is there any use of callin' you at all? This is a nice nine o'clock: do you know what time it is, Mr. Shields?

Seumas [*loudly*]. Yus!

Voice at the Door. Why don't you get up, then, an' not have the house turned into a bedlam tryin' to waken you?

Seumas [*shouting*]. All right, all right, all right! The way these oul' ones bawl at a body! Upon my soul! I'm beginnin' to believe that the Irish People are still in the stone age. If they could they'd throw a bomb at you.

*Davoren.* A land mine exploding under the bed is the only thing that would lift you out of it.

*Seumas* [*stretching himself*]. Oh-h-h. I was fast in the arms of Morpheus—he was one of the infernal deities, son of Somnus, wasn't he?

*Davoren.* I think so.

*Seumas.* The poppy was his emblem, wasn't it?

*Davoren.* Ah, I don't know.

*Seumas.* It's a bit cold this morning, I think, isn't it?

*Davoren.* It's quite plain I'm not going to get much quietness in this house.

*Seumas* [*after a pause*]. I wonder what time is it?

*Davoren.* The Angelus went some time ago.

*Seumas* [*sitting up in bed suddenly*]. The Angelus! It couldn't be that late, could it? I asked them to call me at nine so that I could get Mass before I went on my rounds. Why didn't you give us a rap?

*Davoren.* Give you a rap! Why, man, they've been thundering at the door and hammering at the window for the past two hours, till the house shook to its very foundations, but you took less notice of the infernal din than I would take of the strumming of a grasshopper.

*Seumas.* There's no fear of you thinking of any one else when you're at your poetry. The land of Saints and Scholars 'ill shortly be a land of bloody poets. [*Anxiously*] I suppose Maguire has come and gone?

*Davoren.* Maguire? No, he hasn't been here—why, did you expect him?

*Seumas* [*in a burst of indignation*]. He said he'd be here at nine. 'Before the last chime has struck,' says he, 'I'll be coming in on the door,' and it must be—what time is it now?

*Davoren.* Oh, it must be half-past twelve.

*Seumas.* Did anybody ever see the like of the Irish People? Is there any use of tryin' to do anything in this country? Have everything packed and ready, have everything packed and ready, have . . .

*Davoren.* And have you everything packed and ready?

*Seumas.* What's the use of having anything packed and ready when he didn't come? [*He rises and dresses himself.*] No wonder this unfortunate country is as it is, for you can't depend upon the word of a single individual in it. I suppose he was too damn lazy to get up; he wanted the streets to be well aired first.—Oh, Kathleen ni Houlihan, your way's a thorny way.

*Davoren.* Ah me! alas, pain, pain ever, for ever!

*Seumas.* That's from Shelley's *Prometheus Unbound*. I could never agree with Shelley, not that there's anything to be said against him as a poet—as a poet—but . . .

*Davoren.* He flung a few stones through stained-glass windows.

*Seumas.* He wasn't the first nor he won't be the last to do that, but the stained-glass windows—more than ever of them—are here still, and Shelley is doing a jazz dance down below.

(*He gives a snarling laugh of pleasure.*)

*Davoren* [*shocked*]. And you actually rejoice and are exceedingly glad that, as you believe, Shelley, the sensitive, high-minded, noble-hearted Shelley, is suffering the tortures of the damned.

*Seumas.* I rejoice in the vindication of the Church and Truth.

*Davoren.* Bah. You know as little about truth as anybody else, and you care as little about the Church as the least of those that profess her faith; your religion is simply the state of being afraid that God will torture your soul in the next world as you are afraid the Black and Tans will torture your body in this.

*Seumas.* Go on, me boy; I'll have a right laugh at you when both of us are dead.

*Davoren.* You're welcome to laugh as much as you like at me when both of us are dead.

*Seumas* [*as he is about to put on his collar and tie*]. I don't think I need to wash meself this morning; do I look all right?

*Davoren.* Oh, you're all right; it's too late now to start washing yourself. Didn't you wash yourself yesterday morning?

*Seumas.* I gave meself a great rub yesterday. [*He proceeds to pack various articles into an attaché case—spoons, forks, laces, thread, etc.*] I think I'll bring out a few of the braces too; damn it, they're well worth sixpence each; there's great stuff in them— did you see them?

*Davoren.* Yes, you showed them to me before.

*Seumas.* They're great value; I only hope I'll be able to get enough o' them. I'm wearing a pair of them meself—they'd do Cuchullian, they're so strong. [*Counting the spoons*] There's a dozen in each of these parcels—three, six, nine—damn it, there's only eleven in this one. I better try another. Three, six, nine—my God, there's only eleven in this one too, and one of them bent! Now I suppose I'll have to go through the whole bloody lot of them, for I'd never be easy in me mind thinkin' there'd be more than a dozen in some o' them. And still we're looking for freedom—ye gods, it's a glorious country! [*He lets one fall, which he stoops to pick up.*] Oh, my God, there's the braces after breakin'.

*Davoren.* That doesn't look as if they were strong enough for Cuchullian.

*Seumas.* I put a heavy strain on them too sudden. There's that fellow Maguire never turned up, either; he's almost too lazy to wash himself. [*As he is struggling with the braces the door is hastily shoved in and* MAGUIRE *rushes in with a handbag.*] This is a nice nine o'clock. What's the use of you coming at this hour o' the day? Do you think we're going to work be moonlight? If you weren't goin' to come at nine couldn't you say you weren't. . . .

*Maguire.* Keep your hair on; I just blew in to tell you that I couldn't go to-day at all. I have to go to Knocksedan.

*Seumas.* Knocksedan! An' what, in the name o' God, is bringin' you to Knocksedan?

*Maguire.* Business, business. I'm going out to catch butterflies.

*Seumas.* If you want to make a cod of anybody, make a cod of somebody else, an' don't be tryin' to make a cod o' me. Here I've had everything packed an' ready for hours; you were to be here at nine, an' you wait till just one o'clock to come rushin' in like a mad bull to say you've got to go to Knocksedan! Can't you leave Knocksedan till to-morrow?

*Maguire.* Can't be did, can't be did, Seumas; if I waited till to-morrow all the butterflies might be dead. I'll leave this bag here till this evening. [*He puts the bag in a corner of the room.*] Good-bye . . . ee.

(*He is gone before* SEUMAS *is aware of it.*)

*Seumas* [*with a gesture of despair*]. Oh, this is a hopeless country! There's a fellow that thinks that the four cardinal virtues are not to be found outside an Irish Republic. I don't want to boast about myself—I don't want to boast about myself, and I suppose I could call meself as good as Gael as some of those that are knocking about now—knocking about now—as good a Gael as some that are knocking about now,—but I remember the time when I taught Irish six nights a week, when in the Irish Republican Brotherhood I paid me rifle levy like a man, an' when the Church refused to have anything to do with James Stephens,[1] I tarred a prayer for the repose of his soul on the steps of the Pro-Cathedral. Now, after all me work for Dark Rosaleen, the only answer you can get from a roarin' Republican to a simple question is 'Good-bye . . . ee.' What, in the name o' God, can be bringin' him to Knocksedan?

*Davoren.* Hadn't you better run out and ask him?

*Seumas.* That's right, that's right—make a joke about it! That's the Irish People all over—they treat a joke as a serious thing and a serious thing as a joke. Upon me soul, I'm beginning to believe that the Irish People aren't, never were, an' never will be fit for self-government. They've made Balor of the Evil Eye King of Ireland, an' so signs on it there's neither conscience nor honesty from one end of the country to the other. Well, I hope he'll have a happy day in Knocksedan. [*A knock at the door.*] Who's that? [*Another knock.*]

*Seumas* [*irritably*]. Who's that; who's there?

*Davoren* [*more irritably*]. Halt and give the countersign—damn it, man, can't you go and see?

---

[1] Founder and head of the Irish Republican Brotherhood, not to be confused with the author and poet, James Stephens.

(SEUMAS *goes over and opens the door. A man of about sixty is revealed, dressed in a faded blue serge suit; a half tall hat is on his head. It is evident that he has no love for* SEUMAS, *who denies him the deference he believes is due from a tenant to a landlord. He carries some papers in his hand.*)

*The Landlord* [*ironically*]. Good-day, Mr. Shields; it's meself that hopes you're feelin' well—you're lookin' well, anyhow—though you can't always go be looks nowadays.

*Seumas.* It doesn't matter whether I'm lookin' well or feelin' well; I'm all right, thanks be to God.

*The Landlord.* I'm very glad to hear it.

*Seumas.* It doesn't matter whether you're glad to hear it or not, Mr. Mulligan.

*The Landlord.* You're not inclined to be very civil, Mr. Shields.

*Seumas.* Look here, Mr. Mulligan, if you come here to raise an argument, I've something to do—let me tell you that.

*The Landlord.* I don't come here to raise no argument; a person ud have small gains argufyin' with you—let me tell you that.

*Seumas.* I've no time to be standin' here gostherin' with you—let me shut the door, Mr. Mulligan.

*The Landlord.* You'll not shut no door till you've heard what I've got to say.

*Seumas.* Well, say it then, an' go about your business.

*The Landlord.* You're very high an' mighty, but take care you're not goin' to get a drop. What a baby you are not to know what brings me here! Maybe you thought I was goin' to ask you to come to tea.

*Davoren.* Ah me! alas, pain, pain ever, for ever!

*Seumas.* Are you goin' to let me shut the door, Mr. Mulligan?

*The Landlord.* I'm here for me rent; you don't like the idea of bein' asked to pay your just an' lawful debts.

*Seumas.* You'll get your rent when you learn to keep your rent-book in a proper way.

*The Landlord.* I'm not goin' to take any lessons from you, anyhow.

*Seumas.* I want to have no more talk with you, Mr. Mulligan.

*The Landlord.* Talk or no talk, you owe me eleven weeks' rent, an' it's marked down again' you in black an' white.

*Seumas.* I don't care a damn if it was marked down in green, white, an' yellow.

*The Landlord.* You're a terribly independent fellow, an' it ud be fitter for you to be less funny an' stop tryin' to be billickin'[1] honest an' respectable people.

*Seumas.* Just you be careful what you're sayin', Mr. Mulligan. There's law in the land still.

*The Landlord.* Be me sowl there is, an' you're goin' to get a little of it now. [*He offers the papers to* SEUMAS.] Them's for you.

*Seumas* [*hesitating to take them*]. I want to have nothing to do with you, Mr. Mulligan.

*The Landlord* [*throwing the papers in the centre of the room*]. What am I better? It was the sorry day I ever let you come into this house. Maybe them notices to quit will stop your writin' letters to the papers about me an' me house.

*Davoren.* For goodness' sake, bring the man in, and don't be discussing the situation like a pair of primitive troglodytes.

*Seumas* [*taking no notice*]. Writing letters to the papers is my business, an' I'll write as often as I like, when I like, an' how I like.

*The Landlord.* You'll not write about this house at all events. You can blow about the state of the yard, but you took care to say nothin' about payin' rent: oh no, that's not in your line. But since you're not satisfied with the house, you can pack up an' go to another.

*Seumas.* I'll go, Mr. Mulligan, when I think fit, an' no sooner.

*The Landlord.* Not content with keeping the rent, you're startin' to bring in lodgers—[*to* DAVOREN] not that I'm sayin' anythin' again' you, sir. Bringin' in lodgers without as much as be your leave— what's the world comin' to at all that a man's house isn't his own? But I'll soon put a stop to your gallop, for on the twenty-eight of the next month out you go, an' there'll be few sorry to see your back.

---

[1] Bilking.

*Seumas.* I'll go when I like.

*The Landlord.* I'll let you see whether you own the house or no.

*Seumas.* I'll go when I like!

*The Landlord.* We'll see about that.

*Seumas.* We'll see.

*The Landlord.* Ay, we'll see.

(*The* LANDLORD *goes out and* SEUMAS *shuts the door.*)

*The Landlord* [*outside*]. Mind you, I'm in earnest; you'll not stop in this house a minute longer than the twenty-eight.

*Seumas* [*with a roar*]. Ah, go to hell!

*Davoren* [*pacing the room as far as the space will permit*]. What in the name of God persuaded me to come to such a house as this?

*Seumas.* It's nothing when you're used to it; you're too thin-skinned altogether. The oul' sod's got the wind up about you, that's all.

*Davoren.* Got the wind up about me!

*Seumas.* He thinks you're on the run. He's afraid of a raid, and that his lovely property'll be destroyed.

*Davoren.* But why, in the name of all that's sensible, should he think that I'm on the run?

*Seumas.* Sure they all think you're on the run. Mrs. Henderson thinks it, Tommy Owens thinks it, Mrs. an' Mr. Grigson think it, an' Minnie Powell thinks it too. [*Picking up his attaché case*] I'd better be off if I'm goin' to do anything to-day.

*Davoren.* What are we going to do with these notices to quit?

*Seumas.* Oh, shove them up on the mantel-piece behind one of the statues.

*Davoren.* Oh, I mean what action shall we take?

*Seumas.* I haven't time to stop now. We'll talk about them when I come back. . . . I'll get me own back on that oul' Mulligan yet. I wish to God they would come an' smash his rookery to pieces, for it's all he thinks of, and, mind you, oul' Mulligan would call himself a descendant of the true Gaels of Banba[1]—

---
[1] Ireland.

[*as he goes out*]:

> Oh, proud were the chieftains of famed Inisfail.
> Is truagh gan oidher 'na Vfarradh[1]
> The stars of our sky an' the salt of our soil—

Oh, Kathleen ni Houlihan, your way's a thorny way!

(*He goes out.*)

*Davoren* [*returning to the table and sitting down at the typewriter*]. Oh, Donal Og O'Davoren, your way's a thorny way. Your last state is worse than your first. Ah me, alas! Pain, pain ever, for ever. Like thee, Prometheus, no change, no pause, no hope. Ah, life, life, life! [*There is a gentle knock at the door.*] Another Fury come to plague me now! [*Another knock, a little louder*].

*Davoren*. You can knock till you're tired.

(*The door opens and* MINNIE POWELL *enters with an easy confidence one would not expect her to possess from her gentle way of knocking. She is a girl of twenty-three, but the fact of being forced to earn her living, and to take care of herself, on account of her parents' early death, has given her a force and an assurance beyond her years. She has lost the sense of fear (she does not know this), and, consequently, she is at ease in all places and before all persons, even those of a superior education, so long as she meets them in the atmosphere that surrounds the members of her own class. Her hair is brown, neither light nor dark, but partaking of both tints according to the light or shade she may happen to be in. Her well-shaped figure—a rare thing in a city girl—is charmingly dressed in a brown tailor-made costume, her stockings and shoes are a darker brown tint than the costume, and all are crowned by a silk tam-o'-shanter of a rich blue tint.*)

*Minnie*. Are you in, Mr. Shields?

*Davoren* [*rapidly*]. No, he's not, Minnie; he's just gone out—if you run out quickly you're sure to catch him.

*Minnie*. Oh, it's all right, Mr. Davoren, you'll do just as well; I just come in for a drop o' milk for a cup o' tea; I shouldn't be troublin' you this way, but I'm sure you don't mind.

*Davoren* [*dubiously*]. No trouble in the world; delighted, I'm sure. [*Giving her the milk*] There, will you have enough?

---

[1] It's a pity they have no heir.

*Minnie.* Plenty, lashins, thanks. Do you be all alone all the day, Mr. Davoren?

*Davoren.* No, indeed; I wish to God I was.

*Minnie.* It's not good for you then. I don't know how you like to be by yourself—I couldn't stick it long.

*Davoren* [*wearily*]. No?

*Minnie.* No, indeed; [*with rapture*] there's nothin' I'm more fond of than a Hooley.[1] I was at one last Sunday—I danced rings round me! Tommy Owens was there—you know Tommy Owens, don't you?

*Davoren.* I can't say I do.

*Minnie.* D'ye not? The little fellow that lives with his mother in the two-pair back—[*ecstatically*] he's a gorgeous melodeon player!

*Davoren.* A gifted son of Orpheus, eh?

*Minnie* [*who never heard of Orpheus*]. You've said it, Mr. Davoren: the son of poor oul' Battie Owens, a weeshy,[2] dawny,[3] bit of a man that was never sober an' was always talkin' politics. Poor man, it killed him in the long run.

*Davoren.* A man should always be drunk, Minnie, when he talks politics—it's the only way in which to make them important.

*Minnie.* Tommy takes after the oul' fellow, too; he'd talk from morning till night when he has a few jars in him. [*Suddenly; for like all of her class,* MINNIE *is not able to converse very long on the one subject, and her thoughts spring from one thing to another*] Poetry is a grand thing, Mr. Davoren, I'd love to be able to write a poem—a lovely poem on Ireland an' the men o' '98.

*Davoren.* Oh, we've had enough of poems, Minnie, about '98, and of Ireland, too.

*Minnie.* Oh, there's a thing for a Republican to say! But I know what you mean: it's time to give up the writing an' take to the gun. [*Her roving eye catches sight of the flowers in the vase*] What's Mr. Shields doin' with the oul' weeds?

---

[1] A party.
[2] Small.
[3] Feeble.

*Davoren.* Those aren't Shields', they're mine. Wild flowers is a kindlier name for them, Minnie, than weeds. These are wild violets, this is an *Arum maculatum*, or Wake Robin, and these are Celandines, a very beautiful flower related to the buttercups. [*He quotes*] :

> One day, when Morn's half-open'd eyes
> Were bright with Spring sunshine—
> My hand was clasp'd in yours, dear love,
> And yours was clasp'd in mine—
> We bow'd as worshippers before
> The Golden Celandine.

*Minnie.* Oh, aren't they lovely, an' isn't the poem lovely, too! I wonder, now, who she was.

*Davoren* [*puzzled*]. She, who?

*Minnie.* Why, the . . . [*roguishly*] Oh, be the way you don't know.

*Davoren.* Know? I'm sure I don't know.

*Minnie.* It doesn't matter, anyhow—that's your own business; I suppose I don't know her.

*Davoren.* Know her—know whom?

*Minnie* [*shyly*]. Her whose hand was clasped in yours, an' yours was clasped in hers.

*Davoren.* Oh that—that was simply a poem I quoted about the Celandine, that might apply to any girl—to you, for instance.

*Minnie* [*greatly relieved, coming over and sitting beside* DAVOREN]. But you have a sweetheart, all the same, Mr. Davoren, haven't you?

*Davoren.* I? No, not one, Minnie.

*Minnie.* Oh, now, you can tell that to some one else; aren't you a poet an' aren't all the girls fond o' poets?

*Davoren.* That may be, but all the poets aren't fond of girls.

*Minnie.* They are in the story-books, ay, and fond of more than one, too. [*With a questioning look*] Are you fond of them, Mr. Davoren?

*Davoren.* Of course I like girls, Minnie, especially girls who can add to their charms by the way in which they dress, like you, for instance.

*Minnie.* Oh, now, you're on for coddin' me, Mr. Davoren.

*Davoren.* No, really, Minnie, I'm not; you are a very charming little girl indeed.

*Minnie.* Then if I'm a charmin' little girl, you ought to be able to write a poem about me.

*Davoren* [*who has become susceptible to the attractiveness of* MINNIE, *catching her hand*]. And so I will, so I will, Minnie; I have written about girls not half so pretty as yourself.

*Minnie.* Ah, I knew you had one, I knew you had one now.

*Davoren.* Nonsense. Every girl a poet writes about isn't his sweetheart; Annie Laurie wasn't the sweetheart of Bobbie Burns.

*Minnie.* You needn't tell me she wasn't; 'An' for bonnie Annie Laurie I'd lay me down an' die.' No man ud lay down an' die for any but a sweetheart, not even for a wife.

*Davoren.* No man, Minnie, willingly dies for anything.

*Minnie.* Except for his country, like Robert Emmet.

*Davoren.* Even he would have lived on if he could; he died not to deliver Ireland. The British Government killed him to save the British nation.

*Minnie.* You're only jokin' now; you'd die for your country.

*Davoren.* I don't know so much about that.

*Minnie.* You would, you would, you would—I know what you are.

*Davoren.* What am I?

*Minnie* [*in a whisper*]. A gunman on the run!

*Davoren* [*too pleased to deny it*]. Maybe I am, and maybe I'm not.

*Minnie.* Oh, I know, I know, I know. Do you never be afraid?

*Davoren.* Afraid! Afraid of what?

*Minnie.* Why, the ambushes of course; *I'm* all of a tremble when I hear a shot go off, an' what must it be in the middle of the firin'?

*Davoren* [*delighted at* MINNIE's *obvious admiration; leaning back in his chair, and lighting a cigarette with placid affection*]. I'll admit one does be a little nervous at first, but a fellow gets used to it after a bit, till, at last, a gunman throws a bomb as carelessly as a schoolboy throws a snowball.

Minnie [*fervently*]. I wish it was all over, all the same. [*Suddenly, with a tremor in her voice*] You'll take care of yourself, won't you, won't you, Donal—I mean, Mr. Davoren?

Davoren [*earnestly*]. Call me Donal, Minnie; we're friends, great friends now—[*putting his arm around her*] go on, Minnie, call me Donal, let me hear you say Donal.

Minnie. The place badly needs a tidyin' up . . . Donal—there now, are you satisfied? [*Rapidly, half afraid of* DAVOREN'S *excited emotions*] But it really does, it's in an awful state. To-morrow's a half-day, an' I'll run in an' straighten it up a bit.

Davoren [*frightened at the suggestion*]. No, no, Minnie, you're too pretty for that sort of work; besides, the people of the house would be sure to start talking about you.

Minnie. An' do you think Minnie Powell cares whether they'll talk or no? She's had to push her way through life up to this without help from any one, an' she's not goin' to ask their leave, now, to do what she wants to do.

Davoren [*forgetting his timidity in the honest joy of appreciating the independent courage of* MINNIE]. My soul within art thou, Minnie! A pioneer in action as I am a pioneer in thought. The two powers that shall 'grasp this sorry scheme of things entire, and mould life nearer to the heart's desire.' Lovely little Minnie, and brave as well; brave little Minnie, and lovely as well!

(*His disengaged hand lifts up her bent head, and he looks earnestly at her; he is stooping to kiss her, when* TOMMY OWENS *appears at the door, which* MINNIE *has left partially open.* TOMMY *is about twenty-five years of age. He is small and thin; his words are uttered in a nasal drawl; his voice is husky, due to frequent drinks and perpetual cigarette-smoking. He tries to get rid of the huskiness by an occasional cough.* TOMMY *is a hero-worshipper, and, like many others, he is anxious to be on familiar terms with those who he thinks are braver than he is himself, and whose approbation he tries to win by an assumption equal to their own. He talks in a staccato manner. He has a few drinks taken—it is too early to be drunk—that make him talkative. He is dressed in a suit of dungarees, and gives a gentle cough to draw attention to his presence.*)

Tommy. I seen nothin'—honest—thought you was learnin' to typewrite—Mr. Davoren teachin' you. I seen nothin' else—s'help me God!

*Minnie.* We'd be hard put to it if we minded what you seen, Tommy Owens.

*Tommy.* Right, Minnie, Tommy Owens has a heart—Evenin', Mr. Davoren—don't mind me comin' in—I'm Tommy Owens—live up in the two-pair back, workin' in Ross an' Walpole's—Mr. Shields knows me well; you needn't be afraid o' me, Mr. Davoren.

*Davoren.* Why should I be afraid of you, Mr. Owens, or of anybody else?

*Tommy.* Why should you, indeed? We're all friends here—Mr. Shields knows me well—all you've got to say is, 'Do you know Tommy Owens?' an' he'll tell you the sort of a man Tommy Owens is. There's no flies on Tommy—got me?

*Minnie.* For goodness' sake, Tommy, leave Mr. Davoren alone—he's got enough burgeons on him already.

*Tommy.* Not a word, Minnie, not a word—Mr. Davoren understands me well, as man to man. It's 'Up the Republic' all the time—eh, Mr. Davoren?

*Davoren.* I know nothing about the Republic; I have no connection with the politics of the day, and I don't want to have any connection.

*Tommy.* You needn't say no more—a nod's as good as a wink to a blind horse—you've no meddlin' or makin' with it good, bad, or indifferent, pro nor con; I know it an' Minnie knows it—give me your hand. [*He catches* DAVOREN's *hand*] Two firm hands clasped together will all the power outbrave of the heartless English tyrant, the Saxon coward an' knave. That's Tommy Owens' hand, Mr. Davoren, the hand of a man, a man—Mr. Shields knows me well.

(*He breaks into song.*)

> High upon the gallows tree stood the noble-hearted three,
> By the vengeful tyrant stricken in their bloom;
> But they met him face to face with the spirit of their race,
> And they went with souls undaunted to their doom!

*Minnie* [*in an effort to quell his fervour*]. Tommy Owens, for goodness' sake . . .

*Tommy* [*overwhelming her with a shout*]:

God save Ireland ses the hayros, God save Ireland ses we all,
Whether on the scaffold high or the battle-field we die,
Oh, what matter when for Ayryinn dear we fall!

[*Tearfully*] Mr. Davoren, I'd die for Ireland!

*Davoren.* I know you would, I know you would, Tommy.

*Tommy.* I never got a chance—they never gave me a chance—but all the same I'd be there if I was called on—Mr. Shields knows that—ask Mr. Shields, Mr. Davoren.

*Davoren.* There's no necessity, Tommy; I know you're the right stuff if you got the chance, but remember that 'he also serves who only stands and waits.'

*Tommy* [*fiercely*]. I'm bloody well tired o' waitin'—we're all tired o' waitin'. Why isn't every man in Ireland out with the I.R.A.? Up with the barricades, up with the barricades; it's now or never, now an' for ever, as Sarsfield[1] said at the battle o' Vinegar Hill. Up with the barricades—that's Tommy Owens—an' a penny buys a whistle. Let them as thinks different say different —what do you say, Mr. Davoren?

*Davoren.* I say, Tommy, you ought to go up and get your dinner, for if you wait much longer it won't be worth eating.

*Tommy.* Oh, damn the dinner; who'd think o' dinner an' Ireland fightin' to be free?—not Tommy Owens, anyhow. It's only the Englishman who's always thinkin' of his belly.

*Minnie.* Tommy Owens!

*Tommy.* Excuse me, Miss Powell, in the ardure ov me anger I disremembered there was a lady present.

(*Voices are heard outside, and presently* MRS. HENDERSON *comes into the room, followed by* MR. GALLOGHER, *who, however, lingers at the door, too timid to come any farther.* MRS. HENDERSON *is a massive woman in every way; massive head, arms, and body; massive voice, and a massive amount of self-confidence. She is a mountain of good nature, and during the interview she behaves towards* DAVOREN *with deferential self-assurance. She dominates the room, and seems to occupy the whole of it. She is dressed poorly but tidily, wearing a white apron and a large shawl.* MR. GALLOGHER, *on the other hand, is a spare little man with a spare little grey beard and a thin, nervous voice. He is dressed as well as a faded suit of blue will allow him to be. He is obviously ill at ease during his interview with* DAVOREN. *He carries a hard hat, much the worse for wear, under his left arm, and a letter in his right hand.*)

[1] Patrick Sarsfield, a hero of the Williamite Wars 1690-1691, obviously had no part in the battle of Vinegar Hill, County Wexford, 1798.

*Mrs. Henderson* [*entering the room*]. Come along in, Mr. Gallicker, Mr. Davoren won't mind; it's him as can put you in the way o' havin' your wrongs righted; come on in, man, an' don't be so shy—Mr. Davoren is wan ov ourselves that stands for govermint ov the people with the people by the people. You'll find you'll be as welcome as the flowers in May. Good evenin', Mr. Davoren, an' God an' His holy angels be between you an' all harm.

*Tommy* [*effusively*]. Come on, Mr. Gallicker, an' don't be a stranger—we're all friends here—anything special to be done or particular advice asked, here's your man here.

*Davoren* [*subconsciously pleased, but a little timid of the belief that he is connected with the gunmen*]. I'm very busy just now, Mrs. Henderson, and really . . .

*Mrs. Henderson* [*mistaking the reason of his embarrassment*]. Don't be put out, Mr. Davoren, we won't keep you more nor a few minutes. It's not in me or in Mr. Gallicker to spoil sport. Him an' me was young once, an' knows what it is to be strolling at night in the pale moonlight, with arms round one another. An' I wouldn't take much an' say there's game in Mr. Gallicker still, for I seen, sometimes, a dangerous cock in his eye. But we won't keep you an' Minnie long asunder; he's the letter an' all written. You must know, Mr. Davoren—excuse me for not introducin' him sooner—this is Mr. Gallicker, that lives in the front drawin'-room ov number fifty-five, as decent an' honest an' quiet a man as you'd meet in a day's walk. An' so signs on it, it's them as 'ill be imposed upon—read the letter, Mr. Gallicker.

*Tommy*. Read away, Mr. Gallicker, it will be attended to, never fear; we know our own know, eh, Mr. Davoren?

*Minnie*. Hurry up, Mr. Gallicker, an' don't be keeping Mr. Davoren.

*Mrs. Henderson*. Give him time, Minnie Powell. Give him time. You must know in all fairity, Mr. Davoren, that the family livin' in the next room to Mr. Gallicker—the back drawin'-room, to be particular—am I right or am I wrong, Mr. Gallicker?

*Mr. Gallogher*. You're right, Mrs. Henderson, perfectly right, indeed—that's the very identical room.

*Mrs. Henderson.* Well, Mr. Davoren, the people in the back drawin'-room, or, to be more particular, the residents—that's the word that's writ in the letter—am I right or am I wrong, Mr. Gallicker?

*Mr. Gallogher.* You're right, Mrs. Henderson, perfectly accurate—that's the very identical word.

*Mrs. Henderson.* Well, Mr. Davoren, the residents in the back drawin'-room, as I aforesaid, is nothin' but a gang o' tramps that oughtn't to be allowed to associate with honest, decent, quiet, respectable people. Mr. Gallicker has tried to reason with them, and make them behave themselves—which in my opinion they never will—however, that's only an opinion, an' not legal—ever since they have made Mr. Gallicker's life a HELL! Mr. Gallicker, am I right or am I wrong?

*Mr. Gallogher.* I'm sorry to say you're right, Mrs. Henderson, perfectly right—not a word of exaggeration.

*Mrs. Henderson.* Well, now, Mr. Gallicker, seein' as I have given Mr. Davoren a fair account ov how you're situated, an' ov these tramps' cleverality, I'll ask you to read the letter, which I'll say, not because you're there, or that you're a friend o' mine, is as good a letter as was decomposed by a scholar. Now, Mr. Gallicker, an' don't forget the top sayin'.

(MR. GALLOGHER *prepares to read;* MINNIE *leans forward to listen;* TOMMY *takes out a well-worn note-book and a pencil stump, and assumes a very important attitude.*)

*Tommy.* One second. Mr. Gallicker, is this the twenty-first or twenty-second?

*Mr. Gallogher.* The twenty-first, sir.

*Tommy.* Thanks; proceed, Mr. Gallicker.

*Mr. Gallogher* [*with a few preliminary tremors, reads the letter. Reading*]:

> 'TO ALL TO WHOM THESE PRESENTS COME,
> GREETING
> Gentlemen of the Irish Republican Army . . .'

*Mrs. Henderson.* There's a beginnin' for you, Mr. Davoren.

*Minnie.* That's some swank.

*Tommy.* There's a lot in that sayin', mind you; it's a hard wallop at the British Empire.

*Mrs. Henderson* [*proudly*]. Go on, Mr. Gallicker.

*Mr. Gallogher* [*reading*]:

'I wish to call your attention to the persecution me and my family has to put up with in respect of and appertaining to the residents of the back drawing-room of the house known as fifty-five, Saint Teresa Street, situate in the Parish of St. Thomas, in the Borough and City of Dublin. This persecution started eighteen months ago—or to be precise—on the tenth day of the sixth month, in the year nineteen hundred and eighteen.'

*Mrs. Henderson.* That's the word I was trying to think ov—precise—it cuts the ground from under their feet—so to speak.

*Mr. Gallogher* [*reading*]:

'We, the complainants, resident on the ground floor, deeming it disrespectable . . .'

*Mrs. Henderson* [*with an emphatic nod*]. Which it was.

*Mr. Gallogher* [*reading*]:

'Deeming it disrespectable to have an open hall door, and to have the hall turned into a playground, made a solemn protest, and, in consequence, we the complainants aforesaid has had no peace ever since. Owing to the persecution, as aforesaid specified, we had to take out a summons against them some time ago as there was no Republican Courts then; but we did not proceed again them as me and my wife—to wit, James and Winifred Gallogher—has a strong objection to foreign Courts as such. We had peace for some time after that, but now things have gone from bad to worse. The name calling and the language is something abominable . . .'

*Mrs. Henderson* [*holding out her hand as a constable would extend his to stop a car that another may pass*]. Excuse me, Mr. Gallicker, but I think the word 'shockin'' should be put in there after abominable; for the language used be these tramps has two ways o' bein' looked at—for it's abominable to the childer an' shockin' to your wife—am I right or am I wrong, Mr. Davoren?

*Tommy* [*judicially*]. Shockin' is a right good word, with a great deal o' meanin', an' . . .

*Mrs. Henderson* [*with a deprecating gesture that extinguishes* TOMMY]. Tommy, let Mr. Davoren speak; whatever Mr. Davoren ses, Julia Henderson'll abide be.

*Davoren [afraid to say anything else]*. I think the word might certainly be introduced with advantage.

*Mrs. Henderson.* Go over there, Mr. Gallicker, an' put in the word shockin', as aforesaid.

(GALLOGHER *goes over to the table, and with a great deal of difficulty enters the word.*)

*Tommy [to* MR. GALLOGHER *as he writes]*. Ey, there's two k's in shockin'!

*Mr. Gallogher [reading]*:

'The language is something abominable and shocking. My wife has often to lock the door of the room to keep them from assaulting her. If you would be so kind as to send some of your army or police down to see for themselves we would give them full particulars. I have to be always from home all day, as I work with Mr. Hennessy, the harness maker of the Coombe, who will furnish all particulars as to my unvarnished respectability, also my neighbours. The name of the resident-tenant who is giving all this trouble and who, pursuant to the facts of the case aforesaid, mentioned, will be the defendant, is Dwyer. The husband of the aforesaid Mrs. Dwyer, or the aforesaid defendant, as the case may be, is a seaman, who is coming home shortly, and we beg The Irish Republican Army to note that the said Mrs. Dwyer says he will settle us when he comes home. While leaving it entirely in the hands of the gentlemen of The Republican Army, the defendant, that is to say, James Gallogher of fifty-five St. Teresa Street, ventures to say that he thinks he has made out a Primmy Fashy Case against Mrs. Dwyer and all her heirs, male and female as aforesaid mentioned in the above written schedule.

'*N.B.*—If you send up any of your men, please tell them to bring their guns. I beg to remain the humble servant and devoted admirer of the Gentlemen of the Irish Republican Army.

'Witness my hand this tenth day of the fifth month of the year nineteen hundred and twenty.

'JAMES GALLOGHER.'

*Mr. Gallogher [with a modest cough]*. Ahem.

*Mrs. Henderson.* There's a letter for you, Mr. Davoren!

*Tommy.* It's the most powerfullest letter I ever heard read.

*Minnie.* It wasn't you, really, that writ it, Mr. Gallicker?

*Mrs. Henderson.* Sinn Fein Amhain:[1] him an' him only, Minnie. I seen him with me own two eyes when me an' Winnie—Mrs. Gallicker, Mr. Davoren, aforesaid as appears in the letter—was havin' a chat be the fire.

---
[1] Ourselves alone.

*Minnie.* You'd never think it was in him to do it.

*Mrs. Henderson.* An' to think that the likes ov such a man is to have the sowl-case worried out ov him by a gang o' tramps; but it's in good hands now, an' instead ov them settlin' yous, Mr. Gallicker, it's yous 'ill settle them. Give the letter to Mr. Davoren, an' we'll be goin'.

(GALLOGHER *gives the letter to* DAVOREN.)

*Mrs. Henderson* [*moving towards the door*]. I hope you an' Mr. Shields is gettin' on all right together, Mr. Davoren.

*Davoren.* Fairly well, thanks, Mrs. Henderson. We don't see much of each other. He's out during the day, and I'm usually out during the evening.

*Mrs. Henderson.* I'm afraid he'll never make a fortune out ov what he's sellin'. He'll talk above an hour over a pennorth o' pins. Every time he comes to our place I buy a package o' hairpins from him to give him a little encouragement. I 'clare to God I have as many pins now as ud make a wire mattress for a double bed. All the young divils about the place are beginnin' to make a jeer ov him, too; I gave one ov them a mallavogin' the other day for callin' him oul' hairpins!

*Mr. Gallogher* [*venturing an opinion*]. Mr. Shields is a man of exceptional mental capacity, and is worthy of a more dignified position.

*Mrs. Henderson.* Them words is true, Mr. Gallicker, and they aren't. For to be wise is to be a fool, an' to be a fool is to be wise.

*Mr. Gallogher* [*with deprecating tolerance*]. Oh, Mrs. Henderson, that's a parrotox.

*Mrs. Henderson.* It may be what a parrot talks, or a blackbird, or, for the matter of that, a lark—but it's what Julia Henderson thinks, any . . . whisht, is that a *Stop Press?*

(*Outside is heard the shriek of a newsboy calling 'Stop Press.'*)

*Mrs. Henderson.* Run out, Tommy, an' get it till we see what it is.

*Tommy.* I haven't got a make.

*Mrs. Henderson.* I never seen you any other way, an' you'll be always the same if you keep follyin' your Spearmints, an' your

Bumble Bees an' your Night Patrols. [*Shouting to some one outside*] Is that a *Stop Press*, Mrs. Grigson?

*Voice outside.* Yis; an ambush out near Knocksedan.

*Mrs. Henderson.* That's the stuff to give them. [*Loudly*] Was there anybody hurted?

*Voice outside.* One poor man killed—some chap named Maguire, the paper says.

*Davoren* [*agitated*]. What name did she say?

*Minnie.* Maguire; did you know him, Mr. Davoren?

*Davoren.* Yes—no, no; I didn't know him, no, I didn't know him, Minnie.

*Minnie.* I wonder is it the Maguire that does be with Mr. Shields?

*Davoren.* Oh no, not at all, it couldn't be.

*Mrs. Henderson.* Knocksedan? That's in the County Sligo, now, or I'm greatly mistaken—am I right, Mr. Gallicker, or am I wrong?

*Mr. Gallogher* [*who knows perfectly well that it is in the County Dublin, but dare not correct* MRS. HENDERSON]. That's where it is —Knocksedan, that's the very identical county.

*Mrs. Henderson.* Well, I think we better be makin' a move, Mr. Gallicker; we've kep Mr. Davoren long enough, an' you'll find the letter'll be in good hans.

(MR. GALLOGHER *and* MRS. HENDERSON *move towards the door, which when he reaches it* MR. GALLOGHER *grips, hesitates, buttons his coat, and turns to* DAVOREN.)

*Mr. Gallogher.* Mr. Davoren, sir, on behalf ov meself, James Gallicker, an' Winifred, Mrs. Gallicker, wife ov the said James, I beg to offer, extend an' furnish our humble an' hearty thanks for your benevolent goodness in interferin' in the matter specified, particularated an' expanded upon in the letter, mandamus or schedule, as the case may be. An' let me interpretate to you on behalf ov meself an' Winifred Gallicker, that whenever you visit us you will be supernally positive ov a hundred thousand welcomes—ahem.

*Mrs. Henderson* [*beaming with pride for the genius of her friend*]. There's a man for you, Mr. Davoren! You forgot to mention

Biddy and Shaun, Mr. Gallicker—[*to* DAVOREN] his two children —it's himself has them trained well. It ud make your heart thrill like an alarm clock to hear them singin' 'Faith ov Our Fathers' an' 'Wrap the Green Flag Roun' Me.'

*Mr. Gallogher* [*half apologetically and half proudly*]. Faith an' Fatherland, Mrs. Henderson, Faith and Fatherland.

*Mrs. Henderson.* Well, good-day, Mr. Davoren, an' God keep you an' strengthen all the men that are fightin' for Ireland's freedom.

(*She and* GALLOGHER *go out.*)

*Tommy.* I must be off too; so-long, Mr. Davoren, an' remember that Tommy Owens only waits the call.

(*He goes out too.*)

*Davoren.* Well, Minnie, we're by ourselves once more.

*Minnie.* Wouldn't that Tommy Owens give you the sick—only waitin' to hear the call! Ah, then it'll take all the brass bands in the country to blow the call before Tommy Owens ud hear it. [*She looks at her wristlet watch.*] Sacred Heart, I've only ten minutes to get back to work! I'll have to fly! Quick, Mr. Davoren, write me name in typewritin' before I go—just 'Minnie.'

(DAVOREN *types the name.*)

*Minnie* [*shyly but determinedly*]. Now yours underneath—just 'Donal.' [DAVOREN *does so.*] Minnie, Donal; Donal, Minnie; good-bye now.

*Davoren.* Here, what about your milk?

*Minnie.* I haven't time to take it now. [*Slyly*] I'll come for it this evening.

(*They both go towards the door.*)

*Davoren.* Minnie, the kiss I didn't get.

*Minnie.* What kiss?

*Davoren.* When we were interrupted; you know, you little rogue, come, just one.

*Minnie.* Quick, then.

(DAVOREN *kisses her and she runs out.* DAVOREN *returns thoughtfully to the table.*)

*Davoren.* Minnie, Donal; Donal, Minnie. Very pretty, but very ignorant. A gunman on the run! Be careful, be careful, Donal Davoren. But Minnie is attracted to the idea, and I am attracted to Minnie. And what danger can there be in being the shadow of a gunman?

CURTAIN

## Act II

*The same as in Act I. But it is now night.* SEUMAS *is in the bed that runs along the wall at back.* DAVOREN *is seated near the fire, to which he has drawn the table. He has a fountain-pen in his hand, and is attracted in thought towards the moon, which is shining in through the windows. An open writing-pad is on the table at* DAVOREN's *elbow. The bag left by* MAGUIRE *is still in the same place.*

*Davoren:*

> The cold chaste moon, the Queen of Heaven's bright isles,
> Who makes all beautiful on which she smiles;
> That wandering shrine of soft yet icy flame,
> Which ever is transformed yet still the same.

Ah, Shelley, Shelley, you yourself were a lovely human orb shining through clouds of whirling human dust. 'She makes all beautiful on which she smiles.' Ah, Shelley, she couldn't make this thrice accursed room beautiful. Her beams of beauty only make its horrors more full of horrors still. There is an ugliness that can be made beautiful, and there is an ugliness that can only be destroyed, and this is part of that ugliness. Donal, Donal, I fear your last state is worse than your first.

(*He lilts a verse, which he writes on the pad before him.*)

> When night advances through the sky with slow
> And solemn tread,

> The queenly moon looks down on life below,
>   As if she read
> Man's soul, and in her scornful silence said:
>   All beautiful and happiest things are dead.

*Seumas* [*sleepily*]. Donal, Donal, are you awake? [*A pause.*] Donal, Donal, are you asleep?

*Davoren.* I'm neither awake nor asleep: I'm thinking.

*Seumas.* I was just thinkin', too—I was just thinkin', too, that Maguire is sorry now that he didn't come with me instead of going to Knocksedan. He caught something besides butterflies—two of them he got, one through each lung.

*Davoren.* The Irish people are very fond of turning a serious thing into a joke; that was a serious affair—for poor Maguire.

*Seumas* [*defensively*]. Why didn't he do what he arranged to do? Did he think of me when he was goin' to Knocksedan? How can he expect me to have any sympathy with him now?

*Davoren.* He can hardly expect that now that he's dead.

*Seumas.* The Republicans 'll do a lot for him, now. How am I goin' to get back the things he has belongin' to me, either? There's some of them in that bag over there, but that's not quarter of what he had; an' I don't know where he was stoppin', for he left his old digs a week or so ago—I suppose there's nothing to be said about my loss; I'm to sing dumb.

*Davoren.* I hope there's nothing else in the bag, beside thread and hairpins.

*Seumas.* What else ud be in it? . . . I can't sleep properly ever since they put on this damned curfew. A minute ago I thought I heard some of the oul' ones standin' at the door; they won't be satisfied till they bring a raid on the house; an' they never begin to stand at the door till after curfew. . . . Are you gone to bed, Donal?

*Davoren.* No; I'm trying to finish this poem.

*Seumas* [*sitting up in bed*]. If I was you I'd give that game up; it doesn't pay a working-man to write poetry. I don't profess to know much about poetry—I don't profess to know much about poetry—about poetry—I don't know much about the pearly glint of the morning dew, or the damask sweetness of the rare wild rose, or the subtle greenness of the serpent's eye—but I think a poet's claim to greatness depends upon his power to put passion in the common people.

*Davoren.* Ay, passion to howl for his destruction. The People! Damn the people! They live in the abyss, the poet lives on the mountain-top; to the people there is no mystery of colour: it is simply the scarlet coat of the soldier; the purple vestments of a priest; the green banner of a party; the brown or blue overalls of industry. To them the might of design is a three-roomed house or a capacious bed. To them beauty is for sale in a butcher's shop. To the people the end of life is the life created for them; to the poet the end of life is the life that he creates for himself; life has a stifling grip upon the people's throat—it is the poet's musician. The poet ever strives to save the people; the people ever strive to destroy the poet. The people view life through creeds, through customs, and through necessities; the poet views creeds, customs, and necessities through life. The people . . .

*Seumas* [*suddenly, and with a note of anxiety in his voice*]. Whisht! What's that? Is that the tappin' again?

*Davoren.* Tappin'. What tappin'?

*Seumas* [*in an awed whisper*]. This is the second night I heard that tappin'! I believe it bodes no good to me. There, do you hear it again—a quiet, steady, mysterious tappin' on the wall.

*Davoren.* I hear no tappin'.

*Seumas.* It ud be better for me if you did. It's a sure sign of death when nobody hears it but meself.

*Davoren.* Death! What the devil are you talking about, man?

*Seumas.* I don't like it at all; there's always something like that heard when one of our family dies.

*Davoren.* I don't know about that; but I know there's a hell of a lot of things heard when one of your family lives.

*Seumas.* God between us an' all harm! Thank God I'm where I ought to be—in bed. . . . It's always best to be in your proper place when such things happen—Sacred Heart! There it is again; do you not hear it now?

*Davoren.* Ah, for God's sake go asleep.

*Seumas.* Do you believe in nothing?

*Davoren.* I don't believe in tappin'.

*Seumas.* Whisht, it's stopped again; I'll try to go asleep for fear it ud begin again.

*Davoren.* Ay, do; and if it starts again I'll be sure to waken you up.

(*A pause.*)

*Seumas.* It's very cold to-night. Do you feel cold?

*Davoren.* I thought you were goin' asleep?

*Seumas.* The bloody cold won't let me. . . . You'd want a pair of pyjamas on you. [*A pause.*] Did you ever wear pyjamas, Donal?

*Davoren.* No, no, no.

*Seumas.* What kind of stuff is in them?

*Davoren* [*angrily*]. Oh, it depends on the climate; in India, silk; in Italy, satin; and the Eskimo wears them made from the skin of the Polar bear.

*Seumas* [*emphatically*]. If you take my advice you'll get into bed—that poem is beginnin' to get on your nerves.

*Davoren* [*extinguishing the candle with a vicious blow*]. Right, I'm going to bed now, so you can shut up.

(*Visibility is still maintained from the light of the moon.*)

*Seumas.* I was goin' to say something when you put out the light—what's this it was?—um, um, oh, ay: when I was comin' in this evenin' I saw Minnie Powell goin' out. If I was you I wouldn't have that one comin' in here.

*Davoren.* She comes in; I don't bring her in, do I?

*Seumas.* The oul' ones'll be talkin', an' once they start you don't know how it'll end. Surely a man that has read Shelley couldn't be interested in an ignorant little bitch that thinks of nothin' but jazz dances, fox-trots, picture theatres an' dress.

*Davoren.* Right glad I am that she thinks of dress, for she thinks of it in the right way, and makes herself a pleasant picture to the eye. Education has been wasted on many persons, teaching them to talk only, but leaving with them all their primitive instincts. Had poor Minnie received an education she would have been an artist. She is certainly a pretty girl. I'm sure she is a good girl, and I believe she is a brave girl.

*Seumas.* A Helen of Troy come to live in a tenement! You think a lot about her simply because she thinks a lot about you, an' she thinks a lot about you because she looks upon you as a hero —a kind o' Paris . . . she'd give the world an' all to be gaddin' about with a gunman. An' what ecstasy it ud give her if after a bit you were shot or hanged; she'd be able to go about then— like a good many more—singin', 'I do not mourn me darlin' lost, for he fell in his Jacket Green.' An' then, for a year an' a day, all round her hat she'd wear the Tri-coloured Ribbon O, till she'd pick up an' marry some one else—possibly a British Tommy with a Mons Star. An' as for bein' brave, it's easy to be that when you've no cause for cowardice; I wouldn't care to have me life dependin' on brave little Minnie Powell—she wouldn't sacrifice a jazz dance to save it.

*Davoren* [*sitting on the bed and taking off his coat and vest, preparatory to going to bed*]. There; that's enough about Minnie Powell. I'm afraid I'll soon have to be on the run out of this house, too; it is becoming painfully obvious that there is no peace to be found here.

*Seumas.* Oh, this house is all right; barrin' the children, it does be quiet enough. Wasn't there children in the last place you were in too?

*Davoren.* Ay, ten; [*viciously*] and they were all over forty.

(*A pause as* DAVOREN *is removing his collar and tie.*)

*Seumas.* Everything is very quiet now; I wonder what time is it?

*Davoren.* The village cock hath thrice done salutation to the morn.

*Seumas.* Shakespeare, Richard the III, Act Five, Scene III. It was Ratcliffe said that to Richard just before the battle of Bosworth. . . . How peaceful the heavens look now with the moon in the middle; you'd never think there were men prowlin' about tryin' to shoot each other. I don't know how a man who has shot any one can sleep in peace at night.

*Davoren.* There's plenty of men can't sleep in peace at night now unless they know that they have shot somebody.

*Seumas.* I wish to God it was all over. The country is gone mad. Instead of counting their beads now they're countin' bullets; their Hail Marys and paternosters are burstin' bombs—burstin' bombs an' the rattle of machine-guns; petrol is their holy water; their Mass is a burnin' buildin'; their De Profundis is 'The Soldiers' Song,'[1] an' their creed is, I believe in the gun almighty, maker of heaven an' earth—an' it's all for 'the glory o' God an' the honour o' Ireland.'

*Davoren.* I remember the time when you yourself believed in nothing but the gun.

*Seumas.* Ay, when there wasn't a gun in the country; I've a different opinion now when there's nothin' but guns in the country. . . . An' you daren't open your mouth, for Kathleen ni Houlihan is very different now to the woman who used to play the harp an' sing 'Weep on, weep on, your hour is past', for she's a ragin' divil now, an' if you only look crooked at her you're sure of a punch in th' eye. But this is the way I look at it—I look at it this way: You're not goin'—you're not goin' to beat the British Empire—the British Empire, by shootin' an occasional Tommy at the corner of an occasional street. Besides, when the Tommies have the wind up—when the Tommies have the wind up they let bang at everything they see—they don't give a God's curse who they plug.

*Davoren.* Maybe they ought to get down off the lorry and run to the Records Office to find out a man's pedigree before they plug him.

*Seumas.* It's the civilians that suffer; when there's an ambush they don't know where to run. Shot in the back to save the British Empire, an' shot in the breast to save the soul of Ireland. I'm a Nationalist meself, right enough—a Nationalist right enough, but all the same—I'm a Nationalist right enough; I believe in the freedom of Ireland, an' that England has no right to be here, but I draw the line when I hear the gunmen blowin' about dyin' for

---

[1] Now the National anthem of the Republic of Ireland, written by Peadar Kearney.

the people, when it's the people that are dyin' for the gunmen! With all due respect to the gunmen, I don't want them to die for me.

*Davoren.* Not likely; you object to any one of them deliberately dying for you for fear that one of these days you might accidentally die for one of them.

*Seumas.* You're one of the brave fellows that doesn't fear death.

*Davoren.* Why should I be afraid of it? It's all the same to me how it comes, where it comes, or when it comes. I leave fear of death to the people that are always praying for eternal life; 'Death is here and death is there, death is busy everywhere.'

*Seumas.* Ay, in Ireland. Thanks be to God I'm a daily communicant. There's a great comfort in religion; it makes a man strong in time of trouble an' brave in time of danger. No man need be afraid with a crowd of angels round him; thanks to God for His Holy religion!

*Davoren.* You're welcome to your angels; philosophy is mine; philosophy that makes the coward brave; the sufferer defiant; the weak strong; the . . .

(*A volley of shots is heard in a lane that runs parallel with the wall of the back-yard. Religion and philosophy are forgotten in the violent fear of a nervous equality.*)

*Seumas.* Jesus, Mary, an' Joseph, what's that?

*Davoren.* My God, that's very close.

*Seumas.* Is there no Christianity at all left in the country?

*Davoren.* Are we ever again going to know what peace and security are?

*Seumas.* If this continues much longer I'll be nothing but a galvanic battery o' shocks.

*Davoren.* It's dangerous to be in and it's equally dangerous to be out.

*Seumas.* This is a dangerous spot to be in with them windows; you couldn't tell the minute a bullet ud come in through one of them—through one of them, an' hit the—hit the—an' hit the . . .

*Davoren* [*irritably*]. Hit the what, man?

*Seumas.* The wall.

*Davoren.* Couldn't you say that at first without making a song about it?

*Seumas* [*suddenly*]. I don't believe there's horses in the stable at all.

*Davoren.* Stable! What stable are you talking about?

*Seumas.* There's a stable at the back of the house with an entrance from the yard; it's used as a carpenter's shop. Didn't you often hear the peculiar noises at night? They give out that it's the horses shakin' their chains.

*Davoren.* And what is it?

*Seumas.* Oh, there I'll leave you!

*Davoren.* Surely you don't mean . . .

*Seumas.* But I do mean it.

*Davoren.* You do mean what?

*Seumas.* I wouldn't—I wouldn't be surprised—wouldn't be surprised—surprised . . .

*Davoren.* Yes, yes, surprised—go on.

*Seumas.* I wouldn't be surprised if they were manufacturin' bombs there.

*Davoren.* My God, that's a pleasant contemplation! The sooner I'm on the run out of this house the better. How is it you never said anything about this before?

*Seumas.* Well—well, I didn't want—I didn't want to—to . . .

*Davoren.* You didn't want to what?

*Seumas.* I didn't want to frighten you.

*Davoren* [*sarcastically*]. You're bloody kind!

(*A knock at the door; the voice of* MRS. GRIGSON *heard.*)

*Mrs. Grigson.* Are you asleep, Mr. Shields?

*Seumas.* What the devil can she want at this hour of the night? [*To* MRS. GRIGSON] No, Mrs. Grigson, what is it?

*Mrs. Grigson* [*opening the door and standing at the threshold. She is a woman about forty, but looks much older. She is one of the cave-dwellers of Dublin, living as she does in a tenement kitchen, to which only an occasional sickly beam of sunlight filters through a grating in the yard; the consequent general dimness of her abode has given her a habit of peering through half-closed eyes. She is slovenly dressed in an old skirt and bodice; her face is grimy, not because her habits are dirty—for, although she is untidy, she is a clean woman—but because of the smoky atmosphere of her room. Her hair is constantly falling over her face, which she is as frequently removing by rapid movements of her right hand*]. He hasn't turned up yet, an' I'm stiff with the cold waitin' for him.

*Seumas.* Mr. Grigson, is it?

*Mrs. Grigson.* Adolphus, Mr. Shields, after takin' his tea at six o'clock—no, I'm tellin' a lie—it was before six, for I remember the Angelus was ringin' out an' we sittin' at the table—after takin' his tea he went out for a breath o' fresh air, an' I haven't seen sign or light of him since. 'Clare to God me heart is up in me mouth, thinkin' he might be shot be the Black an' Tans.

*Seumas.* Aw, he'll be all right, Mrs. Grigson. You ought to go to bed an' rest yourself; it's always the worst that comes into a body's mind; go to bed, Mrs. Grigson, or you'll catch your death of cold.

*Mrs. Grigson.* I'm afraid to go to bed, Mr. Shields, for I'm always in dread that some night or another, when he has a sup taken, he'll fall down the kitchen stairs an' break his neck. Not that I'd be any the worse if anything did happen to him, for you know the sort he is, Mr. Shields; sure he has me heart broke.

*Seumas.* Don't be downhearted, Mrs. Grigson; he may take a thought one of these days an' turn over a new leaf.

*Mrs. Grigson.* Sorra leaf Adolphus'll ever turn over, he's too far gone in the horns for that now. Sure no one ud mind him takin' a pint or two, if he'd stop at that, but he won't; nothin' could fill him with beer, an' no matter how much he may have taken, when he's taken more he'll always say, 'Here's the first today.'

*Davoren* [*to* SEUMAS]. Christ! Is she going to stop talking there all the night?

*Seumas.* 'Sh, she'll hear you; right enough, the man has the poor woman's heart broke.

*Davoren.* And because he has her heart broken, she's to have the privilege of breaking everybody else's.

*Mrs. Grigson.* Mr. Shields.

*Seumas.* Yes?

*Mrs. Grigson.* Do the insurance companies pay if a man is shot after curfew?

*Seumas.* Well, now, that's a thing I couldn't say, Mrs. Grigson.

*Mrs. Grigson* [*plaintively*]. Isn't he a terrible man to be takin' such risks, an' not knowin' what'll happen to him. He knows them Societies only want an excuse to do people out of their money—is it after one, now, Mr. Shields?

*Seumas.* Aw, it must be after one, Mrs. Grigson.

*Mrs. Grigson* [*emphatically*]. Ah, then, if I was a young girl again I'd think twice before gettin' married. Whisht! There's somebody now—it's him, I know be the way he's fumblin'.

(*She goes out a little way. Stumbling steps are heard in the hall.*)

*Mrs. Grigson* [*outside*]. Is that you, Dolphie, dear?

(*After a few moments* ADOLPHUS, *with* MRS. GRIGSON *holding his arm, stumbles into the room.*)

*Mrs. Grigson.* Dolphie, dear, mind yourself.

*Adolphus* [*he is a man of forty-five, but looks relatively much younger than* MRS. GRIGSON. *His occupation is that of a solicitor's clerk. He has all the appearance of being well fed; and, in fact, he gets most of the nourishment,* MRS. GRIGSON *getting just enough to give her strength to do the necessary work of the household. On account of living most of his life out of the kitchen, his complexion is fresh, and his movements, even when sober, are livelier than those of his wife. He is comfortably dressed; heavy top-coat, soft trilby hat, a fancy coloured scarf about his neck, and he carries an umbrella*]. I'm all right; do you see anything wrong with me?

*Mrs. Grigson.* Of course you're all right, dear; there's no one mindin' you.

*Adolphus Grigson.* Mindin' me, is it, mindin' me? He'd want to be a good thing that ud mind me. There's a man here—a man, mind you, afraid av nothin'—not in this bloody house anyway.

*Mrs. Grigson* [*imploringly*]. Come on down-stairs, Dolphie, dear; sure there's not one in the house ud say a word to you.

*Adolphus Grigson.* Say a word to me, is it? He'd want to be a good thing that ud say anything to Dolphus Grigson. [*Loudly*] Is there any one wants to say anything to Dolphus Grigson? If there is, he's here—a man, too—there's no blottin' it out—a man.

*Mrs. Grigson.* You'll wake everybody in the house; can't you speak quiet.

*Adolphus Grigson* [*more loudly still*]. What do I care for anybody in the house? Are they keepin' me; are they givin' me anything? When they're keepin' Grigson it'll be time enough for them to talk. [*With a shout*] I can tell them Adolphus Grigson wasn't born in a bottle!

*Mrs. Grigson* [*tearfully*]. Why do you talk like that, dear? We all know you weren't born in a bottle.

*Adolphus Grigson.* There's some of them in this house think that Grigson was born in a bottle.

*Davoren* [*to* SEUMAS]. A most appropriate place for him to be born in.

*Mrs. Grigson.* Come on down to bed, now, an' you can talk about them in the mornin'.

*Grigson.* I'll talk about them, now; do you think I'm afraid of them? Dolphus Grigson's afraid av nothin', creepin' or walkin',—if there's any one in the house thinks he's fit to take a fall out av Adolphus Grigson, he's here—a man; they'll find that Grigson's no soft thing.

*Davoren.* Ah me, alas! Pain, pain ever, for ever.

*Mrs. Grigson.* Dolphie, dear, poor Mr. Davoren wants to go to bed.

*Davoren.* Oh, she's terribly anxious about poor Mr. Davoren, all of a sudden.

*Grigson* [*stumbling towards* DAVOREN, *and holding out his hand*]. Davoren! He's a man. Leave it there, mate. You needn't be afraid av Dolphus Grigson; there never was a drop av informer's blood in the whole family av Grigson. I don't know what you are or what you think, but you're a man, an' not like some of the gougers in this house, that ud hang you. Not referrin' to you, Mr. Shields.

*Mrs. Grigson.* Oh, you're not deludin' to Mr. Shields.

*Seumas.* I know that, Mr. Grigson; go on down, now, with Mrs. Grigson, an' have a sleep.

*Grigson.* I tie meself to no woman's apron strings, Mr. Shields; I know how to keep Mrs. Grigson in her place; I have the authority of the Bible for that. I know the Bible from cover to cover, Mr. Davoren, an' that's more than some in this house could say. And what does the Holy Scripture say about woman? It says, 'The woman shall be subject to her husband,' an' I'll see that Mrs. Grigson keeps the teachin' av the Holy Book in the letter an' in the spirit. If you're ever in trouble, Mr. Davoren, an' Grigson can help—I'm your man—have you me?

*Davoren.* I have you, Mr. Grigson, I have you.

*Grigson.* Right; I'm an Orangeman, an' I'm not ashamed av it, an' I'm not afraid av it, but I can feel for a true man, all the same—have *you* got me, Mr. Shields?

*Seumas.* Oh, we know you well, Mr. Grigson; many a true Irishman was a Protestant—Tone, Emmet an' Parnell.

*Grigson.* Mind you, I'm not sayin' as I agree with them you've mentioned, Mr. Shields, for the Bible forbids it, an' Adolphus Grigson 'll always abide be the Bible. Fear God an' honour the King—that's written in Holy Scripture, an' there's no blottin' it out. [*Pulling a bottle out of his pocket*] But here, Mr. Davoren, have a drink, just to show there's no coolness.

*Davoren.* No, no, Mr. Grigson, it's too late now to take anything. Go on down with Mrs. Grigson, and we can have a chat in the morning.

*Grigson.* Sure you won't have a drink?

*Davoren.* Quite sure—thanks all the same.

*Grigson* [*drinking*]. Here's the first today! To all true men, even if they were born in a bottle. Here's to King William, to the battle av the Boyne; to the Hobah Black Chapter—that's my Lodge, Mr. Davoren; an' to The Orange Lily O.

(*Singing in a loud shout:*)

> An' dud ya go to see the show, each rose an' pinkadilly O,
> To feast your eyes an' view the prize won be the Orange Lily O.
> The Vic'roy there, so debonair, just like a daffadilly O,
> With Lady Clarke, blithe as a lark, approached the Orange Lily O.
>   Heigh Ho the Lily O,
>   The Royal, Loyal Lily O,
> Beneath the sky what flower can vie with Erin's Orange Lily O!

*Davoren.* Holy God, isn't this terrible!

*Grigson* [*singing*]:

> The elated Muse, to hear the news, jumped like a Connaught filly O,
> As gossip Fame did loud proclaim the triumph av the Lily O.
> The Lowland field may roses yield, gay heaths the Highlands hilly O;
> But high or low no flower can show like Erin's Orange Lily O.
>   Heigh Ho the Lily O,
>   The Royal, Loyal Lily O,
> Beneath the sky what flower can vie with Erin's Or . . .

(*While* GRIGSON *has been singing, the sound of a rapidly moving motor is heard, faintly at first, but growing rapidly louder, till it apparently stops suddenly somewhere very near the house, bringing* GRIGSON'S *song to an abrupt conclusion. They are all startled, and listen attentively to the throbbing of the engines, which can be plainly heard.* GRIGSON *is considerably sobered, and anxiously keeps his eyes on the door.* SEUMAS *sits up in bed and listens anxiously.* DAVOREN, *with a shaking hand, lights the candle, and begins to search hurriedly among the books and papers on the table.*)

*Grigson* [*with a tremor in his voice*]. There's no need to be afraid, they couldn't be comin' here.

*Mrs. Grigson.* God forbid! It ud be terrible if they came at this hour ov the night.

*Seumas.* You never know now, Mrs. Grigson; they'd rush in on you when you'd be least expectin' them. What, in the name o' God, is goin' to come out of it all? Nobody now cares a traneen about the orders of the Ten Commandments; the only order that anybody minds now is, 'Put your hands up.' Oh, it's a hopeless country.

*Grigson.* Whisht; do you hear them talking outside at the door? You're sure of your life nowhere now; it's just as safe to go everywhere as it is to go anywhere. An' they don't give a damn whether you're a loyal man or not. If you're a Republican they make you sing 'God save the King,' an' if you're loyal they'll make you sing the 'Soldiers' Song.' The singin' ud be all right if they didn't make you dance afterwards.

*Mrs. Grigson.* They'd hardly come here unless they heard something about Mr. Davoren.

*Davoren.* About me! What could they hear about me?

*Grigson.* You'll never get some people to keep their mouths shut. I was in the Blue Lion this evening, an' who do you think was there, blowin' out av him, but that little blower, Tommy Owens; there he was tellin' everybody that *he* knew where there was bombs; that *he* had a friend that was a General in the I.R.A.; that *he* could tell them what the Staff was thinkin' av doin'; that *he* could lay his hand on tons av revolvers; that they wasn't a mile from where he was livin', but that *he* knew his own know, an' would keep it to himself.

*Seumas.* Well, God blast the little blower, anyway; it's the like ov him that deserves to be plugged! [*To* DAVOREN] What are you lookin' for among the books, Donal?

*Davoren.* A letter that I got to-day from Mr. Gallogher and Mrs. Henderson; I'm blessed if I know where I put it.

*Seumas* [*peevishly*]. Can't you look for it in the mornin'?

*Davoren.* It's addressed to the Irish Republican Army, and, considering the possibility of a raid, it would be safer to get rid of it.

(*Shots again heard out in the lane, followed by loud shouts of Halt, halt, halt!*)

*Grigson.* I think we had better be gettin' to bed, Debby; it's not right to be keepin' Mr. Davoren an' Mr. Shields awake.

*Seumas.* An' what made them give you such a letter as that; don't they know the state the country is in? An' you were worse to take it. Have you got it?

*Davoren.* I can't find it anywhere; isn't this terrible!

*Grigson.* Good-night, Mr. Davoren; good-night, Mr. Shields.

*Mrs. Grigson.* Good-night, Mr. Shields; good-night, Mr. Davoren.

(*They go out.* SEUMAS *and* DAVOREN *are too much concerned about the letter to respond to their good-nights.*)

*Seumas.* What were you thinkin' of when you took such a letter as that? Ye gods, has nobody any brains at all, at all? Oh, this is a hopeless country. Did you try in your pockets?

*Davoren* [*searching in his pockets*]. Oh, thanks be to God, here it is.

*Seumas.* Burn it now, an', for God's sake, don't take any letters like that again. . . . There's the motor goin' away; we can sleep in peace now for the rest of the night. Just to make sure of everything now, have a look in that bag o' Maguire's: not that there can be anything in it.

*Davoren.* If there's nothing in it, what's the good of looking?

*Seumas.* It won't kill you to look, will it?

(DAVOREN *goes over to the bag, puts it on the table, opens it, and jumps back, his face pale and his limbs trembling.*)

*Davoren.* My God, it's full of bombs, Mills bombs!

*Seumas.* Holy Mother of God, you're jokin'!

*Davoren.* If the Tans come you'll find whether I'm jokin' or no.

*Seumas.* Isn't this a nice pickle to be in? St. Anthony, look down on us!

*Davoren.* There's no use of blaming St. Anthony; why did you let Maguire leave the bag here?

*Seumas.* Why did I let him leave the bag here; why did I let him leave the bag here! How did I know what was in it? Didn't I think there was nothin' in it but spoons an' hairpins. What'll we do now; what'll we do now? Mother o' God, grant there'll be no raid to-night. I knew things ud go wrong when I missed Mass this mornin'.

*Davoren.* Give over your praying and let us try to think of what is best to be done. There's one thing certain: as soon as morning comes I'm on the run out of this house.

*Seumas.* Thinkin' of yourself, like the rest of them. Leavin' me to bear the brunt of it.

*Davoren.* And why shouldn't you bear the brunt of it? Maguire was no friend of mine; besides, it's your fault; you knew the sort of a man he was, and you should have been on your guard.

*Seumas.* Did I know he was a gunman; did I know he was a gunman; did I know he was a gunman? Did . . .

*Davoren.* Do you mean to tell me that . . .

*Seumas.* Just a moment . . .

*Davoren.* You didn't know . . .

*Seumas.* Just a moment . . .

*Davoren.* That Maguire was connected with . . .

*Seumas* [*loudly*]. Just a moment; can't . . .

*Davoren.* The Republican Movement? What's the use of trying to tell damn lies!

(MINNIE POWELL *rushes into the room. She is only partly dressed, and has thrown a shawl over her shoulders. She is in a state of intense excitement.*)

*Minnie.* Mr. Davoren, Donal, they're all round the house; they must be goin' to raid the place; I was lookin' out of the window an' I seen them; I do be on the watch every night; have you anything? If you have . . .

(*There is heard at street door a violent and continuous knocking, followed by the crash of glass and the beating of the door with rifle butts.*)

*Minnie.* There they are, there they are, there they are!

(DAVOREN *reclines almost fainting on the bed;* SEUMAS *sits up in an attitude of agonized prayerfulness;* MINNIE *alone retains her presence of mind. When she sees their panic she becomes calm, though her words are rapidly spoken, and her actions are performed with decisive celerity.*)

*Minnie.* What is it; what have you got; where are they?

*Davoren.* Bombs, bombs, bombs; my God! in the bag on the table there; we're done, we're done!

*Seumas.* Hail Mary full of grace—pray for us miserable sinners— Holy St. Anthony, do you hear them batterin' at the door—now an' at the hour of our death—say an act of contrition, Donal—there's the glass gone!

*Minnie.* I'll take them to my room; maybe they won't search it; if they do aself, they won't harm a girl. Good-bye . . . Donal.

(*She glances lovingly at* DONAL—*who is only semiconscious—as she rushes out with the bag.*)

*Seumas.* If we come through this I'll never miss a Mass again! If it's the Tommies it won't be so bad, but if it's the Tans, we're goin' to have a terrible time.

(*The street door is broken open and heavy steps are heard in the hall, punctuated with shouts of "Old the light 'ere,' 'Put 'em up,' etc. An* AUXILIARY *opens the door of the room and enters, revolver in one hand and electric torch in the other. His uniform is black, and he wears a black beret.*)

*The Auxiliary.* 'Oo's 'ere?

*Seumas* [*as if he didn't know*]. Who—who's that?

*The Auxiliary* [*peremptorily*]. 'Oo's 'ere?

*Seumas.* Only two men, mister; me an' me mate in t'other bed.

*The Auxiliary.* Why didn't you open the door?

*Seumas.* We didn't hear you knockin', sir.

*The Auxiliary.* You must be a little awd of 'earing, ay?

*Seumas.* I had rheumatic fever a few years ago, an' ever since I do be a—I do be a little deaf sometimes.

*The Auxiliary* [*to* DAVOREN]. 'Ow is it you're not in bed?

*Davoren.* I was in bed; when I heard the knockin' I got up to open the door.

*The Auxiliary.* You're a koind blowke, you are. Deloighted, like to have a visit from us, ay? Ay? [*Threatening to strike him*] Why down't you answer?

*Davoren.* Yes, sir.

*The Auxiliary.* What's your name?

*Davoren.* Davoren, Dan Davoren, sir.

*The Auxiliary.* You're not an Irishman, are you?

*Davoren.* I-I-I was born in Ireland.

*The Auxiliary.* Ow, you were, were you; Irish han' proud of it, ay? [*To* SEUMAS] What's *your* name?

*Seumas.* Seuma . . . Oh no; Jimmie Shields, sir.

*The Auxiliary.* Ow, you're a selt [*he means a Celt*], one of the seltic race that speaks a lingo of its ahn, and that's going to overthrow the British Empire—I don't think! 'Ere, where's your gun?

*Seumas.* I never had a gun in me hand in me life.

*The Auxiliary.* Now; you wouldn't know what a gun is if you sawr one, I suppowse. [*Displaying his revolver in a careless way*] 'Ere, what's that?

*Seumas.* Oh, be careful, please, be careful.

*The Auxiliary.* Why, what 'ave I got to be careful abaht?

*Seumas.* The gun; it-it-it might go off.

*The Auxiliary.* An' what prawse if it did; it can easily be relowded. Any ammunition 'ere? What's in that press?

(*He searches and scatters contents of press.*)

*Seumas.* Only a little bit o' grub; you'll get nothin' here, sir; no one in the house has any connection with politics.

*The Auxiliary.* Now? I've never met a man yet that didn't say that, but we're a little bit too ikey now to be kidded with that sort of talk.

*Seumas.* May I go an' get a drink o' water?

*The Auxiliary.* You'll want a barrel of watah before you're done with us. [*The* AUXILIARY *goes about the room examining places*] 'Ello, what's 'ere? A statue o' Christ! An' a Crucifix! You'd think you was in a bloomin' monastery.

(MRS. GRIGSON *enters, dressed disorderly and her hair awry.*)

*Mrs. Grigson.* They're turning the place upside-down. Upstairs an' downstairs they're makin' a litter of everything! I declare to God, it's awful what law-abidin' people have to put up with. An' they found a pint bottle of whisky under Dolphie's pillow, an' they're drinkin' every drop of it—an' Dolphie'll be like a devil in the mornin' when he finds he has no curer.

*The Auxiliary* [*all attention when he hears the word whisky*]. A bottle of whisky, ay? 'Ere, where do you live—quick, where do you live?

*Mrs. Grigson.* Down in the kitchen—an' when you go down will you ask them not to drink—oh, he's gone without listenin' to me.

(*While* MRS. GRIGSON *is speaking the* AUXILIARY *rushes out.*)

*Seumas* [*anxiously to* MRS. GRIGSON]. Are they searchin' the whole house, Mrs. Grigson?

*Mrs. Grigson.* They didn't leave a thing in the kitchen that they didn't flitter about the floor; the things in the cupboard, all the little odds an' ends that I keep in the big box, an . . .

*Seumas.* Oh, they're a terrible gang of blaguards—did they go upstairs?—they'd hardly search Minnie Powell's room—do you think would they, Mrs. Grigson?

*Mrs. Grigson.* Just to show them the sort of a man he was, before they come in, Dolphie put the big Bible on the table, open at the First Gospel of St. Peter, second chapter, an' marked the thirteenth to the seventeenth verse in red ink—you know the passages, Mr. Shields—[*quoting*]:

> 'Submit yourselves to every ordinance of man for the Lord's sake: whether it be to the king, as supreme; or unto governors, as unto them that are sent by him for the punishment of evildoers, an' for the praise of them that do well. . . . Love the brotherhood. Fear God. Honour the King.'

An' what do you think they did, Mr. Shields? They caught a hold of the Bible an' flung it on the floor—imagine that, Mr. Shields—flingin' the Bible on the floor! Then one of them says to another—'Jack,' says he, 'have you seen the light; is your soul saved?' An' then they grabbed hold of poor Dolphie, callin' him Mr. Moody an' Mr. Sankey, an' wanted him to offer up a prayer for the Irish Republic! An' when they were puttin' me out, there they had the poor man sittin' up in bed, his hands crossed on his breast, his eyes lookin' up at the ceilin', an' he singin' a hymn—'We shall meet in the Sweet Bye an' Bye'—an' all the time, Mr.

THE SHADOW OF A GUNMAN 289

Shields, there they were drinkin' his whisky; there's torture for you, an' they all laughin' at poor Dolphie's terrible sufferin's.

*Davoren.* In the name of all that's sensible, what did he want to bring whisky home with him for? They're bad enough sober, what'll they be like when they're drunk?

*Mrs. Grigson* [*plaintively*]. He always brings a drop home with him—he calls it his medicine.

*Seumas* [*still anxious*]. They'll hardly search all the house; do you think they will, Mrs. Grigson?

*Mrs. Grigson.* An' we have a picture over the mantelpiece of King William crossing the Boyne, an' do you know what they wanted to make out, Mr. Shields, that it was Robert Emmet, an' the picture of a sacret society!

*Seumas.* She's not listenin' to a word I'm sayin'! Oh, the country is hopeless an' the people is hopeless.

*Davoren.* For God's sake tell her to go to hell out of this—she's worse than the Auxsie.

*Seumas* [*thoughtfully*]. Let her stay where she is; it's safer to have a woman in the room. If they come across the bombs I hope to God Minnie 'll say nothin'.

*Davoren.* We're a pair of pitiable cowards to let poor Minnie suffer when we know that we and not she are to blame.

*Seumas.* What else can we do, man? Do you want us to be done in? If you're anxious to be riddled, I'm not. Besides, they won't harm her, she's only a girl, an' so long as she keeps her mouth shut it'll be all right.

*Davoren.* I wish I could be sure of that.

*Seumas.* D'ye think are they goin', Mrs. Grigson? What are they doin' now?

*Mrs. Grigson* [*who is standing at the door, looking out into the hall*]. There's not a bit of me tha's not shakin' like a jelly!

*Seumas.* Are they gone upstairs, Mrs. Grigson? Do you think, Mrs. Grigson, will they soon be goin'?

*Mrs. Grigson.* When they were makin' poor Dolphie sit up in the bed, I 'clare to God I thought every minute I'd hear their guns goin' off, an' see poor Dolphie stretched out dead in the bed—whisht, God bless us, I think I hear him moanin'!

*Seumas.* You might as well be talking to a stone! They're all hopeless, hopeless, hopeless! She thinks she hears him moanin'! It's bloody near time somebody made him moan!

*Davoren* [*with a sickly attempt at humour*]. He's moaning for the loss of his whisky.

(*During the foregoing dialogue the various sounds of a raid—orders, the tramping of heavy feet, the pulling about of furniture, etc., are heard. Now a more definite and sustained commotion is apparent. Loud and angry commands of 'Go on,' 'Get out and get into the lorry,' are heard, mingled with a girl's voice—it is* MINNIE'S—*shouting bravely, but a little hysterically, 'Up the Republic.'*)

*Mrs. Grigson* [*from the door*]. God save us, they're takin' Minnie, they're takin' Minnie Powell! [*Running out*] What in the name of God can have happened?

*Seumas.* Holy Saint Anthony grant that she'll keep her mouth shut.

*Davoren* [*sitting down on the bed and covering his face with his hands*]. We'll never again be able to lift up our heads if anything happens to Minnie.

*Seumas.* For God's sake keep quiet or somebody'll hear you; nothin'll happen to her, nothin' at all—it'll be all right if she only keeps her mouth shut.

*Mrs. Grigson* [*running in*]. They're after gettin' a whole lot of stuff in Minnie's room! Enough to blow up the whole street, a Tan says! God to-night, who'd have ever thought that of Minnie Powell!

*Seumas.* Did she say anything, is she sayin' anything, what's she sayin', Mrs. Grigson?

*Mrs. Grigson.* She's shoutin' 'Up the Republic' at the top of her voice. An' big Mrs. Henderson is fightin' with the soldiers—she's after nearly knockin' one of them down, an' they're puttin' her into the lorry too.

*Seumas.* God blast her! Can she not mind her own business? What does she want here—didn't she know there was a raid on? Is the whole damn country goin' mad? They'll open fire in a minute an' innocent people'll be shot!

*Davoren.* What way are they using Minnie, Mrs. Grigson; are they rough with her?

*Mrs. Grigson.* They couldn't be half rough enough; the little hussy, to be so deceitful; she might as well have had the house blew up! God to-night, who'd think it was in Minnie Powell!

*Seumas.* Oh, grant she won't say anything!

*Mrs. Grigson.* There they're goin' away now; ah, then I hope they'll give that Minnie Powell a coolin'.

*Seumas.* God grant she won't say anything! Are they gone, Mrs. Grigson?

*Mrs. Grigson.* With her fancy stockins, an' her pompoms, an' her crêpe de chine blouses! I knew she'd come to no good!

*Seumas.* God grant she'll keep her mouth shut! Are they gone, Mrs. Grigson?

*Mrs. Grigson.* They're gone, Mr. Shields, an' here's poor Dolphie an' not a feather astray on him. Oh, Dolphie, dear, you're all right, thanks to God; I thought you'd never see the mornin'.

*Grigson* [*entering without coat or vest*]. Of course I'm all right; what ud put a bother on Dolphie Grigson?—not the Tans anyway!

*Mrs. Grigson.* When I seen you stretched out on the bed, an' you . . . singin' a hymn . . .

*Grigson* [*fearful of possible humiliation*]. Who was singin' a hymn? D'ye hear me talkin' to you—where did you hear me singin' a hymn?

*Mrs. Grigson.* I was only jokin', Dolphie, dear; I . . .

*Grigson.* Your place is below, an' not gosterin' here to men; down with you quick!

(MRS. GRIGSON *hurriedly leaves the room.*)

*Grigson* [*nonchalantly taking out his pipe, filling it, lighting it, and beginning to smoke*]. Excitin' few moments, Mr. Davoren; Mrs. G. lost her head completely—panic-stricken. But that's only natural, all women is very nervous. The only thing to do is to show them that they can't put the wind up you; show the least sign of fright an' they'd walk on you, simply walk on you. Two of them come down— 'Put them up' revolvers under your nose— you know, the usual way. 'What's all the bother about?' says I, quite calm. 'No bother at all,' says one of them, 'only this gun might go off an' hit somebody—have you me?' says he. 'What if it does,' says I, 'a man can only die once, an' you'll find Grigson won't squeal.' 'God, you're a cool one,' says the other, 'there's no blottin' it out.'

*Seumas.* That's the best way to take them; it only makes things worse to show that you've got the wind up. 'Any ammunition here?' says the fellow that come in here. 'I don't think so,' says I, 'but you better have a look.' 'No back talk,' says he, 'or you might get plugged.' 'I don't know of any clause,' says I, 'in the British Constitution that makes it a crime for a man to speak in his own room,'—with that, he just had a look round, an' off he went.

*Grigson.* If a man keeps a stiff upper front—Merciful God, there's an ambush!

(*Explosions of two bursting bombs are heard on the street outside the house, followed by fierce and rapid revolver and rifle fire. People are heard rushing into the hall, and there is general clamour and confusion.* SEUMAS *and* DAVOREN *cower down in the room;* GRIGSON, *after a few moments' hesitation, frankly rushes out of the room to what he conceives to be the safer asylum of the kitchen. A lull follows, punctuated by an odd rifle-shot; then comes a peculiar and ominous stillness, broken in a few moments by the sounds of voices and movement. Questions are heard being asked:* 'Who was it was killed?' 'Where was she shot?' *which are answered by:* 'Minnie Powell'; 'She went to jump off the lorry an' she was shot'; 'She's not dead, is she?'; 'They say she's dead— shot through the buzzom!')

*Davoren* [*in a tone of horror-stricken doubt*]. D'ye hear what they're sayin', Shields, d'ye hear what they're sayin'?—Minnie Powell is shot.

*Seumas.* For God's sake speak easy, an' don't bring them in here on top of us again.

*Davoren.* Is that all you're thinking of? Do you realize that she has been shot to save us?

*Seumas.* Is it my fault; am I to blame?

*Davoren.* It is your fault and mine, both; oh, we're a pair of dastardly cowards to have let her do what she did.

*Seumas.* She did it off her own bat—we didn't ask her to do it.

(MRS. GRIGSON *enters. She is excited and semi-hysterical, and sincerely affected by the tragic occurrence.*)

Mrs. Grigson [*falling down in a sitting posture on one of the beds*]. What's goin' to happen next. Oh, Mr. Davoren, isn't it terrible, isn't it terrible! Minnie Powell, poor little Minnie Powell's been shot dead! They were raidin' a house a few doors down, an' had just got up in their lorries to go away, when they was ambushed. You never heard such shootin'! An' in the thick of it, poor Minnie went to jump off the lorry she was on, an' she was shot through the buzzom. Oh, it was horrible to see the blood pourin' out, an' Minnie moanin'. They found some paper in her breast, with 'Minnie' written on it, an' some other name they couldn't make out with the blood; the officer kep' it. The ambulance is bringin' her to the hospital, but what good's that when she's dead! Poor little Minnie, poor little Minnie Powell, to think of you full of life a few minutes ago, an' now she's dead!

*Davoren.* Ah me, alas! Pain, pain, pain ever, for ever! It's terrible to think that little Minnie is dead, but it's still more terrible to think that Davoren and Shields are alive! Oh, Donal Davoren, shame is your portion now till the silver cord is loosened and the golden bowl be broken. Oh, Davoren, Donal Davoren, poet and poltroon, poltroon and poet!

*Seumas* [*solemnly*]. I knew something ud come of the tappin' on the wall!

CURTAIN

ELIZABETH BOWEN

# An Evening in Anglo-Ireland, with Undertones of War[1]

LOIS, DRESSED for dinner, was tidying her writing-table; two stamped letters, her handiwork, leaned on the clock. She shook out her pink suède blotter and started to sort its contents, but had to re-read everything. Gerald, who had written about a tournament, concluded: 'You have the loveliest soft eyes.' She was perplexed, thought: 'But what can I do?' and snapped the letter, with others, under a rubber band. Then she pulled out a drawer called 'general' and swept the rest into it. She had a waste-paper basket, but only for envelopes. Strokes of the gong, brass bubbles, came bouncing up from the hall. She ran to the glass, changed a necklace, had an apprehensive interchange with her own reflection. What of the night?

Mrs. Montmorency and Laurence were in the drawing-room. They looked anxious, nothing showed the trend of the conversation. The pale room rose to a height only mirrors followed above the level of occupation; this disproportionate zone of emptiness dwarfed at all times figures and furniture. The distant ceiling imposed on consciousness its blank white oblong, and a pellucid silence, distilled from a hundred and fifty years of conversation, waited beneath the ceiling. Into this silence, voices went up in stately attenuation. Now there were no voices; Mrs. Montmorency and Laurence sat looking away from each other.

As Lois came in Laurence slapped his pockets over and saying something about a pipe left the room quickly, leaving Lois in the grip of a *tête-à-tête*. Mrs. Montmorency, seated in a window, held by a corner a copy of the *Spectator*, that had slipped down against the silk of her dress, as though she must be sure to retain this constant refuge from conversation. Vague presence, barely a silhouette, the west light sifting into her fluffy hair and lace wrappings so that she half melted, she gave so little answer to one's inquiry that one did not know how to approach. So Lois stood staring, full in the light.

'Oh, you do look sweet!' exclaimed the visitor. 'Black is so strik-

[1] From *The Last September*, London, 1929.

ing. No, you are not like Laura—I don't know who you're like.'

'Aunt Myra isn't sure about black for girls,' said Lois, sweeping forward for admiration the folds of her dress. 'But a white slip lightens it.'

'And I expect you are having a wonderful time now you're grown up?'

'Oh, well . . .' said Lois. She went across to the fireplace and rose on her tiptoes, leaning her shoulders against the marble. She tried not to look conscious. She still felt a distinct pride at having grown up at all; it seemed an achievement, like marriage or fame. Having a wonderful time, she knew, meant being attractive to a number of young men. If she said, 'Yes, I do,' it implied 'Yes, I am, very——' and she was not certain. She was not certain, either, how much she enjoyed herself. 'Well, yes, I do,' she said finally.

'Tell me,' continued Mrs. Montmorency, 'wasn't that your cousin Laurence?'

'As a matter of fact I am Uncle Richard's niece and he Aunt Myra's nephew.'

'And isn't he very intellectual?'

'I suppose he is, really.'

'I'm afraid,' said Mrs. Montmorency, 'I had no idea how to talk to him. I suppose *you'd* never find that difficult. I expect now, Lois, you're very modern.'

'Oh, well, not really,' said Lois, pleased. Mrs. Montmorency's expression, condensing now from her outline, was of such affection and interest that Lois was moved to go on: 'You could talk to him really about almost anything except about politics. He isn't allowed any here because the ones he brings over from Oxford are all wrong.'

'*Wrong?*' cried the visitor, with a startled flush, putting up a hand to her face as though to press back the mounting colour. 'Wrong—which way? How do you mean, "wrong"?'

'Inconvenient.'

'Oh,' said Mrs. Montmorency. And upon a recurrence of the puzzled silence that had been the note of Lois' entrance, Sir Richard came in. Sir Richard was very much worried by visitors who came down early for dinner: evidently he had not expected this of Francie. 'Oh!' he exclaimed reproachfully, 'this is too bad; I had no idea you were down. Myra's been delayed—you know yourself what happens.'

'Indeed, yes,' said Francie warmly. She would never have been in time herself if she had had a home of her own. Only the little blanks and rifts in her life accounted for her punctuality.

Sir Richard, touching his tie vaguely, wandered about the room, displacing with some irritation the little tables that seemed to spring up in his path, in the pent-up silence of a powerful talker not yet in gear.

'Very fine weather,' he said at last, 'warm at nights—or would you like me to shut that window?' He was bothered; he could not remember how well he had once known Francie, or decide at just what degree of intimacy he was expected to pick her up again. 'Lois has grown up, hasn't she?' he continued, pointing out his niece with an air of inspiration. 'She seems to me to have grown up very fast. Now how long is it since you saw her over in England?'

'But I never did see her.'

'That was extraordinary,' said Sir Richard, looking from one to the other. 'Didn't you meet poor Laura?'

'I did, but Lois was out.'

'That was too bad.' Sir Richard's bother increased, with a suspicion of something somewhere. He observed rather flatly: 'Then it can hardly be such a surprise to you that she's grown up.'

'Not in the same way.'

'We can all sit out on the steps to-night,' said Lois, determined to check the couple in their career of inanity. She went across to a window and folded her arms on the sill.

The screen of trees that reached like an arm from behind the house—embracing the lawns, banks and terraces in mild ascent—had darkened, deepening into a forest. Like splintered darkness, branches pierced the faltering dusk of leaves. Evening drenched the trees; the beeches were soundless cataracts. Behind the trees, pressing in from the open and empty country like an invasion, the orange bright sky crept and smouldered. Firs, bearing up to pierce, melted against the brightness. Somewhere, there was a sunset in which the mountains lay like glass.

Dark had so gained the trees that Lois, turning back from the window, was surprised at how light the room was. Day, still coming in from the fields by the south windows, was stored in the mirrors, in the sheen of the wall-paper, so that the room still shone. Mr.

Montmorency had come in and was standing where she had stood, his shoulders against the mantelpiece.

'We can sit out on the steps to-night, can't we?' persisted Lois. And because no one answered or cared and a conversation went on without her, she felt profoundly lonely, suspecting once more for herself a particular doom of exclusion. Something of the trees in their intimacy of shadow was shared by the husband and wife and their host in the tree-shadowed room. She thought of love with its gift of importance. 'I must break in on all this,' she thought as she looked round the room.

'Do you still go to sleep after dinner?' she asked Mr. Montmorency.

'It's a thing that I never have done,' he said, annoyed.

'But it's what I chiefly remember about you.'

'I'm afraid,' he said, tolerant, 'you are mixing me up with some one else.'

'Listen, Richard,' said Francie: 'are you sure we will not be shot at if we sit out late on the steps?'

Sir Richard laughed and they all shared his amusement. 'We never have yet, not even with soldiers here and Lois dancing with officers up and down the avenue. You're getting very English, Francie! Isn't Francie getting very English? Do you think maybe we ought to put sandbags behind the shutters when we shut up at nights?'

'No, but Richard, seriously——' began Francie, then, as they all stared, laughed and had to give up and go on laughing. Now in County Carlow they had said things were bad round here, that she made a grave mistake in coming at all. But then, as Richard would certainly say, that was County Carlow all over.

Lady Naylor came in arm-in-arm with Laurence and said they were all very punctual. 'The gong's only gone three minutes, also I could be certain I never heard any of you go down. But I was delayed, as I told Richard to tell you. Shall we go in?'

'Francie wants to know,' said Sir Richard, offering Francie his arm, 'if we haven't got a machine-gun?'

'Ah, you're too bad!'

'*Do* you dance on the avenue?' said Mr. Montmorency to Lois.

'Only once, for a bet. I and a man called Mr. Lesworth danced to the white gate, and the man that we had the bet with walked after us carrying the gramophone. But naturally, I don't as a rule.'

'It would come hard on your shoes, I expect,' said Mr. Montmorency distantly.

'And the men we know can't get over here in the evening, now.'

'Still, I expect you have a very gay time,' said Mr. Montmorency, and turned away.

In the dining-room, the little party sat down under the crowd of portraits. Under that constant interchange from the high-up faces staring across—now fading each to a wedge of fawn-colour, and each looking out from a square of darkness tunnelled into the wall—Sir Richard and Lady Naylor, their nephew, niece and old friends had a thin, over-bright look, seemed on the air of the room unconvincingly painted, startled, transitory. Spaced out accurately round the enormous table—whereon, in what was left of the light, damask birds and roses had an unearthly shimmer—each so enisled and distant that a remark at random, falling short of a neighbour, seemed a cry of appeal, the six, in spite of an emphasis of speech and gesture they unconsciously heightened, dwindled personally. While above, the immutable figures, shedding on the wash of dusk smiles, frowns, every vestige of personality, kept only attitude—an outmoded modesty, a quirk or a flare, hand slipped under a ruffle or spread airily over the cleft of a bosom—cancelled time, negatived personality and made of the lower cheerfulness, dining and talking, the faintest exterior friction.

In Laurence's plate of clear soup six peas floated. Six accurate spoonfuls, each with a pea in it, finished the soup. He glanced right in his aunt's direction, left in Mrs. Montmorency's: both were talking. Mr. Montmorency, listening to Lady Naylor, seemed to be looking across at Laurence, but he sat with his back to the light so that Laurence, short-sighted, could not be sure—he preferred uncertainty.

Lady Naylor spoke of the way things were, with her pointed spoon poised over her plate. She noticed the others were waiting, and with a last bright emphatic look in Hugo's direction bent to finish her soup. He said at once to Laurence: 'And what do *you* think of things?'

'Things? Over here?'

'Yes—yes.'

'Seem to be closing in,' said Laurence, crumbling his bread detachedly; 'rolling up rather.'

'Ssh!' exclaimed Lady Naylor, running out a hand at both of them over the cloth. She frowned, with a glance at the parlour-maid. 'Now you mustn't make Laurence exaggerate. All young men from Oxford exaggerate. All Laurence's friends exaggerate: I have met them.'

'If you have noticed it,' said her nephew, 'it is probably so.'

Lois, on his other side, leant eagerly to Mr. Montmorency. 'If you are interested, would you care to come and dig for guns in the plantation? Or if I dig, will you come as a witness? Three of the men on the place here swear there are guns buried in the lower plantation. Michael Keelan swears he was going through there, late, and saw men digging. I asked him, "What were they like?" and he said, "The way they would be," and I said, why didn't he ask them what they were doing, and he said, "Sure, why would I; didn't I see them digging, and they with spades?" So it appears he fled back the way he had come.'

'—Ah, that's nonsense now!' Sir Richard exploded. 'Michael would see anything: he is known to have seen a ghost. I will not have the men talking, and at all accounts I won't have them listened to.'

'All the same,' pursued Lois, 'I feel that one ought to dig. If there is nothing there I can confound Michael for the good of his soul, and if there should be guns, Uncle Richard, just think of finding them! And surely we ought to know.'

'And why would we want to know? You'll have the place full of soldiers, trampling the young trees. There's been enough damage in that plantation with the people coming to sight-see: all Michael's friends. Now I won't have digging at all: do you understand?' said Sir Richard, flushed.

Francie felt torn in herself, dividedly sympathetic. 'I expect one can't be too careful. . . . The poor young little trees . . . and besides,' she added to Lois, 'one might blow oneself up.'

'This country,' continued Sir Richard, 'is altogether too full of soldiers, with nothing to do but dance and poke old women out of their beds to look for guns. It's unsettling the people, naturally. The fact is, the Army's got into the habit of fighting and doesn't know what else to do with itself, and also the Army isn't at all what it used to be. I was held up yesterday for I wouldn't like to say how long, driving over to Ballyhinch, by a thing like a coffee-pot backing in and out of a gate, with a little brute of a fellow bobbing in and out at me from under a lid at the top. I kept my temper, but I couldn't help telling him I didn't know what the country was coming to—and just when we'd got the horses accustomed to motors. "You'll do no good," I told him, "in this unfortunate country by running about in a thing like a coffee-pot." And those patrols in lorries run you into a ditch as soon as look at you. They tell me there's a great deal of socialism now in the British Army.'

'Well, it's difficult for them all,' said his wife, pacific, 'and they're doing their best, I think. The ones who come over here seem quite pleasant.'

'What regiment have you now at Clonmore?'

'The 1st Rutlands.'

'And there are some Field Gunners and Garrison Gunners too,' added Lois. 'Most people seem to prefer the Garrison Gunners.'

'The Garrison Gunners dance better,' said Laurence to Mrs. Montmorency. 'It would be the greatest pity if we were to become a republic and all these lovely troops were taken away.'

'Fool,' said Lois across the flowers. Mr. Montmorency looked at her in surprise.

Lady Naylor continued: 'From all the talk, you might think almost anything was going to happen, but we never listen. I have made it a rule not to talk, either. In fact, if you want rumours, we must send you over to Castle Trent. And I'm afraid also the Careys are incorrigible. . . . Oh, yes, Hugo, it's all very well to talk of disintegration; of course there is a great deal of disintegration in England and on the Continent. But one does wonder sometimes whether there's really much there to disintegrate. . . . I dare say there may have been. . . . And if you talk to the people they'll tell you the whole thing's nonsense: and after all what is a country if it isn't the people? For instance, I had a long conversation this morning with Mrs. Pat Gegan, who came down about the apples—you remember her, Hugo, don't you, she always asks after you: she was really delighted to hear you were coming back—"It is the way the young ones do be a bit wild," she said, and I really agreed with her. She said young people were always the same, and wasn't it the great pity. She is a most interesting woman: she thinks a great deal. But then our people do think. Now have you ever noticed the English? I remember a year ago when I was staying with Anna Partridge in

Bedfordshire—she is always so full of doing things in the village, little meetings and so on. Well, I went to one of her meetings, and really—those village women sitting round in hats and so obviously despising her! And not a move on their faces. I said to her afterwards: "I do think you're splendid, Anna, the way you throw yourself into things—but really what you can do with people with so little brain——" She seemed quite annoyed and said that at least they were loyal. I said they hadn't got any alternative, and if they had an alternative I didn't suppose they'd see it. She said they had hearts of gold if they didn't wear them on their sleeves, and I said I thought it was a pity they didn't—it would have brightened them up a bit. She said that at least one knew where one was with them, and I said I wouldn't live among people who weren't human. Then I thought it seemed a shame to unsettle her, if she really likes living in England. . . . Oh, and I said to Mrs. Gegan this morning: "Some of your friends would like us to go, you know," and she got so indignant she nearly wept. And the Trents were telling me—— Oh, Hugo, the Trents are coming to tennis to-morrow, specially for you and Francie. And the Thompsons are coming, and I believe the Hartigans. The Hartigan girls are still all there, you'll be surprised to hear. Nobody seems to marry them—and oh, a Colonel and Mrs. Boatley are coming, and three or four of the Rutlands——'

'Five,' said Lois.

'Anyhow, several Rutlands. Everyone's so delighted to hear that you and Francie are back.'

'The Trents,' said Lois to Mr. Montmorency, with indignation, 'swear that you and they are related. But you are not, surely? It is a perfect obsession of theirs.'

When he said he supposed that he was, through an aunt's marriage, she became pensive. It seemed odd that even the Trents should have a closer claim than she had. Though it was she who had been humming with agitation the whole morning. The sweetpeas in the urn before them bore evidence to her agitation: they all slanted to the west like a falling haystack. It was true she now hoped nothing more of him, but he still was in shadow, faintly, from the kindly monolith of her childhood. What he might have been, what he persisted in being, met in her mind with a jar, with a grate of disparity. The face she had watched sleeping—wiped clear of complexity, quiet but so communicative in stillness that, watching, she seemed to have shared in some kind of suspense, stayed—like the bright blur from looking too long at a lamp—over the face now turned to her, intelligent, dulled, with its sub-acid smile. She was likely to think of him now as a limitation, Mrs. Montmorency's limitation; something about Mrs. Montmorency that was a pity. The Trents could have him.

'I expect,' she said slightingly, 'you are related to every one.'

'The longer one lives in this country,' he all too agreeably said, 'the more likely that seems.'

Yet she had been certain she felt him looking at her while she argued with Uncle Richard about the guns. Seeking a likeness, perhaps. It was this consciousness that had lent her particular fervour—though she was interested in the guns. Though when she turned round his profile was turned away—in, it seemed, the most scornful repudiation.

He had, as a matter of fact, been looking at her, but without intention and with purely surface observation of detail. When she turned away, light from behind her ran a finger round the curve of her jaw. When she turned his way, light took the uncertain, dinted cheek-line where, under the eyes, flesh was patted on delicately over the rise of the bone. Her eyes, long and soft-coloured, had the intense brimming wandering look of a puppy's; in repose her lips met doubtfully, in a never-determined line, so that she never seemed to have quite finished speaking. Her face was long, her nose modelled down from the bridge, then finished off softly and bluntly as by an upward flick of the sculptor's thumb. Her chin had emphasis, seemed ready for determination. He supposed that unformed, anxious to make an effort, she would marry early.

'Danielstown can't have been so exciting when you were here before,' said Lois to Mrs. Montmorency.

But Mrs. Montmorency, in an absence of mind amounting to exaltation, had soared over the company. She could perform at any moment, discomfitingly, these acts of levitation. She was staring into one of the portraits.

Lois was sent upstairs for the shawls; it appeared that a touch of dew on the bare skin might be fatal to Lady Naylor or Mrs. Montmorency. On the stairs, her feet found their evening echoes; she dawdled, listening. When she came down everybody was on the steps—at the top, on the wide stone plateau—the parlourmaid looking for somewhere to put the coffee tray. Mrs. Montmorency sat in the long chair; her husband was tucking a carriage rug round her knees. 'If you do that,' Lois could not help saying, 'she won't be able to walk about, which is the best part of sitting out.'

No one took any notice: Mr. Montomorency went on tucking.

'Haven't you got a wrap for yourself?' said Lady Naylor. Lois took a cushion and sat on the top step with her arms crossed, stroking her elbows. 'I shouldn't sit there,' her aunt continued; 'at this time of night stone will strike up through anything.'

'If you don't get rheumatism now,' added Francie, 'you will be storing up rheumatism.'

'It will be my rheumatism,' said Lois as gently as possible, but added inwardly: 'After you're both dead.' A thought that fifty years hence she might well, if she wished, be sitting here on the steps—with or without rheumatism—having penetrated thirty years deeper ahead into Time than they could, gave her a feeling of mysteriousness and destination. And she was fitted for this by being twice as complex as their generation—for she must be: double as many people having gone to the making of her.

Laurence, looking resentfully round for somewhere to sit—she had taken the only cushion—said: 'I suppose you think ants cannot run up your legs if you cannot see them?'

Mr. Montmorency surprised her by offering a cigarette. He had a theory, he said, that ants did not like cigarette smoke. The air was so quiet now, the flame ran up his match without a tremble. 'The ants are asleep,' she said, 'they disappear into the cracks of the steps. They don't bite, either; but the idea is horrid.'

'Don't you want a chair?' When she said she didn't, he settled back in his own. Creaks ran through the wicker, discussing him, then all was quiet. He was not due to leave the ship in which they were all rushing out into Time till ten years after the others, though it was to the others that he belonged. Turning half round, she watched light breathe at the tips of the cigarettes; it seemed as though everybody were waiting. Night now held the trees with a toneless finality. The sky shone, whiter than glass, fainting down to the fretted leafline, but was being steadily drained by the dark below, to which the grey of the lawns, like smoke, as steadily mounted. The house was highest of all with toppling immanence, like a cliff.

'I don't think,' said Francie, 'I remember anything so—so quiet as evenings here.'

'Trees,' said Laurence, shifting his pipe. His shirt-front was high above them, he stood by the door with his foot on the scraper.

'This time to-morrow,' said Lady Naylor, 'we shall want to be quiet—after the tennis party.' She let out a sigh that hung in the silence, like breath in cold air.

'Oh yes, the party! The tennis party . . .'

'Francie, did I tell you who were coming?'

'You told her,' said Laurence. 'I heard you.'

'It is the people who don't play tennis who make it so tiring.'

Something about the way, the resigned way, Francie's hands lay out on the rug gave her the look of an invalid. 'It is a good thing,' said Sir Richard, 'you two never went out to Canada. I never liked the idea myself; I was very much against it at the time, if you remember.'

'I was divided about it myself,' said Hugo. 'It seemed worth trying, and yet there was so much against it. I don't know that I should have done very much good—I wonder.'

They wondered with him, with degrees of indifference. Lois stroked her dress—the feel of the stuff was like cobwebs, sticky and damp. There must be dew falling.

'Oh!' cried Francie. '*Listen!*'

She had so given herself to the silence that the birth of sound, after which the others were still straining, had shocked her nerves like a blow. They looked, from the steps, over a bay of fields, between the plantations, that gave on a sea of space. Far east, beyond the demesne: a motor, straining cautiously out of the silence. A grind, an anguish of sound as it took the hill.

'Patrols,' said Laurence.

Hugo reached out and pressed a hand on to Francie's rug. 'Patrols,' he told her, translating the information.

Sir Richard explained severely: 'Out every night—not always in this direction.'

'They're early; it's half-past nine. Now I wonder . . .'

The sound paused, for a moment a pale light showed up the sky in the darkness. Then behind the screen of trees at the skyline, demesne boundary, the sound moved shakily, stoopingly, like some one running and crouching behind a hedge. The jarring echoed down the spines of the listeners. They heard with a sense of complicity.

'A furtive lorry is a sinister thing.'

'Laurence, it isn't furtive!' said Lady Naylor. 'Can't you be ordinary? If it wouldn't be taken in some absurd kind of way as a demonstration, I should ask the poor fellows in to have coffee.'

'They're careful enough,' said Hugo impatiently. It seemed that the lorry took pleasure in crawling with such a menace along the boundary, marking the scope of peace of this silly island, undermining solitude. In the still night sound had a breathlessness, as of intention.

'The roads are so rough,' said Lois: she could see the wary load lurching into the hedges. 'I wonder now,' she added, 'who is with the patrol to-night?'

'Some one you know?' cried Francie. But Sir Richard, who did not like his friends to be distracted from him by lorries any more than by introspection or headaches or the observation of nature, bore this down with one of his major chords:

'The lower tennis court, Hugo'—waving sideways into the darkness—'is not what it used to be. Some cattle got on to it after the rain and destroyed it. It's had rolling enough to level a mountain, but it won't be the same for a long time. D'you remember the fours we had on that court that summer—wasn't it nineteen-six—you and I and O'Donnell and poor John Trent?'

'I do. Now was it James O'Donnell or Peter that went to Ceylon?'

'That was a great summer; I never remember a summer like it. We had the hay in by the end of June.'

The lorry ground off east towards Ballyhinch; silence sifting down on its tracks like sand. Their world was clear of it and a pressure lightened. Once more they could have heard a leaf turn in the trees or a bird shifting along a branch. But they found it was now very dark. Francie shivered, and Lady Naylor, rising formally, said she thought they should go in. 'Poor John Trent,' she added, gathering up her cushions, 'never got over that trouble he had with the Sheehans over the Madder fishing. It went into court, you know, and of course he lost. We always told him to keep it out of court. He was very obstinate.'

'He was indeed,' said Sir Richard. 'He made an enemy of Sheehan and it's not a good thing to have made an enemy. Though of course he's dead nowadays, so it may not matter.'

'It may to the Archie Trents. . . . Laurence, help Uncle Richard in with the long chair, and remember to bring in your own chair afterwards.'

'I never had a chair.'

'Oh, they haven't lighted the lamp in the hall. That is too bad! I am lost without Sarah—do you remember Sarah, Francie? She died, you know.'

Lois, sitting still among rising, passing and vaguely searching figures, cried: 'But it's only just beginning! You're missing the whole point. I shall walk up the avenue.'

Francie went in, groping; trailing her rug. The three men, carrying wicker chairs, converged at the door; the chairs jostled. They all put them down and apologized. Lois repeated: 'I shall walk up the avenue.' But having arranged an order of procedure they all passed on into the house, creaking and bumping. She walked down the steps alone: she wanted to be alone, but to be regretted.

'Mind you don't get locked out!' her uncle shouted after her. The glass doors shut with a rattle.

Lois walked alone up the avenue, where she had danced with Gerald. She thought what a happy night that had been, and how foolish Mr. Montmorency now thought them. He had seemed annoyed at her being young when he wasn't. She could not hope to explain that her youth seemed to her also rather theatrical and that she was only young in that way because people expected it. She had never refused a rôle. She could not forgo that intensification, that kindling of her personality at being considered very happy and reckless, even if she were not. She could not hope to assure him she was not enjoying anything he had missed, that she was now unconvinced and anxious but intended to be quite certain, by the time she was his age, that she had once been happy. For to explain this— were explanation possible to so courteous, ironical and unfriendly a listener—would, she felt, be disloyal to herself, to Gerald, to an illusion both were called upon to maintain.

Just by the lime, in that dancing night, she had missed a step and sagged on his arm, which tightened. His hand slid up between her shoulders; then, as she steadied back to the rhythm, down again.

## AN EVENING IN ANGLO-IRELAND, WITH UNDERTONES OF WAR 307

They had set out laughing, noisy and conscious, but soon had to save their breath. Gerald's cheek, within an inch of her own, was too near to see. All the way up, he had not missed a step; he was most dependable. And remembering how the family had just now gone into the house—so flatly, so unregrettingly, slamming the glass doors—she felt *that* was what she now wanted most—his eagerness and constancy. She felt, like a steady look from him, the perfectness of their being together.

'Oh, I do want you!'

But he was very musical, he conducted a jazz band they had at the barracks; while reaching out in her thoughts she remembered, the band would be practising now. She was disappointed. To a line of tune the thought flung her, she danced on the avenue.

A shrubbery path was solid with darkness, she pressed down it. Laurels breathed coldly and close; on her bare arms the tips of leaves were timid and dank, like tongues of dead animals. Her fear of the shrubberies tugged at its chain, fear behind reason, fear before her birth; fear like the earliest germ of her life that had stirred in Laura. She went forward eagerly, daring a snap of the chain, singing; a hand to the thump of her heart, dramatic with terror. She thought of herself as forcing a pass. In her life—deprived as she saw it—there was no occasion for courage, which like an unused muscle slackened and slept.

High up a bird shrieked and stumbled down through dark, tearing the leaves. Silence healed, but kept a scar of horror. The shuttered-in drawing-room, the family sealed in lamplight, secure and bright like flowers in a paper-weight—were desirable, worth much of this to regain. Fear curled back from the carpet-border. . . . Now, on the path: grey patches worse than the dark: they slipped up her dress knee-high. The laurels deserted her groping arm. She had come to the holly, where two paths crossed.

First, she did not hear footsteps coming, and as she began to notice the displaced darkness thought what she dreaded was coming, was there within her—she was indeed clairvoyant, exposed to horror and going to see a ghost. Then steps, hard on the smooth earth; branches slipping against a trench-coat. The trench-coat rustled across the path ahead, to the swing of a steady walker. She stood by the holly immovable, blotted out in her black, and there passed within reach of her hand, with the rise and fall of a stride, a resolute profile, powerful as a thought. In gratitude for its fleshliness, she felt prompted to make some contact: not to be known seemed like a doom: extinction.

'It's a fine night,' she would have liked to observe; or, to engage his sympathies: 'Up Dublin!' or even—since it was in her uncle's demesne she was straining under a holly—boldly—'What do you want?'

It must be because of Ireland he was in such a hurry; down from the mountains, making a short cut through their demesne. Here was something else that she could not share. She could not conceive of her country emotionally: it was a way of living, an abstract of several landscapes, or an oblique frayed island, moored at the north but with an air of being detached and washed out west from the British coast.

Quite still, she let him go past in contemptuous unawareness. His intentions burnt on the dark an almost visible trail; he might well have been a murderer he seemed so inspired. The crowd of trees, straining up from passive disputed earth, each sucking up and exhaling the country's essence—swallowed him finally. She thought: 'Has he come for the guns?' A man in a trench-coat had passed without seeing her: that was what it amounted to.

She ran back to tell, in excitement. Below, the house waited; vast on its west side, with thin yellow lines round the downstairs shutters. It had that excluded, sad, irrelevant look outsides of houses take in the dark. Inside, they would all be drawing up closer to one another, tricked by the half-revelation of lamp-light. 'Compassed about,' thought Lois, 'by so great a cloud of witnesses. . . .' Chairs standing round dejectedly; upstairs, the confidently waiting beds; mirrors vacant and startling; books read and forgotten, contributing no more to life; dinner-table certain of its regular compulsion; the procession of elephants that throughout uncertain years had not broken file.

But as Lois went up the steps breathlessly, her adventure began to diminish. It held ground for a moment as she saw the rug dropped in the hall by Mrs. Montmorency sprawl like a body across the polish. Then confidence disappeared, in a waver of shadow, among the furniture. Conceivably, she had just surprised life at a significant angle in the shrubbery. But it was impossible to speak of this. At a touch from Aunt Myra adventure became literary, to Uncle Richard it suggested an inconvenience; a glance from Mr. Montmorency or Laurence would make her encounter sterile.

But what seemed most probable was that they would not listen. . . . She lighted her candle and went up to bed—uncivilly, without saying good night to anyone. Her Uncle Richard, she afterwards heard, was obliged to sit up till twelve o'clock. He had not been told she was in, so did not think it right to lock up the house.

SEAN O'FAOLAIN

# Midsummer Night Madness[1]

For a second I looked back into the city, down through the smoke at the clustered chimney-pots and roofs on whose purples and greens and blues the summer night was falling as gently as dust, falling too on the thousand tiny beacons winking and blinking beneath me to their starry counterparts above. It was just the curfew hour and the last few laggard couples went hurrying past me, their lovemaking ended abruptly for the night, lest the Tans in their roaring Lancia patrol-cars should find them conspicuous on the empty white streets of the city. Then I turned to the open fields and drew in a long draught of their sweetness, their May-month sweetness, as only a man could who had been cooped up for months past under one of those tiny roofs, seeing the life of men and women only through a peephole in a window-blind, seeing these green fields only in the far distance from an attic skylight. Mounting my bicycle I left the last gas-lamp behind, and the pavement end, and rode on happily in the open country.

Yet, though the countryside was very sweet to me after all those months among the backyards, worried and watchful lest I should run into a chance patrol or raiding-party, I kept listening, not to the chorus of the birds, not to the little wind in the bushes by the way, but nervously to every distant, tiny sound—the chuckle of a wakeful goose or hen in a near-by farmyard, or the fall of water coming suddenly within earshot, or some animal starting away from the hedge where I surprised its drowsing heavy head, and once I halted dead, my grip tight on the brakes when a donkey brayed suddenly and loudly as if he were laughing at the intense quietness of the night. Fallen hawthorn blossoms splashed with their lime the dust of the road, and so narrow were the boreens in places that the lilac and the dog-rose, hung with wisps of hay, reached down as if to be plucked, and under the over-hanging trees I could smell the pungent smell of the laurel sweating in the damp night-air. And all about me the dead silence of the coming night, unless a little stream trickled over the road and my wheels made a great double splash as they crossed it; then once again the heavy silence, drowsy with the odours of the night-flowers and the cut meadows.

[1] From *Midsummer Night Madness and Other Stories*, New York, 1932.

I was on my way to the townlands of Farrane and Kilcrea, to see why to all appearances the local battalion had been completely inactive for the last three or four months. That portion of my task I did not relish for I had known and been friendly with Stevey Long, the commandant, ever since the chances of revolution threw us together. Still I should be free of the open fields for a few days, and there was enough romance left in the revolution for me to be excited at the thought that I was to stay at a house I had known and wondered at since childhood; I might even see and meet, if he were still alive, its strange mad owner whom as children we thought more terrifying than any of the ogres in the fairy-books—old Henn of Henn Hall.

But I could hardly credit that he was still alive, for even when we were very young my mother always spoke of him as 'that old devil' or 'that old cripple' of a Henn. And an old devil he was, living up there all alone, in what she used to call his 'rooky-rawky' of a house, never married but always in a state of marriage with some woman or other. He began, I could well believe, with women of his own class, officers' wives from the barracks at B——, or Cork, or perhaps with what we used call 'horsey women' from some neighbouring or English hunt. But judging by his later life, he cannot have been over-particular at any time in his choice of women, and many a tinted London beauty must have walked his fields, looking in utter boredom at the gulls flying after the plough or the rain hanging in the bare trees, until finally, like all her predecessors and successors of many years, she in her turn cursed Henn and his Hall, and Ireland and all belonging to it, and went back gladly to the flickering city lights and the back streets, and the familiar loved smells of gas-lit theatres and stuffy hansom-cabs. Clearly, a man who lived by the things of the body—women, wine, hunting, fishing, shooting. My mother often told us how as she and a crowd of schoolgirl friends were returning from their first Communion one cold autumn afternoon they entered his fields to take a short way by the river to their homes, removing their new shoes and stockings as they always did when they left the high road, and they came on Henn—and he was a grown man then—standing in his pelt by the river, ready for a swim. She used shudder as she told how he chased them, and they ran from him, screaming with fear, throwing away the new shoes and stockings as they ran, their legs all torn on the withered rushes of the bog and the furzed hedgetops, not daring to look back to see if the naked 'madman' were catching up with them, until, as she said, they had left his fields 'forty miles behind,' and panting and exhausted they ran into their homes. Henn must have been delighted with his frolic, and I can see him, running back for his swim, his long legs and his long neck that gave him the nickname of 'Henn's Neck,' cutting through the air as he ran. And he must have been especially delighted when in the late evening the fathers and brothers of the children came looking here and there timidly for the little blue or red socks and the black shoes. It was only one of many such escapades that my mother knew, all spreading the name and legend of madness that clung to him through his life. We needed few such warnings to avoid him and his estate, but we used to say to each other, somebody's warning half-understood, that if Henn caught a little girl 'he'd salt her,' and we went in mortal terror of him and his salting for years. No wonder we used say that he had wires hidden under his fields and if you crossed even one of his ditches bells would ring up in the Hall and he would come galloping on a white horse with his hungry hounds to salt you.

It was a wonderful old house to look at, and often we looked at it from far off, sitting up on its own high hill, its two gable chimneys like two cocked ears and all its empty windows gazing wide-eyed down the river-valley—very tall, with a wide door whose steps curled down and around like moustaches. The place was a pale rain-faded pink at the end, but it was often called the Red House, and if it was ever really the *Red* House it must have been visible for miles to anyone driving westward to Crookstown along the valley, following the little river and its dark line of woods. Yet, as I tried to recall it now, only one impression remained, for we came into the city when I was quite young and there I soon forgot the Hall; but at least two or three times afterwards my father took me on an unusually long walk in that direction, and each time when he returned he said to my mother, 'We could just see the Red House up the valley beyond Kilnaglory.' And each time she said, 'Glory be to God, I wonder is that old devil Henn alive yet?' and told us all over again how he chased them in his pelt when they were little children. One of these walks was on a soft wintry day with packed clouds threatening to drop rain every minute, and the Lee and the Bride in flood, and the tall bare beeches with the rooks' nests in their tip-tops swayed and swung in the hard wind. The roads were muddy in places and there were many potholes full of rain or liquid dung and they were all wrinkled in the breeze and the flooded river ran frothing and brown and storm-blown by the very edge of the road. Off up the sodden valley, high on its rounded hill sat Henn's house, and it was really more red than pink that day because of the rain, and as we looked at it one solitary window showed a light. At the same time the cold, yellow sky behind it was turning to a most marvellous red as of blood, and the scarlet light blackened every leafless twig and already rain-black and rain-green tree-trunk that stood against it and every ditch and scooped riverbank, and lastly the road and the very sky itself became swarthy, and there was light only in the waves curling the river, and the pot-holes of the road. When the solitary window shone my father said, 'That's old Henn,' and I pictured him as an old man with a beard and long claw-hands half into the glowing ashes, so that I said, 'I think, father, it's going to be thunder and lightning,' and he looked and said, 'It might,' and to my joy we turned our backs on Henn and his house and faced for the lights and the crowds and the shop-windows of the city.

Really, I am sure, that was not Henn; he would certainly have been down at the bridge-head with his rods and his basket and his gillie. But when those same winter rains streamed down the curtainless windows now, would he not have to stand watching it, back-bent—if indeed he still lived—shivering in the bay, and return to crouch sadly—not so far removed from my childish picture of him—over his perpetual summer-to-summer fire?

You may pity him as I tell you of him, but I, riding along the darkling lanes that night, had nothing in my heart for him but hate. He was one of the class that had battened for too long on our poor people, and I was quite pleased to think that if he lived it was only in name; that if he had any charm at all left he would need it all now to attract even the coarsest women. For no London light-o'-love would be attracted to his ruin of a house now for other reasons.

Perhaps he was beyond all that, and if he was not, he would be like Juan in old age, for the farmers' daughters for miles around would shun him as they would the plague, and for such a man as Henn to descend to the women of the passing tinkers for whom alone his house would appear even yet a big house, was out of the question. And yet not even his maids who came from a distance would be in the house a day without hearing all about him from the neighbours. Perhaps, after all, the tinkers would have to suffice? But, thinking of the big Red House, with its terraced lawns, and its cypresses and its yews, and its great five-mile estate wall, all built by the first Henn, the founder not only of his line but of an industry—glass-making, and long since disappeared from Ireland—I could not believe that even such a house would fall so low.

# I

As I came to a crossways where my road dropped swiftly downhill the tenting chestnuts filled the lanes with darkness as of pitchy night, and under my wheels the lain dust was soft as velvet. Before I took this last turn on my way I looked back the road I had come and saw upthrown behind the hill that distant glow of the city's lights, a furnace-glow that made me realize how near and how far I was to the roofs and chimneys I had left. But as I looked I saw, too, how the clouds were gathering like pale flowers over the inky sky and even as I dropped silently downhill the first drops beat the fronded layers above. On my left, high as two men, rose the estate walls that had once kept the whole countryside at bay but could not now (gapped and crumbling as they were) keep a fox out or a chicken in. I passed two great entrance-gates sunken in the weeds. Then the pale ghostlike pillars of the third gate came in view across a gap in the tunnel where the rain was beating down the dust, gradually changing its pattering blows for the hissing sound of a real downpour. Head bowed I raced across the unsheltered patch and edged my bicycle through the creaking gate and was just abreast of the little Gothic door of the lodge when it swung open and a woman stepped suddenly through the laurels and caught my arm, saying roughly and passionately as she did so:

'Stevey, why did you go away? Henn was down again tonight. Stevey, I . . .'

Astonished, I made no sound. The rain beat down on us, blotting out stars and moon alike.

'Stevey,' she went on, 'I can't help it. . . .'

Then she saw her mistake, and dropped my hand.

'I'm sorry,' she said, 'I thought . . .' I laughed to put her at her ease.

'You thought I was Stevey Long.'

She turned and went back to the door and seeing me from there look after her she cried out roughly:

'Go on!'

And because I was slow in moving for all the falling rain, she cried again:

'Go on about your business. Go on!'

'What a rough, passionate creature!' I was saying to myself, only by degrees recovering from my surprise as I began to wheel my bicycle up the avenue, when I heard her steps behind me and felt her grip on my arm once more. She beckoned and drew me back into the shadow of one of the sheltering trees beside the little house and with the only grace she was capable of leant insinuatingly close to me, fingering my lapel, and said in her hollow mannish voice:

'You know Stevey Long?'

'Yes, of course I do.'

'Are you the boy he was bringing to the Hall to stay?'

'Yes.'

'He told me about you. You know him well, don't you?'

'I know Stevey for a long time.'

'He told me you were in jail with him once.'

'Did he tell you that? I was. Oh, yes! Stevey and I had many a bout together.'

She paused. Then in a low trembling voice she said, 'Do you know his girl?'

'His girl?'

'Yes. He told me all about her. He said you know her too. Tell me . . . where is she?'

Her voice was strained against the leash, became passionately intent in spite of her. I did not want to be caught by her country trickery, and I looked into her face by the light of the little window, as one always looks into the face of a person one doubts, from eye to eye searching for the truth. Seeing me hesitate she caught my arm the more fiercely.

'Tell me!'

'Why, I suppose you are Stevey's girl,' I bantered.

'Tell me, boy! She sent him letters to jail, didn't she? Oh, for Christ's sake, go on and tell me!'

She had me by the two arms now, her full bosom almost touching mine, so close to me that I could see the pouches under her eyes, her mouth dragged down wet and sensual, the little angry furrow between her eye-brows. The wind shook the heavy leaves of the chestnuts and as they scattered benediction on us the light from the little Gothic window shone on their wet leaves, and on her bosom and chest and knees. For a second I thought her blue apron drooped over her too rich, too wide hips. But when I would not speak she shook me like a dog and growled at me so fiercely that I could not refuse to reply.

'I don't know,' I said. 'She just sent letters to us, to Stevey of course, and cigarettes and fruit and things—that's all. I don't know!'

She threw me away so that I all but stumbled over my bike.

'I knew it was true,' she moaned. 'I knew it was true when they said it.'

'But anyone might write him a letter. . . .'

'He denied it. He denied he ever got a letter from her.'

In open country it is surprising how the voice sometimes echoes. Under those trees her voice resounded so that I feared she would be heard up at the Hall or down in the village.

'The liar. He's going to marry that wan. That's the wan he wants. The shcut! And look what he's going to do now.'

Her great bosom rose and fell in rage.

'Do?' I asked. "What is he going to do?'

'Who'd mind Henn? I ought to know. But Stevey. But Stevey, with his grand talk. He said *he'd* never harm me. But I won't marry him. I won't marry him. I won't. I won't!'

And she turned and ran in to the lodge, leaving me with the feeling that this Hall and estate and country-side had an unpleasant, real life of its own, a life that would spoil for me the few days of quietness that I had been dreaming of this last hour as I cycled between the hedgerows. I scarcely noticed that the sudden summer shower had ceased as I made slowly up the mossed drive, dark with unpruned trees and black laurel. Everything here too seemed to send up its sweetness into the soft wet air, even the weeds bursting through the gravel, and when I came to the front of the house the great dark cypresses might in the wet failing light have been plumes of billowy smoke that rose against the sky. I was now on the terrace before the Hall, and as I looked down into the valley to where the sound of the waters of the Bride rose murmuring through the air purified by the shower, I almost expected to see the old libertine come floating up like a spectre or a long-legged ogre through the hills.

I found my way, as I had been instructed to do, to the rear of the house and in by the servants' quarters to the great kitchen. The pale still light of a candle on the table filled the room, and at the foot of the table beneath it was a basin of dusty milk, and before the embers an old sheep-dog yawned and stretched his legs. I sat down by the fire, and, glad of the rest, began to try to understand what it was that so troubled the girl at the lodge, with her passionate raging outburst against Stevey, her cry, 'I won't marry him, I won't marry him.' But almost on my heels I heard the sound of feet mashing the gravel outside and she came into the kitchen.

'Put on some turf, boy,' she said at once. 'And blow up the fire.'

As I laid on the brown peat and sat by the side of the machine turning its handle she began to lay the table for my supper. Then we heard somebody else approach outside, and with a sudden shake of her fist to me by way of warning, she opened the door to Stevey. To her he gave a mere 'Hullo, Gypsy.'

To me he gave a cordial, 'Here we are again,' and he shook my hand several times and told me how glad he was to see me safe and sound. Sullenly the girl broke in on us with:

'Put the kettle on, Stevey, for the boy's supper,' and sent me out to the rain-barrel for some water. I rose and went, and as I passed the window, there she was struggling out of his arms like a wild animal. But when I returned she was again by the table, and he was bending down over the fire, swinging the great iron kettle forward on its crane to be filled. I lay back in the old basket chair and watched him move silently about the kitchen, finding everything where he expected to find it, his fair flock of curls all about his neck and brow like a mountainy sheep, his knees flinging apart at every step as they always did, and his hangdog head and his rounded shoulders more slouched than ever.

Since they would not speak to one another I began to ask random questions; the name of this or that townland; whether this or that family were still alive, and they answered civilly enough but would never talk a word to one another.

A nice companionable house I have come to! I was grumbling to myself; and a nice pair of quarrelsome suspicious lovers! And I was wondering if I should really have come to this house at all, or if I was to have any pleasure in my few days of freedom, when suddenly Gypsy broke silence to say that a lorry-load of Tans had gone past two hours ago on the valley road, 'roaring,' she said 'with the great venom and the drink,' shooting over the thatch of the houses in the village; they had, she even heard, killed a child and gone on without a thought, laughing at the terror of the villagers. At that Stevey burst into a terrible profane rage, but he caught my eye and fell silent. He knew my thought—if he had not been so inactive for the past four months the Tans would not be roaring their way so daringly through his territory now. 'Did anyone come to warn me?' he asked.

'Aye. The girl of the Mullinses.' And she added, 'The boys are wild tonight.'

I wished Stevey would turn to see me sneering at him. I had something to go on already, I thought, and I was looking forward to my talk with him, when the girl would leave us to ourselves. But his mind began to wander from the Tans and he began to hum moodily to himself like a man with something gnawing at his brain, until, at last, unable to keep silent any longer he came out with a very casual:

'Was, eh, was Henn down tonight, Gyp?'

I could see her turn towards me as she answered with a brazen 'No.'

Then she said under her breath to him:

'He knows what he'd get if he came.'

At once everything changed. Stevey burst suddenly into a wild roar of song, his old favourite 'Night of Stars and Night of Love,' the barcarolle from *Hoffman*—and he echoed it through the empty house so that even Gypsy gave me a wry smile as she bade me sit up to supper.

'By God, John,' he cried at me, 'we'll give those bastards of Tans something to think about. Won't we, girl?'

And he caught her up whirling her into a corner of the room so that she screamed with sudden delight and in mock fear of his rough hands. Stevey drew a long comical face at his stupidity, and she smoothed herself down and said she was all right, and so they sat in a corner of the huge fireplace while I, with my back to them, ate my salted rashers and my country bread and butter.

'Ate up, there, John,' he said; and then I heard them kissing secretly.

'I am tired,' I said.

'That's the man,' said Stevey, and they kissed again and she giggled to herself, and turning I found her tousling his already wild mop because he was making too free of her where she sat on his knee.

'She has great titties, John,' said Stevey coarsely, and she slapped his face for that, and as I went on with my supper I heard him kiss her in return. So they made their love in the dark corner, shamelessly, until I was almost finished and ready for Stevey, and then they rose suddenly and left me, to walk, as they said, down to the village now that it was so fine in the heel of the day. Stevey waved me aside when I wanted to detain him, saying the night was long and tomorrow was good too. So I was alone in the Hall, listening to the corncrake at his last dim rattle in the meadows and the doves fluting long and slow in the deep woods through the fallen dark.

As I lit my pipe and smoked under the shadow of the fireplace I began to feel that I should not have come to this house at all. True it was safe because it was the home of one of the 'garrison' people, one of those thousand unofficial blockhouses of the English on Irish soil, the last place to be suspected of harbouring a rebel. But with Stevey's girl—or rather, knowing him as I did—one of his girls in the same house, this was not a suitable place for the investigator of Stevey's short-comings. But, as when I came along the road, the quietness and the peace gradually drove all other thoughts out of my head. The city, I thought, would by now be as empty as if it had been deserted, the Lancias booming along the naked streets, their searchlights shooting down the dark lanes and the side alleys, and the funeral tramp-tramp, tramp-tramp of the patrols taking with them from every door they passed its heavy sigh of suspended fear. All this Stevey had escaped. Not for him as for us, for months on end, the sight of a rusted roof in a city backyard, the stale odour of airless bedrooms. Strange to think that one could work better in that sort of a room than where the walls were deep in lush grass and the springtime rain green-dripping from the trees into the water-butts and the cupped flowers.

The great front door banged, its echoes thundering, and steps clanked in the front hall. Another door opened and was closed again. The night had settled down about the Hall, seeped into the woods, calming the doves, and only the old tireless croaker kept up his ceaseless cry. A door opened again and steps shuffled along the passage and halted; then an old man's voice coughed and called wheedlingly.

'Gypsy?'

I was silent and again the old voice wheedled, now almost at the kitchen door:

'Is he gone, Gypsy? Are you there, my pretty?'

And as I said nothing the shuffling came nearer and the stick-tapping and coughing, and Mad Henn stood peering at me around the candle-flame. I knew him at once by his long collarless neck and his stork's legs, and his madman's face beaked and narrow like a hen.

Even here indoors he wore a little faded bowler-hat cocked airily on one side of his head, and over his shoulders and draping his body a rug. He had the face of a bird, mottled and bead-eyed, and his hair, tawny in streaks with the blister of oil, had one lock at the back that stood out like a cock's comb. As he looked at me for a moment he pulled the loose flesh of his throat or scraped with one finger the tawny scum about his lips as if he were trying to remember whether he might not have asked me to come there or had some business with me that he had forgotten. I stood up awkwardly.

'Gypsy is gone for a walk with Stevey, Mister Henn,' I said.

'And who might you be, young man, if I might ask a polite question?' his eyebrows working up and down with irritation and the strain of having to speak.

'I . . . I'm a friend of Mr. Long's.'

He sniffed so that a drop fell from his beaked nose.

'Mister Long,' he muttered in scorn. 'So you're another of 'em are you? Eh? Are you?'

'I don't quite understand,' I said, and mentally cursed Stevey for not having arranged things better than this for me. For the old fellow began to pound with his heel on the floor and his legs and hands twitched for rage so that I expected him every second to turn me out of his house at the point of his stick.

'I suppose, I say,' he piped sardonically again, 'I suppose you're another one of our new patriots? Eh? Eh? I suppose you think you can walk into any man's house and sit on his armchair and drink his liquor, eh? And threaten him if he protests against you for a cad and a bully, eh? You're another of those, are you?'

He held a decanter in his right hand, and it filled with dancing liquor. I thought it best to humour him.

'I beg your pardon, indeed, Mister Henn,' I said as humbly as I knew how, for I did not want a quarrel with the old devil. 'I'm sorry if I have intruded. But I didn't mean to. I think I have made a mistake—and I'll try if I can find the servant, or . . . find Stevey, that is . . . wherever they are . . . just now.'

It was a very undignified speech, but it seemed to strike the old man with astonishment.

'Ho!' he said. 'This is a new one. Quite polite, in fact. You're not very long on the road, young man,' he added with an air of bitter experience.

'That's all right,' I said, as I turned sullenly to go.

He halted me as I laid my hand on the door-latch—where I was going to I did not know.

'Here! It is all right. Your apology is perfectly all right. Don't go, boy. Don't you go.'

At the word 'here' I noticed how tenderly he said his r's—*here* and *your*, and *perfectly*. It was the last bit of blazonry he preserved, marking him off for all his degradation as one of the conquering race.

'Did you call me?' I asked.

'Yes,' he said.

We looked at one another silently; then, in quite another tone, as coolly and politely as if he were speaking across his decanter in a club:

'Will you have a drink?'

I looked at him in surprise.

'Come along. I should like to talk to you. You are the first of your kind that I have met who seems to have any bit of education. I'd like to talk to you for that reason. We'll have a whisky and soda. Will you join me?'

I returned, no doubt a little flattered, but largely because I did not know what else to do; and our feet went clanking on the hall-flags as if the whole house were a vault, and indeed there was everywhere a musty smell of rooms long abandoned or never tended. His drawing-room was just as I expected, a good room but battered and unkempt like a ragged tramp. At the farther end was a great superfluous fire and standing by it he poured me out a jorum of whisky in a glass whose crevices were brown with the encrustations of years, all the time peering at me around the side of a pink-bowled oil-lamp whose crude unshaded light made everything look even more drab and dirty—the bare uncarpeted floor, the fine marble fireplaces mottled and cracked, the china cabinets with broken glass and no china in them; and I remembered the look of the yards with their rusted churns and staveless barrels, and everywhere and on everything the fur of mildew and green damp.

'Here! Drink that,' he said, pouring himself another glass and throwing it off at a gulp, raw.

'That's the way to take your liquor. I suppose you'll empty the siphon in yours, eh? Hum! If you didn't have a revolver stuck in your back pockets what would you young fellows have over us? Oh, you're stronger—but have you more grit? Let me look at you.'

I stood up for the drink, and he peered at me.

'Ah!' he wailed. 'There's only one thing I regret, one thing I've lost and that's clear eyes. The whole year is all like foggy autumn to me. I see the trees and the woods as if they were clouded in mist. It's a great blessing. I go out on a fine evening like this evening and it's like an evening in winter to me when the light fails at four o'clock in the afternoon and every hill is a valley and every tree is twice as far away as it really is.'

His streaming eyes strayed to the caverns of the fire, but the flames shone dully in the milky cataracts of the old fading pink-shot pupils.

'Why are you in this business, tell me?' he asked of a sudden.

'I . . . I believe in it,' I said awkwardly.

He threw up his hand in disgust.

'I believed in things once,' he said. 'I had ideas about the people, the people on my land. I thought I'd get them to do things with their land—I was ready to help them with loans and advice. I'd tell them how to drain it, how to grow more variety of vegetables, and how to make money out of their gardens selling the produce in the city, and how to make better butter and keep their eggs clean. . . .'

He sniffed in a long sneer at himself and pulled his throat and looked absently into the fire.

'Look at them, today. As dirty as ever, as poor as ever, as backward as ever, and I suppose they blame people like us for it all. If they had my land they'd know how to farm it, they think. But why haven't they done anything with their own? Why? Why?'

He was a hot-tempered old fellow, flying into a temper at a second's warning.

'But you're a city boy, you know nothing of the people. It's people like us who know Ireland. We belong to it—we who've grown up on the land and know it and the people on it.'

'Your people were merchants,' I said rather timidly.

'They made their money on bottles,' he said reaching for the whisky. 'And I've spent their money on bottles,' he added with the air of a man who has often made the same joke and grown serious over it. For as he began to pour the liquor out tremblingly he turned savagely on me.

'And who makes glass in Ireland, now?' he wheezed. 'When we stopped, why didn't somebody else take it up? They could make lovely glass in Ireland at one time. It might have become a great, a distinctive national industry, and everywhere you'd see the men blowing the glass into lovely shapes. People would be coming from abroad to see them. I've seen them as a lad. Pouf! And there you had a globe of glass, shining, coloured, glowing. Oh, no! Oh, no! What do we see in the shop-windows, now?' he cried, leaning forward and baring his rotting, easily-moved teeth. 'Cobblers! Yah! A race of cobblers. That's what we are—a race of cobblers! They hadn't it in them. They hadn't it in them!'

I saw for the first time how deep the hate on his side could be, as deep as the hate on ours, as deep and as terrible, and although he angered me there was so much contempt in his face and voice that I could scarcely muster up the courage to meet his eyes. His whisky was rising in my head.

'Oh, that was all begun two centuries ago,' I cried back at him. 'It was the Union with England that ruined us and our industries. Can't you see that? It ruined you. It ruined your glass-business. Aren't you part of Ireland as much as us?'

'Ach! It's always the same. This ruined us, and that ruined us, and the other ruined us. I tell you I'm ashamed to be called an Irishman, and in fact I'm not an Irishman. I'm a colonist—a planter—whatever you like, one of those that tried to come and do something with you people. Why didn't the people fight for their rights when they had a parliament?'

I tried to answer but he wouldn't let me, spilling his liquor all over the hearth in his rage.

'I know what you'll say. But look at the Welsh, and look at the Scotch. They haven't a parliament and they have prospered. What's to stop us from making our linens and our woven silks, from weaving patterns into them like the Italians and the Slavs? Where are our crafts? What can we show? What have we ever done? Except dig ditches and plough fields? Why haven't we stuffs, yes, stuffs, stuffs,

stuffs, of our own—stuffs' (How he spat it out!) 'that any woman would love to fold around her body, stuffs she'd love to feel against her flesh? Coloured, brilliant, delicate stuffs?'

And he began to rub his little hands down his thighs.

'Oh, fantastic!' I said, and leaned back from him smiling.

'Ah, there's your revolver man talking. But it could be done. Or why don't we export bulbs or cut-flowers like the Dutch and the French and the Channel Islanders?'

'It's impossible—the climate.'

'Pah! It's on our side. The Gulf Stream would do it.'

'The Gulf Stream?'

Mad Henn!

'Yes! It warms our southern shores. You can grow acacias in Kerry in the open air in mid-winter.' (A rush of delicate r's here.) 'I've picked London Pride on the mountains in early March. Jasmine, lilacs, fuchsias . . .'

'Fuchsia isn't a cut-flower,' I taunted. 'Nor a bulb!'

He twitched in every limb, dashed his glass in the fire and banged the hearth with his stick, and stuttered all the rest he had to say to me.

'It grows, it grows, I tell you it grows wild in mid-winter. In the open air. You're a damned obstinate young fellow. And wallflower, lily of the valley, freesia, gardenia, arbutus, mignonette. And all sorts of delicate ferns. A marvelous but a lost opportunity. These things will bring them in more money than potatoes. But they tread on them. It's so silly, really, because it's just like treading on gold.'

'But the people are farmers.'

'What are the Germans, the Dutch, the Belgians? Ah!' (It was a long-drawn-out Ah! of the sweet memories.) 'I know the people. You city fellows don't know them.'

Then his voice fell.

'I know their women,' he said.

He rubbed his little hands again and tapped me on the knee.

'I know every sort of woman: English women, French women, Italians, I've even known a Russian woman. The Russians are like the Irish, you know. But too stubborn and too obstinate and too proud. Prouder even than the Irish. And not one of them all can equal the Irish woman—of the right sort. But they're airy. You have to bind them down with a brutal religion or they'd fly over the fields from you. Don't you feel that too, eh?'

And he cocked his hat even still further over on one ear and laughed a little elfish laugh of delight and his loose lock behind almost curled like a drake's tail. He poked the embers with his stick. He filled my glass in spite of me—delighted like all old bachelors whose clubdays and dancing-days are done to have anyone at all who will talk with them.

'Ah! Yes,' he sighed as he poured my whiskey, 'the women are all right. So lovely and plump. Muscular from the fields. Arms . . . right!' (He moulded them with the bottle in his hand.) 'Breasts like tulips. Lovely! Lovely! But you don't know. You only know the city. The city! Puh! I wouldn't give that much for a city woman.'

I threw off his whisky neat.

'Why shouldn't I know the country?' I cried. 'By damn but I do. As well as you, better than you. I know their women. Many a mouse I moused with their women. What's more than that, I was born in the country and born right here in this townland. My mother was born and is buried and my grandmother and all her people before her down there in Kilcrea churchyard. I lived in the townland of Farrane myself as a child, and my father lived there before me.'

I thought he shrank into himself at that, pulling down his long neck like a snail or a tortoise at the approach of danger.

'What's your name?' he asked quietly.

I told him.

'I remember your mother well,' he said. 'She held land from me. And I remember your father. He was stationed at Kilcrea. I met him first at an eviction on my land. They shoved a red-hot poker through the door at him and he caught it; and by God he pulled it from them, so he did. A fine man.'

'I remember that,' I said, quiet myself, too, now.

'No, boy, no,' he said sadly. 'That was a long time ago.'

'Oh, but I do, well,' I cried. 'I remember the bandage on his hand.'

'Not at all,' and he smacked the stick on the side of the marble fireplace. 'This was a long time ago. Forty years or more. Forty years or more'—and as he said it his eyes strayed, rheum wet, from me to the fire and back to me again as if he were trying to see my father in me and those dead years that were gone from him for ever.

'Where is he now?' he asked.

'He's dead,' I said.

'Ah, and is he dead?'

'Yes.'

'And your mother?'

'She is dead,' I answered quietly.

'Ah!'

He looked into the embers and they seemed to glow but faintly on his all but sightless balls—a quietness more than the night fallen on him secretly and unexpectedly. Just then a step resounded on the hall-flags and the door opened and in came the dark, muscular Gypsy, behind her Stevey, slouching as ever. He did not see me at first, and he approached the old man with a low 'Good night' and I thought the long neck drew into itself again. Henn did not reply, but he raised a feeble hand and took the girl's fingers in his palm. His was as tiny as hers—and the fire shone pink between his bony fingers, ridged with the veins and threaded with the thousand wrinkles of age. As their eyes met the swan's neck curved up to her lovingly.

'Have you had a nice walk, pretty?'

'Yes, down to the bridge at the pub.'

Before him how delicately her lips said, *down,* with a voluptuous upward curve at the corners of her mouth so that they swept into her cheeks as the curved initials on his ring swept into the gold. Her sullen eyes were soft and in this light she almost looked beautiful. His hand wandered over her arm as he asked the next question—a question as familiar as Sunday. She smiled as she replied.

'Was there anything rising?' he asked.

'Down be the bridge they're leppin',' she said.

'It's the breeze. There's always a breeze fluting down that side of the valley.'

Stevey laughed loudly at them both, and his voice was rough and coarse beside the rich voice of the girl and the cultured voice of the old man.

'Leppin'? Rise? Rise, how are you! That was me spittin' when she wasn't looking.'

'Oh, then, there was a rise,' she cried. 'I saw their silver bellies shining as they leaped.'

'Ooh!' mocked Stevey. 'Bellies! Naughty word! Ooh!'

Henn gripped his stick until it trembled and his knuckles strained the skin white. He snapped at Stevey.

'If the girl says there was a rise, there was. Aren't you enough of a gentleman not to contradict her?'

But his voice trembled as if he were half afraid of his own daring. Well he might. In a second Stevey was in one of his violent passions, almost raising his fist over the old bowler-hatted head.

'I don't want any English pimp to tell me what to do or not do with the girl—or any girl. Mind that!'

Henn's hand shook, and all his legs, as he pulled himself up on his stick, taller when he stood than any of us, his bent back straightened, made gigantic by the great shadow that climbed the wall behind him. I could see what a man he was in his heyday, what a figure on a horse, wielding the rod from the top of a rock, wiry, bony giant. There was almost majesty in him as he pointed his trembling stick to the door and faced down to Stevey with:

'Leave my house, sir. I'll not be bullied any longer by you—not an hour.'

'And I'll leave it,' cried Stevey, 'when and only when I choose. I'll not be ordered by *you*. Who the hell do you think you are ordering? Do you think you can order *me*? Ho, and but let me tell you, Mister Alexander Henn, I'm *staying* here.'

I could see he had taken drink while down at the pub, and the devil was in his eyes; he skipped across the hearth by the side of Henn and flopped mockingly into the chair the old man had just left. Then he stretched out his hand for Henn's glass on the mantelpiece, and wiping the side of it on his coat-sleeve raised it in mockery of the old man. There was silence for a second and then Gypsy laughed, and the laugh cut through Henn. He raised his stick and lashed at the hand that held the empty glass in the air, and as the splinters fell I leapt, Henn thrusting his face across my arm into Stevey's face, Gypsy barely holding back Stevey's fist before it crashed into the old rheumy, half-blind eyes. Henn was all but weeping for vanity, for that laughter of the girl at his age and infirmity. All he could say between his sobs was, 'You young ruffian. You ruffian. You ruffian. . . .'

I thrust Stevey back. Henn turned to me.

'This young woman. If anything should happen to her, which God forbid . . .'

'Oh, you hypocrite,' cried Stevey, turning to the empty air for somebody to appeal to. 'Oh, listen to that. God! God forbid! Oh, the hypocrisy of it!'

'Yes, yes, yes,' I appealed and implored Gypsy to take him away and pushed him from us, and the girl dragged him, and pushed him, and persuaded him out of the room. She was strangely cool as if abuse and quarrelling and coarse talk were nothing to her. I put the old man in his chair and filled a glass for him and left him and found Stevey sullenly akimbo on the top of the steps. He was ashamed, I felt, to have played his heroics opposite me and I thought he might not have quarrelled with old Henn if he knew I was there. So I stood beside him without speaking until he said he was sorry he had broken out like that since it would ruin my chances of staying at the Hall. I could not tell of what else he was thinking, but I was thinking to myself: Where shall I go now? For I could neither remain in the Hall nor go with Stevey. My hopes of a quiet, serene night were already vanished, and I felt to Stevey as one feels towards some hooligan who breaks in on lovely music with his loud shouting and laughter. We stood in silence and looked down into the night. A frightened bird fluttered in the woods; a star fell in a graceful, fatal swoop, vanishing in mid-air as if a mighty hand had scratched the sky with light.

Biting his nails, Stevey said, 'Tell Gypsy I want her.'

I went back to the drawing-room where the girl and the old man stood by the window.

'Stevey wishes to speak to you,' I said; and when she went tramping wearily, heavily, from the room I looked at Henn and he looked back at me and neither of us spoke. As I looked away again through the shining window I could see the old man's eyes fixed on me. At last I buttoned my coat about me and turned to him.

'I suppose I'd better be going,' I said.

'Going? Where are you going?'

'I don't know really, but . . .'

'Hum! You were to stay here, I take it, eh?'

After a long hesitation I answered, 'Yes—I was. I was. I may even stay in your hay-barn yet, for all you know. Good night,' I concluded, 'I'm glad to have met you.'

'No, boy. I won't say good night. And you won't stay in my hay-barn, because I have none. Stay where you intended to stay. Even though you didn't choose to ask me, stay. If not for your own sake, for your father's and mother's sake.'

He rose and went slowly and feebly to the door, his half-emptied bottle in his hand.

'Could I stop you,' he said, 'if you wanted to stay here a month? Stay! And be damned to ye!'

'I won't,' I said.

He turned to me at the door.

'Please do stay,' he pleaded, nodding his head many times to encourage me. 'Stay, stay, stay.'

He was maudlin with the excitement and the liquor.

'Will you stay?' he asked again.

I looked out into the dark.

Stay! I thought to myself it must be near to eleven or midnight.

'Thanks very much,' I said; and being satisfied he waved his bony hand, slipping his bottle into the great pocket of his swallow-tailed coat; then he turned and went, his little hat perched on one side of his head and his rug trailing after him on the uncarpeted floor.

I sat by the table and looked about me again: at the tablecloth like a gypsy's shawl, at the threadbare carpet on the floor, at the dusty lace curtains dragged to the ends of their poles, and everything my eyes fell on mocked him and his desires. Lovely woven silks, he had said, and woven linens, and stuffs such as women might love to feel? And such strange flowers and bulbs as the Dutch and the Channel Islanders grew, as freesia, gardenia, mignonette? What a liar, I thought; and bitterly I was pleased to end the triad, calling him (as the farming folk had called him for fifty years) a lunatic; and he would not deny he was a libertine as well.

Gypsy returned, and I told her I was staying in the house, and once more she went and returned. We heard Stevey's steps vanish down the drive, and then silently she took a candle and lit me upstairs to bed. As we went I asked her what her name was, and she said:

'My name is Gammle.'

'Indeed,' I said, thoughtlessly.

'Why *indeed?*' she asked, halting in her step and looking at me.

'Nothing,' I said, 'It's just a strange name.'

But I did not tell her I was thinking that the name was well known in North Cork for a tinker tribe, in Charleville and Doneraile and the borders of Limerick and up into Clare, a name few decent men or women ever bore.

'Good night,' she said, and left me in a great empty musty room, the bed all tousled and the bed-clothes soiled and yellow. I lay down as I stood, and to the sound of the branches of the trees tapping on the bare window I dozed and slept.

## II

I awoke, wide-eyed of a sudden insomnia, to the rusted, wailing drone of an old phonograph in the room below me. By the light of the moon I looked at my watch, it was past twelve o'clock, an hour when cities begin to live and the fields are fast asleep. How many times had I not lain awake for hours listening to the quietness of the city, or to late parties singing their way homeward, before the war and curfew sent us all to our beds? I would be awake now almost until the dawn broke. Rising peevishly I went to the door, opening it in time to hear a new record begin its nasal introductory speech —This is an Edison Bell recawrd; number one seven nine nine; songs from the Awpera of Dawn Giovanni by Mozart. And then through the hollow-sounding house the stifled music of one of the loveliest of all operas; and humming with the singer, or rather behind the singer, came old blear-eyed, maudlin Henn's cracked and drunken voice:

'Batti; batti . . .'

I bade sleep good night, and dragging on my pants sat on the edge of the bed, my coat about my shoulders, smoking a cigarette. Or watched the branches beating on the panes, or the laurels shivering and shining in the tangled garden beneath my window, or the Bride rain-laden far below glinting between its ancient gall black alders under the starry sky.

> 'Questo è il fin di chi fa mal,
> E de' perfidi la morte alla vita è sempre ugual!'

The pair and their song died slowly, and when silence fell Henn kicked his enamel chamber-pot until it rang. Croaking and humming the love-song he shuffled out on his landing. From my door I watched him almost stumble headlong down the stairs, out of the house, on to the gravelled drive and out of sight into the dark.

One by one I began to hear them—those innumerable, inexplicable sounds that are to be heard at night in a house when all the casual day-sounds are still; timbers that stretch and contract, little insects that make a great creaking noise. And feeling that I had rather be in the open air than alone in this empty house I pulled on my boots and went down to the open door and out on the avenue and down towards the cottage in the track of Henn. Here a chill wind was blowing last year's leaves high in the air, but near the lodge where the drive fell sharply down to the gates between the trees on their high ditches the dust lay in soft whispering drifts— soft and white as snow under the moon, so soft that as I stood by the little deserted lodge peering curiously in through one of the windows I might have been a rabbit or a fox for all the warning I gave anyone who might be inside. Only a shaft of wavering light lay thrown across the tiny hallway from another room. Moving cautiously to the other window I peered in again. There they were, Gypsy and Henn: she with her skirt drawn above her knees, an old coat over the warm skin of her bare shoulders, toasting her shins to a little flickering fire—Henn, as he did the first time I saw them together, holding her fingers in his palm and leaning forward over her round knee to see into her eyes.

Strange to watch the unequal pair looking at one another so long, so silently, seeming not to say one word to each other, her dark head bowed sidelong to his lips, her fallen lashes on her cheeks, her parted lips that never moved, he, with a smile, foolish yet tender, sagging his quivering mouth apart, his old hat cocked forward on eyes that streamed their water to his cheeks; and yet, though Henn was old and decaying, and she warm-fleshed, white to her teeth, full of the pride of youth, and—Henn was right—her breasts like tulips fully blown, if anything too magnificently full, too Jewess soft, yet he could for all that, raise his hand now with so much languid grace to feel their roundness, hold the precious globe for one moment so lightly, so fondly on his fingers before his withered hand fell as if in despair into her lap, that finer women than Gypsy might well have smiled, even as she smiled now, with head turning slow from that flattering gesture of the epicure, with long slow-drawn sighs at the uselessness of such praise from him. To which of these men, I wondered, had this girl given herself? For now with her hair dragged on the ridge of her chair and her head falling lower and lower on her bosom until her eyes caught in the embers of the fire, she permitted him to move aside her skirt, ever so little, from her bare knee, and caress it with his withered hand as softly as if it were swansdown, caress it even after the glow of the fire shone on her eyes drowned in tears, caress it while she sat rigid with misery, her moans breaking out in trembling waves to the whispering night outside. And yet not a stir or word from Henn, but as if hoping that his old hand could quiet her child-like sobs, he caressed and caressed and looked and looked dog-like into her face. Alas! each exhausted sigh was but the prelude to a new shuddering burst of tears like waves that are silent for a while and then burst suddenly and inevitably on the shore.

I could not bear those dog-like eyes of the old libertine, nor those sighs and sobs of the young girl; and stumbling away from the light of the little window and out of the creaking gate I found myself walking on and on under the tenting chestnuts in the windy dust-blown land, up and along the highway I had come that evening, too moved to return and sit alone in my unkempt bedroom in the Hall. For somehow country and freedom seemed a small thing under this austere darkness with that pair, heavy with one another's sorrow, down in the weather-streaked decaying cottage; and with the memory of those drooping mother's breasts and that large mother's belly on the young girl, and the look of pity on the old libertine's face I find myself walking aimlessly on and on.

But suddenly across the black valley there rises a leaping yellow flame, and through the night air on the night wind comes the crackle of the burning timber, joists moist with the damp of years, burning the vermin in their cracks and the resinous veins.

The flames through the trees flickered like a huge bonfire and running down the lanes toward Henn Hall I could see from time to time as I ran the outline of windows, of a gable-end, of a chimney silhouetted against the glowing air about it. At the lodge the little light was still shining in the window but without looking through I knocked and knocked until bare padding feet came along the floor and the girl's voice said:

'Who is it? Who's there?'

'A fire,' I cried. 'What can we do? Across the valley, a big house.' And in my excitement I cried out, 'Where's Mad Henn?'

She answered through the door.

'He's not here. Isn't he at the Hall?'

I was, I admit, a fool that night.

'I don't know,' I shouted back to her.

'You don't know?'

She opened an inch or two of the door and looked out at me with frightened eyes.

'Whose house is it?' she asked.

'I don't know. It's straight over the river—straight across there.'

Holding her clothes about her body she stepped to the corner of the lodge and looked across at the blazing house.

'It's Blake's,' she said. 'We can't do anything. They may come over here. Where's Henn?' she asked then, suddenly terrified.

'I thought he was here.'

She stared at me, astonished, yet full of cunning that was mingled with fright for Henn.

'Isn't he at the Hall?' she insisted nervously.

'Maybe,' I stuttered, 'yes—perhaps he is—I suppose he *is* at the Hall.'

'Did you try?'

'I was out walking,' I said.

'Walking!'

There was a pause.

'What time is it?' she asked.

As I peered at my watch, saying, 'It's well after one o'clock,' I could see her eyes looking at me with fear and suspicion, and having spied on her I was ashamed to look up. But slowly I understood why she was watching me in that way; she thought that my coming there that night, a man 'on the run,' had something to do with this burning house, that I had caused it, as a reprisal, an act of revenge, and that in some way Henn too would suffer by it, and that Stevey, probably, had been the man who carried it out. How stupid I had been—but such reprisals were as yet rare in the country and it had never occurred to me that this was one until in her eyes I saw fear and distrust and hate.

'A nice time for walking,' she said shortly, and raced down the slope of the ditch and up to the Hall and there she knocked on the heavy hen's-head knocker until the countryside resounded and even a dog, somewhere across the fields, began to bark-bark at our knock-knock on the echoing door. I tried to explain myself.

' 'Tis why I came to the country—to sleep. I get insomnia. So I got up and came out.'

'How did you get out? Henn keeps the key in his room.'

'The door was open.'

But I was now concealing something from her and she would not believe me.

'My God,' she moaned, 'what's happened to him?'

Then in her fear and rage and suspicion she turned on me, a tigress robbed of her mate—and even in that instant I remember saying to myself, Oho! So it's Henn, is it?

'Where is he?' she cried. 'What did ye do with him? Christ blast ye all, ye set of——s. What did ye do to him?'

Her voice was echoed by the stony face of the house, thrown back into the fields and echoed there again and again by the barking dog.

'I know nothing about him,' I said angrily. 'He's probably dead drunk. Knock him up.'

And I clouted the hen's head until my hand ached. Not a sound replied but the dog over the fields, now thoroughly aroused, and crackling of the flames across the valley, and, within, the old sheepdog, who stirred and howled mournfully.

The girl caught my arm in fear.

'Oh, it's the dog crying before somebody dies.'

'Ssh! Is that a window?'

'Is it the I.R.A. that burnt it?' she asked, looking up and then over her shoulder.

'I know nothing about it. How can we get in?'

'It's for the child the Tans killed. Oh! Ye've done something to Henn. Ye've surely done something to Henn.'

We found a little scullery window open and through it I clambered and let her in at the front door. Up we climbed the dark stairs, the dog flopping along behind, and up to his room, and into it. We found him there in his bed, snoring on his stomach with the weight of drink, his nightshirt crumpled above his bare knees, and on his head a fluff-laden night-cap of scarlet wool. Ashamed of the sight of him with his dirty toes and the engrimed creases across the base of his neck and half-way up his skull, Gypsy shook him madly into a gasping wakefulness; and seeing me, in the faint glow that filled the room, smile at his comically stupid look she straightened his cap on his head as if he were a child, and covered his shoulders as he sat up in bed looking about him at the angry waving light—like a picture of Juan in hell.

'Are you all right?' she asked.

'I—yes—oh, I'm all right. But . . .'

'Look.' She pointed, and he looked.

'My God!' he cried. 'Totty Blake's.'

His eyes bulged as he looked, and trying to master himself he scrambled across the floor to stoop in the open window in his shirt.

'Oh! My God! My God!' was all he could say, and then, 'Do you hear them? Do you hear the noise?'

'The flames?' I said.

'No! The rooks. They'll never nest there again. They're ruined with the heat.'

And he began to tousle his cap and sank on his knees crying like a child. Gypsy stood over him where he knelt.

'The Blakes will be likely coming here for the night.'

He stood up at once like a hardened toper, and turned to us.

'Go down,' he said, 'and lay the table for them, and set the fire going. And you, boy, go, like a good fellow, and give her a hand.'

Gypsy went but I thought he was unable to look after himself and tried to coax him from the window.

'I'll stay here,' I whispered. 'It's cold, you know. You must dress, now. I'll help you. Come on.'

But when I tried to lead him back to the bed he flung my arm aside, peevishly.

'Am I a child?' he cried.

So I left him in a palsy of trembling, dragging his nightshirt over his head, rump-naked, fumbling for his clothes by the pale light of the candle and the fluttering light of the burning house.

In silence we set about blowing the seed of fire on the hearth into flame, and I dipped the kettle in the dark water of the butt and the crane swung it slowly over the fire. The false dawn of the fire and the distant rooks cawing with fright had awakened the doves and all the birds on this side of the valley and the night was sweet with their music. From time to time as we passed from kitchen to parlour with ware or food we halted to look at the fire that sometimes seemed to have died away and sometimes flared up more madly than ever before. There Henn joined me and we waited there, wondering if the Blakes would come or if we should go back to bed and try to sleep out the end of the night. At last he drew me into the room and filled out a drink for himself, while I yawned, dry-eyed for lack of sleep.

'I don't know where else the Blakes can go,' he said. 'Though if there was another house within three miles of them they'd rather die than come under my roof. I'm sorry for his two tits of sisters, though.'

'Only two women?' I asked wearily.

'Philamena and Agatha. Two sour tits. And the Captain, their father. That's all that's there. Oh, but Philamena *is* a sour creature. I chalked that very word on the door of the church about her when I was six—got whipped for it too. And she never spoke a word to me after. And I gave Agatha a penny at the age of eight if she'd let me swing her so high that I could see her drawers. They would never let her see me after that. I once went,' he said throwing back his liquor, 'I once went to church to a Handel service, and I had to run out of it when I saw the two virgins singing away *"To us a child is born; to us a son is given."* But, ah!' he snarled, 'they're sour titties. Vinegar for milk they have. Sour and old and virginal.'

He was getting angry with them, I could see.

'They'd just raise their hands in horror at a girl like . . . at a girl that would, that would . . .'

I stood in the corner of the window watching the sparks rising and falling endlessly like fireflies, silenced as one is always silenced by a raging fire, to think of calamity on one's doorstep.

'Gypsy,' says Henn, suddenly rising and going to another window, 'Gypsy was sick tonight.'

'Bad?' I asked sleepily.

'Bad? Oh, no! Not yet.'

'Not yet?'

'That's what I said. Didn't you hear me?'

'Yes.'

He came shuffling over to me on his stick.

'The girl is ruined,' he said, peering into my eyes that filled with shame as he looked at them.

'What do you mean by that?'

'Gypsy is going to be a mother next month or after.'

I answered his stare.

'Who do you think is to blame?' he asked.

For answer I looked angrily over the valley at the house. What did it matter to him what I thought? What would all the country think when they heard it? Another servant of Henn's—it was an old story —about to bear a child.

'I'll not be blamed;' he cried and his tubes were hoarse with passion. 'I am not to be blamed.'

'What does the girl say?'

'How does she know?'

And he went back to his glass and his fire.

And then up the avenue in a shadowy mass, singing and shouting, came the incendiaries, Stevey at their head, ready for anything, drunk with the whisky and triumph. Had it been six months later, he could safely have burnt half the houses in the district and we should not have dared, nor cared, nor had the time, nor even wished in the heat of passion—for things grew very hot by then—to question any such act of his. But tonight I ran to the door determined to thwart him. He faced up the steps and shouted for Henn, Henn the whore, Henn the cock, the Henn's neck, and all about him shouted with him out of the dark in their rough, country accents:

'Henn! Henn! Come out, you whore. Henn! Come out, Henn!'

There was a glint of a revolver in one man's hand as I ran down the steps and faced up to Stevey.

'What rotten sort of soldier are you?' I shouted at him.

'What do you mean?' he cried.

'Is that what you call soldiering?' I shouted into his face, pointing across the valley at the burning ruin. For an instant he looked at it, and then to his men and at me.

'Ah,' he shouted. 'We burnt the bastards out; didn't we boys? And damn right well they deserved it.'

They shouted it back to him, their memories full of the days when their people died of starvation by the roadsides and the big houses looked on in portly indifference. Again and again they echoed it back to him.

'And we'll burn Henn out,' cried Stevey, and made a drive for the steps. I caught him and swung him about while Henn hung over the iron railings and croaked down at us:

'If I had a gun. Oh, if I only had a gun.'

'Shut up,' I shouted at him. The crowd was nasty enough without this.

'Oh, for a gun,' he persisted. 'Just for one minute. . . .'

'Go in, blast you,' I shouted at him while Gypsy tried to drag him from the steps.

'You're fine fellows. Oh, you're great fellows,' I taunted them.

'You haven't, between the lot of you, fired a single shot in all this district for four months. Unless you shot a sitting hare or a tame fox. It's what you'd do by the look of you. And now you go and burn a couple of women out in the middle of the night. Oh, you're grand soldiers entirely. You cowardly mob!'

'You keep your tongue quiet'; from Stevey. He was a head higher than me.

'I'm here to talk to you,' I said, 'and I'll give you and your men my talk now, if you want it. Let me tell you you have the reputation of being the tamest commandant . . .'

He flew into a passion at once and drew his revolver at me. At once the country fellows skipped aside—they didn't at all like this business of drawing a gun on one of their own, and they began to mutter and pluck at Stevey, and to signal me to hold my peace; but I knew my man.

'Now, now, Long,' they muttered. 'Be aisy now, Long.'

'You won't bully me,' I said. 'Why don't you use your gun on the Tans?'

He turned to them.

'Are you going to be stopped by a city caffler?'

And to me:

'We know what Henn is.'

'What am I?' croaked Henn who was still grasping the railings, with Gypsy trying to persuade him to come in.

'What did Henn ever do to *you*?' I asked.

'Ay, what did I ever do to you?' gasped Henn, hoarse with excitement, sweeping his little hat off his head and leaning down over the railings like a man giving a speech. 'What did I do to you? What did I ever do to you or yours?'

'Ah,' shouted Stevey up to him. 'Ah, you whore-master'—and I thought he'd blow the old man's brains out. 'What do you know what's mine or yours? You blasted father of thousands.'

Utterly beyond himself he pointed with his gun at Gypsy, and shook his fist in the old man's eyes.

'Look at that girl. What did you do to her? Answer that or you'll not have a house by morning.'

Then quite without warning the rest of them turned and raced over the lawn into the surrounding night. Only one waited to pluck Stevey by the arm and whisper:

'It's the Blakes. They're coming. Come away out of this. They'll know us.'

'I don't care about the Blakes,' said Stevey, too intent on having his way with Henn that night to care about anything else. 'Ask him,' he said to me, 'ask him what did he do to that girl! Ask him that!'

'Stevey, Stevey,' implored the girl as she tried still to induce Henn to move.

I drew Stevey to one side as Henn, who had also seen the Blakes come up the drive swaying with the weight of the bundles they bore, stood down on the steps to meet them, his hat in his hand like an ambassador or a prince receiving his guests, his head like a gander's head, jigging up and down as he bowed them in; and as the two old maids came timidly up to him, peering here and there in their fear, and the portly captain, their father, brought up the rear, peeping over their shoulders because he was almost as blind as Henn, they all looked more like frightened ganders and geese than human beings able to look to themselves. They clustered together on their way up the steps, Henn wheezing about not being 'quite up to the tip-top of readiness,' and saying, 'You have me at a disadvantage, Miss Blake. But come in. A cup of hot tea, now. A shot of Martell's, Captain? Most regrettable! Terrible! This way, now. Allow me. This way. That's right—there we are. . . .' And so into the hall with his visitors.

When they were gone the dark figures gathered about us again, like wolves, or tormenting flies that had been driven aside for the moment.

'I'll make that man marry the girl,' said Stevey under his breath to me, 'or I'll burn this house to the very ground.'

'We'll burn him out,' they growled, the lust for destruction in their blood.

'He'll marry the girl, or he'll have no house over his head by morning.'

'But the man is eighty if he's a day,' I implored, 'and the girl is a mere slip of a girl. Is she twenty itself?'

'Well, he ruined her,' said Stevey up to my mouth as if he would force the words into it.

'I do not believe it,' I said.

Another shower had begun to fall by now, growing heavier drop by drop, dimming the starlight and shimmering dark about the distant fire. Stevey waved his hand to his fellows.

'The city fellows are a lot of help to us,' he said. 'But I'll show you. I'm not going to stand here all night in the rain talking with you.'

He rushed past me up the steps and into the house with his mob after him. I managed to stop him at the door of the drawing-room and we parleyed there for a while, whispering as we peeped through the cracked door. There, where fifty years ago he had leant across the shining walnut to his perfumed lights-o'-love, smiling quizzically down on them from his swan's neck, approving the painted lips, the tilted eyebrows, always gracious to them, however cynical, perpetually on the smile, only leaning back from his scandalous whispering when the butler laid a new course or refilled his glass—there, now, he offered his smoke-tainted tea, with the airs of fifty years ago, though they creaked and stuttered a little from lack of use, to the two silent, miserable old maids.

'Oh, yes, do drink a cup of tea, Miss Blake,' and he puffs out his cheeks to encourage her. 'Just one?'

'Thank you. I don't believe I really want one, Mr. Henn.'

'Oh, just one cup. Just one.'

But they sat very straight-backed and unbending, trying hard not to keep looking over the valley at their ruined home. They looked instead at the soiled tablecloth, the unequal ware, the tarnished silver, or at one another, or at the old captain, their father, who sat sucking his brandy, heavy jowled and heavy bodied, by Henn's fire. Or they looked at Gypsy, who, careless of her ungainly, ungirlish shape, danced superfluous attendance on them, full of pity for their misfortune, glad to be in the presence of real ladies even for an hour.

So they were sitting when Stevey burst in on them, calling on Henn so loudly that they almost screamed.

'Henn,' he said. 'We want you.'

'Don't go, Henn,' said the captain at once, as if he felt as much for his own sake as for Henn's that it was better they should cling together now.

'What do you want, now?' stuttered Henn.

'I want you to come too, Gypsy,' said Stevey.

'Oh, Stevey, Stevey,' said the girl, utterly ashamed before the company.

'Come on, Henn,' bullied Stevey. 'Or will I tell my business here?'
'Out with it,' says the captain.
'One minute now,' pleaded Henn.

I thought it best to get the matter over, and went up to the old man and whispered that it would be best to come—I could not keep those fellows in hand for him any longer.

'Don't go, Henn,' said the captain again.

'No, no,' said the old maids, with the same thought as their father in their minds that even Henn was better than nothing in their extremity, homeless as they were at this hour of the morning.

But he rose and went into the kitchen and Stevey and Gypsy and I after him. There he turned and faced us, looking down over us all, even over Stevey himself. And Stevey alone returned his glare, for the girl sat with her head in her hands by the fire and I looked at the rain spitting on the dark window. When Stevey had finished, all Henn could say was, 'You liar, you liar!' And all the girl could do was weep and say, 'My misfortune. My misfortune. My misfortune.' Even when I went to her and put my hand on her shoulder she only burst away from me and cried to let her alone, let her alone in her misfortune; for God's sake to let her alone in her misfortune, and sat at the table hiding her face in her hands, shaken with tears.

'You liar!' muttered Henn.

'I'm no liar,' cried Stevey.

As the girl wept with renewed shame that no man would own now that he ever loved her, Henn looked at her and said very gently to me:

'Supposing I won't marry her?'

'No harm will come to your person,' I said, and faced Stevey on that.

'Your house will go the way of Blake's,' said Stevey and faced me on that. 'If not tonight, tomorrow night; and if not then, the night after. But if I have to wait a year to do it, up it will go.'

I shook the wretched girl by the shoulder.

'Do you want to marry this old man?' I cried into her ear.

She gave no reply.

'Speak up, Gypsy,' said Stevey. 'You will marry him, won't you? You said you would.'

She said not a word now.

'I'll not marry her,' said Henn.

Stevey had cunning enough to play his last card.

'Then tell your Blake friends to get out of this house, if they have sense. Or, you needn't—I'll do it.'

Henn stopped him at the door.

'Stop. Don't! Don't!'

And thereupon he sank into a chair with a sudden dizziness, and I had to hold him up from falling sidelong to the floor.

'Gypsy,' I said. 'Get a sup of whisky.'

'Alec!' she said, going to him, and he took her hand, her little hand in his when she stood by his side and said his name. 'Alec! Will I get a sup of brandy?'

There was silence for a few minutes, with only the noise of the rain cat-pattering against the window and the three of us over Henn. At last he began to whisper through his fingers, and I leaned down to hear him.

'Will she marry me?' he was whispering while the spittle dropped like a cow's spittle between his fingers to the flagged floor.

'Now!' cried Stevey triumphantly. 'Gypsy! Will you have him?'

In her deep man's voice she replied:

'And who else would have me now? Since others won't—others that have their own life and their own plans and plots?'

And seeing that the old man was not in need of help she went out of the kitchen, holding her stomach in her little palms, murmuring as she went:

'I will, if he will.'

I pushed Stevey before me from the kitchen and leaving Henn to himself we drove the rest of the herd before us from the hall, into the darkness, so rain-arrowy and cold. From the great front door I watched them go tramping down the avenue and as I, too, turned to go upstairs to my bed I heard Henn, back in the drawing-room, trying once more to play the host, after his fifty years' interval, with his smoky tea and his patched ware. I wondered as I tramped upstairs if he was thinking that, with this young wife, he might begin life again.

From my bed I heard the summer downpour drip about the house and occasionally spit down the chimney on the damp papers stuffed in the grate, tainting all the room with their sooty reek. Not until late noon did I hear another sound, and then it was the birds singing and the croaking corncrake and the doves in the high woods, and when I rose the whole house was radiant with sunshine reflected from the fields and the trees. There was nobody about the house but

Gypsy. The Blakes had gone since early morning and Henn did not leave his bed for several days. Stevey I could find nowhere and the local men said he was gone into Kerry, swearing he would only return to make Henn keep to his promise. Two days I waited for him and searched about for news of him, and then I called a meeting of his battalion and replaced him by a new commandant.

One evening I left Henn Hall as I had come, but before I went I visited Henn in his room to say good-bye and I found him sitting over his fire, drinking punch and reading an *Anglers' Annual* of thirty years ago.

'Be careful of yourself, boy,' he warned as I turned to leave him.
'Oh, yes,' I said. 'I'll be careful.'
'Do you believe Long's story?' he said then, leaning forward to me.
'I have no cause,' I parried, 'to believe or disbelieve anybody.'
He leaned back and stared at the fire.

'Anyway,' he said after a while, 'I'm going to marry her. She's as good as the next, and better than some, even though she *is* only a tinker's daughter. Besides,' he added proudly, 'if it's a boy 'twill keep the name alive.'

As if he were a Hapsburg or a Bourbon!

One night two months or so later we heard in our backyard bedroom that a strange pair left Cork for Dublin that afternoon on the Mail Express, all their dozen or so of trunks and bags labelled forward to an address in Paris. The woman, in a massive hat with a scarlet feather, had flaunted her way to her carriage—the old man, her husband, hobbling and shuffling along yards behind her. His travelling coat almost completely hid him, its tail touching the ground, its coat-collar up about his ears, and so weak did his eyes appear to be that even in the dim filtered light of the station he had cocked his hat forward over his eyebrows and shaded his eyes with his withered hand as he walked. But I find it too painful to think of him, there in Paris, with his scraps of governess-French, guiding his tinker wife through the boulevards, the cafés, the theatres—seeing once more the lovely women and the men gay in their hour. Life is too pitiful in these recapturings of the *temps perdu*, these brief intervals of reality.

EDWARD SHEEHY

# God Send Sunday[1]

AT MIDDAY Padna found himself outside; heard the iron gate clang behind him; stood for a while listening to the keys jangling in time with the heavy tread of the porter returning to his lodge. The sky wide and blue, white roads going three ways made him want to call the porter and ask to be let in again. Then he remembered the village and Sunday. It's better for a man, Padna thought, to be with people you know in a place you are used to than among strangers. In the village the creamery said honk-honk-honk-honk all day long and the men played twenty-five in the yard behind Dorney's. Mr. Dorney said: How are we to-day, Padna? Everybody said Padna. Hello, Padna! Get to hell out of the way, Padna! But in there they were all too busy thinking of themselves and their own importance. Of course they had to be that way to be famous like the man who made all the railways in the world, or like the man who married the Indian princess and had one hundred and twenty-seven children the first year. There was no use in being in there unless you had some call to fame. A simple fellow like Padna might forget who he was entirely and forget the village. That would be a bad thing.

He took the middle road and padded along through the soft dust, going back in his mind over the morning and the good thing that had happened. The chaplain gave him a black suit that hadn't a single hole anywhere, not even at the elbows. People would take him for an important person with the kind of suit a doctor would wear, or a stationmaster if it had silver buttons, and a gentleman's shirt to go with it, white as writing paper. Yea, now, wouldn't they get the start of their lives in the village to see the toff Padna had become? With money in his pocket too, silver.

The man with the glasses was ferreting around among the papers on the desk; then he looked up and said:

'This is your train fare, Sweeney. Do you understand?'

Sure Padna understood; but he didn't like trains. There was no use in saying that though. There was no use in saying: I don't like this or that or the other. It only landed you in trouble.

'Sweeney, your train starts in half an hour. You know the sta-

---

[1] Number Five of The Tower Press Booklets (Third Series), Dublin, 1939.

tion? At the ticket office ask for a single to Coolnamanac. Remember that, a single to Coolnamanac.'

'Yea, sir, a single to Coolnamanac.' It wasn't any trouble to say and saying it didn't take you there.

'I'll be worried about you, Sweeney,' the man with the glasses said, 'but I can't spare a man to go with you. But I ask you, what in God's name can a man do when half his staff turns out to be brigadiers and commandants and the devil knows what else?'

You didn't have to answer a man who was talking to himself.

'At the station Padna says a single to Coolnamanac? Yea?'

'You'll do,' the man said, 'and take care you don't become a general. They're looking for men like you.'

'So long,' Padna said, 'see you in blighty.' The man who kept the aeroplanes had taught him that. It was a good saying; it made people laugh. Even though the man himself was a bloody liar, he had good sayings.

The village was behind miles of country to the northwest. He knew that without having to think. First there was level country for a long way, then the hills, then level country again for a while and then the village. And now it was pleasant to walk the white, dusty road with no one to say: Don't go there, Sweeney! Don't do that, Sweeney! People with quiet voices were saving hay in the meadows. The sound of the mowing-machine was bigger than the sound of the grasshopper in the meadowsweet of the ditches. No one said Padna until the village. When the haymakers said: Padna is back! Hi lads, Padna is back, then he could lie in the hay and they would give him porter and yallabuck at noon. But not till then. He must be in the village all the time and at the same time he was here with a long way to walk yet. Some things were impossible to understand. A man itches when he has fleas. There's reason in that. But some things have no reason. There must be things that even the priest wouldn't know the reason of.

The road was straight and white and grew narrow away from you. Away from you the telegraph-poles grew smaller and closer together. But the one near you was always the same and the road always the same width. A lorry coming along behind was kicking clouds of grey dust into the hedges. He got up on the bank to let it pass. But instead of passing, the lorry slowed down and stopped. There were two men in the cabin, the driver who had a square, freckled face and hair the colour of hay, and a small dark fellow with bright black eyes and a flat nose.

'Want a lift, Mister?' the driver said.

'Thanks,' Padna said.

They made room for him in the cabin and he sat up next to Flatnose. There was a sound under his feet like a giant bee in a jamjar. The lorry jerked forward. They moved faster and faster.

After a while they came to a bridge; you could see that the bridge was broken. The lorry stopped. Flatnose got down and took two planks from the back of the lorry. He laid the planks across the gap in the bridge. While he was at that the driver said:

'The country's in a nice state, Mister.'

'Yea,' Padna said, 'Fine.'

'Hell,' the driver said, 'You wouldn't talk like that if you had to jack this bus out of trenches a couple of times a day. Yea, and how would you like to find yourself at four in the bloody morning with the biggest tree in Ireland across the road in front of you and turn back and find they'd dropped another a couple of miles behind you? Hell,' the driver said, 'It's a fine bloody job, all right.' Slowly he drove forward across the planks.

'How would you like to be commandeered by one side today and the other to-morrow and never know the minute some bloody idiot'll let a gun off in your ribs? Yea, it's all very well for them but a man has to make a living and I've a wife and three kids. Yea!'

'Three kids,' Padna said. 'I like kids, you know, when they're small, before they shout and throw stones.'

'Yea,' the driver said, 'kids is all right; but they've got to be fed. See? And they've got to have boots. See? And them three of mine, they're only fly-weight, but they're harder on boots than this bus is on tyres.'

'Kids don't care about boots,' Padna said.

'Sure,' the driver said, 'but you don't know my missis. She's got notions.'

Flatnose was stowing away the planks in the back of the lorry.

'Do you know, Mister,' the driver said, 'the only job for a man at the present time?'

'What's that?' Padna said.

'Patriotism,' the driver said, 'if you're a patriot you can do anything; if you're not you're only in the way.'

'Sure,' Padna said. The redcoats pointed their guns and the patriot had a green coat standing there waiting for the bang to fall. Then the people cheered.

'Say, Mister,' the driver said, 'isn't it kind of unusual, the beard I mean. You wouldn't be an artist now?'

'I'm Padna, Mister.'

'I thought you might be an artist,' the driver said.

'No, Mister, just Padna.'

'Padna!' The driver looked hard at him.

'Yea,' Padna said, 'they all know that in the village where I'm going. Padna lives in the village and the old one washes out the chapel and goes to the doctor's and Dorney's other days.'

'That's fine,' the driver said. 'So your old one washes out the chapel.'

'Yea. On Sunday though she stays home and there's pig's cheek.'

'That's fine,' the driver said.

Flatnose climbed back into the cabin.

They started off again and soon the road was coming up and up and suddenly disappearing under you. The telegraph poles kept shooting up . . . prp . . . prp . . . into the sky. Fat green trees were whipped past your ear. The driver and Flatnose were talking but he couldn't hear what they said with the roar of the engine. Flatnose was laughing.

After a while the driver leaned across and shouted:

'Say, Padna, where do you want to get to?'

Padna smiled; he loved to hear the name; there couldn't be trouble with anyone who knew the name.

'Home,' he said, 'in the village. That's where.'

'Home,' Flatnose said.

'Yea, home,' Padna said.

'But where?' Flatnose said. 'What's the name of the place? We're not a pair of bloody mind-readers.'

'In the lane behind Mr. Dorney's,' Padna said. 'They play cards there in the yard. The old one lives behind there. I'll show you. Maybe there'll be pig's cheek. Maybe she'll give ye some if 'tis Sunday.'

'No bon,' the driver said, 'the poor bastard . . .'

'Yea,' Flatnose said, 'he's nuts all right. He might know himself where to get down though. Them looneys has instincts, like homing pigeons, or even you might say like drunks. Did you ever find yourself at home after a skite without knowing how you got there?'

'Did I hell?' the driver said.

How soon is Sunday, Padna wondered, with mass in the morning and all the people dressed up and maybe a play in the hall that night. If he wasn't Padna he'd like to be the patriot in the play and wait for the bang and fall, only first he'd speak and all the people would listen. But Padna had to stay at the back and promise to be quiet.

He nudged Flatnose and asked:

'When is Sunday, Mister?'

'He wants to know when is Sunday,' Flatnose grinned.

'Tomorrow,' Flatnose said. 'To-day's Saturday, to-morrow's Sunday.' Padna nodded and smiled.

'I'd like to know where he's going though,' the driver said. 'I don't like the idea of taking the poor bastard miles out of his way.'

'Yerra, he don't care,' Flatnose said. 'That kind don't know the meaning of time.'

'All the same,' the driver said.

In front was a low hill capped with pines. Under the pines a wheatfield was between green and gold and under that a red-roofed house half-hid among trees. What, thought Padna, happens here? He knew when he saw the side-road, the triangle of dusty grass. But already the lorry had heeled away round the bend. He tugged Flatnose by the sleeve. He shook his head in Flatnose's face and pointed towards the right. The lorry slowed down and stopped.

'I told you,' Flatnose said, 'they has instincts.'

'Is that the way you go?' the driver asked.

'Yea,' Padna said, scrambling down to the road. He put a hand in his pocket and took out one of the half-crowns. Smiling he handed it to Flatnose who took it in spite of the driver's vicious elbow in his ribs.

'Buy a drink,' Padna said, 'buy two drinks.'

'Sure,' Flatnose said, 'we'll give you all the best.'

'So long and thanks,' Padna said. 'See you in blighty,' and disappeared.

'You shouldn't have taken that dough,' the driver said.

'He'd take you in all right in them togs,' Flatnose said, 'the spit of Parnell.'

'You shouldn't have taken that dough,' the driver said.

'Aw,' Flatnose said, 'that kind don't know the value of money. They has instincts all right, but they're innocent.'

'All the same,' the driver said, revving up and slipping in the clutch.

Travelling was easy in fine weather. You could sleep anywhere. When you got hungry you went to the door of the next house and said: For the love of God, for the sake of your nearest and dearest in purgatory this day, that the Lord may grant them a lessening of their pains and a short term. That was a good saying; it nearly always meant a bite and a sup. 'Twas the best the old one knew, she always said. Anyway it got him the plateful of potatoes and a bowl of buttermilk from the young woman in the slate house. The milk was straight from the churn and had primrose blobs of butter in it. The men coming in from the hayfield wanted news of the election. How were the people feeling to the south? Was it true that Mr. Connaughton was going to address a meeting in Coolnamanac that very Sunday? Padna nodded and smiled. '*Duine le Dia*,'[1] they said, pityingly. They gave him a square of yallabuck to take on his road.

That night he slept in a hayfield, the mountains still between him and the village. With the crimson daybreak he was on the road again, the narrow hill road through heath and rock and twisted bushes. The cock-grouse crowed and the hens said *go-back, go-back*. It was Sunday already and his legs weren't quick enough for his hurry.

Soon everyone would say Padna. In the window of the medical hall were the father and mother of all the bottles, red and yellow. He would promise not to make a sound and they would let him sit at the back of the hall. That was where he wanted to be listening to the crowd cheering, clapping, shouting, the grand words of the patriot ready to die for Ireland.

The sun was high and white. The lowlands stretched to meet the sky. The hay was cut in the meadows. The corn was turning gold. As he came down out of the hill he met the people going to mass. They too were going to the village, black-coated men in twos and threes, fawn-shawled women perched high in red carts. The men

---

[1] Literally 'a person with God,' a half-wit.

bade him good-day; the young women giggled under their shawls. Padna smiled at them and kept on his way. It was Sunday and he would go to mass. At home the old one always said: Come here, Padna, till I wash your face if you're going to be in time for mass.

The chapel was hidden among trees, pines straight as brush-handles to which the country-men were hitching their horses. The bell clanged. The women hurried; the men sauntered towards the door. The bell hammering away above his head had a good sound, a sound that he knew. Inside he threw a handful of holy water over himself and the floor, bobbed his knee and slipped back into the corner behind the baptismal font. His lips kept saying: Hail-Mary-full-of-grace-the-Lord-is-with-thee, as he looked round the chapel wondering if the old one was at this mass. As the priest came out on the altar about twenty men stamped into the porch and stacked their rifles in the corner. All the people turned round in their places to look at them as they came in and crowded in Padna's corner, leaning back against the wall, crouching on one knee on the board floor.

Padna was glad because it was the village. When the priest turned round it was Father Gogarty saying: 'Your prayers are requested for the repose of the souls of . . .' They were Sunday words. Now he was looking straight at Padna down the whole length of the chapel. The people were turning to see who the priest was talking to. 'There are men here in this church,' the priest was saying, 'who should be ashamed to show their faces in the house of God.'

Padna was suddenly afraid with words like that at his throat. Only for the men about him he would have made for the door. They were angry too, muttering among themselves. He shrank back into his corner from so much anger around him. 'Men,' Father Gogarty went on, 'who are doing the work of Anti-Christ, who are in the pay of the red menace of Moscow, traitors and renegades to the religion and the country of their forefathers.'

What makes him talk like that to me, Padna wondered; is it because I didn't take the train, single for Coolnamanac, like the man with the glasses said? Here is another thing without reason.

Near him a man with a hook nose and a long face said:

'Come on, boys, I've had enough of this.'

Hooknose turned; the others crowded after him, tramping out into the porch. The way was clear; he could get away now from the voice and the eyes of all the people. In a few quick steps he was through the door, through the porch, standing in front of the men who were slinging the rifles across their shoulders. He had to stop.

'So you couldn't stand it either,' Hooknose said.

Padna nodded.

'He's Connaughton's man all right,' Hooknose said, jerking his head towards the chapel where the voice was beating against the walls trying to follow them out.

'Yea,' Padna said.

Hooknose stiffened and said:

'I'm Commandant Michael Caffrey, Coolnamanac Number One Brigade.'

The whole world is talking about this Coolnamanac, Padna thought.

Hooknose was waiting for Padna to say something; they were all waiting.

'Well,' Hooknose said, 'and who might you be, Mister?'

'Oh, I'm Padna,' Padna said.

'Padna!' Hooknose said. 'I can't say I know the name. It isn't by any chance an alias, Mr. Padna?'

'Not Mister,' Padna said, 'just Padna.'

'Well then, would you mind telling me what's your connection with the movement?' Hooknose said. He was getting angry. Padna had nothing to say to a question he didn't know the meaning of.

'Come on,' Hooknose barked, 'what are you?'

That was easy; the men who played cards in the yard behind Dorney's had taught him the answer to that.

'Padna's a fool,' he said. It was a good answer because it made them all laugh, all except Hooknose. But the others laughed and joked.

'Who did you think you had, Mick? Trotsky?'

Then a fat red-cheeked fellow slapped his thighs and laughed:

'Boys-o-boys, 'tis Padna Sweeney. Judy's Padna. 'Twas the beard put me out.'

Padna smiled at him eagerly. In the fat fellow's eyes he saw the old look of the village.

'Yea, sure, 'tis Padna. Sure. Padna Sweeney,' the men said. Hooknose was moving off.

'Come on,' he said. 'Don't stay there all day with that idiot.' The others turned to follow him.

'Wait, Mister,' Padna said, following at the fat fellow's side. 'Tell me a thing, Mister.'

'Sure,' the fat fellow said. 'Anything you like, Padna, anything you bloody well like.'

'Will there be a play at the hall, Mister, as 'tis Sunday?'

The fat fellow's laughter went jittering through the hollow air under the pines. The others turned.

'He wants to know will there be a play at the hall to-night. Will there be a play at the hall to-night?'

They all laughed, except Hooknose.

'Yea,' Hooknose said, 'a play and a half, a farce with a bloody fine finish.'

'Fine,' Padna said. 'That's fine.'

They were on the road now, going towards the village.

'Say, Padna,' the fat fellow asked, 'what kind of a play do you like?'

Padna raised his right arm above his head, clenched his fist, turned his eyes to heaven and said: 'Death to the Saxon foe!' He took up the position of a man aiming a rifle . . . 'Bang-bang.' Then he came erect, looked at them. 'You know,' he said, 'like that.'

'Then Padna, you couldn't wish to see a better play than the one to-night,' the fat fellow said, 'especially as you seem to be a bit of a patriot yourself.'

'Do you mean that, Mister? Honest?' Padna blurted out, holding the fat fellow to a standstill by the sleeve. 'You're not just taking a rise out of me?'

'Do I mean what?' They moved on, after the others.

'About Padna being a bit of a patriot, Mister.'

'Sure I mean it. Didn't you say yourself: "Death to the Saxon foe?" Didn't you register a protest by going again' the priest when he insulted the national ideals? What more do you want?'

'I don't know,' Padna said.

'Well, I'm telling you,' the fat fellow said.

'Thanks, Mister,' Padna said. 'When I go home I'll tell the old one.'

'Don't, Padna,' he spoke solemnly. 'She wouldn't like it.'

'But why, Mister? She was always at me to be something.'

'Don't ask me why,' the fat fellow said. 'Only take my advice and don't. And remember another thing,' he winked knowingly, 'patriots never ask questions. They just go right ahead. That's what they do.'

'Thanks, Mister,' Padna said.

They crossed the bridge over the railway-line. Across the village street a dog sauntered, stopping to gaze at his shadow every now and then. A distant, wavering drone came up from the valley. Hooknose stopped and held up his hand. They all stooped, listening.

'Come on,' Hooknose said. The men were unslinging their rifles. After Hooknose they scrambled across the stone wall on the left. On the other side of the wall the fat fellow turned and said:

'Go home, Padna. Quick! Go on, hurry.'

'See you in blighty,' Padna said, smiling. That was a nice fellow.

Padna went up the empty street. There in the window of the medical hall were the bottles, but not so big, not so wonderful after all. The shutters were up in Dorney's for the Sunday. Hurrying, he turned the corner into the lane. From the yard came the smell of horsedung and stale porter, the sound of a horse-hoof striking concrete to wound the dull murmur of the flies.

The last of three low houses was the house, the same, only grown down with age like an old fellow who'd be leaning on a stick. He pushed in the half-door and stooped into the brown dusk of the kitchen. There was the old one sitting in the basket-chair by the fire, looking at him with her mouth as wide as a sluice.

'I'm giving her the surprise of her life,' Padna thought, 'coming in like this with a suit on me that hasn't a single hole anywhere, not even at the elbows, and a shirt, the like of which only a toff would wear on a Sunday, it's that fine and white.'

'Padna,' Judy Sweeney said, 'Padna.' She got slowly to her feet and came towards him. 'Is it you, my poor boy? Is it you, *alannah*? Tell me because the sight's not too good at me, *alannah*.'[1]

She took his hands and moved hers up along his arms, gripping him.

'What are you crying for, Ma, and I home now?'

'Thanks be to You, God,' Judy Sweeney said, 'sure You're too good to me.'

'You're very small, Ma, terrible small.'

''Tis the age, *alannah*.'

'And thin, Ma, I can feel your bones.'

'Never mind that, *alannah*. That's a fine piece of serge you're wearing wherever you got it.'

'The priest at the place gave it to me, Ma, and the shirt too.'

'God bless him for that,' Judy Sweeney said, 'And now, *alannah*,

---
[1] Child.

put your breath to the fire and bring that kettle to the boil and we'll have a cup of tea.'

'Tell me, Ma.'

'What is it, *alannah?*'

'Is it pig's cheek to-day?'

'Maybe, now, maybe. But first go and blow that fire.'

'Wait, Ma. There's another thing.' He took the second half-crown out of his pocket. 'Here, Ma, silver.'

She rubbed the coin between her fingers.

'We'll have tea, now, *alannah*, and for dinner you'll have your pig's cheek.'

'That's fine, Ma. That's what I wanted all the time.'

As he blew on the red turf, there came the sound of gunfire. He stopped blowing to listen to the snap of the rifles, the laconic conversation of the machine-guns. What was it all about? He would like to go out and see, but as soon as he moved Judy said:

'Stay where you are, Padna, boy. The country is upside down with half the people out of their senses. Stay there and mind what you're at!'

After a while the air became heavy and quiet again. While he puffed at the fire she hobbled across the mud floor, to and fro between the table and the dresser. When the kettle boiled she scalded the pot and Padna watched her dark, bony hands spooning the tea out of the caddie. Everything was the same, Ma stooping over the blue tea-pot, taking the kettle from the crane, the throaty gush of bubbling water. Everything slow and fine. While they were eating she said:

'They sent me a letter and Mairead Grace read it to me. But how could I be going fifty miles and back in the train without a copper? Tell me, *alannah*, how did they treat you in that place?'

'Fine, Ma,' Padna said, 'fine and decent only not being able to go abroad. Some of them used to get mad and have to be tied, especially the general. Me and the general used to be weeding together. For a high-up man like him he was a sweet hand at weeding.'

'God between us and all harm,' Judy Sweeney said.

'Yea,' Padna said, 'a sweet hand. But he used to get mad at not being able to go back to his battles, real battles, with thousands of men dead at the end.'

'God help us,' Judy Sweeney said, 'sure we all has our misfortunes.'

## GOD SEND SUNDAY

The kitchen darkened suddenly with the bulk of a woman standing in the doorway.

'Is that you, Mairead?' Judy asked.

'Can I come in?' the woman said, pushing open the half-door.

'Come on in, *achree*,'[1] Judy said. 'My Padna is home.'

A big bare-armed, huge-breasted woman stooped into the kitchen and the light followed her across the floor. It was Mairead Grace.

'Yerra, Padna,' Mairead Grace said, 'give us a look at you.'

Padna stood up. Everything about the woman was big. She looked him up and down; she sighed; pulled a chair to the fire and sat down. 'He looks like a two-year-old,' she said. 'God between us and all harm, but you'd never think from the look of him he was a natural.'

'There are worse things than being simple, Mairead,' Judy said.

'So there are,' Mairead said. 'So there are, *achree*.'

'And he's a gentle soul, gentle as a child,' Judy said.

The chair complained every time Mairead drew her breath. She was big and red. Beside her his Ma looked like the moon after the sun is up. Padna smiled at the two old ones talking about him like that. Fat lot they knew about him.

'Padna,' Judy Sweeney said, 'go on out to the yard and bring me in a few sods of turf.'

When he had gone she turned to Mairead and said:

'Mairead, would you run over to Dorney's and get me half a pig's head? They'll give it to you at the back door and here's the money. I'd go myself only for being too much on his books already and he'd be wanting to take this off the bill. It's for the boy,' she said, 'the first thing he asked for.'

Evening darkened the kitchen and Padna sat with a full belly, his chair tilted back against the wall, thinking over everything. In a way it seemed as if he had never been away at all with everything the same, slow and fine, only smaller, as if the whole place had shrunk in the wash and his Ma along with it. If he went out now the people would say: Padna is back! Hello Padna! That's an elegant suit you're wearing, Padna, you look as if you'd been left a fortune. But the old one didn't want him to go out. Every time he made for the door she said: 'Stay with me, *alannah*. Sure you're only just back. Stay in to-day and to-morrow you'll see the place.'

---

[1] My dear, darling.

Anyway with your belly full you didn't really want to do anything but listen to the flies and think over things and watch the old one nodding her head, down, down, down, until her chin dropped on her chest and you knew by the sound that she was asleep in the chair, the same basket-chair as always, that would whisper for a long time, remembering the last person that sat in it. If he wanted he could go now, only it was nicer to sit and watch the fire going to sleep. Later on when the time for the play came . . . They would say: with a suit like that he should be far up among the important people. They might even. . . .

At first he thought the sound was in his head. Then he knew that the sound was in the street and that he'd been asleep. Brum-brum-brum, brum-brum-brum. It was dark and he couldn't see the old one's face to know if she was still asleep. Now the shrilling fifes went curling round the solid blocks of the drumbeats. Softly he rose and softly he crossed the floor. She didn't stir.

The air in the lane was like cool, green water. The street outside was boiling with sound. The music grew louder as the band swung round the corner into the main street and marched, brum-brum-brum-brum, up the street with small kids running bare-legged on both sides and bigger ones with boots marching in time with the band. Torches over the heads of the crowd coming along behind. The torches kept losing odd ribbons of flame in the air. A motor-car, like a big, black box with windows, crawled along very slowly in the middle of the crowd. The band stopped opposite the hall. It looks as if the fat fellow's right, Padna thought, and it's going to be a very important play. Indeed, I'm lucky to be back for it and at the very least they'll let me sit far at the back and I'll promise not to make a sound.

The band kept on playing as several gentlemen got out of the car and went through the door into the hall. The men with the torches were putting them out by stamping them into the dust. All the time people in ones and twos were going into the hall, all the time. But a lot were just standing round near the fountain, just standing still. Policemen kept wandering round among them looking into the people's faces. There was a woman lugging her kids off by the ears to put them to bed. Padna kept back in the thick of the crowd hoping that the old one wouldn't wake up and send someone to look for him. There was Mr. Dorney now, all dressed up, talking to the man at the door, a man Padna didn't know. But that didn't matter because this was the village and everyone knew Padna. The band stopped playing and started moving towards the hall; one by one they disappeared through the door. Still the people around Padna didn't make the slightest move until the policemen wandering around began to say: 'Move on there! Move on! Come on now, keep on the move!' and prod the people in the ribs with their batons.

Slowly, as if they didn't like taking orders from the policemen, the people moved up the street and down the street away from the hall. Padna had to move too because the policemen were like sheepdogs worrying the people all round him and he had to move with them. The policemen touched their caps to the priest who came down the street. They touched their caps as he passed and went on with their 'Keep moving!' It must be a very important play or the priest wouldn't be going. But all this talk about moving on was queer. Nobody liked policemen anyway. Long ago there used to be one or two holding up the wall at the post-office corner sucking straws. Now they were all over the place.

Soon there were very few people around and those were far from the hall. The policemen were just lounging against the walls and against the doctor's railings, their batons back in the holders. Suddenly in the hall the people cheered and clapped. If I don't go now, I'll be late entirely, Padna thought. He walked quickly towards the hall. The policemen swung slowly round to look at him and slowly away again. He rapped softly on the door. Even before it opened he could hear the big important voice. The door opened a few inches and a face, long like a billy-goat's, appeared in the crack. The voice of the man speaking was louder and Padna could hear the words: 'the folly of pinning our faith in a pack of moonstruck idealists.' Grand words!

'Let us in, Mister,' Padna whispered.

'Are you a member of the organisation?' the face asked.

'I don't know that,' Padna said, 'but I'll be quiet at the back. Honest, Mister.'

'You can't come in if you're not a member of the organisation,' the face said. 'Them's my instructions.'

'Honest, Mister,' Padna said, 'I'll be quiet as you like. I'm Padna and they always lets me sit at the back.'

'Them's my orders, I tell you,' the face said. 'Produce your membership card or off you go.'

While Padna was trying to think of something else to say the gap closed and left him staring at the blank wood of the door.

'Come on, now. Come on. None of that,' a heavy voice said behind him. 'Off with you now,' the policeman said.

Padna felt sick. He moved off, but not towards the lane. He went towards the railway bridge, trying to remember something he had done before, long ago, one night they wouldn't let him into the hall. Everything was fine until now; but now things were not so good.

When he came to the gap in the hedge, he remembered. He climbed through the gap and on to the railway embankment. The high grass was wet with dew as he worked his way along the slope until he came to another gap. The field on the other side was grey under the stars so that you couldn't make out the yellow of the *geosadawns*.[1] But across the field the window at the back of the hall shone through the trees, throwing shadows of their branches sprawling across a lighted square of grass. Quickly and silently he reached the trees and beyond them the wall. He hoisted himself to the top of the wall. There was no one about. The big voice was in the hall. He dropped to the ground and moved crouching along until he was under the second window. Looking up he saw the festoons of coloured paper spanning the brown wood of the ceiling. Level with his knees was a ventilator covered with a metal grid. He remembered. He smiled as he took out the grid, pleased at having remembered. As he stooped to lay the grid on the ground he heard a sound, tic-tic-tic-tic, like a clock, the image of a clock. The sound was in the hole, near his head. It was too dark to see into the hole. He put his hand into the hole and found something, a box, it felt like. He took it out; it was a box and the tic-tic-tic was in it all right. He tried to open it but the cover was stiff. Never mind now, he thought, I'll take it away with me after.

He laid the box on the ground and with his toe in the hole raised himself until his head and shoulders were above the sill. But here he found that he could only see the ceiling, the top half of Daniel O'Connell and a piece of the wall opposite, because coloured paper had been pasted on the inside of the lower panes. The sill was too narrow to sit on; when he tried he fell back to the ground with a bump, nearly on top of the box with the tic-tic going on all the time as he lay beside it. There might be something good in the box, he thought, I'll find out when I take it home. Finders, keepers! He

[1] A kind of weed.

picked up the box and moved out towards the street. Only when he saw the black, strolling shadows did he realise that he had forgotten all about the policemen. And it was too late now to turn back. And it was worse now with this box that didn't belong to him. No use in saying: finders, keepers, to a policeman.

The first one didn't take any notice of him, nor the second, nor the third. He had nearly reached the fountain when he heard: 'Come here, you. What are you hanging around for?'

Padna stopped and turned. The policeman stalked towards him and squinted into his face. Padna shivered.

'What are you up to?' the policeman growled. 'Come on. Out with it.'

'Nothing, sir.' He pulled his coat closer to hide the box.

'Come on. Come on. Don't try to pull that stuff on me. What's the game? I could run you in, y' know, for refusing to answer.'

'I found it, Mister. Honest I did,' Padna said.

'Found what?'

'The box,' Padna said, ' I found it in the hole under the window. Sure you can keep a thing if you find it.'

'What the hell are you talking about?' the policeman said. 'Where's this box?'

'Here, Mister,' Padna said, producing the box from inside his coat. 'Only I found it. Honest.'

The policeman turned the box over in his hands.

'Where did you find it? Come on, out with it.'

'At the back of the hall, Mister. First I heard the tick and then I found it.

'What tick? What are you talking about?'

'Listen, Mister.'

The policeman held the box to his ear.

'Cripes,' he said, flinging it away from him, 'a bloody mine.'

The box landed with a clatter on the wet flagstone under the pump. There's no reason in that kind of thing, Padna thought, if he didn't want it he could have given it back to me.

'Can I have it back, so, Mister?' he asked, looking to where the box lay on its edge on the flagstone, leaning against the wall of the fountain. Under his eyes the box disappeared in a wild explosion of flame and smoke. The fountain shook and split. Stones began to fall out of the air. In Padna's head a rush of sparks was quenched in sudden blackness.

Far away, on the other side of a pain in his head, men were talking. He couldn't make out what they were saying. He was lying on the ground and someone was holding his head. There was a bang, and . . . Padna fell . . . maybe he was a real patriot. What were the people saying?

The policeman was saying:

'He stated that he found the object behind the village hall, sir.'

'He didn't seem to be aware of the lethal nature of the object, sir. The locals say he's a natural, sir.'

'A what, Sergeant?' a heavy voice said gruffly.

'A natural, sir, that is to say a foolish person, sir.'

'A foolish person,' the heavy voice burst out. 'Good God, Sergeant, the man saved all our lives. Do you agree with whatever degraded section of local opinion considers that to be the act of a foolish person? The man is a hero, Sergeant. And I'll see to it that his action receives proper recognition.' The heavy voice came nearer, saying, gently now, 'How is he, Doctor?'

'He's coming to,' a voice said behind Padna's ear.

Padna raised himself to one elbow and found himself in a forest of dark, trousered legs. A big man, hatless, was bending a smooth, heavy-jowled face down towards him. Out of his mouth the same heavy voice was saying:

'Let me thank you, sir. I'm John J. Connaughton. I hope you're better, sir. What's your opinion, Doctor?'

'Just a contusion, I think,' the voice behind said, 'but of course, I can't be absolutely sure. Superficially, it's slight.'

'I'm glad of that, Doctor,' John J. Connaughton said. 'I say, Sergeant, couldn't we manage to let him have some air?'

Then the policeman started saying: 'Move back, there. Move back,' and the legs kept shuffling back and back from Padna.

With hands under his armpits, two of the policemen helped Padna to his feet in the centre of the crowd and they all looking, all the people with their eyes on Padna. There was Father Gogarty talking to John J. Connaughton, waving their arms about like people in a play. Maybe suddenly the priest would turn into the yeoman captain with fiery glare. That would be a good thing because then Padna would be able to tell what came next.

Then John J. Connaughton stepped forward and said:

'We'll resume the meeting.' He said it to all the people and then he stepped forward and took Padna by the hand. The people cheered. The cheering got mixed up with the noise in Padna's head, like the purring of a cat. Mr. Connaughton took Padna's arm and together they walked slowly between lines of people towards the door of the hall. All the people were looking at Padna, even while they stepped back from the policemen saying: 'Make way there. Make way, will ye?' they kept on looking and smiling and talking like a flock of starlings.

Behind them walked Father Gogarty and the doctor, their heads bowed close to one another's, the priest saying: '. . . the man is stubborn as a mule. He won't lead nor drive. If we'd known sooner . . . As for that idiot . . . I'll see to it that he shaves off that beard. It's . . . it's almost blasphemous.'

Now they were in the hall, marching up between the empty seats, up, up to the top where Padna had never been. He could hear the crowding feet of the people pouring into the hall behind.

On the platform was a long table with chairs along the far side. And here he was, sitting on the platform itself with the priest and Mr. Dorney and the doctor and Samuel Horton of the mills, as well as Mr. Connaughton, keeping still until all the people were in their seats. And the people were all looking at Padna as if they wanted him to do something. But what could he do until the red coats came in with guns saying: We hold this house for our lord the king, amen, say I, may all traitors swing? Only where was Anne Devlin[1] who would go down on her bended knees to plead for mercy with the cruel Yeos?[2] And the bang was already when he fell by the pump and where he got the pain in his head . . . and got the lovely suit, that hadn't a single hole anywhere, not even at the elbows, all covered with dust and dried horse-dung. It was all very mixed being a patriot with all those faces looking up at him like a lot of yobs without a smile anywhere. It might have been better almost if he stayed as he was instead of wanting to be an important person.

Father Gogarty was on his feet, clearing his throat with little coughs through a hole in his fist and beginning to talk to the people: 'I'm ashamed of ye,' he was saying in a voice that turned the faces like an east wind, 'I'm ashamed of Coolnamanac. A dastardly outrage has been perpetrated that should be a lesson to ye, that should teach ye once and for all that the only way to save this coun-

---

[1] Robert Emmet's heroic housekeeper, whom even torture could not force to inform against him.

[2] Short for the Yeomanry, 'a British volunteer cavalry force first embodied in 1794' (N.E.D.), notorious for their brutality in Ireland.

try from Red and Godless anarchy is to place her destiny in the hands of men like Mr. John J. Connaughton here. 'Twill teach ye not to be misled from yeer bounden duty by the ravings of lunatics and fly-by-nights. 'Twill teach ye that the only way to set our house in order after the madness and folly of a fratricidal civil war, is to put men of sound business instincts at the head of affairs. If I ask a man: "Where were you in nineteen-sixteen?" and if he says to me: "I was minding my business, Father," he's my man. And he's yeer man too. Remember that. I'll say no more now except to tell the candidate that every decent man in the community regrets the incident and to thank God for making a simple man His instrument to avert what might have been one of the gravest tragedies and a lasting dishonour to the name of Coolnamanac. And now, if he has recovered sufficiently from such a harrowing experience, I'll ask Mr. Connaughton to resume his interrupted address. Mr. John J. Connaughton.'

Father Gogarty sat down, slowly lowering himself into his chair while the people clapped, gently, with the decorum of *Tenebrae*.

That, Padna thought, was a grand speech, with grand words, but no word of me, not a single word. And nothing happening. Wait though! John J. Connaughton was getting up, his waistcoat creaking as he straightened and swelled his chest through a long pause during which his eyes moved over the people like a shepherd counting.

'People of Coolnamanac,' he said, 'before I continue my speech, I have a duty to perform, and that is, to pay tribute to the heroic patriotism of a fellow-citizen of yours . . . Padna Sweeney.'

At the back of the hall the people cheered, their faces back there a murky red in the dimmer lamplight.

'Padna!' the men shouted. 'Hurra for Padna! Hurra!'

At last, Padna thought, it is all coming out, at last. Please God he'll say more, only plainer, just to show them for sure.

'And though,' Mr. Connaughton was saying, 'opinion, I regret to say, doesn't seem to be unanimous in appreciating his courage and daring, to me, his action is heartening proof that the spirit of patriotism, which, in days of yore, animated men like Michael O'Dwyer, still lives in the hearts of Wicklowmen. Padna Sweeney is a patriot . . . who will be remembered . . .'

A burst of cheering from the back carried his words away. In front they only smiled. They were jealous; that was it, jealous.

'... by risking his life in an attempt to preserve the liberty of democratic institutions ...'

Father Gogarty was pulling Mr. Connaughton by the sleeve. Mr. Connaughton, bending down, was using his cupped palm as a funnel to catch the quick words about an undesirable element having gained admittance when the meeting was resumed.

From the tumult at the back, compounded of stamping feet, clapping hands, cheers, laughter and cat-calls, a voice shot up:

'Speech, Padna! Speech!'

A dozen voices took up the cry:

'Speech, Padna! Speech! Speech! Padna, speech!'

It was all coming out now. At last he was standing up to speak to the people. He mustn't smile, though; the patriot doesn't smile. Yea, he remembered now. He raised his clenched right hand above his head and shouted to the ceiling:

'Up the republic! Death to the Saxon foe!'

And at that the people at the back cheered and clapped fit to wake the dead. The people in the front seats only smiled. Jealous, they were, jealous.

Father Gogarty jumped to his feet. His hands fluttered over the people. The cheering wavered and stopped.

'There are men here who have no right here,' he said, 'men who seem to have no sense of the dignity of the proceedings. I'm asking them to leave this hall at once.'

Someone opened the door. The policemen started to move towards the back of the hall. The crowd at the back started to move with a stamping and a shuffling of heavy feet.

Outside the door they stopped and shouted back into the hall: 'Come on, Padna. Come on out, Padna.'

Padna looked around him at the faces. They were all very quiet, as if the fun was over. He looked at Father Gogarty and the priest nodded and looked towards the door. He looked at John J. Connaughton, but Mr. Connaughton was looking at the row of buttons along the bulge of his waistcoat. They were waiting for him to go; it must be the right thing to do. He smiled at the men round the table.

'See you in blighty,' he said ... and went down the steps and straight for the door. The faces of the people swung round with him as he walked.

The men carried him on their shoulders and cheered as they carried him up the street. They were decent fellows enough, but rough and without any education. They praised the grand way he behaved at the meeting. That was all right; that was fine. But soon he wanted to go home and tell the old one. You got tired of listening to a lot of fellows laughing and talking. The old one would be glad. She always wanted him to be something, like Micky Grace being a carpenter . . . only being a patriot was better.

At last he got away from them and made for the lane behind Dorney's. Everything would be fine now. There was a light in the window. He unlatched the door and stooped through into the kitchen. There, the old one was rising slowly out of her creaking chair by the fire. She turned her face to him, saying:

'God forgive you, Padna Sweeney, for tormenting me like this. May God forgive you, that's all I say.'

She was mad with him about something; but she wouldn't when she knew. His mouth was open to tell her as she went on:

'Didn't I tell you to stay at home? Didn't I? And instead of that you go gallivanting out into the night that is like bedlam with them and their politics.'

'Ma, Ma, don't mind that. Let me tell you a thing.'

'Don't talk to me. I'm going to bed.'

'Listen to me, Ma. I'm a patriot,' he shouted. 'I'm a patriot.'

'Ssh, boy. Don't talk like that, boy.' Judy Sweeney was frightened.

'But I tell you I am, Ma. The man at the hall said it. They all said it.'

'May God forgive them,' Judy Sweeney said. 'May God forgive them.'

She didn't believe him. She actually didn't believe him. The whole world said he was a patriot and here his own Ma wouldn't let him.

'Be easy, boy, be easy,' she said gently. 'Come on now, boy, I've the bed made for you. Be easy or you'll bring another attack on yourself.'

He must make her believe him.

' 'Tis true, I tell you,' he shouted. 'I'm a patriot, I tell you. That's what I am.'

'Easy, Padna boy. For the love of God. Don't look like that, *alannah*, and me your mother that bore you.' Judy Sweeney saw that the door was still open. The whole village would be listening. She must close that door, quick. Already there were faces leaning out of the dark to catch the red of the lamplight.

There she is, Padna thought, going out to tell them all that I'm not.

'Stop,' he shouted. 'Stop!'

She didn't stop. She didn't even look at him.

Before her slow shuffle had taken her half way to the door, he stepped up to her, caught her up in his arms and carried her across to the bed. He dropped her onto the bed. Around the door the people whipped in their breaths. Padna turned to see the cluster of red faces. The faces sank in the darkness and two policemen rose and stepped into the kitchen. The only sound in the world was his heart, dum-dum-dum-dum, filling the kitchen with red.

'For God's sake, have pity,' his Ma was saying. 'Leave him to me, whatever he done. Don't take him. For God's sake. It's the excitement.'

'But he doesn't look safe, Mam,' one of the policemen was saying.

'Oh, leave him to me, sir. After a while he'll be like a lamb. It's the excitement.'

'Well, Mam, if you think . . .'

'For the love of God, sir,' his Ma was saying, pleading for mercy with the cruel Yeos. It was all coming out. The lights were red like new blood. Padna was not afraid. They just go right ahead, that's what they do. He was big and they could never hold him. With a blow he could smash them up, like that. Easy as easy, and lovely to hear it ring like a bell in your head. They were both coming now, step by step. Padna jumped and sent one of them flying into the dresser. Plates and cups fell crashing on top of him. Padna smiled. Lovely.

But the old one was complaining as usual, far away.

Ah, now the place was full of them, swimming about in the redness with faces all the time in front of his fists. Only they started to hang on to him, to weigh down his legs and his shoulders so that he couldn't move any more. He couldn't do any more. The red was going out of the air and why was the old one keening? She couldn't think he was dead when he didn't even fall. The old one didn't know a good fight when she saw one.

'Have pity, Sergeant, for the love of God, don't take him. He's all I've got, Sergeant. Have pity.'

'I'm sorry, Mam,' the Sergeant said, 'but he's not safe. He'll want a while under observation.'

At the door, Padna turned and said:

'So long, Ma. See you in blighty.'

But the old one didn't even smile.

*Part IV*

# TURN ASIDE AND BROOD

*And no more turn aside and brood
Upon love's bitter mystery;
For Fergus rules the brazen cars . . .*
                    W. B. YEATS

LIAM O'FLAHERTY

# Going into Exile[1]

Patrick Feeney's cabin was crowded with people. In the large kitchen men, women, and children lined the walls, three deep in places, sitting on forms, chairs, stools, and on one another's knees. On the cement floor three couples were dancing a jig and raising a quantity of dust, which was, however, soon sucked up the chimney by the huge turf fire that blazed on the hearth. The only clear space in the kitchen was the corner to the left of the fireplace, where Pat Mullaney sat on a yellow chair, with his right ankle resting on his left knee, a spotted red handkerchief on his head that reeked with perspiration, and his red face contorting as he played a tattered old accordion. One door was shut and the tins hanging on it gleamed in the firelight. The opposite door was open and over the heads of the small boys that crowded in it and outside it, peering in at the dancing couples in the kitchen, a starry June sky was visible and, beneath the sky, shadowy grey crags and misty, whitish fields lay motionless, still and sombre. There was a deep, calm silence outside the cabin and within the cabin, in spite of the music and dancing in the kitchen and the singing in the little room to the left, where Patrick Feeney's eldest son Michael sat on the bed with three other young men, there was a haunting melancholy in the air.

The people were dancing, laughing and singing with a certain forced and boisterous gaiety that failed to hide from them the real cause of their being there, dancing, singing and laughing. For the dance was on account of Patrick Feeney's two children, Mary and Michael, who were going to the United States on the following morning.

Feeney himself, a black-bearded, red-faced, middle-aged peasant, with white ivory buttons on his blue frieze shirt and his hands stuck in his leather waist belt, wandered restlessly about the kitchen, urging the people to sing and dance, while his mind was in agony all the time, thinking that on the following day he would lose his two eldest children, never to see them again perhaps. He kept talking to everybody about amusing things, shouted at the dancers and behaved in a boisterous and abandoned manner. But every now and then he had to leave the kitchen, under the pretence of going to

[1] From *Spring Sowing and Other Stories*, London, 1924.

369

the pigsty to look at a young pig that was supposed to be ill. He would stand, however, upright against his gable and look gloomily at some star or other, while his mind struggled with vague and peculiar ideas that wandered about in it. He could make nothing at all of his thoughts, but a lump always came up his throat, and he shivered, although the night was warm.

Then he would sigh and say with a contraction of his neck: 'Oh, it's a queer world this and no doubt about it. So it is.' Then he would go back to the cabin again and begin to urge on the dance, laughing, shouting and stamping on the floor.

Towards dawn, when the floor was crowded with couples, arranged in fours, stamping on the floor and going to and fro, dancing the 'Walls of Limerick,' Feeney was going out to the gable when his son Michael followed him out. The two of them walked side by side about the yard over the grey sea pebbles that had been strewn there the previous day. They walked in silence and yawned without need, pretending to be taking the air. But each of them was very excited. Michael was taller than his father and not so thickly built, but the shabby blue serge suit that he had bought for going to America was too narrow for his broad shoulders and the coat was too wide around the waist. He moved clumsily in it and his hands appeared altogether too bony and big and red, and he didn't know what to do with them. During his twenty-one years of life he had never worn anything other than the homespun clothes of Inverara, and the shop-made clothes appeared as strange to him and as uncomfortable as a dress suit worn by a man working in a sewer. His face was flushed a bright red and his blue eyes shone with excitement. Now and again he wiped the perspiration from his forehead with the lining of his grey tweed cap.

At last Patrick Feeney reached his usual position at the gable end. He halted, balanced himself on his heels with his hands in his waist belt, coughed and said, 'It's going to be a warm day.' The son came up beside him, folded his arms and leaned his right shoulder against the gable.

'It was kind of Uncle Ned to lend the money for the dance, father,' he said. 'I'd hate to think that we'd have to go without something or other, just the same as everybody else has. I'll send you that money the very first money I earn, father . . . even before I pay Aunt Mary for my passage money. I should have all that money paid off in four months, and then I'll have some more money to send you by Christmas.'

And Michael felt very strong and manly recounting what he was going to do when he got to Boston, Massachusetts. He told himself that with his great strength he would earn a great deal of money. Conscious of his youth and his strength and lusting for adventurous life, for the moment he forgot the ache in his heart that the thought of leaving his father inspired in him.

The father was silent for some time. He was looking at the sky with his lower lip hanging, thinking of nothing. At last he sighed as a memory struck him. 'What is it?' said the son. 'Don't weaken, for God's sake. You will only make it hard for me.' 'Fooh!' said the father suddenly with pretended gruffness. 'Who is weakening? I'm afraid that your new clothes make you impudent.' Then he was silent for a moment and continued in a low voice: 'I was thinking of that potato field you sowed alone last spring the time I had the influenza. I never set eyes on the man that could do it better. It's a cruel world that takes you away from the land that God made you for.'

'Oh, what are you talking about, father?' said Michael irritably. 'Sure what did anybody ever get out of the land but poverty and hard work and potatoes and salt?'

'Ah yes,' said the father with a sigh, 'but it's your own, the land, and over there'—he waved his hand at the western sky— 'you'll be giving your sweat to some other man's land, or what's equal to it.'

'Indeed,' muttered Michael, looking at the ground with a melancholy expression in his eyes, 'it's poor encouragement you are giving me.'

They stood in silence fully five minutes. Each hungered to embrace the other, to cry, to beat the air, to scream with excess of sorrow. But they stood silent and sombre, like nature about them, hugging their woe. Then they went back to the cabin. Michael went into the little room to the left of the kitchen, to the three young men who fished in the same curragh[1] with him and were his bosom friends. The father walked into the large bedroom to the right of the kitchen.

The large bedroom was also crowded with people. A large table

---
[1] A light, keelless boat used in the West of Ireland.

was laid for tea in the centre of the room and about a dozen young men were sitting at it, drinking tea and eating buttered raisin cake. Mrs. Feeney was bustling about the table, serving the food and urging them to eat. She was assisted by her two younger daughters and by another woman, a relative of her own. Her eldest daughter Mary, who was going to the United States that day, was sitting on the edge of the bed with several other young women. The bed was a large four poster bed with a deal canopy over it, painted red, and the young women were huddled together on it. So that there must have been about a dozen of them there. They were Mary Feeney's particular friends, and they stayed with her in that uncomfortable position just to show how much they liked her. It was a custom.

Mary herself sat on the edge of the bed with her legs dangling. She was a pretty, dark-haired girl of nineteen, with dimpled, plump, red cheeks and ruminative brown eyes that seemed to cause little wrinkles to come and go in her little low forehead. Her nose was soft and small and rounded. Her mouth was small and the lips were red and open. Beneath her white blouse that was frilled at the neck and her navy blue skirt that outlined her limbs as she sat on the edge of the bed, her body was plump, soft, well-moulded and in some manner exuded a feeling of freshness and innocence. So that she seemed to have been born to be fondled and admired in luxurious surroundings instead of having been born a peasant's daughter, who had to go to the United States that day to work as a servant or maybe in a factory.

And as she sat on the edge of the bed crushing her little handkerchief between her palms, she kept thinking feverishly of the United States, at one moment with fear and loathing, at the next with desire and longing. Unlike her brother she did not think of the work she was going to do or the money that she was going to earn. Other things troubled her, things of which she was half ashamed, half afraid, thoughts of love and of foreign men and of clothes and of houses where there were more than three rooms and where people ate meat every day. She was fond of life, and several young men among the local gentry had admired her in Inverara. But . . .

She happened to look up and she caught her father's eyes as he stood silently by the window with his hands stuck in his waist belt. His eyes rested on hers for a moment and then he dropped them without smiling, and with his lips compressed he walked down into the kitchen. She shuddered slightly. She was a little afraid of her father, although she knew that he loved her very much and he was very kind to her. But the winter before he had whipped her with a dried willow rod, when he caught her one evening behind Tim Hernon's cabin after nightfall, with Tim Hernon's son Bartly's arms around her waist and he kissing her. Ever since, she always shivered slightly when her father touched her or spoke to her.

'Oho!' said an old peasant who sat at the table with a saucer full of tea in his hand and his grey flannel shirt open at his thin, hairy, wrinkled neck. 'Oho! indeed, but it's a disgrace to the island of Inverara to let such a beautiful woman as your daughter go away, Mrs. Feeney. If I were a young man, I'd be flayed alive if I'd let her go.'

There was a laugh and some of the women on the bed said: 'Bad cess to you, Patsy Coyne, if you haven't too much impudence, it's a caution.' But the laugh soon died. The young men sitting at the table felt embarrassed and kept looking at one another sheepishly, as if each tried to find out if the others were in love with Mary Feeney.

'Oh, well, God is good,' said Mrs. Feeney, as she wiped her lips with the tip of her bright, clean, check apron. 'What will be must be, and sure there is hope from the sea, but there is no hope from the grave. It is sad and the poor have to suffer, but . . .' Mrs. Feeney stopped suddenly, aware that all these platitudes meant nothing whatsoever. Like her husband she was unable to think intelligently about her two children going away. Whenever the reality of their going away, maybe for ever, three thousand miles into a vast unknown world, came before her mind, it seemed that a thin bar of some hard metal thrust itself forward from her brain and rested behind the wall of her forehead. So that almost immediately she became stupidly conscious of the pain caused by the imaginary bar of metal and she forgot the dread prospect of her children going away. But her mind grappled with the things about her busily and efficiently, with the preparation of food, with the entertaining of her guests, with the numerous little things that have to be done in a house where there is a party and which only a woman can do properly. These little things, in a manner, saved her, for the moment at least, from bursting into tears whenever she looked at her daughter and whenever she thought of her son, whom she loved most of all her children, perhaps because she nearly died giving birth to him and he had been very delicate until he was twelve years old. So she laughed down in her breast a funny laugh she had that made her heave where her check apron rose out from the waist band in a deep curve. 'A person begins to talk,' she said with a shrug of her shoulders sideways, 'and then a person says foolish things.'

'That's true,' said the old peasant, noisily pouring more tea from his cup to his saucer.

But Mary knew by her mother laughing that way that she was very near being hysterical. She always laughed that way before she had one of her fits of hysterics. And Mary's heart stopped beating suddenly and then began again at an awful rate as her eyes became acutely conscious of her mother's body, the rotund, short body with the wonderful mass of fair hair growing grey at the temples and the fair face with the soft liquid brown eyes, that grew hard and piercing for a moment as they looked at a thing and then grew soft and liquid again, and the thin-lipped small mouth with the beautiful white teeth and the deep perpendicular grooves in the upper lip and the tremor that always came in the corner of the mouth, with love, when she looked at her children. Mary became acutely conscious of all these little points, as well as of the little black spot that was on her left breast below the nipple and the swelling that came now and again in her legs and caused her to have hysterics and would one day cause her death. And she was stricken with horror at the thought of leaving her mother and at the selfishness of her thoughts. She had never been prone to thinking of anything important but now, somehow for a moment, she had a glimpse of her mother's life that made her shiver and hate herself as a cruel, heartless, lazy, selfish wretch. Her mother's life loomed up before her eyes, a life of continual misery and suffering, hard work, birth pangs, sickness and again hard work and hunger and anxiety. It loomed up and then it fled again, a little mist came before her eyes and she jumped down from the bed, with the jaunty twirl of her head that was her habit when she set her body in motion.

'Sit down for a while, mother,' she whispered, toying with one of the black ivory buttons on her mother's brown bodice. 'I'll look after the table.' 'No, no,' murmured the mother with a shake of her whole body, 'I'm not a bit tired. Sit down, my treasure. You have a long way to travel to-day.'

And Mary sighed and went back to the bed again.

At last somebody said: 'It's broad daylight.' And immediately everybody looked out and said: "So it is, and may God be praised.'

The change from the starry night to the grey, sharp dawn was hard to notice until it had arrived. People looked out and saw the morning light sneaking over the crags silently, along the ground, pushing the mist banks upwards. The stars were growing dim. A long way off invisible sparrows were chirping in their ivied perch in some distant hill or other. Another day had arrived and even as the people looked at it, yawned and began to search for their hats, caps and shawls preparing to go home, the day grew and spread its light and made things move and give voice. Cocks crew, blackbirds carolled, a dog let loose from a cabin by an early riser chased madly after an imaginary robber, barking as if his tail were on fire. The people said goodbye and began to stream forth from Feeney's cabin. They were going to their homes to see to the morning's work before going to Kilmurrage to see the emigrants off on the steamer to the mainland. Soon the cabin was empty except for the family.

All the family gathered into the kitchen and stood about for some minutes talking sleepily of the dance and of the people who had been present. Mrs. Feeney tried to persuade everybody to go to bed, but everybody refused. It was four o'clock and Michael and Mary would have to set out for Kilmurrage at nine. So tea was made and they all sat about for an hour drinking it and eating raisin cake and talking. They only talked of the dance and of the people who had been present.

There were eight of them there, the father and mother and six children. The youngest child was Thomas, a thin boy of twelve, whose lungs made a singing sound every time he breathed. The next was Bridget, a girl of fourteen, with dancing eyes and a habit of shaking her short golden curls every now and then for no apparent reason. Then there were the twins, Julia and Margaret, quiet, rather stupid, flat-faced girls of sixteen. Both their upper front teeth protruded slightly and they were both great workers and very obedient to their mother. They were all sitting at the table, having just finished a third large pot of tea, when suddenly the mother hastily gulped down the remainder of the tea in her cup, dropped the cup with a clatter to her saucer and sobbed once through her nose.

'Now mother,' said Michael sternly, 'what's the good of this work?'

'No, you are right, my pulse,' she replied quietly. 'Only I was just thinking how nice it is to sit here surrounded by all my children, all my little birds in my nest, and then two of them going to fly away made me sad.' And she laughed, pretending to treat it as a foolish joke.

'Oh, that be damned for a story,' said the father, wiping his mouth on his sleeve; 'there's work to be done. You Julia, go and get the horse. Margaret, you milk the cow and see that you give enough milk to the calf this morning.' And he ordered everybody about as if it were an ordinary day of work.

But Michael and Mary had nothing to do and they sat about miserably conscious that they had cut adrift from the routine of their home life. They no longer had any place in it. In a few hours they would be homeless wanderers. Now that they were cut adrift from it, the poverty and sordidness of their home life appeared to them under the aspect of comfort and plenty.

So the morning passed until breakfast time at seven o'clock. The morning's work was finished and the family was gathered together again. The meal passed in a dead silence. Drowsy after the sleepless night and conscious that the parting would come in a few hours, nobody wanted to talk. Everybody had an egg for breakfast in honour of the occasion. Mrs. Feeney, after her usual habit, tried to give her egg first to Michael, then to Mary, and as each refused it, she ate a little herself and gave the remainder to little Thomas who had the singing in his chest. Then the breakfast was cleared away. The father went to put the creels on the mare so as to take the luggage into Kilmurrage. Michael and Mary got the luggage ready and began to get dressed. The mother and the other children tidied up the house. People from the village began to come into the kitchen, as was customary, in order to accompany the emigrants from their home to Kilmurrage.

At last everything was ready. Mrs. Feeney had exhausted all excuses for moving about, engaged on trivial tasks. She had to go into the big bedroom where Mary was putting on her new hat. The mother sat on a chair by the window, her face contorting on account of the flood of tears she was keeping back. Michael moved about the room uneasily, his two hands knotting a big red handkerchief behind his back. Mary twisted about in front of the mirror that hung over the black wooden mantelpiece. She was spending a long time with the hat. It was the first one she had ever worn, but it fitted her beautifully, and it was in excellent taste. It was given to her by the schoolmistress, who was very fond of her, and she herself had taken it in a little. She had an instinct for beauty in dress and deportment.

But the mother, looking at how well her daughter wore the cheap navy blue costume and the white frilled blouse, and the little round black hat with a fat, fluffy, glossy curl covering each ear, and the black silk stockings with blue clocks in them, and the little black shoes that had laces of three colours in them, got suddenly enraged with . . . She didn't know with what she got enraged. But for the moment she hated her daughter's beauty, and she remembered all the anguish of giving birth to her and nursing her and toiling for her, for no other purpose than to lose her now and let her go away, maybe to be ravished wantonly because of her beauty and her love of gaiety. A cloud of mad jealousy and hatred against this impersonal beauty that she saw in her daughter almost suffocated the mother, and she stretched out her hands in front of her unconsciously and then just as suddenly her anger vanished like a puff of smoke, and she burst into wild tears, wailing: 'My children, oh, my children, far over the sea you will be carried from me, your mother.' And she began to rock herself and she threw her apron over her head.

Immediately the cabin was full of the sound of bitter wailing. A dismal cry rose from the women gathered in the kitchen. 'Far over the sea they will be carried,' began woman after woman, and they all rocked themselves and hid their heads in their aprons. Michael's mongrel dog began to howl on the hearth. Little Thomas sat down on the hearth beside the dog and, putting his arms around him, he began to cry, although he didn't know exactly why he was crying, but he felt melancholy on account of the dog howling and so many people being about.

In the bedroom the son and daughter, on their knees, clung to their mother, who held their heads between her hands and rained kisses on both heads ravenously. After the first wave of tears she had stopped weeping. The tears still ran down her cheeks, but her eyes gleamed and they were dry. There was a fierce look in them as she searched all over the heads of her two children with them, with her brows contracted, searching with a fierce terror-stricken expression, as if by the intensity of her stare she hoped to keep a living photograph of them before her mind. With her quivering lips she made a queer sound like 'im-m-m-m' and she kept kissing. Her right hand clutched at Mary's left shoulder and with her left she fondled the back of Michael's neck. The two children were sobbing freely. They must have stayed that way a quarter of an hour.

Then the father came into the room, dressed in his best clothes. He wore a new frieze waistcoat, with a grey and black front and a white back. He held his soft black felt hat in one hand and in the other hand he had a bottle of holy water. He coughed and said in a weak gentle voice that was strange to him, as he touched his son: 'Come now, it is time.'

Mary and Michael got to their feet. The father sprinkled them with holy water and they crossed themselves. Then, without looking at their mother, who lay in the chair with her hands clasped on her lap, looking at the ground in a silent tearless stupor, they left the room. Each hurriedly kissed little Thomas, who was not going to Kilmurrage, and then, hand in hand, they left the house. As Michael was going out the door he picked a piece of loose whitewash from the wall and put it in his pocket. The people filed out after them, down the yard and on to the road, like a funeral procession. The mother was left in the house with little Thomas and two old peasant women from the village. Nobody spoke in the cabin for a long time.

Then the mother rose and came into the kitchen. She looked at the two women, at her little son and at the hearth, as if she were looking for something she had lost. Then she threw her hands into the air and ran out into the yard.

'Come back,' she screamed; 'come back to me.'

She looked wildly down the road with dilated nostrils, her bosom heaving. But there was nobody in sight. Nobody replied. There was a crooked stretch of limestone road, surrounded by grey crags that were scorched by the sun. The road ended in a hill and then dropped out of sight. The hot June day was silent. Listening foolishly for an answering cry, the mother imagined she could hear the crags simmering under the hot rays of the sun. It was something in her head that was singing.

The two old women led her back into the kitchen. 'There is nothing that time will not cure,' said one. 'Yes. Time and patience,' said the other.

# The Wounded Cormorant[1]

Beneath the great grey cliff of Clogher Mor there was a massive square black rock, dotted with white limpets, sitting in the sea. The sea rose and fell about it frothing. Rising, the sea hoisted the seaweed that grew along the rock's rims until the long red winding strands spread like streams of blood through the white foam. Falling, the tide sucked the strands down taut from their bulbous roots.

Silence. It was noon. The sea was calm. Rock-birds slept on its surface, their beaks resting on their fat white breasts. Tall sea-gulls standing on one leg dozed high up in the ledges of the cliff. On the great rock there was a flock of black cormorants resting, bobbing their long necks to draw the food from their swollen gullets.

Above on the cliff-top a yellow goat was looking down into the sea. She suddenly took fright. She snorted and turned towards the crag at a smart run. Turning, her hoof loosed a flat stone from the cliff's edge. The stone fell, whirling, on to the rock where the cormorants rested. It fell among them with a crash and arose in fragments. The birds swooped into the air. As they rose a fragment of the stone struck one of them in the right leg. The leg was broken. The wounded bird uttered a shrill scream and dropped the leg. As the bird flew outwards from the rock the leg dangled crookedly.

The flock of cormorants did not fly far. As soon as they passed the edge of the rock they dived headlong into the sea. Their long black bodies, with outstretched necks, passed rapidly beneath the surface of the waves, a long way, before they rose again, shaking the brine from their heads. Then they sat in the sea, their black backs shimmering in the sunlight, their pale brown throats thrust forward, their tiny heads poised on their curved long necks. They sat watching, like upright snakes, trying to discover whether there were any enemies near. Seeing nothing, they began to cackle and flutter their feathers.

But the wounded one rushed about in the water flapping its wings in agony. The salt brine stung the wound, and it could not stand still. After a few moments it rose from the sea and set off at a terrific rate, flying along the face of the cliff, mad with pain. It circled the face of the cliff three times, flying in enormous arcs, as if

---

[1] From *The Tent and Other Stories*, London, 1926.

it were trying to flee from the pain in its leg. Then it swooped down again towards the flock and alighted in the water beside them.

The other birds noticed it and began to cackle. It swam close to one bird, but that bird shrieked and darted away from it. It approached another bird, and that bird prodded it viciously with its beak. Then all the birds screamed simultaneously and rose from the water, with a great swish of their long wings. The wounded one rose with them. They flew up to the rock again and alighted on it, bobbing their necks anxiously and peering in all directions, still slightly terrified by the stone that had fallen there. The wounded one alighted on the rocks with them, tried to stand up, and immediately fell on its stomach. But it struggled up again and stood on its unwounded leg.

The other birds, having assured themselves that there was no enemy near, began to look at the wounded one suspiciously. It had its eyes closed, and it was wobbling unstably on its leg. They saw the wounded leg hanging crookedly from its belly and its wings trailing slightly. They began to make curious screaming noises. One bird trotted over to the wounded one and pecked at it. The wounded bird uttered a low scream and fell forward on its chest. It spread out its wings, turned up its beak, and opened it out wide, like a young bird in a nest demanding food.

Immediately the whole flock raised a cackle again and took to their wings. They flew out to sea, high up in the air. The wounded bird struggled up and also took flight after them. But they were far ahead of it, and it could not catch up with them on account of its waning strength. However, they soon wheeled inwards towards the cliff, and it wheeled in after them, all flying low over the water's surface. Then the flock rose slowly, fighting the air fiercely with their long thin wings in order to propel their heavy bodies upwards. They flew half-way up the face of the cliff and alighted on a wide ledge that was dotted with little black pools and white feathers strewn about.

The wounded bird tried to rise too, but it had not gone out to sea far enough in its swoop. Therefore it had not gathered sufficient speed to carry it up to the ledge. It breasted the cliff ten yards below the ledge, and being unable to rise upwards by banking, it had to wheel outwards again, cackling wildly. It flew out very far, descending to the surface of the sea until the tips of its wings touched the water. Then it wheeled inwards once more, rising gradually, making a tremendous effort to gather enough speed to take it to the ledge where its comrades rested. At all costs it must reach them or perish. Cast out from the flock, death was certain. Sea-gulls would devour it.

When the other birds saw it coming towards them and heard the sharp whirring of its wings as it rose strongly, they began to cackle fiercely, and came in a close line to the brink of the ledge, darting their beaks forward and shivering. The approaching bird cackled also and came headlong at them. It flopped on to the ledge over their backs and screamed, lying on the rock helplessly with its wings spread out, quite exhausted. But they had no mercy. They fell upon it fiercely, tearing at its body with their beaks, plucking out its black feathers and rooting it about with their feet. It struggled madly to creep in farther on the ledge, trying to get into a dark crevice in the cliff to hide, but they dragged it back again and pushed it towards the brink of the ledge. One bird prodded its right eye with its beak. Another gripped the broken leg firmly in its beak and tore at it.

At last the wounded bird lay on its side and began to tremble, offering no resistance to their attacks. Then they cackled loudly, and, dragging it to the brink of the ledge, they hurled it down. It fell, fluttering feebly through the air, slowly descending, turning round and round, closing and opening its wings, until it reached the sea.

Then it fluttered its wings twice and lay still. An advancing wave dashed it against the side of the black rock and then it disappeared, sucked down among the seaweed strands.

AUSTIN CLARKE

# Gormlai and Cormac[1]

EVERY NIGHT of the week she had searched among ecclesiastical tracts and vellums, because she had suddenly determined to discover, once and for all, the meaning and mystery of matrimony. Cormac had given her permission to use this quiet room above the chapel while he was absent. But she had explored the book-racks at first with a sense of guilt. Searching among those moral treatises, she felt indeed that she was craving for a knowledge forbidden to women. She fought the unreasonable fear, for it was no sinful curiosity that impelled her, but a need of mind that she must obey whatever the cost. Even as a girl she had felt that clear urgency of mind, had rebelled secretly at her convent when the Abbess reproved her and sent word to the *Ri*.[2] She thought of those pious virgins, in their cells there, following the example of Saint Ita, living in simple faith, untouched by the toil of intellect. But was not the intellect the highest work of the Creator? Even as a youngster she had despised those recluses, their ignorance, their docile obedience, and she had felt proud of her own mind.

She had worked feverishly for five nights, dipping into the pages of Tertullian, Jerome and others whose names she forgot almost as soon as she had read them. She had come to a bewildering world of vehement opinions, of strange anger, of stern ordinances. But it was the real world, despite its ugliness, and she knew that she must face its facts. Sentences which she could scarcely understand confronted her, horrible words that she knew instinctively referred to some terrible evil at the very root of life. Woman was denounced by the Early Fathers, arraigned as the temptress, the bringer of spiritual evil and disease. She read with growing indignation and horror. But she must not yield to the emotion of revolt. She must read calmly, coldly, submitting all to her intelligence. The sacrament of matrimony was not what she had thought of it in her innocence, it was not what the uneducated laity thought of it. Cormac had been correct though she had doubted his word. It was an inferior spiritual state, a refuge from concupiscence, and as some schoolmen and theologians held, a state that was no more than tolerable. She read of

---

[1] From *The Singing-Men at Cashel*, London, 1936, Clarke's imaginative reconstruction of a chapter from Irish medieval history.
[2] King.

the widespread reign of lust in ancient cities, the multiplying sins of the flesh. Those who were married did not always escape from horrible sins that blotched both body and soul. The very intimacy of the married state brought with it the occasion of unnatural sins, and a slow demoralization could be brought on by the uxoriousness of that state.

The more she read, the more her mind was bewildered. Fornication, adultery, concupiscence, uncleanliness of thought and act—the ominous words leaped loudly from the pages as from a pulpit, but their meaning was as vague to her as it was alarming. There was some shame in womanhood and its periods, some mysterious corruption due to the Fall which she could not ascertain. Still in ignorance of the meaning of matrimony, she raced from page to page, skipping or turning back, ever in the hope of finding some precise definition that would reveal all to her.

This night she read wildly, frantically, for the time was short. She must know, she could not remain any longer in the torment of doubt and suspicion. This might be her last chance of discovering the dread secret before Cormac returned.

Among the Latin manuscripts on the desk, she found some transcriptions in Gaelic from a Life of Saint Scothín, and seeing that they were in her husband's hand, she turned to them curiously. A passage dealing with the saint's nightly temptation caught her attention and she read on: 'Now two maidens with pointed breasts used to lie with him every night that the battle with the Devil might be the greater for him. And it was proposed to accuse him on that account. So Brennain came to test him and Scothín said: "Let you lie in my bed to-night." So when he reached the hour of resting the girls came into the house where Brennain was, with lapfuls of glowing embers in their chasubles and the fire did not harm them. They spilled the embers in front of Brennain and got into the bed with him. "What is this?" asked Brennain. "This is what we do every night," said the girls. They lay down with Brennain and he could not find sleep because of his burning. "That is imperfect, Father," said the girls, "he who is here every night feels nothing at all. Why not go, Father, to the tub of cold water if it be easier for you? Tis often that the holy Father, even Scothín, pays a visit to it." "Well," said Brennain, "it is wrong for us to make this test for he is better than we are." After that they made their union and covenant and the saints part *feliciter*.'

Hastily she put aside the manuscript with a little shudder of disgust. She did not understand entirely what the passage meant, but a dim suspicion was stirring in her mind, and she remembered Cormac's conversation with her on the question of temptation. Somehow it all seemed like a mocking commentary on her own marriage.

Ill at ease, she got up and wandered along the bookracks with a taper. The stern voices hidden in those leaves challenged her across the centuries, the authority of all those saints and churchmen warned her. She felt dispirited and lone in her struggle. She knew even less than when she started, she would never pierce the ignorance that darkened her mind.

A small ancient volume bound in withered neatskin caught her attention. It looked mysterious and secretive. She picked it up cautiously and bore it back to the desk as if at last she had found what she wanted. But when she opened it she found to her disappointment that it was only a treatise on Digamy and other matters. She was about to replace it on the rack when a passage from St. Gregory Nazianzen held her eye. It was a commentary on a text from Saint Paul which she had read the previous night and she read rapidly, translating the ecclesiastical Latin into her own words: 'If there are two Christs there may be two husbands or two wives. If there is but one Christ, one Head of the Church, there is but one flesh, a second is repelled. But if He forbids a second, what is to be said of third marriages? The first is law, the second is pardon and indulgence, the third is iniquity.' On the margin a later scribe had scribbled a phrase from Athenagoras: 'Second marriage is but a decent adultery.' Farther down was another quotation, this time from the blessed Clement of Alexandria: 'Fornication is a lapse from one marriage into many.' She pushed aside the book in despair: she was appalled by the complication of the subject. It was useless to read of second or third marriages when she knew nothing about first marriages. There must be some kind of spiritual deterioration, some evil latent in marriage which grew worse if the sacrament were repeated.

Suddenly she remembered her stepmother. She had always felt that there was something strange about that marriage. Was it some instinct even as a child which had caused her to feel that her father's second marriage was unblessed? Nial had felt the same, too, though he had only mentioned it to her once. The thought of her home life at Ardnaree depressed her. She leaned her elbows on the desk, staring into the shadows.

Was she right in pursuing the subject which was avoided by all? Was she merely yielding to an impulse of sinful curiosity? Even in her dreams she had been tormented ever since she came to Cashel. Another self that she hated and resented seemed to become active when she was asleep. Only the other night, she dreamed that she was back again in the wood above Glenalua. She relived that awful moment of evil knowledge. She saw again that hermit, his eyes glittering through his tangled glib,[1] the rags and twisted pelts hanging across his matted chest. She knew he was really the Devil in disguise because of the snake sign.

Overcome at once by the vividness of that horrible image of evil, she sprang to her feet and walked up and down, wringing her hands. Her mind was polluted, she would never forget that sight. Heaven was punishing her for her contumacy.

There were long wasters at the sides of the candles. The turves were greyer, and bending down she drew them together with a charred stick. She calmed herself and sat on the low stool beside the last embers. It must be very late, but she was afraid to go to bed even though she was tired. Horrible dreams were waiting to seize her mind when it was defenceless in sleep.

She must have fallen into a light doze by the hearth, for she found herself awake again, alert, trembling. Had she heard the far sound of hooves or dreamed she had heard them?

She ran to the fenestrelle and listened.

She was not mistaken. In the silence of the night below, she could hear clearly the beat of hooves coming across the plain. The sounds were approaching from the north and Dysart was in that direction.

'Cormac is coming back.'

She must not delay. She dared not see him to-night, she could not endure it. She would have time to reach her room, to get into bed. But she would have to pretend to be asleep when he came into the room. She hated the thought of that petty deception but she could not face him to-night. She was in despair—never, never would she escape from this furtive, double existence into which she was driven by circumstance. She extinguished the tapers, all except one which she took with her.

---

[1] 'A thick mass of matted hair hanging over the eyes, formerly worn by the Irish.' N.E.D.

She closed the great door, but when she had gone down a few of the steps, she stopped and listened again at a loophole. Even if her husband and his attendants were coming up the hill-road, she would still have time to reach her bed. To her surprise she could not hear a sound, the silence was intense again. She waited for a minute on the stone stairs, but there was still no sound. Her suspicion had been wrong. She had only heard some lategoers returning to their homes. She was relieved at the thought that she would be alone for another night, even though she feared the hours of sleep.

*Be on your guard for the Airseoir[1] has many wiles!*

Cormac heard again the valedictory warning which the aged Colman had given to him at Dysart. It was almost midnight for the moon was high in the south-west and the trotting of the horses had made him drowsy. But the holy whisper came back to his ear with such startling distinctness that he raised his head in surprise. Dimna, the cleric, was nodding beside him, the heavy hood drawn down to conceal his features. Cormac turned to watch the passing shadows of branch and night-eared bush, fantastic and unreal in the moonlight.

Colman had hinted that in the next few weeks the Adversary of souls might attempt to defeat him. Even at the threshold the saint had paused to repeat his last warning in a whisper.

The horses swung into an easy pace. Corra, the driver, glanced over his shoulder, pointing ahead as they came from the shadows of a wood-edge.

Little more than a mile away was the summit of Cashel, its peaked roofs and round tower against the moon.

'We are almost there, Father Dimna.' The other stirred and looked up as Cormac spoke.

In a few minutes they came to a small oratory, half hidden by quicksets.

'I shall see you early in the morning. God be with you.'

'And with you, *A Tierna!*'[2]

---
[1] Adversary, i.e. Satan.
[2] My Lord.

Both spoke gravely as if they realized the solemn purpose of the morrow. The priest paused for a moment, then bowed and went down the path among the trees.

Cormac called to the driver as they came to the embankment. The lesser settlements and outhouses, clustered under the pale limestone cliffs of Cashel, were deep in shadow.

'I'll walk up. It is a fair night and I need exercise after the day's journey. The horses are tired.'

He stopped to pat their manes. He did not add that Corra himself looked weary and that he wished to spare him the additional journey.

Slowly the *Ri* paced up the wide road, his hands behind his back. He lingered half-way and leaned on the low stone wall to gaze at the plain below him. The fields, the long pastures were prosperous in the moonlight; the distant woods were heavy and still under their fruit; all that land was at peace.

He mused beside a slender rowan growing from a fissure outside the rough wall. Its patterned, fernlike leaves were dark against the sky. They began to stir faintly, finding for themselves a freshet in the air, but the thick clusters of berries remained still.

'Wonderful are the works of the Creator,' he thought, as the leaves, after that faint sighing, became still again. He resumed his walk until at the turn of the road, he saw, spread below, all the three plains of Munster.

On so calm a night, evil might well seem a dream of the disturbed senses. All who trusted in Heaven had nothing to fear in this mortal world. Creation was lulled by its own wonder and loveliness, manifest as when it came from the hand and word of God. Even the warning of his old master and soul-preceptor seemed a remote fancy. Cormac went slowly, glancing at the harvests below, at the firmament beyond, his heart praising the wonder of field and sky. But for the violence and greed in the nature of man, the earth might be as peaceful as it is in the contemplation of the saints. But his own land, small as it was, he would preserve in peace, in holiness: and that resolution, as he repeated it to himself, filled him with exaltation and at the same time with calmness. Those days and nights at Dysart had brought certainty to his mind. Since that hour when he was crossing the courtyard to his scriptorium and a voice spoke from the air, commanding him to go to Dysart, he had not wavered.

From that moment his mind was enlightened, by the direct grace of Heaven, and his purpose, so long obscure to him, was at last clear.

Colman had known of his coming, for he had heard holy beings astir in the eaves of his house. He knew, too, the purpose of the visit and had awaited him, among his clergy, at the threshold. It was plain, indeed, that Heaven was guiding him and Cormac's heart filled once more with gratitude.

At the entrance-gate, a few soldiers started up from a bench, yawning and stretching. They looked startled when they saw the tall, majestic figure of the *Ri* standing before them.

But Cormac, with a smile and an involuntary blessing to the fellows, passed into the inner quadrangle under the shadow of the dormer-houses.

Half in moonlight, half in dark, he saw the High Cross, its inter-knotted figures and Eastern symbols obscure, mysterious. Cormac gazed at the sacred spot which the Cross marked, for there the Talkend[1] had baptized King Aongus and that event was the first set down in the annals of Cashel. As Patric was administering the sacrament of holy water, the spike of his heavy crozier pierced the foot of the king. But he uttered no sound despite the grievous pain which the sharp point caused him. The saint expressed his concern when he discovered what had happened and asked him why he had not complained.

'But I thought it was part of the ceremony,' the royal neophyte replied and even Patric had to smile tenderly at the simplicity of the great man.

Cormac meditated for a few moments on that holy spot and then passed within the shadows of the buildings. Much had happened at Cashel since then and dark events were recorded in the annals. Cruelty and rapine had disturbed its peace, dim sacrilege and the unnamed sin. As he went into the shadows, he remembered those long years of wantonness and luxury which had brought shame to Cashel in the past. The darkness seemed astir with memories of indolence and chambering, the raising of languid arms and of faces pale with desire, in secret rooms. He shut away those thoughts of the past and with a prayer turned to the doorway.

'But we perceive only through the mind,' he paused on the doorstep. 'All is entelechy. The cravings of desire, the sensations of its

---
[1] St. Patrick.

attainment, are communicated to us by the mind, even the pleasures of the senses, however acutely felt, are primarily a mental experience.'

He realized that he was thinking strangely and dismissed the train of thought abruptly. The Evil One was subtile in his attacks and was inveigling him into sophistry. Experience had long ago rendered him suspicious of those debates in which the mind argues with itself as with an unseen disputant.

Inside the house, he made his way quickly along a dim passage into which a faint ray of moonlight penetrated. He went quietly, knowing that his household was asleep, until he came to the curtain of the great chamber.

He paused cautiously for his wife would be asleep and he must not disturb her. There would be plenty of time to-morrow to tell her of his great decision. The thought of her virtue and noble nature filled him with gratitude to Heaven. Gormlai would understand at once when he explained his purpose to her. As he drew apart the curtains a few inches, he noticed to his surprise that there was a light still burning within. Believing that in his absentmindedness he had come to the wrong bed-division, he was about to turn away in confusion, when his eye was attracted by a strange glittering in the room. Before he realized what he was doing, his eye was held, his hand stayed, in horror.

A young woman was standing completely naked in the middle of the room and, despite the shame of her state, she remained idle in the clear candlelight. Her hands were clasped in mock modesty over her face as though she would beguile her watcher into sin. But it was the strange glitter of her body that held the scholar's amazed attention so that he doubted his own senses. The Tempter had suddenly fashioned out of darkness a deceptive image of desire and so cunningly that no human eye could withhold itself in time. Even the loosened plait of hair which might have served to conceal her breasts, was gathered carefully over her left shoulder, so that they were fully exposed and the tiny dark summit of each teat was erect, eager to defend its mistress from the invasive chill of night. Her bright body curved from the haunch as if she were about to turn and, by a single wily action, both defeat and increase his sight. *Look, look, quickly!* the Evil One spoke in an urgent whisper and his captive's glance sped of its own volition towards her impatient to satisfy its lust. Nature itself has modestly endeavoured ever since the Fall to conceal by dark or fair posy as best it might, that poor attraction which has caused many a man to lose his immortal soul, but now the very night hastened to defeat mortal eye and the gleamer disappeared.

The curtain swung back and the *Ri* was in darkness again. His eye could not have deceived him, but who could be this glittering being hidden in Cashel, how long had she been there unkown to him? Almost in superstitious terror, the scholar reeled from the doorpost, his memory alive with strange adulterous tales of the past hidden in the annals.

But only for a few seconds did those memories race through his mind. His face was burning with shame, his temples throbbing with the assault of passion. The words of Colman repeated themselves loudly in his mind, those warning words which he had put from him in his spiritual pride. He gripped the doorpost in his anguish. He had, indeed, been outwitted: he had gone instantly to the toils of temptation.

His eyes, despite the first impulse of horror, had disobeyed him; he had taken pleasure in sight. He had dreamed of leading his people into holiness, of reviving the ancient fame of his land, yet fallen into common sin. Not only had he taken pleasure in curiosity, in seeing a naked woman for the first time in his life, he had been unfaithful in impulse to the very marriage vows which he had so lately taken. He had kept his own marriage inviolate and spiritual, yet he succumbed to the first temptation which was presented to him.

But as he struggled against his anguish in the darkness, another thought came slowly, fighting its way into his mind until it held all his attention. He had not been mistaken about the room, he had not seen a strange woman or an eidolon of the senses.

'I saw my own wife.'

Amazed by that revelation, his mind began to debate with itself. It could not be a sin for him to look on his wife's body even with curiosity or desire since they were one flesh in the sight of Heaven. Certainly it was to be avoided by all who wished to lead the higher life, but it would be no more than a venial fault. It was a practice in which young couples were wont to indulge in the first weeks of marriage, though ridiculous and unseemly at his age. Nevertheless, the thought brought him little consolation. He knew in his heart that he was trying to deceive himself with specious excuses. He had not known that it was his wife at the time. He had taken pleasure in her nakedness as if she were a strange woman. Since the commission of sin is in the intention, his guilt remained as great.

But the thought that it was his own wife brought back the temptation in a fiercer degree. He saw her grave smile, heard her low voice, a little hoarse, yet delicious, as if there were honey at the roots of her tongue. Many times since their marriage when she was asleep late at night, he had to combat his inclination. But now his passion became intenser.

*Go back. She is your wife!* whispered Iafer Niger, the most cunning of the fallen spirits, for it was he who stood beside Cormac. He hesitated in the dark and his grasp on the doorpost tightened: his will was shaken and within his mind, now feverish and confused, the cunning one went with prompts and prurience. The thought of the nuptial pleasure, unknown to him and yet acutely familiar to his senses, filled his veins with soft flows of desire. He was clasping his wife in his arms, she was yielding to him obediently, for her first alarms were over.

'No. No. For a mortal pleasure, for the comfort of a few minutes, I am to sacrifice my duties, defeat the very purposes of Heaven.' Instinctively he knew that remorse would immediately overcome him if he yielded to the passion which dimmed his intellect, being thought's enemy. If the marriage were consummated that night, it could never be annulled. The fact remained chill amid his burning emotions and brought back all his intentions. Fortified by the advice of Colman, he had resolved to take Holy Orders and assume the hereditary Bishopric of his land. In that way the ecclesiastical kingdom of Cashel would be restored. Moreover, a secret delegation of clergy had urged him to accept the supreme position as Head of the Church in the south. His marriage had been a preliminary test, sent by Heaven itself and to his shame he had proved unworthy. For the sake of mere physical relief, a few minutes' play, he was ready to destroy the work of his life.

'No. No!' urged the Airseoir, 'it is more than a passing pleasure, more than the happiness of one night. Why should you not experience those pleasures, those tender touchings for which even learned men have cast away their books?' Instinct revealed to him the pleasures which he might find with his wife, not once but repeatedly, those pleasures which the married learn by practice to prolong, the feverish abandonment of midnight, the warmth of mingling limbs at morning: of that tenderness and power would come their sturdy offspring.

'Possess your wife. Many Irish Bishops have been married. The first order of saints, founded by Patric, were all husbands,' urged the black fellow.

'Patric chose married men, because none chaste enough was found among the single at that time. The custom of clerical marriage which lingers in remote dioceses must not be encouraged now. I cannot set a bad example.'

To aid him, the *Ri* called to mind the innocence, the virginity of his wife. He saw her, after the annullment of their marriage, as an Abbess, ruling a great community, and by her devotion, her self-sacrifice, helping him even more truly in his designs than when she was his wife. She had consented gladly, willingly to the idea of spiritual marriage. Prayer would reveal to her a vocation for the religious life. Was it not, indeed, the example of her spiritual nature which had helped him to avoid and despise his own impulses? In horror, now, he thought of his designs against her, his lust for that maidenhead which she would preserve as a treasure for Heaven.

The depths of his impious desire appalled him. He had been on the verge of what could not, in the circumstances, be less than sacrilege. But even as he shrank back, the horrible thought began to fascinate his numbed mind, and he saw himself under cover of the darkness committing the vile deed, robbing Christ of that treasure. So had Saint Enda, before his conversion from sin, planned to deflower a virgin who had taken the veil. Fearful of himself now, he made his way through the darkness fighting against the promptings of the unclean spirit at his elbow. He came at last to the outer threshold, but the cold air of night did not diminish the torment in his veins.

'There is but one remedy!' Grimly, with clenched hand and knitted brows, he hurried across the moonlit quadrangle to a small dark doorway which was opposite to him.

Gormlai had not yet gone to bed although it was more than a quarter of an hour since she had left the scriptorium. She felt wakeful and her mind was confused by the many pages she had turned in vain. She was alone for another night but there was little use in staying up any longer. She undressed slowly and hid her face in her hands for a moment as she stepped from her last garment. But in that moment she became aware that she was being watched. It was the same intuition that she had felt upon the first night of her marriage and though she knew that it was a spirit that looked at her she raised her head quickly and glanced towards the curtain.

'It is only my own imagining. I am disturbed to-night. My mind is upset.'

She blew out the candle and got into bed, but as she lay in the darkness, restlessly turning on the pillow, she found that she could not sleep. She was fearful of surrendering herself to that inner darkness, fearful of submitting herself to its mystery and meaninglessness. For weeks she had had difficulty in composing herself to rest. She imagined herself slowly descending into unknown regions. Far down in that darkness was that other self which had only appeared since she came to Cashel—a darker self that she scarcely recognized, and yet could not deny, a self troubled by intimations and a guilt of which she herself was innocent. As she felt her consciousness beginning to yield, to disappear into the first nothingness of sleep, she resisted the dread spell and clung desperately to a passing thought of the previous night.

But despite herself she must have succumbed to sleep, for she found herself alert once more listening intently. She had heard a voice calling her gently, persistently in the darkness. She could not tell how long she had been asleep, but she knew that the voice had been calling her for some time.

*Gormlai! Gormlai!*

Even in that confused state of half waking she knew that the voice, though little more than a whisper, was familiar to her. But her memory was dim and she could not remember where she had heard it before. Suddenly her mind was clear again and she knew it was her husband's voice.

'Cormac is calling me. He has been calling me for a long time.'

Vaguely she knew that he was in some trouble or distress and the thought afflicted her in a strange way. She must get up and go to him, for if she did not something terrible might happen. But she could not remember where she was, the darkness was so great around her. She thought at first that she was back in the scriptorium though she could not remember how she had got there. She tried to stir and was unable. Yet she knew instinctively that the scriptorium was changed, if indeed she were in it, and there was some dread power in the darkness that kept her even from stretching out her hand.

*Gormlai!*

It was the same voice again and yet was different. She knew that she had been mistaken. It could not be Cormac who was calling. The clear whisper coming from a great distance and yet strangely near was yet, nevertheless, familiar to her. But where had she heard that voice before? It was so gentle—the guarded echo of a whisper and so sorrowful, so lonely that it penetrated to the inmost privacy of her being. It was the voice of One Who calls to the soul in its darkness, Who is despised and neglected by mankind. It was that gentle voice from which the soul, though it hide or delay, cannot escape.

She knew that she must obey that summons, gentle and yet reproachful, and she struggled against her own reluctance and the weariness of effort. Suddenly she found herself hurrying through the darkness lest she be too late. . . .

She was in the chill air and there was now a pale phosphorescence in the sky which enabled her to see her way. She was straying in a wilderness of rocks, some of which were hewn into the shape of great slabs and tilted strangely. Among the rocks were small flickerings that came and went. People were moving about and she saw that some among them carried small bronze or stone lamps.

'But why are they coming up from the rocks?'

She was puzzled for the people seemed to be emerging from the ground. Then she saw that they were coming up the steps from small underground dwellings, the stone doors of which were wide open. The wicks of lamps were burning with a feeble, bluish flame in those chambers and she could see that the rock-walls were glistening with damp. She found herself at the threshold of one of the underground rooms and saw, to her surprise, a low stone table at which a hooded figure was seated. There was bread and wine upon the table and the stranger, as if expecting her, held out the bread to her.

She felt hunger but, even as she put out her hand, a warning voice was at her ear.

*Do not eat anything here or you will never escape.*

But the stooping figure picked up the wine cup and held it to her.

She felt a great thirst but, just as she was about to take the chalice, the invisible warner spoke again.

*Do not drink or you will never escape from here.*

As if aware of the presence of that warning spirit, the stranger at the table looked up. There was no face beneath the hood but a mass of leprous corruption.

'Christ save me!' With a sob of terror, Gormlai stumbled up the steps from the tomb. . . .

She was running across a waste, dimly lighted by the moon. Glancing back over her shoulder, she could see at a distance those people in their long grey robes, still coming up among the rocks or going down steps again into the sepulchres, as if they had forgotten something. She had gone a little way when she noticed a long line of people moving slowly and with weary gestures along the ridges of a hill. Some among them raised pale faces towards the sky, stopping in numb despair, and then went on again. A dim memory stirred in her mind, but it was too faint for her to hold its significance. She only knew that it was part of a great affliction. Those people were escaping from a terrible invasion. They had left behind them the blackened fields and charred homesteads. So she saw the people of Munster going past. Then she knew that some terrible grief had happened to her too—some shock that had numbed her mind with pain so that she could not even remember what had occurred. But as she came towards the desolate crowd, several moved their lips silently and pointed to her to go back.

They were trying to tell her something and they were afraid to speak. Someone had forbidden her to go with them. She must remember. She must remember what it was that she had forgotten.

'I have been called.'

That was it. She knew at last. She had been called and she would be too late. Something terrible would happen to her if she did not get there in time. But where was it she was to go and what was she to do?

'Poor Gormlai! Poor Gormlai!' The voice was so near, so full of pity that it surprised her and for a moment she did not realize that it was her own voice, that she was speaking to herself. But her voice was no longer young. It was old and thin, sighing, sighing to itself so that she could not keep from bursting into tears. Never had she known so terrible a loneliness. Around her was a moonlit desert, chill and shadowed but by its own endless furrows. Looking down she noticed for the first time the grey, ugly robe that hid her limbs. She was clad as a penitent. She was here in the wilderness because of some sin she had committed long ago. . . .

It seemed as if she had been wandering for years in that wilderness for she could remember nothing of her past life. Then suddenly her attention was caught by a curious glittering in the distance. At first she thought that the moon had become brighter. Then she saw that the glittering was caused by a threefold mountain in the north. The mountain, like a great jewel, emitted its own radiance and yet its rays did not explore the darkness surrounding it.

*Hurry! Hurry!* Her guardian angel beside her was again protecting her, aiding her so that quicker than her own thought she was approaching the glittering tiers of that mountain.

She could not tell how it happened. The next moment she found herself immediately below a small plat. People were moving to and fro along the plat and because of their astonishing radiance she thought at first they were living jewels.

On the fair grass that was of a substance more precious than particoloured enamels those people were moving joyfully among themselves in slowly circling patterns and the loveliness of their glances held her in fascination. Never had she seen such noble faces, such glances lost in their own light. The rich shapely robes which those men and women wore must be the cause of their radiance for they seemed of a pure crystalline substance that she had never seen before. She was staring at those happy people as they came and went, examining their bodies with a curiosity, with a darting minuteness that was unusual to her. It was some time before she realized that those people were entirely naked and that it was their own bodies which were so radiant. Gracefully, with beatific faces, those men and women moved in ever-changing circles, rejoicing among themselves without shame or embarrassment. They were as immortals who live in regions of bliss, untouched by memory or mortal cares.

To and fro those men and women moved as in a ceremonial dance, with glimmering brow and limbs. All were similar in grace, in form, and there were no shameful differences between them. They were sexless as our first parents in Eden. To and fro the everliving moved in delight along the lustres of grass.

'They are the Blessed,' she thought. 'It is the first night of the

Resurrection and such are the bodies of the glorified, those whose flesh has been made holy by the righteousness of their lives.'

Even as the thought crossed her mind, she saw one of the blessed approach her and she knew by the stranger's smile that it was a woman. With a look of pity, the bright one bent down and held out to her a silver beaker.

*Do not drink!* Gormlai heard the faithful warning. But her lips were parching and temptation overcame her. She was about to take the glittering vessel when she saw the woman looking down at her in horror. In confusion, Gormlai realized that her penitential garment was torn and that her breasts, heavy and dull, were exposed. She stepped back in shame as all those dazzling faces turned towards her in surprise.

The next moment the plat and its gleaming figures was far behind. Once more she was running in the middle of the desert plain. She was approaching the ridges of the triplicate mountain and its rocks were already astir with glittering multitudes of beings. They were watching her and she could not cease from running towards them. She bent down as she ran, trying to grasp her torn robe, to hold it against her thigh. But, to her horror, the weft was crumbling between her fingers as fast as she plucked at it. Frantically she clutched at the dwindling rags, the last threads. But they disappeared into fine dust in her fists and in a few seconds she was a naked biped before that silent throng of noble beings. She tried to hide her shame by pulling down her locks around her. But she could not conceal the coarse hips, thickened by middle age, the flabby paunch, wrinkled and seamed as if by childbirth. She crouched as she stumbled onward, in a wild attempt to escape from the glittering mountain of eyes.

*Gormlai!*

The voice which she had tried to forget was now an imperious summons. She dared no longer disobey the anger in its tone. It prolonged itself and lesser voices took up her name like echoes and bandied it throughout the hollows of the air. . . .

All had changed.

She was standing in the centre of a vast pavement. Light beat on her lids so that she could scarcely see the ranks of watching genii on each side. The radiance which was before her exceeded all shape and form, preceding them, as she thought, and known to her by its opposite. For she was lost now in the very darkness of light and knew that the seven nights of which that blackness was composed were the Great Wounds.

Voices were taking their places on both sides of her.

'Gormlai, daughter of Flann Siona.'

'I am here.'

Her lips uttered the words of their own accord.

'Let her life be shown.'

The presences around her were astir. She was lost. Her last chance of salvation was gone for ever. It was too late to repent.

A rustling sound was approaching, the crisping of forests when the wind begins to awaken them, the angry gossip of fire finding its own strength, growing gigantic as the mental fear of it. In the darkness the mind can see more clearly. She was aware of a great Book, its pages descending into many sounds.

Her mind was whirling with those pages, her senses racing with and through them—red-purple, green and silver illuminations, unending scrolls were revolving around each other, expanding and contracting within their reappearing circles, while glittering animals whisked into them glancing at her with small, startled eyes as they passed. Great capitals sprang with their retinues into word shapes and vanished more quickly than their own ink, so that she had no time to catch their meanings. All was racing towards her and receding in a dim, confused roar, as if she were held in the delirium of a great brain.

'It is the Book of Life.'

To her astonishment, she was quietly watching minute simulacra that were vaguely familiar to her. But each was so small that it seemed less in span than the imaging on a retina. Five tiny children were running towards her hand in hand. She was behind a tree, but the children stopped and screamed with terror as she beckoned to them. When she turned she was in a room, for the evening sunlight was shining on the edges of a high table. A woman was seated at the table, her head bowed with grief. 'Mother, it is you at last,' Gormlai went towards her but the woman looked up in alarm and pointed to the door. Next moment Gormlai was in the darkness, hammering in fear at the locked door, trying desperately to get out.

'Attend,' whispered a voice. The faithful spirit was warning her again. She was still standing in the middle of the pavement and all were watching her.

'Yes, yes. I am listening.'

The voices were so rapid that she could not hear what they were saying. They were accusing her and her mind could not keep pace with their words. With a despairing effort, she caught at the meaning as it fled past her.

'Was this woman married?'

'Yes.'

'More than once.'

'Yes.'

'How many times?'

She tried to cry out, to contradict those interlocutory voices, those false answers, but her lips failed her. There was some dreadful error. They had mistaken her for someone else. They were condemning her and she was innocent.

'How many times?'

She had not heard the answer to that question. She had been thinking of something else. She had been unwary, tricked into inattention. It was too late and she would never know now.

But she must tell them that they were wrong. She had only been married once. Truly it was so. She could not remember to whom she had been married, but she knew somehow that her husband was mild and pious.

The voices had hurried ahead of her and she could not catch up with them.

'What happened that night at Knockmore?'

'Was she unfaithful to her marriage vows that night?'

*Adulteress!*—the words wrote themselves across her mind searing it with anguish.

'No. No. I was not there. I swear that I am innocent.'

The spirit at her shoulder restrained her quietly so that she did not know whether the wild denial had crossed her lips.

The rustle of leaves was around her and she knew that the Book was living again. She peered into a room, housed somewhere in a forest, for the trees were still whispering outside. Then she saw her own face in the moonlight. She was lying in a bed but she could not see clearly the man who was beside her.

'Let her husbands come forward.'

The summons rang out and she trembled alone in the centre of the pavement. Steps were coming slowly, gravely towards her. The steps hesitated and stopped, making a little silence of their own. She was triumphant. Her accusers had been wrong—she had only been married once. But her gladness was brief for heavier steps were approaching from the opposite direction and she listened with an agony of realization. They stopped and she heard the footsteps of yet another, quick, impulsive and vaguely familiar to her. How long must she endure the suspense?

*Do not look back.* The warning came from her own mind. She must not look on the faces of the strangers who were waiting or she would be trapped into some admission.

'Turn and face your husbands.'

'No. No.' Her self-will sprang up dark and monstrous as she refused the command. It exulted in its darkness, in its savage power. The next instant she knew that she had been tricked into condemning herself. In that dark flush of wilfulness she had laid bare her true nature, she had shown her rebelliousness against the subservient position of womankind. There was silence all around her. The genii were waiting to see what she would do. But the mounting, despairing flush filled her soul.

'The trial is unjust. I protest. I protest.'

The gentle spirit that had guided her was weeping beside her. But she pushed past it sullenly in the night of will, her voice harsh and violent.

Then, for one awful second of revelation, she saw a bright form like that of Lu the Sun God, rising up while the winged beings abased themselves.

All had changed.

She was clinging frantically to a Tarpeian rock somewhere near a dim-lit sky. Far below a river was descending in seven falls that seemed like weirs. 'This is the ransom of the world,' said a voice, 'Titus seeks more.' She saw that the river was of blood and she screamed as the rock slowly parted, carrying her down to the gulf.

Gormlai was awakened by the echo of her own scream ringing in her ears. She sat up and listened, but the silence of the night was so intense that she found it difficult to believe that her cry had pierced it the moment before. She waited for the quick running steps of the housewomen coming to her assistance. She would have to reassure them, answer their startled enquiries, but a minute elapsed and no one came.

'I must have dreamed that I cried out.'

The moonlight shone fully on the counterpane. She could have read by its brilliant ray and its calmness was soothing to her agitated mind. The moon must have been shining on her face while she lay asleep: she had been in the midst of its cold radiance while her mind was struggling through darkness and terror. But how long had she been asleep? The question brought back confused impressions of her ordeal and she shivered. Little wonder that she had feared to go asleep that night, feared to explore those mysterious regions in which the mind can suffer so much woe. The wild uproar of the nightmare had become confused and meaningless as she fought her way back to consciousness, but she must remember all that had happened to her in her sleep before it was too late. That dream had been sent to her as a warning.

'No. No. It was nothing more than fantasy. I have been reading too much during the last week.'

But her conscience was uneasy, and as she concentrated on the fleeting images of her dream, recalling its last awful moments, she could not resist the thought that she had been in the power of evil. In that way she was punished for tampering with the forbidden knowledge. But why should knowledge be corrupting, if one sought it with a pure motive? Why should her mind be stained and a torment to itself?

She caught sight of her breasts in the moonlight and the anguish of her dream returned. Once more she was snatching at the disappearing robe that she might hide herself from a multitude of peering eyes. Never again would she be herself, happy among her thoughts, delighting in the ever-fair promises of existence.

It must be long after midnight, but she dared not sleep again. She would go back to the scriptorium and remain there until daybreak. The fire would still be smouldering and she remembered that there was plenty of fuel in the basket. She would be safe there. She got up and dressed herself hastily by the light of the room.

She felt calmer when she was dressed and stopped to gaze from the sill at the plain below. The distant fields were greyly luminous in the moonlight. Far away were the low mountain ranges and the dim edges of the Great Forest in the south-west. She stared at the calm idle land below in wonder and perplexity. Often she had stolen from her bed in the past and watched such meadowlands under the moonlight. Poets taught long ago that field and wood hid an inner, secret land, lovelier than the visible world where moon and sun shone on apple blossom, where fruit and bud prospered side by side on the one branch. But now the far plains seemed blank and vacant, meaningless as the cold moon shining to itself in the empty abyss of the air. All was indifferent to the hot turmoil and agitation of her mind. The lovely imaginings of the past, the beliefs that ennobled life were all gone. But where was that grim world of sin and retribution that hid behind the mystery of sleep, that no waking eye could detect?

She wrapped herself in a winter cloak, for the chills of the night made her shiver. She left the room and moved quietly down the passages, fearful lest her footstep be heard. All in that great house were asleep. In the darkness she fancied she could hear, like a single breath, a great recurrent sigh, the breathing of all the sleepers in that house. Soon she was at the threshold in the moonlight once more.

She drew the hood of the cloak, concealing her features as she crossed the bright courtyard. As she glanced back at the walls of the dormer-house, her attention was caught by the shadow she cast. It seemed to her like the shadow of a tall Abbess.

She entered the doorway of the chapel tower, and looked around her cautiously.

A dim light filtered through a high fenestrelle, and as she turned to hurry up the stairs to the scriptorium, she glanced towards the archway that led to the chapel. The pavement of the chapel was flooded with moonlight and the rich carvings of coign and pillar were strangely clear. The holiness and peace of that place filled her heart. Often as a young girl she had stolen alone into some quiet chapel at evening and cried to herself in her happiness. But she had hardened her heart and turned from God. She felt again that emotion of trust and longing which she had tried to forget, even to stifle. If she knelt in prayer she would find peace again. The grace of Heaven had led her there that night.

She went slowly towards the arch, but she had not gone more than a few steps when her foot struck something on the ground. She almost started back in alarm, then quickly recovered herself. Scarcely realizing what she was doing, she stooped and carefully picked up the slender object lying at her feet. For a moment she fingered it absentmindedly in the dim light but could not make out what it was. It might be an asperge of some kind which had been overlooked by the sacristan. Even as she gripped the leather handle she knew that she was mistaken. It must be a goad, left by some careless driver. She was stupid not to have noticed at first that it was sticky and that her fingers were wet. Suddenly she guessed what it was and with a shudder of horror she dropped the awful thing and ran to a high fenestrelle. She held up her hands to the ray. She was right. The dark streaks on her fingers were blood-stains.

She leaned against the wall until she had overcome her inclination to vomit. Then she moved towards the archway as far as possible from the flagellum lying there in the darkness. She wanted to escape to the book-room but she was afraid of stepping again on that horrid thing in the darkness. Somebody must have been using it a short time ago and at once she thought of the ascetic, Fernan. She had heard hints of his austerities. It was said that he wore chains knotted around his limbs and that the rusted iron had eaten into his flesh under the glossy soutane. She had only seen him once or twice at a distance near the chapel. He must have come there in the dead of the night after she had left the scriptorium. Perhaps he had been interrupted by a step and was hiding somewhere near. She had stumbled accidentally upon his secret and it oppressed her. She almost imagined she could see his small, wry figure, stooping in the shadowy corner opposite her when she drew back. She was standing on the moon-lit pavement beyond the arch and she turned in astonishment. She had stepped into peace and rare loveliness. Never had she been in the chapel by moonlight and she was entranced. Gazing at the arcaded walls with their delicate pilasters and mouldings, enriched by deeper shadow, she forgot for a moment her agitation. Beyond the massive central arch was the chancel stilled by a brighter radiance so that its fair pierced stonework, its simple altar table, had become pure silver.

As she glided forward, anxious to get away from the atrium, she noticed the serried heads carven on the chancel arch above her. She fancied that those stern male faces were watching her, were leaning forward to prevent her passing them. They were like the horrible heads of unfortunate hostages decapitated in time of war. If she turned to the right or the left she would see a bearded manhead bending towards her from either cornice.

'No. No. I must pray. I must not look at them.'

She moved towards the chancel, keeping her eyes down as she passed under that arch of mocking heads. She knelt down, but even as she did so, she was aware that she was not alone in the chapel.

There was someone in the tiny aisle in front of her. It was the priest, Fernan, and as she rose hastily to her feet, she realized her folly. She was chilled, she was trembling, but her eyes were drawn to him in horror. In the mingled light and shadow of that corner she saw him abased on the flags. His robe was stripped from his back and there were long, dark weals on his flesh. As she was about to steal away, he raised himself slowly and something familiar in the movement of his shoulders caught her attention. The man was bigger than Fernan. The next moment his voice rose in anguish.

But she had known even before he raised his voice that it was Cormac who knelt there. In that moment everything was clear—utterly clear to her. She understood why he had avoided her during the last months, why he had gone away suddenly to Dysart. She felt all the force of that which had come between them and the shock of seeing him there was less than that new knowledge. He had returned to Cashel secretly without telling her of his arrival. Their ways were apart now, their marriage was destroyed and she must keep the secret of this night all the rest of her life.

She scarcely knew how she reached the threshold again. She could not remember running through the moonlight to the dormer-house. Thoughts rushed and clamoured in her feverish imagination. Her instinct had been right all along and ever since that fatal day at Glenalua she had been trying to deceive herself.

The grim denunciations of womankind which she had been reading every night that week in tracts and ancient volumes rang around her. Stories of the saints which had frightened her as a child in the Sunday class raced back into her memory. There were still enclosed anchorites in remote places of Ireland. They were immured in pits beneath the church wall. Hard food was handed down to them through the grill daily and they were huddled there in darkness and chill, in rags and excrement. Saint Kiernan slept on the flags even in winter, with a stone for bolster. Saint Fernan slept beside his own open grave every night of his life. Saint Baithin was accustomed to stretch beside every new corpse that was brought into the mortuary chapel. Others tortured themselves in thorny brakes and suspended themselves in bog-pools by means of scythe-blades placed beneath their armpits. They fasted for forty days at a time and carried great boulders in order that they might be worthy of the example of the Crucified One. Heaven demanded these sacrifices from the elect, so that they might atone for the sins of the wicked. Hundreds of pale youths and virgins went gladly to cell or desert that, by their self-inflicted mortifications, they might save others from the anger of Heaven. Even in marriage must that sacrifice be demanded?

She was back again in her room. She was sitting on the edge of the bed staring into the moonlight, but she did not see its peaceful gleams—she was staring into the darkness of her own fate.

FRANK O'CONNOR

# The Bridal Night[1]

IT WAS SUNSET, and the two great humps of rock made a twilight in the cove where the boats were lying high up the strand. There was one light only in a little whitewashed cottage. Around the headland came a boat, and the heavy dipping of its oars was like a heron's flight. The old woman was sitting on the low stone wall outside her cottage.

' 'Tis a lonesome place,' said I.

' 'Tis so,' she agreed, 'a lonesome place, but any place is lonesome without one you'd care for.'

'Your own flock are gone from you, I suppose?' I asked.

'I never had but the one,' she replied, 'the one son only,' and I knew because she did not add a prayer for his soul that he was still alive.

'Is it in America he is?' I asked. (It is to America all the boys of the locality go when they leave home.)

'No, then,' she replied simply. 'It is in the asylum in Cork he is on me these twelve years.'

I had no fear of trespassing on her emotions. These lonesome people in wild places, it is their nature to speak; they must cry out their sorrows like the wild birds.

'God help us!' I said. 'Far enough!'

'Far enough,' she sighed. 'Too far for an old woman. There was a nice priest here one time brought me up in his car to see him. All the ways to this wild place he brought it, and he drove me into the city. It is a place I was never used to, but it eased my mind to see poor Denis well-cared-for and well-liked. It was a trouble to me before that, not knowing would they see what a good boy he was before his madness came on him. He knew me; he saluted me, but he said nothing until the superintendent came to tell me the tea was ready for me. Then poor Denis raised his head and says, "Leave ye not forget the toast. She was ever a great one for her bit of toast." It seemed to give him ease and he cried after. A good boy he was and is. It was like him after seven long years to think of his old mother and her little bit of toast.'

'God help us,' I said, for her voice was like the birds', hurrying

[1] From *Crab Apple Jelly*, New York. Copyright 1944 by Alfred A. Knopf, Inc.

high, immensely high, in the coloured light, out to sea to the last islands where their nests were.

'Blessed be His Holy Will,' the old woman added, 'there is no turning aside what is in store. It was a teacher that was here at the time. Miss Regan her name was. She was a fine big jolly girl from the town. Her father had a shop there. They said she had three hundred pounds to her own cheek the day she set foot in the school, and—'tis hard to believe but 'tis what they all said: I will not belie her—'twasn't banished she was at all, but she came here of her own choice, for the great liking she had for the sea and the mountains. Now, that is the story, and with my own eyes I saw her, day in day out, coming down the little pathway you came yourself from the road, and sitting beyond there in a hollow you can hardly see, out of the wind. The neighbours could make nothing of it, and she being a stranger, and with only the book Irish, they left her alone. It never seemed to take a peg out of her, only sitting in that hole in the rocks, as happy as the day is long, reading her little book or writing her letters. Of an odd time she might bring one of the little scholars along with her to be picking posies.

'That was where my Denis saw her. He'd go up to her of an evening and sit on the grass beside her, and off and on he might take her out in the boat with him. And she'd say with that big laugh of hers, "Denis is my beau." Those now were her words and she meant no more harm by it than the child unborn, and I knew it and Denis knew it, and it was a little joke we had, the three of us. It was the same way she used to joke about her little hollow. "Mrs. Sullivan," she'd say, "leave no one near it. It is my nest and my cell and my little prayer-house, and maybe I would be like the birds and catch the smell of the stranger and then fly away from ye all." It did me good to hear her laugh, and whenever I saw Denis moping or idle I would say it to himself, "Denis, why wouldn't you go out and pay your attentions to Miss Regan and all saying you are her intended?" It was only a joke. I would say the same thing to her face, for Denis was such a quiet boy, no way rough or accustomed to the girls at all —and how would he in this lonesome place?

'I will not belie her; it was she saw first that poor Denis was after more than company, and it was not to this cove she came at all then but to the little cove beyond the headland, and 'tis hardly she would go there itself without a little scholar along with her. "Ah," says I, for I missed her company, "isn't it the great stranger Miss Regan is becoming?" and Denis would put on his coat and go hunting in the dusk till he came to whatever spot she was. Little ease that was to him, poor boy, for he lost his tongue entirely, and lying on his belly before her, chewing an old bit of grass, is all he would do till she got up and left him. He could not help himself, poor boy. The madness was on him, even then, and it was only when I saw the plunder done that I knew there was no cure for him only to put her out of his mind entirely. For 'twas madness in him and he knew it, and that was what made him lose his tongue—he that was maybe without the price of an ounce of 'baccy—I will not deny it: often enough he had to do without it when the hens would not be laying, and often enough stirabout and praties was all we had for days. And there was she with money to her name in the bank! And that wasn't all, for he was a good boy; a quiet, good-natured boy, and another would take pity on him, knowing he would make her a fine steady husband, but she was not the sort, and well I knew it from the first day I laid eyes on her, that her hand would never rock the cradle. There was the madness out and out.

'So here was I, pulling and hauling, coaxing him to stop at home, and hiding whatever little thing was to be done till evening the way his hands would not be idle. But he had no heart in the work, only listening, always listening, or climbing the *cnuceen*[1] to see would he catch a glimpse of her coming or going. And oh, Mary, the heavy sigh he'd give when his bit of supper was over and I bolting the door for the night, and he with the long hours of darkness forninst him—my heart was broken, thinking of it. It was the madness, you see. It was on him. He could hardly sleep or eat, and at night I would hear him, turning and groaning as loud as the sea on the rocks.

'It was then when the sleep was a fever to him that he took to walking in the night. I remember well the first night I heard him lift the latch. I put on my few things and went out after him. It was standing here I heard his feet on the stile. I went back and latched the door and hurried after him. What else could I do, and this place terrible after the fall of night with rocks and hills and water and streams, and he, poor soul, blinded with the dint of sleep. He travelled the road apace, and then took to the hills, and I followed him with my legs all torn with briers and furze. It was over by the doctor's house beyond that he gave up. He turned to me then the way a little child that is running away turns and clings to your knees; he

[1] Little hill.

turned on me and said, "Mother, we'll go home now. It was the bad day for you ever you brought me into the world." And as the day was breaking I got him back to bed and covered him up to sleep.

'I was hoping in time he would wear himself out, but it was worse he was getting. I was a strong woman then, a mayen-strong woman. I could cart a load of seaweed or dig a field with any man, but the night walking broke me. I knelt one night before the Blessed Virgin and I prayed whatever was to happen, it would happen while the light of life was in me, the way I would not be leaving him lonesome like that in a wild place.

'And it happened the way I prayed. Blessed be God, he woke that night or the next night on me and he roaring. I went in to him but I could not hold him. He had the strength of five men. So I went out and locked the door behind me. It was down the hill I faced in the starlight to the little house above the cove. The Donoghues came with me; I will not belie them; they were fine powerful men and good neighbours. The father and the two sons came with me and brought the rope from the boats. It was a hard struggle they had of it and a long time before they got him on the floor, and a longer time before they got the ropes on him. And when they had him tied they put him back into bed for me, and I covered him up, nice and decent, and put a hot stone to his feet to take the chill of the cold floor off him.

'Sean Donoghue spent the night sitting beside the fire with me, and in the morning he sent one of the boys off for the doctor. Then Denis called me in his own voice and I went in to him. Sean Donoghue came with me. "Mother," says Denis, "will you leave me this way against the time they come for me?" I hadn't the heart. God knows I hadn't. "Don't do it Peg," says Sean. "If 'twas a hard job trussing him before, it will be harder the next time and I won't answer for it."

'"You're a kind neighbour, Sean," says I, "and I would never make little of you, but he is the only son I ever reared and I'd sooner he'd kill me now than to shame him at the last."

'So I loosened the ropes on him and he lay there very quiet all day without breaking his fast. Coming on to evening he asked me for the sup of tea and he drank it, and soon after the doctor and another man came in the car. They said a few words to Denis but he made them no answer, and the doctor gave me the bit of writing. "It will be tomorrow before they come for him," says he, "and 'tisn't right for you to be alone in the house with the man." But I said I would stop with him and Sean Donoghue said the same.

'When darkness came on there was a little bit of a wind blew up from the sea and Denis began to rave to himself, and it was her name he was calling all the time. "Winnie," that was her name, and it was the first time I heard it spoken. "Who is that he is calling?" says Sean. "It is the schoolmistress," says I, "for though I do not recognise the name, I know 'tis no one else he would be asking for." "That is a bad sign," says Sean. "He will get worse as the night goes on and the wind rises. 'Twould be better for me to go down and get the boys to put the ropes on him again while he's quiet." And it was then something struck me and I said, "Maybe if she came to him herself for a minute he would be quiet after." "We can try it anyway," says Sean, "and if the girl has a kind heart she will come."

'It was Sean that went up for her. I would not have the courage to ask her. Her little house is there on the edge of the hill; you can see it as you go back the road with the bit of garden before it the new teacher left grow wild. And it was a true word Sean said, for 'twas worse Denis was getting, shouting out against the wind for us to get Winnie for him. Sean was a long time away, or maybe I felt it long, and I thought it might be the way she was afeared to come. There are many like that, small blame to them. Then I heard her step I knew so well on the boreen beside the house and I ran to the door, meaning to say I was sorry for the trouble we were giving her, but when I opened the door Denis called out her name in a loud voice, and the crying fit came on me, thinking how light-hearted we used to be together.

'I couldn't help it and she pushed in past me into the bedroom with her face as white as that wall. The candle was lighting on the dresser. He turned to her roaring with the mad look in his eyes, and then went quiet all of a sudden, seeing her like that overright him with her hair all tumbled in the wind. I was coming behind her. I heard it. He put up his two poor hands and the red mark of the ropes on his wrists and whispered to her, "Winnie, *asthore*,[1] isn't it the long time you were away from me?"

' "It is, Denis, it is indeed," says she, "but you know I couldn't help it."

' "Don't leave me any more now, Winnie," says he, and then he said no more, only the two eyes lighting out on her as she sat by the

[1] My treasure.

bed. And Sean Donoghue brought in the little stooleen for me, and there we were, the three of us talking, and Denis paying us no attention, only staring at her. Then all at once he got excited and sat up in the bed.

'"Winnie," says he, "lie down here beside me."

'"Oye," says Sean, humouring him, "don't you know the poor girl is played out after her day's work? She must go home to bed."

'"No, no, no," says Denis, and the terrible mad light in his eyes. "There is a high wind blowing and 'tis no night for one like her to be out. Leave her sleep here beside me. Leave her creep under the clothes to me the way I'll keep her warm."

'"Oh, oh, oh, oh," says I, "indeed and indeed, Miss Regan, 'tis I'm sorry for bringing you here. 'Tisn't my son is talking at all but the madness in him. I'll go now," says I, "and bring Sean's boys to put the ropes on him again."

'"No, Mrs. Sullivan," says she in a quiet voice, "don't do that at all. I'll stop here with him and he'll go fast asleep. Won't you, Denis?"

'"I will, I will," says he, "but come under the clothes to me. There does a terrible draught blow under that door."

'"I will indeed, Denis," says she, "if you'll promise me you'll go to sleep."

'"Oye, whisht, girl!" says I. "'Tis you that's mad. While you're here you're in my charge, and how would I answer to your father if you stopped here by yourself?"

'"Never mind about me, Mrs. Sullivan," she said. "I'm not a bit in dread of Denis. I promise you there will no harm come to me. You and Mr. Donoghue can sit outside in the kitchen and I'll be all right here."

'She had a worried look, but there was something about her there was no mistaking. I wouldn't take it on myself to cross the girl. We went out to the kitchen, Sean and myself, and we heard every whisper that passed between them. She got into the bed beside him: I heard her. He was whispering into her ear the sort of foolish things boys do be saying at that age, and then we heard no more, only the pair of them breathing. I went to the room door and looked in. He was lying with his arm about her and his head on her bosom, sleeping like a child, sleeping like he slept in his good days with no worry at all on his poor face. She did not look at me and I did not speak to her. My heart was too full. God help us, it was an old song of my father's that was going through my head: "Lonely Rock is the one wife my children will know."

'Later on the candle went out and I did not light another. I wasn't a bit afraid of her then. The storm blew up and he slept through it all, breathing nice and even. When it was light I made a cup of tea for her and beckoned her from the room door. She loosened his hold and slipped out of bed. Then he stirred and opened his eyes.

' "Winnie," says he, "where are you going?"

' "I'm going to work, Denis," says she. "Don't you know I must be at the school early?"

' "But you'll come back to me tonight, Winnie?" says he.

' "I will, Denis," says she. "I'll come back, never fear."

'And he turned on his side and went fast asleep again.

'When she walked into the kitchen I went on my two knees before her and kissed her hands. I did so. There would no words come to me, and we sat there, the three of us, over our tea, and I declare for the time being I felt 'twas nearly worth it all, all the troubles of his birth and rearing and all the lonesome years ahead.

'It was a great ease to us. Poor Denis never stirred, and when the police came he went along with them without commotion or handcuffs or anything that would shame him and all the words he said to me was, "Mother, tell Winnie I'll be expecting her."

'And isn't it a strange and wonderful thing? From that day to the day she left us there did no one speak a bad word about what she did, and the people couldn't do enough for her. Isn't it a strange thing, and the world as wicked as it is, that no one would say the bad word about her?'

Darkness had fallen over the Atlantic, blank grey to its farthest reaches.

MICHAEL MCLAVERTY

# Six Weeks On and Two Ashore[1]

IN THE EARLY HOURS of the night it had rained and the iron gate that led to the lightkeepers' houses had rattled loose in the wind, and as it cringed and banged it disturbed Mrs. O'Brien's spaniel where he lay on a mat in the dark draughty hallway. Time and again he gave a muffled growl, padded about the hall, and scratched at the door. His uneasiness and the noise of the wind had wakened Mrs. O'Brien in the room above him, and she lay in bed wondering if she should go down and let him into the warm comfort of the kitchen. Beside her her husband was asleep, snoring loudly, unaware of her wakefulness or of the windows shaking in their heavy frames. The rain rattled like hailstones against the panes and raced in a flood into the zinc tank at the side of the house. God in Heaven, how anybody could sleep through that, she said—it was enough to waken the dead and there he was deep asleep as if it were a calm summer night. What kind of a man was he at all! You'd think he'd be worrying about his journey to the Rock in the morning and his long six weeks away from her. He was getting old—there was no mistake about that. She touched his feet—they were cold, as cold as a stone you'd find on a wintry beach.

The dog growled again, and throwing back the bedclothes she got up and groped on the table for the matchbox. She struck one match but it was a dead one, and she clicked her tongue in disapproval. She was never done telling Tom not to be putting his spent matches back into the box but he never heeded her. It was tidy he told her; it was exasperating if she knew anything. She struck three before coming upon a good one, and in the spurt of flame she glanced at the alarm-clock and saw that it was two hours after midnight. She slipped downstairs, lit the lamp, and let the dog into the kitchen. She patted his head and he jumped on the sofa, thumped it loudly with his tail and curled up on a cushion. On the floor Tom's hampers lay ready for the morning when the boatmen would come to row him out to the lighthouse to relieve young Frank Coady. She looked at the hampers with sharp calculation, wondering if she had packed everything he needed. She was always sure to forget something—

---

[1] From *The Game Cock and Other Stories*, London, 1949. First published in *Irish Writing*, (Cork), No. 4, 1948.

boot polish or a pullover or a corkscrew or soap—and he was always sure to cast it up to her as soon as he stepped ashore for his two weeks leave. She could never remember a time when he arrived back without some complaint or other. But this time she was sure she had forgotten nothing for she had made a list and ticked each item off as she packed them into the cases. Yes, he wouldn't be able to launch any of his ill-humour on her this time!

She quenched the lamp, and returning to her room she stood at the window for a moment and saw the lighthouse beam shine on the clouds and sweep through the fine wire of falling rain. Tom was still asleep, heedless of his coming sojourn on that windy stub of rock. But maybe if the wind would hold during the night the boatmen would be unable to row him out in the morning. But even that would be no comfort—waiting, and waiting, and watching the boatmen sheltering all day in the lea of the boathouse expecting the sea to settle. It'd be better, after all, that they'd be able to take him. She got into bed and turned her back to him, and as she listened to the rain she thought of how it would wash the muddy paw-marks from the cement paths and save her the trouble of getting down on her hands and knees in the morning.

She awoke without aid of the alarm-clock, and from her bed she saw the washed blue of the sky, and in the stillness heard the hollow tumult of the distracted sea. He'd have to go out this morning—there was no doubt about that! But God grant he'd return to her in better form! She got up quietly, and buttoning her frock at the window she gazed down at the Coady's house. The door was open to the cold sun and Delia Coady was on her knees freshly whitening the doorstep that had been streaked in the night's rain. All her windows were open, the curtains bulging in the uneasy draught. Delia raised her head and looked round but Mrs. O'Brien withdrew to the edge of the window and continued to watch her. Delia was singing now and going to the zinc tank at the side of the house for a bucket of water.

Tom stirred in his bed and threw one arm across the pillow.

'Do you hear her?' his wife said.

'Hear who?' he mumbled crossly and pulled the clothes up round his chest.

'Delia Coady is singing like a lark.'

'Well, let her sing. Isn't it a free country?'

The alarm-clock buzzed on the table and she let it whirl out to the end of its spring.

Tom raised his head from the pillow and stared at her. 'Isn't it a great wonder you didn't switch that damned thing off and you up before it?'

'You better get up, Tom. Delia will think you're in no hurry to take her Frank off the Rock.'

'I'll go when it suits me—not a second faster. When young Coady's as long on the lights as I am he'll not hurry much. The way to get on in my job is to go slow, slow, slow—dead slow, snail slow, and always slow. Do you remember what one of the Commissioners said to me on the East Light in Rathlin? "Mister O'Brien," he said, "there's not as much dust in the whole place as would fill a matchbox." And the secret is—slow.'

'No Commissioner would use such a word as "matchbox".'

'And do you think, woman, that I'm making up that story? What would you have him say?' and he affected a mincing feminine accent: ' "Lightkeeper O'Brien, there is not as much elemental dust in the hallowed precincts of this Lighthouse as would fill a silver snuff-box." Is that what you would have him say?' he added crossly.

'I don't think he'd pass any remark about dust or dirt.'

'You don't think! You don't think! It's a wonder you didn't think of switching off the damned alarm-clock and you knowing I hate the sound of it.'

She said nothing. All their quarrels seemed to arise out of the simplest remarks—one remark following another, spreading out and involving them, before they were aware, in a quarrel of cold cruelty. She, herself, was to blame for many of them. She should have let him have his little story of 'the matchbox'. What on earth possessed her to turn a word on him and this the last day she'd be speaking to him for six long weeks. She checked a long sigh, tidied the things in the room quietly, and all the time tried to find something to say that would soften her last words to him. She crossed to the window and put her hand to the snib to lower it. Delia was still singing and standing out from the door the better to see the freshly whitened window-sills and doorstep.

'She has a blue frock on,' she said over her shoulder. 'I never saw her in that before; it fairly becomes her.'

'Didn't I tell you she was married in blue! It'll be the same frock.'

'She has a nice voice.'

'I think you're jealous of her.'

'Hm, I used to be able to sing very well myself.'

'I must say I heard precious little of it.'

'Maybe you didn't! Maybe you'd be interested to know I gave that up shortly after we were married—some twelve years ago.'

'And whose fault was that?'

'Oh, I don't know,' she said, controlling herself.

He pulled the clothes over his shoulder and she pleaded with him to get up and not be the sort that'd deprive another man of even one hour of his leave on shore.

'Is it Frank Coady I'd hurry for! Not me! I'll take my time. I'm over thirty years on the lights and he's a bare half-dozen. He doesn't rush much if he's coming out to relieve me.'

'You can't blame him and he not long married,' she said, scarcely knowing what she was saying as she spoke into the mirror and brushed her hair.

'Last time he came out to relieve me I was waiting for the boat all morning and it didn't come till the afternoon. And what did he say as he stepped ashore: "God, Tom, I'm sorry the boat's late. I took a hellish pain in my stomach and had to lie down for a couple of hours." That's what the scamp said to me instead of offering to give me an extra day on account of his hellish pains. Well, I feel tired this morning and I'm not stirring hand or foot for another hour at least!'

She turned round in her chair from the mirror: 'I'm beginning to get tired of that word "tired" of yours. You were tired last night, tired the night before—always tired. You've said nothing else since you stepped ashore two weeks ago. Tired!—it's not out of any consideration you show me. Going off to the pub of an evening and waiting there till somebody gives you a lift home.'

'And what do you want me to do? What do you want off me?'

'Oh, nothing,' she almost cried, 'nothing! I'm used to loneliness now! I'm used to my married widowhood—in my marriage! You won't come for a game of bridge of an evening. You're tired—you always say. And if I go you won't wait up till I come back. You lower the lamp and go to your bed. Oh, it's no wonder my hair is beginning to turn grey at the temples.'

'My own is white!'

'What do you expect and you nearing sixty.'

'You're lovely company!'

'Company! Only for the companionship of the old dog I'd go out of my mind.'

'If you'd go out of this room I might think of getting up.'

'Oh, if I'd thought I was keeping you back I'd have gone long ago,' and she lifted the alarm-clock, the box of matches, and hastened from the room.

He stretched his arms and looked at the glass of water on the table. He'd not drink that! The stale taste of it would upset him—and what with his stomach upset and his mind upset he'd be in a nice fix for a journey on the sea. He'd smoke a cigarette—and stretching out to the chair for his coat, he lit one, and lay back on the pillows, frowning now and then at the cold air that blew through the open window. He could hear Delia singing and he wondered if Mag sang when she was expecting him home. He doubted it! She was more attached to that damned old dog, and she thought nothing of walking five miles of an evening for a game of cards and bringing the old dog with her. If she were on the Rock for awhile it'd soon tether her, soon take the skip out of her step. Ah, he should have married somebody less flighty, somebody a bit older and settled, somebody that'd enjoy a glass of stout with you of an evening and not be wanting to drag you over the whole blasted country in search of a game of bridge.

Downstairs he heard Mag opening the front door and letting out the dog for a run, and he heard her speak across to Delia and say how glad she was that it had cleared up in time for Frank's homecoming. Hm, he thought, she's greatly concerned about the neighbours. He looked at the cigarette in his hand, and from the bed he tried to throw it through the open window but it struck the pane and fell on the floor, and he had to get up and stamp on the lighted end.

His clothes were folded neatly for him on the edge of the table: a clean white shirt, his trousers creased and the brass buttons on his jacket brightly polished. He pulled on the cold, starched shirt and gave a snort of contempt. He wished she'd be less particular—ye'd think he was expecting a visit from the Commissioners on the Rock. Damn the thing you ever saw out there except an exhausted pigeon or a dead cormorant that you'd have to kick into the sea to keep the blowfly from stalking around it. It's remarkable the nose a blowfly has for decaying flesh—flying two or three miles out to sea to lay its eggs on a dead sea-bird. Nature's remarkable when you come to think about it—very remarkable!

Mag tapped the stairs with her knuckles and called out that his breakfast was ready, and when he came down, she glanced at him furtively, trying to read from his face the effect of her remark to him about his white hair. If only she could tell him that she was sorry. But it was better not to—it was better to let it pass and speak to him as if nothing had happened.

'Oh, Tom,' she said brightly, 'Delia was over to see what time you expected to go.'

'And how the hell do I know at what time I'm expected to go. I'll wait till the boatmen call—and to my own slow and unhurried time.'

'She has plenty of paint on, this morning,' she added to restore ease.

'Who has?'

'The old boat, I mean,' she lashed back.

There it was again: they were back to where they started from—chilling one another with silent hostility or with words that would spurt in bitter fury. Oh, she thought, if only he had shown some of his old love for her during the past two weeks they would not now be snapping at one another, and there would be ease and satisfaction and longing in this leave-taking.

She brought a hot plate of rashers and eggs from the range and poured out tea for him.

'Maybe, Tom, I should run over and tell Delia you'll be ready as soon as the boatmen arrive. I'd like to take the full of my eyes of her place as she does of ours. I always think there's a heavy smell of paraffin in her kitchen. Do you ever find it, Tom?'

'That smell's been in my nose ever since I joined the Lights. Do you know what I'm going to tell you,' and he raised the fork in his hand as she sat down opposite him. 'There's nothing as penetrating and as permanent as the smell of paraffin. It's remarkable. It seeps into the walls and it would ooze out again through two coats of new paint. It's in my nose and I wouldn't know the differs between it and the smell of a flower.'

She smiled, for she at that moment caught sight of two cases of Guiness's stout on the floor and she yearned to tell him jokingly that he had a fine perfume for something else. But she repressed that desire and turned to the dog as he laid his nose on her lap. She threw him a few scraps from the table and he snapped at them greedily. She fondled his head and toyed with one of his ears, turning it inside out.

'It's a great wonder you wouldn't put out that dog and let me get my breakfast in some sort of Christian decency. There's a bad smell from him.'

'And you said a moment ago that you could smell nothing only paraffin.'

'Well, I get the smell of him—and that's saying something.'

At that moment the dog walked under the table to his side and he made a kick at it and it yelped and ran under the sofa.

'Come here, Brian,' she called coaxingly, and the dog came out and walked timorously towards her.

'Either he goes out of this or I don't finish my breakfast!'

Without a word she got up and let the dog out.

'Maybe that'll please you,' she said, coming back to the table. 'Anything I love, you despise.'

'That's a damned lie!'

'It's true—and because you thought I was jealous of Delia you praised her.'

'That's another infernal lie!'

'It's too true, Tom. Nothing pleases you—and you used to be so different. You used to be so jolly—one could joke and laugh with you. But of late you've changed.'

'It's you that's changed!'

She took her handkerchief and blew her nose. She felt the tears rising to her eyes and she held her head, trying to regain her self-control.

A shadow passed the window. There was a knock at the door and she opened it to admit three of the boatmen.

'We'd like to catch the tide, Mister O'Brien,' they said, and lifting the hampers they shuffled out of the house.

Tom finished his breakfast slowly and went upstairs. He came down after a short time, dressed, and ready for the road. In a glance she saw that he hadn't a breast-pocket handkerchief, and telling him to wait for a minute she ran upstairs to get one, and coming down again she found he was gone. She hurried after him and overtook him at the iron gate.

'Don't keep me back,' he said, 'didn't you hear as well as I did that we've to catch the tide!' But she held him, and as he tried to wrench himself free she folded the handkerchief into his pocket.

'Tom, don't go away from me like that!' and she looked up at him with an anxious pleading face.

'You're making a fine laughing-stock of me!' he said, and pushing the handkerchief out of sight into his pocket he walked off.

She stood at the gate waiting for him to turn and wave his hand to her but he went on stolidly, erect, along the loose sandy road to the shore. He smoked his pipe, the road sloping before him, its sand white in places from the feet of the boatmen and dark with rain where it was untrodden.

The men were already in the boat, baling out the night's rain-water, and as Tom picked his steps over the piles of slabby wrack on the shore they kept calling out to him to be careful. They assisted him into the boat and he sat in the stern, his legs apart, and his arms dangling between his knees. The boatmen spat on their hands, gripped the oars, and in a few minutes were out from the shelter of the cove and saw ahead of them the black rock with its stub of a lighthouse like a brooding sea-bird. The men rowed with quick, confident strokes, and the boat rose and fell, cutting swathes on the green sward of the sea.

'Take your time,' Tom said, 'take your time. You're not paid for sweating yourselves. We'll be there soon enough.'

They said nothing, and as they came nearer to the rock they saw the white path curving from the top to the water's edge and saw the waves jabbling and shouldering one another in mad confusion. They dipped their oars now with short, snappy strokes, their eyes on the three lightkeepers who awaited them.

'Ye'll have to jump for it, Mister O'Brien, when we give the word. We'll get the cases landed first,' and while one held off the boat with a boat hook, two stood at the stern with a case waiting their chance to hoist it on to the out-stretched hands of those on shore. When the cases were roped and landed Frank Coady jumped and alighting on the gunwale he balanced himself on one leg as lightly as a ballet dancer. 'The fairy godmother!' he said, and folding his arms he spun round on his toe with emphatic daintiness, and then bowing he kissed his fingers to those on shore.

Tom O'Brien lumbered up to him, putting his pipe in his pocket.

'Now, Tom, my lad, let me give you a hand,' said Coady, stretching out his hand to him.

'Get away from me, you bloody fool!' said O'Brien, steadying one foot on the gunwale.

'Be careful now, Mister O'Brien, be careful!' the boatmen shouted. 'Wait till that big fellow passes. Take him on the rise!'

But O'Brien wasn't listening to them. He took his leap on the descent of the wave, missed the path, and was all but disappearing into the sea when the lightkeepers gripped him and hauled him ashore.

'I'm all right! I'm all right!' he said, as they laughed at his soaked trousers, the knee-cap cut and the blood oozing out of it.

'Are you O.K., Tom?' shouted Coady from the boat.

'Ah, go to hell, you!' said O'Brien.

'He's a cranky oul divil,' Coady said to the boatmen as he took off his coat and lifted an oar. 'Now my hearties let us see how you can make her leap!' He pulled on his oar with all his strength: 'Up, my hearty fellows! Up she jumps! That's the way to make her skip! I'll leave a pint for all hands in the pub! A pint from Frank Coady!'

Near the shore he turned his head and saw his wife awaiting him.

'There she is, my hearty men! Knitting and waiting for her darling Frank!' He threw down his oar and perched himself on the bow ready to jump ashore.

'Take care you don't go like O'Brien,' they laughed.

'O'Brien's as stiff as a man on stilts! Here she goes!' and he jumped lightly on to the rock and spinning round he warded off the boat with his foot.

In a minute he was in his wife's arms, and linked together they went off slowly along the sandy road, and for a long time the boatmen could hear him laughing and they knew he was laughing at O'Brien.

Through the iron gate they went arm in arm. Mag O'Brien was outside her house with the dog and as Frank drew near he told her with much relish how Tom had cut the knee of his trousers.

'He wasn't hurt?' she said.

'Hurt—not a bit! He strode up the path after it like a man in training for the half-mile. The only thing you need to worry about is to get a nice patch.' And taking Delia by the hand they swung across to their own house, stood for a minute admiring the whitened doorstep, and going inside they closed the door.

Mag withdrew and sat for a minute at her own window that overlooked their house. Her head ached, and she thought how careless she was in forgetting to pack a bandage or a taste of iodine that he could daub on his bruised knee. One can't think of everything, she said, and she laid her hands on her lap and gazed across at Coady's house that was now silent and still. With an effort she got to her feet and withdrew from the window, and taking a stick she called her dog and set off through the iron gate and away to the shore that was nearest to the rock.

She scanned the rock and the white path down to the sea. If only he saw her and came out on the parapet as he used to do and signaled to her she'd be content—her mind would be eased. She sat down on a green slope and waited. There was no stir about the rock, only a gull or two tilting and gliding above the sea. She got up and waved her hand. The dog scratched at the ground, leapt sideways, impatient to be off. She waved again—still there was no sign that she was being seen. She turned and felt the soft wind—it was light and tired: exhausted after its rampage. She stretched herself and stood facing it but it was too weak even to shake her hair. If only it were strong, blowing against her with force she would delight in it. But there was no strength in it—it was indolent and inert, as tired as an old man. She looked once more at the Rock, and seeing a black whorl of smoke rising from it she knew that it was Tom putting on a good fire. He would take a book now, or a bottle of Guinness and his pipe, and after that he would close his eyes and sleep.

The dog barked and ran up the slope after a rabbit. She followed after him and looking to the right she saw the iron gate and the clump of houses she had just left. There was nothing there but silence and sunlight, and behind her the stir of the cold sea.

FRANCIS STUART

# The Varied Shapes of Violence[1]

A couple of weeks later Ezra was sitting with Kavanagh in the parlour above the fish-shop. It was Kavanagh's first visit to Altamont since the week-end of the picnic, and they were drinking Guinness while Annie prepared a fish supper in the small kitchen. She was no longer working for Kavanagh in his shop. The sergeant had spoken to her about the scandal of her relationship to her employer and had wanted to send her as maid to a family in another town. But she had run round to Father Mellowes. She had arrived one morning in her Sunday clothes and sat down heavily on the sofa.

'Don't send me out of the town,' she had said. 'All my friends are here.'

Father Mellowes did not know what she was talking about. And when she realised that, she did not say anything about her interview with the sergeant. A look of complete innocence came into her violet eyes that had the freshness of flowers in her plump, freckled face.

'I lost my job,' she said.

'I'm sorry for that. It's a pity losing a good job,' said Father Mellowes. He knew nothing of the scandal. He heard very little of the town gossip.

'It's not that,' she answered. She wasn't sure how much he knew about her. But when he waited she added: 'I was used to him.'

'You mean as an employer?' asked Father Mellowes.

'As a man, Father. That's what I mean.'

'You were living together?' he asked.

'That's so,' she said.

'Ah, my poor child,' said the priest, his big face tilted down at her, regarding her.

'I'm in trouble,' she went on.

'Ah, little one, you're going to have a child, is that it? And you've lost your job. And these two things that seem like the worst blows to you are the ways that our Lord shows His loving care for you. And was that the reason that Mr. Kavanagh gave you notice?' he added.

'No. He doesn't know about that.'

---
[1] From *Redemption*, New York, 1950.

'And I suppose if you told him he wouldn't marry you?'

'It isn't his,' the girl said. She saw that she could confide in Father Mellowes. She had an instinct that there were depths in him in which all her worries and burdens could be swallowed up.

'There was another man, then?' he asked her.

'Yes.'

'Wait a minute. We'll have a cup of tea,' the priest said. He went out on to the landing and called down to Mrs. Bamber to make them a pot of tea. Annie had regarded the lithograph of St. Francis with the rays from the crucified Seraph piercing his own hands and feet. The dead white rays, the crimson wounds and the blue-black, stormy sky were beautiful to her. She had enjoyed sitting there drinking the hot, sweet tea and listening to Father Mellowes. She did not try to understand what he was saying to her. Sin and repentance were not real to her. The lithograph was real, and the large stuffed fish in a glass case in the window of Kavanagh's shop. Each meant to her a certain atmosphere, a certain kind of life, the life of the flesh and the life of the spirit and she was quite ready to shift over from one to the other. The priest had asked her a question!

'Eh?' she said, starting.

'Ah, I'm sorry. You were thinking,' he said.

'Oh, don't mind me, Father. I'm a terror for manners.'

'If you'll excuse me now, Annie, I've got to go into the town. There are plenty of books there if you'd care to read till I come back at dinner-time.'

'If you've any mending or washing, I'd rather do that, Father.'

There had been a tap on the door and Sergeant Foley had come in with his greyhound, Rainbow Cutlet, covered from head to tail in a linen coat that hung down on each side to the ground. The priest's little dog hurled himself at this strange intruder. There was a mêlée of snarls and snapping and Annie burst out laughing. 'The Cutlet,' as he was locally called, had been out at exercise, the day of the great race was almost at hand, and the sergeant had come to ask Father Mellowes if he might use the sink in the kitchen in which to immerse his champion in a mustard bath, as the one at the barracks was too shallow.

'You'll find the very thing you want in the kitchen, sergeant. I've seen Mrs. Bamber bathing the children in it; and Miss Lee here won't mind giving you a hand, will you, Annie?' Father Mellowes said.

She did not mind. She had no resentment against the sergeant.

Kavanagh was now repeating this story to Ezra. He had heard it all from Annie when she had come secretly to the flat the night before. She was now temporarily taken on by Father Mellowes as a kind of housekeeper and had a small attic room at Mrs. Bamber's. But she had not told Kavanagh about how well she had got on with the sergeant. Or how, after they had dried 'The Cutlet,' she had mended the dog's coat for him that had been torn by the teeth of the priest's little mongrel, or that the sergeant had asked her to meet him on the night of the dog-races.

'That's freedom for you; that's democracy,' Kavanagh was saying. 'The girl can't sleep where she likes and I can't spend a week-end in my own flat with one of my own employees. But I'm not going to lie down and let them walk over me. I'll raise bloody hell in this gimcrack town before I'll let them go sneaking round taking my employees away from me.'

Ezra drank the Guinness and listened. The crude, vulgar energy of Kavanagh, his anger and his lust gave him a reality. To be in a room with most people was like being in a room with a ghost. So many people here struck Ezra as ghostly, their coming and going, their talk and expressions were ghostly and when he looked at them he saw nothing, or he saw something else. People who were not in pain, not in love, not angry, not in the grip of desire or of some secret vision; they were ghosts. He couldn't talk to them because the breath of his mouth would blow through them without touching them. But Kavanagh was ready to be touched and to be kindled, his little anger kindled by Ezra's greater anger. He seemed to sense Ezra's greater anger and to bow to it.

'I could bring business to this town. I could bring a bit of life to it,' Kavanagh said. 'But they'd sooner go to pot in their own petty way. They're scared of people like us, that's what. They're scared. And they'll be more scared when I'm done with them. And do you know what, if this town's finished, it's not the only one. There's many other towns all over the country that are going the same way. I've got branches in eight or ten other places and I know what's going on. I can smell it in the air. The good times are over for them, the times when you could look out of your hotel window on a fine Sunday morning and see the townspeople strolling up the main street to Mass and pull down the blind again and go back to bed and have another snooze in peace and security, knowing that the day was long and there was a well-stocked larder downstairs and good company in the private bar, quiet knowledgeable fellows who could tell you the winners of the big races for the past twenty years and more. But now it's another story. No one remembers anything beyond the week before last, and if you sleep late they come rattling at the door wanting to do out the room. There's no ease and quiet. Everyone's nervous, with one eye on the next day or the next meal or the next drink. It's as if they were afraid that their new gimcrack houses and cars and wireless sets were going to go phut! Perhaps it's another war they're afraid of, one that they wouldn't be able to sit out on Guinness and rashers as pretty as they did the last. What say, Arrigho, is there going to be another bust-up?'

'Well, it can't last for ever,' said Ezra. 'No world has ever lasted very long. They all go down one after another and there's not much left, only a fish or a deer scratched on the wall of a cave, or some marble statues without arms, or a bit of red brick wall in a jungle somewhere. Perhaps our going down has begun and perhaps nothing can stop it. Sometimes it looks like that all right; you get the smell of it, like you said, in the air.'

'You're right. We're going down,' Kavanagh repeated, leaning heavily over the table, looking into the black beer. 'This town's going down and it's the same tale in the others. And there's no use them blaming it on people like me. "Kavanagh's one of those fellows who make trouble in the town and bring down its morals." That's what the sergeant said to Annie. Hey, Annie,' he called. 'What was it the sergeant said?'

Annie put her head in the door. She wore a dirty white apron and had rolled up her sleeves. She smiled her slight, placid smile.

'I disremember exactly, Mr. Kavanagh. It doesn't signify. I'm here, anyhow, aren't I?'

'You're here, my girl, and they couldn't stop you,' repeated Kavanagh, leaning far over the table and laughing into his glass of black stout. 'And I'm going to let you into a secret, Arrigho; not now, though, wait till we've had a bit of supper. I'm going to throw a stone into their duck-pond that'll make a walloping big splash, me boy.'

Ezra remembered how he had written home from the foreign city, the bombed, dying city, to his wife during the war about Margareta. He had written about bringing her back with him if they were alive after this particular catastrophe passed over. He had thought in his innocence that there would be no difficulties, that she would have found shelter and refuge with his own people. His wife had understood and agreed. But later, after she had spoken to some of the officials whose permission would have had to be had, she had written that it was impossible. She had spoken to their local priest. He had discussed with Ezra's wife the implications of letting Ezra bring Margareta back into their fold. And they had confused her with their complacent, duck-pond arguments. But in the end they had overcome her and she had written to him that she could not have Margareta. But by then Margareta was lying with a huge pile of rubble on her heart. And he could not go home. He felt no bitterness against his wife. On the contrary, she had, alone and with nothing but the words of his letters to help her, stood out as long as she could. As his wife, she was powerless; the family love, the duck-pond love was too much for her. And now he could not go back. She did not even know that he was in Ireland. She was all right. She had the house and enough money, but he could not go back and live with her.

'Let's have a bite to eat. What say?' Kavanagh said.

Annie brought in a huge plate of fish and some more bottles of Guinness. She had tidied herself up and dusted her plump, freckled face with powder.

'Have a drink with us, Annie,' Kavanagh said to her.

'You know I don't take anything, Mr. Kavanagh.'

'Very well. Don't call me Mr. Kavanagh, but. That's not called for among friends. Have some port. Have something.'

'All right. I don't mind a glass of port.'

She was glad to be back here in the cosy, familiar atmosphere. She had often felt homesick in the past week for the little flat above the shop with its smell of stale, spilt stout and fish.

The three of them were sitting at the table; Kavanagh pulled Annie's chair nearer his own so that she was within handreach of him. He wanted to touch her, to lay his big hand on her. Ezra felt himself floating on a sea of black Guinness, lit by the violet eyes of Annie and scented by the greasy slab of fried fish crumbling open in white flakes on his plate. Kavanagh was opposite him, a big, smouldering shadow in the dusk of the room, leaning over the white table-cloth with an old-fashioned watch-chain strung across his broad, waistcoated torso. Ezra saw the glint of the gold chain as Kavanagh leant forward, overshadowing the bottles and Annie, brooding over them with his smouldering fire engendered by the black stout, anger, lust, and some confused vision of revenging himself.

He began to speak in a low voice to Annie. She listened with her blank passivity, only turning her head slightly away from his hot, beery breath.

'Ah,' she said. 'I could never abide the sight of blood.'

'A drop of blood, that's nothing, girl.' He turned to Ezra. 'Did you ever remark the holy picture that Father Mellowes has in his room?'

'I dread cutting myself,' said Annie.

'Tcha! What a baby! Just a pin-prick somewhere where it won't be noticed. Here I'll show you. Give us a bit of light.'

She switched on the light and came back to the table. Kavanagh took a needle from inside the lapel of his coat. He pulled up her dress over her knees and jabbed in the needle. She gave a little gasp and a drop of ruby blood appeared on her bluish white thigh.

She liked things to happen, even the sting of the needle; and she liked the thought of the bleeding picture. She liked the smell of drink on the breath of men. Heavy and passive in herself, she was like a sponge that soaked up sensation, excitement. But she pretended to be afraid of him and quickly pulled down her dress with a little squeal. He began to try to mollify her with pats and caresses, calling her a baby and holding the glass of port to her lips that were greasy from the fried fish. She drank the sweet wine passively, doing nothing beyond making the lazy movement of swallowing now and then, her head bent back and resting in the big palm of Kavanagh's hand. When he had emptied the glass into her mouth, he put it down and leant over her, looking at her.

'Don't mind any of them, Annie,' Kavanagh said. He turned to Ezra. 'The damned busybodies came round and spoke to her. They told her that by staying here in the flat with me over the week-ends she was causing a scandal in a respectable town.' He could not get over it. He went on brooding on it.

Ezra had begun by listening, amused and detached. The quarrel between the toping fishmonger and the town had no real concern for him. But gradually he began to speak too, to be caught into the controversy in spite of himself. Whether Kavanagh followed him or not, he did not care. He spoke for the first time in all these years of the shape of the cataclysm through which he had been.

'When I walk down the main street of this town,' he said, 'past the small busy shops and the pubs with Guard Higgins on point duty at the corner and Father Mellowes coming down the steps from the church after hearing confessions, for a moment I too breathe a breath of sweetness. I am tempted to believe that this is peace and righteousness and that they're justified in protecting it. But it's no good. Because I know where this street leads and where all streets lead. Your sergeant and the others can't see beyond the end of their street. The words that they speak in this street would be meaningless in the other street, in the street in which I was.'

'What street was that?' asked Kavanagh, fondling Annie with one hand while he held his glass of Guinness in the other.

'The street of a great city. It had been a street like the others, with tailors' dummies draped in the newest fashions in the shop-windows and restaurants with table lamps on the white cloths and a big, ugly church on the square at one end and hotels where they changed the towels in your bedroom every morning, and if a child fell and cut its knee on the pavement there was a great to-do and its mummy brought out her hanky and dabbed away the blood.'

'Ha!' said Kavanagh blankly. He did not know what Ezra was getting at.

'As long as there were clean handkerchiefs to dab at scratched knees and glass in the shop-windows,' Ezra went on, 'the same sermons were being preached in the church at the corner as Father Mellowes preaches here.

'I knew that street as I know this street. I had been into each restaurant along it at one time or other. I had sat in the summer nights on the terraces of the cafés and seen the lights shining on to the leaves of the lime trees planted along it when it was still secure and sheltered between its shops and houses, leading to all the other streets of the world. But slowly there was a change along it. Not only that I was now alone in it, or that the bombs had ground down many of the houses to piles of rubble. A street between walls of rubble is still a street and the shape of the ruins becomes as familiar and homely as the shape of the houses was. But now I began to know where it led.

'The street had its own air, its own atmosphere. Even when the houses collapsed they lay in their own dust, in their own light. Everything moves or stands in its own light or shadow, I suppose, a tree, a street, a rock, and the earth itself, and the final violation is the stripping from a thing of its own air. That is what happens to you when you're arrested; the little protective sanctum around you is violated—strange hands feel in your pockets, strange voices strip away the protective layer of space around you.

'I knew this first when the shells began to fall into the street. Shells are different from bombs. Shells are the first touch of the *others*, the sign of their presence; shells begin to strip away the familiar air and bring the first breath of the unknown darkness with them.

'It was the growing strangeness of the street that is what I remember of those days. I felt it turning into something different. Along part of it a column of tanks and heavy guns had been abandoned—for want of petrol, I suppose. I came on them there one evening, grey hulks of steel, like strange monsters washed up on a shore during a night of storm. I wasn't allowed in the streets because I was a foreigner, but I came out at night to look around. I came up out of the cellar where we were waiting, and each evening there was a new darkness in the street. It wasn't the same darkness through which the lights from the shops had shone and the buses rattled or even the darkness in which the houses had burnt after the raids. The street was being stripped of its own light and its own darkness and it lay there like the dead lie, without the halo of their own beings around them any more, exposed.

'I didn't know what was coming. There were no more newspapers and no wireless. There were only rumours, words in the darkness, names. But there were no names for the unknown shape; when they had spoken the strange names of Russian generals and Russian armies, there was still something that had not been given a name, the thing that would appear in the street at a certain coming hour of the day or of the night. There was another name being spoken like an incantation against the unknown horror: the army Wenck. In the cellars under the street and along the street at night there was this name spoken, in a question, an assertion or in irony. The army Wenck. That was the name of all that was familiar, the known, the past, fighting its way back to the city and the street. The army Wenck was the name of all that was known and familiar, the familiar pain, the familiar ruins and the familiar hunger and the small familiar joys and securities still left amid the ruins and the hunger. And the other names were the names of death, of the angel of death, of Ashtoreth, and they had the sound of the last trumpet. The horribly strange sound of something announcing the unknown doom.

'And in the street at night there were always new signs and new portents. No one knew what they meant, except that they meant the end coming nearer. There were the German lieutenant and sergeant hanging under the bridge of the elevated railway with a placard with words on it that confirmed the hopelessness of those who read it furtively as they passed. "Found without arms in face of the enemy."

'In face of the enemy. Those too were words that were mysterious and horrible. The street was now in face of the enemy! The street that had led to a bridge across the railway and beyond that to a leafy avenue that in its turn went out to a suburb now led only into the jaws of the enemy.

'I as a neutral might not have any enemy, but I had lived for five years in the street; through the war I had lived there and its smells and its ruins were familiar to me and I too was touched by the passing of that world. For a street is a world, with its air and its shape and its order. And it is a great shock, no matter how detached one may be, to see the actual hour in which order passes away and chaos appears. It is a shock in the depth of the heart. The heart cannot absorb the shapelessness of chaos, it is shocked, it is like a great scandal to it.'

'That was what he said to Annie,' Kavanagh interrupted. 'That we were causing a scandal in this town.'

'There were a couple of days and nights when I didn't leave the cellar,' Ezra went on, 'because we heard that foreign workers had been shot for being out in the street. All the people of the house were living in the cellars, Germans and foreigners together. The cellar had become a thoroughfare; holes had been broken through into the cellars of the next-door houses and it was possible to go from street to street through the cellars. I stayed two or three days in the cellar with the others from the house, sometimes in the dark and sometimes with a bit of candle burning. There in the cellar there were no more pretences; I had a glimpse of how a tribe must live in their huts in the depth of an African forest. All the escapes, the cinemas and radios and books, were gone and privacy was gone; no one lived any more in the little civilised isolation of his own room and his own possessions. There was no more dressing up or washing. If we stank, we stank. At least it was the stench of life and not the other stench that was beginning to drift through the streets.

'We were a little tribe in the midst of the forest on the edge of death. There were no more differences between us except what could be seen or felt. We were not Germans or Poles or Irish or railway officials or dressmakers or schoolteachers, but we were still men and women because the man and woman difference is a thing of shape and sensation and shape and sensation were left. Indeed, there was only shape and sensation. The shape of the shadows in the dark cellar, the new shape of time, flowing slower and slower, like a river at its mouth beginning to meet the pressure of the sea, and the shape of our own cramped bodies. The underground darkness was full of sensation as the day or the night up above in the world seldom is. The two dry slices of black bread which we could eat once every twelve hours were a sensation, they were sweeter than manna, and the quivering of the darkness from the bombs and the shower of shells that they called Stalin organs was a sensation in the spine and in the guts, like a tree whose roots are shaken by a storm. And when we prayed it was a different praying to most of the church praying; it was a turning of our dirty, pale faces to the face of darkness beyond the cellar-darkness; it was the feeling in the trembling of the cellar and the falling of the plaster, the passing of the angel of death and the angel of the end. And if a man took the hand of the girl huddled next to him it was another touch from the old touching, the old mechanical caressing.

'But even down there we could sense the progress of the battle.

'Soldiers came through, passing down the street through the cellars, their dull-painted, steel helmets like dark hoods over their faces in the shine of their electric torches. And they were questioned, questioned. And the same blank look in reply, tinged with impatience, and then the long, empty, noisy hours again with no one coming through, with whispers and only the minute break of going out into the passage to make water.

'It was about the third night that I went up and out into the street again. Now it had changed again. In two days there was a change that normally would have taken centuries. There were corpses lying in the street and no one paying any attention to them. Even two days before, when someone was killed they were picked up and carried away. Death had still been an accident, a part of disorder to be quickly tidied up. Now there was only disorder; chaos and death were beginning to be in the street, not as something accidental, but as part of the street. There were women with basins and buckets and a few men with knives cutting up a dead horse in the middle of the street. I went back to the cellar and got a basin and a knife and hacked away between the white bones, filling the basin with slabs of dark flesh. That was the treasure of those nights, the dark slabs of flesh, and it was lusted after more than the flesh of women. There were many living women and girls in the streets and only a few horses. There was a crowd round the horses with buckets and basins, and those who had not basins took the wet chunks of meat in their arms, hugging them to their breasts. In the morning the dead were still lying in the street in the full light of day and I stood and looked at a group of four or five bodies in their dusty sleep, a child and young woman and an old woman, drinking in this new shape, the shape of death that was strange and shocking and fascinating at first, as the shape of a woman's naked body at a window had been to me long ago as a boy. But as I walked down the street I had learnt this new shape, death-in-the-street, the dead sharing the street with the living and making again something different out of the street, signing it with their dusty, still and huddled sign.

'We feasted on the meat in the candle-lit cellar and the girl next me kissed my hands and pressed them to her breast in rapture at satiating her hunger.

'That night I was out in the street again. There were a lot of shells falling, and while I was sheltering under the remains of the bridge of the elevated railway I got a piece of shrapnel through my shoulder. There was a dressing-station further up the street and although it was a military station I went there with a sergeant who had been wounded in the leg and, as I was helping him, they let us both in. They couldn't do much for us; there were no bandages, no antiseptics, only the candlelit rooms with the shadowy, blanket-covered forms. There was only one sister, and as she was washing the sergeant's leg wound he talked to her. He was a small, thick-set little fellow of forty-five and he had a way with him, an air of knowing a great deal of what was going on.

' "What are they holding out for? Do you really expect the army Wenck to break through from the West?" the sister asked. She could hardly hold the basin of water for tiredness.

'The sergeant shrugged his shoulders and smiled his weary, knowing smile.

' "We heard the capitulation would come to-night," said the nurse. "They are said to be discussing terms."

' "Terms!" said the little sergeant with his thin smile. "All I know is they have thrown in the Norwegian S.S. Division, all big, young fellows of twenty or so. I saw some of them in the Friedrichstrasse area."

' "There's no sense in it; no sense," said the girl, slopping water from the basin to the floor in her weariness.

'Afterwards the sergeant and I sat in the hall. The outer door was ajar and the street was just beyond, and we were both drawn towards it, not wanting to be far from it. We sat in the hall and through the door came the night air from the street with the smoky tang that had been in it for weeks. And there was a faint smell of excrement; it had been there, too, for days, like the scent of savoury, slightly rotten cooking, and I did not know whether it was only a memory in my nose lingering from the cellar or whether here, too, there was no sanitation. Now and then the sergeant asked me to go to the door and have a look out; he couldn't move so easily because of his leg wound.

'It was a clear night with a waning moon and I could see along the street. The smooth black surface of the wide street gleamed and it seemed very quiet. There was always the background of noise, but that we were used to and there were no new noises and no shells. Only the street lying empty with its dark, traffic-polished surface leading away into the night. Such a moment of quiet there had not been in these weeks, and I stood there alone and came to myself as I had not in all that time. In the long hours in the cellar I had only been capable of waiting with the others, dreaming of food, of a bed, waiting for the hour of eating the two slices of bread or the two cold potatoes, drinking in every scrap of rumour. But now in the street outside the dressing-station I felt a change in myself. I had strength again, and not drifting here and there with each pang of hunger, each wave of sleeplessness, each new whispered announcement. It was as if I had got strength at the last minute. But so it is with me; all happens to me at the last minute.

'When I came back the sergeant had got hold of an old civilian suit and was putting it on, slowly drawing the trousers on over his stiff leg.

' "How's it look?" he asked.

' "Worn. But that doesn't matter if it fits."

' "Not the suit, man, the street."

' "It's quiet," I said. "It's quieter than it's been for a long time."

'He was taking papers and things out of the pocket of his uniform, tearing them up, tearing up his soldiers' *soldbuch*, and laying a few things aside, a comb and some money and a small tattered New Testament. There was an envelope stuck in it as a marker and he opened it and said to me: "Do you know that all this was prophesied in the Bible? Listen." He held the small book close to the hurricane lamp on the table and began to read: "Then he said unto them: Nation shall rise against nation and kingdom against kingdom and great earthquakes shall be in divers places, and famines and pestilences; and fearful sights and great signs shall there be from heaven. . . . For these be the days of vengeance, that all things which are written may be fulfilled. . . ."

'And these words were themselves a sign to me,' Ezra went on, 'coming in and hearing these words I knew what it was that I had seen in the street.'

'What was it?' Kavanagh asked. Annie, too, was listening with her big, freckled face against Kavanagh's shoulder.

'I had seen how these things must be if we were not to go on swimming round our duck-pond. We dare not be given too much security. As soon as we have a little security, we settle down by our duck-ponds, and it doesn't matter whether it's a religious duck-pond, a cultural duck-pond or an economic duck-pond. It's all the same old mud. The little duck-pond writers, the duck-pond reformers, and the little white duck-pond God with its neat crown of thorns. That's our great genius: to tame! We have our tame God and our tame art, and it is only when the days of vengeance come that there's a flutter around the pond.'

'A flutter around the pond!' repeated Kavanagh with a cackle. Ezra looked at the big, slightly bemused face with a momentary dislike. He knowing nothing of the price paid in horror, in starving and sweating and bleeding, had no call to use the words that Ezra might use without offence.

'After the days of vengeance there comes a new breath. Here and there, among those who have survived, comes a new vision, further than the duck-pond vision. That's the only hope for us now: a new vision and a new god. That's what I saw that last hour before the end, with the wide, empty street waiting under the moon. It was a strange moon, the colour of flesh bled bluish-white. And then I went back to the dressing-station and the little sergeant was reading those words out of the book he had come across emptying out his uniform pockets: "And there shall be signs in the sun and in the moon . . . and upon the earth distress of nations, with perplexity, the sea and waves roaring."'

Ezra stopped speaking to take a swill of the black stout. By now Kavanagh was slightly drunk. Not really drunk, though, because what Ezra was saying kept him from drifting down on the dark tide of Guinness in his blood.

'At midnight the sergeant and I were still sitting in the hall of the flat that had been turned into a hospital,' Ezra was saying. 'I was thinking of going back to the cellar. "Hold on a bit," the sergeant would say. "You've got all night, haven't you?" But I had seen the sign in the moon and I wanted to be back in my own corner——'

'What sign was that?' asked Kavanagh.

'That's only a way of speaking. It was a sign in myself,' Ezra said; 'the sign that I was ripe for what was coming. And the moment you are ripe for what is coming, it comes. Death, pain, love, whatever it may be.'

'That's a queer word,' said Kavanagh. 'What about all the others who weren't ripe, as you call it?'

'I don't know. There are two faces to reality, and I have seen them both. There was the bloody face of the sister as I saw her a little later, one of all the faces of the raped, the dying, the horror-stricken and the other face, the face of "Not a sparrow falls without the Father——" and whoever has seen these two faces as one is finally delivered and at peace. But I haven't. And now I never shall.

'I wanted to go but I kept staying on to keep the sergeant company. We had been talking and we stopped talking. There was a new sound from the street, a soft, even sound after all the loud and intermittent sounds of the time before. I peered out from behind the door. I saw dimly a column of men pass down the other side of the street.

' "What is it?" asked the sergeant. I didn't know, and yet I knew. I did not want to give it a name. To name the hour for which all had been waiting in fear and trembling.

' "Well, what is it, man?"

' "The Russians," I said.

'We were speaking lower. "Did you see them?" he asked. I thought that in spite of all his air of knowingness even he had still a hope about the army Wenck. We heard more of them passing and then the door was pushed open and some of them came in, in their baggy, belted uniforms. They had come. The Apocalyptic rider on the pale horse had dismounted and come through the door into the hall and gone on into the wards. There was a sentry at the door, and the sergeant and I went back into the ward, where a Russian colonel was standing talking in German to the chief orderly and a soldier with a tommy-gun stood just behind him. Then the officer went into the small room where we had had our wounds dressed by the sister, and the soldier stood outside the closed door. In a few minutes they came out again and the colonel went upstairs with his bodyguard and the sister went about her duties, silent. I was spoken to by a big, slouching fellow in German and I showed my passport which, being printed in English, French and Gaelic, he could not read. But he did not want to read it. That was the first thing I learnt about these Apocalyptic hordes. They had not yet come to the complete faith in documents and documentation that the Germans and Americans and English have. He looked at me out of his small, peasant eyes and repeated after me, "Irländer," and seemed to think it over and think me over. He handed me back my papers and slouched off down the room, the gun dangling from his big hand, stooping over a mattress now and then as the fancy took him and demanding the papers of the man lying on it, but then hardly looking at them, dangling the gun and kicking the straw of the mattress with his big boot.

'The colonel's orderly came down and went back upstairs with the sister. All the time I wanted to get back to the cellar. My few belongings were there. I felt that the end had come and caught me far from home.

' "Wait a bit," the sergeant told me. "Wait an hour or two and let things settle down." I would have been still waiting if I'd waited for that,' Ezra went on.

'An hour or two,' repeated Kavanagh in his own slow way, wiping his mouth. 'An hour or two, ha!'

'The little sergeant and I went back and sat in the hall. "This is the best place to be, in a hospital," he said.

'The long, long waiting was over; the end had come. The sergeant had heard that the city had capitulated. No more bombs would fall, no more shells; the rocking of the earth that loosened the roots of the heart in your breast was over; the earth was still. I could see out into the street past the sentry lounging at the half-open door and it was still. But it was not the beginning of peace. "There was silence in heaven and on earth for the space of half an hour."

'The sister came downstairs. Her face was scratched and bitten and bloody. I went to the door and stood outside it, looking up and down the street. I did not want to seem to be in a hurry. I must move like these men moved, easily, slouching without haste. There were two of them outside the door talking and I stood beside them. I felt the breath of violence in which we stood and moved and had our being. The former, explosive violence had passed away and there was this new, quieter, more intimate violence in the air of the street. All these years we had moved in and breathed the air of hatred, of violence and the threat of violence. Not only the explosive violence, the violence that came down out of heaven, but the other soft-footed, official violence. I knew much about the shape of violence and I could sniff it around me, in all its different shapes and forms. If you have a kind of quietness and suppleness in you you can often slip through under the very jaws of violence, but if you haven't, if you're nervous and excitable and if your movements of body and of soul are too quick or too set in one direction, then you're lost from the start. I had lived with it, in a city where all the offices in all the official buildings were ante-rooms of violence, and, waiting outside them, waiting for one's turn, however quiet you tried to be, your armpits got damp. That was the mechanical, statistical violence, and you couldn't escape it if, because of your papers, you came into one of the doomed categories. That was the violence of order, the terrible statistical violence of the great machine of order and it had its lair in every street, in dusty corridors and offices and its threat was in every ring of the bell, in every strange voice.

'In the street as long as I had lived there there had always been the unseen presence and pressure of violence like an invisible hand laid on the heart. Even in my room it was there, the slight pressure always there, subtly altering the shape of everything, squeezing everything a little bit smaller. Just as long before I had sometimes been in another great city and I had lived in the pressure of another hand laid on me, the hand of sex. Sex was then the great mystery for me; it was in the belly, in the house and in the streets. And later in this other city and in this other street it was violence.

'I thought about this as I stood at the door of the dressing-station and tried to sense the new violence that had come to replace the old. And I felt that this new violence was not so statistical, and you might escape it not so much by having the right papers, the right signatures, but by the way you moved and looked, by keeping a small centre of quiet in you.

'As I say, I know all about violence and its different shapes. I have sat waiting in corridors with violence hidden on the other side of a door and known it there, known in my stomach that it was there, unseen, and waited, gone dead and numb between chest and belly with the touch of its invisible hand in my guts. You get so that you can sniff it from far away, when it's hidden away behind doors and walls. You can walk down a street full of shops and traffic and the sun shining and the old women calling the latest editions of the papers, and you can know in a slight sensation below the ribs that behind all this, like a boy who has wound up his train and sits back watching it go, there is violence. I got so that I could sense it in the very stone of the houses, in the reflection of the windows. And I hadn't completely escaped it, either. For some months I had been locked away with the others, though later I had been let out again to walk in the street or sit in the cafés and restaurants, moving in the pseudo-freedom of a world in which everyone is numbered and registered and summoned from time to time into one of the ante-rooms of the great machine. I had lived all this time in this order of brooding, hidden violence that was broken through from time to time by the other violence, the open violence of destruction. It had a different face, but from its mouth came the same breath of the pit, and when the cellar rocked you knew it was the same hand that rocked it as the cold hand that grabbed you in the guts as you waited for your turn outside one of the closed doors in the big building down the street.

'And to-night the hand of violence had another grip. So far I had only caught a glimpse of it in the night air and in the marks of its claws on the face of the nurse, which was no more than a touch in passing. I leant up against the door lintel and smoked my cigarette to the end, and as I threw the butt down I moved off into the street, trying to make my movements quiet and familiar as I think I would try to move in a lion's cage. The two soldiers stopped talking together. I did not look back, but strolled on very slowly, and I heard them talking again and at that moment I had a kind of love for them, because they had left me alone.

'I walked down the street. It had changed since I had walked up it with the little sergeant limping on my arm some hours before. There had been that silence, as for the space of half an hour, and in that space the last wall had fallen that had surrounded it, that had made it, in spite of all, still a street in a city with still some faint air of being sheltered, as towns and cities were once shelters. But now it was a space open to all the winds that blew.

'I knew this even more certainly when I reached the cellar. It was no more a shelter. It was a ravaged pit. But how easily and subtly the body accepts all so long as it can still breathe and stretch itself and talk. Some get over it in talking and some in silence; the ones who talk, quicker. The girl who had shared my corner for the last weeks showed me the scratches on her arm and began to talk to me. She huddled up close to me and I put my arm around her and listened to the quick, warm words against my cheek. They had taken her and raped her in the flat above. But already rape, that a few hours ago had the shape of the unknown horror, similar to the shape of death, was something familiar, a thing like the corpses lying in the street, that after all could be in some way come to terms with, and turned out not to be the final horror. You adapt yourself to it, you become a girl-who-has-been-raped. You pass in a short time, in that "space of half an hour," from being one thing to being the other. As the street did. It is the moment of passing over, of giving up what you were, and knew and which was the form and sign under which you had lived, almost the *you*. But not quite the *you*. Even under the other form, the new raped form there was still the *you*, and quite quickly it conformed itself and was chattering, making the same gestures, pouring out tea made from the packet the soldier had given. But the hand trembled. She spilled some tea on the blanket that she had pulled over us, and she showed me her bare wrist. "They are taking all the wrist watches and jewellery," she said.

"Their arms are covered with watches to the elbow. As long as I don't get a dose," she went on, "I don't mind getting pregnant. I can cure that, but I'm afraid of getting a dose. You're lucky your girl is lying under the ruins," she said. "She's better off."

'She was being a little false, a little sentimental. I knew I was not lucky and that I would never be lucky again. If I had had Margareta with me there in the cellar, then I would have been lucky, let her have been twenty times raped, let her be scratched and bitten and raped, but there under the same blanket, pouring the tea, or with no tea, with nothing, then I would have known the unfathomable gift of luck. But I let the girl go on, chattering in her quick whisper with my arm around her, her breath on my cheek: "I know of a place in the ruins," she said, "and I'm going out there to hide as soon as it begins to get light. I'm too sore to stay here and have that done to me again."

'In the next days I got to know what rape looks like as you can't know it from hearsay, as you can't know what raids are and death-from-explosion is from hearsay. Violence never takes the shape that you imagine it will. The first rape I saw was the body of a young girl on the floor of the cellar, spread-eagled, not like a girl any more, like something nailed to a wall, a skin or a rug or some rags with the bare legs sticking out of them. But not a girl's body; and what they were doing to her wasn't like what you had thought it would be like. It was like some mechanical operation, pumping up a tyre or like the drilling that goes on in the street, with a little group of workmen standing round; only all went silently, quite silent and against flesh instead of concrete.'

Kavanagh was listening, rapt in the dark miasma produced by the Guinness against which appeared the varying face of violence that Ezra had conjured up for him into the quiet parlour. One heavy arm lay across the table-cloth, which was already stained with stout and grease, and the other arm encircled Annie. When Ezra paused to drink from his glass or light a cigarette or go to the lavatory, Kavanagh leant over the girl, whispering. He was stirred by this tale of Nineveh. Why had his path not led down that street? Why was he condemned to walk down these mean streets of Altamont and the other towns where he was frustrated and diminished? He should have been there, where Ezra had been, there at the beginning of the end. He saw himself there in the foreign darkness, among ruins. He did not know what ruins were, what a razed street looked like. He knew he had only his small vision of darkness; the constricted night in which he sometimes moved through the back streets of Dublin, visiting mean houses in the rain, leaving again later in the deserted night, limping home past the rows of shuttered shops with the thirst in his bowels damped but unslaked. He turned savagely to Annie: 'You know what you have to do, eh? Take a needle and prick yourself like I showed you—or if you can't manage to draw enough blood like that, take a safety-razor blade. And then with a match or a pencil dab a drop or two of the blood on the holy picture, see? On the hands and the feet of St. Francis, that's the ticket. That's all. Then wait, lie low. I'll do the rest. All you've got to think of is to keep the blood on the holy picture. There'll be a to-do, there'll be a holy, bloody fiesta when the word gets round, as it will, first through the urchins who are always in and out of the Reverend Father's room. As soon as he washes off the blood, you wait till the stage is clear and on you dab it again.'

He got up and limped into the bathroom to fetch a blade.

'Ah, me bould Moss Kavanagh,' said the voice within him, mocking, 'what a bloody, great fellow you are with your needles and matches. Matches! Jaysus! Matches!'

He fetched the blade all the same. He laid it on the table. He wanted to go on listening to the words of Ezra. But Ezra had not much more to say. One picture remained, for some reason, still at the surface of his consciousness, ready to be told among all the others that had sunk into him and were too absorbed into him to be told.

On the last evening that he had been in the cellar before he had moved back up to his room in the flat above, the second evening after the end of the war, a figure had appeared in the doorway. It had stood there in a long, well-fitting coat, with pale leather gloves and a cane in one hand, exuding a faint fragrance of eau-de-Cologne in the evil-smelling cellar. It had stood looking at them and had nodded to them and then turned and gone, followed by the little group of soldiers who accompanied it. Not one of them huddled in the cellar had known what to make of it. There was a hum of talk around it. Did it herald the end of the war? For at that time they had not known that the war was over. Or the end of the sack of the city? And then there was the question whether it had really nodded at all.

Kavanagh was standing at the window. The house was at a corner and the windows at which he stood looked out on a side street and over the roofs of Altamont towards the hills. The other window faced on to the main street. From where he was, Kavanagh saw the cold, grey flush of dawn. The blackness of night had turned to ash piled on the hills and dully reflecting the still far-away flame of day. He limped to the other window. When he had drunken a few pints of stout, his limp always became more noticeable. From this window there was nothing to be seen but the oceanic darkness. That was better. Kavanagh did not yet want the dawn. He did not yet want the day that would bring him back to the shop, to the mean street of the provincial town from the other street down which he had followed Ezra in the Doomsday darkness. His heart had expanded as Ezra's words had touched it. He felt it would burst if it could not be stilled. It needed darkness; he had been brought by Ezra to a place on the edge of depths that seemed half-familiar to him. Had he seen them in dreams? There was still the night left. From this window the night was still long—long enough for him to go down into it with Annie and be stilled. Be stilled? That was a queer word, too. He stood staring out at the darkness that already seemed a shade less profound. He could see the low roofs of the shops in Main Street. Was there still enough of the night left in which to do that that would save him from the drabness of the coming day?

Yet when Ezra rose to go, Kavanagh tried to keep him. He knew that when he went he would take with him some of the breath of darkness, of the *Dies Irae* darkness, and that what was left of the night would be lessened and diminished. They split one more bottle of stout together, and then Ezra crossed the street to Flood's hotel.

Kavanagh sat on at the table. He heard Annie washing at the sink. He would show them! He would desecrate their little pieties with her body and blood. He would slake his lust by befouling their miserable altars!

When she had finished washing, she walked naked through the parlour to the bedroom. 'Going to bed,' she murmured.

'You might remember that this is the parlour, girl, and put something on when you're going through it,' he said. He hated her for taking him so much for granted, for taking this night for granted, for not being affected by Ezra's words, for not being afraid of him.

'What for? Aren't you used to the sight of me?' she said.

'More than used. I'm sick of it and that's a fact.' But it was not true. He was seeing her for the first time.

In this smouldering, mouldering way, the quarrel which on his part was only a polite pretence had dragged on as he undressed and got into bed with her. He smelt the kitchen soap that she had used. She lay quite still and breathed through her mouth. Kavanagh had turned to her savagely in the dark. Tomorrow he must return to Dublin, and there was so little darkness left between him and the long, drab day that would dawn. He had other nights, of course, but each night it would be more difficult to wrest from her what he wanted. He thought of the soldiers sacking the city, their arms covered in watches. What was there left for him to do, to get? He could not sack a city. But he could at least raise quite a little bit of trouble in this town.

He would smear their holy pictures for them with the blood from her big, bluish-white thigh! He was a little drunk; not with the stout though. That was a surface drunkenness. Dawn was at the window; but now he had no more fear of the sober, pious light of the small-town day. Let the light fall on the street, on the black clothes of Father Mellowes clip-clopping down the steps of the church from saying Mass, *Dominus vobiscum, ite Missa est*, on the women doing their shopping, the bacon machine slicing the rashers while they waited, thin, thick or medium, fat, streaky or lean, the jingle of the till, of the bicycle bells in the street, of the bell rung by the servers at Mass. All the tinkling, clinking, chattering day that was ebbing back into the street, but before which there were still these hours of silence. In the grey silence he had yet time to burrow into the secret flower of chaos whose pollen was blood.

*Part V*

# WHERE MOTLEY IS WORN

*Being certain that they and I
But lived where motley is worn . . .*
W. B. YEATS

SOMERVILLE AND ROSS

# The Holy Island[1]

For three days of November a white fog stood motionless over the country. All day and all night smothered booms and bangs away to the south-west told that the Fastnet gun was hard at work, and the sirens of the American liners uplifted their monstrous female voices as they felt their way along the coast of Cork. On the third afternoon the wind began to whine about the windows of Shreelane, and the barometer fell like a stone. At 11 p.m. the storm rushed upon us with the roar and the suddenness of a train; the chimneys bellowed, the tall old house quivered, and the yelling wind drove against it, as a man puts his shoulder against a door to burst it in.

We none of us got much sleep, and if Mrs. Cadogan is to be believed—which experience assures me she is not—she spent the night in devotional exercises, and in ministering to the panic-stricken kitchen-maid by the light of a Blessed candle. All that day the storm screamed on, dry-eyed; at nightfall the rain began, and next morning, which happened to be Sunday, every servant in the house was a messenger of Job, laden with tales of leakages, floods, and fallen trees, and inflated with the ill-concealed glory of their kind in evil tidings. To Peter Cadogan, who had been to early Mass, was reserved the crowning satisfaction of reporting that a big vessel had gone on the rocks at Yokahn Point the evening before, and was breaking up fast; it was rumoured that the crew had got ashore, but this feature, being favourable and uninteresting, was kept as much as possible in the background. Mrs. Cadogan, who had been to America in an ocean liner, became at once the latest authority on shipwrecks, and was of opinion that 'whoever would be dhrownded, it wouldn't be thim lads o' sailors. Sure wasn't there the greatest storm ever was in it the time meself was on the say, and what'd thim fellows do but to put us below entirely in the ship, and close down the doors on us, the way theirselves'd leg it when we'd be dhrownding!'

This view of the position was so startlingly novel that Philippa withdrew suddenly from the task of ordering dinner, and fell up the kitchen stairs in unsuitable laughter. Philippa has not the most rudimentary capacity for keeping her countenance.

[1] From *Some Experiences of an Irish R. M.*, London, 1897.

That afternoon I was wrapped in the slumber, balmiest and most profound, that follows on a wet Sunday luncheon, when Murray, our D.I. of police, drove up in uniform, and came into the house on the top of a gust that set every door banging and every picture dancing on the walls. He looked as if his eyes had been blown out of his head, and he wanted something to eat very badly.

'I've been down at the wreck since ten o'clock this morning,' he said, 'waiting for her to break up, and once she does there'll be trouble. She's an American ship, and she's full up with rum, and bacon, and butter, and all sorts. Bosanquet is there with all his coastguards, and there are five hundred country people on the strand at this moment, waiting for the fun to begin. I've got ten of my fellows there, and I wish I had as many more. You'd better come back with me, Yeates, we may want the Riot Act before all's done!'

The heavy rain had ceased, but it seemed as if it had fed the wind instead of calming it, and when Murray and I drove out of Shreelane, the whole dirty sky was moving, full sailed, in from the south-west, and the telegraph wires were hanging in a loop from the post outside the gate. Nothing except a Skebawn car-horse would have faced the whooping charges of the wind that came at us across Corran Lake; stimulated mysteriously by whistles from the driver, Murray's yellow hireling pounded woodenly along against the blast, till the smell of the torn seaweed was borne upon it, and we saw the Atlantic waves come towering into the bay of Tralagough.

The ship was, or had been, a three-masted barque; two of her masts were gone, and her bows stood high out of water on the reef that forms one of the shark-like jaws of the bay. The long strand was crowded with black groups of people, from the bank of heavy shingle that had been hurled over on to the road, down to the slope where the waves pitched themselves and climbed and fought and tore the gravel back with them, as though they had dug their fingers in. The people were nearly all men, dressed solemnly and hideously in their Sunday clothes; most of them had come straight from Mass without any dinner, true to that Irish instinct that places its fun before its food. That the wreck was regarded as a spree of the largest kind was sufficiently obvious. Our car pulled up at a publichouse that stood askew between the road and the shingle; it was humming with those whom Irish publicans are pleased to call 'Bona feeds,'[1] and sundry of the same class were clustered round the door. Under the wall on the lee side was seated a bagpiper, droning out *The Irish Washerwoman* with nodding head and tapping heel, and a young man was cutting a few steps of a jig for the delectation of a group of girls.

So far Murray's constabulary had done nothing but exhibit their imposing chest measurement and spotless uniforms to the Atlantic, and Bosanquet's coastguards had only salvaged some spars, the debris of a boat, and a dead sheep, but their time was coming. As we stumbled down over the shingle, battered by the wind and pelted by clots of foam, someone beside me shouted 'She's gone!' A hill of water had smothered the wreck, and when it fell from her again nothing was left but the bows, with the bowsprit hanging from them in a tangle of rigging. The clouds, bronzed by an unseen sunset, hung low over her; in that greedy pack of waves, with the remorseless rocks above and below her, she seemed the most lonely and tormented of creatures.

About half an hour afterwards the cargo began to come ashore on the top of the rising tide. Barrels were plunging and diving in the trough of the waves, like a school of porpoises; they were pitched up the beach in waist-deep rushes of foam; they rolled down again, and were swung up and shouldered by the next wave, playing a kind of Tom Tiddler's ground with the coastguards. Some of the barrels were big and dangerous, some were small and nimble like young pigs, and the bluejackets were up to their middles as their prey dodged and ducked, and the police lined out along the beach to keep back the people. Ten men of the R.I.C.[2] can do a great deal, but they cannot be in more than twenty or thirty places at the same instant; therefore they could hardly cope with a scattered and extremely active mob of four or five hundred, many of whom had taken advantage of their privileges as 'bona-fide travellers,' and all of whom were determined on getting at the rum.

As the dusk fell the thing got more and more out of hand; the people had found out that the big puncheons held the rum, and had succeeded in capturing one. In the twinkling of an eye it was broached, and fifty backs were shoving round it like a football scrummage. I

---

[1] In Ireland a *bona-fide* traveller is still entitled to a drink at any pub after closing hours or on Sundays. In the good old days a 3-mile trip made one a licensed toper.
[2] Royal Irish Constabulary.

have heard many rows in my time: I have seen two Irish regiments—one of them Militia—at each other's throats in Fermoy barracks; I have heard Philippa's water-spaniel and two fox-terriers hunting a strange cat round the dairy; but never have I known such untrammelled bedlam as that which yelled round the rum-casks on Tralagough strand. For it was soon not a question of one broached cask, or even of two. The barrels were coming in fast, so fast that it was impossible for the representatives of law and order to keep on any sort of terms with them. The people, shouting with laughter, stove in the casks, and drank rum at thirty-four degrees above proof, out of their hands, out of their hats, out of their boots. Women came fluttering over the hillsides through the twilight, carrying jugs, milk-pails, anything that would hold the liquor; I saw one of them, roaring with laughter, tilt a filthy zinc bucket to an old man's lips.

With the darkness came anarchy. The rising tide brought more and yet more booty: great spars came lunging in on the lap of the waves, mixed up with cabin furniture, seamen's chests, and the black and slippery barrels, and the country people continued to flock in, and the drinking became more and more unbridled. Murray sent for more men and a doctor, and we slaved on hopelessly in the dark; collaring half-drunken men, shoving pig-headed casks up hills of shingle, hustling in among groups of roaring drinkers—we rescued perhaps one barrel in half a dozen. I began to know that there were men there who were not drunk and were not idle; I was also aware, as the strenuous hours of darkness passed, of an occasional rumble of cart wheels on the road. It was evident that the casks which were broached were the least part of the looting, but even they were beyond our control. The most that Bosanquet, Murray, and I could do was to concentrate our forces on the casks that had been secured, and to organize charges upon the swilling crowds in order to upset the casks that they had broached. Already men and boys were lying about, limp as leeches, motionless as the dead.

'They'll kill themselves before morning, at this rate!' shouted Murray to me. 'They're drinking it by the quart! Here's another barrel; come on!'

We rallied our small forces, and after a brief but furious struggle succeeded in capsizing it. It poured away in a flood over the stones, over the prostrate figures that sprawled on them, and a howl of reproach followed.

'If ye pour away any more o' that, Major,' said an unctuous voice in my ear, 'ye'll intoxicate the stones and they'll be getting up and knocking us down!'

I had been aware of a fat shoulder next to mine in the throng as we heaved the puncheon over, and I now recognised the ponderous wit and Falstaffian figure of Mr. James Canty, a noted member of the Skebawn Board of Guardians, and the owner of a large farm near at hand.

'I never saw worse work on this strand,' he went on. 'I considher these debaucheries a disgrace to the counthry.'

Mr. Canty was famous as an orator, and I presume that it was from long practice among his fellow P.L.G.'s[1] that he was able, without apparent exertion, to out-shout the storm.

At this juncture the long-awaited reinforcements arrived, and along with them came Dr. Jerome Hickey, armed with a black bag. Having mentioned that the bag contained a pump—not one of the common or garden variety—and that no pump on board a foundering ship had more arduous labour to perform, I prefer to pass to other themes. The wreck, which had at first appeared to be as inexhaustible and as variously stocked as that in the *Swiss Family Robson*, was beginning to fail in its supply. The crowd were by this time for the most part incapable from drink, and the fresh contingent of police tackled their work with some prospect of success by the light of a tar barrel, contributed by the owner of the public-house. At about the same time I began to be aware that I was aching with fatigue, that my clothes hung heavy and soaked upon me, that my face was stiff with the salt spray and the bitter wind, and that it was two hours past dinner time. The possibility of fried salt herrings and hot whisky and water at the public-house rose dazzlingly before my mind, when Mr. Canty again crossed my path.

'In my opinion ye have the whole cargo under conthrol now, Major,' he said, 'and the police and the sailors should be able to account for it all now by the help of the light. Wasn't I the finished fool that I didn't think to send up to my house for a tar barrel before now! Well—we're all foolish sometimes! But indeed it's time for us to give over, and that's what I'm saying to the Captain and Mr. Murray. You're exhausted now, the three of ye, and if I might make so bold, I'd suggest that ye'd come up to my little place and

---

[1] Poor Law Guardians.

have what'd warm ye before ye'd go home. It's only a few perches up the road.'

The tide had turned, the rain had begun again, and the tar barrel illumined the fact that Dr. Hickey's dreadful duties alone were pressing. We held a council and finally followed Mr. Canty, picking our way through wreckage of all kinds, including the human variety. Near the publichouse I stumbled over something that was soft and had a squeak in it; it was the piper, with his head and shoulders in an overturned rum-barrel, and the bagpipes still under his arm.

I knew the outward appearance of Mr. Canty's house very well. It was a typical southern farmhouse, with dirty white-washed walls, a slated roof, and small, hermetically-sealed windows staring at the morass of manure which constituted the yard. We followed Mr. Canty up the filthy lane that led to it, picked our way round vague and squelching spurs of the manure heap, and were finally led through the kitchen into a stifling best parlour. Mrs. Canty, a vast and slatternly matron, had evidently made preparations for us; there was a newly-lighted fire pouring flame up the chimney from layers of bogwood, there were whisky and brandy on the table, and a plateful of biscuits sugared in white and pink. Upon our hostess was a black silk dress which indifferently concealed the fact that she was short of boot-laces, and that the boots themselves had made many excursions to the yard and none to the blacking-bottle. Her manners, however, were admirable, and while I live I shall not forget her potato cakes. They came in hot and hot from a pot-oven, they were speckled with caraway seeds, they swam in salt butter, and we ate them shamelessly and greasily, and washed them down with hot whisky and water; I knew to a nicety how ill I should be next day, and heeded not.

'Well, gentlemen,' remarked Mr. Canty later on, in his best Board of Guardians' manner, 'I've seen many wrecks between this and the Mizen Head, but I never witnessed a scene of more disgraceful excess than what was in it to-night.'

'Hear, hear!' murmured Bosanquet with unseemly levity.

'I should say,' went on Mr. Canty, 'there was at one time to-night upwards of one hundhred men dead dhrunk on the strand, or anyway so dhrunk that if they'd attempt to spake they'd foam at the mouth.'

'The craytures!' interjected Mrs. Canty sympathetically.

'But if they're dhrunk to-day,' continued our host, 'it's nothing at all to what they'll be to-morrow and afther to-morrow and it won't be on the strand they'll be dhrinkin' it.'

'Why, where will it be?' said Bosanquet, with his disconcerting English way of asking a point-blank question.

Mr. Canty passed his hand over his red cheeks.

'There'll be plenty asking that before all's said and done, Captain,' he said, with a compassionate smile, 'and there'll be plenty that could give the answer if they'll like, but by dam I don't think ye'll be apt to get much out of the Yokahn boys!'

'The Lord save us, 'twould be better to keep out from the likes o' thim!' put in Mrs. Canty, sliding a fresh avalanche of potato cakes on to the dish; 'didn't they pull the clothes off the gauger and pour potheen[1] down his throath till he ran screeching through the streets o' Skebawn!'

James Canty chuckled.

'I remember there was a wreck here one time, and the undherwriters put me in charge of the cargo. Brandy it was—cases of the best Frinch brandy. The people had a song about it, what's this the first verse was—

> One night to the rocks of Yokahn
> Came the barque *Isabella* so dandy,
> To pieces she went before dawn,
> Herself and her cargo of brandy,
> And all met a wathery grave
> Excepting the vessel's car*pen*ther,
> Poor fellow, so far from his home.

Mr. Canty chanted these touching lines in a tuneful if wheezy tenor. 'Well, gentlemen, we're all friends here,' he continued, 'and it's no harm to mention that this man below at the publichouse came askin' me would I let him have some of it for a consideration. "Sullivan," says I to him, "if ye ran down gold in a cup in place of the brandy, I wouldn't give it to you. Of coorse," says I, "I'm not sayin' that if a bottle was to get a crack of a stick, and it to be broken, and a man to drink a glass out of it, that would be no more than an accident." "That's no good to me," says he, "but if I had twelve gallons of that brandy in Cork," says he, "by the Holy German!" says he, saying an awful curse, "I'd sell twenty-five out of it!" Well, indeed, it was true for him; it was grand stuff. As the saying is, it would make a horse out of a cow!'

---

[1] Illegally distilled whiskey.

'It appears to be a handy sort of place for keeping a pub,' said Bosanquet.

'Shut to the door, Margaret,' said Mr. Canty with elaborate caution. 'It'd be a queer place that wouldn't be handy for Sullivan!'

A further tale of great length was in progress when Dr. Hickey's Mephistophelian nose was poked into the best parlour.

'Hullo, Hickey! Pumped out? eh?' said Murray.

'If I am, there's plenty more like me,' replied the doctor enigmatically, 'and some of them three times over! James, did these gentlemen leave you a drop of anything that you'd offer me?'

'Maybe ye'd like a glass of rum, Doctor?' said Mr. Canty with a wink at his other guests.

Dr. Hickey shuddered.

I had next morning precisely the kind of mouth that I had anticipated, and it being my duty to spend the better part of the day administering justice in Skebawn, I received from Mr. Flurry Knox and other of my brother magistrates precisely the class of condolences on my 'Monday head' that I found least amusing. It was unavailing to point out the resemblance between hot potato cakes and molten lead, or to dilate on their equal power of solidifying; the collective wisdom of the Bench decided that I was suffering from contraband rum, and rejoiced over me accordingly.

During the next three weeks Murray and Bosanquet put in a time only to be equalled by that of the heroes in detective romances. They began by acting on the hint offered by Mr. Canty, and were rewarded by finding eight barrels of bacon and three casks of rum in the heart of Mr. Sullivan's turf rick, placed there, so Mr. Sullivan explained with much detail, by enemies, with the object of getting his licence taken away. They stabbed potato gardens with crowbars to find the buried barrels, they explored the chimneys, they raided the cowhouses; and in every possible and impossible place they found some of the cargo of the late barque *John D. Williams*, and, as the sympathetic Mr. Canty said, 'For as much as they found, they left five times as much afther them!'

It was a wet, lingering autumn, but towards the end of November the rain dried up, the weather stiffened, and a week of light frosts and blue skies was offered as a tardy apology. Philippa possesses, in common with many of her sex, an inappeasable passion for picnics, and her ingenuity for devising occasions for them is only equalled by her gift for enduring their rigours. I have seen her tackle a moist chicken pie with a splinter of slate and my stylograph pen. I have known her to take the tea-basket to an auction, and make tea in a four-wheeled inside car, regardless of the fact that it was coming under the hammer in ten minutes, and that the kettle took twenty minutes to boil. It will therefore be readily understood that the rare occasions when I was free to go out with a gun were not allowed to pass uncelebrated by the tea-basket.

'You'd much better shoot Corran Lake to-morrow,' my wife said to me one brilliant afternoon. 'We could send the punt over, and I would meet you on Holy Island with——'

The rest of the sentence was concerned with ways, means, and the tea-basket, and need not be recorded.

I had taken the shooting of a long snipe bog that trailed from Corran Lake almost to the sea at Tralagough, and it was my custom to begin to shoot from the seaward end of it, and finally to work round the lake after duck.

To-morrow proved a heavenly morning, touched with frost, gilt with sun. I started early, and the mists were still smoking up from the calm, all-reflecting lake, as the Quaker stepped out along the level road, smashing the thin ice on the puddles with his big feet. Behind the calves of my legs sat Maria, Philippa's brown Irish water-spaniel, assiduously licking the barrels of my gun, as was her custom when the ecstasy of going out shooting was hers. Maria had been given to Philippa as a wedding-present, and since then it had been my wife's ambition that she should conform to the Beth Gelert standard of being 'a lamb at home, a lion in the chase.' Maria did pretty well as a lion: she hunted all dogs unmistakably smaller than herself, and whenever it was reasonably possible to do so she devoured the spoils of the chase, notably jack snipe. It was as a lamb that she failed; objectionable as I have no doubt a lamb would be as a domestic pet, it at least would not snatch the cold beef from the luncheon-table, nor yet, if banished for its crimes, would it spend the night in scratching the paint off the hall door. Maria bit beggars (who valued their disgusting limbs at five shillings the square inch), she bullied the servants, she concealed ducks' claws and fishes' backbones behind the sofa cushions, and yet, when she laid her brown snout upon my knee, and rolled her blackguard amber eyes upon me, and smote me with her feathered paw, it was impossible to remember her iniquities against her. On shooting mornings Maria ceased to be a buccaneer, a glutton, and a hypocrite. From the moment when I put my gun together her breakfast stood untouched until it suffered the final degradation of being eaten by the cats, and now in the trap she was shivering with excitement, and agonizing in her soul lest she should even yet be left behind.

Slipper met me at the cross-roads from which I had sent back the trap; Slipper, redder in the nose than anything I had ever seen off the stage, very husky as to the voice, and going rather tender on both feet. He informed me that I should have a grand day's shooting, the head-poacher of the locality having, in a most gentlemanlike manner, refrained from exercising his sporting rights the day before, on hearing that I was coming. I understood that this was to be considered as a mark of high personal esteem, and I set to work at the bog with suitable gratitude.

In spite of Mr. O'Driscoll's magnanimity, I had not a very good morning. The snipe were there, but in the perfect stillness of the weather it was impossible to get near them, and five times out of six they were up, flickering and dodging, before I was within shot. Maria became possessed of seven devils and broke away from heel the first time I let off my gun, ranging far and wide in search of the bird I had missed, and putting up every live thing for half a mile round, as she went splashing and steeple-chasing through the bog. Slipper expressed his opinion of her behaviour in language more appallingly picturesque and resourceful than any I have heard, even in the Skebawn court house; I admit that at the time I thought he spoke very suitably. Before she was recaptured every remaining snipe within earshot was lifted out of it by Slipper's steam-engine whistles and my own infuriated bellows; it was fortunate that the bog was spacious and that there was still a long tract of it ahead, where beyond these voices there was peace.

I worked my way on, jumping treacle-dark drains, floundering through the rustling yellow rushes, circumnavigating the bog-holes, and taking every possible and impossible chance of a shot; by the time I had reached Corran Lake I had got two and a half brace, retrieved by Maria with a perfection that showed what her powers were when the sinuous adroitness of Slipper's woodbine stick was fresh in her mind. But with Maria it was always the unexpected that happened. My last snipe, a jack, fell in the lake, and Maria, bursting through the reeds with kangaroo bounds, and cleaving the water like a torpedo-boat, was a model of all the virtues of her kind.

She picked up the bird with a snake-like dart of her head, clambered with it on to a tussock, and there, well out of reach of the arm of the law, before our indignant eyes crunched it twice and bolted it.

'Well,' said Slipper complacently, some ten minutes afterwards, 'divil such a bating ever I gave a dog since the day Prince killed owld Mrs. Knox's paycock! Prince was a lump of a brown tarrier I had one time, and faith I kicked the toes out o' me owld boots on him before I had the owld lady composed!'

However composing Slipper's methods may have been to Mrs. Knox, they had quite the contrary effect upon a family party of duck that had been lying in the reeds. With horrified outcries they broke into flight, and now were far away on the ethereal mirror of the lake, among strings of their fellows that were floating and quacking in preoccupied indifference to my presence.

A promenade along the lake-shore demonstrated the fact that without a boat there was no more shooting for me; I looked across to the island where, some time ago, I had seen Philippa and her punt arrive. The boat was tied to an overhanging tree, but my wife was nowhere to be seen. I was opening my mouth to give a hail, when I saw her emerge precipitately from among the trees and jump into the boat; Philippa had not in vain spent many summers on the Thames: she was under way in a twinkling, sculled a score of strokes at the rate of a finish, then stopped at the peaceful island. I called to her, and in a minute or two the punt had crackled through the reeds, and shoved its blunt nose ashore at the spot where I was standing.

'Sinclair,' said Philippa in awestruck tones, 'there's something on the island!'

'I hope there's something to eat there,' said I.

'I tell you there *is* something there, alive,' said my wife with her eyes as large as saucers; 'it's making an awful sound like snoring.'

'That's the fairies, ma'am,' said Slipper with complete certainty; 'sure I known them that seen fairies in that island as thick as the grass, and every one o' them with little caps on them.'

Philippa's wide gaze wandered to Slipper's hideous pug face and back to me.

'It was not a human being, Sinclair!' she said combatively, though I had not uttered a word.

Maria had already, after the manner of dogs, leaped, dripping, into the boat: I prepared to follow her example.

'Major,' said Slipper, in a tragic whisper, 'there was a man was a night on that island one time, watching duck, and Thim People cot him, and dhragged him through Hell and through Death, and threw him in the tide——'

'Shove off the boat,' I said, too hungry for argument.

Slipper obeyed, throwing his knee over the gunwale as he did so, and tumbling into the bow; we could have done without him very comfortably, but his devotion was touching.

Holy Island was perhaps a hundred yards long, and about half as many broad; it was covered with trees and a dense growth of rhododendrons; somewhere in the jungle was a ruined fragment of a chapel, smothered in ivy and briars, and in a little glade in the heart of the island there was a holy well. We landed, and it was obviously a sore humiliation to Philippa that not a sound was to be heard in the spell-bound silence of the island, save the cough of a heron on a tree-top.

'It *was* there,' she said, with an unconvinced glance at the surrounding thickets.

'Sure, I'll give a thrawl through the island, ma'am,' volunteered Slipper with unexpected gallantry, 'an' if it's the divil himself is in it, I'll rattle him into the lake!'

He went swaggering on his search, shouting 'Hi, cock!' and whacking the rhododendrons with his stick, and after an interval returned and assured us that the island was uninhabited. Being provided with refreshments he again withdrew, and Philippa and Maria and I fed variously and at great length, and washed the plates with water from the holy well. I was smoking a cigarette when we heard Slipper addressing the solitudes at the farther end of the island, and ending with one of his whisky-throated crows of laughter.

He presently came lurching towards us through the bushes, and a glance sufficed to show even Philippa—who was as incompetent a judge of such matters as many of her sex—that he was undeniably screwed.

'Major Yeates!' he began, 'and Mrs. Major Yeates, with respex to ye, I'm bastely dhrunk! Me head is light since the 'fluenzy, and the docther told me I should carry a little bottle-een o' sperrits——'

'Look here,' I said to Philippa, 'I'll take him across, and bring the boat back for you.'

'Sinclair,' responded my wife with concentrated emotion, 'I would rather die than stay on this island alone!'

Slipper was getting drunker every moment, but I managed to stow him on his back in the bows of the punt, in which position he at once began to uplift husky and wandering strains of melody. To this accompaniment we, as Tennyson says,

> moved from the brink, like some full-breasted swan,
> That, fluting a wild carol ere her death,
> Ruffles her pure cold plume, and takes the flood
> With swarthy webs.

Slipper would certainly have been none the worse for taking the flood, and, as the burden of *Lannigan's Ball* strengthened and spread along the tranquil lake, and the duck once more fled in justifiable consternation, I felt much inclined to make him do so.

We made for the end of the lake that was nearest Shreelane, and, as we rounded the point of the island, another boat presented itself to our view. It contained my late entertainer, Mrs. Canty, seated bulkily in the stern, while a small boy bowed himself between the two heavy oars.

'It's a lovely evening, Major Yeates,' she called out. 'I'm just going to the island to get some water from the holy well for me daughter that has an impression on her chest. Indeed, I thought 'twas yourself was singing a song for Mrs. Yeates when I heard you coming, but sure Slipper is a great warrant himself for singing.'

'May the divil crack the two legs undher ye!' bawled Slipper in acknowledgment of the compliment.

Mrs. Canty laughed genially, and her boat lumbered away.

I shoved Slipper ashore at the nearest point; Philippa and I paddled to the end of the lake, and abandoning the duck as a bad business, walked home.

A few days afterwards it happened that it was incumbent upon me to attend the funeral of the Roman Catholic bishop of the diocese. It was what is called in France *un bel enterrement*, with inky flocks of tall-hatted priests, and countless yards of white scarves, and a repast of monumental solidity at the bishop's residence. The actual interment was to take place in Cork, and we moved in long and imposing procession to the railway station, where a special train awaited the cortège. My friend Mr. James Canty was among the mourners: an important and active personage, exchanging condolences with the priests, giving directions to porters, and blowing his nose with a trumpeting mournfulness that penetrated all the other noises of the platform. He was condescending enough to notice my presence, and found time to tell me that he had given Mr. Murray 'a sure word' with regard to some of *'the wreckage'*— this with deep significance, and a wink of an inflamed and tearful eye. I saw him depart in a first-class carriage and the odour of sanctity; seeing that he was accompanied by seven priests, and that both windows were shut, the latter must have been considerable.

Afterwards, in the town, I met Murray, looking more pleased with himself than I had seen him since he had taken up the unprofitable task of smuggler-hunting.

'Come along and have some lunch,' he said, 'I've got a real good thing on this time! That chap Canty came to me late last night, and told me that he knew for a fact that the island on Corran Lake was just stiff with barrels of bacon and rum, and that I'd better send every man I could spare to-day to get them into the town. I sent the men out at eight o'clock this morning; I think I've gone one better than Bosanquet this time!'

I began to realize that Philippa was going to score heavily on the subject of the fairies that she had heard snoring on the island, and I imparted to Murray the leading features of our picnic there.

'Oh, Slipper's been up to his chin in that rum from the first,' said Murray. 'I'd like to know who his sleeping partner was!'

It was beginning to get dark before the loaded carts of the salvage party came lumbering past Murray's windows and into the yard of the police-barrack. We followed them, and in so doing picked up Flurry Knox, who was sauntering in the same direction. It was a good haul, five big casks of rum, and at least a dozen smaller barrels of bacon and butter, and Murray and his Chief Constable smiled seraphically on one another as the spoil was unloaded and stowed in a shed.

'Wouldn't it be as well to see how the butter is keeping?' remarked Flurry, who had been looking on silently, with, as I had noticed, a still and amused eye. 'The rim of that small keg there looks as if it had been shifted lately.'

The sergeant looked hard at Flurry; he knew as well as most people that a hint from Mr. Knox was usually worth taking. He turned to Murray.

'Will I open it, sir?'

'Oh! open it if Mr. Knox wishes,' said Murray, who was not famous for appreciating other people's suggestions.

The keg was opened.

'Funny butter,' said Flurry.

The sergeant said nothing. The keg was full of black bog-mould. Another was opened, and another, all with the same result.

'Damnation!' said Murray, suddenly losing his temper. 'What's the use of going on with those? Try one of the rum casks.'

A few moments passed in total silence while a tap and a spigot were sent for and applied to the barrel. The sergeant drew off a mugful and put his nose to it with the deliberation of a connoisseur.

'Water, sir,' he pronounced, 'dirty water, with a small indication of sperrits.'

A junior constable tittered explosively, met the light blue glare of Murray's eye, and withered away.

'Perhaps it's holy water!' said I, with a wavering voice.

Murray's glance pinned me like an assegai, and I also faded into the background.

'Well,' said Flurry in dulcet tones, 'if you want to know where the stuff is that was in those barrels, I can tell you, for I was told it myself half an hour ago. It's gone to Cork with the bishop by special train!'

Mr. Canty was undoubtedly a man of resource. Mrs. Canty had mistakenly credited me with an intelligence equal to her own, and on receiving from Slipper a highly coloured account of how audibly Mr. Canty had slept off his potations, had regarded the secret of Holy Island as having been given away. That night and the two succeeding ones were spent in the transfer of the rum to bottles, and the bottles and the butter to fish boxes; these were, by means of a slight lubrication of the railway underlings, loaded into a truck as 'Fresh Fish, Urgent,' and attached to bishop's funeral train, while the police, decoyed far from the scene of action, were breaking their backs over barrels of bog-water. 'I suppose,' continued Flurry pleasantly, 'you don't know the pub that Canty's brother has in Cork. Well, I do. I'm going to buy some rum there next week, cheap.'

'I shall proceed against Canty!' said Murray, with fateful calm.

'You won't proceed far,' said Flurry, 'you'll not get as much evidence out of the whole country as'd hang a cat.'

'Who was your informant?' demanded Murray.

Flurry laughed. 'Well, by the time the train was in Cork, yourself and the Major were the only two men in the town that weren't talking about it.'

JAMES STEPHENS

# The Unworthy Princess[1]

His mother finished reading the story of the Beautiful Princess, and it was surely the saddest story he had ever heard. He could not bear to think of that lovely and delicate lady all alone in the huge, black castle, waiting, waiting until the giant came back from killing her seven brothers. He would come back with their seven heads swinging pitifully from his girdle, and when he reached the castle gates he would gnash his teeth through the keyhole with a noise like the grinding together of great rocks, and would poke his head through the fanlight of the door and say fee-faw-fum in a voice of such exceeding loudness that the castle would be shaken to its foundations.

Thinking of this his throat grew painful with emotion, and his heart swelled to the most uncomfortable dimensions, and he resolved to devote his whole life to the rescue of the Princess and, if necessary, die in her defence.

Such was his impatience that he could wait for nothing more than his dinner, and this he ate so speedily as to cause his father to call him a Perfect-Young-Glutton and a Disgrace-To-Any-Table. He bore these insults in a meek and heroic spirit, whereupon his mother said he was ill, and it was only by a sustained and violent outcry that he escaped being sent to bed.

Immediately after dinner, he set out in search of the Giant's-Castle. Now, a Giant's-Castle is one of the most difficult things in the world to find; that is because it is so large that one can only see it through the wrong end of a telescope, and further, he did not even know this giant's name; and so he might never have found the way if he had not met a certain Old-Woman on the common. She was a very nice Old-Woman: she had three teeth and a red shawl, and an umbrella with groceries inside it; so he told her of the difficulty he was in. She replied that he was in luck's way, and that she was the only person in the world who could assist him. She said her name was Really-and-Truly, and that she had a magic head, and that if he cut off her head it would answer any questions he asked it. So he stropped his penknife on his boot and said he was ready. The

---

[1] From *Here Are Ladies*, London, 1913. First published in *The Irish Homestead*, December 17, 1910.

Old-Woman then told him that in all affairs of this delicate nature it was customary to take the will for the deed, and that he might now ask her head anything he wanted to know, so he asked the head what was the way to the nearest giant, and the head replied that if he took the first turning to the left, the second to the right and then the first to the left again, and knocked at the fifth door on the right-hand side, he would see the giant.

He thanked the Old-Woman very much for the use of her head, and she permitted him to lend her one threepenny piece, one pocket handkerchief, one gun-metal watch, and one bootlace. She said that she never took two of anything because that was not fair, and that she wanted these for a very particular secret purpose about which she dare not speak and as to which she trusted he would not press her, and then she took a most affectionate leave of him and went away.

He followed her directions with the utmost fidelity and soon found himself opposite a house which, to the eye of anyone over seven years of age, looked very like any other house, but to the searching eye of six and three-quarters it was palpably and patently a Giant's-Castle. He tried the door, but it was locked, as, indeed, he expected it would be, and then he crept very cautiously and peeped through the first-floor window. He could see in quite plainly. There was a Polar-Bear crouching on the floor, and the head looked at him so directly and vindictively that if he had not been a hero he would have fled. The unexpected is always terrible, and when one goes forth to kill a Giant it is unkind of Providence to complicate one's adventure with a gratuitous and wholly unnecessary Polar-Bear. He was, however, reassured by the sight of a heavy chair standing on the Polar-Bear's stomach, and in the chair there sat the Most-Beautiful-Woman-In-The-World.

An ordinary person would not have understood, at first sight, that she was the Most-Beautiful-Woman-In-The-World, because she looked very stout and much older than is customary with Princesses—but that was because she was under an Enchantment and she would become quite young again when the giant was slain and three drops of his blood had been sprinkled on her Brow.

She was leaning forward in her chair staring into the fire, and she was so motionless that he was certain she must be under an enchantment. From the very instant he saw the Princess he loved her, and his heart swelled with pity to think that so beautiful a damsel should be subject to the tyranny of a giant, and these twin passions of pity and love grew to so furious a strength within him that he could no longer contain himself, but wept in a loud and very sudden voice which lifted the damsel out of her enchantment and her chair and hurled her across the room as though she had been propelled by a powerful spring.

He was so overjoyed at seeing her move that he pressed his face against the glass and wept with great strength, and in a few moments the Princess came timidly to the window and looked out. She looked right over his head at first and then she looked down and saw him, and her eyebrows went far up on her forehead and her mouth opened, and so he knew she was delighted to see him. He nodded to give her courage and shouted three times—Open Sesame, Open Sesame, Open Sesame, and then she opened the window and he climbed in. The Princess tried to push him out again, but she was not able, and he bade her put all her jewels in the heel of her boot and fly with him. But she was evidently the victim of a very powerful enchantment, for she struggled violently and said incomprehensible things to him, such as—'Is it a fire, or were you chased?' and 'Where *is* the cook?' But after a little time she listened to the voice of reason and knew that these were legitimate and heroic embraces from which she could not honourably disentangle herself.

When her first transports of joy were somewhat abated she assured him that excessive haste had often undone great schemes, and that one should look before one leaped, and that one should never be rescued all at once, but gradually, in order that one might become accustomed to the severe air of freedom, and he was overjoyed to find that she was as wise as she was beautiful. He told her that he loved her dearly, and she admitted, after some persuasion, that she was not insensible to the charms of his heart and intellect, but that her love was given to Another. At these tidings his heart withered away within him, and when the Princess admitted that she loved the Giant his amazement became profound and complicated. There was a rushing sound in his ears, the debris of his well-known world was crashing about him and he was staring upon a new planet the name of which was Astonishment. He looked around with a queer feeling of insecurity. At any moment the floor might stand up on one of its corners or the walls might begin to flap and waggle. But none of these things happened. Before him sat the Princess in an attitude of deep dejection and her lily-white hands rested helplessly in her lap. She told him in a voice that trembled that she would have married him if he had asked ten years earlier and said she could not fly with him because, in the first place, she had six children, and, in the second place, it would be against the Law, and, in the third place, his mother might object. She admitted that she was Unworthy of his love and that she should have Waited, and she bore his reproaches with a meekness that finally disarmed him.

He stropped his penknife on his boot and said that there was nothing left but to kill the giant, and that she had better leave the room while he did so because it was not a sight for a weak woman, and he wondered how much hasty-pudding would fall out of the giant if he Stabbed Him Right To The Heart. The Princess begged him not to kill her husband, and assured him that this giant had not got any hasty-pudding in his heart, and stated that he was really the nicest giant who ever lived, and that he had *not* killed her seven brothers but the seven brothers of quite another person entirely, which was a reasonable thing to do in the circumstances; and she continued in a strain which proved to him that this unnatural woman really loved the giant.

It was more in pity than in anger that he recognised the impossibility of rescuing this person. He saw at last that she was Unworthy of Being Rescued, and told her so. He said bitterly that he had grave doubts of her being a Princess at all and that if she was married to a giant it was no more than she deserved, and that he had a good mind to rescue the giant from her, and he would do it in a minute only that it was against his principles to rescue giants. And saying so he placed his penknife between his teeth and climbed out through the window.

He stood for a moment outside the window with his right hand extended to the sky and the moonlight blazing on his penknife—a truly formidable figure and one which the Princess never forgot, and then walked slowly away, hiding behind a cold and impassive demeanour a mind that was tortured, and a heart that had plumbed most of the depths of human suffering.

SEUMAS O'KELLY

# The Man with the Gift[1]

For twenty-five years the Boss had gone up and down the worn cabin steps without a worry. His fists had grown accustomed to the feel of ropes, to the rolling up and down of barrels, and the swinging of boxes, at the loading and discharging of *The Golden Barque*.[2] The motion of his limbs had come to be part of the ritual of the deck. He exhaled an odour of tar. His feet had flattened, his hands had rounded, his neck had developed a curve, throwing his face forward. His eyes were palely yellow, like the water of the canal. His vision had become concentrated, drilling through the landscape like canals. His temperament was placid. His emotions rose and fell as mechanically as if they were regulated by invisible locks. He was as tame as a duck. His name was Martin Coughlan, and he was known, by stray words that followed his speech like a memory, to have come from the North.

That torch of democracy—organisation—one day reached the backwash of existence. It found by its strange devices, of all people, Martin Coughlan. Up to that he had no sense of responsibility for the wrongs of the world, no brooding of the spirit in the problems of his day. His interests began at one harbour and ended at another. The things that he saw from the deck made up his world. They were good, and he was satisfied.

But then they came to him and told him he had been elected on the Committee. He beamed at the announcement, for he grasped, though vaguely, that he was a man chosen, one to whom honour was paying her respects. He walked into the shed where they held the Committee meetings with his slow lurch, his mind a blank as to the purpose of the assembly. He made no inquiries. He sat down with the others and looked around him. A man at a table read something out of a book. Martin Coughlan laughed, and felt the others staring at him.

A deep voice, with a note of admonition, if not tragedy, called out 'Order.' Martin Coughlan poked the ribs of a neighbour to show that he appreciated the humour of the situation.

---

[1] From *The Golden Barque and The Weaver's Grave*, Dublin, 1919. First published in the *Irish Weekly Independent*, 1912.
[2] *The Golden Barque* is a canal barge.

Then a man rose at the head of the table. He was a spare man with drooping mustachios, a penetrating eye, a voice that sounded high and sharp in the shed.

Martin Coughlan stared at the speaker. Something rare and unsuspected had touched his life. He wondered where this spare man had got all the words. They came out in a steady flow. He was obviously aiming at something, but what it was Martin Coughlan did not know, and, indeed, did not care. It was sufficient for him that the words came on and on. He had never heard any mortal before keeping up such a sustained flood of speech. Martin Coughlan leaned back, delight on his face.

Another man rose. He spoke even better. He gesticulated with energy. The others began to slap their limbs with their hands. Martin Coughlan slapped his limbs, feeling he was privileged. He had begun to live.

A thick-set man followed. His voice wakened echoes all over the place. His eyes flashed around, seeking one face now, another again. Suddenly the eyes fell on Martin Coughlan; the man addressed him as if he were appealing to an intelligence! He argued with him, made gestures at him, deposited all his logic at his feet.

Martin Coughlan's blood began to heat. He felt a tingle at the curve on the back of his neck. He coughed to relieve the tension. Then the speaker's gaze wandered to somebody else.

The talk went on for some hours. Men grew excited. Several spoke at the same time for pregnant minutes. Martin Coughlan began to perspire. Once he shouted, 'Hear, hear,' because the words had begun to sound familiar.

When the Committee meeting broke up he went back to the boat, his cheeks flaming, feeling that he had done it all himself. He passed Hike on the way. The little driver looked up at him with respect. The dark-faced man was sitting on a box by the stern.

'The meeting over?' he asked.

'Yes,' Martin Coughlan said.

His voice sounded hoarse. His throat felt dry. He went down to the keg and drank a mug of water.

Afterwards Martin Coughlan paced the deck with a new air. He became preoccupied. Once they saw him gesticulating at a bush on the bank. He took a new tone to the lock-keepers. He was always clearing his throat.

A few times at the meals they thought he was about to make a speech. But something always overcame him. When they sounded him as to the Committee proceedings his face beamed.

'There was speech-making,' he would say.

'What did they say?'

Martin Coughlan rose. He caught the lapel of his coat; struck an attitude. An inspired look came into his face. But no words followed. Instead he took up a bucket and went on deck.

'He's a great man for the Committee,' they said. 'He won't give the show away.'

'Aye, man, but that fellow is knowing. He could hold a Cabinet secret.'

One day the dark-faced man loaned a paper at a village.

'They don't give the speeches,' he said, 'but there is the name right enough—Martin Coughlan.'

Martin Coughlan took the paper. His eyes swam as he spelled out his name. He pored over the sheet for long spells throughout the rest of the evening. When the men were turning in he said: 'Boys, but she's a brave wee paper.'

He got a candle, and sat over it, spelling everything out, including the advertisements. Then he sat up, delight on his face, the look in his eyes of a man who knew he had achieved something. 'Men,' he said, 'I've overhauled her, beam and aft, stem to stern.'

But the only answer was a chorus of heavy snores. He turned in with a grumble.

There was another Committee meeting soon after. The speeches fell on his head like dew from the heavens. Language! Why, the world had never yet heard the like. Moreover, he became conscious that the other men were deferring to him in their views. He sat there as solemn as a judge, the greatest listener who had ever arrived in the shed. The speakers felt that they had at last got hold of an audience, a man of appreciation. Now and then he nodded his head in approval. It was worth a yard of debate. When he shook his head in disapproval it excited the speakers. They went on and on, fighting, arguing, playing for his opinion. But Martin Coughlan held to his silent views with wonderful pugnacity. He was not to be cajoled.

'What were they at last night, Martin?' one of them asked afterwards.

'That,' said Martin, after a pause, 'is a secret.'

'He's too close-minded,' they said. 'He keeps it all in for the Committee. It must be something to hear him when the cork is off.'

The dark-faced man was fond of the paper. He got it regularly in the village. 'Here we are,' he said, with satisfaction. 'They give us the speeches this time. Now we'll know what Martin Coughlan had to say for himself.'

But there was no speech from Martin Coughlan. Everybody had said something except the representative from *The Golden Barque*.

The dark-faced man made a complaint.

'Don't mind the paper,' Martin Coughlan said. 'She is no good. I knew from the first she had sprung a leak.'

But he felt that the men were dissatisfied. He struck an attitude on the deck, and said: 'Mr. Chairman and gentlemen—I venture to think.' He paused. 'To my mind,' he added. There was another pause. 'I say, standing here to-night.' He looked vaguely over the landscape. 'I beg to propose.' And then he took a little run up and down the deck, rubbing his hands with delight.

'He's too clever,' one of the men said. 'He thinks to put us off by play-acting. It won't do.'

Before the proceedings of the next Committee meeting began, Martin Coughlan took the secretary aside. The secretary was a shrewd person. There was a motion on the agenda to give him a salary.

'John,' said Martin Coughlan, with familiarity, 'I want you to tell me how it is done.'

'How is what done?'

'The speeches, you know; the language, the words, the talk they do have.'

John was puzzled. Then a light broke upon him.

'Well,' he said, 'a man must have it in him.'

'Have what in him?'

John hesitated, thought, and said, 'The gift.'

Martin Coughlan was crestfallen. He felt there was something in life he had let slip.

'Where would there be likelihood of getting the gift?' he asked at last.

'I don't know,' the other replied. 'It comes from within.'

'Oh, I see,' Martin Coughlan said, more cheerfully. Then he con-

# THE MAN WITH THE GIFT

fided. 'John, I have it within in the inside of me. Language, great language. But I can't get it out.'

'Have courage,' the other said. 'Take your chance. Get up on your legs. Face them. When you do that the words will flow out of you.'

'Do you think they will, John?'

'Sure.' John was a man persuasive, one who carried conviction, inspired hope—and drew salaries.

'Then there is that wee paper, John. If I'd come out with the words, they would be there, of course. They do be reading her, looking out for what a man might say.'

'Oh, that's it, is it, Martin?' John asked, then patted the other on the back. 'That will be all right, old man. Leave that to me. Vote straight on the salary question, and the goods will be delivered to you on the paper.'

'Thanks, John; I will.'

At a critical moment in the debate, Martin Coughlan rose. He went over to the table, rapped his knuckles upon it to command attention, jerked the collar of his coat about his neck. He struck the attitude he had rehearsed aboard. It was reminiscent of various statues erected to the memory of great orators.

He looked up and down the shed. A hush fell upon the assembly. Men leaned back to hear what the silent man, the audience, the one man of reticence among them, had to say at this crisis.

'Mr. Chairman and Mr. Gentlemen,' Martin Coughlan began, blundering through nervousness.

There was a laugh. Martin Coughlan moistened his lips with his tongue, for they were dry and inclined to stick. One of his knees struck against the other. Then he had to clear a lump from his throat.

'John, our secretary,' he said at last, 'told me that if I stood up on me legs the words would flow out from within the inside of me.'

He hesitated, looking about him in a panic, a queer feeling of collapse in his brain. He smiled a ghastly smile.

'Go on,' said the chairman.

'He said,' Martin Coughlan resumed, his voice falling to an echo, 'that if I faced you they would flow out of me. But—by heavens—they won't.' He sat down. There was a burst of laughter and applause.

The men stared at Martin Coughlan. There was that mixture of scepticism, enjoyment, malicious delight, in their glances that fastens upon all fallen gods. They were taking their fun out of an exposure, the showing up of an emptiness that wore a mask, the betrayal of that discretion which is only a dullness.

Martin Coughlan was too heated, too full of confusion, to notice their crude levity. By the time he had recovered himself they had dropped him. They no longer deferred to him. He was no longer appealed to as an intelligence. He drew back instinctively to the shadows, and he sat there until the meeting broke up.

When he reached his boat the men greeted him with deference. He muttered something and went down to the cabin. He stayed there for the rest of the night.

'The Committee,' he said to the dark-faced man next day, 'is a rotten Committee.'

'I thought that all along,' the other replied. 'But I didn't like to say it, seeing you were a great one on it.'

'And an ignorant Committee,' Martin Coughlan added.

'It is that.'

But by the end of the week the paper was out. The dark-faced man, after reading it, looked up at Martin Coughlan and then went to him.

'Look here, Boss,' he said, putting out his hand, 'shake hands.'

They shook hands, Martin Coughlan nervously.

'It was a great speech,' the dark-faced man said. 'You're wasting your time on this boat.'

Martin Coughlan blushed; his gaze was uncertain. The other left him the paper.

He sat on a barrel and opened the sheet. There was his name in print again! He spelled it out slowly. 'Mr. Martin Coughlan, who was received with loud applause, said ———,' and there followed over a column of type, of words, of language, of a speech. He read it over with a thumping heart. It was dotted with 'hear, hear,' 'applause,' and 'cheers.' When he finished, he stood up and walked the deck, his thick limbs outspread, his flat feet solid on the planks, his chest out.

'Is it a good report, Boss?' they asked.

'It is very fair, very fair, men,' he said, with toleration.

'Man, but I'd like to hear it coming out.'

'No doubt you would.'

'We'll hear you some time.'

'You will, why not, to be sure.'

He ran his fingers through his hair. He drilled spaces, vague spaces, through the familiar landscape with his gaze. His blood rose gradually, eventually flooding his face until it grew purple in colour, rising as steadily as if somebody had lifted the sluice of a flood-gate.

'God, the language of it,' he repeated to himself over and over again throughout the day.

For the first time in his life, he refused to go into *The Haven* when they had made the journey across the bog. Instead he went into the cabin, and alone spelt the speech over and over again.

Gradually his mind got over the habit of thinking of it as something apart, something outside his own life. He no longer said, 'God, the language of it.' Instead he muttered, 'Great language; splendid talk; just the thing. That's it. That's what I'd say. That's the very word I'd say. I declare I think it was the word I said. It was going through my head at the time. I must have said that very word. If I did not, I intended it. But I forget what I said. Maybe I said it. To be sure I said it. Of course I said it. Why not? The very word; no, but the very words. If I said one word I must have said another. I could not help following up one word with another. What was to stop me? Nothing. I went on that very way. One word borrowed another. What else could it do. To be sure I said it. In fact, it's all what I said, word for word.'

He went on persuading himself until the others came back from *The Haven*.

He went up to the dark-faced man.

'I tell you what it is, it's a very fine report; a very good report; a tip-top report. Word for word there it is, in black and in white.' He struck one fist in the other.

'Boss,' the other said, something almost approaching reverence in his long, narrow face, 'you're a great one, a gifted one. For to turn round and say the like of what you said, a man must have the gift.'

'To be sure he must,' Martin Coughlan agreed, taking some steps along by the cargo covered with great oil-cloths. 'I told John, the secretary, I had it within in the inside of me. And what had I within in the inside of me, I ask you, men? The gift!'

'Well, thank God we'll all hear you soon,' the dark-faced man said. 'There's a public meeting coming on.'

Martin Coughlan drew a long breath. 'You don't tell me so?'

'I do. We had word of it in *The Haven*. There is to be speech-making, and great speech-making. We'll expect you that day to show the great gift that's in you.'

'You will, to be sure,' Martin Coughlan said, but without enthusiasm. He ran his fingers through his hair. Then he walked away from the others, standing at the prow of the boat, his sturdy figure solid against the water.

'A great one he is for the gab,' the grotesque-looking man said irreverently. 'Look at the two powerful limbs he has holding him up from the ground.'

After that Martin Coughlan grew very subdued, silent, avoiding the topic of the coming meeting. The men said he was bottling himself up for the big occasion. They noted that he still pored over the paper that contained his speech. He would lie back in his bunk at night, a candle fixed by his side, drilling through the speech. Once or twice the men heard him muttering to himself like a boy grappling with a lesson. In these days it was noted that some of the colour left his face. A certain pensiveness crept into his expression.

'Boss,' one of the men asked him, 'are you in pain?'

'I am,' Martin Coughlan answered, and walked sadly away.

Once the men wakened to hear him pacing the deck in the middle of the night. The dark-faced man went up the ladder and popped his vignette over the hold. He came back after a time.

'He's on deck in his shirt,' he said. 'The moon is shining on him, his legs are like two white pillars under the tiller. He has that paper with him. I heard him giving out a few words. He was losing them, trying to catch them up again, stumbling and staggering over them like a man that would be raving. Then he would run his hands through his hair, and the wind blowing the shirt about the white pillars.'

'Be the powers,' said the grotesque man, turning over in his bunk, 'It's a chilly sort of a night, and I'm glad I have not the gift.'

As the day of the meeting approached, and it became more and more a topic of conversation, Martin Coughlan's depression increased. Something seemed to weigh him down. He took the dark-faced man aside.

'You know this meeting is got up by the Committee?' he said.

'I do.'

'And you can call to mind what I told you of that Committee a long while ago. I said it was a rotten Committee.'

'You did. I remember that.'

'And I said it was an ignorant Committee.'

'You did, right enough.'

'You agreed with me. We were at one as regards this Committee. Very well, I'm not going to give that Committee the satisfaction of making a speech for them.'

'Now, that would be a pity and you having the gift.'

'There you are! That's what makes me do it. How can a man of gift speak for a rotten, ignorant Committee?'

To the dark-faced man this was a poser. Perhaps in that moment of expediency, of pressure, Martin Coughlan showed that he had, after all, some talent for politics.

He walked down the deck with a stride.

'Never!' he exclaimed with decision, waving his arms.

The meeting came off without Martin Coughlan. He did not even attend. He 'sent word' to strike his name off the Committee.

'We will, indeed,' one of the men said. 'Little good any such tame ducks is to anyone.'

The men from *The Golden Barque* were disappointed that Martin Coughlan did not pour forth his eloquence at the assembly. They somehow regarded him as in some way wronged. But he became more cheerful himself. He began to whistle again as he moved around the boat. His flat feet became more than ever a part of the ritual of the deck. The curve at the back of his neck threw out his head another degree. His eyes became more palely yellow. They went on digging imaginary canals in the landscape. He was as happy as a duck in the water. Once the dark-faced man asked: 'Boss, what became of the paper with your speech in it?'

'Oh, yon rag!' Martin Coughlan made answer. 'I rolled her up in a stone, and she's at the bottom a wheen of weeks.'

OLIVER ST. JOHN GOGARTY

# Tall Hats and Churns[1]

TODAY I WILL be a millionaire. I will do just as I please. Have I come into millions? Yes. The heavens have endowed me: it is a fine day in Dublin, and my tastes are more than money can buy. I have never confused money with wealth, that is why I am a millionaire: I am as wealthy as any, though not as monied as the least. What are my wants? Already I have the first of them gratified—it is a fine day in Dublin; and the second, which needs a high barometric pressure to fulfill, has got it. Freedom from the tyranny of meals, appointments and even friends, any man can have by embracing Sister Poverty; but there is one thing that she must give me in return for my attentions, and that she cannot give—the power of unimpeded movement. Her vehicles are the ambulance or the Black Maria. I would desert her for a Baby Ford.

A child has an extra appetite; one in addition at least to those a grown person has—it is the necessity for movement. To keep a child motionless would as assuredly kill it as it would kill an old man to confine him to bed. Young and old must move; and the desire for movement is overflowing into the hunger for speed. The eternal feminine, the female force in Nature, led the men of old upward; speed is taking her place in this generation. What is at the back of this hunger for and need of speed?

Just as there are tribes who are unacquainted with the facts of parenthood, with children who do not know their fathers, so we are unaware of our heavenly descent, our cosmic relationship. And yet the thrill of the electric atoms which make up the substance of our bodies is slowly being felt and interpreted in terms of Speed. Our bodies are desirous of swift movement now: Speed for speed's sake. Soon our minds will realise the electric nature of our being and deliberately direct our bodies' movements towards the All-mover, the *Primum Mobile* whose glory thrills and penetrates the universe.

Call them profanely protons and electrons, these are but names for matter in the immeasurable Mystery of Being which vibrates through the whole of space, or rather of creation. The body is vibrating in harmony with the universe. The more we grow conscious of this, the more we will to move. Movement is the ritual and recog-

[1] From *As I Was Going Down Sackville Street*, New York, 1937.

nition of the divine nature of our substance. It is a recoil from that which is dead, an act of life. To satisfy the desire and to make an action of recognition, the power to move must be provided. Else we remain still as death.

My motor, therefore, takes me far to-day from the Eternal Feminine of the Viceregal Lodge with her *gentil babil,* into the hills or even into the air. I will arise and go into the granite mountains, and sit on a stone in the middle of a little yard-wide rill, and watch the water move over the clean golden sands, or by a heathery stream watch the sub-aqueous grasses wave, while far above go the high cumulus clouds that look down upon it all.

I remember once Talbot Clifton asking me, 'What the devil were you doing on that hill? You had no gun.'

There was not the least use in trying to answer him. The answer would, for peace and for understanding's sake, have to be 'nothing.' And that would seem an offensive and unsatisfactory reply. He did not know that I was a millionaire and can let others shoot my imaginary birds and catch all my fish but the Salmon of Knowledge.

With these blanketing clouds there will be a warm dell above Ticknock, where I can do nothing until it is time to fall down on Dundrum and give Yeats the Governor-General's invitation. Will he accept it? Of course not, at first; but a little strategy, a little strategy. I have already in my mind a little scheme to endow him with the necessary distinction. He must be made to see that he has an opportunity to take up the position which he likes beyond all others: the position from which he can both dominate and endow.

His mind provides me with a realm of beauty beyond the beauty of Woman. It will be a relief to be independent in thought for an hour or two while I sail in the shadowy waters or sit with Cuchullain grown old. Seven lean years he endured of love, only to win at the end emancipation from—what was it the aged Sophocles called Love?—'a relentless master.'

Now he leaves to Love the perfervid sunlight. He has refracted his rays, as it were, through the pearl of Paradise, and they fall with so gentle a softness that they are only visible under the moon. How different this from George Moore, caught in the ugly snare and wry-twisted with curiosity; how different even from Keats, whom he makes to appear somewhat treacly and relaxed. Keats, Gates, Yeats: etymologically these three names are one and the same. They are names found in Cornwall. So Keats and Yeats are neither English nor Irish originally, but Cornish. And Yeats' mother being a Pollexfen makes Yeats closer to Cornwall than Keats, and closer to Parnassus as it rises to our modern eyes. I must remember that: Cornish! He will be delighted to hear it. He is growing somewhat tired of being irretrievably Irish, which has come lately to mean Gaelic, which means nothing. He wants a change. But with Yeats a Cornishman! He shall have sailed with Tristram, sung hopelessly of Iseult for seven long years and reproved the facetious Dinadan. And he shall disapprove of present times before I have done with him. Already I hear the sailors singing the oldest sea chanties as they near Tintagel, where Yeats is waiting beside King Mark.

> They rowed hard, and sung thereto
> With Heveloe, and Rumbaloo!

It's enough to give him, with this new outlook, a new lease of life. And that is the function of anyone who is a wellwisher of the Muses' mighty son. And he can find an excuse to escape from boredom, which is the only thing that ages, an excuse to get out of the Kildare Street Club.

I will gather myself up and hurry down. I can see the old grey mole of De Lacy's Castle from here, and past it the Yellow House; a mile this side is Yeats. Yes. Yes. How pleased he will be! But, of course, he has to discover this lineage for himself.

Why did I not think of this before? There could not be a Gaelic Yeats. It won't take 'O' or 'Mac' as a prefix. Now that he is recovering from a cold, is the very time for a change to complete the cure and put him up for the Round Table. He will elect himself. Merlin will not be in it with me as a magician! He had better be Sir Lancelot than Sir Tristram, for 'Lancelot was better breathed.'

Yeats lives in Rathfarnham in an old house in lovely grounds, a house built before cement took the place of stone and thin-walled clangour for the stately repose and long silence of continuous dwelling. His gate is on a bridge which spans a stream fresh from the golden granite of the hills. The walk rises through a well-gardened wilderness of flowering shrubs, and the old grey house is screened by a blossoming orchard. His croquet lawn is beside it, and the hills form an ever-changing picture as deep and as glowing in colour as a picture by his brother, Jack Yeats, in his latest style. The door faces you. 'Yeats' on a heart-shaped brass knocker. As it used to be simply 'Yeats' on his London house in Woburn Place before the place was demolished.

'I am glad you have come,' he said, 'you are the very man I want to see. I have just been reading George Moore's *Memoirs of My Dead Life*. And a question keeps rising in my mind which you can answer. Take that seat there. This is the question: Do you think George Moore was impotent?'

The great Cornishman was sitting up among his pillows, his magnificent head, with its crown of white hair and satin-like brown skin, toning well with the fawn dressing-gown he wore. His nose, like an eagle's, was broadest between the eyes. At the foot of the bed a gas-fire burned; outside the open window birds were seeking food in a coconut shell which he had fastened to the sill. He was recovering from a cold and 'enjoying his illness' for the peace it provided and for the immunity it gave him from his friends.

Good Lord! but aloud: 'I don't know. It is rare for a man to be impotent. He may be unable to propagate, but organic impotence must be very rare.'

'Was he a man?'

'He had the pelvis of a woman, as artists are said to have. There is little to be deduced from that. The only arguments that come to my mind are based on deduction more than on facts physical or otherwise.'

'Well, go on.'

'Take the evidence of women. Susan Mitchell sensed something lacking. Women are like that. She wrote, "Some men kiss and do not tell, some kiss and tell; but George Moore told and did not kiss." Kiss may mean . . . Well, she was hardly likely to say more.'

'Go on.'

'You remember Goethe says'—how well Yeats remembered, I knew, for I remembered long ago mentioning Goethe to Moore, and Moore pointing to Beckermann's *Life of Goethe* and saying with a snigger: 'That's where Yeats gets all his information. That's his text-book'—'that the "passing of a genius is measured by the woman it leaves behind." Now, where are Moore's surviving lady friends?'

'There's one.'

'Oh, we all know! But did Moore hold her exclusive affection? He did not. She was faithful to him only in her infidelities, *splen-*

*dide mendax.* "I could not love thee, Moore, so much, loved I not others more." That's argument number one. Then, one evening I sat with him in his bedroom in Ebury Street. He was recounting with a reminiscence so devoid of melancholy that I suspected it was but a work of the creative imagination. Suddenly he looked at the rug in front of the fire and addressed it and me: "O rug, thou could'st tell many a pleasant tale of love!" What's wrong with the bed? thought I.'

'Exactly,' Yeats exclaimed, with the excitement of a triumphant detective, jerking himself up in the bed. 'Exactly! His accounts of his adventures are all one-sided. There never is— he never gives one a distinct feeling for the woman in the case. I have just been reading these Memoirs, and I am wondering more than ever what form his impotence took. I remembered this: He was passing along Merrion Square one night with Best and he saw couples standing upright, standing immobile, speechless, with heads on one another's shoulders. "But they are not saying a word!" he exclaimed. "I wish I could do that! Best, could you do that?" Best laughed and said that it was about the only thing anybody could do. But psychologically it reveals that Moore never felt the all sufficing silence of Love. His scenes leave you with no account of the woman. It is only of his own sensations he talks. Now we all know a woman has far fiercer sensations than a man. She cannot conceal them. She cries out. Moore never tells what the woman did. Why?'—pointing and shaking his finger at me—'Because she was not there!'

'A woman in Paris told me that the earlier emotions are apt to become obliterated by the later. Moore only recounts his earlier emotions!'

I said: 'I consulted a woman novelist about the Moore problem and I put the objection regarding the one-sidedness of his love scenes. "The Lovers of Orelay," for instance, where there is more writing about the locale than the love.'

'What did she say?'

'That Moore was an artist and was both sided, woman and man, as artists should be.'

'She was a woman novelist, you say? That accounts for her defending him. His works are admired particularly by women.'

'Wait! I begin to see a further argument for your thesis in that. Women admire him because they feel instinctively that he can never give them away.'

'Admirable!'

'Love must have ever been to Moore "All a wonder and a wild desire." His curiosity was undiminished, and yet, it could be argued that that was chiefly a proof that his interest in women was undiminished. An argument in his favour.'

'Would you mind closing that window? The birds will not come back until it's down. I interrupted you?'

'Not at all. I remember since we spoke of the absence of the woman from Moore's description of his love scenes, his telling me of something a lover—no, he preferred to call her a mistress—of his was supposed to remark . . . it is so much on the lines of the ignorance he revealed to Best that I forbear telling it; but you may take it that now I come to think of it, it bears out the conclusion we come to from what he said to Best.'

'What was that?'

'Oh, never mind. But don't you remember the way in which he tried to make me personate him in Vienna shortly after I had returned from that most delightful of cities?'

'When the lady that admired his work theatened to come to Dublin so that she might bear a child of his?'

'Precisely. She was, according to Moore, a beautiful Viennese . . .'

'And you had just come back from Vienna. That's what gave him the idea. The idea of the Viennese admirer. You had been extolling Vienna?'

'Very likely.'

'Go on.'

' "How am I to know her? And do you imagine for a moment that she will not find me out?" I objected.

' "My dear fellow, I will show you her photograph. And as for finding you out, she only admires my work, she does not know me, and that is why she insists on bearing a child to me." '

'Yes! Yes! Go on.'

'Having, so to speak, screwed my courage to the sticking-place, I asked to see the photograph.'

'And did you see it?'

'I cannot remember.'

'Try to think.'

'I did see a photograph, but he might have forgotten that he had shown it to me before I left for Vienna the year before. It may have been the photograph he used for Pearl Craigie . . .'

'Now, listen to me. I saw that photograph, yellow with age. It had become, when I saw it, the photograph of a beautiful Virginian who was threatening to come to him from America desirous of his services. He wrote a play about it. That was all.'

Yeats lit the lamp beside his bed. The birds were twittering in his apple-trees, settling for the night. I might open the window now.

'After all, he was a great artist and greatly loved art,' I said. 'He was a devotee to that and creative in that sphere at all events. He was a great person and he never forgot it. His air of perpetual cantankerousness was to defend himself from rational little critics "while the work was in progress"; to defend himself from Reality and common-sense. Had he not said, "We must keep up the illusion?" And while he attended to his garden, the garden of his prose, he resented what anyone can have if they bear fools gladly—comments.'

But while Moore wrote much about Yeats, Yeats remained silent about his contemporary. Why was this? I think that Moore's inordinate jealousy, a jealousy which flew at the fame of Hardy like a pettish child, realised a greater genius in Yeats than he possessed, and so he tried to subject by ridicule what he could never have outshone. Yeats disliked Moore, first of all for his 'position'—a landlord—and then because he was attacked by Moore before his friends. Also, Yeats feels that his words may easily confer fame, since he has never allowed his literary judgment to be persuaded. Making your rival ridiculous is the chief aim of Irish opponents since the duel was abolished. And in his trilogy *Ave, Salve, Vale*, Moore mocked at Yeats. *Ave atque Vale*, I have recorded it was at first, until he pilloried Professor Tyrrell, who aware of Moore's ignorance, remarked on hearing of his portrait drawn by Moore, 'Moore is one of those fellows who think that "Atque" is a Roman centurion.'

The problems that confront the mind of man are innumerable, some of them incalculable. My problem was not one of those which may be described somewhat hyperbolically as vital; nevertheless it was, considered from the point of view of Art, a cardinal one on which much hinged. And I was nearly forgetting it! I had to persuade a real poet to accept an invitation to a pseudo court. Yeats is the greatest poet of this and of most of the last generation. Tennyson, his predecessor, built a world of song on ready-made foundations. Yeats had to create it all from 'airy nothing'; and to protect it from marauding hands. I had to persuade him to accept a word-of-mouth invitation to the opening ceremony of the Spring Show.[1] The Show might have opened itself, but its success was contributed to by the presence of His Majesty's representative. Dublin is loyal at Ballsbridge. Horses connote knights, 'Men who ride upon horses' (I will quote Yeats to himself), and therefore courtliness. This may help me to persuade the poet to join the 'Distinguished Visitors' in the 'Royal' box.

'By the way, Yeats, the Governor-General has asked me to invite you to the opening of the Spring Show. He will be in his private box, and we can go up to it or take tea under it in his private apartments.'

'I will not go. I am suffering from a cold.'

'You are not, but you are making your friends suffer from your cold.'

'I will not abet this trumpery mockery of a throne. I will not meet Tim Healy[2] or Lady Lavery in the Royal box. Really I am surprised that you take this mummery of kingship seriously.'

'No. I do not; but I think that in the Decline and Fall of the British Empire in Ireland, and Ireland with it, you and I should stand like your Triton in the stream, and resist the lapse from grandeur with dignity. I am going in a tall hat, as if I were crowned by remembering happier things. I am sure that mine will be the only tall hat at the Spring Show. Half the Kildare Street Club will be there, but they will hesitate to honour the King lest they offend Democracy by meeting his Viceroy suitably attired. I, as you know, have not the least concern for popular opinion.'

'Neither have I!'

'I am going in what I hope will be the only silk hat to be seen at the first official function of the Free State. We must not conform to the unceremonious.'

This aroused him. 'Look here, I think you are right. Unless we are to let the country drift without a protest into the loutish ways of the bog, we must stand for the observances of good manners. We must wear tall hats.' The grandeur innate in the man was coming out. Quietly now! Leave him the tiller.

'You are quite right. If we do not give our countrymen the lead, who is there left courageous enough to sport a tall hat?'

---

[1] The Spring agricultural fair of the Royal Dublin Society at its exhibition grounds, Ballsbridge, Dublin.
[2] First Governor-General of the Irish Free State.

I hope, I said to myself, that the proposition will not appear to his mind as 'Silk hats save Ireland!'

He was agreeing, but it did not mean that he was coming to the Show.

'Quite so. But it is neither here nor there, this mock court held by a barrister, in what is no more important than an agricultural show in one of the shires. I will not go. I am not well enough. It is a travesty: a revolution in a palace.'

My last card: 'Yeats, we need not ascend the grandstand at all. As poet of the Lake Isle, you ought to see the country girls producing the island's fare. It is a goodly sight. I saw some of the dairy-maids at work in the last Spring Show, and they were very comely. The butter-girls are so clean and wholesome you would think that they were personally selected by Dr. Russell of the Department of Public Health. Wonderful sight, the churning! Lassies of seventeen, with white elbows.'

'Why white elbows?'

'You must know that the skin of the elbow retains to the last any trace of pigment that there may be in the racial species. If there is the least Eurasian, Arabian or Semitic blood, for instance, it shows in the browning of the skin of the elbow: some skin diseases are diagnosed by a spot or two at the elbows. Now the dairy-maids I saw churning have snow-white and ruddy arms like strawberries and cream. Their work at the churning had made them rosy, and still they kept on with the old-fashioned churns, plunging up and down the long handle. It is a very graceful attitude. I wonder why your brother Jack has not caught them at their work. In a year or two there will be no more churns with long upright handles, nothing but revolving barrels with glass windows. The old and homely things are ebbing away, ebbing away.'

'You do not expect me to rise from my bed to see Tim Healy; and a few country girls churning?'

'Whoever suggested it? I merely threw out a hint that you and I could attend the Spring Show, wear silk hats where no one else dared, and slip away from the Royal box in time for the butter-making competition. I will drive you home.'

'Perfectly preposterous!'

'Very well—you are missing a lot.'

'What am I missing?'

# TALL HATS AND CHURNS

'Oh nothing, perhaps. But I am deep in the folk-lore of the churn. Most of the treasure trove from Irish bogs is butter, and we get that unique and beautiful form of vessel the mether from the bogs. The three- or four-handed goblet. The descendants of those who made the mether and put butter into firkins are churning at the present moment, unconscious of the long tradition of the churn; and the awful tragedy of it is that no one realises what is being lost. The sea chanties were nearly all gone until a few late-comers collected half-a-dozen Bowdlerised stanzas or so. But the churn! Only one song of butter-making remains.'

'Have you got it?'

'Father Claude overheard it in Tipperary, when a buxom maid was churning as she thought all alone. She had buttocks like a pair of beautiful melons. Her sleeves were rolled up. She had churned from early morning. Her neck was pink with exercise. Her bosom laboured, but she could not desist, for the milk was at the turn. Up and down, desperately she drove the long handle: up and down, up and down and up and up for a great drive. The resistance grew against the plunger. Her hips and bosom seemed to increase in size while her waist grew thin. In front of her ears the sweat broke into drops of dew. She prayed in the crisis to old forgotten gods of the homestead! Twenty strokes for ten! Gasping, she sang:

> 'Come, butter!
> Come, butter!
> Come, butter,
> Come!
> Every lump
> As big as
> My bum!

'You are missing not one, but many milk-maids' songs. And when we are dead, they too shall be; and the folk-lore lost forever of the dairy and the byre.'

'How does it go?'—He beat time to recall the rhythm.

'"Every lump As big as My Bum!"'

'Yes. You are correct. But my proposal is that we get these chants at first-hand and be not depending on Father Claude for such songs.'

'When does Tim expect us?'

'Any time from four to six.'

'"Come, butter, come butter,"' he murmured. 'I think I will join you. Let me know when you can send a car. And there's my hat to be brushed.'

PATRICK KAVANAGH

# The Grey Dawn[1]

A COUNTY COUNCIL QUARRY WAS OPENED IN OUR VICINITY. Among the quarry-men was one man named Bob. He was a stout fellow of thirty, brown-eyed and very quiet. For three months he passed our house on his way to work before we spoke to each other. He was usually reading a book—an Irish grammar. He was studying Gaelic.

Then one evening he came in to have his boot repaired. Bob was a flame. He touched the damp wood of my mind till sparks began to dance.

He talked on unusual themes. He mentioned Canon Law, syphilis, and irregular verbs. He recited verse, bad verse by critical standards, perhaps; Longfellow's *Evangeline* and a translation of Dante by—I think—Cary.

He had tried his skill at verse-making himself. One poem of eleven lines he gave me; there were meant to be twelve lines, but he couldn't get the last line. 'For the past six months I've been trying to find that line,' he told me.

'Beside an Irish rath,' was the nearest he could get.

'It's a great poem as it is,' I told him, 'a real masterpiece.' And I thought so at the time. We were then standing in the shadow of Rocksavage wall, close to the crossroads from which the wild laughter of young men came. It was a moonlit evening in October and the air was filled with the fragrance of over-ripe blackberries and alderberries.

'Aren't they the gets?' I said, referring to the boys at the crossroads.

'They're true Irishmen,' he said.

Bob gave me a long lecture on the beauty of *Alice in Wonderland* and *Gil Blas*.

Down among the slabs of basalt rock, when Bob was in the quarry, thought took wing. The listeners in this academy of stone hunger were fed.

'What is God?'

'God's a man.'

Bob's conception of God, whatever it was, must have been a million-forked tongue of truth.

---
[1] From *The Green Fool*, New York, 1939.

'What would the priest say if he heard us?' some fool was sure to say. And Bob would tell them that their conversation was truly religious. Bob was asked a long time afterwards who was the cleverest man he had ever met; he said I was. Lucky for me I didn't hear of this opinion till my mind had developed a resistance to vanity.

A neighbour of mine—a young fellow who lived alone in a fine house—had a large stock of inherited books. I used to visit him in the winter evenings. He loaned me books. We would sit by his fire long hours discussing literature. I did most of the talking, and I shudder when I think of the flood of poetic silliness I let loose on my friend. We agreed that *The Siege of Corinth*, by Byron, was sublime. I it was who suggested the word 'sublime.'

'Sublime, that's exactly the word,' my host said. I envied this fellow his stock of books. The fine old volumes lay blue-moulded around the floor and on tables. Burns's poems and a huge history of Rome stood on the hob. On top of a bag of flour lay—in the company of some copies of the *Wide World Magazine*—Shelley's *The Cenci*. It was the fashion in fancy houses to have a big book on the parlour table. This man had several big books on his parlour table, but it wasn't for vanity.

Two is company, three is a crowd, the saying goes. There is deep intimacy when two men sit by a winter fire. When a third enters—though he be of close spiritual kindred—the whole fabric of familiar sweetness and innocence comes to pieces.

This often happened to us. Some fellow was sure to come rumbling in his hob-nailed boots up the cobbled yard to our door. A bull to the china-shop of the angels.

'Anybody inside?'

'Come in.'

If the fellow who entered had leprosy or was a lunatic with a gun I wouldn't be half as vexed. And he would more than likely be breezy with good humour. He would be entirely unconscious that he was treading on holy ground. He would be sure to lift a book and turn over the pages before he sat down.

'Aw, holy fiddlesticks! What the divil does that mane?'

It might be Milton's *Paradise Lost*, for that chunk of poetic theology was in my friend's library.

We wouldn't tell him what the book was.

'Take a sate,' the man of the house would say.

Then the talk would turn on the loud wheel of present day. I could talk that kind of talk, too, but it went against the grain of my soul. So that when I talked everyday talk I was the most vulgar man in the company.

This man's house was quite close to my own. I was lucky, for had it been miles distant I should have gone there to read the books, and more than that to unload myself of my poetic whimsies. There were so few to whom I could talk.

He gave me the works of Pope. In this edition the poet was given as Mr. Pope. I liked Pope. His essays on Man and on Criticism were good strong truths in rhyme. At the cross-roads on Sunday afternoon I recited with enthusiasm to a crowd of farm-folk.

> 'Of all the causes which conspire to blind
> Man's erring judgment and misguide the mind,
> What the weak head with strongest bias rules
> Is pride, the never-failing vice of fools.'

My hearers understood and appreciated this. Some of them were very eager for knowledge. We might have had some very metaphysical debates if there were not always in the crowd one of those ridicule-making fellows whom poor Ireland still continues to produce.

My sister was attending the convent school. She had many books dealing with the craft of verse.

*Intermediate Poetry and Prose*, by Father Corcoran, D. Litt., was one I remember. I thumb-marked that book. I studied iambics, trochees, rhyme, and stanza. I counted the feet in the verses I read. I tried to write verse myself, but the number of feet per line varied to break my heart. Once I wrote a complete poem and sent it to a weekly paper which had a Poet's Corner. I was in wonderful humour the next week when I saw my initials among the list of those whose poems had been rejected. It was recognition. I never imagined that the editor would as much as recognise that my writing was verse, even for the waste-paper basket. I was getting on.

I made a lot of ballads. I sang them at dances, and part of one at a wake. I remember at the wake how I had just the first verse sung when the Rosary broke out in the room of the corpse.

> 'Thou, O Lord, wilt open my lips
> And my tongue shall announce Thy praise.'

We all dropped on our knees.

Some of the girls at the dances got romantic about me. I really believe that one of them fell in love with me. The boys laughed at my songs, though not all. Some of them said I 'was the makings of a very good comic.'

My first song celebrated the drinking of a half-barrel of stout. I remember four lines.

> Farrelly fell over the barrow
> At the gable-end of the house
> And the singing and ructions were awful
> Around the half-barrel of stout.

To relations in America I wrote letters in rhyme. 'I see you have a new Tom Moore,' one of the Yankees wrote to my father.

As I wandered about the roads and fields I composed my verses. I was spreading dung in drills for turnips in a field belonging to Red Pat. Red Pat was not at home. I was alone. I got my tea in the field. Sitting beside a heap of steaming dung I drank the tea and afterwards felt in great poetic form. I had lately been reading of a poet who made a poem about a telegraph pole. I started making a poem on an old wooden gate which guarded a field I knew. For every drill of dung I spread I made a line of verse. I kept adding to the poem till it was of grand size. I sent it to the editor of the local paper. The next week my poem appeared.

> ADDRESS TO AN OLD WOODEN GATE
> Battered by time and weather, scarcely fit
> For firewood. There's not a single bit
> Of paint to hide those wrinkles, and such scringes
> Tear hoarsely down the silence—rusty hinges.
> A barbed-wire clasp around one withered arm
> Replaces the old latch with wanton charm.
> This gap ere long must find another sentry
> If the cows are not to roam the open country.

There was a whole column of similar quality. I cannot remember the rest. It wasn't too bad. The readers of the paper didn't like it. They wanted sentimental verse about the gallant sons of Erin or something like that.

Everyone who had an old wooden gate—and that was half the parish—claimed that it was their gate I had slandered.

I sent some verse to the Poet's Corner of a Dublin paper. It was published. Part of the rules of the Corner was that the author's address as well as name must be at the bottom of each poem. This rule left the poets open to a lot of fan-mail. I got books of tickets to sell for charitable purposes. From priests and nuns these tickets came.

An Irish woman in Wigan, England, wrote asking if I would do some research into her family history for her. Her mother's people were natives of Monaghan, she said, and she would love to know if there were any of the name in the place now.

A fellow wrote to me from Chicago:

DEAR FRIEND,
I read your poem entitled 'A Memory' in the Irish paper. I have never found this sense in writing before.
The weather here is very bad for the past two weeks, but I think we will have a dry spell soon.
Wishing you great success in your writing,
I remain,
Yours sincerely,
HARRY J. MILLIN.

I replied to this letter. Then my distant admirer began to flood me with letters and piles of comic papers. Some days I got half a dozen letters from him. He sent me a Sunday-school paper in which he had inserted an advertisement in praise of me. It was a double-column advertisement about six inches square:

GREETINGS:
FROM HARRY J. MILLIN TO PATRICK KAVANAGH,
POET, IRELAND.

It was headed thus in heavy black type. There was a lot of small print which said big things about my poetic genius. I was suffering from chronic poverty at this time and I wrote to H. J. M. for money. I had hopes that he might be a mad millionaire. He replied:

DEAR FRIEND,
This is the first letter of this description I have ever received. I can only afford to send you one dollar. I am only a poor lift-man in a hotel at fifteen dollars a week.
Yours sincerely,
H. J. M.

I lost contact with him shortly afterwards.

Verse-writing was getting a grip on me. It grew unawares like an insidious disease. But I wasn't satisfied. There was something dead and rotten about the verse-world in which I moved.

Of Yeats I had not heard. Not one of the contributors to our Corner had heard of him either. Yeats, A. E., Colum, Stephens, and all that crowd, if their names ever came through the dense wall of prejudice to us, would have been just a gang of evil men who were out for a destruction of the Catholic Faith. No nun or priest would send books of lottery tickets to such men.

We were very pious poets. Many of the poems in the Corner were religious. The Blessed Virgin, Saint Patrick, Saint Bridget, the Sacred Heart, and others of lesser nimbus power provided themes for our verse. From Brian Boru to Dan O'Connell we sang the praises of the saints of Irish Nationalism as well.

We were the biddable children of Kathleen Mavourneen—but for me at least the grey dawn was breaking.

It was the last days of August, nineteen twenty-seven. We had grass-seed for sale. I had cut the hay with a scythe and scutched in on the bottom of a tub. It yielded me four bags, which I had sieved and winnowed in the breeze and sun. I was proud of my grass-seed—it was white and clean. My father, who was in his second childhood then, seemed as proud of me as I was of the grass-seed. Second childhood is like that.

'Ye'll be takin' it to Dundalk,' he said.

'Tomorrow,' I answered.

Selling the grass-seed was my special prerogative. I could do as I liked with myself and the money.

A man passing looked at the seed. 'Very dirty,' he said, 'a lot of hair-grass in it.'

This after all my sieving.

I went to get the loan of Carr's ass on the evening of Sunday—the market was next day. The ass was already promised.

'The "Charger" has him,' I was informed. 'Charger' was the nickname of a neighbour.

'Get Maggy Quigley's ass,' they advised me; 'he's a very good stepper.'

Maggy lived up a long lane. Her ass was an old creature and the cart was still older. 'It's a danger to be safe in Maggy's cart,' people used to say.

'We don't lend the ass to anybody,' she stated when I declared my business. She waited till the importance of the ass and cart should have time to sink into my mind. 'But on account of who ye are we'll let ye have Darby.'

The ass was lying before Maggy's door with his two forepaws stretched out in front and his eyes closed. He wasn't a promising beast to drive to Dundalk.

'Do ye see that pole there?' Maggy said, pointing out to me a long pole laid across the gap in the stone ditch. 'If Darby gets an aisy day he jumps that pole during the night, but if he's abused he lies out there on the rock.'

I promised to treat Darby well.

It was considered a good-stepping horse could make Dundalk from our district in two and a half hours. I left at five o'clock in the morning as I calculated getting in around nine. I over-rated Darby's powers; he was nearly as bad as the ass of the song:

> With blood-stained powers
> It took him two hours
> To travel each mile of the road.

Darby wasn't just as bad as that, though he was bad enough.

Sitting on top of my four bags of grass seed, I jogged down the Mucker Road between the tall poplars at a pretty speed. I had given the ass two full porringers of oats, a temporary rejuvenation to his old blood. He cocked his ears and swayed pleasantly between the shafts. It must have been an early harvest that year for much of the corn was gathered, and in one or two haggards the threshing mills were set up.

The morning was chill, still, and the crevices of the land were grey. There were two stars in the western sky. When I turned eastwards for Dundalk, leaving the poplar-lined road, the dawn was before me, a grey dawn breaking above the Irish Sea, and in my mind a grey passionate dawn was breaking too. I was becoming aware of new beauty.

For the first two miles Darby travelled on the steam of the oats. Then the weariness of age returned to his bones. It took him half an hour to climb Mahera Hill. I got down and pushed at the tail board.

'Foolish fella,' a man who was yoking a horse to a cart said when he saw me. 'Don't ye know,' he explained, 'that the more you push the less the ass will pull?' I might have known, for I had wide experience of the ass-temperament. The man who spoke was getting ready for the market himself.

'How's the time going?' I inquired.

'It's hittin' round half-six,' he said, 'but ye'll have lavings of time.'

Darby trotted down the hills passing out horse-carts drawn by hairy-legged Clydesdales. Short and sweet like an ass's gallop, is a good saying: the hairy-legged Clydesdales recovered the lost ground and passed out of our sight on the top of the next hill.

The sun was up before I got to the town. A double row of carts laden with grass-seed was queued up in Park Street. I tried to get in before a woman who was holding an ass by the head. She looked quiet enough but was far from it as I soon found out.

'Ye brat,' she sort of squealed, 'is it tryin' to knock dacent people outa their turn ye are? People that's after losin' a night's sleep.'

'I have only the bare four bags,' I pleaded.

'Four or twenty-four, it's all the same to me,' and she pulled on the rein to narrow the gap between her and the cart in front. There was nothing for it but go to the end of the row and learn patience.

The rows of carts moved very slowly towards the market crane because of late arrivals, whom well-wishers were letting cut in further up. Around me people were complaining. 'It's a damn shame, that's what it is.'

I strongly supported the speaker. 'It's all that,' I said, 'and a good deal more.'

There was a lot of talk about politics, and right behind me two young men were confabing about last night's dance.

'I think I could go with her if I went all-out.'

'I think you might.'

'I seen Tom on the job again.'

'Aye, the oul' clown, some people wouldn't know when they were insulted. Paddy Kirk tried his hardest for Josie Duffy and he might as well be idle.'

'No go for Paddy.'

I came opposite a newsagent's shop, and was glad. 'Keep an eye on that ass,' I told the fellow before me.

Searching among the papers on the counter I came across a periodical dated a few weeks back. 'What kind of a paper is this?' I asked the newsagent.

'Something like *John Bull*,' he said.

It was the *Irish Statesman*. Returning to my ass I opened the paper and read.

The first thing my eye fell upon was a review of a book by Gertrude Stein. I read a quotation and found it like a foreign language, partly illuminated by the Holy Spirit. There was mention of a man called Joyce. I was a little surprised to find that his Christian name was James and not P. W. or Robert Dwyer. P. W. Joyce had written a History of Ireland which I had read at school and his brother Robert Dwyer Joyce, whom I knew from a song of his—three lines of which I remember:

> Where the stream leaps down
> From the moorland brown
> And all on a May-day morning.

'Any stir on the paper?' a fellow asked me.

'Plenty,' I replied. 'Gertrude Stein is after writing a new book.'

'Quit the coddin'. How's the markets goin'? My sowl, this looks like a bad pit to-day.'

> They shall sink under water
> They shall rise up again,
> They shall be peopled
> By myriads of men.
> Paris and Babel
> London and Tyre
> Re-born from the darkness
> Shall sparkle like fire.

I didn't understand AE's poem except, in a vague way, the last line: 'Shall sparkle like fire.' Later I heard from AE himself that that poem had a commonsensical meaning, but for me on that August morning in Dundalk Grass-seed Market it had a meaning and a message that had come from hills of the imagination far beyond the flat fields of common-sense.

On that day the saints of Ireland, political and theological, lost a strong supporter. I never wrote for the holy poets again. How I fared with my four bags of grass-seed hardly matters. Sufficient to say I sold it, afterwards visited an eating-house, viewed the sights of the town from the gaol to the distillery chimney and down to the quays, bought a packet of cigarettes, yoked Darby to the cart and gave him his head. How long it took us to get home I do not know, for I was wandering among the hills of a timeless world. It was an Eden time and Eve not violated. Men were not subject to death. I was happy.

> Paris and Babel
> London and Tyre
> Re-born from the darkness
> Shall sparkle like fire. . . .
> Faery shall dance in
> The streets of the town
> And from sky headlands
> The gods looking down.

MARGARET BARRINGTON

# Village Without Men[1]

WEARY AND DISTRAUGHT the women listened to the storm as it raged around the houses. The wind screamed and howled. It drove suddenly against the doors with heavy lurchings. It tore at the straw ropes which anchored the thatched roofs to the ground. It rattled and shook the small windows. It sent the rain in narrow streams under the door, through the piled-up sacks, to form large puddles on the hard stamped earthen floors.

At times when the wind dropped for a moment to a low whistling whisper and nothing could be heard but the hammering of the sea against the face of Cahir Roe, the sudden release would be intolerable. Then one or another would raise her head and break into a prayer, stumbling words of supplication without continuity or meaning. Just for a moment a voice would be heard. Then the screaming wind would rise again in fury, roaring in the chimney and straining the roof-ropes, the voice would sink to a murmur and then to nothing as the women crouched again over the smouldering sods, never believing for a moment in the miracle they prayed for.

Dawn broke and the wind dropped for a while. The women wrapped their shawls tightly round them, knotted the ends behind them and tightened their headcloths. They slipped out through cautiously opened doors. The wind whipped their wide skirts so tightly to their bodies it was hard to move. They muttered to themselves as they clambered over the rocks or waded through the pools down to the foaming sea.

To the right Cahir Roe sloped upward, smothered in storm clouds, protecting the village from the outer sea. The ears of the women rang with the thunder of the ocean against its giant face. Salt foam flecked their faces, their clothes, as they struggled along in knots of three or four, their heads turned from the wind as they searched the shore and looked out over the rolling water. But in all that grey-green expanse of churning sea, nothing. Not even an oar. All day long they wandered.

It was not until the turn of the tide on the second day that the bodies began to roll in, one now, another again, over and over in

---

[1] From *They Go, The Irish: A Miscellany of War-time Writing*, compiled by Leslie Daiken, London, 1944.

the water like dark, heavy logs. Now a face showed, now an outstretched hand rose clear of the water. John Boyle's face had been smashed on the rocks, yet his wife knew him as an incoming wave lifted his tall lean body to hurl it to shore.

For two days the women wandered until the ocean, now grown oily but still sullen with anger, gave up no more. Niel Boylan, Charley Friel and Dan Gallagher were never found.

The women rowed across the bay to the little town of Clonmullen for the priest. After the heavy rain the road across the bog was dangerous, and the village was cut off by land. The young curate, Father Twomey, came across. When he looked at the grey haggard faces of these women, all words of comfort deserted the young priest. His throat went dry and his eyes stung as if the salt sea had caught them. What comfort could words bring to women in their plight? He could with greater ease pray for the souls of the drowned than encourage the living to bear their sorrow in patience.

The women had opened the shallow graves in the sandy graveyard. They lowered the bodies and shovelled back the sand. Then for headstones, to mark the place where each man was laid before the restless sand should blot out every sign, they drove an oar which he had handled into each man's grave and dropped a stone there for every prayer they said. The wind blew the sand into the priest's vestments, into his shoes, into his well-oiled hair and into his book. It whirled the sand around the little heaps of stones.

As the women rowed him home across the bay, the priest looked back at the village. The oars in the graves stood out against the stormy winter sky like the masts of ships in harbour.

The midwife was the first to leave the village.

As they brought each dead man up from the sea, she stripped him and washed his body. For most of them she had done this first service. From early youth, first with her mother, then alone, she had plied her trade on this desolate spit of land. These same bodies which once warm, soft, tender and full of life, had struggled between her strong hands, now lay cold and rigid beneath them. She washed the cold sea-water from these limbs from which she had once washed the birth-slime. Silently she accomplished her task and retired to her cottage. Of what use was a midwife in a village without men?

She wrote to her married daughter in Letterkenny who replied that there was work in plenty for her there. Then two weeks later when the hard frosts held the bog road, she loaded her goods on a cart and set out for Clonmullen from where she could get the train to Letterkenny. She took with her young Laurence Boyle, John Boyle's fourteen-year-old son, to bring the donkey and cart.

The women watched her go. A few called God-speed but the others, thin-lipped, uttered no word. Silently they went back to their houses and their daily tasks. From now on their bodies would be barren as fields in winter.


All the winter the village lay dumb and still. The stores of potatoes and salt fish were eaten sparingly. The fish might run in the bay now, followed by the screaming sea-gulls, but there were no men to put out the boats or draw in the gleaming nets. The children gathered mussels to feed the hens.

Then in the early spring days, the women rose from their hearths, and tightly knotted their head-cloths and shawls. They took down the wicker creels from the lofts, the men's knives from the mantelshelves and went down to the rocks below Cahir Roe to cut the seawrack for the fields. The children spread it on the earth. Then with fork and spade the women turned the light sandy soil, planted their potatoes, oats and barley. The work was heavy and backbreaking but it had to be done. If they did not work now with all their strength, their children would be crying for food in the coming winter.

Driven, bone-tired, sick at heart, they rose early and worked all day, stopping at midday as their husbands had stopped, to rest in the shelter of a stone wall, to drink some milk or cold tea and to eat some oatbread the children brought to them in the fields. At night they dragged their bodies to bed. There was no joy, no relief to be got there now. Nothing but sleep, the easing of weary muscles.

Their work in the house was neglected. Their hearths went untended, their clothes unwashed. They no longer whitewashed the walls of the cottages or tended the geraniums they grew in pots. They did not notice when the flowers died.

The next to leave the village was Sally Boyle. She was to have married young Dan Gallagher after the next Lent. There at the end of the straggling village was the half-built ruin of the house he had been getting ready with the help of the other men in the village. All winter she moped over the fire, only rousing herself when her mother's voice rose sharp and angry. Now in the spring she began to wander about restlessly. She would leave her work and climb the great headland of Cahir Roe, there to look out to where Tory rose like a fortress from the sea—out there across the sea in which Dan Gallagher had been drowned, the sea which had refused to surrender what should have been hers. At night in bed she could not control the wildness of her body. She pitched from side to side, moaning and muttering. Her whole mind was darkened by the memory of soft kisses on warm autumn nights, of strong hands fondling her. She felt bereft, denied.

She slipped away one day and joined the lads and lasses in Clonmullen who were off to the hiring fair at Strabane. Later her mother got a letter and a postal order for five shillings. Sally was now hired girl on a farm down in the Lagan.

Then in ones and twos the young girls began to leave. With the coming of spring their eyes brightened, their steps grew lighter. They would stop and look over their shoulders hurriedly, as if someone were behind. They would rush violently to work and then leave their tasks unfinished to stand and look out over the landscape, or out to sea from under a sheltering hand. They became irritable, quarrelsome and penitent by turns. Somewhere out there across the bog, across the sea, lay a world where men waited; men who could marry them, love them perhaps, give them homes and children.

The women objected to their going and pleaded with them. Every hand was needed now. The turf must be cut in the bog, turned and stacked for the coming winter. Surely they could go when the crops were gathered in. But tears and pleading were in vain. Nature fought against kindness in their young bodies. Here no men were left to promise these girls life, even the hazardous life of this country. They gathered their few garments together and departed, promising to send back what money they could. But their mothers knew that it was not to get money they left. It was the blood in their veins which drove them forth. And though the women lamented, they understood.

No use now to give a dance for the departing girls. There were no men with whom they could dance. No use to gather the neighbours into the house to sing. The voices of women are thin and shrill without men's voices to balance them.

Larry Boyle found himself the only lad in the village. The other boys were many years younger and those who were older had been lost with their fathers in the storm. The winter gloom, the silence of the women and his loneliness drove him to day-dreaming, to the creation of a fantasy world. He saw himself, in coming years, stronger and taller than any man, towering over humanity as Cahir Roe towered over the sea, impregnable, aloof. Boats, fields, cattle, houses, everything in the village would belong to him. For as yet the outside world meant nothing to him and women had no power over his dreams. They existed but to serve him.

At first the women paid no more attention to him than they did to the other children. He ate what food was set before him—some potatoes, a piece of dried fish, a bowl of buttermilk. He performed such tasks as were set him, helping with the few cows, carrying the sea-wrack, heeling the turf. Indeed, he was rather despised than otherwise for the girls of his age were more nimble and less absent-minded than he.

But slowly, as if in answer to his dreams, his position changed. In every house he entered he was welcomed and given the seat by the fire. He was never allowed to depart without food and drink. The older women baked and cooked for him, kept the best for him, gave him small presents from their hoard; a husband's knife; a son's trousers. They began to compliment him at every turn on his strength and growth. No one asked him to work.

Now he allowed his hair to grow like a man's. The stubby quiff vanished and a crop of thick, fair curls crowned his forehead, giving him the obstinate look of a fierce young man. He became particular about the cleanliness of his shirt, refused to wear old patched trousers and coat. Gradually he dominated the whole village. Even the dogs owned him sole master, and snarled savagely at one another when he called them to heel. The younger boys were his slaves, to fetch and carry for him. He scarcely noticed the girls of his own age, never called them by name, never spoke directly to them. Unlike them, he had no wish to leave the village.

A day came when Larry Boyle went from house to house and collected the fishing lines, hooks and spinners which had belonged to the drowned men. They were granted him as if by right. He took them to the rock behind the village where formerly the fish had been dried and where the men had then met in the summer evenings to talk, away from their women folk. It was a day of shifting sun and shadow and the wind from the west broken by the headland.

He sang as he carefully tested, cut and spliced each line. He rubbed the hooks and spinners clean of rust with wet sand from the stream. He made a long line, tested each length and wound it in a coil between hand and elbow. He fastened the hooks and the lead weight. Then, satisfied, he went down to the shore to dig bait.

He swung his can of bait over his shoulder, picked up his line and made for Cahir Roe. He was going to fish for rock fish.

A deep shelf ran round part of the headland and from this the men had fished in the drowsy heat of summer days when they could spare time from the fields. He clambered along the shelf and stood on the edge. The sea heaved and foamed beneath him. Far out, Tory rose, a castle against the white line of the horizon.

He fixed his bait carefully and placed the loose end of the line beneath his heel. Then, clear of the beetling rock behind, he swung the coil of line above his head and threw it far out. His body, balanced over the edge, seemed to follow it as his eye watched the untwisting of the cord, the drop of the lead towards the sea. He bent down and gathered up the end.

He could feel the movement as the length of line ran through the sea and the weight sank slowly through the heavy water. His hand knew what was happening down there beneath the surface of the water. He felt the lead strike the bottom. His fingers, born to a new delicacy, held the line firmly so that the bait should float free. He could feel the gentle nibbling of the fish at the bait, nibbling cautiously, daintily as sheep nibble grass. Twice he drew in his line to re-bait the hook. Then one struck.

Excited, breathing heavily, his eyes distended, he drew in the line slowly, letting it fall in careful coils at his feet. Then the fish left the water and the full weight hung on the line. It plunged about madly in the air, twisting and flapping. The cord rubbed against the edge of the shelf as it passed from hand to hand, dislodging small stones and dirt from the crumbling surface. He had to lean out to jerk the fish over the edge, at that moment unaware of everything but the twisting, flapping fish. He threw it well behind him so that it could not leap back into the water. It lay there, twisting and turning, its brilliant orange and green colouring coming and going, its belly heaving, its panting gills shining red. Then it lay still and from its open mouth the brick-red blood flowed over the stones. Another leap, another twitch. It was dead.

Larry passed the back of his hand across his forehead to wipe away the sweat. Before he stooped to disengage the hook from the jaws of the fish, he looked around him, at Tory on the far horizon, at the towering cliff above, the heaving sea beneath. For a moment his head reeled as he felt the turning of the world.


The women liked the new schoolmistress. They liked her modesty and reserve. Though young, she knew how to keep the children in order, teach them their lessons and their manners. They looked after her with approval when they saw her walk precisely from the school to the cottage where she lived, her hands stiffly by her sides, her eyes lowered. They admired her round, rosy face, her light hair, her neat figure. She appeared so young and lovely to these women whose bodies were lean and tired from hard work and poor food.

She never stopped at the half-door for a chat, nor delayed for a moment to pass the time of day with a neighbour on the road. She never played with the younger children. She walked around encased in herself.

Every Saturday while the road held, she would mount her clean, well-oiled bicycle and cycle to Clonmullen. On the way she did not speak to anyone nor answer a greeting. With gaze fixed on the road before her, she pedaled furiously. In Clonmullen she would make one or two purchases, post her letters and cycle back home. All attempts at conversation were firmly repulsed. She did not even stop to have tea at the hotel.

She lived alone in a small cottage built on the rise of ground just beyond the village. For an hour at a time she would kneel in the shelter of the fuchsia hedge and gaze hungrily at the houses she did not wish to enter, at the women to whom she did not care to speak. She knew all their comings and goings, all the details of their daily life. She watched them at their work, in their conversation. She watched the children at play. She watched Larry Boyle as he wandered along the shore towards Cahir Roe to fish, or passed her cottage on his way to set rabbit snares in the burrows.

The July heat beat down on the earth and the blue-grey sea moved sleepily under a mist. He was returning home when he saw her, standing in the shelter of the bushes that grew over the gateway. She was looking at him with fierce intentness. He stood still and gazed back, his eyes wide and startled. The fear of unknown lands, of uncharted seas took hold of him. His mouth dropped open, his skin twitched. His throat hurt and there was a hammering in his ears like the heavy pounding of the surf on Cahir Roe. He could not move hand nor foot. With a sudden movement her hand darted out and caught his wrist. She drew him towards her, in the shelter of the thick fuchsia hedge. Frightened by her intent stare, her pale face, her quick uneven breathing, when she put out her other hand to fondle him, he pulled away and burst through the bushes. Quietly, with lowered eyes, she listened as his boots clattered over the rocky road. She sighed and turned back into her house.

The first time he ran away. But he came back. Furtively. He would steal into her kitchen when she was at school and leave some offering; a freshly caught fish, a rabbit, some rock pigeon's eggs. He had so little to give.

She did not seem to notice. She did not stop him to thank him when they met. She passed without even a greeting, once again encased in her rigid calm. Then one evening, as darkness fell, he lifted the latch of her door. She was seated on her hearthrug, gazing at the glowing turf fire. He approached in silent desperation and with the same wild desperation she answered.

Such happenings do not long remain hidden in a small world. Without a word spoken the women came to know. Primitive anger seized hold on them. They said nothing to Larry. Their belief in man's place in life and the fact that they had denied him nothing, shut their mouths. All their rage turned against the young teacher whom they had thought so modest and gentle. They became as fierce as hawks at the theft of their darling.

They ceased work. They came together in groups, muttering. They buzzed like angry bees. Their lips spoke words to which their ears were long unaccustomed as they worked themselves into an ancient battle fury. They smoothed their hair back from their foreheads with damp and trembling hands. They drew their small shawls tightly round their shoulders.

From behind the fuchsia hedge the girl saw them coming like a flock of angry crows. Their wide dark skirts, caught by the light summer breeze, billowed out behind them. Their long, thin arms waved over their heads like sticks in the air. Their voices raised in some primitive battle cry, they surged up the road towards her.

Terrified of this living tidal wave, she rushed out. Her eyes dimmed with terror, her limbs shook. The uneven road caught her feet. It seemed to her that she made no headway as she ran, that the surging mass of women came ever nearer. Stones rattled at her heels. She ran on in blind panic, unaware of where she was going. Her chest began to ache, her throat to burn. A stone caught her shoulder but she scarcely felt the blow. Then another hit her on the back and she stumbled. Still she ran on, not daring to look back. A stone struck her head. She reeled and fell. Over the edge of the narrow bog road, down the bank towards the deep watery ditch. Briars caught her clothes. Her hands grasped wildly at the tufts of rough grass. There she lay, half in, half out of the water, too frightened to move or struggle.

When they saw her fall, the women stopped and stood there in the road, muttering. Then they turned back. They burst into her neat little cottage. They threw the furniture about, broke the delft, hurled the pots out of doors, tore the pretty clothes to ribbons. Then they left, still muttering threats, like the sea after storm.

Later, shivering, aching, sick, the girl dragged herself back on to the road. There was no one there now. The flock of crows had gone. She stood alone on the empty road. There was no sound but the lonely call of a moor bird overhead.

The next day Larry, too, left the village.

The war when it came meant little to these women. The explosions of mines on the rocks could not harm them now that there were no men to risk their lives on the water. The aeroplanes which from time to time circled over the coast seemed to them no more than strange birds, at first matter for wonder and then taken for granted. Sometimes the sea washed up an empty ship's boat, some timbers or empty wooden cases. One morning scores of oranges came dancing in on the waves. The children screamed with delight and not knowing what they were played ball with them. But since the oranges did not bounce they soon tired of them and left them along the shore to rot. The women only realised that the war could touch them when the supplies of Indian meal ran out.

All that winter storms lashed the coast. Snow whirled around the houses, blotting out the sight of the fierce sea which growled savagely against the headland of Cahir Roe day and night. Not once during the bitter months did the snow melt on the mountains beyond Clonmullen. The wind tore at the ropes which tethered the thatched roofs, rotting and grass-grown from neglect. The northeast wind drove under the doors, roared in the chimneys; it hardened the earth until it was like a stone.

Yet now it seemed that the silence was broken, that terrible silence they had kept in mourning for their dead. Now in the evenings they gathered round one another's firesides. They told stories, old Rabelaisian tales heard when they were children from the old men of the village. Such tales as lie deep in the minds of a people and are its true history. Tales of old wars, of great slaughter of men, of the survival of the women and children, of tricks to preserve the race. They told of the Danes and their love of the dark-haired Irishwomen. They laughed quietly and spoke in whispers of the great power of the Norsemen's bodies, of the fertility of their loins.

Over and over again they told the story of the women of Monastir, who, when widowed and alone, lured with false lights a ship to their shore. What matter that their victims were dark-skinned Turks. Their need was great.

The eyes of the women grew large and full of light as they repeated these tales over the dying embers of their fires. A new ferocity appeared in their faces. Their bodies took on a new grace, grew lithe and supple, as the body of the wild goat becomes sleek and lovely in the autumn.

Spring came suddenly. After the weeks of fierce winds and wild seas, followed days of mild breezes and scampering sunshine. The women threw open their doors and stepped out with light hearts. As they cut the sea-wrack for their fields, they called to one another and sang snatches of old songs. Sometimes one or another would stop in her work and look out over the water at the sea-swallows dipping and skimming over the surface of the water, at the black shags as they swam and dived, at old Leatherwing standing in his corner in wait. The older children laughed and shouted as they helped to spread out the wrack on the fields. The younger ones screamed as they ran along the shore and searched under the rocks for crabs. They called and clapped their hands at the sea-pies as they bobbed up and down on the waves.

On and on the children ran, their toes pink in the sea-water. They chattered together like pies over each fresh discovery. They travelled along the shore until they found themselves out on the point of land beside Cahir Roe, facing the open sea. There they stood and looked out to sea from under sheltering hands.

For some minutes they stood and stared. Then in a body they turned and ran towards the women, shouting all together that out there, coming in closer every minute, was a strange boat.

The women straightened their backs and listened. Even before they understood what the children were shouting, they let down their petticoats and started for the point. There they stood in a group and stared, amazed that a boat should put in on that inhospitable shore. Close in now, with flapping sail, the boat came.

They could make out only one man and their eyes, used to long searching over the water, could see that he was lying across the tiller. Was he alive or dead? Could he not see where he was going? If he did not change his course now he would fetch up on the reef below Cahir Roe. They rushed forward to the water's edge and shouted. The man bent over the tiller did not move. They continued to shout. They waded into the sea until the water surged against their bodies and threatened to overbalance them. Their dark skirts swirled round them in the heavy sea as they shouted and waved their arms.

Then the man at the tiller slowly raised his head. He looked around him, at the sea, at the screaming women, at the great red granite face of Cahir Roe. With great effort he pulled his body upright and swung the tiller over. Then he fell forward again. Even before the keel had grounded on the gravel the women had seized the boat and dragged it up on to the beach.

Six men lay huddled in the bottom of the boat. Great strong men, now helpless. The women turned to the helmsman. He looked at them with dull, sunken eyes. He moved. He tried to speak. His grey face was stiff, his lips cracked.

'Scotland?' he asked and his voice was hoarse.

The women shook their heads. Then the man slowly lifted one hand, pointed to the men at his feet and then to himself.

'Danes. Torpedoed. Ten days.'

The women cried aloud as they lifted the heavy bodies of the men. Their voices sang out in wild exultation:

The Danes. The Danes were come again.

MYLES na gCOPALEEN

# Drink and Time in Dublin[1]

A RECORDED STATEMENT

—Did you go to that picture 'The Lost Weekend'?
—*I did.*
—I never seen such tripe.
—*What was wrong with it?*
—O it was all right, of course—bits of it was good. Your man in the jigs inside in the bed and the bat flying in to kill the mouse, that was *damn* good. I'll tell you another good bit. Hiding the bottles in the jax. And there was no monkey business about that because I tried it since meself. It works but you have to use the half pint bottles. Up the chimbley is another place I thought of and do you know the ledge affair above windows?
—*I do.*
—That's another place but you could get a hell of a fall reaching up there on a ladder or standing on chairs with big books on them. And of course you can always tie the small bottles to the underneath of your mattress.
—*I suppose you can.*
—But what are you to do with the empties if you stop in bed drinking? There's a snag there. I often thought they should have malt in lemonade syphons.
—*Why didn't you like the rest of 'The Lost Weekend'?*
—Sure haven't I been through far worse weekends meself—you know that as well as I do. Sure Lord save us I could tell you yarns. I'd be a rich man if I had a shilling for every morning I was down in the markets at seven o'clock[2] in the slippers with the trousers pulled on over the pyjamas and the overcoat buttoned up to the neck in the middle of the summer. Sure don't be talking man.
—*I suppose the markets are very congested in the mornings?*
—With drunks? I don't know. I never looked round any time I was there.
—*When were you last there?*
—The time the wife went down to Cork last November. I won't

---

[1] From *Irish Writing*, Cork, No. 1, 1946.
[2] The public houses near the Dublin Cattle Market are permitted to open at 7 A.M. instead of 10:30 A.M. for the convenience of the cattle men.

forget that business in a hurry. That was a scatter and a half. Did I never tell you about that? O be God, don't get me on to *that* affair.

—*Was it the worst ever?*

—It was and it wasn't but I got the fright of me life. I'll tell you a damn good one. You won't believe this but it's a true bill. This is one of the best you ever heard.

—*I'll believe anything you say.*

—In the morning I brought the wife down to Kingsbridge in a taxi. I wasn't thinking of drink at all, hadn't touched it for four months, but when I paid the taxi off at the station instead of going back in it, the wife gave me a look. Said nothing, of course—after the last row I was for keeping off the beer for a year. But somehow she put the thing into me head. This was about nine o'clock, I suppose. I'll give you three guesses where I found meself at ten past nine *in another taxi?*

—*Where?*

—Above in the markets. And there wasn't a more surprised man than meself. Of course in a way it's a good thing to start at it early in the morning because with no food and all the rest of it you're finished at four o'clock and you're home again and stuffed in bed. It's the late nights that's the killer, two and three in the morning, getting poisoned in shebeens and all classes of hooky stuff, wrong change, and a taxi man on the touch. After nights like that it's a strong man that'll be up at the markets in time next morning.

—*What happened after the day you got back at four?*

—Up at the markets next morning *before* they were open. There was another chap there but I didn't look at him. I couldn't tell you what age he was or how bad he was. There was no four o'clock stuff that day. I was around the markets till twelve or so. Then off up town and I have meself shaved be a barber. Then up to a certain hotel and straight into the bar. There's a whole crowd there that I know. What are you going to have and so on. No no, have a large one. So-and-so's getting married on Tuesday. Me other man's wife has had a baby. You know the stuff? Well Lord save us I had a terrible tank of malt in me that day! I had a feed in the middle of it because I remember scalding myself with hot coffee and I never touch the coffee at all only after a feed. Of course I don't remember what happened me but I was in the flat the next morning with the clothes half off. I was supposed to be staying with the brother-in-law, of course, when the wife was away. But sure it's the old dog for the hard road. Drunk or sober I went back to me own place. As a matter of fact I never went near the brother-in-law at all. Be this time I was well into the malt. Out with me again feeling like death on wires and I'm inside in the local curing meself for hours, spilling stuff all over the place with the shake in the hand. Then into the barber's and after that off up again to the hotel for more malt. I'll give you a tip. Always drink in hotels. If you're in there you're in for a feed, or you've just had a feed, or you've an appointment there to see a fellow, and you're having a small one to pass the time. It looks very bad being in bars during the daytime. It's a thing to watch, that.

—*What happened then?*

—What do you think happened? What could happen? I get meself into a quiet corner and I start lowering them good-o. I don't know what happened me, of course. I met a few pals and there is some business about a greyhound out in Cloghran. It was either being bought or being sold and I go along in the taxi and where we were and where we weren't I couldn't tell you. I fall asleep on a chair in some house in town and next thing I wake up perished with the cold and as sick as I ever was in me life. Next thing I know I'm above in the markets. Taxis everywhere of course, no food only the plate of soup in the hotel, and be this time the cheque-book is in and out of the pocket *three or four times a day,* standing drinks all round, kicking up a barney in the lavatory with other drunks, looking for me 'rights' when I was refused drink—O, blotto, there's no other word for it. I seen some of the cheques since. *The writing!* A pal carts me home in a taxi. How long this goes on I don't know. I'm all right in the middle of the day but in the mornings I'm nearly too weak to walk and the shakes getting worse every day. Be this time I'm getting frightened of meself. Lookat here, mister-me-man, I say to meself, this'll have to stop. I was afraid the heart might give out, that was the only thing I was afraid of. Then I meet a pal of mine that's a doctor. This is inside in the hotel. There's only one man for you, he says, and that's sleep. Will you go home and go to bed if I get you something that'll make you sleep? Certainly, I said. I suppose this was about four or half four. Very well, says he, I'll write you out a prescription. He writes one out on hotel notepaper. I send for a porter. Go across with this, says I, to the nearest chemist shop and get this stuff for me and here's two bob for yourself. Of course I'm at the whiskey all the time. Your man comes back with a box of long-shaped green pills. You'll want to be careful with that stuff, the doctor says, that stuff's very dangerous. If you take one now and take another when you get home, you'll get a very good sleep but don't take any more till to-morrow night because that stuff's very dangerous. So I take one. But I know the doctor doesn't know how bad I am. I didn't tell him the whole story, no damn fear. So out with me to the jax where I take another one. Then back for a drink, still as wide-awake as a lark. You'll have to go home now, the doctor says, we can't have you passing out here, that stuff acts very quickly. Well, I have one more drink and off with me, *in a bus*, mind you, to the flat. I'm very surprised on the bus to find meself so wide-awake, looking out at people and reading the signs on shops. Then I begin to get afraid that the stuff is too weak and that I'll be lying awake for the rest of the evening and all night. To hell with it, I say to meself, we'll chance two more and let that be the end of it. Down went two more in the bus. I get there and into the flat. I'm still wide-awake and nothing will do me only one more pill for luck. I get into bed. I don't remember putting the head on the pillow. I wouldn't go out quicker if you hit me over the head with a crow-bar.

—*You probably took a dangerous over-dose.*

—Next thing I know I'm awake. It's dark. I sit up. There's matches there and I strike one. I look at the watch. The watch is stopped. I get up and look at the clock. Of course the clock is stopped, hasn't been wound for days. I don't know what time it is. I'm a bit upset about this. I turn on the wireless. It takes about a year to heat up and would you believe me I try a dozen stations all over the place and not one of them is telling what the time is. Of course I knew there was no point in trying American stations. I'm very disappointed because I sort of expected a voice to say 'It is now seven thirty p.m.' or whatever the time was. I turn off the wireless and begin to wonder. I don't know what time it is. *Then*, bedamnit, another thing strikes me. *What day is it?* How long have I been asleep with that dose? Well lookat, I got a hell of a fright when I found I didn't know what day it was. I got one hell of a fright.

—*Was there not an accumulation of milk-bottles or newspapers?*

—There wasn't—all that was stopped because I was supposed to be staying with the brother-in-law. What do I do? On with all the clothes and out to find what time it is and what day it is. The funny thing is that I'm not feeling too bad. Off with me down the street. There's lights showing in the houses. That means it's night-time and not early in the morning. Then I see a bus. That means it's not yet half-nine, because they stopped at half-nine that time. Then I see a clock. It's twenty past nine! But I still don't know what day it is and it's too late to buy an evening paper. There's only one thing—into a pub and get a look at one. So I march into the nearest, very quiet and correct and say a bottle of stout please. All the other customers look very sober and I think they are all talking very low. When the man brings me the bottle I say to him I beg your pardon but I had a few bob on a horse today, could you give me a look at an evening paper? The man looks at me and says what horse was it? It was like a blow in the face to me, that question! I can't answer at all at first and then I stutter something about Hartigan's horses. None of them horses won a race today, the man says, and there was a paper here but it's gone. So I drink up the bottle and march out. It's funny, finding out about the day. You can't stop a man in the street and say have you got the right day please? God knows what would happen if you done that. I know be now that it's no use telling lies about horses, so in with me to another pub, order a bottle and ask the man has he got an evening paper. The missus has it upstairs, he says, there's nothing on it anyway. I now begin to think the best thing is to dial O on the phone, ask for Inquiries and find out that way. I'm on me way to a call-box when I begin to think that's a very bad idea. The girl might say hold on and I'll find out, I hang on there like a mug and next thing the box is surrounded by Guards and ambulances and attendants with ropes. No fear, says I to meself, there's going to be no work on the phone for me! Into another pub. I have the wind up now and no mistake. How long was I knocked out be the drugs? A day? Two days? Was I in the bed *for a week?* Suddenly I see a sight that gladdens me heart. Away down at the end of the pub there's an oul' fellow reading an evening paper with a magnifying glass. I take a mouthful of stout, steady meself, and march down to him. Me mind is made up: if he doesn't hand over the paper, I'll kill him. Down I go. Excuse me, says I, snatching the paper away from him and he still keeps looking through the glass with no paper there, I think he was deaf as well as half blind. Then I read the date—I suppose it was the first time the date was the big news on a paper. It says 'Thursday, 22nd November, 1945.' I never enjoyed a bit of news so much. I hand back the paper and says thanks very much, sir, for the loan of your paper. Then I go back to finish me stout, very happy and pleased with me own cuteness. Another man, I say to meself, would ask people, make a show of himself and maybe get locked up. But not me. I'm smart. Then begob I nearly choked.

—*What was the cause of that?*

—To-day is Thursday, I say to meself. Fair enough. But *what . . . day did I go to bed?* What's the use of knowing to-day's Thursday if I don't know when I went to bed? I still don't know whether I've been asleep for a day or a week! I nearly fell down on the floor. I am back where I started. Only I am feeling weaker and be now I have the wind up in gales. The heart begins to knock so loud that I'm afraid the man behind the counter will hear it and order me out.

—*What did you do?*

—Lookat here, me friend, I say to meself, take it easy. Go back now to the flat and take it easy for a while. This'll all end up all right, everything comes right in the latter end. Worse than this happened many's a man. And back to the flat I go. I collapse down into a chair with the hat still on me head, I sink the face down in me hands, and try to think. I'm like that for maybe five minutes. Then, *suddenly*, I know the answer! Without help from papers or clocks or people, I know how long I am there sleeping under the green pills! How did I know? Think that one out! How would *you* know if you were in the same boat?

(Before continuing, readers may wish to accept the sufferer's challenge.)

—*I am thinking.*

—Don't talk to me about calendars or hunger or anything like that. It's no use—you won't guess. You wouldn't think of it in a million years. Look. My face is in my hands—like this. Suddenly I notice the face is smooth. I'm not badly in need of a shave. That means it *must* be the same day I went to bed on! Maybe the stomach or something woke me up for a second or so. If I'd stopped in bed, I was off asleep again in a minute. But I got up to find the time and that's what ruined me! Now do you get it? Because when I went back to bed that night, I didn't waken till the middle of the next day.

—*You asked me how I would have found out how long I had been there after finding that the day was Thursday. I have no guarantee that a person in your condition would not get up and shave in his sleep. There was a better way.*

—There was no other way.

—*There was. If I were in your place I would have looked at the date on the prescription!*

FRANK O'CONNOR

# First Confession[1]

ALL THE TROUBLE began when my grandfather died, and my grandmother—my father's mother—came to live with us. Relations in the one house are a trial at the best of times, but, to make it worse, my grandmother was a real old countrywoman, and quite unsuited to the life in town. She had a fat, wrinkled old face, and, to my mother's indignation, went round the house in bare feet—the boots had her crippled, she said. For dinner she had a jug of porter and a pot of potatoes, with, sometimes, a bit of salt fish, and she poured out the potatoes on the table and ate them slowly, with great enjoyment, using her fingers by way of a fork.

Now, girls are supposed to be fastidious, but I was the one who suffered from that. Nora, my sister, just sucked up to the old woman for the penny she got every Friday out of the old age pension, a thing I could not do. I was too honest; that was my trouble; and when I was playing with Bill Connell, the sergeant-major's son, and saw my grandmother steering up the path with the jug of porter sticking out from beneath her shawl, I was mortified. I made excuses not to let him come into the house, because I could never be sure what she would be up to when we went in.

When my mother was at work, and my grandmother made the dinner I wouldn't even touch it. Nora tried to make me once, but I hid under the table from her, and took the bread-knife with me for safety. Nora let on to be very indignant (she wasn't, of course, but she knew that mother saw through her and sided with father and Gran) and came after me. I lashed out at her with the knife, and after that she left me alone. I stayed there till my mother came in from work, and she made dinner for me; but then my father came home and Nora said in a shocked voice: 'Oh, dadda, do you know what Jackie did at dinner-time?' Then, of course, it all came out, and he gave me a leathering and the mother interfered, and for days after he wouldn't even look at me. God knows, I was heart-scalded!

Then, to crown my misfortunes, I had to make my first confession and communion. It was an old woman called Ryan who prepared us for that. She was about the one age with Gran, only she was well-to-do, lived in a big house on Montenotte, wore a black cloak and

[1] From *Traveller's Samples*, New York. Copyright 1951 by Frank O'Connor.

# FIRST CONFESSION

bonnet, and came every day to the school at three o'clock, when we should have been going home, to talk to us about Hell. She may have mentioned the other place as well, but that could only have been by accident for Hell had the first place in her heart.

She lit a candle and took out a new half-crown and offered it to the first fellow who would hold one finger—only one finger!—in the flame for five minutes by the school clock. I was always very ambitious, and was tempted to volunteer, only as no one else did, I thought it might look greedy. Then she asked were we afraid of holding one finger—only one finger!—in a little bit of candle for five minutes, and not afraid of burning all over in roasting hot furnaces for all eternity. 'All eternity! Just think of that! A whole lifetime goes by, and it's nothing; only a drop in the ocean of your sufferings.' The woman was really interesting about Hell, but I had very little attention to spare from the half-crown which was still on the desk beside her. At the end of the lesson she put it back in her purse. It was a great disappointment in a religious woman like that.

Another day she said she knew a priest who woke one night to find a fellow he didn't recognise leaning over the end of his bed. The priest was a bit frightened—naturally enough—but he asked the fellow what he wanted, and the fellow said in a low, husky voice that he wanted to go to confession. The priest said it was an awkward time and wouldn't it do in the morning? but the other chap said the last time he went to confession there was one sin he kept back because he was ashamed to mention it, and now it was always on his mind. Then the priest knew it was a serious case, because the fellow was after making a bad confession and committing a mortal sin. He got up to dress, and just then the cock crew in the yard outside, and lo and behold! when the priest looked round there was no sign of the fellow at all, only an awful smell like burning timber, and when the priest looked at the bed didn't he see the print of two hands burned in it? That was because the fellow had made a bad confession. This story made a shocking impression on me.

But the worst of all was when she showed us how to examine our consciences. Did we take the name of God in vain? Did we honour our father and our mother? (I asked her did this include grandmothers and she said it did.) Did we love our neighbour as ourselves? Did we covet our neighbour's goods? They seemed to include every blooming thing down to the penny that Nora got on Fridays. I think, between one thing and another, I must have broken all the commandments, all on account of that old woman, and, as far as I could see as long as she was in the house I had no hope of ever doing anything else.

I was scared to death of confession. The day the whole class went I let on to have the toothache, hoping my absence from school wouldn't be noticed, but at three o'clock, just when I was feeling safe, along came a chap with a message from Mrs. Ryan to say I was to go to confession myself and be at the chapel for Communion on Sunday morning. To make it worse, my mother couldn't come with me and sent Nora instead.

Now, that girl had ways of tormenting me that my mother never knew. She held my hand as we went down the hill, smiling and saying how sorry she was for me.

'Oh, God help us!' she said. 'Isn't it a terrible pity you weren't a good boy? Oh, Jackie, my heart bleeds for you! How will you think of all your sins? Do you remember the time you kicked Gran on the shin?'

'Lemme go!' I wailed, trying to drag myself away from her. 'I won't go to confession at all.'

'Sure, you'll have to go, Jackie,' she replied in the same regretful tone. 'Sure, if you didn't the parish priest would be up to the house, looking for you. 'Tisn't, God knows, that I'm not sorry for you! Do you remember the time you tried to kill me with the bread-knife under the table? And the language you used to me? Oh, I don't know what'll he do to you at all. He might send you up to the Bishop.'

I remember thinking that she didn't know the half of what I had to tell, if I did tell it. There is very little about that day that I don't remember—the steep hill down to the church, and the sunlit hillsides at the other side of the river-valley seen between gaps in the houses, like Adam's last glimpse of Paradise.

Then, as she got me down the long flight of steps into the chapel yard and under the big limestone portico Nora suddenly changed her tune.

'There you are!' she said with a yelp of triumph, hurling me from her through the church door. 'And I hope he'll give you the penitential psalms, you dirty little caffler!'

I knew then I was lost. The door with the coloured glass panels swung shut behind me; the sunlight went out and gave place to deep shadow, and the wind whistled outside so that the silence seemed to be frozen and to crackle like ice under my feet as I tiptoed up the aisle. Nora sat in front of me beside the confession box. There were a couple of old women ahead of her, and then a miserable-looking poor devil came and wedged me in at the other side, so that I couldn't escape even if I wanted to. He joined his hands and rolled his eyes in the direction of the roof, muttering aspirations in an anguished tone, and I wondered had he a grandmother too. That, I felt, was the way you'd expect a fellow with a grandmother to behave, but I was worse off than he, for I knew that just like the man in the story, I'd never have the nerve to tell all my sins; that I should make a bad confession and then die in the night and be continually coming back and burning people's furniture.

Nora's turn came, and I heard the sound of something slamming, and then I heard her voice as if butter wouldn't melt in her mouth, and the thing slammed again and it was all over. God, the hypocrisy of women! Her eyes were lowered, her hands were joined on her stomach, and she walked up the aisle to the side-altar as if she was treading on egg-shells. I remembered the devilish malice with which she had tormented me all the way from home, and I wondered if all religious people were like that. It was my turn now. I went in with the fear of damnation in my soul, and the confessional door closed of itself behind me.

It was pitch-black inside. I couldn't see priest or anything else. Then I really began to be frightened. In the darkness it was a matter between God and me, and God had all the odds. He knew what my intentions were even before I started. I had no chance at all. All I had ever been told about confession got mixed up in my mind, and I knelt to one wall and said, 'Bless me, father, for I have sinned; this is my first confession.' I waited for a few minutes but nothing happened, so I tried it on the other wall. Nothing happened there either. He had me spotted all right.

It must have been then that I noticed the shelf at about the one height with my head. It struck me that it was probably the place you were supposed to kneel. Of course, it was on the high side, and not very deep, but by this time I was beyond all rational considerations. Mind you, it took some climbing, but I was always good at that, and I managed to get up all right. The trouble was to stay up. There was just room for my knees, but, apart from a sort of moulding in the outer wall, nothing you could get a grip on. I held on to the moulding and repeated the words a little louder, and this time something happened all right. A slide was slammed back and a man's voice asked after a moment: 'Who's there?'

' 'Tis me, father,' said I, for fear he mightn't see me and go away again. I couldn't see him at all. The place his voice came from was under the moulding, about level with my knees, so I took a good grip of the moulding and swung myself down till I saw the astonished face of a young priest looking up at me. He had to put his head on one side to see me, and I had to put mine on one side to see him, so we were more or less talking to one another upside down. It struck me as a very queer way to hear confessions, but I didn't feel it was my place to criticise.

'Bless me, father, for I have sinned; this is my first confession,' I rattled off, all in one breath, and swung myself down the least shade more to make it easier for him.

'What are you doing up there?' he shouted in an angry voice, and the strain the politeness was putting on my hold of the moulding, and the shock of being addressed in that uncivil way were too much for me. Down I tumbled and hit the door an unmerciful wallop before I found myself on the flat of my back in the middle of the aisle. The priest opened the door of the middle box and came out, pushing the biretta back from his forehead. He looked something terrible. Then Nora came scampering down the aisle from the altar.

'Oh, you dirty little caffler!' she said. 'I might have known you'd do it! I might have known you'd disgrace me! I can't leave you out of my sight for a minute.'

Before I even got to my feet she bent down and gave me a smack across the ear. This reminded me that I was so stunned I had even forgotten to cry, so that people might think I wasn't hurt at all, when, as a matter of fact, I was probably crippled for life.

'What's all this about?' said the priest, getting angrier than ever, and pushing her off me. 'How dare you hit the child like that, you little vixen?'

'But I can't do my penance with him, father,' cried Nora, cocking an outraged eye up at him.

'Well, go on and do it,' he said, giving me a hand up, 'or I'll give you some more to do. . . . Was it coming to confession you were, my poor man?' he asked me.

' 'Twas, father,' said I with a sob.

# FIRST CONFESSION

'Oh,' he said in a respectful tone, 'a big, hefty fellow like you must have terrible sins. Is this your first?'

' 'Tis, father,' said I.

'Worse and worse,' he said, shaking his head gloomily. 'You have the crimes of a lifetime to tell. I don't know will I get rid of you at all today. You'd better sit down here and wait till I'm finished with these old ones. You can see by the looks of them they haven't much to tell.'

'I will so, father,' I said with something approaching joy.

The relief of it was enormous. Nora stuck out her tongue at me behind his back, but I couldn't even be bothered noticing it. I knew from the very moment that man opened his mouth that he was exceptionally intelligent. It only stood to reason that a fellow confessing his sins after seven years would have more to tell than people that went every week. That was what the priest expected, and the rest was only old women and girls and their talk about Hell and the penitential psalms—people with no experience of life. I started to make my examination of conscience, and, barring the things about the grandmother, it didn't seem too bad.

The next time the priest steered me into the confession box himself and left the shutter back the way I'd see him sitting down at the other side with his biretta pulled well down over his eyes.

'Well now,' he said, 'what do they call you?'

'Jackie, father,' said I.

'And what's a-trouble to you, Jackie?' he said.

'Father,' I said, feeling I might as well get it over while I had him in good humour, 'I had it all arranged to kill my grandmother!'

He seemed a bit shaken by that all right, because he didn't say anything for a while.

'My goodness,' he said at last, 'that'd be a shocking thing to do. What put that into your head?'

'Father,' I said, feeling very sorry for myself, 'she's an awful woman.'

'Is she?' he asked. 'What way is she awful?'

'She takes porter, father,' said I, knowing well from the way the mother talked of porter that it must be a mortal sin, and hoping it might make the priest see my point of view.

'Oh, my!' he said.

'And snuff, father,' said I.

'She's a bad case all right, Jackie,' he said.

'And she goes round in her bare feet, father,' said I. 'And she knows I don't like her, and she gives pennies to Nora and none to me, and my da sides with her and beats me, so one night I was so heart-scalded I made up my mind I'd have to kill her.'

'And what would you do with the body?' he asked with great interest.

'I was thinking I could cut it up and carry it away in a barrow I have,' said I.

'Begor, Jackie,' said he, 'do you know, you're a terrible child?'

'I know, father,' said I. (I was thinking the same thing myself.) 'I tried to kill Nora too, with a bread-knife, under the table, only I missed her.'

'Is that the little girl that was beating you just now?' he asked.

' 'Tis, father,' said I.

'Someone will go for her with a bread-knife one day, and he won't miss her,' he said. 'But you must have great courage. There's lots of people I'd like to do the same to, between ourselves, but I'd never have the nerve. Hanging is an awful death.'

'Is it, father?' said I with the deepest interest. (I was always very keen on hanging.) 'Did you ever see a fellow hanged?'

'I saw dozens of them,' he assured me solemnly, 'and they all died roaring.'

'Jay!' said I.

'Oh, 'tis a horrible death,' he said with great satisfaction. 'Lots of the fellows I saw killed their grandmothers too, but any of them I asked said 'twas never worth it.'

He had me there for a full ten minutes, talking, and then walked out to the chapel yard with me. I was quite sorry to part with him because he was the most entertaining man I'd ever met in the religious line. Outside, the sunlight after the shadow of the church was like the roaring of waves on a beach; it dazzled me, and when the frozen silence melted and I heard the scream of trams on the road, the heart rose in me. But the best of all was to know I wouldn't die that night and come back leaving marks on my poor mother's furniture. I knew it would be a great worry to her and the poor soul had enough.

Nora was sitting on the railing, waiting for me, and she put on a very sour puss when she saw the priest along with me. She was mad jealous because a priest had never come out of the church with her.

'Well,' she asked coldly after he parted me, 'what did he give you?'

'Three Hail Marys,' said I.

'Three Hail Marys?' she repeated incredulously. 'You mustn't have told him anything.'

'I told him everything,' I said confidently.

'About Gran and all?'

'About Gran and all.'

(All she wanted was to be able to go home and say I had made a bad confession.)

'Did you tell him you went for me with the bread-knife?' she asked with a frown.

'I did to be sure,' said I.

'And he only gave you three Hail Marys?'

'That's all.'

She got down off the railing slowly with a baffled air. Clearly, this was beyond her. As we mounted the steps to the main road she looked at me suspiciously.

'What are you sucking?' she asked.

'Bulls' eyes,' I said.

'Was it the priest gave them to you?'

' 'Twas.'

'Lord God!' she wailed bitterly. 'Some people have all the luck! 'Tis no advantage to anybody trying to be good. I might just as well be a sinner like you.'

*Part VI*

# NO COUNTRY FOR OLD MEN

*That is no country for old men. The young
In one another's arms, birds in the trees . . .*
W. B. YEATS

JAMES JOYCE

# The Sirens[1]

Bronze by gold heard the hoofirons, steelyringing.
Imperthnthn thnthnthn.
Chips, picking chips off rocky thumbnail, chips.
Horrid! And gold flushed more.
A husky fifenote blew.
Blew. Blue bloom is on the
Gold pinnacled hair.
A jumping rose on satiny breasts of satin, rose of Castille.
Trilling, trilling: Idolores.
Peep! Who's in the . . . peepofgold?
Tink cried to bronze in pity.
And a call, pure, long and throbbing. Longindying call.
Decoy. Soft word. But look! The bright stars fade. O rose!
Notes chirruping answer. Castille. The morn is breaking.
Jingle jingle jaunted jingling.
Coin rang. Clock clacked.
Avowal. *Sonnez*. I could. Rebound of garter. Not leave thee.
Smack. *La cloche!* Thigh smack. Avowal. Warm. Sweetheart, goodbye!
Jingle. Bloo.
Boomed crashing chords. When love absorbs. War! War! The tympanum.
A sail! A veil awave upon the waves.
Lost. Throstle fluted. All is lost now.
Horn. Hawhorn.
When first he saw. Alas!
Full tup. Full throb.
Warbling. Ah, lure! Alluring.
Martha! Come!
Clapclop. Clipclap. Clappyclap.
Goodgod heneverheard inall
Deaf bald Pat brought pad knife took up.
A moonlit nightcall: far: far.
I feel so sad. P. S. So lonely blooming.

---
[1] From *Ulysses*, Paris, 1922; the most helpful elucidation of this passage and of the entire work may be found in Stuart Gilbert's *James Joyce's Ulysses* and Richard M. Kain's *Fabulous Voyager*. See also our note, p. 562, after this selection.

Listen!

The spiked and winding cold seahorn. Have you the? Each and for other plash and silent roar.

Pearls: when she. Liszt's rhapsodies. Hissss.

You don't?

Did not: no, no: believe: Lidlyd. With a cock with a carra.

Black.

Deepsounding. Do, Ben, do.

Wait while you wait. Hee hee. Wait while you hee.

But wait!

Low in dark middle earth. Embedded ore.

Naminedamine. All gone. All fallen.

Tiny, her tremulous fernfoils of maidenhair.

Amen! He gnashed in fury.

Fro. To, fro. A baton cool protruding.

Bronzelydia by Minagold.

By bronze, by gold, in oceangreen of shadow. Bloom. Old Bloom.

One rapped, one tapped with a carra, with a cock.

Pray for him! Pray, good people!

His gouty fingers nakkering.

Big Benaben. Big Benben.

Last rose Castille of summer left bloom I feel so sad alone.

Pwee! Little wind piped wee.

True men. Lid Ker Cow De and Doll. Ay, ay. Like you men. Will lift your tschink with tschunk.

Fff! Oo!

Where bronze from anear? Where gold from afar? Where hoofs?

Rrrpr. Kraa. Kraandl.

Then, not till then. My eppripfftaph. Be pfrwritt.

Done.

Begin!

Bronze by gold, Miss Douce's head by Miss Kennedy's head, over the crossblind of the Ormond bar heard the viceregal hoofs go by, ringing steel.

—Is that her? asked Miss Kennedy.

Miss Douce said yes, sitting with his ex, pearl grey and *eau de Nil*.

—Exquisite contrast, Miss Kennedy said.

When all agog Miss Douce said eagerly:

—Look at the fellow in the tall silk.

—Who? Where? gold asked more eagerly.

—In the second carriage, Miss Douce's wet lips said, laughing in the sun. He's looking. Mind till I see.

She darted, bronze, to the backmost corner, flattening her face against the pane in a halo of hurried breath.

Her wet lips tittered:

—He's killed looking back.

She laughed:

—O wept! Aren't men frightful idiots?

With sadness.

Miss Kennedy sauntered sadly from bright light, twining a loose hair behind an ear. Sauntering sadly, gold no more, she twisted twined a hair. Sadly she twined in sauntering gold hair behind a curving ear.

—It's them has the fine times, sadly then she said.

A man.

Bloowho went by by Moulang's pipes, bearing in his breast the sweets of sin, by Wine's antiques in memory bearing sweet sinful words, by Carroll's dusky battered plate, for Raoul.

The boots to them, them in the bar, them barmaids came. For them unheeding him he banged on the counter his tray of chattering china. And

—There's your teas, he said.

Miss Kennedy with manners transposed the teatray down to an upturned lithia crate, safe from eyes, low.

—What is it? loud boots unmannerly asked.

—Find out, Miss Douce retorted, leaving her spyingpoint.

—Your *beau*, is it?

A haughty bronze replied:

—I'll complain to Mrs de Massey on you if I hear any more of your impertinent insolence.

—Imperthnthn thnthnthn, bootsnout sniffed rudely, as he retreated as she threatened as he had come.

Bloom.

On her flower frowning Miss Douce said:

—Most aggravating that young brat is. If he doesn't conduct himself I'll wring his ear for him a yard long.

Ladylike in exquisite contrast.

—Take no notice, Miss Kennedy rejoined.

She poured in a teacup tea, then back in the teapot tea. They cowered under their reef of counter, waiting on footstools, crates upturned, waiting for their teas to draw. They pawed their blouses, both of black satin, two and nine a yard, waiting for their teas to draw, and two and seven.

Yes, bronze from anear, by gold from afar, heard steel from anear, hoofs ring from afar, and heard steelhoofs ringhoof ringsteel.

—Am I awfully sunburnt?

Miss bronze unbloused her neck.

—No, said Miss Kennedy. It gets brown after. Did you try the borax with the cherry laurel water?

Miss Douce halfstood to see her skin askance in the barmirror gildedlettered where hock and claret glasses shimmered and in their midst a shell.

—And leave it to my hands, she said.

—Try it with the glycerine, Miss Kennedy advised.

Bidding her neck and hands adieu Miss Douce

—Those things only bring out a rash, replied, reseated. I asked that old fogey in Boyd's for something for my skin.

Miss Kennedy, pouring now fulldrawn tea, grimaced and prayed:

—O, don't remind me of him for mercy'sake!

—But wait till I tell you, Miss Douce entreated.

Sweet tea Miss Kennedy having poured with milk plugged both two ears with little fingers.

—No, don't, she cried.

—I won't listen, she cried.

But Bloom?

Miss Douce grunted in snuffy fogey's tone:

—For your what? says he.

Miss Kennedy unplugged her ears to hear, to speak: but said, but prayed again:

—Don't let me think of him or I'll expire. The hideous old wretch! That night in the Antient Concert Rooms.

She sipped distastefully her brew, hot tea, a sip, sipped sweet tea.

—Here he was, Miss Douce said, cocking her bronze head three quarters, ruffling her nosewings. Hufa! Hufa!

Shrill shriek of laughter sprang from Miss Kennedy's throat. Miss Douce huffed and snorted down her nostrils that quivered imperthnthn like a shout in quest.

—O! shrieking, Miss Kennedy cried. Will you ever forget his goggle eye?

Miss Douce chimed in in deep bronze laughter, shouting:

—And your other eye!

Bloowhose dark eye read Aaron Figatner's name. Why do I always think Figather? Gathering figs I think. And Prosper Loré's huguenot name. By Bassi's blessed virgins Bloom's dark eyes went by. Bluerobed, white under, come to me. God they believe she is: or goddess. Those today. I could not see. That fellow spoke. A student. After with Dedalus' son. He might be Mulligan. All comely virgins. That brings those rakes of fellows in: her white.

By went his eyes. The sweets of sin. Sweet are the sweets.

Of sin.

In a giggling peal young goldbronze voices blended, Douce with Kennedy your other eye. They threw young heads back, bronze gigglegold, to let freefly their laughter, screaming, your other, signals to each other, high piercing notes.

Ah, panting, sighing. Sighing, ah, fordone their mirth died down.

Miss Kennedy lipped her cup again, raised, drank a sip and gigglegiggled. Miss Douce, bending again over the teatray, ruffled again her nose and rolled droll fattened eyes. Again Kennygiggles, stooping her fair pinnacles of hair, stooping, her tortoise napecomb showed, spluttered out of her mouth her tea, choking in tea and laughter, coughing with choking, crying:

—O greasy eyes! Imagine being married to a man like that, she cried. With his bit of beard!

Douce gave full vent to a splendid yell, a full yell of full woman, delight, joy, indignation.

—Married to the greasy nose! she yelled.

Shrill, with deep laughter, after bronze in gold, they urged each each to peal after peal, ringing in changes, bronzegold goldbronze, shrilldeep, to laughter after laughter. And then laughed more. Greasy I knows. Exhausted, breathless their shaken heads they laid, braided and pinnacled by glossycombed, against the counterledge. All flushed (O!), panting, sweating (O!), all breathless.

Married to Bloom, to greaseaseabloom.

—O saints above! Miss Douce said, sighed above her jumping rose. I wished I hadn't laughed so much. I feel all wet.

—O, Miss Douce! Miss Kennedy protested. You horrid thing!

And flushed yet more (you horrid!), more goldenly.

By Cantwell's offices roved Greaseabloom, by Ceppi's virgins, bright of their oils. Nannetti's father hawked those things about, wheedling at doors as I. Religion pays. Must see him about Keyes's par. Eat first. I want. Not yet. At four, she said. Time ever passing. Clockhands turning. On. Where eat? The Clarence, Dolphin. On. For Raoul. Eat. If I net five guineas with those ads. The violet silk petticoats. Not yet. The sweets of sin.

Flushed less, still less, goldenly paled.

Into their bar strolled Mr Dedalus. Chips, picking chips off one of his rocky thumbnails. Chips. He strolled.

—O welcome back, Miss Douce.

He held her hand. Enjoyed her holidays?

—Tiptop.

He hoped she had nice weather in Rostrevor.

—Gorgeous, she said. Look at the holy show I am. Lying out on the strand all day.

Bronze whiteness.

—That was exceedingly naughty of you, Mr Dedalus told her and pressed her hand indulgently. Tempting poor simple males.

Miss Douce of satin douced her arm away.

—O go away, she said. You're very simple, I don't think.

He was.

—Well now, I am, he mused. I looked so simple in the cradle they christened me simple Simon.

—You must have been a doaty, Miss Douce made answer. And what did the doctor order today?

—Well now, he mused, whatever you say yourself. I think I'll trouble you for some fresh water and a half glass of whisky.

Jingle.

—With the greatest alacrity, Miss Douce agreed.

With grace of alacrity towards the mirror gilt Cantrell and Cochrane's she turned herself. With grace she tapped a measure of gold whisky from her crystal keg. Forth from the skirt of his coat Mr Dedalus brought pouch and pipe. Alacrity she served. He blew through the flue two husky fifenotes.

—By Jove, he mused. I often wanted to see the Mourne mountains. Must be a great tonic in the air down there. But a long threatening comes at last, they say. Yes, yes.

Yes. He fingered shreds of hair, her maidenhair, her mermaid's, into the bowl. Chips. Shreds. Musing. Mute.

None not said nothing. Yes.

Gaily Miss Douce polished a tumbler, trilling:

# THE SIRENS

*—O, Idolores, queen of the eastern seas!*
—Was Mr Lidwell in today?

In came Lenehan. Round him peered Lenehan. Mr Bloom reached Essex bridge. Yes, Mr Bloom crossed bridge of Yessex. To Martha I must write. Buy paper. Daly's. Girl there civil. Bloom. Old Bloom. Blue Bloom is on the rye.

—He was in at lunchtime, Miss Douce said.

Lenehan came forward.

—Was Mr Boylan looking for me?

He asked. She answered:

—Miss Kennedy, was Mr Boylan in while I was upstairs?

She asked. Miss voice of Kennedy answered, a second teacup poised, her gaze upon a page.

—No. He was not.

Miss gaze of Kennedy, heard not seen, read on. Lenehan round the sandwichbell wound his round body round.

—Peep! Who's in the corner?

No glance of Kennedy rewarding him he yet made overtures. To mind her stops. To read only the black ones: round o and crooked ess.

Jingle jaunty jingle.

Girlgold she read and did not glance. Take no notice. She took no notice while he read by rote a solfa fable for her, plappering flatly:

—Ah fox met ah stork. Said thee fox too thee stork: Will you put your bill down inn my troath and pull upp ah bone?

He droned in vain. Miss Douce turned to her tea aside.

He sighed, aside:

—Ah me! Oh my!

He greeted Mr Dedalus and got a nod.

—Greetings from the famous son of a famous father.

—Who may he be? Mr Dedalus asked.

Lenehan opened most genial arms. Who?

—Who may he be? he asked. Can you ask? Stephen, the youthful bard.

Dry.

Mr Dedalus, famous father, laid by his dry filled pipe.

—I see, he said. I didn't recognise him for the moment. I hear he is keeping very select company. Have you seen him lately?

He had.

—I quaffed the nectar bowl with him this very day, said Lenehan. In Mooney's *en ville* and in Mooney's *sur mer*. He had received the rhino for the labour of his muse.

He smiled at bronze's teabathed lips, at listening lips and eyes.

—The *élite* of Erin hung upon his lips. The ponderous pundit, Hugh MacHugh, Dublin's most brilliant scribe and editor and that minstrel boy of the wild wet west who is known by the euphonious appellation of the O'Madden Burke.

After an interval Mr Dedalus raised his grog and

—That must have been highly diverting, said he. I see.

He see. He drank. With faraway mourning mountain eye. Set down his glass.

He looked towards the saloon door.

—I see you have moved the piano.

—The tuner was in today, Miss Douce replied, tuning it for the smoking concert and I never heard such an exquisite player.

—Is that a fact?

—Didn't he, Miss Kennedy? The real classical, you know. And blind too, poor fellow. Not twenty I'm sure he was.

—Is that a fact? Mr Dedalus said.

He drank and strayed away.

—So sad to look at his face, Miss Douce condoled.

God's curse on bitch's bastard.

Tink to her pity cried a diner's bell. To the door of the diningroom came bald Pat, came bothered Pat, came Pat, waiter of Ormond. Lager for diner. Lager without alacrity she served.

With patience Lenehan waited for Boylan with impatience, for jingle jaunty blazes boy.

Upholding the lid he (who?) gazed in the coffin (coffin?) at the oblique triple (piano!) wires. He pressed (the same who pressed indulgently her hand), soft pedalling a triple of keys to see the thicknesses of felt advancing, to hear the muffled hammerfall in action.

Two sheets cream vellum paper one reserve two envelopes when I was in Wisdom Hely's wise Bloom in Daly's Henry Flower bought. Are you not happy in your home? Flower to console me and a pin cuts lo. Means something, language of flow. Was it a daisy? Innocence that is. Respectable girl meet after mass. Tanks awfully muchly. Wise Bloom eyed on the door a poster, a swaying mermaid smoking mid nice waves. Smoke mermaids, coolest whiff of all. Hair streaming: lovelorn. For some man. For Raoul. He eyed and saw afar on Essex bridge a gay hat riding on a jauntingcar. It is. Third time. Coincidence.

Jingling on supple rubbers it jaunted from the bridge to Ormond quay. Follow. Risk it. Go quick. At four. Near now. Out.

—Twopence, sir, the shopgirl dared to say.

—Aha . . . I was forgetting . . . Excuse . . .

—And four.

At four she. Winsomely she on Bloohimwhom smiled. Bloo smi qui go. Ternoon. Think you're the only pebble on the beach? Does that to all. For men.

In drowsy silence gold bent on her page.

From the saloon a call came, long in dying. That was a tuningfork the tuner had that he forgot that he now struck. A call again. That he now poised that it now throbbed. You hear? It throbbed, pure, purer, softly and softlier, its buzzing prongs. Longer in dying call.

Pat paid for diner's popcorked bottle: and over tumbler tray and popcorked bottle ere he went he whispered, bald and bothered, with Miss Douce.

—*The bright stars fade . . .*

A voiceless song sang from within, singing:

— *. . . the morn is breaking.*

A duodene of birdnotes chirruped bright treble answer under sensitive hands. Brightly the keys, all twinkling, linked, all harpsichording, called to a voice to sing the strain of dewy morn, of youth, of love's leavetaking, life's, love's morn.

—*The dewdrops pearl . . .*

Lenehan's lips over the counter lisped a low whistle of decoy.

—But look this way, he said, rose of Castille.

Jingle jaunted by the curb and stopped.

She rose and closed her reading, rose of Castille. Fretted forlorn, dreamily rose.

—Did she fall or was she pushed? he asked her.

She answered, slighting:

—Ask no questions and you'll hear no lies.

Like lady, ladylike.

Blazes Boylan's smart tan shoes creaked on the barfloor where he strode. Yes, gold from anear by bronze from afar. Lenehan heard and knew and hailed him:

—See the conquering hero comes.

Between the car and window, warily walking, went Bloom, unconquered hero. See me he might. The seat he sat on: warm. Black wary hecat walked towards Richie Goulding's legal bag, lifted aloft saluting.

—*And I from thee* . . .

—I heard you were round, said Blazes Boylan.

He touched to fair Miss Kennedy a rim of his slanted straw. She smiled on him. But sister bronze outsmiled her, preening for him her richer hair, a bosom and a rose.

Boylan bespoke potions.

—What's your cry? Glass of bitter? Glass of bitter, please, and a sloegin for me. Wire in yet?

Not yet. At four he. All said four.

Cowley's red lugs and Adam's apple in the door of the sheriff's office. Avoid. Goulding a chance. What is he doing in the Ormond? Car waiting. Wait.

Hello. Where off to? Something to eat? I too was just. In here. What, Ormond? Best value in Dublin. Is that so? Diningroom. Sit tight there. See, not be seen. I think I'll join you. Come on. Richie led on. Bloom followed bag. Dinner fit for a prince.

Miss Douce reached high to take a flagon, stretching her satin arm, her bust, that all but burst, so high.

—O! O! jerked Lenehan, gasping at each stretch. O!

But easily she seized her prey and led it low in triumph.

—Why don't you grow? asked Blazes Boylan.

Shebronze, dealing from her jar thick syrupy liquor for his lips, looked as it flowed (flower in his coat: who gave him?), and syrupped with her voice:

—Fine goods in small parcels.

That is to say she. Neatly she poured slowsyrupy sloe.

—Here's fortune, Blazes said.

He pitched a broad coin down. Coin rang.

—Hold on, said Lenehan, till I . . .

—Fortune, he wished, lifting his bubbled ale.

—Sceptre will win in a canter, he said.

—I plunged a bit, said Boylan winking and drinking. Not on my own, you know. Fancy of a friend of mine.

# THE SIRENS

Lenehan still drank and grinned at his tilted ale and at Miss Douce's lips that all but hummed, not shut, the oceansong her lips had trilled. Idolores. The eastern seas.

Clock whirred. Miss Kennedy passed their way (flower, wonder who gave), bearing away teatray. Clock clacked.

Miss Douce took Boylan's coin, struck boldly the cashregister. It clanged. Clock clacked. Fair one of Egypt teased and sorted in the till and hummed and handed coins in change. Look to the west. A clack. For me.

—What time is that? asked Blazes Boylan. Four?
O'clock.

Lenehan, small eyes ahunger on her humming, bust ahumming, tugged Blazes Boylan's elbowsleeve.

—Let's hear the time, he said.

The bag of Goulding, Collis, Ward led Bloom by ryebloom flowered tables. Aimless he chose with agitated aim, bald Pat attending, a table near the door. Be near. At four. Has he forgotten? Perhaps a trick. Not come: whet appetite. I couldn't do. Wait, wait. Pat, waiter, waited.

Sparkling bronze azure eyed Blazure's skyblue bow and eyes.

—Go on, pressed Lenehan. There's no-one. He never heard.

— *... to Flora's lips did hie.*

High, a high note, pealed in the treble, clear.

Bronzedouce, communing with her rose that sank and rose, sought Blazes Boylan's flower and eyes.

—Please, please.

He pleaded over returning phrases of avowal.

—*I could not leave thee ...*

—Afterwits, Miss Douce promised coyly.

—No, now, urged Lenehan. *Sonnez la cloche!* O do! There's no-one.

She looked. Quick. Miss Kenn out of earshot. Sudden bent. Two kindling faces watched her bend.

Quavering the chords strayed from the air, found it again, lost chord, and lost and found it faltering.

—Go on! Do! *Sonnez!*

Bending, she nipped a peak of skirt above her knee. Delayed. Taunted them still, bending, suspending, with wilful eyes.

—*Sonnez!*

Smack. She let free sudden in rebound her nipped elastic garter smackwarm against her smackable woman's warmhosed thigh.

—*La cloche!* cried gleeful Lenehan. Trained by owner. No sawdust there.

She smilesmirked supercilious (wept! Aren't men?), but, lightward gliding, mild she smiled on Boylan.

—You're the essence of vulgarity, she in gliding said.

Boylan, eyed, eyed. Tossed to fat lips his chalice, drank off his tiny chalice, sucking the last fat violet syrupy drops. His spellbound eyes went after her gliding head as it went down the bar by mirrors, gilded arch for ginger ale, hock and claret glasses shimmering, a spiky shell, where it concerted, mirrored, bronze with sunnier bronze.

Yes, bronze from anearby.

— . . . *Sweetheart, goodbye!*

—I'm off, said Boylan with impatience.

He slid his chalice brisk away, grasped his change.

—Wait a shake, begged Lenehan, drinking quickly. I wanted to tell you. Tom Rochford . . .

—Come on to blazes, said Blazes Boylan, going.

Lenehan gulped to go.

—Got the horn or what? he said. Wait. I'm coming.

He followed the hasty creaking shoes but stood by nimbly by the threshold, saluting forms, a bulky with a slender.

—How do you do, Mr. Dollard?

—Eh? How do? How do? Ben Dollard's vague bass answered, turning an instant from Father Cowley's woe. He won't give you any trouble, Bob. Alf Bergan will speak to the long fellow. We'll put a barleystraw in that Judas Iscariot's ear this time.

Sighing, Mr Dedalus came through the saloon, a finger soothing an eyelid.

—Hoho, we will, Ben Dollard yodled jollily. Come on, Simon, give us a ditty. We heard the piano.

Bald Pat, bothered waiter, waited for drink orders, Power for Richie. And Bloom? Let me see. Not make him walk twice. His corns. Four now. How warm this black is. Course nerves a bit. Refracts (is it?) heat. Let me see. Cider. Yes, bottle of cider.

—What's that? Mr Dedalus said. I was only vamping, man.

—Come on, come on, Ben Dollard called. Begone, dull care. Come, Bob.

He ambled Dollard, bulky slops, before them (hold that fellow with the: hold him now) into the saloon. He plumped him Dollard on the stool. His gouty paws plumped chords. Plumped stopped abrupt.

Bald Pat in the doorway met tealess gold returning. Bothered he wanted Power and cider. Bronze by the window watched, bronze from afar.

Jingle a tinkle jaunted.

Bloom heard a jing, a little sound. He's off. Light sob of breath Bloom sighed on the silent bluehued flowers. Jingling. He's gone. Jingle. Hear.

—Love and war, Ben, Mr Dedalus said. God be with old times.

Miss Douce's brave eyes, unregarded, turned from the crossblind, smitten by sunlight. Gone. Pensive (who knows?), smitten (the smiting light), she lowered the dropblind with a sliding cord. She drew down pensive (why did he go so quick when I?) about her bronze, over the bar where bald stood by sister gold, inexquisite contrast, contrast inexquisite nonexquisite, slow cool dim seagreen sliding depth of shadow, *eau de Nil*.

—Poor old Goodwin was the pianist that night, Father Cowley reminded them. There was a slight difference of opinion between himself and the Collard grand.

There was.

—A symposium all his own, Mr Dedalus said. The devil wouldn't stop him. He was a crotchety old fellow in the primary stage of drink.

—God, do you remember? Ben bulky Dollard said, turning from the punished keyboard. And by Japers I had no wedding garment.

They laughed all three. He had no wed. All trio laughed. No wedding garment.

—Our friend Bloom turned in handy that night, Mr Dedalus said. Where's my pipe by the way?

He wandered back to the bar to the lost chord pipe. Bald Pat carried two diners' drinks, Richie and Poldy. And Father Cowley laughed again.

—I saved the situation, Ben, I think.

—You did, averred Ben Dollard. I remember those tight trousers too. That was a brilliant idea, Bob.

Father Cowley blushed to his brilliant purply lobes. He saved the situa. Tight trou. Brilliant ide.

—I knew he was on the rocks, he said. The wife was playing the piano in the coffee palace on Saturdays for a very trifling consideration and who was it gave me the wheeze she was doing the other business? Do you remember? We had to search all Holles street to find them till the chap in Keogh's gave us the number. Remember?

Ben remembered, his broad visage wondering.

—By God she had some luxurious opera cloaks and things there.

Mr. Dedalus wandered back, pipe in hand.

—Merrion square style. Balldresses, by God, and court dresses. He wouldn't take any money either. What? Any God's quantity of cocked hats and boleros and trunkhose. What?

Ay, ay, Mr. Dedalus nodded. Mrs. Marion Bloom has left off clothes of all descriptions.

Jingle jaunted down the quays. Blazes sprawled on bounding tyres.

Liver and bacon. Steak and kidney pie. Right, sir. Right, Pat.

Mrs Marion met him pike hoses. Smell of burn of Paul de Kock. Nice name he.

—What's this her name was? A buxom lassy. Marion . . .

—Tweedy.

—Yes. Is she alive?

—And kicking.

—She was a daughter of . . .

—Daughter of the regiment.

—Yes, begad. I remember the old drummajor.

Mr Dedalus struck, whizzed, lit, puffed savoury puff after.

—Irish? I don't know, faith. Is she, Simon?

Puff after stiff, a puff, strong, savoury, crackling.

—Buccinator muscle is . . . What? . . . Bit rusty . . . O, she is . . . My Irish Molly, O.

He puffed a pungent plumy blast.

—From the rock of Gibraltar . . . all the way.

They pined in depth of ocean shadow, gold by the beerpull, bronze by maraschino, thoughtful all two, Mina Kennedy, 4 Lismore terrace, Drumcondra with Idolores, a queen, Dolores, silent.

Pat served uncovered dishes. Leopold cut liverslices. As said before he ate with relish the inner organs, nutty gizzards, fried cods' roes while Richie Goulding, Collis, Ward ate steak and kidney, steak then kidney, bite by bite of pie he ate Bloom ate they ate.

Bloom with Goulding, married in silence, ate. Dinners fit for princes.

# THE SIRENS

By Bachelor's walk jogjaunty jingled Blazes Boylan, bachelor, in sun, in heat, mare's glossy rump atrot, with flick of whip, on bounding tyres: sprawled, warmseated, Boylan impatience, ardentbold. Horn. Have you the? Horn. Have you the? Haw haw horn.

Over their voices Dollard bassooned attack, booming over bombarding chords:

—*When love absorbs my ardent soul* . . .

Roll of Bensoulbenjamin rolled to the quivery loveshivery roofpanes.

—War! War! cried Father Cowley. You're the warrior.

—So I am, Ben Warrior laughed. I was thinking of your landlord. Love or money.

He stopped. He wagged huge beard, huge face over his blunder huge.

—Sure, you'd burst the tympanum of her ear, man, Mr Dedalus said through smoke aroma, with an organ like yours.

In bearded abundant laughter Dollard shook upon the keyboard. He would.

—Not to mention another membrane, Father Cowley added. Half time, Ben. *Amoroso ma non troppo*. Let me there.

Miss Kennedy served two gentlemen with tankards of cool stout. She passed a remark. It was indeed, first gentleman said, beautiful weather. They drank cool stout. Did she know where the lord lieutenant was going? And heard steelhoofs ringhoof ring. No, she couldn't say. But it would be in the paper. O, she needn't trouble. No trouble. She waved about her outspread *Independent*, searching, the lord lieutenant, her pinnacles of hair slowmoving, lord lieuten. Too much trouble, first gentleman said. O, not in the least. Way he looked that. Lord lieutenant. Gold by bronze heard iron steel.

— .. .. .. .. *my ardent soul*
*I care not foror the morrow.*

In liver gravy Bloom mashed mashed potatoes. Love and war someone is. Ben Dollard's famous. Night he ran round to us to borrow a dress suit for that concert. Trousers tight as a drum on him. Musical porkers. Molly did laugh when he went out. Threw herself back across the bed, screaming, kicking. With all his belongings on show. O, saints above, I'm drenched! O, the women in the front row! O, I never laughed so many! Well, of course, that's what gives him the base barreltone. For instance eunuchs. Wonder who's playing. Nice touch. Must be Cowley. Musical. Knows whatever note you play. Bad breath he has, poor chap. Stopped.

Miss Douce, engaging, Lydia Douce, bowed to suave solicitor, George Lidwell, gentleman, entering. Good afternoon. She gave her moist, a lady's, hand to his firm clasp. Afternoon. Yes, she was back. To the old dingdong again.

—Your friends are inside, Mr Lidwell.

George Lidwell, suave, solicited, held a lydiahand.

Bloom ate liv as said before. Clean here at least. That chap in the Burton, gummy with gristle. No-one here: Goulding and I. Clean tables, flowers, mitres of napkins. Pat to and fro, bald Pat. Nothing to do. Best value in Dub.

Piano again. Cowley it is. Way he sits into it, like one together, mutual understanding. Tiresome shapers scraping fiddles, eye on the bowend, sawing the 'cello, remind you of toothache. Her high long snore. Night we were in the box. Trombone under blowing like a grampus, between the acts, other brass chap unscrewing, emptying spittle. Conductor's legs too, bagstrousers, jiggedy jiggedy. Do right to hide them.

Jiggedy jingle jaunty jaunty.

Only the harp. Lovely gold glowering light. Girl touched it. Poop of a lovely. Gravy's rather good fit for a. Golden ship. Erin. The harp that once or twice. Cool hands. Ben Howth, the rhododendrons. We are their harps. I. He. Old. Young.

—Ah, I couldn't, man, Mr Dedalus said, shy, listless.

Strongly.

—Go on, blast you, Ben Dollard growled. Get it out in bits.

—*M'appari*, Simon, Father Cowley said.

Down stage he strode some paces, grave, tall in affliction, his long arms outheld. Hoarsely the apple of his throat hoarsed softly. Softly he sang to a dusty seascape there: *A Last Farewell*. A headland, a ship, a sail upon the billows. Farewell. A lovely girl, her veil awave upon the wind upon the headland, wind around her.

Cowley sang:

—*M'appari tutt'amor:*
*Il mio sguardo l'incontr* . . .

She waved, unhearing Cowley, her veil to one departing, dear one, to wind, love, speeding sail, return.

—Go on, Simon.

—Ah, sure my dancing days are done, Ben . . . Well . . .

Mr Dedalus laid his pipe to rest beside the tuningfork and, sitting, touched the obedient keys.

—No, Simon, Father Cowley turned. Play it in the original. One flat.

The keys, obedient, rose higher, told, faltered, confessed, confused.

Up stage strode Father Cowley.

—Here, Simon, I'll accompany you, he said. Get up.

By Graham Lemon's pineapple rock, by Elvery's elephant jingle jogged. Steak, kidney, liver, mashed at meat fit for princes sat princes Bloom and Goulding. Princes at meat they raised and drank Power and cider.

Most beautiful tenor air ever written, Richie said: *Sonnambula*. He heard Joe Maas sing that one night. Ah, what M'Guckin! Yes. In his way. Choirboy style. Maas was the boy. Massboy. A lyrical tenor if you like. Never forget it. Never.

Tenderly Bloom over liverless bacon saw the tightened features strain. Backache he. Bright's bright eye. Next item on the programme. Paying the piper. Pills, pounded bread, worth a guinea a box. Stave it off awhile. Sings too: *Down among the dead men*. Appropriate. Kidney pie. Sweets to the. Not making much hand of it. Best value in. Characteristic of him. Power. Particular about his drink. Flaw in the glass, fresh Vartry water. Fecking matches from counters to save. Then squander a sovereign in dribs and drabs. And when he's wanted not a farthing. Screwed refusing to pay his fare. Curious types.

Never would Richie forget that night. As long as he lived, never. In the gods of the old Royal with little Peake. And when the first note.

Speech paused on Richie's lips.

Coming out with a whopper now. Rhapsodies about damn all. Believes his own lies. Does really. Wonderful liar. But want a good memory.

Which air is that? asked Leopold Bloom.

—*All is lost now*.

Richie cocked his lips apout. A low incipient note sweet banshee murmured all. A thrush. A throstle. His breath, birdsweet, good teeth he's proud of, fluted with plaintive woe. Is lost. Rich sound. Two notes in one there. Blackbird I heard in the hawthorn valley. Taking my motives he twined and turned them. All most too new call is lost in all. Echo. How sweet the answer. How is that done? All lost now. Mournful he whistled. Fall, surrender, lost.

Bloom bent leopold ear, turning a fringe of doyley down under the vase. Order. Yes, I remember. Lovely air. In sleep she went to him. Innocence in the moon. Still hold her back. Brave, don't know their danger. Call name. Touch water. Jingle jaunty. Too late. She longed to go. That's why. Woman. As easy stop the sea. Yes: all is lost.

—A beautiful air, said Bloom lost Leopold. I know it well.

Never in all his life had Richie Goulding.

He knows it well too. Or he feels. Still harping on his daughter. Wise child that knows her father, Dedalus said. Me?

Bloom askance over liverless saw. Face of the all is lost. Rollicking Richie once. Jokes old stale now. Wagging his ear. Napkinring in his eye. Now begging letters he sends his son with. Crosseyed Walter sir I did sir. Wouldn't trouble only I was expecting some money. Apologise.

Piano again. Sounds better than last time I heard. Tuned probably. Stopped again.

Dollard and Cowley still urged the lingering singer out with it.

—With it, Simon.

—It, Simon.

—Ladies and gentlemen, I am most deeply obliged by your kind solicitations.

—It, Simon.

—I have no money but if you will lend me your attention I shall endeavour to sing to you of a heart bowed down.

By the sandwichbell in screening shadow, Lydia her bronze and rose, a lady's grace, gave and withheld: as in cool glaucous *eau de Nil* Mina to tankards two her pinnacles of gold.

The harping chords of prelude closed. A chord longdrawn, expectant drew a voice away.

—*When first I saw that form endearing.*

Richie turned.

—Si Dedalus' voice, he said.

Braintipped, cheek touched with flame, they listened feeling that flow endearing flow over skin limbs human heart soul spine. Bloom signed to Pat, bald Pat is a waiter hard of hearing to set ajar the door of the bar. The door of the bar. So. That will do. Pat, waiter, waited, waiting to hear, for he was hard of hear by the door.

—*Sorrow from me seemed to depart.*

Through the hush of air a voice sang to them, low, not rain, not leaves in murmur, like no voice of strings of reeds or whatdoyoucallthem dulcimers, touching their still ears with words, still hearts of their each his remembered lives. Good, good to hear: sorrow from them each seemed to from both depart when first they heard. When first they saw, lost Richie, Poldy, mercy of beauty, heard from a person wouldn't expect it in the least, her first merciful lovesoft oftloved word.

Love that is singing: love's old sweet song. Bloom unwound slowly the elastic band of his packet. Love's old sweet *sonnez la* gold. Bloom wound a skein round four forkfingers, stretched it, relaxed, and wound it round his troubled double, fourfold, in octave, gyved them fast.

—*Full of hope and all delighted* . . .

Tenors get women by the score. Increase their flow. Throw flower at his feet when will we meet? My head it simply. Jingle all delighted. He can't sing for tall hats. Your head it simply swurls. Perfumed for him. What perfume does your wife? I want to know. Jing. Stop. Knock. Last look at mirror always before she answers the door. The hall. There? How do you? I do well. There? What? Or? Phial of cachous, kissing comfits, in her satchel. Yes? Hands felt for the opulent.

Alas! The voice rose, sighing, changed: loud, full, shining, proud.

—*But alas, 'twas idle dreaming* . . .

Glorious tone he has still. Cork air softer also their brogue. Silly man! Could have made oceans of money. Singing wrong words. Wore out his wife: now sings. But hard to tell. Only the two themselves. If he doesn't break down. Keep a trot for the avenue. His hands and feet sing too. Drink. Nerves overstrung. Must be abstemious to sing. Jenny Lind soup: stock, sage, raw eggs, half pint of cream. For creamy dreamy.

Tenderness it welled: slow, swelling. Full it throbbed. That's the chat. Ha, give! Take! Throb, a throb, a pulsing proud erect.

Words? Music? No: it's what's behind.

Bloom looped, unlooped, noded, disnoded.

Bloom. Flood of warm jimjam lickitup secretness flowed to flow in music out, in desire, dark to lick flow, invading. Tipping her tepping her tapping her topping her. Tup. Pores to dilate dilating. Tup. The joy the feel the warm the. Tup. To pour o'er sluices pouring gushes. Flood, gush, flow, joygush, tupthrop. Now! Language of love.

— . . . *ray of hope* . . .

Beaming. Lydia for Lidwell squeak scarcely hear so ladylike the muse unsqueaked a ray of hope.

*Martha* it is. Coincidence. Just going to write. Lionel's song. Lovely name you have. Can't write. Accept my little pres. Play on her heartstrings pursestrings too. She's a. I called you naughty boy. Still the name: Martha. How strange! Today.

The voice of Lionel returned, weaker but unwearied. It sang again to Richie Poldy Lydia Lidwell also sang to Pat open mouth ear waiting, to wait. How first he saw that form endearing, how sorrow seemed to part, how look, form, word charmed him Gould Lidwell, won Pat Bloom's heart.

Wish I could see his face, though. Explain better. Why the barber in Drago's always looked my face when I spoke his face in the glass. Still hear it better here than in the bar though farther.

—*Each graceful look* . . .

First night when first I saw her at Mat Dillon's in Terenure. Yellow, black lace she wore. Musical chairs. We two the last. Fate. After her. Fate. Round and round slow. Quick round. We two. All looked. Halt. Down she sat. All ousted looked. Lips laughing. Yellow knees.

—*Charmed my eye* . . .

Singing. *Waiting* she sang. I turned her music. Full voice of perfume of what perfume does your lilactrees. Bosom I saw, both full, throat warbling. First I saw. She thanked me. Why did she me? Fate. Spanishy eyes. Under a peartree alone patio this hour in old Madrid one side in shadow Dolores shedolores. At me. Luring. Ah, alluring.

—*Martha! Ah, Martha!*

Quitting all languor Lionel cried in grief, in cry of passion dominant to love to return with deepening yet with rising chords of harmony. In cry of lionel loneliness that she should know, must Martha feel. For only her he waited. Where? Here there try there here all try where. Somewhere.

—*Co-me, thou lost one!*
*Co-me thou dear one!*

'Twas rank and fame: in Ned Lambert's 'twas. Good God he never heard in all his life a note like that he never did *then false one we had better part* so clear so God he never heard *since love lives not* a clinking voice ask Lambert he can tell you too.

Goulding, a flush struggling in his pale, told Mr Bloom, face of the night, Si in Ned Lambert's, Dedalus house, sang *'Twas rank and fame*.

He, Mr Bloom, listened while he, Richie Goulding, told him, Mr Bloom of the night he, Richie, heard him, Si Dedalus, sing *'Twas rank and fame* in his, Ned Lambert's house.

Brothers-in-law: relations. We never speak as we pass by. Rift in the lute I think. Treats him with scorn. See. He admires him all the more. The night Si sang. The human voice, two tiny silky cords. Wonderful, more than all the others.

That voice was a lamentation. Calmer now. It's in the silence you feel you hear. Vibrations. Now silent air.

Bloom ungyved his crisscrossed hands and with slack fingers plucked the slender catgut thong. He drew and plucked. It buzzed, it twanged. While Goulding talked of Barraclough's voice production, while Tom Kernan, harking back in a retrospective sort of arrangement, talked to listening Father Cowley who played a voluntary, who nodded as he played. While big Ben Dollard talked with Simon Dedalus lighting, who nodded as he smoked, who smoked.

Thou lost one. All songs on that theme. Yet more Bloom stretched his string. Cruel it seems. Let people get fond of each other: lure them on. Then tear asunder. Death. Explos. Knock on the head. Outtohelloutofthat. Human life. Dignam. Ugh, that rat's tail wriggling! Five bob I gave. *Corpus paradisum.* Corncrake croaker: belly like a poisoned pup. Gone. They sing. Forgotten. I too. And one day she with. Leave her: get tired. Suffer then. Snivel. Big Spanishy eyes goggling at nothing. Her wavyavyeavyheavyeavyevyevy hair un comb: 'd.

Yet too much happy bores. He stretched more, more. Are you not happy in your? Twang. It snapped.

Jingle into Dorset street.

Miss Douce withdrew her satiny arm, reproachful, pleased.

—Don't make half so free, said she, till we are better acquainted.

George Lidwell told her really and truly: but she did not believe.

Alone. One love. One hope. One comfort me. Martha, chestnote, return.

—*Come!*

It soared, a bird, it held its flight, a swift pure cry, soar silver orb it leaped serene, speeding, sustained, to come, don't spin it out too long long breath he breath long life, soaring high, high resplendent, aflame, crowned, high in the effulgence symbolistic, high, of the ethereal bosom, high, of the high vast irradiation everywhere all soaring all around about the all, the endlessnessnessness . . .

—*To me!*

Siopold!

Consumed.

Come. Well sung. All clapped. She ought to. Come. To me, to him, to her, you too, me, us.

—Bravo! Clapclap. Goodman, Simon. Clappyclapclap. Encore! Clapclipclap. Sound as a bell. Bravo, Simon! Clapclopclap. Encore, enclap, said, cried, clapped all, Ben Dollard, Lydia Douce, George Lidwell, Pat, Mina, two gentlemen with two tankards, Cowley, first gent with tank and bronze Miss Douce and gold Miss Mina.

Blazes Boylan's smart tan shoes creaked on the barfloor, said before. Jingle by monuments of sir John Gray, Horatio one-handled Nelson, reverend father Theobald Matthew, jaunted as said before just now. Atrot, in heat, heatseated. *Cloche. Sonnez la. Cloche. Sonnez la.* Slower the mare went up the hill by the Rotunda, Rutland square. Too slow for Boylan, Blazes Boylan, impatience Boylan, joggled the mare.

An afterclang of Cowley's chords closed, died on the air made richer.

And Richie Goulding drank his Power and Leopold Bloom his cider drank, Lidwell his Guinness, second gentleman said they would partake of two tankards if she did not mind. Miss Kennedy smirked, disserving, coral lips, at first, at second. She did not mind.

—Seven days in jail, Ben Dollard said, on bread and water. Then you'd sing, Simon, like a garden thrush.

Lionel Simon, singer, laughed. Father Bob Cowley played. Mina Kennedy served. Second gentleman paid. Tom Kernan strutted in; Lydia, admired, admired. But Bloom sang dumb.

Admiring.

Richie, admiring, descanted on that man's glorious voice. He remembered one night long ago. Never forget that night. Si sang

# THE SIRENS

First gentleman told Mina that was so. She asked him was that so. And second tankard told her so. That that was so.

Miss Douce, Miss Lydia, did not believe: Miss Kennedy, Mina, did not believe: George Lidwell, no: Miss Dou did not: the first, the first: gent with the tank: believe, no, no: did not, Miss Kenn: Lidlydiawell: the tank.

Better write it here. Quills in the postoffice chewed and twisted.

Bald Pat at a sign drew nigh. A pen and ink. He went. A pad. He went. A pad to blot. He heard, deaf Pat.

—Yes, Mr Bloom said, teasing the curling catgut fine. It certainly is. Few lines will do. My present. All that Italian florid music is. Who is this wrote? Know the name you know better. Take out sheet notepaper, envelope: unconcerned. It's so characteristic.

—Grandest number in the whole opera, Goulding said.

—It is, Bloom said.

Numbers it is. All music when you come to think. Two multiplied by two divided by half is twice one. Vibrations: chords those are. One plus two plus six is seven. Do anything you like with figures juggling. Always find out this equal to that, symmetry under a cemetery wall. He doesn't see my mourning. Callous: all for his own gut. Musemathematics. And you think you're listening to the ethereal. But suppose you said it like: Martha, seven times nine minus x is thirty-five thousand. Fall quite flat. It's on account of the sounds it is.

Instance he's playing now. Improvising. Might be what you like till you hear the words. Want to listen sharp. Hard. Begin all right: then hear chords a bit off: feel lost a bit. In and out of sacks over barrels, through wirefences, obstacle race. Time makes the tune. Question of mood you're in. Still always nice to hear. Except scales up and down, girls learning. Two together nextdoor neighbours. Ought to invent dummy pianos for that. *Blumenlied* I bought for her. The name. Playing it slow, a girl, night I came home, the girl. Door of the stables near Cecilia street. Milly no taste. Queer because we both I mean.

Bald deaf Pat brought quite flat pad ink. Pat set with ink pen quite flat pad. Pat took plate dish knife fork. Pat went.

It was the only language Mr Dedalus said to Ben. He heard them as a boy in Ringabella, Crosshaven, Ringabella, singing their barcaroles. Queenstown harbour full of Italian ships. Walking, you know, Ben, in the moonlight with those earthquake hats. Blending their voices. God, such music, Ben. Heard as a boy. Cross Ringabella haven mooncarole,

Sour pipe removed he held a shield of hand beside his lips that cooed a moonlight nightcall, clear from anear, a call from afar, replying.

Down the edge of his *Freeman* baton ranged Bloom's your other eye, scanning for where did I see that. Callan, Coleman, Dignam Patrick. Heigho! Heigho! Fawcett. Aha! Just I was looking . . .

Hope he's not looking, cute as a rat. He held unfurled his *Freeman*. Can't see now. Remember write Greek ees. Bloom dipped, Bloo mur: dear sir. Dear Henry wrote: dear Mady. Got your lett and flow. Hell did I put? Some pock or oth. It is utterl imposs. Underline *imposs*. To write today.

Bore this. Bored Bloom tambourined gently with I am just reflecting fingers on flat pad Pat brought.

On. Know what I mean. No, change that ee. Accept my poor little pres enclos. Ask her no answ. Hold on. Five Dig. Two about here. Penny the gulls. Elijah is com. Seven Davy Byrne's. Is eight about. Say half a crown. My poor little pres: p. o. two and six. Write me a long. Do you despise? Jingle, have you the? So excited. Why do you call me naught? You naughty too? O, Mairy lost the pin of her. Bye for today. Yes, yes, will tell you. Want to. To keep it up. Call me that other. Other world she wrote. My patience are exhausted. To keep it up. You must believe. Believe. The tank. It. Is. True.

Folly am I writing? Husbands don't. That's marriage does, their wives. Because I'm away from. Suppose. But how? She must. Keep young. If she found out. Card in my high grade ha. No, not tell all. Useless pain. If they don't see. Women. Sauce for the gander.

A hackney car, number three hundred and twenty-four, driver Barton James of number one Harmony avenue, Donnybrook, on which sat a fare, a young gentleman, stylishly dressed in an indigoblue serge suit made by George Robert Mesias, tailor and cutter, of number five Eden quay, and wearing a straw hat very dressy, bought of John Plasto of number one Great Brunswick street, hatter. Eh? This is the jingle that joggled and jingled. By Dlugacz' porkshop bright tubes of Agendath trotted a gallant-buttocked mare.

—Answering an ad? keen Richie's eyes asked Bloom.

—Yes, Mr Bloom said. Town traveller. Nothing doing, I expect.

# THE SIRENS

Bloom mur: best references. But Henry wrote: it will excite me. You know now. In haste. Henry. Greek ee. Better add postscript. What is he playing now? Improvising intermezzo. P. S. The rum tum tum. How will you pun? You punish me? Crooked skirt swinging, whack by. Tell me I want to. Know. O. Course if I didn't I wouldn't ask. La la la ree. Trails off there sad in minor. Why minor sad? Sign H. They like sad tail at end. P. P. S. La la la ree. I feel so sad today. La ree. So lonely. Dee.

He blotted quick on pad of Pat. Envel. Address. Just copy out of paper. Murmured: Messrs Callan, Coleman and Co, limited. Henry wrote:

>    Miss Martha Clifford
>    c/o P.O.
>    Dolphin's barn lane
>    Dublin.

Blot over the other so he can't read. Right. Idea prize titbit. Something detective read off blottingpad. Payment at the rate of guinea per col. Matcham often thinks the laughing witch. Poor Mrs Purefoy. U. p.: up.

Too poetical that about the sad. Music did that. Music hath charms Shakespeare said. Quotations every day in the year. To be or not to be. Wisdom while you wait.

In Gerard's rosery of Fetter lane he walks, greyedauburn. One life is all. One body. Do. But do.

Done anyhow. Postal order stamp. Postoffice lower down. Walk now. Enough. Barney Kiernan's I promised to meet them. Dislike that job. House of mourning. Walk. Pat! Doesn't hear. Deaf beetle he is.

Car near there now. Talk. Talk. Pat! Doesn't. Settling those napkins. Lot of ground he must cover in the day. Paint face behind on him then he'd be two. Wish they'd sing more. Keep my mind off.

Bald Pat who is bothered mitred the napkins. Pat is a waiter hard of his hearing. Pat is a waiter who waits while you wait. Hee hee hee hee. He waits while you wait. Hee hee. A waiter is he. Hee hee hee hee. He waits while you wait. While you wait if you wait he will wait while you wait. Hee hee hee hee. Hoh. Wait while you wait.

Douce now. Douce Lydia. Bronze and rose.

She had a gorgeous, simply gorgeous, time. And look at the lovely shell she brought.

To the end of the bar to him she bore lightly the spiked and winding seahorn that he, George Lidwell, solicitor, might hear.

—Listen! she bade him.

Under Tom Kernan's ginhot words the accompanist wove music slow. Authentic fact. How Walter Bapty lost his voice. Well, sir, the husband took him by the throat. *Scoundrel*, said he. *You'll sing no more lovesongs*. He did, sir Tom. Bob Cowley wove. Tenors get wom. Cowley lay back.

Ah, now he heard, she holding it to his ear. Hear! He heard. Wonderful. She held it to her own and through the sifted light pale gold in contrast glided. To hear.

Tap.

Bloom through the bardoor saw a shell held at their ears. He heard more faintly that that they heard, each for herself alone, then each for other, hearing the plash of waves, loudly, a silent roar.

Bronze by a weary gold, anear, afar, they listened.

Her ear too is a shell, the peeping lobe there. Been to the seaside. Lovely seaside girls. Skin tanned raw. Should have put on coldcream first make it brown. Buttered toast. O and that lotion mustn't forget. Fever near her mouth. Your head it simply. Hair braided over: shell with seaweed. Why do they hide their ears with seaweed hair? And Turks their mouth, why? Her eyes over the sheet, a yashmak. Find the way in. A cave. No admittance except on business.

The sea they think they hear. Singing. A roar. The blood is it. Souse in the ear sometimes. Well, it's a sea. Corpuscle islands.

Wonderful really. So distinct. Again. George Lidwell held its murmur, hearing: then laid it by, gently.

—What are the wild waves saying? he asked her, smiled.

Charming, seasmiling and unanswering Lydia on Lidwell smiled.

Tap.

By Larry O'Rourke's, by Larry, bold Larry O', Boylan swayed and Boylan turned.

From the forsaken shell Miss Mina glided to her tankard waiting. No, she was not so lonely archly Miss Douce's head let Mr Lidwell know. Walks in the moonlight by the sea. No, not alone. With whom? She nobly answered: with a gentleman friend.

Bob Cowley's twinkling fingers in the treble played again. The landlord has the prior. A little time. Long John. Big Ben. Lightly

# THE SIRENS

he played a light bright tinkling measure for tripping ladies, arch and smiling, and for their gallants, gentlemen friends. One: one, one, one: two, one, three, four.

Sea, wind, leaves, thunder, waters, cows lowing, the cattle market, cocks, hens don't crow, snakes hissss. There's music everywhere. Ruttledge's door: ee creaking. No, that's noise. Minuet of *Don Giovanni* he's playing now. Court dresses of all descriptions in castle chambers dancing. Misery. Peasants outside. Green starving faces eating dockleaves. Nice that is. Look: look, look, look, look: you look at us.

That's joyful I can feel. Never have written it. Why? My joy is other joy. But both are joys. Yes, joy it must be. Mere fact of music shows you are. Often thought she was in the dumps till she began to lilt. Then know.

M'Coy valise. My wife and your wife. Squealing cat. Like tearing silk. When she talks like the clapper of a bellows. They can't manage men's intervals. Gap in their voices too. Fill me. I'm warm, dark, open. Molly in *quis est homo:* Mercadante. My ear against the wall to hear. Want a woman who can deliver the goods.

Jog jig jogged stopped. Dandy tan shoe of dandy Boylan socks skyblue clocks came light to earth.

O, look we are so! Chamber music. Could make a kind of pun on that. It is a kind of music I often thought when she. Acoustics that is. Tinkling. Empty vessels make most noise. Because the acoustics, the resonance changes according as the weight of the water is equal to the law of falling water. Like those rhapsodies of Liszt's, Hungarian, gipsyeyed. Pearls. Drops. Rain. Diddle iddle addle addle oodle oodle. Hiss. Now. Maybe now. Before.

One rapped on a door, one tapped with a knock, did he knock Paul de Kock, with a loud proud knocker, with a cock carracarracarra cock. Cockcock.

Tap.

—*Qui sdegno,* Ben, said Father Cowley.

—No, Ben, Tom Kernan interfered, *The Croppy Boy.* Our native Doric.

—Ay do, Ben, Mr Dedalus said. Good men and true.

—Do, do, they begged in one.

I'll go. Here, Pat, return. Come. He came, he came, he did not stay. To me. How much?

—What key? Six sharps?

—F sharp major, Ben Dollard said.

Bob Cowley's outstretched talons gripped the black deepsounding chords.

Must go prince Bloom told Richie prince. No, Richie said. Yes, must. Got money somewhere. He's on for a razzle backache spree. Much? He seehears lipspeech. One and nine. Penny for yourself. Here. Give him twopence tip. Deaf, bothered. But perhaps he has wife and family waiting, waiting Patty come home. Hee hee hee hee. Deaf wait while they wait.

But wait. But hear. Chordsdark. Lugugugubrious. Low. In a cave of the dark middle earth. Embedded ore. Lumpmusic.

The voice of dark age, of unlove, earth's fatigue made grave approach, and painful, come from afar, from hoary mountains, called on good men and true. The priest he sought, with him would he speak a word.

Tap.

Ben Dollard's voice barreltone. Doing his level best to say it. Croak of vast manless moonless womoonless marsh. Other comedown. Big ships' chandler's business he did once. Remember: rosiny ropes, ships' lanterns. Failed to the tune of ten thousand pounds. Now in the Iveagh home. Cubicle number so and so. Number one Bass did that for him.

The priest's at home. A false priest's servant bade him welcome. Step in. The holy father. Curlycues of chords.

Ruin them. Wreck their lives. Then build them cubicles to end their days in. Hushaby. Lullaby. Die, dog. Little dog, die.

The voice of warning, solemn warning, told them the youth had entered a lonely hall, told them how solemn fell his footstep there, told them the gloomy chamber, the vested priest sitting to shrive.

Decent soul. Bit addled now. Thinks he'll win in *Answers* poets' picture puzzle. We hand you crisp five pound note. Bird sitting hatching in a nest. Lay of the last minstrel he thought it was. See blank tee what domestic animal? Tee dash ar most courageous mariner. Good voice he has still. No eunuch yet with all his belongings.

Listen. Bloom listened. Richie Goulding listened. And by the door deaf Pat, bald Pat, tipped Pat, listened.

The chords harped slower.

The voice of penance and of grief came slow, embellished tremulous. Ben's contrite beard confessed: *in nomine Domini,* in God's name. He knelt. He beat his hand upon his breast, confessing: *mea culpa.*

Latin again. That holds them like birdlime. Priest with the communion corpus for those women. Chap in the mortuary, coffin or coffey, *corpusnomine*. Wonder where that rat is by now. Scrape.

Tap.

They listened: tankards and Miss Kennedy, George Lidwell eyelid well expressive, fullbusted satin, Kernan, Si.

The sighing voice of sorrow sang. His sins. Since easter he had cursed three times. You bitch's bast. And once at masstime he had gone to play. Once by the churchyard he had passed and for his mother's rest he had not prayed. A boy. A croppy boy.

Bronze, listening by the beerpull, gazed far away. Soulfully. Doesn't half know I'm. Molly great dab at seeing anyone looking.

Bronze gazed far sideways. Mirror there. Is that best side of her face? They always know. Knock at the door. Last tip to titivate.

Cockcarracarra.

What do they think when they hear music? Way to catch rattlesnakes. Night Michael Gunn gave us the box. Tuning up. Shah of Persia liked that best. Remind him of home sweet home. Wiped his nose in curtain too. Custom his country perhaps. That's music too. Not as bad as it sounds. Tootling. Brasses braying asses through uptrunks. Doublebasses, helpless, gashes in their sides. Woodwinds mooing cows. Semigrand open crocodile music hath jaws. Woodwind like Goodwin's name.

She looked fine. Her crocus dress she wore, lowcut, belongings on show. Clove her breath was always in theatre when she bent to ask a question. Told her what Spinoza says in that book of poor papa's. Hypnotised, listening. Eyes like that. She bent. Chap in dresscircle, staring down into her with his operaglass for all he was worth. Beauty of music you must hear twice. Nature woman half a look. God made the country man the tune. Met him pike hoses. Philosophy. O rocks!

All gone. All fallen. At the siege of Ross his father, at Gorey all his brothers fell. To Wexford, we are the boys of Wexford, he would. Last of his name and race.

I too, last my race. Milly young student. Well, my fault perhaps. No son. Rudy. Too late now. Or if not? If not? If still?

He bore no hate.

Hate. Love. Those are names. Rudy. Soon I am old.

Big Ben his voice unfolded. Great voice, Richie Goulding said, a flush struggling in his pale, to Bloom, soon old but when was young.

Ireland comes now. My country above the king. She listens. Who fears to speak of nineteen four? Time to be shoving. Looked enough.

—*Bless me, father,* Dollard the croppy cried. *Bless me and let me go.*

Tap.

Bloom looked, unblessed to go. Got up to kill: on eighteen bob a week. Fellows shell out the dibs. Want to keep your weathereye open. Those girls, those lovely. By the sad sea waves. Chorusgirl's romance. Letters read out for breach of promise. From Chickabiddy's own Mumpsypum. Laughter in court. Henry. I never signed it. The lovely name you.

Low sank the music, air and words. Then hastened. The false priest rustling soldier from his cassock. A yeoman captain. They know it all by heart. The thrill they itch for. Yeoman cap.

Tap. Tap.

Thrilled, she listened, bending in sympathy to hear.

Blank face. Virgin should say: or fingered only. Write something on it: page. If not what becomes of them? Decline, despair. Keeps them young. Even admire themselves. See. Play on her. Lip blow. Body of white woman, a flute alive. Blow gentle. Loud. Three holes all women. Goddess I didn't see. They want it: not too much polite. That's why he gets them. Gold in your pocket, brass in your face. With look to look: songs without words. Molly that hurdygurdy boy. She knew he meant the monkey was sick. Or because so like the Spanish. Understand animals too that way. Solomon did. Gift of nature.

Ventriloquise. My lips closed. Think in my stom. What?

Will? You? I. Want. You. To.

With hoarse rude fury the yeoman cursed. Swelling in apoplectic bitch's bastard. A good thought, boy, to come. One hour's your time to live, your last.

Tap. Tap.

Thrill now. Pity they feel. To wipe away a tear for martyrs. For all things dying, want do, dying to, die. For that all things born. Poor Mrs Purefoy. Hope she's over. Because their wombs.

# THE SIRENS

A liquid of womb of woman eyeball gazed under a fence of lashes, calmly, hearing. See real beauty of the eye when she not speaks. On yonder river. At each slow satiny heaving bosom's wave (her heaving embon) red rose rose slowly, sank red rose. Heartbeats her breath: breath that is life. And all the tiny tiny fernfoils trembled of maidenhair.

But look. The bright stars fade. O rose! Castille. The morn. Ha. Lidwell. For him then not for. Infatuated. I like that? See her from here though. Popped corks, splashes of beerfroth, stacks of empties.

On the smooth jutting beerpull laid Lydia hand lightly, plumply, leave it to my hands. All lost in pity for croppy. Fro, to: to, fro: over the polished knob (she knows his eyes, my eyes, her eyes) her thumb and finger passed in pity: passed, repassed and, gently touching, then slid so smoothly, slowly down, a cool firm white enamel baton protruding through their sliding ring.

With a cock with a carra.

Tap. Tap. Tap.

I hold this house. Amen. He gnashed in fury. Traitors swing.

The chords consented. Very sad thing. But had to be.

Get out before the end. Thanks, that was heavenly. Where's my hat. Pass by her. Can leave that *Freeman*. Letter I have. Suppose she were the? No. Walk, walk, walk. Like Cashel Boylo Connoro Coylo Tisdall Maurice Tisntdall Farrell. Waaaaaaalk.

Well, I must be. Are you off? Yrfmstbyes. Blmstup. O'er rychigh blue. Bloom stood up. Ow. Soap feeling rather sticky behind. Must have sweated: music. That lotion, remember. Well, so long. High grade. Card inside, yes.

By deaf Pat in the doorway, straining ear, Bloom passed.

At Geneva barrack that young man died. At Passage was his body laid. Dolor! O, he dolores! The voice of the mournful chanter called to dolorous prayer.

By rose, by satiny bosom, by the fondling hand, by slops, by empties, by popped corks, greeting in going, past eyes and maidenhair, bronze and faint gold in deepseashadow, went Bloom, soft Bloom, I feel so lonely Bloom.

Tap. Tap. Tap.

Pray for him, prayed the bass of Dollard. You who hear in peace. Breathe a prayer, drop a tear, good men, good people. He was the croppy boy.

Scaring eavesdropping boots croppy bootsboy Bloom in the Ormond hallway heard growls and roars of bravo, fat backslapping, their boots all treading, boots not the boots the boy. General chorus off for a swill to wash it down. Glad I avoided.

—Come on, Ben, Simon Dedalus said. By God, you're as good as ever you were.

—Better, said Tomgin Kernan. Most trenchant rendition of that ballad, upon my soul and honour it is.

—Lablache, said Father Cowley.

Ben Dollard bulkily cachuchad towards the bar, mightily praisefed and all big roseate, on heavyfooted feet, his gouty fingers nakkering castagnettes in the air.

Big Benaben Dollard. Big Benben. Big Benben.

Rrr.

And deepmoved all, Simon trumping compassion from foghorn nose, all laughing, they brought him forth, Ben Dollard, in right good cheer.

—You're looking rubicund, George Lidwell said.

Miss Douce composed her rose to wait.

—Ben machree, said Mr Dedalus, clapping Ben's fat back shoulderblade. Fit as a fiddle, only he has a lot of adipose tissue concealed about his person.

Rrrrrrsss.

—Fat of death, Simon, Ben Dollard growled.

Richie rift in the lute alone sat: Goulding, Collis, Ward. Uncertainly he waited. Unpaid Pat too.

Tap. Tap. Tap. Tap.

Miss Mina Kennedy brought near her lips to ear of tankard one.

—Mr Dollard, they murmured low.

—Dollard, murmured tankard.

Tank one believed: Miss Kenn when she: that doll he was: she doll: the tank.

He murmured that he knew the name. The name was familiar to him, that is to say. That was to say he had heard the name of Dollard, was it? Dollard, yes.

Yes, her lips said more loudly, Mr Dollard. He sang that song lovely, murmured Mina. And *The last rose of summer* was a lovely song. Mina loved that song. Tankard loved the song that Mina.

'Tis the last rose of summer dollard left Bloom felt wind wound round inside.

Gassy thing that cider: binding too. Wait. Postoffice near Reuben J's one and eightpence too. Get shut of it. Dodge round by Greek street. Wish I hadn't promised to meet. Freer in air. Music. Gets on your nerves. Beerpull. Her hand that rocks the cradle rules the. Ben Howth. That rules the world.

Far. Far. Far. Far.

Tap. Tap. Tap. Tap.

Up the quay went Lionelleopold, naughty Henry with letter for Mady, with sweets of sin with frillies for Raoul with met him pike hoses went Poldy on.

Tap blind walked tapping by the tap the curbstone tapping, tap by tap. Cowley, he stuns himself with it; kind of drunkenness. Better give way only half way the way of a man with a maid. Instance enthusiasts. All ears. Not lose a demisemiquaver. Eyes shut. Head nodding in time. Dotty. You daren't budge. Thinking strictly prohibited. Always talking shop. Fiddlefaddle about notes.

All a kind of attempt to talk. Unpleasant when it stops because you never know exac. Organ in Gardiner street. Old Glynn fifty quid a year. Queer up there in the cockloft alone with stops and locks and keys. Seated all day at the organ. Maunder on for hours, talking to himself or the other fellow blowing the bellows. Growl angry, then shriek cursing (want to have wadding or something in his no don't she cried), then all of a soft sudden wee little wee little pippy wind.

Pwee! A wee little wind piped eeee. In Bloom's little wee.

—Was he? Mr Dedalus said, returning, with fetched pipe. I was with him this morning at poor little Paddy Dignam's . . .

—Ay, the Lord have mercy on him.

—By the by there's a tuningfork in there on the . . .

Tap. Tap. Tap. Tap.

—The wife has a fine voice. Or had. What? Lidwell asked.

—O, that must be the tuner, Lydia said to Simonlionel first I saw, forgot it when he was here.

Blind he was she told George Lidwell second I saw. And played so exquisitely, treat to hear. Exquisite contrast: bronzelid minagold.

—Shout! Ben Dollard shouted, pouring. Sing out!

—'lldo! cried Father Cowley.

Rrrrrr.

I feel I want . . .

Tap. Tap. Tap. Tap. Tap.

—Very, Mr Dedalus said, staring hard at a headless sardine.

Under the sandwichbell lay on a bier of bread one last, one lonely, last sardine of summer. Bloom alone.

—Very, he stared. The lower register, for choice.

Tap. Tap. Tap. Tap. Tap. Tap. Tap. Tap.

Bloom went by Barry's. Wish I could. Wait. That wonderworker if I had. Twenty-four solicitors in that one house. Litigation. Love one another. Piles of parchment. Messrs Pick and Pocket have power of attorney. Goulding, Collis, Ward.

But for example the chap that wallops the big drum. His vocation: Micky Rooney's band. Wonder how it first struck him. Sitting at home after pig's cheek and cabbage nursing it in the armchair. Rehearsing his band part. Pom. Pompedy. Jolly for the wife. Asses' skins. Welt them through life, then wallop after death. Pom. Wallop. Seems to be what you call yashmak or I mean kismet. Fate.

Tap. Tap. A stripling, blind, with a tapping cane, came taptaptapping by Daly's window where a mermaid, hair all streaming (but he couldn't see), blew whiffs of a mermaid (blind couldn't), mermaid coolest whiff of all.

Instruments. A blade of grass, shell of her hands, then blow. Even comb and tissuepaper you can knock a tune out of. Molly in her shift in Lombard street west, hair down. I suppose each kind of trade made its own, don't you see? Hunter with a horn. Haw. Have you the? *Cloche. Sonnez la!* Shepherd his pipe. Policeman a whistle. Locks and keys! Sweep! Four o'clock's all's well! Sleep! All is lost now. Drum? Pompedy. Wait, I know. Towncrier, bumbailiff. Long John. Waken the dead. Pom. Dignam. Poor little *nomine-domine.* Pom. It is music, I mean of course it's all pom pom pom very much what they call *da capo.* Still you can hear. As we march we march along, march along. Pom.

I must really. Fff. Now if I did that at a banquet. Just a question of custom shah of Persia. Breathe a prayer, drop a tear. All the same he must have been a bit of a natural not to see it was a yeoman cap. Muffled up. Wonder who was that chap at the grave in the brown mackin. O, the whore of the lane!

A frowsy whore with black straw sailor hat askew came glazily in the day along the quay towards Mr Bloom. When first he saw that form endearing. Yes, it is. I feel so lonely. Wet night in the lane. Horn. Who had the? Heehaw. Shesaw. Off her beat here. What is she? Hope she. Psst! Any chance of your wash. Knew Molly. Had me decked. Stout lady does be with you in the brown costume. Put you off your stroke. That appointment we made. Knowing we'd never, well hardly ever. Too dear too near to home sweet home. Sees me, does she? Looks a fright in the day. Face like dip. Damn her! O, well, she has to live like the rest. Look in here.

In Lionel Marks's antique saleshop window haughty Henry Lionel Leopold dear Henry Flower earnestly Mr Leopold Bloom envisaged candlestick melodeon oozing maggoty blowbags. Bargain: six bob. Might learn to play. Cheap. Let her pass. Course everything is dear if you don't want it. That's what good salesman is. Make you buy what he wants to sell. Chap sold me the Swedish razor he shaved me with. Wanted to charge me for the edge he gave it. She's passing now. Six bob.

Must be the cider or perhaps the burgund.

Near bronze from anear near gold from afar they chinked their clinking glasses all, brighteyed and gallant, before bronze Lydia's tempting last rose of summer, rose of Castille. First Lid, De, Cow, Ker, Doll, a fifth: Lidwell, Si Dedalus, Bob Cowley, Kernan and Big Ben Dollard.

Tap. A youth entered a lonely Ormond hall.

Bloom viewed a gallant pictured hero in Lionel Marks's window. Robert Emmet's last words. Seven last words. Of Meyerbeer that is.

—True men like you men.

—Ay, ay, Ben.

—Will lift your glass with us.

They lifted.

Tschink. Tschunk.

Tip. An unseeing stripling stood in the door. He saw not bronze. He saw not gold. Nor Ben nor Bob nor Tom nor Si nor George nor tanks nor Richie nor Pat. Hee hee hee hee. He did not see.

Seabloom, greaseabloom viewed last words. Softly. *When my country takes her place among.*[1]

Prrprr.

Must be the bur.

Ff. Oo. Rrpr.

*Nations of the earth.* No-one behind. She's passed. *Then and not*

---

[1] This and the following phrases in italics are the concluding sentences of Robert Emmet's speech from the dock.

*till then.* Tram. Kran, kran, kran. Good oppor. Coming Krandlkrankran. I'm sure it's the burgund. Yes. One, two. *Let my epitaph be.* Karaaaaaaa. *Written. I have.*

Pprrpffrrppfff

Done.

NOTE: *In the above episode from* Ulysses, *given in its entirety, the two barmaids correspond to the Sirens whose singing tempted Ulysses. Appropriately, Joyce has chosen to illustrate in this episode the art of music: the technic of the episode as a whole is that of a* fuga per canonem; *musical terms and the names of musical instruments abound in the text; a great number of musical devices are imitated by the repetition and distortion of words and sentences.*

*A brief outline of the events that occur in this episode follows: Mr. Bloom (Ulysses) dines in the Ormond Hotel while Blazes Boylan has a drink in the bar and departs on a jaunting-car to an assignation with Mrs. Bloom (Penelope). Bloom knows about the appointment and cannot keep his mind off it for long. Meanwhile in the music room of the hotel, Simon Dedalus sings the aria* M'appari *from Flotow's* Martha *and Ben Dollard follows with a pathetic patriotic ballad,* The Croppy Boy. *Mr. Bloom after dinner writes a 'lonely hearts' letter to Martha Clifford, signing himself 'Henry Flower.' Upon leaving the hotel to post his letter, he avoids two minor embarrassments, one social, the other intestinal, with the resourcefulness of a true Ulysses.*

FLANN O'BRIEN

# Mad Sweeny versus Jem Casey[1]

SYNOPSIS, *being a summary of what has gone before, FOR THE BENEFIT OF NEW READERS:* DERMOT TRELLIS, an eccentric author, conceives the project of writing a salutary book on the consequences which follow wrong-doing and creates for the purpose

THE POOKA FERGUS MACPHELLIMEY, a species of human Irish devil endowed with magical powers. He then creates

JOHN FURRISKEY, a depraved character, whose task is to attack women and behave at all times in an indecent manner. By magic he is instructed by Trellis to go one night to Donnybrook where he will by arrangement meet and betray

PEGGY, a domestic servant. He meets her and is much surprised when she confides in him that Trellis has fallen asleep and that her virtue has already been assailed by an elderly man subsequently to be identified as

FINN MACCOOL, a legendary character hired by Trellis on account of the former's venerable appearance and experience, to act as the girl's father and chastise her for her transgressions against the moral law; and that her virtue has also been assailed by

PAUL SHANAHAN, another man hired by Trellis for performing various small and unimportant parts in the story, also for running messages, &c. &c. Peggy and Furriskey then have a long discussion on the roadside in which she explains to him that Trellis's powers are suspended when he falls asleep and that Finn and Shanahan were taking advantage of that fact when they came to see her because they would not dare to defy him when he is awake. Furriskey then inquires whether she yielded to them and she replies that indeed she did not. Furriskey then praises her and they discover after a short time that they have fallen in love with each other at first sight. They arrange to lead virtuous lives, to simulate the immoral actions, thoughts and words which Trellis demands of them on pain of the severest penalties. They also arrange that the first of them who shall be free shall wait for the other with a view to marriage at the earliest opportunity. Meanwhile Trellis, in order to show how an evil man can debase the highest and the lowest in the same story, creates a very beautiful and refined girl called

[1] From *At Swim-Two-Birds*, London, 1939. First published in U. S., 1951.

563

SHEILA LAMONT, whose brother,

ANTONY LAMONT he has already hired so that there will be somebody to demand satisfaction off John Furriskey for betraying her—all this being provided for in the plot. Trellis creates Miss Lamont in his own bedroom and he is so blinded by her beauty (which is naturally the type of beauty nearest to his heart), that he so far forgets himself as to assault her himself. Furriskey in the meantime returns to the Red Swan Hotel where Trellis lives and compels all those working for him to live also. He (Furriskey) is determined to pretend that he faithfully carried out the terrible mission he was sent on. Now read on.

*Further extract from Manuscript. Oratio recta:* With a key in his soft nervous hand, he opened the hall door and removed his shoes with two swift spells of crouching on the one leg. He crept up the stairs with the noiseless cat-tread of his good-quality woollen socks. The door of Trellis was dark and sleeping as he passed up the stairs to his room. There was a crack of light at Shanahan's door and he placed his shoes quietly on the floor and turned the handle.

The hard Furriskey, said Shanahan.

Here was Shanahan stretched at the fire, with Lamont on his left and the old greybeard seated beyond dimly on the bed with his stick between his knees and his old eyes staring far into the red fire like a man whose thought was in a distant part of the old world or maybe in another world altogether.

By God you weren't long, said Lamont.

Shut the door, said Shanahan, but see you're in the room before you do so. Shut the door and treat yourself to a chair, Mr. F. You're quick off the mark all right. Move up there, Mr. L.

It's not what you call a full-time occupation, said Furriskey in a weary way. It's not what you call a life sentence.

It is not, said Lamont. You're right there.

Now don't worry, said Shanahan in a pitying manner, there's plenty more coming. We'll keep you occupied now, don't you worry, won't we, Mr. Lamont?

We'll see that he gets his bellyful, said Lamont.

You're decent fellows the pair of ye, said Furriskey.

He sat on a stool and extended his fan to the fire, the fan of his ten fingers.

You can get too much of them the same women, he said.

Is that a fact, said Shanahan in unbelief. Well I never heard that said before. Come here, Mr. Furriskey, did you. . . .

O it was all right, I'll tell you sometime, said Furriskey.

Didn't I tell you it was all right? Didn't I?

You did, said Furriskey.

He took a sole cigarette from a small box.

I'll tell you the whole story sometime but not now, he said. He nodded towards the bed.

Is your man asleep or what?

Maybe he is, said Shanahan, but by God it didn't sound like it five minutes ago. Mr. Storybook was wide awake.

He was wide awake, said Lamont.

Five minutes ago he was giving out a yarn the length of my arm, said Shanahan. Right enough he is a terrible man for talk. Aren't you now? He'd talk the lot of us into the one grave if you gave him his head, don't ask me how I know, look at my grey hairs. Isn't that a fact, Mr. Lamont?

For a man of his years, said Lamont slowly and authoritatively, he can do the talking. By God he can do the talking. He has seen more of the world than you or me, of course, that's the secret of it.

That's true, said Furriskey, a happy fire-glow running about his body. He carefully directed the smoke of his cigarette towards the flames and up the chimney. Yes, he's an old man, of course.

His stories are not the worst though. I'll say that, said Lamont, there's always a head and a tail on his yarns, a beginning and an end, give him his due.

O I don't know, said Furriskey.

O he can talk, he can talk, I agree with you there, said Shanahan, credit where credit is due. But you'd want what you'd call a grain of *salo* with more than one of them if I know anything.

A pinch of salt? said Lamont.

A grain of *salo*, Mr. L.

I don't doubt it, said Furriskey.

Relate, said hidden Conán, the tale of the Feasting of Dún na nGedh.

Finn in his mind was nestling with his people.

I mean to say, said Lamont, whether a yarn is tall or small I like to hear it well told. I like to meet a man that can take in hand to tell a story and not make a balls of it while he's at it. I like to know where I am, do you know. Everything has a beginning and an end.

It is true, said Finn, that I will not.

O that's right too, said Shanahan.

Relate then, said Conán, the account of the madness of King Sweeny and he on a madman's flight through the length of Erin.

That's a grand fire, said Furriskey, and if a man has that, he can't want a lot more. A fire, a bed, and a roof over his head, that's all. With a bite to eat, of course.

It's all very fine for you to talk, now, said Lamont, you had something for your tea to-night that the rest of us hadn't, eh, Mr. Shanahan. Know what I mean?

Keep the fun clean, said Shanahan.

I beg, Mr. Chairman, said Furriskey, to be associated with them sentiments. What's clean, keep it clean.

There was a concerted snigger, harmonious, scored for three voices.

I will relate, said Finn.

We're off again, said Furriskey.

The first matter that I will occupy with honey-words and melodious recital, said Finn, is the reason and the first cause for Sweeny's frenzy.

Draw in your chairs, boys, said Shanahan, we're right for the night. We're away on a hack.

Pray proceed, Sir, said Lamont.

Now Sweeny was King of Dal Araidhe and a man that was easily moved to the tides of anger.[1] Near his house was the cave of a saint called Ronan—a shield against evil was this gentle generous friendly active man, who was out in the matin-hours taping out the wall-steads of a new sun-bright church and ringing his bell in the morning.

Good for telling, said Conán.

Now when Sweeny heard the clack of the clergyman's bell, his brain and his spleen and his gut were exercised by turn and together with the fever of a flaming anger. He made a great run out of the house without a cloth-stitch to the sheltering of his naked nudity, for he had run out of his cloak when his wife Eorann held it

---

[1] The story of Mad Sweeny, which Finn proceeds to relate, is a virtual translation of a 12th century text, *Buile Shuibni*.

for restraint and deterrence, and he did not rest till he had snatched the beauteous light-lined psalter from the cleric and put it in the lake, at the bottom; after that he took the hard grip of the cleric's hand and ran with a wind-swift stride to the lake without a halting or a letting go of the hand because he had a mind to place the cleric by the side of his psalter in the lake, on the bottom, to speak precisely. But, evil destiny, he was deterred by the big storm-voiced hoarse shout, the shout of a scullion calling him to the profession of arms at the battle of Magh Rath. Sweeny then left the cleric sad and sorrowful over the godless battery of the king and lamenting his psalter. This, however, an otter from the murk of the lake returned to him unharmed, its lines and its letters unblemished. He then returned with joyous piety to his devotions and put a malediction on Sweeny by the uttering of a lay of eleven melodious stanzas.

Thereafter he went himself with his acolytes to the plain of Magh Rath for the weaving of concord and peace between the hosts and was himself taken as a holy pledge, the person of the cleric, that fighting should cease at sun-down and that no man should be slain until fighting would be again permitted, the person of the cleric a holy hostage and exchange between the hosts. But, evil destiny, Sweeny was used to violating the guarantee by the slaughter of a man every morning before the hour when fighting was permitted. On the morning of a certain day, Ronan and his eight psalmists were walking in the field and sprinkling holy water on the hosts against the incidence of hurt or evil when they sprinkled the head of Sweeny with the rest. Sweeny in anger took a cast and reddened his spear in the white side of a psalmist and broke Ronan's bell whereupon the cleric uttered this melodious lay:

> My curse on Sweeny!
> His guilt against me is immense,
> he pierced with his long swift javelin
> my holy bell.
>
> The holy bell that thou hast outraged
> will banish thee to branches,
> it will put thee on a par with fowls—
> the saint-bell of saints with sainty-saints.
>
> Just as it went prestissimo
> the spear-shaft skyward,
> you too, Sweeny, go madly mad-gone
> skyward.

> Eorann of Conn tried to hold him
> by a hold of his smock
> and though I bless her therefore,
> my curse on Sweeny.

Thereafter when the hosts clashed and bellowed like stag-herds and gave three audible world-wide shouts till Sweeny heard them and their hollow reverberations in the sky-vault, he was beleaguered by an anger and a darkness, and fury and fits and frenzy and fright-fraught fear, and he was filled with a restless tottering unquiet and with a disgust for the places that he knew and with a desire to be where he never was, so that he was palsied of hand and foot and eye-mad and heart-quick and went from the curse of Ronan bird-quick in craze and madness from the battle. For the nimble lightness of his tread in flight he did not shake dewdrops from the grass-stalks and staying not for bog or thicket or marsh or hollow or thick-sheltering wood in Erin for that day, he travelled till he reached Ros Bearaigh in Glenn Earcain where he went into the yew-tree that was in the glen.

In a later hour his kin came to halt beneath the tree for a spell of discourse and melodious talk about Sweeny and no tidings concerning him either in the east or the west; and Sweeny in the yew-tree above them listened till he made answer in this lay:

> O warriors approach,
> warriors of Dal Araidhe,
> you will find him in the tree he is
> the man you seek.
>
> God has given me life here,
> very bare, very narrow,
> no woman, no trysting,
> no music or trance-eyed sleep.

When they noticed the verses from the tree-top they saw Sweeny in branches and then they talked their honey-words, beseeching him that he should be trustful, and then made a ring around the tree-bole. But Sweeny arose nimbly and away to Cell Riagain in Tir Conaill where he perched in the old tree of the church, going and coming between branches and the rain-clouds of the skies, trespassing and wayfaring over peaks and summits and across the ridge-pole of black hills, and visiting in dark mountains, ruminating and searching in cavities and narrow crags and slag-slits in rocky hidings, and lodging in the clump of tall ivies and in the cracks of hillstones, a year of time from summit to summit and from glen to glen and from river-mouth to river till he arrived at ever-delightful Glen Bolcain. For it is thus that Glen Bolcain is, it has four gaps to the four winds and a too-fine too-pleasant wood and fresh-banked wells and cold-clean fountains and sandy pellucid streams of clear water with green-topped watercress and brooklime long-streamed on the current, and a richness of sorrels and wood-sorrels, *lus-bian* and *biorragan* and berries and wild garlic, *melle* and *miodhbhun*,[1] inky sloes and dun acorns. For it was here that the madmen of Erin were used to come when their year of madness was complete, smiting and lamming each other for choice of its watercress and in rivalry for its fine couches.

In that glen it was hard for Sweeny to endure the pain of his bed there on the top of a tall ivy-grown hawthorn in the glen, every twist that he would turn sending showers of hawy thorns into his flesh, tearing and rending and piercing him and pricking his blood-red skin. He thereupon changed beds to the resting of another tree where there were tangles of thick fine-thorned briars and a solitary branch of blackthorn growing up through the core of the brambles. He settled and roosted on its slender perch till it bowed beneath him and bent till it slammed him to the ground, not one inch of him from toe to crown that was not red-prickled and blood-gashed, the skin to his body being ragged and flapping and thorned, the tattered cloak of his perished skin. He arose death-weak from the ground to his standing for the recital of this lay.

> A year to last night
> I have lodged there in branches
> from the flood-tide to the ebb-tide
> naked.

> Bereft of fine women-folk,
> the brooklime for a brother—
> our choice for a fresh meal
> is watercress always.

> Without accomplished musicians
> without generous women,
> no jewel-gift for bards—
> respected Christ, it has perished me.

---

[1] These Gaelic names of plants presumably have no identifiable English equivalents.

> The thorntop that is not gentle
> has reduced me, has pierced me,
> it has brought me near death
> the brown thorn-bush.
>
> Once free, once gentle,
> I am banished for ever,
> wretch-wretched I have been
> a year to last night.

He remained there in Glen Bolcain until he elevated himself high in the air and went to Cluain Cille on the border of Tir Conaill and Tir Boghaine. He went to the edge of the water and took food against the night, watercress and water. After that he went into the old tree of the church where he said another melodious poem on the subject of his personal hardship.

After another time he set forth in the air again till he reached the church at Snámh-dá-én (or Swim-Two-Birds) by the side of the Shannon, arriving there on a Friday, to speak precisely; here the clerics were engaged at the observation of their nones, flax was being beaten and here and there a woman was giving birth to a child; and Sweeny did not stop until he had recited the full length of a further lay.

For seven years, to relate precisely, was Sweeny at the air travel of all Erin, returning always to his tree in charming Glen Bolcain, for that was his fortress and his haven, it was his house there in the glen It was to this place that his foster-brother Linchehaun came for tidings concerning him, for he carried always a deep affection for Sweeny and had retrieved him three times from madness before that. Linchehaun went seeking him in the glen with shouts and found toe-tracks by the stream-mud where the madman was wont to appease himself by the eating of cresses. But track or trace of Sweeny he did not attain for that day and he sat down in an old deserted house in the glen till the labour and weariness of his pursuit brought about his sleep. And Sweeny, hearing his snore from his tree-clump in the glen, uttered this lay in the pitch darkness.

> The man by the wall snores
> a snore-sleep that's beyond me,
> for seven years from that Tuesday at Magh Rath
> I have not slept a wink.
>
> O God that I had not gone
> to the hard battle!

> thereafter my name was Mad—
> Mad Sweeny in the bush.
>
> Watercress from the well at Cirb
> is my lot at terce,
> its colour is my mouth,
> green on the mouth of Sweeny.
>
> Chill chill is my body
> when away from ivy,
> the rain torrent hurts it
> and the thunder.
>
> I am in summer with the herons of Cuailgne
> with wolves in winter,
> at other times I am hidden in a copse—
> not so the man by the wall.

And thereafter he met Linchehaun who came visiting to his tree and they parleyed there the two of them together and the one of them talkative and unseen in branches and prickle-briars. And Sweeny bade Linchehaun to depart and not to pursue or annoy him further because the curse of Ronan stopped him from putting his trust or his mad faith in any man.

Thereafter he travelled in distant places till he came at the black fall of a night to Ros Bearaigh and lodged himself in a hunched huddle in the middle of the yew-tree of the church in that place. But being besieged with nets and hog-harried by the caretaker of the church and his false wife, he hurried nimbly to the old tree at Ros Eareain where he remained hidden and unnoticed the length of a full fortnight, till the time when Linchehaun came and perceived the murk of his shadow in the sparse branches and saw the other branches he had broken and bent in his movements and in changing trees. And the two of them parleyed together until they had said between them these fine words following.

Sad it is Sweeny, said Linchehaun, that your last extremity should be thus, without food or drink or raiment like a fowl, the same man that had cloth of silk and of satin and the foreign steed of the peerless bridle, also comely generous women and boys and hounds and princely people of every refinement; hosts and tenants and men-at-arms, and mugs and goblets and embellished buffalo-horns for the savouring of pleasant-tasted fine liquors. Sad it is to see the same man as a hapless air-fowl.

Cease now, Linchehaun, said Sweeney, and give me tidings.

Your father is dead, said Linchehaun.

That has seized me with a blind agony, said Sweeny.

Your mother is likewise dead.

Now all the pity in me is at an end.

Dead is your brother.

Gaping open is my side on account of that.

She has died too your sister.

A needle for the heart is an only sister.

Ah, dumb dead is the little son that called you pop.

Truly, said Sweeny, that is the last blow that brings a man to the ground.

When Sweeney heard the sorry word of his small son still and without life, he fell with a crap from the middle of the yew to the ground and Linchehaun hastened to his thorn-packed flank with feters and handcuffs and manacles and locks and black-iron chains and he did not achieve a resting until the lot were about the madman, and through him and above him and over him, roundwise and about. Thereafter there was a concourse of hospitallers and knights and warriors around the trunk of the yew, and after melodious talk they entrusted the mad one to the care of Linchehaun till he would take him away to a quiet place for a fortnight and a month, to the quiet of a certain room where his senses returned to him, the one after the other, with no one near him but the old mill-hag.

Oh hag, said Sweeny, searing are the tribulations I have suffered; many a terrible leap have I leaped from hill to hill, from fort to fort, from land to land, from valley to valley.

For the sake of God, said the hag, leap for us now a leap such as you leaped in the days of your madness.

And thereupon Sweeny gave a bound over the top of the bedrail till he reached the extremity of the bench.

My conscience indeed, said the hag, I could leap the same leap myself.

And the hag gave a like jump.

Sweeny then gathered himself together in the extremity of his jealousy and threw a leap right out through the skylight of the hostel.

I could vault that vault too, said the hag and straightway she vaulted the same vault. And the short of it is this, that Sweeny travelled the length of five cantreds of leaps until he had penetrated to Glenn na nEachtach in Fiodh Gaibhle with the hag at her hag's leaps behind him; and when Sweeny rested there in a huddle at the top of a tall ivy-branch, the hag was perched there on another tree beside him. He heard there the voice of a stag and he thereupon made a lay eulogizing aloud the trees and the stags of Erin, and he did not cease or sleep until he had achieved these staves.

> Bleating one, little antlers,
> O lamenter we like
> delightful the clamouring
> from your glen you make.
>
> O leafy-oak, clumpy-leaved,
> you are high above trees,
> O hazlet, little clumpy-branch—
> the nut-smell of hazels.
>
> O alder, O alder-friend,
> delightful your colour,
> you don't prickle me or tear
> in the place you are.
>
> O blackthorn, little thorny-one,
> O little dark sloe-tree;
> O watercress, O green-crowned,
> at the well-brink.
>
> O holly, holly-shelter,
> O door against the wind,
> O ash-tree inimical,
> you spearshaft of warrior.
>
> O birch clean and blessed,
> O melodious, O proud,
> delightful the tangle
> of your head-rods.
>
> What I like least in woodlands
> from none I conceal it—
> stirk of a leafy-oak,
> at its swaying.
>
> O faun, little long-legs,
> I caught you with grips,
> I rode you upon your back
> from peak to peak.
>
> Glen Bolcain my home ever,
> it was my haven,
> many a night have I tried
> a race against the peak.

I beg your pardon for interrupting, said Shanahan, but you're after reminding me of something, brought the thing into my head in a rush.

He swallowed a draught of vesper-milk, restoring the cloudy glass swiftly to his knee and collecting little belated flavourings from the corners of his mouth.

That thing you were saying reminds me of something bloody good. I beg your pardon for interrupting, Mr. Storybook.

In the yesterday, said Finn, the man who mixed his utterance with the honeywords of Finn was the first day put naked into the tree of Coill Boirche with nothing to his bare hand but a stick of hazel. On the morning of the second day thereafter. . . .

Now listen for a minute till I tell you something, said Shanahan, did any man here ever hear of the poet Casey?

Who did you say? said Furriskey.

Casey. Jem Casey.

On the morning of the second day thereafter, he was taken and bound and rammed as regards his head into a black hole so that his white body was upside down and upright in Erin for the gazing thereon of man and beast.

Now give us a chance, Mister Storybook, yourself and your black hole, said Shanahan fingering his tie-knot with a long memory-frown across his brow. Come here for a minute. Come here till I tell you about Casey. Do you mean to tell me you never heard of the poet Casey, Mr. Furriskey?

Never heard of him, said Furriskey in a solicitous manner.

I can't say, said Lamont, that I ever heard of him either.

He was a poet of the people, said Shanahan.

I see, said Furriskey.

Now do you understand, said Shanahan. A plain upstanding labouring man, Mr. Furriskey, the same as you or me. A black hat or a bloody ribbon, no by God, not on Jem Casey. A hard-working well-made block of a working man, Mr. Lamont, with the handle of a pick in his hand like the rest of us. Now say there was a crowd of men with a ganger all working there laying a length of gas-pipe on the road. All right. The men pull off their coats and start shovelling and working there for further orders. Here at one end of the hole you have your men crowded up together in a lump and them working away and smoking their butts and talking about the horses and one thing and another. Now do you understand what I'm telling you. Do you follow me?

I see that.

But take a look at the other end of the hole and here is my brave Casey digging away there on his own. Do you understand what I mean, Mr. Furriskey?

Oh I see it all right, said Furriskey.

Right. None of your horses or your bloody blather for him. Not a bit of it. Here is my nabs saying nothing to nobody but working away at a pome in his head with a pick in his hand and the sweat pouring down off his face from the force of his work and his bloody exertions. That's a quare one!

Do you mind that now, said Lamont.

It's a quare one and one that takes a lot of beating. Not a word to nobody, not a look to the left or right but the brainbox going there all the time. Just Jem Casey, a poor ignorant labouring man but head and shoulders above the whole bloody lot of them, not a man in the whole country to beat him when it comes to getting together a bloody pome—not a poet in the whole world that could hold a candle to Jem Casey, not a man of them fit to stand beside him. By God I'd back him to win by a canter against the whole bloody lot of them give him his due.

Is that a fact, Mr. Shanahan, said Lamont. It's not every day in the week you come across a man like that.

Do you know what I'm going to tell you, Mr. Lamont, he was a man that could give the lot of them a good start, pickaxe and all. He was a man that could meet them . . . and meet the best . . . and beat them at their own game, now I'm telling you.

I suppose he could, said Furriskey.

Now I know what I'm talking about. Give a man his due. If a man's station is high or low he is all the same to the God I know. Take the bloody black hats off the whole bunch of them and where are you?

That's the way to look at it, of course, said Furriskey.

Give them a bloody pick, I mean, Mr. Furriskey, give them the shaft of a shovel into their hand and tell them to dig a hole and have the length of a page of poetry off by heart in their heads before the five o'clock whistle. What will you get? By God you could take off your hat to what you'd get at five o'clock from that crowd and that's a sure sharkey.

You'd be wasting your time if you waited till five o'clock if you ask me, said Furriskey with a nod of complete agreement.

You're right there, said Shanahan, you'd be waiting around for bloody nothing. Oh I know them and I know my hard Casey too. By Janey he'd be up at the whistle with a pome a yard long, a bloody lovely thing that would send my nice men home in a hurry, home with their bloody tails between their legs. Yes, I've seen his pomes and read them and . . . do you know what I'm going to tell you, I have loved them. I'm not ashamed to sit here and say it, Mr. Furriskey. I've known the man and I've known his pomes and by God I have loved the two of them and loved them well, too. Do you understand what I'm saying, Mr. Lamont? You, Mr. Furriskey?

Oh that's right.

Do you know what it is, I've met the others, the whole lot of them. I've met them all and know them all. I have seen them and I have read their pomes. I have heard them recited by men that know how to use their tongues, men that couldn't be beaten at their own game. I have seen whole books filled up with their stuff, books as thick as that table there and I'm telling you no lie. But by God, at the heel of the hunt, there was only one poet for me.

On the morning of the third day thereafter, said Finn, he was flogged until he bled water.

Only the one, Mr. Shanahan? said Lamont.

Only the one. And that one poet was a man . . . by the name . . . of Jem Casey. No 'Sir', no 'Mister', no nothing. Jem Casey, Poet of the Pick, that's all. A labouring man, Mr. Lamont, but as sweet a singer in his own way as you'll find in the bloody trees there of a spring day, and that's a fact. Jem Casey, an ignorant God-fearing upstanding labouring man, a bloody navvy. Do you know what I'm going to tell you, I don't believe he ever lifted the latch of a school door. Would you believe that now?

I'd believe it of Casey, said Furriskey, and

I'd believe plenty more of the same man, said Lamont. You haven't any of his pomes on you, have you, Mr. Shanahan?

Now take that stuff your man was giving us a while ago, said Shanahan without heed, about the green hills and the bloody swords and the bird giving out the pay from the top of the tree. Now that's good stuff, it's bloody nice. Do you know what it is, I liked it and liked it well. I enjoyed that certainly.

It wasn't bad at all, said Furriskey, I have heard worse, by God, often. It was all right now.

Do you see what I'm getting at, do you understand me, said Shanahan. It's good, very good. But by Christopher it's not every man could see it, I'm bloody sure of that, one in a thousand.

Oh that's right too, said Lamont.

You can't beat it, of course, said Shanahan with a reddening of the features, the real old stuff of the native land, you know, stuff that brought scholars to our shore when your men on the other side were on the flat of their bellies before the calf of gold with a sheepskin around their man. It's the stuff that put our country where she stands to-day, Mr. Furriskey, and I'd have my tongue out of my head by the bloody roots before I'd be heard saying a word against it. But the man in the street, where does he come in? By God he doesn't come in at all as far as I can see.

What do my brave men in the black hats care whether he's in or out, asked Furriskey. What do they care? It's a short jump for the man in the street, I'm thinking, if he's waiting for that crowd to do anything for him. They're a nice crowd, now, I'm telling you.

Oh that's the truth, said Lamont.

Another thing, said Shanahan, you can get too much of that stuff. Feed yourself up with that tack once and you won't want more for a long time.

There's no doubt about it, said Furriskey.

Try it once, said Shanahan, and you won't want it a second time.

Do you know what it is, said Lamont, there are people who read that . . . and keep reading it . . . and read damn the bloody thing else. Now that's a mistake.

A big mistake, said Furriskey.

But there's one man, said Shanahan, there's one man that can write pomes that you can read all day and all night and keep reading them to your heart's content, stuff you'd never tire of. Pomes written by a man that is one of ourselves and written down for ourselves to read. The name of that man . . .

Now that's what you want, said Furriskey.

The name of that man, said Shanahan, is a name that could be christened on you or me, a name that won't shame us. And that name, said Shanahan, is Jem Casey.

And a very good man, said Lamont.

Jem Casey, said Furriskey.

Do you understand what I mean, said Shanahan.

You haven't any of his pomes on you, have you, said Lamont. If there's one thing I'd like. . . .

I haven't one *on* me if that's what you mean, Mr. Lamont, said Shanahan, but I could give one out as quick as I'd say my prayers. By God it's not for nothing that I call myself a pal of Jem Casey.

I'm glad to hear it, said Lamont.

Stand up there and recite it man, said Furriskey, don't keep us waiting. What's the name of it now?

The name or title of the pome I am about to recite, gentlemen, said Shanahan with leisure priest-like in character, is a pome by the name of the 'Workman's Friend.' By God you can't beat it. I've heard it praised by the highest. It's a pome about a thing that's known to all of us. It's about a drink of porter.[1]

Porter!

Porter.

Up on your legs man, said Furriskey. Mr. Lamont and myself are waiting and listening. Up you get now.

Come on, off you go, said Lamont.

Now listen, said Shanahan clearing the way with small coughs. Listen now.

He arose holding out his hand and bending his knee beneath him on the chair.

> When things go wrong and will not come right,
> Though you do the best you can,
> When life looks black as the hour of night—
> A PINT OF PLAIN IS YOUR ONLY MAN.

By God there's a lilt in that, said Lamont.

Very good indeed, said Furriskey. Very nice.

I'm telling you it's the business, said Shanahan. Listen now.

> When money's tight and is hard to get
> And your horse has also ran,
> When all you have is a heap of debt—
> A PINT OF PLAIN IS YOUR ONLY MAN.

> When health is bad and your heart feels strange,
> And your face is pale and wan,
> When doctors say that you need a change,
> A PINT OF PLAIN IS YOUR ONLY MAN.

There are things in that pome that make for what you call *permanence*. Do you know what I mean, Mr. Furriskey?

---

[1] The Irish working man's drink, a black ale somewhat weaker and cheaper than stout. Also known as 'plain porter' or just 'plain.'

There's no doubt about it, it's a grand thing, said Furriskey. Come on, Mr. Shanahan, give us another verse. Don't tell me that is the end of it.

Can't you listen? said Shanahan.

> When food is scarce and your larder bare
> And no rashers grease your pan,
> When hunger grows as your meals are rare—
> A PINT OF PLAIN IS YOUR ONLY MAN.

What do you think of that now?

It's a pome that'll live, called Lamont, a pome that'll be heard and clapped when plenty more . . .

But wait till you hear the last verse, man, the last polish-off, said Shanahan. He frowned and waved his hand.

Oh it's good, it's good, said Furriskey.

> In time of trouble and lousy strife,
> You have still got a darlint plan,
> You still can turn to a brighter life—
> A PINT OF PLAIN IS YOUR ONLY MAN!

Did you ever hear anything like it in your life, said Furriskey. A pint of plain, by God, what! Oh I'm telling you, Casey was a man in twenty thousand, there's no doubt about that. He knew what he was at, too true he did. If he knew nothing else, he knew how to write a pome. A pint of plain is your only man.

Didn't I tell you he was good? said Shanahan. Oh by Gorrah you can't cod me.

There's one thing in that pome, *permanence*, if you know what I mean. That pome, I mean to say, is a pome that'll be heard wherever the Irish race is wont to gather, it'll live as long as there's a hard root of an Irishman left by the Almighty on this planet, mark my words. What do you think, Mr. Shanahan?

It'll live, Mr. Lamont, it'll live.

I'm bloody sure it will, said Lamont.

A pint of plain, by God, eh? said Furriskey.

Tell us, my Old Timer, said Lamont benignly, what do you think of it? Give the company the benefit of your scholarly pertinacious fastidious opinion, Sir Storybook. Eh, Mr. Shanahan?

Conspirators' eyes were winked smartly in the dancing firelight. Furriskey rapped Finn about the knees.

Wake up!

And Sweeny continued, said corn-yellow Finn, at the recital of these staves.

> If I were to search alone
> the hills of the brown world,
> better would I like my sole hut
> in Glen Bolcain.
>
> Good its water greenish-green
> good its clean strong wind,
> good its cress-green cresses,
> best its branching brooklime.

Quick march again, said Lamont. It'll be a good man that'll put a stop to that man's tongue. More of your fancy kiss-my-hand, by God.

Let him talk, said Furriskey, it'll do him good. It has to come out somewhere.

I'm a man, said Shanahan in a sententious fashion, that could always listen to what my fellowman has to say. I'm telling you now, it's a wise man that listens and says nothing.

Certainly said Lamont. A wise old owl once lived in a wood, the more he heard the less he said, the less he said the more he heard, let's emulate that wise old bird.

There's a lot in that, said Furriskey. A little less of the talk and we were right.

Finn continued with a patient weariness, speaking slowly to the fire and to the six suppliant shoes that were in devotion around it, the voice of the old man from the dim bed.

> Good its sturdy ivies,
> good its bright neat sallow,
> good its yewy yew-yews,
> best its sweet-noise birch.
>
> A haughty ivy
> growing through a twisted tree,
> myself on its true summit,
> I would loth leave it.
>
> I flee before skylarks,
> it is the tense stern-race,
> I overleap the clumps
> on the high hill-peaks.

When it rises in front of me
the proud turtle-dove,
I overtake it swiftly
since my plumage grew.

The stupid unwitting woodcock
when it rises up before me,
methinks it red-hostile,
and the blackbird that cries havoc.

Small foxes yelping
to me and from me,
the wolves tear them—
I flee their cries.

They journeyed in their chase of me
in their swift courses
so that I flew away from them
to the tops of mountains.

On every pool there will rain
a starry frost;
I am wretched and wandering
under it on the peak.

The herons are calling
in cold Glen Eila
swift-flying flocks are flying,
coming and going.

I do not relish
the mad clack of humans
sweeter warble of the bird
in the place he is.

I like not the trumpeting
heard at morn;
sweeter hearing is the squeal
of badgers in Benna Broc.

I do not like it
the loud bugling;
finer is the stagbelling stag
of antler-points twice twenty.

There are makings for plough-teams
from glen to glen;
each resting-stag at rest
on the summit of the peaks.

Excuse me for a second, interposed Shanahan in an urgent manner, I've got a verse in my head. Wait now.
 What!

Listen, man. Listen to this before it's lost. When stags appear on the mountain high, with flanks the colour of bran, when a badger bold can say good-bye, A PINT OF PLAIN IS YOUR ONLY MAN!

Well, by God Shanahan, I never thought you had it in you, said Furriskey, turning his wide-eyed smile to the smile of Lamont, I never thought you had it in you. Take a look at the bloody poet, Mr. Lamont. What?

The hard Shanahan by God, said Lamont. The hard man. That's a good one all right. Put it there, Mr. Shanahan.

Hands were extended till they met, the generous grip of friendship in front of the fire.

All right, said Shanahan laughing in the manner of a proud peacock, don't shake the handle off me altogether. Gentlemen, you flatter me. Order ten pints a man till we celebrate.

My hard bloody Shanahan, said Lamont.

That'll do you now the pair of ye, said Shanahan. Silence in the court now.

The droning from the bed restarted where it stopped.

> The stag of steep Slieve Eibhlinne,
> the stag of sharp Slieve Fuaid,
> the stag of Eala, the stag of Orrery,
> the mad stag of Loch Lein. . . .

WILLIAM BUTLER YEATS

# The Resurrection[1]

Before *I had finished this play I saw that its subject-matter might make it unsuited for the public stage in England or in Ireland. I had begun it with an ordinary stage scene in the mind's eye, curtained walls, a window and door at back, a curtained door at left. I now changed the stage directions and wrote songs for the unfolding and folding of the curtain that it might be played in a studio or a drawing-room like my dance plays, or at the Peacock Theatre[2] before a specially chosen audience. If it is played at the Peacock Theatre the Musicians may sing the opening and closing songs, as they pull apart or pull together the proscenium curtain; the whole stage may be hung with curtains with an opening at the left. While the play is in progress the Musicians will sit towards the right of the audience; if at the Peacock, on the step which separates the stage from the audience, or one on either side of the proscenium.*

Song for the Unfolding and Folding of the Curtain

I

I saw a staring virgin stand
Where holy Dionysus died,
And tear the heart out of his side,
And lay the heart upon her hand
And bear that beating heart away;
And then did all the Muses sing
Of Magnus Annus at the spring,
As though God's death were but a play.

II

Another Troy must rise and set,
Another lineage feed the crow,
Another Argo's painted prow
Drive to a flashier bauble yet.
The Roman Empire stood appalled:

---

[1] First performed July 30, 1934 at the Abbey Theatre, Dublin.
[2] A small playhouse opened by the Abbey Theatre in 1928 for training actors and experimenting with new plays.

It dropped the reins of peace and war
When that fierce virgin and her Star
Out of the fabulous darkness called.

*(The HEBREW is discovered alone upon the stage; he has a sword or spear. The Musicians make faint drum-taps, or sound a rattle; the GREEK enters through the audience from the left.)*

*The Hebrew.* Did you find out what the noise was?

*The Greek.* Yes, I asked a Rabbi.

*The Hebrew.* Were you not afraid?

*The Greek.* How could he know that I am called a Christian? I wore the cap I brought from Alexandria. He said the followers of Dionysus were parading the streets with rattles and drums; that such a thing had never happened in this city before; that the Roman authorities were afraid to interfere. The followers of Dionysus have been out among the fields tearing a goat to pieces and drinking its blood, and are now wandering through the streets like a pack of wolves. The mob was so terrified of their frenzy that it left them alone, or, as seemed more likely, so busy hunting Christians it had time for nothing else. I turned to go, but he called me back and asked where I lived. When I said outside the gates, he asked if it was true that the dead had broken out of the cemeteries.

*The Hebrew.* We can keep the mob off for some minutes, long enough for the Eleven to escape over the roofs. I shall defend the narrow stair between this and the street until I am killed, then you will take my place. Why is not the Syrian here?

*The Greek.* I met him at the door and sent him on a message; he will be back before long.

*The Hebrew.* The three of us will be few enough for the work in hand.

*The Greek* [*glancing towards the opening at the left*]. What are they doing now?

*The Hebrew.* While you were down below, James brought a loaf out of a bag, and Nathaniel found a skin of wine. They put them on the table. It was a long time since they had eaten anything. Then they began to speak in low voices, and John spoke of the last time they had eaten in that room.

*The Greek.* They were thirteen then.

*The Hebrew.* He said that Jesus divided bread and wine amongst them. When John had spoken they sat still, nobody eating or drinking. If you stand here you will see them. That is Peter close to the window. He has been quite motionless for a long time, his head upon his breast.

*The Greek.* Is it true that when the soldier asked him if he were a follower of Jesus he denied it?

*The Hebrew.* Yes, it is true. James told me. Peter told the others what he had done. But when the moment came they were all afraid. I must not blame. I might have been no braver. What are we all but dogs who have lost their master?

*The Greek.* Yet you and I if the mob come will die rather than let it up that stair.

*The Hebrew.* Ah! That is different. I am going to draw that curtain; they must not hear what I am going to say. [*He draws curtain.*]

*The Greek.* I know what is in your mind.

*The Hebrew.* They are afraid because they do not know what to think. When Jesus was taken they could no longer believe him the Messiah. We can find consolation, but for the Eleven it was always complete light or complete darkness.

*The Greek.* Because they are so much older.

*The Hebrew.* No, no. You have only to look into their faces to see they were intended to be saints. They are unfitted for anything else. What makes you laugh?

*The Greek.* Something I can see through the window. There, where I am pointing. There, at the end of the street. [*They stand together looking out over the heads of the audience.*]

*The Hebrew.* I cannot see anything.

*The Greek.* The hill.

*The Hebrew.* That is Calvary.

*The Greek.* And the three crosses on the top of it. [*He laughs again.*]

*The Hebrew.* Be quiet. You do not know what you are doing. You have gone out of your mind. You are laughing at Calvary.

*The Greek.* No, no. I am laughing because they thought they were nailing the hands of a living man upon the Cross, and all the time there was nothing there but a phantom.

*The Hebrew.* I saw him buried.

*The Greek.* We Greeks understand these things. No god has ever been buried; no god has ever suffered. Christ only seemed to be born, only seemed to eat, seemed to sleep, seemed to walk, seemed to die. I did not mean to tell you until I had proof.

*The Hebrew.* Proof?

*The Greek.* I shall have proof before nightfall.

*The Hebrew.* You talk wildly, but a masterless dog can bay the moon.

*The Greek.* No Jew can understand these things.

*The Hebrew.* It is you who do not understand. It is I and those men in there perhaps who begin to understand at last. He was nothing more than a man, the best man who ever lived. Nobody before him had so pitied human misery. He preached the coming of the Messiah because he thought the Messiah would take it all upon himself. Then some day when he was very tired, after a long journey perhaps, he thought that he himself was the Messiah. He thought that because of all destinies it seemed the most terrible.

*The Greek.* How could a man think himself the Messiah?

*The Hebrew.* It was always foretold that he would be born of a woman.

*The Greek.* To say that a god can be born of woman, carried in her womb, fed upon her breast, washed as children are washed, is the most terrible blasphemy.

*The Hebrew.* If the Messiah were not born of a woman he could not take away the sins of man. Every sin starts a stream of suffering, but the Messiah takes it all away.

*The Greek.* Every man's sins are his property. Nobody else has a right to them.

*The Hebrew.* The Messiah is able to exhaust human suffering as

## THE RESURRECTION

though it were all gathered together in the spot of a burning glass.

*The Greek.* That makes me shudder. The utmost possible suffering as an object of worship! You are morbid because your nation has no statues.

*The Hebrew.* What I have described is what I thought until three days ago.

*The Greek.* I say that there is nothing in the tomb.

*The Hebrew.* I saw him carried up the mountain and the tomb shut upon him.

*The Greek.* I have sent the Syrian to the tomb to prove that there is nothing there.

*The Hebrew.* You knew the danger we were all in and yet you weakened our guard?

*The Greek.* I have risked the apostles' lives and our own. What I have sent the Syrian to find out is more important.

*The Hebrew.* None of us is in our right mind to-day. I have got something in my own head that shocks me.

*The Greek.* Something you do not want to speak about?

*The Hebrew.* I am glad that he was not the Messiah; we might all have been deceived to our lives' end, or learnt the truth too late. One had to sacrifice everything that the divine suffering might, as it were, descend into one's mind and soul and make them pure. [*A sound of rattles and drums at first in short bursts that come between sentences, but gradually growing continuous.*] One had to give up all worldly knowledge, all ambition, do nothing of one's own will. Only the divine could have any reality. God had to take complete possession. It must be a terrible thing when one is old, and the tomb round the corner, to think of all the ambitions one has put aside; to think, perhaps, a great deal about women. I want to marry and have children.

*The Greek* [*who is standing facing the audience, and looking out over their heads*]. It is the worshippers of Dionysus. They are under the window now. There is a group of women who carry upon their shoulders a bier with an image of the dead god upon it. No, they are not women. They are men dressed as women. I have seen something like it in Alexandria. They are all silent, as if something were going to happen. My God! What a spectacle! In Alexandria a few men paint their lips vermilion. They imitate women that they may obtain in worship a woman's self-abandonment. No great harm comes of it—but here! Come and look for yourself.

*The Hebrew.* I will not look at such madmen.

*The Greek.* Though the music has stopped, some men are still dancing, and some of the dancers have gashed themselves with knives, imagining themselves, I suppose, at once the god and the Titans that murdered him. A little further off a man and woman are coupling in the middle of the street. She thinks the surrender to some man the dance threw into her arms may bring her god back to life. All are from the foreign quarter to judge by face and costume, and are the most ignorant excitable class of Asiatic Greeks, the dregs of the population. Such people suffer terribly and seek forgetfulness in monstrous ceremonies. Ah, that is what they were waiting for. The crowd has parted to make way for a singer. It is a girl. No, not a girl; a boy from the theatre. I know him. He acts girls' parts. He is dressed as a girl, but his fingernails are gilded and his wig is made of gilded cords. He looks like a statue out of some temple. I remember something of the kind in Alexandria. Three days after the full moon, a full moon in March, they sing the death of the god and pray for his resurrection.

*(One of the Musicians sings the following song)*

Astrea's holy child!
A rattle in the wood
Where a Titan strode!
His rattle drew the child
Into that solitude.

**Barrum, barrum, barrum.** [*Drum-taps accompany and follow the words.*]

We wandering women,
Wives for all that come,
Tried to draw him home;
And every wandering woman
Beat upon a drum.

Barrum, barrum, barrum. [*Drum-taps as before.*]

> But the murderous Titans
> Where the woods grow dim
> Stood and waited him.
> The great hands of those Titans
> Tore limb from limb.

Barrum, barrum, barrum. [*Drum-taps as before.*]

> On virgin Astrea
> That can succour all
> Wandering women call;
> Call out to Astrea
> That the moon stood at the full.

Barrum, barrum, barrum. [*Drum-taps as before.*]

*The Greek.* I cannot think all that self-surrender and self-abasement is Greek, despite the Greek name of its god. When the goddess came to Achilles in the battle she did not interfere with his soul, she took him by his yellow hair. Lucretius thinks that the gods appear in the visions of the day and night but are indifferent to human fate; that, however, is the exaggeration of a Roman rhetorician. They can be discovered by contemplation, in their faces a high keen joy like the cry of a bat, and the man who lives heroically gives them the only earthly body that they covet. He, as it were, copies their gestures and their acts. What seems their indifference is but their eternal possession of themselves. Man, too, remains separate. He does not surrender his soul. He keeps his privacy. [*Drum-taps to represent knocking at the door.*]

*The Hebrew.* There is someone at the door, but I dare not open with that crowd in the street.

*The Greek.* You need not be afraid. The crowd has begun to move away. [*The* HEBREW *goes down into the audience towards the left.*] I deduce from our great philosophers that a god can overwhelm man with disaster, take health and wealth away, but man keeps his privacy. If that is the Syrian he may bring such confirmation that mankind will never forget his words.

*The Hebrew* [*from amongst the audience*]. It is the Syrian. There is something wrong. He is ill or drunk. [*He helps the* SYRIAN *on to the stage.*]

*The Syrian.* I am like a drunken man. I can hardly stand upon my feet. Something incredible has happened. I have run all the way.

*The Hebrew.* Well?

*The Syrian.* I must tell the Eleven at once. Are they still in there? Everybody must be told.

*The Hebrew.* What is it? Get your breath and speak.

*The Syrian.* I was on my way to the tomb. I met the Galilean women, Mary the mother of Jesus, Mary the mother of James, and the other women. The younger women were pale with excitement and began to speak all together. I did not know what they were saying; but Mary the mother of James said that they had been to the tomb at daybreak and found that it was empty.

*The Greek.* Ah!

*The Hebrew.* The tomb cannot be empty. I will not believe it.

*The Syrian.* At the door stood a man all shining, and cried out that Christ had arisen. [*Faint drum-taps and the faint sound of a rattle.*] As they came down the mountain a man stood suddenly at their side; that man was Christ himself. They stooped down and kissed his feet. Now stand out of my way that I may tell Peter and James and John.

*The Hebrew* [*standing before the curtained entrance of the inner room*]. I will not stand out of the way.

*The Syrian.* Did you hear what I said? Our master has arisen.

*The Hebrew.* I will not have the Eleven disturbed for the dreams of women.

*The Greek.* The women were not dreaming. They told you the truth, and yet this man is in the right. He is in charge here. We must all be convinced before we speak to the Eleven.

*The Syrian.* The Eleven will be able to judge better than we.

*The Greek.* Though we are so much younger we know more of the world than they do.

*The Hebrew.* If you told your story they would no more believe it than I do, but Peter's misery would be increased. I know him longer than you do and I know what would happen. Peter would remember that the women did not flinch; that not one amongst them denied her master; that the dream proved their love and faith. Then he would remember that he had lacked both, and imagine that John was looking at him. He would turn away and bury his head in his hands.

*The Greek.* I said that we must all be convinced, but there is another reason why you must not tell them anything. Somebody else is coming. I am certain that Jesus never had a human body; that he is a phantom and can pass through that wall; that he will so pass; that he will pass through this room; that he himself will speak to the apostles.

*The Syrian.* He is no phantom. We put a great stone over the mouth of the tomb, and the women say that it has been rolled back.

*The Hebrew.* The Romans heard yesterday that some of our people planned to steal the body, and to put abroad a story that Christ had arisen; and so escape the shame of our defeat. They probably stole it in the night.

*The Syrian.* The Romans put sentries at the tomb. The women found the sentries asleep. Christ had put them asleep that they might not see him move the stone.

*The Greek.* A hand without bones, without sinews, cannot move a stone.

*The Syrian.* What matter if it contradicts all human knowledge?— another Argo seeks another fleece, another Troy is sacked.

*The Greek.* Why are you laughing?

*The Syrian.* What is human knowledge?

*The Greek.* The knowledge that keeps the road from here to Persia free from robbers, that has built the beautiful humane cities, that has made the modern world, that stands between us and the barbarian.

*The Syrian.* But what if there is something it cannot explain, something more important than anything else?

*The Greek.* You talk as if you wanted the barbarian back.

*The Syrian.* What if there is always something that lies outside knowledge, outside order? What if at the moment when knowledge and order seem complete that something appears? [*He has begun to laugh.*]

*The Hebrew.* Stop laughing.

*The Syrian.* What if the irrational return? What if the circle begin again?

*The Hebrew.* Stop! He laughed when he saw Calvary through the window, and now you laugh.

*The Greek.* He too has lost control of himself.

*The Hebrew.* Stop, I tell you. [*Drums and rattles.*]

*The Syrian.* But I am not laughing. It is the people out there who are laughing.

*The Hebrew.* No, they are shaking rattles and beating drums.

*The Syrian.* I thought they were laughing. How horrible!

*The Greek* [*looking out over heads of audience*]. The worshippers of Dionysus are coming this way again. They have hidden their image of the dead god, and have begun their lunatic cry, 'God has arisen! God has arisen!'

(*The Musicians who have been saying* 'God has arisen!' *fall silent.*)

They will cry 'God has arisen!' through all the streets of the city. They can make their god live and die at their pleasure; but why are they silent? They are dancing silently. They are coming nearer and nearer, dancing all the while, using some kind of ancient step unlike anything I have seen in Alexandria. They are almost under the windows now.

*The Hebrew.* They have come back to mock us, because their god arises every year, whereas our god is dead for ever.

*The Greek.* How they roll their painted eyes as the dance grows quicker and quicker! They are under the window. Why are they all suddenly motionless? Why are all those unseeing eyes turned upon this house? Is there anything strange about this house?

*The Hebrew.* Somebody has come into the room.

*The Greek.* Where?

*The Hebrew.* I do not know; but I thought I heard a step.

*The Greek.* I knew that he would come.

*The Hebrew.* There is no one here. I shut the door at the foot of the steps.

*The Greek.* The curtain over there is moving.

*The Hebrew.* No, it is quite still, and besides there is nothing behind it but a blank wall.

*The Greek.* Look, look!

*The Hebrew.* Yes, it has begun to move. [*During what follows he backs in terror towards the left-hand corner of the stage.*]

*The Greek.* There is someone coming through it.

(*The figure of Christ wearing a recognisable but stylistic mask enters through the curtain. The* SYRIAN *slowly draws back the curtain that shuts off the inner room where the apostles are. The three young men are towards the left of the stage, the figure of Christ is at the back towards the right.*)

*The Greek.* It is the phantom of our master. Why are you afraid? He has been crucified and buried, but only in semblance, and is among us once more. [*The* HEBREW *kneels.*] There is nothing here but a phantom, it has no flesh and blood. Because I know the truth I am not afraid. Look, I will touch it. It may be hard under my hand like a statue—I have heard of such things—or my hand may pass through it—but there is no flesh and blood. [*He goes slowly up to the figure and passes his hand over its side.*] The heart of a phantom is beating! The heart of a phantom is beating! [*He screams. The figure of Christ crosses the stage and passes into the inner room.*]

*The Syrian.* He is standing in the midst of them. Some are afraid. He looks at Peter and James and John. He smiles. He has parted the clothes at his side. He shows them his side. There is a great wound there. Thomas has put his hand into the wound. He has put his hand where the heart is.

*The Greek.* O Athens, Alexandria, Rome, something has come to destroy you! The heart of a phantom is beating! Man has begun to die. Your words are clear at last, O Heraclitus. God and man die each other's life, live each other's death.

(*The Musicians rise, one or more singing the following words. If the performance is in a private room or studio, they unfold and fold a curtain as in my dance plays; if at the Peacock Theatre, they draw the proscenium curtain across.*)

## I

In pity for man's darkening thought
He walked that room and issued thence
In Galilean turbulence;
The Babylonian starlight brought
A fabulous, formless darkness in;
Odour of blood when Christ was slain
Made all Platonic tolerance vain
And vain all Doric discipline.

## II

Everything that man esteems
Endures a moment or a day.
Love's pleasure drives his love away,
The painter's brush consumes his dreams;
The herald's cry, the soldier's tread
Exhaust his glory and his might:
Whatever flames upon the night
Man's own resinous heart has fed.

# NOTES ON THE AUTHORS

AE (George Russell) was born in Lurgan, County Armagh, April 10, 1867. Like Yeats, with whom he attended The High School, Dublin, AE's early interests in painting and the esoteric remained with him for the rest of his life. But as secretary and chief organizer of the Irish Agricultural Organization Society and editor of the leading Irish agricultural journal, *The Irish Homestead,* which later merged with *The Irish Statesman,* AE became an agricultural economist whose books *Cooperation and Nationality* 1912 and *The National Being* 1916 were read by Gandhi and had influence upon The New Deal through Henry Wallace, then Secretary of Commerce. However, it was as a poet and a discoverer of poets that AE achieved his significance in the Literary Revival. The performance of his play *Deirdre,* along with Yeats' *Cathleen Ni Houlihan,* by The Irish National Theatre Society in 1902 marks the real beginning of the Irish national theatre. His biographer, John Eglinton, tells us that AE got his famous *nom de plume* when a compositor had difficulty in making out the word AEON with which Russell had signed an article. Although AE worked for most of his life in the public eye as journalist, agrarian economist, and agricultural organizer, his poems, with few exceptions, are private in their subject matter and subtle in their method. In explaining why he did not include a personal description of AE in *Hail and Farewell,* along with the portraits of other famous Dubliners of the time, George Moore said that AE 'exists rather in one's imagination, dreams, sentiments, feelings, than in one's ordinary sight and hearing, and try as I will to catch the fleeting outlines, they escape me; and all I remember are the long gray, pantheistic eyes that have looked so often into my soul and with such a kindly gaze.' AE died in Bournemouth, England, July 17, 1935. His *Collected Poems* was published in 1927 and *Selected Poems* in 1933.

MARGARET BARRINGTON (Mrs. Liam O'Flaherty), born in 1896, was educated at the Royal School, Dungannon, Co. Tyrone, and at Trinity College, Dublin. Her first husband was Professor Edmund Curtis, the celebrated Irish historian. In 1926, after her divorce, she married Liam O'Flaherty, by whom she has one daughter. The author of one novel, *Look Ever Northward,* she is by profession a free-lance journalist and has written for Irish, English, and American newspapers and periodicals. Her varied and original short stories have never been collected. She now lives a quiet country life at Castletownshend, Co. Cork (also the home of Edith Œ. Somerville), where she can indulge her tastes for walking, collecting wild flowers, bird-watching and fishing.

ELIZABETH BOWEN was born in Dublin on June 7, 1899. Her barrister father came from an Anglo-Irish Cork family, whose ancestral home, Bowen's Court, was built in the 18th century upon land given to the first Bowen for his services to Cromwell a century earlier. Elizabeth Bowen's home for most of her youth was Dublin, but she went to school in Kent, and spent most of her summers and holidays in Cork. She began to write seriously when she was nineteen. She has for some time lived in London with her husband Alan Cameron, but still vacations annually in Cork. Her best-known novels are *To the North* 1932, *The House in Paris* 1936, *The Death of the Heart* 1939; her latest is *The Heat of the Day* 1950. *Look at All Those Roses* 1941 and *Ivy Gripped the Steps* 1945 are collections of her short stories. *Bowen's Court* 1942 is the story of her family, centered on the family estate in Cork.

SHAN F. BULLOCK—christened John William—was born 1865, the eldest son of Thomas Bullock, Killynick House, Co. Fermanagh. Though his father later became a Justice of the Peace, he was no landlord, but a farmer, and a struggling one for all his large holding. Young Bullock was educated at Farra School, Co. Westmeath; failed the Entrance Examination to Trinity College, Dublin; tried a year's farming; and entered the British Civil Service in 1884. The rest of his life was passed in London. In 1889 he married Emma Mitchell, by whom he had a son and a daughter. 1893 saw the publication of his first book, *The Awkward Squads*, a collection of short stories, while his first novel, *By Thrasna River*, followed in 1895. In all, he wrote over 20 books; most were novels and tales about County Fermanagh and the shores of lovely Upper Lough Erne, the last being *The Loughsiders* 1924. He returned yet again to his life-long subject-matter in *After Sixty Years* 1930, a memoir of his Fermanagh days. He remained a civil servant until his retirement, being a member of the Secretariat at the Irish Convention, Dublin, 1917-18. In recognition of his faithful service, he was made a member of the Order of the British Empire before 1925; just before his death in 1935 he was elected to the Irish Academy of Letters.

AUSTIN CLARKE was born in Dublin in 1896, his family on both sides having lived there for generations. Like James Joyce, he received his secondary education from the Jesuits at Belvedere College, Dublin, where his experiences were rather similar to those described in *A Portrait of the Artist as a Young Man*. Still following in Joyce's steps, he graduated B.A. from University College, Dublin, where he was taught Irish by Douglas Hyde and heard of the Literary Revival from Thomas MacDonagh, one of the signers of the Proclamation of the Irish Republic in Easter Week, 1916. MacDonagh was executed by the British for his part in the Rising, and Clarke succeeded him as Lecturer in English at U.C.D. Encouraged and helped by AE, he published his first book, *The Vengeance of Fionn*, a long narrative poem, in 1917. Some years later he found himself in London earning a fugitive livelihood as a critic and reviewer for the more intelligent newspapers and periodicals. In 1937 he returned to Ireland for good, settling in Templeogue, a village close to Dublin. He has since organized the Dublin Verse Speaking Society and the Lyric Theatre; the former gives weekly broadcasts of verse on Radio Eireann, while the latter keeps alive the tradition of Irish verse drama. His early lyric and narrative poetry will be found in *Collected Poems* 1936. Since his return to Ireland, dramatic poetry for stage and radio has almost monopolized his creative powers; *Sister Eucharia* 1939, *Black Fast* 1941, *As the Crow Flies* 1943, *The Viscount of Blarney and Other Plays* 1944, have all appeared in small, semi-private editions, as has *Night and Morning* 1938, his most recent volume of lyrics. More than any other writer he has made medieval Ireland—with its comedies and tragedies of conscience—his creative theme, always casting a sly glance at modern Ireland the while. His two published novels, *The Bright Temptation* 1932 and *The Singing-Men at Cashel* 1936, complement his poetry in this respect; he has just written a third.

# NOTES ON THE AUTHORS

PADRAIC COLUM was born in the town of Longford, 1881, son of the master of the local workhouse. He grew up in Dun Laoghaire, Co. Dublin, receiving his education in National Schools. His first poems were published in Arthur Griffith's *United Irishman*, and his first play, *Broken Soil*, was first performed on December 3, 1903, by the Irish Literary Theatre. *The Land* followed at the Abbey in 1905 and *Thomas Muskerry* in 1910. The patient realism of these three plays has won their author a permanent place in the history of the Irish theatre, but it is as a lyric poet that he has won worldwide recognition. *Wild Earth* 1907 contains most of his best-known poems, though he has published many volumes since. In 1912 he married Mary Maguire, who as Mary Colum has become a well-known author and critic. An aunt of his in Pittsburgh asked them to visit her for their honeymoon, but they did not take up her offer until August 1914. Mr. Colum found his lecturing engagements multiplying, America entered the war, and ultimately it was 1922 before they returned to Ireland—for a visit only. *The King of Ireland's Son* 1916 was the first of a long line of books by Padraic Colum retelling old tales for children and adults; these led to his being invited to Hawaii in 1923 to collect the Island legends and retell them in the same way. The years 1930-33 were spent mainly in England and France, and there have been vacation visits to Ireland and elsewhere, but the Colums have in effect been residents of the U.S. since 1914. They have written, they have lectured, they have taught at Columbia and the University of Miami. Among the more important prose works of Mr. Colum's American phase are a novel, *Castle Conquer* 1923, and *The Road Round Ireland* 1926. He and his wife now make their home in New York for most of the year.

JAMES CONNOLLY was born in Clones, County Monaghan, in 1870, but spent his childhood and early youth in Edinburgh, Scotland, where he earned his living from the age of eleven. He returned to Ireland as a Socialist organizer and founded in 1896 the Irish Socialist Republican Party. In America from 1903 to 1910 he worked as an organizer for the IWW and the Socialist Labor Party. He returned to Ireland in 1910 and became the editor of the first Socialist newspaper to be published in Ireland, *The Workers' Republic*. A student of revolution for most of his life, he became the spokesman of Irish revolutionary ideals in the labor movement. In 1913 he was in Ulster, working as an organizer for the Irish Transport and General Workers Union, when he was summoned to aid Jim Larkin in directing the great Dublin strike. Out of the strike came the Irish Citizen Army which he and Larkin organized. When his famous editorial 'What Is Our Programme?' came out in *The Workers' Republic* on January 22, 1916, Connolly's demands for an immediate rising, 'the time for Ireland's Battle is NOW, the place for Ireland's Battle is HERE,' so embarrased the Supreme Council of the Irish Republican Brotherhood, who were laying plans for Easter Week, that Connolly was kidnapped and sworn in as a member of the Military Council and the plans were revealed to him so that he should preserve a discreet silence thenceforward. He and Pearse, more than any others, emerged as the dominant figures of the Easter Week Rising, for his part in which he was executed by the British on May 13, 1916. Connolly was aware of the apparent inconsistency in his dual role of nationalist and socialist, for he said to his daughter the night before his execution. 'The Socialists will never understand why I am here. They forget I am an Irishman.'

MYLES na gCOPALEEN (Myles of the Little Horses) and FLANN O'BRIEN are two of the pseudonyms of BRIAN O'NOLAN (or in Gaelic Ó NUALLÁIN), born 1912 in Co. Tyrone. At 23, having graduated from University College,

Dublin, he entered the Irish Civil Service and became a permanent resident of Dublin. The publication of *At Swim-Two-Birds* 1939 under the pseudonym Flann O'Brien gained him little fame at home or abroad, though this extravaganza seemed to some readers a perfect blend of the techniques of Stephens and Joyce. In 1940, however, the supposedly conservative *Irish Times* employed him, as Myles na gCopaleen (the name of a character in Gerald Griffin's *The Collegians*), to write a daily humorous column in Gaelic. His puns and neologisms horrified the Simon Pures of the Gaelic League, but delighted many who were tired of the humorless platitudes that had hitherto passed for Gaelic journalism. In time the column came to be half-English, half-Gaelic, and then wholly English. It now appears thrice weekly, in English. An officer of the Department of Local Government and Public Health, O'Nolan was private secretary to the Minister, Mr. Seán MacEntee, until the fall of Mr. DeValera's government in 1948. His publications as Myles na gCopaleen include: *Cruiskeen Lawn*, a bilingual selection from his column of the same name; *An Béal Bocht* (The Poor Mouth), a Gaelic parody of such autobiographies as Maurice O'Sullivan's *Twenty Years A-Growing;* and *Faustus Kelly*, a play about an Irish politician who sells himself to the Devil, first performed at the Abbey Theatre, January 25, 1943. Mr. O'Nolan is married and lives in Blackrock, a suburb of Dublin. For other facts (and fables) about this author see *Time* magazine, August 23, 1943.

DANIEL CORKERY, born 1878 in Cork City, has spent his entire life there or in the surrounding County of Cork. He was educated by the Presentation Brothers and became a National School (elementary school) teacher in 1898. In 1922, having studied art in his spare time for some years, he became an art teacher under the County Cork Technical Education Committee. Later he organized Gaelic classes under the same committee. From 1931 to 1947 he was Professor of English at University College, Cork, receiving on his retirement the degree of Doctor of Literature of the National University of Ireland. In his early twenties he joined the Gaelic League, learned Gaelic, and then began to teach it to other enthusiasts. In 1909 he founded the Cork Dramatic Society, which proposed to write all its own plays as well as perform them. Corkery, who had written nothing but verse previously, wrote *King and Hermit* in a great hurry to round out an evening of one-act plays. In 1912 he began his only novel, *The Threshold of Quiet* 1917, which may well be his masterpiece; at present he is better known for his volumes of short stories—*A Munster Twilight* 1916, *The Hounds of Banba* 1920 (stories of the Anglo-Irish War), *The Stormy Hills* 1929, *Earth Out of Earth* 1939. The Abbey Theatre has performed three of his plays—*The Labour Leader* 1919, *The Yellow Bittern* 1920, and *Fohnam the Sculptor* 1939. *The Hidden Ireland: A Study of Gaelic Munster in the Eighteenth Century* 1925 won him a unique place among modern Irishmen as a literary historian and critic; *Synge and Anglo-Irish Literature* 1931, a much more controversial work, in no way reduced his stature. A bachelor, Dr. Corkery lives with his sister in a suburb of Cork and spends much of his summers in the country sketching landscapes in water colors. This brief biography must not conclude without a reference to Dr. Corkery's influence, both directly and through his writings, on such younger Corkmen as Sean O'Faolain, Frank O'Connor, and the gifted sculptor Seamus Murphy, author of *Stone Mad*.

OLIVER ST JOHN GOGARTY was born in Dublin on August 17, 1878. He was educated at Stonyhurst and Trinity College, Dublin, from which he received his medical degree. Despite his fame as one of Dublin's better-known surgeons, and his fourteen years of service as a Free State Senator, Gogarty has become known to a wider audience as one of Dublin's foremost wits. A friend of Joyce, Moore, AE, and Yeats, Gogarty was in fact known as a literary man long before he actually published his first book of poems when he was in his forties. Consequently it is no surprise that Moore named the hero of *The Lake* after Gogarty —to irritate Gogarty's mother, it was rumored—and that Joyce modelled Buck Mulligan in *Ulysses* upon Gogarty. Although his ability as a poet is without question, his best-known work, *As I Was Going Down Sackville Street* 1937, is a hilarious account of life in Dublin which has established his reputation as a wit, a *raconteur*, and a man whose ability to quote Greek poetry lends truth to the remark that he tried to Hellenize Ireland. Recently he has retired from medical practice and lives in the United States. He has continued to write novels, articles about Ireland, and reminiscences of Yeats, AE, and Joyce.

LADY ISABELLA AUGUSTA GREGORY was born in Roxborough, County Galway, March 5, 1852. She was a widow in her forties with a son at Harrow when, through her neighbor Edward Martyn, she met Moore and Yeats and was drawn into their plans for founding The Irish Literary Theatre. By the time the group had gone through two reorganizations, in 1903 and 1905, Moore and Martyn had withdrawn completely and Lady Gregory had assumed a position in the dramatic movement that was second in importance only to Yeats'. In fact from 1905, when she became co-director with Yeats and Synge of the Abbey Theatre, until her death in May 23, 1932, the practical business of managing the theatre and establishing its policies was as much hers as Yeats'. In addition to her business contribution to the Abbey Theatre, she wrote over thirty short plays and adaptations for it and she encouraged numerous young dramatists, notably Sean O'Casey. But Lady Gregory's influence upon the Literary Revival was broader than her contributions to the dramatic movement. Her popular retellings in Kiltartan dialect of the traditional stories centering upon Ireland's two great epic heroes, Cuchulain and Finn, in *Cuchulain of Muirthemne* 1902 and *Gods and Fighting Men* 1904, gave the early writers of the Revival what one of them (J. M. Synge) described as 'part of my daily bread.' It may be said that in Standish O'Grady's histories of bardic Ireland, Douglas Hyde's translations of the love songs of Connacht, and Lady Gregory's books on Ireland's heroic past, the Literary Revival had its origin.

DOUGLAS HYDE, born at French Park, Co. Roscommon, in 1862, was the third son of the Rev. Arthur Hyde, Canon of Elphin. He received a classical education from his father at home, learned Gaelic from his father's workmen and others, and entered Trinity College, Dublin, with the intention of becoming a clergyman like his father, grandfather, great-grandfather and great-great-grandfather. However, he gave up that idea, graduated B.A. in 1884 at the top of his class, and went on to take the Doctor of Laws degree. Next he taught English Literature and studied the American Indian in Canada for a year. Shortly after his return to Ireland he met and married a German girl, Lucy Kurtz. In 1893 he founded the Gaelic League, of which he remained President until 1915, when he resigned because he felt the League had ceased to be non-political. In 1901 the League battled to obtain a permanent place for Gaelic in Irish secondary education; by 1908 it had reached its peak of 550 branches; in 1909 Gaelic was made compulsory for matriculation at the new National University of Ireland through the League's efforts. Hyde had spent more than six months in the United States in 1905-6 collecting over $60,000 for the League. From 1909 to 1932 he was Professor of Modern Irish at University College,

Dublin; then he retired and moved from Dublin to Ratra, the house at French Park presented to him by his admirers after the American tour. Having been twice an Irish Free State Senator, he was nominated in May 1938, by both the leading Irish parties, for the post of First President of Ireland. In spite of ill-health he served the full seven-year term, retired again to Ratra, and died there in July 1949. The majority of his writings are in Gaelic, and include original poetry and plays, besides editions of folk-tales and folk poetry. The translations from Gaelic poetry in *Love Songs of Connacht* 1893, *Songs Ascribed to Raftery* 1903, and *The Religious Songs of Connacht* 1906 are extremely important. Many other translations appear in his *A Literary History of Ireland* 1899. His *Casadh an tSúgáin* (The Twisting of the Rope) was the first Gaelic play performed by the Irish Literary Theatre. Lady Gregory translated or adapted this and others of his one-act plays; *The Workhouse Ward* is the best-known. His literal rendering of Gaelic idioms in *Love Songs of Connacht* showed the way to Lady Gregory and Synge.

JAMES JOYCE was born in Rathgar, a Dublin suburb, on February 2, 1882. His father, John Stanislaus Joyce, is described in *A Portrait of the Artist as a Young Man* as 'a medical student, an oarsman, a tenor, an amateur actor, a shouting politician, a small landlord, a small investor, a drinker, a good fellow, a storyteller, somebody's secretary, something in a distillery, a taxgatherer, a bankrupt and at present a praiser of his own past,' a description which would seem to be factual. Joyce's formal education at Clongowes Wood College, Belvedere College, and University College, Dublin, was at the hands of the Jesuits, a fact which explains his indoctrination in Thomistic philosophy. In 1904 the young Joyce left Ireland for good, and for the rest of his life lived in Italy, Switzerland, and France. He worked as a teacher in a Berlitz school in Trieste, but later accepted contributions from friends in order to support his family. His first book, *Dubliners*, a collection of short stories about his native city, was published in 1914 only after years of heartbreaking disappointments at the hands of publishers who objected to his realism. His only play, *Exiles* 1918, was written in the same naturalistic style as *Dubliners* and was imitative of Ibsen, Joyce's first model. In *A Portrait of the Artist as a Young Man* 1916 Joyce attempted, for the first time and on a simple scale, the stream-of-consciousness method which he was to perfect in *Ulysses* 1922 and which, among other things, was to stamp him as unquestionably the foremost technician among modern novelists. His last work, *Finnegans Wake*, published two years before his death in Zurich on January 13, 1941, has been called the most original, if the least comprehensible, of modern novels. In it Joyce was apparently attempting to invade not just the dreamworld of the individual but the collective unconscious of the race.

PATRICK KAVANAGH was born some forty years ago in County Monaghan in a townland called Mucker, a corrupted Gaelic word, he writes, meaning a place where pigs breed in abundance. His father was a shoe-maker, but Patrick and his brothers worked the farm. At eighteen he won fourth place in a poetry competition in the *Weekly Independent*. In 1939 he went to London where he was befriended by Helen Waddell, who encouraged him to write his first book, an autobiography, *The Green Fool* 1939, which he now claims is less factual than his novel *Tarry Flynn* 1948. His volume of verse, *A Soul for Sale* 1949, contains his chief work, the long narrative poem 'The Great Hunger.' He lives in Dublin where he writes tart criticisms of his contemporaries and has contributed the 'Diary' to *Envoy* magazine. His poem 'The Paddiad,' which appeared in *Horizon,* August, 1949, is a Popean satire on contemporary Irish letters.

MICHAEL McLAVERTY was born in Monaghan, 1907, but his family had to migrate from the country to the city of Belfast while he was still a child; the experience provided him with the theme of his first novel, *Lost Fields.* Part of his boyhood was spent on Rathlin Island, off the coast of County Antrim. He received his secondary education at St. Malachy's College, Belfast, and then entered Queen's University in the same city, where he studied Mathematics and Experimental Physics, taking his Master of Science degree in 1933. The same year saw the publication of his first short story. He became a school-teacher in Belfast, but has found time to write four novels, each of which has contributed its share to a steadily growing reputation; the last two are *In This Thy Day* 1945 and *The Three Brothers* 1948; all have been published in America. His output of short stories is small, but their exceptionally high quality has been recognized by Edward J. O'Brien and several other anthologists; see *The Game Cock and Other Stories* 1947. After the editors had chosen 'Six Weeks On and Two Ashore' for the present collection, Mr. McLaverty wrote to say that he felt it was one of the best of his short stories so far. It has not been previously published in the U.S.A. Mr. McLaverty is unique among the authors included here in that he is the only Roman Catholic who continues to make his home in Northern Ireland.

GEORGE MOORE was born on February 24, 1852 at Moore Hall, County Mayo. His family were Catholic, had been in Ireland since the end of the 17th century, and had some claim to descent, in the male line, from Saint Thomas More. The latest heir to Moore Hall became an absentee landlord because he was interested in an artistic career removed from the turbulent Ireland of Land League days. An unsuccessful period as art student in Paris, where he arrived in 1873 with an Irish valet, was not without value since it enabled him to meet a good many of the great Impressionist artists and gave him the background for writing, twenty years later, some very respectable art criticism, as well as sensitive impressions of Monet, Manet, Degas, Renoir, and Pissarro. For most of his adult life Moore lived in London; and when he, Yeats, and Edward Martyn decided in 1898 to found an Irish theatre and to initiate a new literary movement, he was the only one of the founders who had an established literary reputation both in England and on the continent. He had by that time written *A Drama in Muslin* 1886, *Confessions of a Young Man* 1888, *Impressions and Opinions* 1891, *Modern Painting* 1893, and the famous *Esther Waters* 1894. From 1901 to 1910 he lived in Dublin and wrote his volume of short stories *The Untilled Field* 1903, his sensitive novel *The Lake* 1905, and his masterpiece, the three-volume unofficial history of the early years of the Literary Revival, *Hail and Farewell* 1911-1914. In addition to these books, which represent a peak in prose writing for the Revival, Moore's contribution to the movement must be measured by the fact that the influence upon later Irish novelists of such European writers as Dujardin and the Russians, notably Moore's master Turgeniev, must be largely attributed to him. He died in London, January 21, 1933.

SEAN O'CASEY was born of Protestant parents in the slums of Dublin in 1880. In his autobiography O'Casey tells a grim story of a boyhood full of bitterness and humiliation engendered by poverty, ill health, notably weak eyes, and hard work as a pick-and-shovel laborer, dock worker, and hod-carrier. As a young man in Dublin he was fully aware of the Abbey Theatre, but had actually been in it to see a play only twice before he went to see the performance of his own *The Shadow of a Gunman*. 'The fact is,' he writes, 'I couldn't afford to pay for a seat. My pay for the full week's work then, from six in the morning till five in the evening, was nineteen shillings, three and a half pence. Out of that I had to keep myself and mother, pay subs to Gaelic League, the IRB, plus "rifle levy" and *Irish Freedom* levy—*Irish Freedom* was the monthly paper of the movement—supply myself with hurleys, and pay subs to the Hurling Club; so you can guess how much money I had to spare, not to mention the buying of an odd book in Gaelic and English.' After writing three realistic plays of Dublin slum life, *The Shadow of a Gunman, Juno and the Paycock*, and *The Plough and the Stars*, and seeing them performed at the Abbey respectively in 1923, 1924, and 1926, O'Casey turned to symbolism and expressionism with *The Silver Tassie*. When Yeats and his fellow directors of the Abbey rejected it, O'Casey, who had just moved to London, decided to offer no more of his work to the Abbey Theatre. From that point on in his career he has followed in the same direction of symbolism and fantasy. Most of his subsequent plays, *Within the Gates, The Star Turns Red, Purple Dust, Red Roses for Me, Oak Leaves and Lavender*, and *Cock A Doodle Dandy* are expressionistic in method. Except for *Within the Gates*, which had a successful New York run in 1934, none of his later plays has had the success or drawn the critical acclaim that was given to his early work. But his finest writing since he left Ireland in the late twenties has unquestionably been his four volumes of highly imaginative autobiography, *I Knock at the Door, Pictures in the Hallway, Drums Under the Window*, and *Inishfallen Fare Thee Well*. These books, obviously written under the influence of the stream of consciousness, with their brilliantly subjective style and outlook, are a justification of O'Casey's desertion of his early style.

FRANK O'CONNOR (Michael O'Donovan) was born in Cork City in 1903. Like his fellow Corkonian Sean O'Faolain, with whom he is often linked, O'Connor was drawn into the troubles as a Republican and spent some time in an Irish Free State jail, where he studied Irish and became proficient enough to write, on his release, a prize-winning study of Turgeniev in Irish. AE gave O'Connor his first real chance, however, when he published some of his poems, stories, and translations in *The Irish Statesman*. A director of the Abbey Theatre until 1939, O'Connor was dismissed by his associate directors in a policy squabble in which he refused to yield to the demands of the Gaelic enthusiasts who wanted to use the theatre as a propagandist device for furthering the government's language program. This incident, plus his brush with the government censors, who banned his translation of Brian Merriman's bawdy eighteenth-century poem *The Midnight Court*, possibly accounts for O'Connor's waspish attitude toward Ireland evident in his latest books, *The Common Chord* 1948, *Leinster, Munster and Connaught* 1950 and *Traveller's Samples* 1951. O'Connor's fine translations from the Irish include *The Wild Bird's Nest* 1932, *Three Old Brothers and Other Poems* 1936, *Lords and Commons* 1938, and *The Fountain of Magic* 1939. He has written a readable biography of Michael Collins published in America as *Death in Dublin* 1937; a novel, *The Saint and Mary Kate* 1932; a novel built up out of short narratives, *Dutch Interior* 1940, and three other volumes of short stories—*Guests of the Nation* 1931, *Bones of Contention* 1936, and *Crab Apple Jelly* 1944.

SEAN O'FAOLAIN was born in 1900 in Dublin. He was brought up, however, in Cork, where he early fell under the influence of Daniel Corkery, who was then a national schoolteacher. After taking a B.A. and M.A. from University College, Dublin, O'Faolain came to the United States on a Commonwealth Fellowship in 1926. During his three-year stay here he earned an M.A. from Harvard and lectured at Boston College. From 1929 to 1933 he lived in England and taught at St. Mary's College, Strawberry Hill, Middlesex. In 1933 he returned to Ireland and taught school in County Wicklow. Sometime in the '30's O'Faolain gave up teaching and embarked on a full-time writing career. Since the publication of his first book of short stories, *Midsummer Night Madness*, in 1932, O'Faolain has written three novels, *A Nest of Simple Folk* 1933, *Bird Alone* 1936, *Come Back to Erin* 1940; biographies of Hugh O'Neill, Daniel O'Connell, Constance Markievicz, Eamon DeValera and Cardinal Newman; two more volumes of short stories; *The Silver Branch* 1938, a collection of translations from the Irish; and *The Irish* 1949, a study of the growth of the racial mind. *The Short Story* 1950 concerns the art of writing. *An Irish Journey* and *A Summer in Italy*, travel books, complete the list. Quite apart from his significance as a novelist and biographer, O'Faolain has been a force in Irish letters. As editor of *The Bell*, for example, he was outspoken against the government's administration of the censorship law.

LIAM O'FLAHERTY was born in the Aran Islands in 1897, just one year before Synge's first visit. He early showed exceptional intelligence and was educated free by the Holy Ghost Fathers from his thirteenth year, as a postulant for the priesthood. His studies took him from Rockwell College, Co. Tipperary, to Blackrock College, Co. Dublin, then to the Dublin diocesan seminary (Holy Cross College, Clonliffe), where he finally gave up the idea of taking Orders. After a short time at University College, Dublin, he joined the crack Irish Guards. He spent six months in France, was shell-shocked at Langemarck in September 1917 and, after many months of hospital, was discharged with a disability pension. He spent some time at home and then set out in search of himself once more. This time his journey took him most of the way round the world, as a stoker and deckhand, a beachcomber, hobo and lumberjack. Back in Ireland after two or three years of wandering, he rested and recuperated once more on Aran. In 1922 he seized a public building in Dublin at the head of a group of unemployed workers and hoisted the red flag. Driven out by Government forces, he soon after fled to England. There his first novel, *Thy Neighbour's Wife* 1923, was written, and accepted by Edward Garnett, D. H. Lawrence's editor. *The Black Soul*, a Laurentian novel, and *Spring Sowing* (short stories) followed in 1924. In Dublin that year he first met Margaret Barrington, whom he married in 1926. *The Informer* 1925 took the world by storm, as did its movie version ten years later. *Skerrett* 1932 and *Famine* 1937 are far finer novels. Some of his very best work is contained in his four collections of short stories. These are *Spring Sowing*, *The Tent* 1926, *The Mountain Tavern* 1929, *Two Lovely Beasts* 1948. Since he went to Hollywood to help John Ford film *The Informer* O'Flaherty has written little by comparison with his earlier prodigious output. He has, too, lived in the U.S., visiting France in 1938 for the making of a French film from his novel *The Puritan* and returning to Aran periodically for fresh contact with his first and best subject-matter, the fauna—human and otherwise—of his native place. His recently completed *Insurrection* is his fourteenth novel.

STANDISH JAMES O'GRADY was born in Castletown Berehaven, Co. Cork, on September 18, 1846, the son of a Church of Ireland clergyman. He entered Trinity College, Dublin, from Tipperary Grammar School and graduated B.A. in 1868 after a distinguished undergraduate career, during which he won a Scholarship in Classics, and also shone in oratory, essay-writing, and practically every game and sport then popular. He next studied law and was called to the Irish Bar in 1872, but did not practise for long. His true life-work first called him in 1869, when a wet day spent in the library of a country house introduced him to the first History of Ireland he had ever read—O'Halloran's. Years of eager reading in Irish history and legend—especially the latter—followed. Meanwhile he turned from law to critical writing, and from that to an attempt to recreate ancient Irish literature in a readable form. His *History of Ireland: Heroic Period* 1878 and *History of Ireland: Cuculain and his Contemporaries* 1880 became the foundation stones of the literary revival, though his *History of Ireland: Critical and Philosophical* 1881 never got beyond the first volume (probably no satisfactory evaluation of the authenticity of the Old Irish 'historical' writings is possible even today). *Cuculain: An Epic* 1882 reprinted the relevant portions of the earlier *History*, which ought to have been classified as epic rather than history from the first. In the next decade he wrote many fine novels and tales based mainly on Irish history of the Elizabethan period. *The Bog of Stars* 1893 and *The Flight of the Eagle* 1897 are probably the best-known of these. O'Grady was also, among other things, a working journalist and an ardent student of politics. Beginning as a Tory who urged that the landlords take the lead once again in Irish affairs (*Toryism and the Tory Democracy* 1886), he ended as an advocate of Guild Socialism in A. R. Orage's magazine, *The New Age*. As owner and editor of the *Kilkenny Moderator*, a small-town newspaper, he printed and published his own and others' books, and, from 1900 to 1906, the *All Ireland Review*, a literary weekly. His career is full of odd ironies: though he brought Old Irish literature to life for the unlearned reader, he himself hardly knew Gaelic at all, unlike his kinsman Standish Hayes O'Grady, who was an accomplished Celtic scholar; he objected to the Irish Literary Theatre's dramatizations of the legends he had helped to popularize as 'degrading Irish ideals'; finally, though so true an Irish patriot, he left Ireland permanently many years before his death, which occurred at Shanklin, Isle of Wight, May 18, 1928.

SEUMAS O'KELLY was born in Loughrea, Co. Galway, where his father was a grain-buyer and carrier. He was educated at the local Catholic secondary school, St. Brendan's College. When he grew up he started to write for a nearby country newspaper, and in 1903 became editor of *The Southern Star*, published in Skibbereen, Co. Cork. Soon he moved nearer Dublin to become editor of *The Leinster Leader*, Naas, Co. Kildare. Already a member of the Gaelic League, he now met Arthur Griffith and other leading Dublin authors and journalists, and joined Sinn Féin on its foundation. His first book, a collection of short stories and sketches entitled *By the Stream of Killmeen* 1906, showed little promise, but by 1908-9 he was writing some admirable short stories for the *Irish Weekly Independent*. Though at first ignored by the Abbey Theatre, he won their approval of his third play, *The Shuiler's Child*, in 1910. Other Abbey plays by O'Kelly are *The Bribe* 1913, *The Parnellite* 1917, *Meadowsweet* 1919. In or around 1911 O'Kelly had a long and severe bout of rheumatic fever which permanently weakened his heart; he resigned from *The Leinster Leader* in 1912 to become editor of *The Dublin Saturday Post*, had to give up this position owing to ill health, and soon after he accepted a similar editorship which he had to relinquish for the same reason. Finally, in 1915, he settled down in Naas with an elder sister and a young nephew to make a living as a free-lance writer. To this period belong his book of short stories, *Waysiders* 1917, and his fine novel, *The Lady of Deerpark* 1917. In May 1918 Arthur Griffith was imprisoned; O'Kelly at once went to Dublin at the risk of his health to edit the Sinn Féin paper *Nationality*. On November 13 some British soldiers celebrating the Armistice broke into the *Nationality* office with their girl friends; O'Kelly's efforts to resist their vandalism were too much for his overstrained heart, and he died at his desk in a matter of hours. Three collections of early short stories were published after his death, as well as an inferior, unrevised novel, *Wet Clay* 1922. His last completed work (and his masterpiece) is the long short story *The Weaver's Grave*.

PADRAIC PEARSE was born in Dublin in 1879, educated by the Christian Brothers, graduated from the Royal (now the National) University, and became the founder of St Enda's, a school for boys at Rathfarnham which gave its students a Gaelic and Irish outlook and education. In 1913 he entered the secret revolutionary organization, the Irish Republican Brotherhood, and became a leading member of its Supreme Council. He and James Connolly, more than any others, were responsible for the Rising of 1916; and the impact which it had upon the popular imagination was largely due to his influence. His biographer and friend, Desmond Ryan, writes, 'Pearse had travelled the road to insurrection through his Gaelic idealism. He had been the educationalist of the Gaelic League. He became the orator of the Irish Volunteer movement, an orator of ultimate revolution, and his power of gripping the rank and file of the Volunteers was due to his mastery of language, his sincerity, his personality, his fire.' He was executed by a British firing squad in Dublin on May 3, 1916.

EDWARD SHEEHY, born in Tralee, Co. Kerry, some forty years ago, holds an M.A. degree from the National University of Ireland. He was Book Editor of the magazine *Ireland To-day* from December 1936 to its demise in March 1938, contributing many articles and short stories to the magazine besides. He has been art critic of *The Dublin Magazine* since 1943. Though he has completed at least one novel, *God Send Sunday* 1939 is his only creative work to be separately published. Another of his tales, reprinted from *Horizon*, will be found in *Horizon Stories*. He has done some teaching. For many years he lived in a peasant cottage in the Dublin mountains, whence he descended upon the city wearing a black goatee beard and black leather leggings. He now lives at Phrompstown House, Enniskerry, Co. Wicklow. He is married to Anna Kelly, a Dublin painter, and has two children.

EDITH ŒNONE SOMERVILLE and MARTIN ROSS (Violet Florence Martin), who for twenty-six years were associated in one of the most successful of literary partnerships, were born respectively in Corfu on May 2, 1858 and in Ross, County Galway, on June 11, 1862. Although the two cousins were brought up in County Galway, they did not meet until 1886. Miss Somerville writes, 'almost immediately they were aware that Chance, or Fate, had done them a good turn, and that to the marriage of true minds there would be no impediment.' Their first book, *An Irish Cousin* 1889, was successful enough to encourage them to continue their collaboration. From this date until the death of Martin Ross on December 21, 1915, they wrote travel books, essays, sporting and children's picture books, the incomparable *Experiences of an Irish R. M.*, immortalised in 1944 by its inclusion in Everyman's Library, and *The Real*

*Charlotte* 1894, reissued in 1948 in The World's Classics. Miss Somerville, up to her death, Oct. 8, 1949, maintained the myth of collaboration by continuing to write over the familiar names of Somerville and Ross, and she admitted only that since her collaborator's death 'our technique of writing together has had to be changed, and, to a certain extent, modified.' Her desire to continue the collaboration in name at least was recognised in 1932 when Trinity College, Dublin, tactfully bestowed honorary Litt.D.'s on both the dead and the living collaborator. Although writing at a time when Irish literature was being transformed by the ideals of the new nationalism and the Celtic revival, Somerville and Ross continued to write in the Ascendancy tradition established by Maria Edgeworth, Samuel Lover, and Charles Lever, who have been described as Irish colonial writers. But the Ireland of Somerville and Ross, which is neither the realistic Ireland of Synge and O'Flaherty nor the 'hidden Ireland' of Daniel Corkery, is no less true for being an Ireland of Big Houses and fox hunts; and their achievement should be measured in the terms of the Ascendancy tradition in which they excelled and not by the ideals of the Literary Revival by which they remained untouched, and of which they were apparently oblivious.

JAMES STEPHENS was born in Dublin in 1882. He was trying to support a wife and child on a meagre salary as a typist in a lawyer's office in Dublin when AE discovered him and introduced him to Yeats, Lady Gregory, and George Moore. His first volume of verse, *Insurrections* 1909, received scant critical approval, probably because it did not deal with leprechauns, fairies and, as Ernest Boyd pointed out, 'the other adjuncts of accepted Celticism.' But *The Crock of Gold* 1912 was a book to silence all such criticisms and its success was immediate. The popularity of *The Crock of Gold* today, just forty years since it was first published, is attested by the fact that it is currently in its nineteenth printing. Stephens has been a successful prose writer in such novels as *The Charwoman's Daughter* 1912, *The Demi-Gods* 1914, *Deirdre* 1923, and *In the Land of Youth* 1924, and in such a collection of short stories as *Here Are Ladies* 1912. But despite the fame of *The Crock of Gold*, Stephens is most likely to be remembered as a poet. In his poems he seldom descends to the sentimentality of *The Charwoman's Daughter*, or the 'sophisticated infantilism' of *The Crock of Gold*. After his *Collected Poems* was published in 1926, he published two more thin volumes of verse, *Strict Joy* 1931 and *Kings and the Moon* 1938. He died in London, 1950.

FRANCIS STUART was born in Australia in 1902. Except for several years when he was attending Rugby School, he spent his youth in Ireland. At twenty he fought in the Irish Civil War as a Republican, was captured in a street fight, spent over nine months in prison and internment camp, and went on an eleven-day hunger strike. He married Iseult Gonne, daughter of Maude Gonne; they have two children. During the war years he lived in Germany and saw the Russians enter Berlin in 1945. He is at present living in Paris. Stuart's second novel, *Pigeon Irish*, published when he was thirty, a curious blending of mysticism, sex, and violence, won him immediate critical acclaim. Two plays performed at the Abbey Theatre—*Men Crowd Me Round* in 1933 and *Strange Guest* in 1940 —two volumes of autobiographical reveries—*Things to Live For* 1935 and *The Angel of Pity* also 1935—and thirteen novels represent his entire published work. The most successful of his latest novels is *Redemption* 1949, a brilliant study of the sexual and spiritual urges which Stuart sees as the motivating forces of human conduct.

JOHN MILLINGTON SYNGE was born in Rathfarnham, a suburb of Dublin, on January 16, 1871. Descended from landed English gentry who had come to Ireland in the 17th century, he had among his ancestors five bishops, including the famous 18th-century Archbishop Synge of Tuam. Educated mostly at home by private tutor, he was graduated from Trinity College, Dublin, in 1892. After college he went to Europe, not in the tradition of the Irish *vagantes*, but merely to put the finishing touches to an Irish gentleman's education before embarking on a musical career. By 1894 he had decided against music, settled in Paris, and was deliberating about earning his living as a journalist in France. When the famous meeting with Yeats took place, in which Yeats said, 'Give up Paris, you will never create anything by reading Racine. . . . Go to the Aran Islands. Live there as if you were one of the people themselves; express a life that has never found expression,' Synge was living comfortably, though frugally, on regular contributions from his family. The story assumed all the proportions of a Yeatsian myth in which Synge's quarters in the Hotel Corneille became a garret and Synge himself took on the features of a bohemian. Synge, at any rate, took the advice. In 1898 he paid his first visit to Aran, equipped with his notebooks, his fiddle, and a Gaelic dictionary to help him brush up on Irish, which he had not read since his undergraduate days at Trinity College. Synge's brief career as a member of the Literary Revival, which began with this visit to Aran, ended on March 24, 1909, when he died of cancer at a nursing home in Dublin. In those eleven years he wrote *In the Shadow of the Glen, Riders to the Sea, The Playboy of the Western World, The Well of the Saints, The Tinker's Wedding,* and the unfinished *Deirdre of the Sorrows,* and established himself as the greatest dramatist of modern Ireland.

WILLIAM BUTLER YEATS was born in Sandymount, a suburb of Dublin, on June 13, 1865. His mother's people were country gentry from Sligo, where the poet spent a good deal of his youth. Yeats, in his early twenties, was editing stories from Carleton and Irish fairy tales for an English publisher when he wrote what he later called his first properly Irish poem, 'The Lake Isle of Innisfree.' His early editorial work is not without significance, however, because his *Poems and Ballads of Young Ireland* 1888, a slim anthology containing the work of several of his young contemporaries, is now considered the first collective offering of the Literary Revival. Shortly after the publication of his first volume of verse in 1889, he met Maude Gonne, to whom he wrote love lyrics almost to the end of his life. He helped inaugurate the Literary Revival by founding, with others, The Irish Literary Society of London in 1891 and The Irish National Literary Society of Dublin in 1892. In 1899, with George Moore and Edward Martyn, he launched The Irish Literary Theatre by the performance in Dublin of his play *The Countess Cathleen* and Martyn's *The Heather Field.* From that point on it was Yeats who formulated the ideals and objectives of the movement and became its most significant figure. In 1917 he married an Englishwoman who shared his interest in spiritualism. He had two children by her. In 1923 his importance as a world figure in literature was signalised by his receiving the Nobel Prize for poetry. He died, while in France with his wife, on January 28, 1939. His *Collected Poems,* first published in 1933, is the standard collection of his best poems. His *Collected Plays,* now unfortunately out of print, was published in 1934.